Expert Oracle RAC Performance Diagnostics and Tuning

Murali Vallath

Apress®

Expert Oracle RAC Performance Diagnostics and Tuning

ISBN-13 (pbk): 978-1-4302-6709-6

ISBN-13 (electronic): 978-1-4302-6710-2

Publisher: Heinz Weinheimer
Acquisitions Editor: Jonathan Gennick
Developmental Editor: Chris Nelson
Technical Reviewer: Arup Nanda
Editorial Board: Steve Anglin, Mark Beckner, Ewan Buckingham, Gary Cornell, Louise Corrigan, James DeWolf,
    Jonathan Gennick, Robert Hutchinson, Michelle Lowman, James Markham, Matthew Moodie,
    Jeff Olson, Jeffrey Pepper, Douglas Pundick, Ben Renow-Clarke, Dominic Shakeshaft, Gwenan Spearing,
    Matt Wade, Steve Weiss
Coordinating Editor: Rita Fernando
Copy Editor: Deanna Hegle
Compositor: SPi Global
Indexer: SPi Global
Cover Designer: Anna Ishchenko

Distributed to the book trade worldwide by Springer Science+Business Media New York, 233 Spring Street, 6th Floor, New York, NY 10013. Phone 1-800-SPRINGER, fax (201) 348-4505, e-mail orders-ny@springer-sbm.com, or visit www.springeronline.com. Apress Media, LLC is a California LLC and the sole member (owner) is Springer Science + Business Media Finance Inc (SSBM Finance Inc). SSBM Finance Inc is a Delaware corporation.

For information on translations, please e-mail rights@apress.com, or visit www.apress.com.

Apress and friends of ED books may be purchased in bulk for academic, corporate, or promotional use. eBook versions and licenses are also available for most titles. For more information, reference our Special Bulk Sales–eBook Licensing web page at www.apress.com/bulk-sales.

Any source code or other supplementary materials referenced by the author in this text is available to readers at www.apress.com. For detailed information about how to locate your book's source code, go to www.apress.com/source-code/.

To Jaya, Grishma, and Nabhas—you are my dearest and everything to me.

Contents at a Glance

About the Author xxi

About the Technical Reviewer xxiii

Acknowledgments xxv

Introduction xxvii

■Chapter 1: Methodology 1

■Chapter 2: Capacity Planning and Architecture 21

■Chapter 3: Testing for Availability 55

■Chapter 4: Testing for Scalability 87

■Chapter 5: Real Application Testing 111

■Chapter 6: Tools and Utilities 145

■Chapter 7: SQL Tuning 201

■Chapter 8: Parallel Query Tuning 235

■Chapter 9: Tuning the Database 277

■Chapter 10: Tuning Recovery 319

■Chapter 11: Tuning Oracle Net 339

■Chapter 12: Tuning the Storage Subsystem 355

■Chapter 13: Tuning Global Cache 387

■Chapter 14: Tuning the Cluster Interconnect 451

■Chapter 15: Optimize Distributed Workload 495

■**Chapter 16: Oracle Clusterware Diagnosis**..**545**

■**Chapter 17: Waits, Enqueues, and Latches**..**585**

■**Chapter 18: Problem Diagnosis**...**615**

■**Appendix A: The SQL Scripts Used in This Book**..**653**

■**Bibliography**..**661**

Index..**665**

Contents

About the Author xxi

About the Technical Reviewer xxiii

Acknowledgments xxv

Introduction xxvii

■Chapter 1: Methodology 1

Performance Requirements 2

Tuning the System 4

Step 1: Optimizing Workload 4

Step 2: Finding and Eliminating Contention 4

Step 3: Reduce Physical I/O 5

Step 4: Optimize Logical I/O 5

Methodology 6

Performance Tuning Methodology 7

Getting to the Obvious 11

Divide Into Quadrants 11

Looking at Overall Database Performance 13

Oracle Unified Method 13

Testing and Performance Management 14

RAP Testing 16

RAP Testing Phase I—Stability Testing of the Cluster 17

RAP Testing Phase II—Availability and Load Balancing 17

RAP Testing Phase III—High Availability 17

RAP Testing Phase IV—Backup and Recovery 17

RAP Testing Phase V—Hardware Scalability 17

RAP Testing Phase VI—Database Scalability 17

RAP Testing Phase VII—Application Scalability 17

RAP Testing Phase VIII—Burnout Testing 18

Creating an Application Testing Environment 18

How Much to Tune? 18

Conclusion 19

■Chapter 2: Capacity Planning and Architecture 21

Analyzing the Stack 22

Capacity Planning 23

How to Measure Scaling 26

Estimating Size of Database Objects 26

Architecture 28

Oracle Single-Instance vs. Clustered Configuration 29

RAC Architecture 29

Conclusion 54

■Chapter 3: Testing for Availability 55

Points of Failure (Gaps) 55

Interconnect Failure 56

Node Failure 65

Instance Failure 67

Oracle Component Failure 67

Media Failure 68

Protecting the Database 69

Testing Hardware for Availability 69

RAP Phase I 69

Testing Application for Availability 75

RAP Phase II—Availability and Load Balancing 76

RAP Phase III—HA 79

RAP Phase IV—Backup and Recovery 82

Conclusion 85

■**Chapter 4: Testing for Scalability** **87**

Scale-Up or Scale-Out..87

Scale-Up 87

Scale-Out...88

Scalable Components...89

Interconnect...89

ASM 92

Instance 92

SQL*Net 92

Testing Hardware for Scalability 93

RAP Phase V Hardware Scalability 93

Testing the Database for Scalability...102

Testing Application for Scalability 102

RAP Phase VII Application Scalability 102

End-to-End Testing..107

RAP Testing Phase VIII Burnout Tests 107

Conclusion...110

■**Chapter 5: Real Application Testing** **111**

Testing Methods 112

Method I—Using Homegrown Utilities 112

Method II—Using Real Application Testing..113

Conclusion...143

■**Chapter 6: Tools and Utilities**...**145**

Oracle Enterprise Manager..145

Performance Manager..147

SQL Advisory...148

Automatic Workload Repository 150

Automatic Workload Repository Warehouse..155

Automatic Database Diagnostic Monitor 156

Active Session History..159

Tools and Utilities from Oracle Support 160

OSWATCHER 160

Light Onboard Monitor (LTOM) 165

Cluster Health Monitor (CHM) 171

Architecture 172

CHM Statistics 173

EXPLAIN PLAN 176

DBMS_SQLTUNE 177

SQL Trace 180

Event 10046 182

Level 1 182

Level 4 183

Level 8 184

Level 12 184

Event 10053 185

Service-Module-Action 191

The trcsess Utility 195

Oracle's Wait Interface 196

Conclusion 199

■Chapter 7: SQL Tuning 201

SQL Execution Life Cycle 201

Step 1: Create a Cursor 203

Step 2: Parse the Statement 203

Step 3: Describe the Results 207

Step 4: Define Query Output 207

Step 5: Bind Any Variables 207

Step 6: Parallelize the Statement 207

Step 7: Execute the Statement 208

Step 8: Fetch Rows 208

Step 9: Close the Cursor 208

Capturing Execution Times 208

TIMED_STATISTICS 208

STATISTICS_LEVEL 209

V$STATISTICS_LEVEL 209

TIMED_OS_STATISTICS 210

What Are Consistent Gets? 211

Logical Reads 212

Physical Reads 215

Why Tune? 216

Optimizer 216

Optimizer Statistics 231

Conclusion 234

■Chapter 8: Parallel Query Tuning 235

Why Parallel Processing? 236

Oracle and Parallel Processing 237

Parallel Query Architecture 238

Methods of Applying Parallelism 240

Parallel Processing in RAC... 250

Parallel Recovery.. 262

Optimizing Parallel Operations 263

Data Dictionary Views to Monitor Parallel Operations 265

Wait Events Related to Parallel Operations 272

Troubleshooting Using Oracle Event Interface.. 274

Conclusion 275

■Chapter 9: Tuning the Database 277

Data Partitioning 278

Partitioned Indexes 279

Local Indexes 280

Global Indexes 280

Benefits of Partitioning 280

Partition Pruning 280

Partition-wise Joins 281

Sequence Numbers 281

Sequences and Index Contention 281

Undo Block Considerations 293

Hard Parses 293

Result Cache 295

Query Result Cache 295

Function Result Cache 306

Limitations of the Result Cache 311

In-Memory Cache 311

How Does This Work? 312

Workshop 5 313

Conclusion 318

■Chapter 10: Tuning Recovery 319

Instance Recovery 320

How Does Oracle Know That Recovery Is Required for a Given Data File? 320

The Instance Recovery Process 321

Tuning Instance Recovery 326

Redo Log Sizing Advisory 330

Crash Recovery 333

Thread Recovery 333

Online Block Level Recovery 333

Media Recovery..333

Fast Recovery Area...335

Conclusion...337

■**Chapter 11: Tuning Oracle Net**...**339**

Making the Connection...339

Connectivity Drivers...340

Oracle Net Foundation Layer (ONFL)..340

Oracle Protocol Support Layer...341

Listeners..341

Load Balancing..342

Tracing the Load Metric Capture..344

Connection Throughput...345

Workshop...346

Wait Events related to SQL*Net...351

Conclusion...353

■**Chapter 12: Tuning the Storage Subsystem**...**355**

Choosing Storage..355

Transaction-Based Workload...356

Throughput-Based Workload..356

Mixed Workload..356

Choosing the Storage Array...357

Storage-Wide Considerations for Performance..357

Disk Drive Performance...358

Storage Contention...360

Oracle Files and RAID..365

Datafiles..365

Redolog Files..368

Testing to Determine Performance...368

Types of I/O Operations..369

Oracle and I/O Characteristics..371

Oracle-Supported Access Types 374

    Clustered File System 374

    Automatic Storage Management 374

    ASM Clustered File System 375

ASM Architecture 376

Allocation Units 377

How Many Diskgroups? 379

Monitoring ASM 379

    Data Dictionary Views to Monitor Storage 380

    Enterprise Manager to Monitor Storage 382

Conclusion 385

■ **Chapter 13: Tuning Global Cache** 387

Global Cache 387

RAC Specific Background Processes 388

    LMSn 389

    LMON 389

    LMDn 390

    LCK0 390

    LMHB 390

    ACMS 390

    RMSn 391

    RSMN 391

    PING 391

    IPC0 391

    LDDn 391

    Resource Availability 391

Think Outside the Interconnect 398

    Scenario 1: Block Request Involving Two Instances 399

    Scenario 2: Block Request Involving Three Instances 402

    Prepare Phase 405

Transfer Phase 406

Workshop 407

Mastering and Remastering 414

Monitoring Remastering 416

Manual Remastering 422

Global Cache Optimization 424

Queries with High Cluster Overhead 427

Blockers and Deadlocks 429

Identifying Hot Blocks 429

Data Dictionary Views to Monitor Global Cache 434

Enterprise Manager to Monitor Global Cache 445

Troubleshooting Using Oracle Event Interface 447

Conclusion 449

■Chapter 14: Tuning the Cluster Interconnect 451

Cluster Interconnect 451

Block Transfer 453

Types of Interconnects 454

Network Throughput and Bandwidth 455

Verifying the Interconnect 458

Check 1 458

Check 2 462

Check 3 463

Check 4 463

Check 5 465

Think Inside the Interconnect 465

Prepare Phase 466

Transfer Phase 466

Workshop 467

Linear Scalability of Private Interconnect 478

Interconnect Monitoring 482

    Workshop 482

    Data Dictionary Views to Monitor Cluster Interconnect 487

    Enterprise Manager to Monitor Cluster Interconnect 490

Conclusion 493

■**Chapter 15: Optimize Distributed Workload** **495**

Service Framework 495

    Manageability 495

    Availability 496

    Performance 496

Server Pools 497

Distributed Workload Management (DWM) 498

    Resource Manager 498

    Fast Application Notification (FAN) 498

    Fast Connect Failover (FCF) 507

Load Balancing 510

    Client Load Balancing 510

    Connection Load Balancing 511

    Applications Using Connection Pooling 513

Locating the Problem 527

    Workshop 531

    Troubleshooting Using Oracle Event Interface 542

Conclusion 543

■**Chapter 16: Oracle Clusterware Diagnosis** **545**

Oracle Clusterware 545

    The Oracle Cluster Registry (OCR) 546

    The Oracle Local Registry (OLR) 547

    High Availability Service (HAS) 553

    The Cluster Synchronization Service (CSS) 556

    Cluster/Node Failures/Evictions.. 559

OCR Administration Utilities 570

   OCR Verification (ocrcheck) Utility 570

   OCR Configuration (ocrconfig) Utility 571

   OCR Dump (ocrdump) Utility 574

   Workshop.. 574

EVMD Verification 578

Grid Plug and Play 579

Monitoring Resource Utilization in the Cluster 582

   Step 1 583

   Step 2 583

   Step 3 583

Conclusion...583

■Chapter 17: Waits, Enqueues, and Latches..585

Latches...585

   Willing-to-Wait Mode.. 585

   No-Wait Mode 586

   Cache Buffers Chains 587

   gc element 591

   Redo Allocation 592

   Classes 593

Enqueues..596

   TX—Transaction 599

   TM—DML (Table)... 601

   ST—Space Management Transaction 601

   HW—Segment High Water Mark 601

   SQ—Sequence Number 602

   CF—Control File Transaction.. 603

Waits 603

   Consistent Read vs. Current 606

   Cluster Waits 607

   Mutex Waits 613

Conclusion 614

■ **Chapter 18: Problem Diagnosis** **615**

Health Monitor 615

   V$HM_CHECK 616

   Running Checks 617

   HM Using EM 621

Automatic Diagnostic Repository 622

   ADR Actions 623

   ADR Configuration 625

   Retention Policy 626

   Workshop—Monitoring Incidents and Problems.. 630

   SQL Test Case Builder 634

ORADEBUG Utility 638

Critical ORA Errors 643

   ORA-600: Internal error code, arguments: [...], [...]... 643

   ORA-7445: exception encountered core dump [...][...] 645

DBA Support Utilities 645

   Remote Diagnostic Agent (RDA) 645

   RAC DIAG 646

   ORACHK 646

   OLS 649

Conclusion 652

■ **Appendix A: The SQL Scripts Used in This Book** **653**

Chapter 3—Testing for Availability 653

Chapter 4—Testing for Scalability 653

Chapter 6—Tools and Utilities 654

Chapter 9—Tuning the Database 654

Chapter 11—Tuning Oracle Net 655

Chapter 12—Tuning the Storage Subsystem 655

Chapter 13—Tuning Global Cache 655

Chapter 14—Tuning the Cluster Interconnect..657

Chapter 15—Optimizing Distributed Workload 657

Chapter 17—Waits, Enqueues, and Latches 658

Chapter 18—Problem Diagnostics..658

■Bibliography 661

Index...665

About the Author

Murali Vallath has more than 25 years of IT experience, including over 20 years using Oracle products. Murali Vallath has in-depth experience in the IT segment. His work spans industries such as broadcasting, manufacturing, telephony and transportation logistics, finance, trading, and tools development. Vallath is no stranger to the software development life cycle; his solid understanding of IT covers requirement analysis, architecture, database design, application development, performance tuning, and implementation.

Vallath has been an Oracle ACE Director and is an Oracle Certified Database Administrator. He has worked on a variety of database platforms from small to very large implementations, designing databases for high volume, machine critical, real time online transaction processing (OLTP) systems. His expertise is with Oracle Real Application Clusters (RAC), and Vallath released his second book titled *Oracle 10g RAC, Grid, Services & Clustering* in March 2006 and has coauthored his third book, *Oracle Automatic Storage Management: Under-the-Hood & Practical Deployment Guide* (Automatic Storage Management [ASM]) November 2007, from Oracle Press.

Vallath has held several voluntary positions: (a) Founder, President of the All India Oracle Users Group (www.aioug.org), 2007–2014; (b) International Chair of the Oracle RAC SIG (special interest group), 2008–2010 (www.oracleracsig.org); (c) Founder and President of the Oracle RAC SIG, 2003–2008; (d) President of Charlotte Oracle Users Group (www.cltoug.org), 1998–2004; and (e) Contributing editor to the IOUG (Independent Oracle Users Group) *SELECT Journal*, 2006–2008. Vallath is known for his dedication and leadership. He has been an active participant in the Oracle Beta programs, including participating in the invitation-only IOUC Beta testing at the Oracle Head Quarters in Redwood Shores, CA.

Vallath is a regular speaker at industry conferences, including the Oracle Open World; Oracle Technology Network (OTN) Tours' UKOUG, AUSOUG, IOUG, and AIOUG on Oracle RAC; and Oracle RDBMS (Relational Database Management System) Performance and Tuning related topics. He has conducted several seminars across the four continents for Oracle University under the "Oracle Celebrity" series.

Vallath has successfully completed over 200 small-, medium-, and terabyte-sized RAC implementations (Oracle 9i, 10g, 11gR2, and 12cR1) for reputed corporate firms.

When Vallath is not working on complex databases or writing books, his hobbies include photography and playing on the tabla, an Indian instrument. Vallath maintains a technical blog of his Oracle RAC and ASM discoveries at www.muralivallath.com.

About the Technical Reviewer

Arup Nanda has been an Oracle database administrator (DBA) since 1993, dealing with everything from modeling to security, and has a lot of gray hairs to prove it. He has coauthored five books, written 500+ published articles, presented 300+ sessions, delivered training sessions in 22 countries, and actively blogs at arup.blogspot.com. He is an Oracle ACE Director, a member of Oak Table Network, an editor for *SELECT Journal* (the IOUG publication), and a member of the Board for Exadata SIG. Oracle awarded him the DBA of the Year in 2003 and Architect of the Year in 2012. He lives in Danbury, CT, with his wife Anu and son, Anish.

Acknowledgments

In James Patterson's book, *Suzanne's Dairy for Nicholas*, he writes on the importance of life and compares it to a game in which you are juggling five balls. "Imagine life is a game in which you are juggling five balls. The balls are called work, family, health, friends, and integrity. And you're keeping all of them in the air. But one day you finally come to understand that work is a rubber ball. If you drop it, it will bounce back. The other four balls…are made of glass. If you drop one of these, it will be irrevocably scuffed, nicked, perhaps even shattered." What a simple but valuable example for the importance of life and family values.

In spite of my assignments spread across different regions of the world or being actively involved in organizing events for the Oracle user group and having to be away for several weeks, my family has been very supportive during the periods of ups and downs of life. With all of these activities, the book project took a great hit in keeping up with the schedule, which meant spending even more time at home trying to complete it. I am beyond words in expressing my thanks to my wife Jaya and my two children, Grishma and Nabhas, for their patience and sacrifices during the unbelievable number of days we have missed each other either because I was away on some assignment, spending time for user groups, speaking at a conference, or working on my book at home. I love you all so much.

My parents have always been the inspiration to find new venues and opportunities to improve. My passion for being actively involved with user groups comes from my father, who has always shown my sister and me the right directions in life. They have taught us that giving back to society in ways possible within your circle of interest is important to make life complete. Thank you, achha and amma; you have provided the true light and directions: You just don't know how much you have helped me.

Many of the practical examples and outputs contained in this book are based on my troubleshooting and optimization projects. During this process, I have met with several intelligent minds whose knowledge and enthusiasm have always told me that education never stops and opportunities are endless. Life is short and is an everyday challenge because so much has to be learned in a short span. The book would be incomplete if I did not thank friends like Erik Petterson, Sar Maoz, Tom Kyte, Jonathan Lewis, Krishnadev Telikicherla, Srikanth Kalluri, K. Gopalakrishnan, Gopal Subramanian, P.S. Janakiram, Ganesh Jayaraman, Syed Ahmed, and Baldev Marepally, who have in several ways provided content to this book either in the form of knowledge sharing or by helping to conduct some of the tests required, or even more importantly by providing encouragement with their words: "this is a great thing you are doing for the Oracle community by sharing your knowledge." On many occasions, I have felt this book would not have been possible without Baldev's help. Every time I wanted a configuration to retest an issue for the workshops, he would have the server and environment available.

No matter how many years of experience you have in the field and how many problem-solving situations you have encountered, when dumping your thoughts into paper you need those extra eyes to make sure your thoughts are written down with accuracy. In a technical book, a small error could change the complete context give it a negative spin. Thanks to Michael Zoll from the RAC performance tuning team at Oracle, USA, for the informal reviews of the material during the very early phases of writing this book; and to Arup Nanda, who carries a wealth of knowledge in this Oracle technology space, for reviewing and providing criticism and suggestions to improve on the material.

All through this process, it has been the efforts and pursuance of Jonathan Hassell, Jonathan Gennick, Rita Fernando, Chris Nelson, and the entire team at Apress who have worked through different stages to make publishing the book even possible.

I am proud to have been involved in such an incredible project, and I hope my readers benefit from the efforts of so many to bring this book to life. Enjoy.

—Murali Vallath

Introduction

Working for several years across several industries on various RAC projects, there have been several occasions to troubleshoot performance issues in a production environment. Applications and databases that where moved from a single-instance Oracle environment to a two or more node RAC environment to hide a performance problem. An example that comes to mind, which I have encountered in the field on several occasions, is when the database was moved to a RAC environment because the single instance was running at 100% CPU and it was hoped that by moving to a RAC configuration, the 100% CPU overload would be distributed between the various instances in the cluster. This really does not happen this way; RAC cannot do magic to fix poorly written structured query language (SQL) statements or SQL statements that have not been optimized. The general best practice or rule of thumb to follow is when an application can scale from one CPU to multiple CPUs on a single node/instance configuration, it could potentially scale well in a RAC environment. The outcome of migrating applications that perform poorly to a RAC environment is to roll back to a single-instance configuration (by disabling the RAC/cluster parameters), testing/ tuning the application and identifying problem SQL statements, and when the application is found to successfully scale (after SQL statement tuning), it is moved to a RAC environment.

Moving to a RAC environment for the right reasons (namely, availability and scalability) should be done only when the application and environments that have been tested and proven to meet the goals. Almost always the reason for a RAC environment to crash on the third, fourth or sixth day after it's rolled into a production environment is lack of proper testing. This is either because testing was never considered as part of the project plan or because testing was not completed due to project schedule delays. Testing the application through the various phases discussed in this book helps identify the problem areas of the application; and tuning them helps eliminate the bottlenecks. Not always do we get an opportunity to migrate a single-instance Oracle database into a RAC environment. Not always is an existing RAC environment upgraded from one type of hardware configuration to another. What I am trying to share here is the luxury to test the application and the RAC environment to get the full potential happens only once before it's deployed into production. After this point, its primary production calls for poor response time, node evictions, high CPU utilization, faulty networks, chasing behind run of processes, and so on and so forth.

During the testing phase, taking the time to understand the functional areas of the application, how these functional areas could be grouped into database services, or mapping an application service to a database service would help place a single service or a group of services on an instance in the cluster. This would help in the distribution of workload by prioritizing system resources such as CPU, I/O, and so forth. This mapping could also help in availability partially by disabling a specific database service during a maintenance window when application changes need to be deployed into production, thus avoiding shutting down the entire database.

About This Book

The book is primarily divided into two sections: testing and tuning. In the testing section of the book, various phases of testing grouped under a process called "RAP" (Recovery, Availability, & Performance) have been defined. The second section discusses troubleshooting and tuning the problems. The style followed in the book is to use workshops through performance case studies across various components of a RAC environment.

Almost always, when a performance engineer is asked a question such as why the query is performing badly, or why the RAC environment is so slow, or why did the RAC instance crash, the expected answer should be "it depends." This is because there could be several pieces to the problem, and no one straight answer could be the reason. If the answers are all straight and if there is one reason to a problem, we would just need a Q&A book and we would not need the mind of a technical DBA to troubleshoot the issue. Maybe a parameter "ORACLE_GO_FASTER" (OGF) could be set and all the slow-performing queries and the database would run faster. Similar to the "it depends" answer, in this book I have tried to cover most of the common scenarios and problems that I have encountered in the field, there may or may not be a direct reference to the problem in your environment. However, it could give you a start in the right direction.

How to Use This Book

The chapters are written to follow one another in a logical fashion by introducing testing topics in the earlier chapters and building on them to performance and troubleshooting various components of the cluster. Thus, it is advised that you read the chapters in order. Even if you have worked with clustered databases, you will certainly find a nugget or two that could be an eye opener.

Throughout the book, examples in the form of workshops are provided with outputs, followed by discussions and analysis into problem solving.

The book contains the following chapters:

Chapter 1—Methodology

Performance tuning is considered an art and more recently a science. However, it is definitely never a gambling game where guesswork and luck are the main methods of tuning. Rather, tuning should be backed by reasons, and scientific evidence should be the determining factor. In this chapter, we discuss methodologies to approach performance tuning of the Oracle database in a precise, controlled method to help obtain successful results.

Chapter 2—Capacity Planning and Architecture

Before starting the testing phase, it is important to understand how RAC works, how the various components of the architecture communicate with each other. How many users and workload can a clustered solution handle? What is the right capacity of a server? The cluster that is currently selected may be outgrown due to increased business or high data volume or other factors. In this chapter, we discuss how to measure and ascertain the capacity of the systems to plan for the future.

Chapter 3—Testing for Availability

The primary reason for purchasing a RAC configuration is to provide availability. Whereas availability is the immediate requirement of the organization, scalability is to satisfy future needs when the business grows. When one or more instances fail, the others should provide access to the data, providing continuous availability within a data center. Similarly, when access to the entire data center or the clustered environment is lost, availability should be provided by a standby location. When components fail, one needs to ensure that the redundant component is able to function without any hiccups. In this chapter, we cover just that:

- Testing for failover
- Simulating failover
- Test criteria to be adopted
- User failover
- Tuning the failover to achieve maximum availability

Chapter 4—Testing for Scalability

One of the primary reasons in purchasing a RAC configuration is to provide scalability to the environment. However, such scalability is not achievable unless the hardware and the application tiers are scalable. Meaning that unless the hardware itself is scalable, the application or database cannot scale. In this chapter, we discuss the methods to be used to test the hardware and application for scalability:

- Testing for data warehouse
- Testing for OLTP
- Testing for mixed workload systems
- Operating system parameter tuning
- Diagnosis and problem solving at the hardware level
- Verification of the RAC configuration at the hardware and O/S levels
- Using tools such as SwingBench, Hammerora, and other utilities

Chapter 5—Real Application Testing

Once the hardware has been tested and found to be scalable, the next step is to ensure that the application will scale in this new RAC environment. Keeping the current production numbers and the hardware scalability numbers as a baseline, one should test the application using the database replay feature of the RAT tool to ensure that the application will also scale in this new RAC environment.

Chapter 6—Tools and Utilities

There are several tools to help tune an Oracle database, tools that are bundled with the Oracle RDBMS product and others that are provided by third party vendors. In this chapter, we discuss some of the key tools and utilities that would help the database administrators and the performance analysts. A few of the popular tools are Oracle Enterprise Cloud Control, SQLT (SQL Trace), AWR (Automatic Workload Repository), AWR Warehouse, ASH (Active Session History), and ADDM (Automatic Database Diagnostic Monitor).

Chapter 7—SQL Tuning

The application communicates with the database using SQL statements. This includes both storage and retrieval. If the queries are not efficient and tuned to retrieve and or store data efficiently, it directly reflects on the performance of the application. In this chapter, we go into detail on the principles of writing and tuning efficient SQL statements, usage of hints to improve performance, and selection and usage of the right indexes. Some of the areas that this chapter will cover are the following:

- Reducing physical IO
- Reducing logical IO
- Tuning based on wait events
- Capturing trace to analyze query performance
- SQL tuning advisory
- AWR and ADDM reports for query tuning in a RAC environment

Chapter 8—Parallel Query Tuning

Queries could be executed sequentially in which a query attaches to the database as one process and retrieves all the data in a sequential manner. They could also be executed using multiple processes and using a parallel method to retrieve all the required data. Parallelism could be on a single instance in which multiple CPUs will be used to retrieve the required data or by taking advantage of more than one instance (in a RAC environment) to retrieve data. In this chapter, we cover the following:

- Parallel queries on a single node

- Parallel queries across multiple nodes

- Optimizing parallelism

- Tracing parallel operations

- Parameters to tune for parallel operations

- SQL tuning advisory

- AWR and ADDM reports for parallel query tuning in a RAC environment

Chapter 9—Tuning the Database

The database cache area is used by Oracle to store rows fetched from the database so that subsequent requests for the same information is readily available. Data is retained in the cache based on the usage. In this chapter, we discuss efficient tuning of the shared cache, the pros and cons of logical I/O operations versus physical I/O operations, and how to tune the cache area to provide the best performance. In this chapter, we discuss some of the best practices to be used when designing databases for a clustered environment.

Chapter 10—Tuning Recovery

No database is free from failures; RAC that supports multiple instances is a solution for high availability and scalability. Every instance in a RAC environment is also prone for failures. When an instance fails in a RAC configuration, another instance that detects the failure performs the recovery operation. Similarly, the RAC database also can fail and have to be recovered. In this chapter, we discuss the tuning of the recovery operations.

Chapter 11—Tuning Oracle Net

The application communicates with the database via SQL statements; these statements send and receive information from the database using the Oracle Net interface provided by Oracle. Depending on the amount of information received and sent via the Oracle Net layer, there could be a potential performance hurdle. In this chapter, we discuss tuning the Oracle Net interface. This includes tuning the listener, TNS (transparent network substrate), and SQL Net layers.

Chapter 12—Tuning the Storage Subsystem

RAC is an implementation of Oracle in which two or more instances share a single copy of the physical database. This means that the database and the storage devices that provide the infrastructure should be available for access from all the instances participating in the configuration. Efficiency of the database to support multiple instances depends on a good storage subsystem and an appropriate partitioning strategy. In this chapter, we look into the performance measurements that could be applied in tuning the storage subsystem.

Chapter 13—Tuning Global Cache

Whereas the interconnect provides the mechanism for the transfer of information between the instances, the sharing of resources is managed by Oracle cache fusion technology. All instances participating in the clustered configuration share data resident in the local cache of one instance with other process on other instances. Locking, past images, current images, recovery, and so forth normally involved in a single-instance level can also present at a higher level across multiple instances. In this chapter, we discuss tuning of the global cache.

Chapter 14—Tuning the Cluster Interconnect

The cluster interconnect provides the communication link between two or more nodes participating in a clustered configuration. Oracle utilizes the cluster interconnect for interinstance communication and sharing of data in the respective caches of the instance. This means that this tier should perform to its maximum potential, providing efficient communication of data between instances. In this chapter, we discuss the tuning of the cluster interconnect.

Chapter 15—Optimization of Distributed Workload

One of the greatest features introduced in Oracle 10g is the distributed workload functionality. With this databases can be consolidated; and by using services options, several applications could share an existing database configuration utilizing resources when other services are not using them. Efficiency of the environment is obtained by automatically provisioning services when resources are in demand and automatically provisioning instances when an instance in a cluster or server pool is not functioning.

Chapter 16—Tuning the Oracle Clusterware

Oracle's RAC architecture places considerable dependency on the cluster manager of the operating system. In this chapter, we discuss tuning the various Oracle clusterware components:

- Analysis activities performed by the clusterware

- Performance diagnosis for the various clusterware components, including ONS (Oracle notification services), EVMD (Event Manager Daemon), and LISTENER

- Analysis of AWR, ADDM reports and OS-level tools to tune the Oracle clusterware

- Debugging and tracing clusterware activity for troubleshooting clusterware issues

Chapter 17—Enqueues, Waits, and Latches

When tuned and optimized SQL statements are executed, there are other types of issues such as contention, concurrency, locking, and resource availability that could cause applications to run slow and provide slow response times to the users. Oracle provides instrumentation into the various categories of resource levels and provides methods of interpreting them. In this chapter, we look at some of these critical statistics that would help optimize the database. By discussing enqueues, latches, and waits specific to a RAC environment, in this chapter we drill into the contention, concurrency, and scalability tuning of the database.

Chapter 18—Problem Diagnosis

To help the DBA troubleshoot issues with the environment, Oracle provides utilities that help gather statistics across all instances. Most of the utilities that focus on database performance-related statistics were discussed in Chapter 5. There are other scripts and utilities that collect statistics and diagnostic information to help troubleshoot and get to the root cause of problems. The data gathered through these utilities will help diagnose where the potential problem could be. In this chapter, we discuss the following:

- Health monitor

- Automatic Diagnostic Repository

Appendix A—The SQL Scripts Used in This Book

The appendix provides a quick reference to all the scripts used and referenced in the book.

CHAPTER 1

■ ■ ■

Methodology

Performance tuning is a wide subject, probably a misunderstood subject; so it has become a common practice among technologists and application vendors to regard performance as an issue that can be safely left for a tuning exercise performed at the end of a project or system implementation. This poses several challenges, such as delayed project deployment, performance issues unnoticed and compromised because of delayed delivery of applications for performance optimization, or even the entire phase of performance optimization omitted due to delays in the various stages of the development cycle. Most important, placing performance optimization at the end of a project life cycle basically reduces opportunities for identifying bad design and poor algorithms in implementation. Seldom do they realize that this could lead to potentially rewriting certain areas of the code that are poorly designed and lead to poor performance.

Irrespective of a new product development effort or an existing product being enhanced to add additional functionality, performance optimization should be considered from the very beginning of a project and should be part of the requirements definition and integrated into each stage of the development life cycle. As modules of code are developed, each unit should be iteratively tested for functionality and performance. Such considerations would make the development life cycle smooth, and performance optimization could follow standards that help consistency of application code and result in improved integration, providing efficiency and performance.

There are several approaches to tuning a system. Tuning could be approached artistically like a violinist who tightens the strings to get the required note, where every note is carefully tuned with the electronic tuner to ensure that every stroke matches. Similarly, the performance engineer or database administrator (DBA) could take a more scientific or methodical approach to tuning. A methodical approach based on empirical data and evidence is a most suitable method of problem solving, like a forensic method that a crime investigation officer would use. Analysis should be backed by evidence in the form of statistics collected at various levels and areas of the system:

- From functional units of the application that are performing slowly

- During various times (business prime time) of the day when there is a significant user workload

- From heavily used functional areas of the application, and so forth

The data collected would help to understand the reasons for the slowness or poor performance because there could be one or several reasons why a system is slow. Slow performance could be due to bad configuration, unoptimized or inappropriately designed code, undersized hardware, or several other reasons. Unless there is unequivocal evidence of why performance is slow, the scientific approach to finding the root cause of the problem should be adopted. The old saying that "tuning a computer system is an art" may be true when you initially configure a system using a standard set of required parameters suggested by Oracle from the installation guides; but as we go deeper into testing a more scientific approach of data collection, mathematical analysis and reasoning must be adopted because tuning should not be considered a hit-or-miss situation: it is to be approached in a rigorous scientific manner with supporting data.

Problem-solving tasks of any nature need to be approached in a systematic and methodical manner. A detailed procedure needs to be developed and followed from end to end. During every step of the process, data should be collected and analyzed. Results from these steps should be considered as inputs into the next step, which in turn is performed in a similar step-by-step approach. A methodology should be defined to perform the operations in a rigorous manner. Methodology (*a body of methods, rules, and postulates employed by a discipline: a particular procedure or set of procedures*) is the procedure or process followed from start to finish, from identification of the problem to problem solving and documentation. A methodology developed and followed should be a procedure or process that is repeatable as a whole or in increments through iterations.

During all of these steps or iterations, the causes or reasons for a behavior or problem should be based on quantitative analysis and not on guesswork. Every system deployed into production has to grow in the process of a regression method of performance testing to determine poorly performing units of the application. During these tests, the test engineer would measure and obtain baselines and optimize the code to achieve the performance numbers or service-level agreements (SLA) requirements defined by the business analysts.

Performance Requirements

As with any functionality and business rule, performance needs are also (to be) defined as part of business requirements. In organizations that start small, such requirements may be minimal and may be defined by user response and feedback after implementation. However, as the business grows and when the business analyst defines changes or makes enhancements to the business requirements, items such as entities, cardinalities, and the expected response time requirements in use cases should also be defined. Performance requirements are every bit as important as functional requirements and should be explicitly identified at the earliest possible stage. However, too often, the system requirements will specify what the system must do, without specifying how fast it should do it.

When these business requirements are translated into entity models, business processes, and test cases, the cardinalities, that is, the expected instances (aka records) of a business object and required performance levels should be incorporated into the requirements analysis and the modelling of the business functions to ensure these numbers could be achieved. Table 1-1 is a high-level requirement of a direct-to-home broadcasting system that plans to expand its systems based on the growth patterns observed over the years.

Table 1-1. Business Requirements

Entity	Current Count	Maximum Count	Maximum Read Access (trans/sec)	Maximum Update Access (trans/sec)	Average Growth Rate (per year)
Smartcards	16,750,000	90,000,000	69	73	4,250,000
Products	43,750,000	150,000,000	65	65	21,250,000
Transmission logs	400,000 records/day	536,000,000	N/A	138	670,000,000
Report back files	178,600 records/day	390,000,000 records processed/year	N/A	N/A	550,000,000

Note: trans/sec. = transactions per second; N/A = not applicable.

1. It will store for 15 million subscriber accounts.

2. Four smart cards will be stored per subscriber account.

3. Average growth rate is based on the maximum number of active smart cards.

4. The peak time for report back transactions is from midnight to 2 AM.

5. Peak times for input transactions are Monday and Friday afternoons from 3 PM to 5 PM.

6. The number of smart cards is estimated to double in 3 years.

Based on an 18-hour day (peak time = 5 times average rate), today 3.5 messages are processed per second. This is projected to increase over the next 2 years to 69 messages per second.

Table 1-1 gives a few requirements that help in

1. sizing the database (Requirement 1 and 6);

2. planning on the layout of the application to database access (Requirement 5); and

3. allocation of resources (Requirements 4 and 5).

These requirements with the expected transaction rate per second helps the performance engineer to work toward a goal.

It's a truism that errors made during requirements definition are the most expensive to fix in production and that *missing* requirements are the hardest requirements errors to correct. That is, of all the quality defects that might make it into a production system, those that occur because a requirement was unspecified are the most critical. To avoid these surprises, the methodology should take into consideration testing the application code in iterations from complex code to the least complex code and step-by-step integration of modules when the code is optimal.

Missing detailed requirements lead to missing test cases: if we don't identify a requirement, we are unlikely to create a performance test case for the requirement. Therefore, application problems caused by missing requirements are rarely discovered prior to the application being deployed.

During performance testing, we should create test cases to measure performance of every critical component and module interfacing with the database. If the existing requirements documents do not identify the performance requirements for a business-critical operation, they should be flagged as "missing requirement" and refuse to pass the operation until the performance requirement is fully identified and is helpful in creating a performance test case.

In many cases, we expect a computer system to produce the same outputs when confronted with the same inputs—this is the basis for most test automation. However, the inputs into a routine can rarely be completely controlled. The performance of a given transaction will be affected by

- The number of rows of data in the database

- Other activity on the host machine that might be consuming CPU, memory, or performing disk input/output (I/O)

- The contents of various memory caches—including both database and operating system (O/S) cache (and sometimes client-side cache)

- Other activity on the network, which might affect network round-trip time

Unless there is complete isolation of the host that supports the database and the network between the application client (including the middle tier if appropriate), you are going to experience variation in application performance.

Therefore, it's usually best to define and measure performance taking this variation into account. For instance, transaction response times maybe expressed in the following terms:

1. In 99% of cases, Transaction X should complete within 5 seconds.

2. In 95% of cases, Transaction X should complete within 1 second.

The end result of every performance requirement is to provide throughput and response times to various user requests.

Within the context of the business requirements the key terminologies used in these definitions should also be defined: for instance, 95% of cases; Transaction X should complete within 1 second. What's a transaction in this context? Is it the time it takes to issue the update statement? Or is it the time it takes for the user to enter something and press the "update" or "commit" button? Or yet, is it the entire round-trip time between the user pressing the "OK" button and the database completing the operation saving or retrieving the data successfully and returning the final results back to the user?

Early understanding of the concepts and terminology along with the business requirements helps all stack holders of the project to have the same viewpoint, which helps in healthy discussions on the subject.

- *Throughput*: Number of requests processed by the database over a period of time normally measured by number of transactions per second.

- *Response time*: Responsiveness of the database or application to provide the requests results over a stipulated period of time, normally measured in seconds.

In database performance terms, the response time could be measured as database time or db time. This is the amount of time spent by the session at the database tier performing operations and in the process of completing its operation, waiting for resources such as CPU, disk I/O, and so forth.

Tuning the System

Structured tuning starts by normalizing the application workload and then reducing any application contention. After that is done, we try to reduce physical I/O requirements by optimizing memory caching. Only when all of that is done do we try to optimize physical I/O itself.

Step 1: Optimizing Workload

There are different types of workloads:

- Workloads that have small quick transactions returning one or few rows back to the requestor

- Workloads that return a large number of rows (sequential range scan of the database) back to the requestor

- A mixed workload where the users sometimes request for small random rows; however, they can also request a large number of rows

The expectations are for applications to provide good response to various types of workloads. Optimization of database servers should be in par with the workloads they can support. Overcomplicating the tuning effort to extract the most out of the servers may not give sufficient results. Therefore, before looking at resource utilization such as memory, disk I/O, or upgrading hardware, it's important to ensure that the application is making optimal demands on the database server. This involves finding and tuning the persistence layer consuming excessive resources. Only after this layer is tuned should the database or O/S level tuning be considered.

Step 2: Finding and Eliminating Contention

Most applications making requests to the database will perform database I/O or network requests, and in the process of doing this consumes CPU resources. However, if there is contention for resources within the database, the database and its resources may not scale well. Most database contention could be determined using Oracle's wait interface by querying V$SESSION, V$SESSION_WAIT, V$SYSTEM_WAIT, V$EVENT_NAME, and V$STATNAME. High wait events related to latches and buffers should be minimized. Most wait events in a single instance (non-Real Application Clusters [RAC]) configuration represent contention issues that will be visible in RAC as global events, such as global cache gc buffer busy. Such issues should be treated as single instance issues and should be fixed before moving the application to a RAC configuration.

■ **Note**   Oracle wait interface is discussed in Chapters 6, 8, and 17.

Step 3: Reduce Physical I/O

Most database operations involve disk I/Os, and it can be an expensive operation relative to the speed of the disk and other I/O components used on the server. Processing architectures have three major areas that would require or demand a disk I/O operation:

1. A logical read by a query or session does not find data in the cache and hence has to perform a disk I/O because the buffer cache is smaller than the working set.

2. SORT and JOIN operations cannot be performed in memory and need to spill to the TEMP table space on disk.

3. Sufficient memory is not found in the buffer cache, resulting in the buffers being prematurely written to disk; it is not able to take advantage of the lazy writing operation.

Optimizing physical I/O (PIO) or disk I/O operations is critical to achieve good response times. For disk I/O intensive operations, high-speed storage or using storage management solutions such as Automatic Storage Management (ASM) will help optimize PIO.

Step 4: Optimize Logical I/O

Reading from a buffer cache is faster compared to reading from a physical disk or a PIO operation. However, in Oracle's architecture, high logical I/O (LIOs) is not so inexpensive that it can be ignored. When Oracle needs to read a row from buffer, it needs to place a lock on the row in buffer. To obtain a lock, Oracle has to request a latch; for instance, in the case of a consistent read (CR) request, a latch on buffer chains has to be obtained. To obtain a latch, Oracle has to depend on the O/S. The O/S has limitations on how many latches can be made available at a given point in time. The limited number of latches are shared by a number of processes. When the requested latch is not available, the process will go into a sleep state and after a few nanoseconds will try for the latch again. Every time a latch is requested there is no grantee that the requesting process may be successful in getting the latch and may have to go into a sleep state again. The frequent trying to obtain a latch leads to high CPU utilization on the host server and cache buffer chains latch contention as sessions try to access the same blocks. When Oracle has to scan a large number of rows in the buffer to retrieve only a few rows that meet the search criteria, this can prove costly. LIO should be reduced as much as possible for efficient use of CPU and other resources. In a RAC environment this becomes even more critical because there are multiple instances in the cluster, and each instance may perform a similar kind of operation. For example, another user maybe executing the very same statement retrieving the same set of rows and may experience the same kind of contention. In the overall performance of the RAC, environment will indicate high CPU usage across the cluster.

■ **Note**   LIO is discussed in Chapter 7 and Latches are discussed in Chapter 17.

Methodology

Problem-solving tasks of any nature need to be approached in a systematic and methodical manner. A detailed procedure needs to be developed and followed from end to end. During every step of the process, data should be collected and analyzed. Results from these steps should be considered as inputs into the next step, which in turn is performed in a similar systematic approach. Hence, methodology is the procedure or process followed from start to finish, from identification of the problem to problem solving and documentation.

During all this analysis, the cause or reasons for a behavior or problem should be based on quantitative analysis and not on guesswork or trial and error.

USING DBMS_ APPLICATION INFO

A feature that could help during all the phases of testing, troubleshooting, and debugging of the application is the use of the DBMS_APPLICATION_INFO package in the application code. The DBMS_APPLICATION_INFO package has procedures that will allow modularizing performance data collection based on specific modules or areas within modules.

Incorporating the DBMS_APPLICATION_INFO package into the application code helps the administrators to easily track the sections of the code (module/action) that are high resource consumers. When the user/application session registers a database session, the information is recorded in V$SESSION and V$SQLAREA. This helps in easy identification of the problem areas of the application.

The application should set the name of the module and name of the action automatically each time a user enters that module. The name given to the module could be the name of the code segment in an Oracle pre-compiler application or service within the Java application. The action name should usually be the name or description of the current transaction within a module.

Procedures

Procedure	Description
SET_CLIENT_INFO	Sets the CLIENT_INFO field of the session.
SET_MODULE	Sets the name of the module that is currently running.
SET ACTION	Sets the name of the current action within the current module.
SET_SESSION_LONGOPS	Sets a row in the GV$SESSION_LONGOPS table.

When the application connects to the database using a database service name (either using a Type 4 client or a Type 2 client) then even a granular level of resource utilization for a given service, module, and/or action could be collected. Database service names are also recorded in GV$SESSION.

One of the great benefits of enabling the DBMS_APPLICATION_INFO package call in the application code is that the database performance engineer can enable statistics collection or enable tracing when he/she feels it's needed and at what level it's needed.

Methodologies could be different depending on the work involved. There could be methodologies for

- Development life cycle
- Migration
- Testing
- Performance tuning

Performance Tuning Methodology

The performance tuning methodology can be broadly categorized into seven steps.

Problem Statement

Identify or state the specific problem in hand. This could be different based on the type of application and the phase of the development life cycle. When a new code is being deployed into production, the problem statement is to meet the requirements for response time and transaction per second and the recovery time. The business analysts, as we have discussed earlier, define these requirements. Furthermore, based on the type of requirement being validated, the scope may require some additional infrastructure such as data guard configuration for disaster recovery.

On the other hand, if the code is already in production, then the problem statement could be made in terms of slow response time that the users have been complaining about; a dead lock situation that has been encountered in your production environment; an instance in a RAC configuration that crashes frequently, and so forth.

A clear definition of the tuning objective is a very important step in the methodology because it basically defines what is going to be achieved in the testing phase or test plan that is being prepared.

Information Gathering

Gather all information relating to the problem identified in step one. This depends on the problem being addressed. If this is a new development rollout, the information gathering will be centered on the business requirements, the development design, entity model of the database, the database sizing, the cardinality of the entities, the SLA requirements, and so forth. If this is an existing application that is already in production, the information-gathering phase may be around collecting statistics, trace, log, or other information. It is important to understand the environment, the configuration, and the circumstances around the performance problem. For instance, when a user complains of poor performance, it may be a good idea to interview the user. The interview can consist of several levels to understanding the issue.

What kind of functional area of the application was used, and at what time of the day was the operation performed? Was this consistently occurring every time during the same period in the same part of the application (it is possible that there was another contending application at that time, which may be the cause of the slow performance)? This information will help in collecting data pertaining to that period of the day and will also help in analyzing data from different areas of the applications, other applications that access the database, or even applications that run on the same servers.

Once user-level information is gathered, it may be useful to understand the configuration and environment in general:

- Does the application use database services? Is the service running as SINGLETON on one instance or more than one instance (UNIFORM)? What other services are running on these servers?
- Is the cluster configured to use server pools?
- What resource plans have been implemented to prioritize the application (if any)?

Similarly, if the problem statement is around the instance or node crashing frequently in a RAC environment, the information that has to be gathered is centered on the RAC cluster:

- Collecting data from the /var/log/messages from the system administrators

- Adding additional debug flags to the cluster services to gather additional information in the various GRID (Cluster Ready Services [CRS]) infrastructure log files and so forth

In Oracle Database 11g Release 2, and recently in Oracle Database 12c Release 1, there are several additional components added to the clusterware, which means several more log files (illustrated in Figure 1-1) to look into when trying to identify reasons for problems.

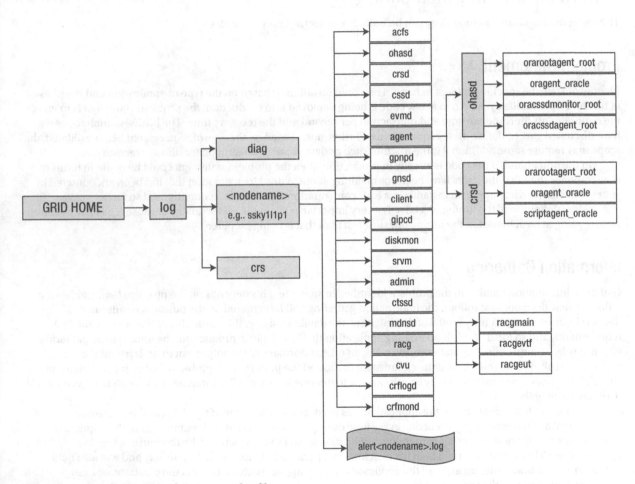

Figure 1-1. *Oracle 11g R2 grid component log files*

Area Identification

Once the information concerning the performance issue is gathered, the next step is to identify the area of the application system that is reported to have a performance issue. Most of the time, the information gathered during the previous step of the methodology is sufficient. However, this may require a fine-grained look at the data and statistics collected.

If the issue was with the instance or a server crashing in the RAC environment, data related to specific modules, such as the interconnect, data related to the heartbeat verification via the interconnect, and the heartbeat verification against the voting disks have to be collected. For example, a detailed look at the data in the GRID infrastructure log files may have to be analyzed after enabling debug (crsctl debug log css "CSSD:9") to get the clusterware to write more data into these log files. If this is a performance-related concern, then collecting data using a trace from the user session would be really helpful in analyzing the issue. Tools such as Lightweight Onboard Monitor (LTOM[1]), or at the minimum collecting trace using event 10046, would be really helpful.

Several times instance or server crashes in a RAC environment could be due to overload on the system affecting the overall performance of the system. In these situations, the directions could shift to availability or stability of the cluster. However, the root cause analysis may indicate other reasons.

Area Drilldown

Drilling down further to identify the cause or area of a performance issue is probably the most critical of the steps because with all the data collected, it's time to drill down to the actual reason that has led to the problem. Irrespective of whether this is an instance/server crash because of overload or poorly performing module or application, the actual problem should be identified at this stage and documented. For example, what query in the module or application is slowing down the process, or is there a contention caused by another application (batch) that is causing the online application to slow down?

At this level of drilldown, the details of the application area need to be identified: what service, what module, and what action was the reason for this slowness. To get this level of detail, the DBMS_APPLICATION_INFO package discussed earlier is a very helpful feature.

Problem Resolution

Working to resolve the performance issue is probably the most critical step. When resolving problems, database parameters may have to be changed, host bus adaptor (HBA) controllers or networks or additional infrastructure such as CPU or memory may have to be added, or maybe it all boils down to tuning a bad performing structured query language (SQL) query, or making sure that the batch application does not run in the same time frame as the primary online application, or even better if the workload can be distributed using database services to reduce resource contention on any one server/instance causing poor response times. It is important that when fixing problems the entire application is taken into consideration; making fixes to help one part of the application should not affect the other parts of the application.

Testing Against Baseline

Once the problem identified has been fixed and unit tested, the code is integrated with the rest of the application and tested to see if the performance issue has been resolved. In the case of hardware related changes or fixes, such a test may be very hard to verify; however, if the fix is done over the weekend or during a maintenance window, the application could be tested to ensure it is not broken due to these changes. Depending on the complexity of the situation and maintenance window available, it will drive how extensive these tests can be. Here is a great benefit of using database services that allow disabling usage of a certain server or database instance from regular usage or allowing limited access to certain part of the application functionality, which could be tested using an instance or workload until such time as it's tested and available for others to use.

---

[1]Usage and implementation of LTOM will be discussed in Chapter 6.

Repeating the Process

Now that the identified problem has been resolved, it's time to look at the next issue or problem reported. As discussed, the methodology should be repeatable through all the cases. Methodology also calls for documentation and storing the information in a repository for future review, education, and analysis.

Whereas each of the previous steps is very broad, a methodical approach will help identify and solve the problem in question, namely, performance.

Which area of the system is having a performance problem? Where do we start? Should the tuning process start with the O/S, network, database, instance, or the application? Probably the users of the application tier are complaining that the system is slow. Users access the application, and the application in turn through some kind of persistence layer communicates to the database to store and retrieve information. When the user who makes the data request using an application does not get a response in a sufficiently fair amount of time, they complain that the system is slow.

Although the top-down methodology of tuning the application and then looking at other components works most of the time, sometimes one may have to adopt a bottom-up approach: that is, starting with the hardware platform, tuning the storage subsystem, tuning the database configuration, tuning the instance, and so forth. Addressing the performance issues using this approach could bring some amount of change or performance improvement to the system with less or no impact to the actual application code. If the application is poorly written (for example, a bad SQL query), it does not matter how much tuning is done at the bottom tier; the underlying issue will remain the same.

The top-down or bottom-up methodology just discussed is good for an already existing production application that needs to be tuned. This is true for several reasons:

1. Applications have degraded in performance due to new functionality that was not sufficiently tuned.

2. The user base has increased and the current application does not support the extended user base.

3. The volume of data in the underlying database has increased; however, the storage has not changed to accept the increased I/O load.

Whereas these are issues with an existing application and database residing on existing hardware, a more detailed testing and tuning methodology should be adopted when migrating from a single instance to a clustered database environment. Before migrating the actual application and production enabling the new hardware, the following basic testing procedure should be adopted.

Testing of the RAC environment should start with tuning a single instance configuration. Only when the performance characteristics of the application are satisfactory should the tuning on the clustered configuration begin. To perform these tests, all nodes in the cluster except one should be shut down and the single instance node should be tuned. Only after the single instance has been tuned and the appropriate performance measurements equal to the current configuration or more are obtained should the next step of tuning be started. Tuning the cluster should be done methodically by adding one instance at a time to the mix. Performance should be measured in detail to ensure that the expected scalability and availability is obtained. If such performance measurements are not obtained, the application should not be deployed into production, and only after the problem areas are identified and tuned should deployment occur.

■ **Note** RAC cannot perform any magic to bring performance improvements to an application that is already performing poorly on a single instance configuration.

■ **Caution**   The rule of thumb is if the application cannot scale on a single instance configuration when the number of CPUs on the server is increased from two to four to eight, the application will not scale in a RAC environment. On the other hand, due the additional overhead that RAC gives, such as latency of interconnect, global cache management, and so forth, such migration will negate performance.

Getting to the Obvious

Not always do we have the luxury of troubleshooting the application for performance issues when the code is written and before it is taken into production. Sometimes it is code that is already in production and in extensive use that has performance issues. In such situations, maybe a different approach to problem solving may be required. The application tier could be a very broad area and could have many components, with all components communicating through the same persistence layer to the Oracle database. To get to the bottom of the problem, namely, performance, each area of the application needs to be examined and tuned methodically because it may be just one user accessing a specific area of the application that is causing the entire application to slow down. To differentiate the various components, the application may need to be divided into smaller areas.

Divide Into Quadrants

One approach toward a very broad problem is to divide the application into quadrants, starting with the most complex area in the first quadrant (most of the time the most complex quadrant or the most commonly used quadrant is also the worst-performing quadrant), followed by the area that is equally or less complex in the second quadrant, and so on. However, depending on how large the application is and how many areas of functionality the application covers, these four broad areas may not be sufficient. If this were the case, the next step would be to break each of the complex quadrants into four smaller quadrants or functional areas. This second level of breakdown does not need to be done for all the quadrants from the first level and can be limited to only the most complex ones. After this second level of breakdown, the most complex or the worst performing functionality of the application that fits into the first quadrant is selected for performance testing.

Following the methodology listed previously, and through an iterative process, each of the smaller quadrants and the functionality described in the main quadrant will have to be tested. Starting with the first quadrant, the various areas of the application will be tuned; and when the main or more complex or most frequently used component has been tuned, the next component in line is selected and tuned. Once all four quadrants have been visited, the process starts all over again. This is because after the first pass, even though the findings of the first quadrant were validated against the components in the other quadrants, when performance of all quadrants improves, the first quadrant continues to show performance degradation and probably has room to grow.

Figure 1-2 illustrates the quadrant approach of dividing the application for a systematic approach to performance tuning. The quadrants are approached in a clockwise pattern, with the most critical or worst performing piece of the application occupying Quadrant 1. Although intensive tuning may not be the goal of every iteration in each quadrant, based on the functionality supported and the amount of processing combined with the interaction with other tiers, it may have room for further tuning or may have areas that are not present in the component of the first quadrant and hence may be a candidate for further tuning.

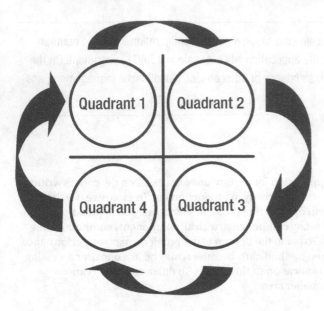

Figure 1-2. *Quadrant approach*

Now that we have identified which component of the application needs immediate attention, the next step would be, where do we start? How do we get to the numbers that will show us where the problem exists? There are several methods to do this. One is a method that some of us would have used in the old days: embedding times calls (timestamp) in various parts of the code and logging them when the code is executed to a log file. From the timestamp outputs in the log files, it would provide analysis of the various areas of the application that are consuming the largest execution times. Another method, if the application design was well thought out, would be to allow the database administrator to capture performance metrics at the database level by including DBMS_APPLICATION_INFO definitions (discussed earlier) of identifying modules and actions within the code; this could help easily identify which action in the code is causing the application to slow down.

Obviously the most important piece is where the rubber meets the road. Hence, in the case of an application that interacts with the database, the first step would be to look into the persistence layer. The database administrator could do this by tracing the database calls.

The database administrator can create trace files at the session level using the DBMS_MONITOR.SESSION_TRACE_ENABLE procedure. For example

```
SQL> exec dbms_monitor.session_trace_enable(session_id=>276,
                                serial_num =>1449,
                                waits=>TRUE,
                                binds=>TRUE);
```

The trace file will be located in the USER_DUMP_DEST directory. The physical location of the trace file can be obtained by checking the value of the parameter (or by querying V$PARAMETER):

```
SQL> SHOW PARAMETER USER_DUMP_DEST
```

Once the required session has been traced, the trace can be disabled using the following:

```
SQL> exec dbms_monitor.session_trace_disable(session_id=>276,
                                 serial_num =>1449,
                                 waits=>TRUE,
                                 binds=>TRUE);
```

From a database tuning perspective, the persistence layer would be the first layer to which considerable attention should be given. However, areas that do not have any direct impact on the database such as application partitioning, looking at the configuration of the application server (e.g., Web Logic, Oracle AS, Web Sphere, and so forth).

Tuning the various parameters of the application tier, such as the number of connections, number of threads, or queue sizes of the application server, could also be looked at.

The persistence layer is the tier that interacts with the database and comprises SQL statements, which communicate with the database to store and retrieve information based on users' requests. These SQL statements depend on the database, its tables, and other objects that it contains and store data to respond to the requests.

Looking at Overall Database Performance

It's not uncommon to find that database performance overall is unsatisfactory during performance testing or even in production.

When all database operations are performing badly, it can be the result of a number of factors, some interrelated in a complex and unpredictable fashion. It's usually best to adopt a structured tuning methodology at this point to avoid concentrating your tuning efforts on items that turn out to be symptoms rather than causes. For example, excessive I/O might be due to poor memory configuration; it's therefore important to tune memory configuration before attempting to tune I/O.

Oracle Unified Method

Oracle Unified Method (OUM) is life cycle management process for information technology available from Oracle. Over the years the methodology that is being used in IT has been the waterfall methodology. In the waterfall method, each stage follows the other. Although this method has been implemented and is being used widely, it follows a top-down approach and does not allow flexibility with changes. In this methodology, one stage of the process starts after the previous stage has completed.

OUM follows an iterative and incremental method for IT life cycle management, meaning iterate through each stage of the methodology, each time improving the quality compared to the previous run. However, while iterating through the process, the step to the next stage of the process is in increments.

Figure 1-3 illustrates the five phases of IT project management: inception, elaboration, construction, transition, and production. As illustrated in Figure 1-3, at the end of each phase there should be a defined milestone that needs to be achieved or met:

- The milestone during the Inception phase is to have a clear definition of life cycle objectives (LO).

- The milestone during the Elaboration phase is to have a clear understanding of the life cycle architecture (LA) that would help build the system.

- The milestone during the Construction phase is to have the initial operational capability (IOC) has been reached.

- The goal or milestone of the Transition phase is to have the System ready for production (SP).

- To milestone of the Production phase is to ensure the system is deployed and a signoff (SO) from the customer or end user is obtained.

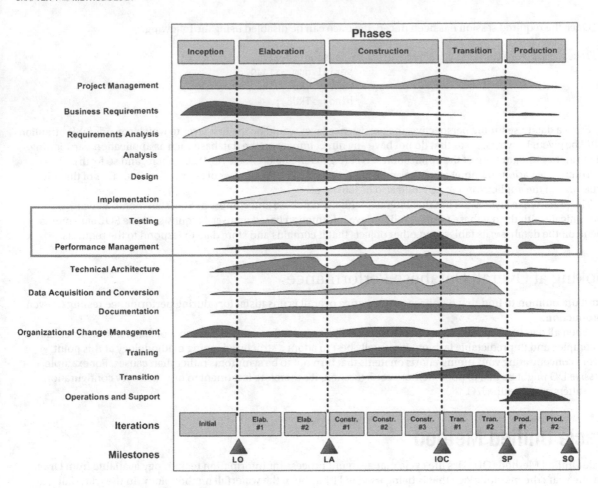

Figure 1-3. *OUM IT life cycle management phases*[2]

The definition and discussions of the various phases of all stages of an IT life cycle management is beyond the scope of this book.

The two stages, Testing and Performance Management, are stages of the development life cycle that are very crucial for the success of any project, including migrating from a single instance to a RAC configuration.

Testing and Performance Management

Testing and performance management go hand in hand with any product development or implementation. Whereas testing also focuses on functional areas of the system, without testing performance-related issues cannot be identified. The objective of both these areas is to ensure that the performance of the system or system components meet the user's requirements and justifies migration from a single instance to a RAC environment.

As illustrated in Figure 1-3, effective performance management must begin with identifying the key business transactions and associated performance expectations and requirements early in the Inception and Elaboration phases and implementing the appropriate standards, controls, monitoring checkpoints, testing, and metrics to ensure

---

[2]Source: Oracle Corporation.

that transactions meet the performance expectations as the project progresses through elaboration, construction, transition, and production. For example, when migrating from a single instance to RAC, performance considerations such as scalability requirements, failover requirements, number of servers, resource capacity of these servers, and so forth will help in the Inception and Elaboration phases.

Time spent developing a Performance Management strategy and establishing the appropriate controls and checkpoints to validate that performance has been sufficiently considered during the design, build, and implementation (Figure 1-4) will save valuable time spent in reactive tuning at the end of the project while raising user satisfaction. The Performance Management process should not end with the production implementation but should continue after the system is implemented to monitor performance of the implemented system and to provide the appropriate corrective actions in the event that performance begins to degrade.

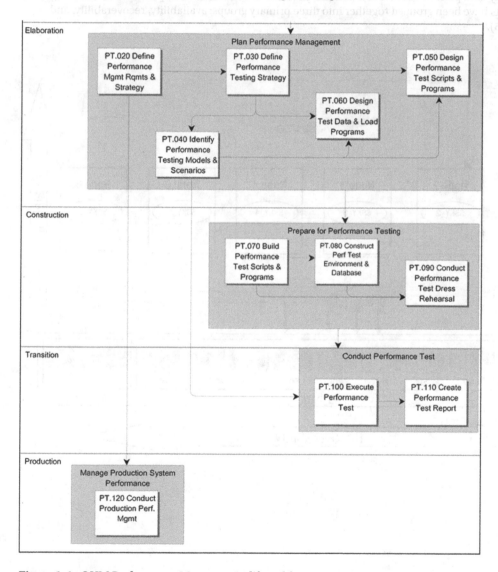

Figure 1-4. OUM Performance Management life cycle[3]

---

[3]Source: Oracle Corporation.

RAP Testing

Migration from a single instance to a RAC configuration should be for the right reasons, namely, scalability of the enterprise systems and availability. Scalability is achieved through optimal performance of the application code, and availability is achieved by redundant components of the hardware configuration. Both these reasons should be thoroughly tested from end to end for optimal performance and stability of the environment. Methodologies we discussed in the previous sections are just guidelines to have a systematic approach to testing and tuning the system; the actual tests and plans will have to prepared and customized based on the environment, O/S, number of nodes in the cluster, storage components, and the workload of the application. Testing should cover three major areas of RAC: recovery, availability, and performance (RAP). In this section, we discuss the various phases of RAP testing. Just like the acronym, the tests have been grouped together into three primary groups: availability, recoverability, and scalability (see Figure 1-5).

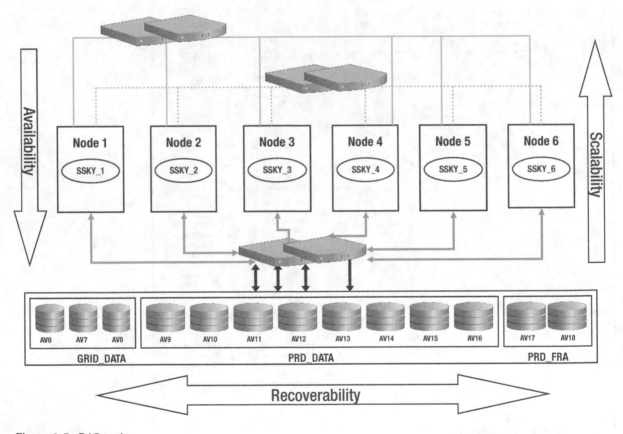

Figure 1-5. *RAP testing*

RAP Testing Phase I—Stability Testing of the Cluster

During this phase of the test, the cluster is verified for failure of components and the stability of the other components in the cluster. This is performed with the help of the system administrator by manually creating physical component failure during database activity.

RAP Testing Phase II—Availability and Load Balancing

During this phase of the test, the user application creates constant load; servers are crashed randomly; and the user failover from one instance to the other is observed. The purpose of this test is to ensure that the application and SQL*Net connections are configured for user failover with minimal transaction loss. During this phase of the test, RAC functionality such as TAF (Transparent Application Failover), FAN (Fast Application Notification), FCF (Fast Connection Failover), and RTLB (run-time load balancing) features are all tested.

If the proposed configuration also includes disaster recovery, failover and switchover between the primary site and the secondary site should also be incorporated in this phase of the tests.

RAP Testing Phase III—High Availability

Whereas RAC provides availability within the data center, it does not provide availability if the entire data center was to fail due to disasters from earthquake, floods, and so forth. Implementing a disaster recovery (DR) location, which is normally of a similar configuration, provides this level of availability; and to keep the databases identical to the primary site, a physical standby database is implemented. Testing between the primary site and DR sites should also be included as part of RAP testing. Both failover and switchover testing between primary and DR sites should be tested. Along with this testing the application should also be tested against both the sites.

RAP Testing Phase IV—Backup and Recovery

During this phase of the tests, the database backup and recovery features are tested. As part of the recovery testing, recovery scenarios from database corruption, loss of control file, or losses of server parameter file (spfile) are tested. This phase of testing also includes tuning the recovery functionality, taking into account the mean time to failure (MTTF), mean time between failures (MTBF), and so forth and includes sizing of redo logs and tuning the instance recovery parameters.

RAP Testing Phase V—Hardware Scalability

The hardware components are tested and tuned to get maximum scalability. Using third party load testing tools, the servers and the database are put to high loads and the various scalable components—for example, interconnect, memory, and so forth—are sized and tuned. The results from these tests are used as baselines for the next step.

RAP Testing Phase VI—Database Scalability

Test the scalability of the configuration using the application to generate the required workload. These tests help determine the maximum user workload that the clustered configuration can accommodate.

RAP Testing Phase VII—Application Scalability

Test the scalability of the configuration using the application to generate the required workload. These tests help determine the maximum user workload that the clustered configuration can accommodate.

RAP Testing Phase VIII—Burnout Testing

This phase of the testing is to verify the overall health of both the application and the databases when the database is constantly receiving transactions from the application. Using tools such as LoadRunner, a typical workload is generated against the database for a period of 40–60 hours and the stability of the environment is monitored. This phase of the testing is to verify any issues with application and database software components for memory leaks and other failures. The data and statistics collected from the tests can also help in the final tuning of the database and network parameters.

Creating an Application Testing Environment

One of the common mistakes found in the industry is not to have an environment similar to production for development and performance testing of the application, as the performance of all database interactions is affected by the size of the underlying database tables. The relationship between performance and table sizes is not always predictable and is all based on the type of application and the functionality of the application being executed. For example, in a data warehouse type of application, the database could be static between two data load periods; and depending on how often data feeds are received, the performance of the database could be predictable. On the other hand, the database could be linear in an OLTP (online transaction processing) application because data is loaded in small quantities.

It is essential to ensure that database tables are as close to production size as possible. It may not be always possible to create full replicas of production systems for performance testing; in these cases, we need to at least create volumes sufficient to reveal any of the unexpected degradations caused by execution patterns. In such situations, importing database optimizer statistics from the production environment could help produce similar execution plans and similar response times.

When migrating from single instance configuration to a RAC environment or when making upgrades either to the database version or the application version a use of Oracle Real Application Testing (RAT) should be considered. RAT provides functionalities such as database replay and SQL Performance Analyzer, which allow replaying production workloads in a test environment.

■ **Note**   Oracle RAT is discussed in detail in Chapter 5.

How Much to Tune?

Several database administrators or performance engineers look at the performance statistics with a high-powered lens to find details that could be tuned. They spend countless hours day and night over performance issues, microtuning the system. In spite of achieving response times stipulated by the business requirements, the DBA or performance engineer goes into tuning the database to the nth degree with no return on improved performance. Such micromanagement of the performance tier is what is referred to as compulsive tuning disorder (CTD; *Oracle Performance Tuning 101* by Gaja Krishna Vidyanathan, Kirtikumar Deshpande, and John Kostelac [Oracle Press, 1998]). CTD is caused by an absence of complete information that would allow you to prove conclusively whether the performance of a given user action has any room for improvement (*Optimizing Oracle Performance* by Carry Millsap and Jeff Holt [O'Reilly, 2003]). If repeated tuning creates a disorder, how much is too much? This should not be hard to define. Tuning should be made with goals in perspective, a good place to start is the SLA defined by business; then, based on tests and user response or feedback, reasonable goals could be defined. Tuning should not be an endless loop with no defined goals. When it's approached with no defined goals, then the DBA may get infected by the CTD syndrome.

Conclusion

Tuning of applications and databases is a very important task for optimal performance and for providing good response times to user requests for data from the database. Performance tuning tasks could be highly intensive during initial application development and may be less intensive or more of a routine when monitoring and tuning the database and/or application after the code is moved to production. Similarly, when migrating from a single instance to a RAC environment, the test phases maybe extensive for enterprise resource planning (ERP), Systems Applications and Products in Data Processing (SAP) software, and so forth and may be less intensive when migrating smaller home-grown applications. Either way, the testing and migration process should adhere to a process or methodology for smooth transitions and for easily tracing the path. When such methodologies are followed, success for most operations is certain.

Performance testing is not a process of trial and error; it requires a more scientific approach. To obtain the best results, it is important that a process or method is followed to approach the problem statement or performance issue in a systematic manner. A process or methodology that is repeatable and allows for controlled testing with options to create baselines through iterations should be followed.

The primary goal of any performance workshop or exercise is to tune the application and database or system to provide better throughput and response times. Response times and throughputs of any system are directly related to the amount of resources that the system currently has and its capacity to make available the resources to the requestors. In the next chapter, we will look at capacity planning.

CHAPTER 2

■ ■ ■

Capacity Planning and Architecture

RAC provides normal features such as recoverability, manageability, and maintainability found in a stand-alone (single instance) configuration of Oracle Relational Database Management System (RDBMS). Among the business requirements supported by Oracle RDBMS, availability and scalability are naturally derived from the architecture of the RAC configuration.

Using database built-in features such as Fast Application Notification (FAN), Transparent Application Failover (TAF) and Fast Connection Failover (FCF), RAC provides failover and scalability options. Features introduced in Oracle 11g Release 2 provide additional features such as dynamic provisioning of instances. Such features are a step toward eliminating the need to physically map a database instance to a specific server and to treat each instance as a service within a pool of servers available. Further to this, Oracle provides scalability features through implementation of load balancing based on demand in the pool distributing workload and effectively utilizing resources also through the implementation of FAN.

Although RAC does provide availability and scalability features, such features can also be obtained through alternative methods. Availability of the database environment could be obtained by implementing a standby environment using Oracle Data Guard (ODG). Similarly scalability of the database environment could be achieved by providing additional resources such as CPU, memory to the existing hardware, or scaling the servers up (vertical scalability). If all these alternate solutions can help meet the business requirements, why do we need RAC? It's a good question and it's encouraged that an answer satisfies the business goals and justifies a RAC implementation.

The alternate solutions just mentioned, such as the data guard or the options to vertically scale the servers, have limitations and do not provide a complete flexible solution to meet the ever-increasing demands of today's business. For example, when failing over from the primary location/database to the secondary/data guard location, it is possible that all the data that were generated by the primary site might not have reached the secondary site. Other complexities may occur as well, such as applications having to be moved from the current locations so they point to the new data guard locations and users having to disconnect or close the sessions and start their activities again. Similarly, vertical scalability has its limitations, such as how much additional memory or CPU can be added to the existing servers. This is limited by how much increase in such resources these servers can physically accommodate. What happens when these limits are reached? These servers have to be replaced with a higher model, which brings downtime and possible changes to the application and adds to the additional testing that would have to be included.

With the increased growth of customers and users, businesses face an everyday challenge in providing system response time. The day-to-day challenge is how these additional users can utilize the limited resources available on the servers. The capacity of the servers and resources such as CPU, processing power, memory, and network bandwidths are all limited.

When deciding on the servers and the related infrastructure for the organization, it is critical that the capacity measured in terms of power to support the user workload be determined.

Analyzing the Stack

Typically, the computer system stack consists of the layers illustrated in Figure 2-1. The application communicates with the software libraries, which in turn communicate with the operating system (O/S), and the O/S depends on system resources. Layers 1 to 4 in Figure 2-1 are primarily pass-through layers, and most of the activity happens when the application or user session tries to get the result or compute the end results requested by the operation. Such computations require resources, and obviously resources are not in abundance. Because there are limited resources, this can cause several types of delays based on what resources are currently not available, causing processing delays, transmission delays, propagation delays, and retransmission delays, to name a few. When processes are not able to complete operations in time or there are delays in any of the layers illustrated in Figure 2-1, the requests are queued. When these processes don't release the resources on time, queuing delays are formed. When multiple requests for resources are sent, over and above what is available, to obtain the right resource, large queues are formed (illustrated in step 5), causing significant delays in response time.

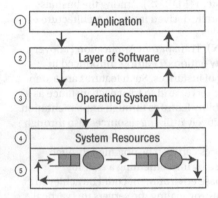

Figure 2-1. *System stack*

Queuing is primarily due to lack of resources, or overutilization, or processes holding on to resources for long periods of time.

To better understand this, we look at a simple metaphor of a restaurant where a customer spends a fair amount of time inside to obtain service. The restaurant service time depends on how many customers come into the restaurant and how soon a customer obtains the required service and leaves the restaurant. If the number of customers coming into the restaurant increases or doubles, but the time required to service a customer remains the same, the customer spends the same amount or an increased amount of time at the restaurant. This can best be understood using Little's theorem. Little's theorem states that the average number of customers (N) can be determined from the following equation:

$$N = \lambda T$$

Here lambda (λ) is the average customer arrival rate and T is the average service time for a customer. Applying the preceding formula to the our restaurant situation and relating the same to a computer system model illustrated in Figure 2-1, the queuing will depend on

- How many customers arrive at the restaurant? Customers can arrive one by one or can arrive in batches. In information technology, it could be related to the number of requests received and getting added to the queue.

- How much time do customers spend in the restaurant? Customers are willing to wait or customers could be in hurry. In information technology, it could be related to the time required to process a request.

- How many tables does the restaurant have to service the customers? This also depends on the discipline followed in the restaurant, for example, FIFO, random order, and priorities based on age (senior citizens). In information technology, it could be related to the number of servers available to process the request.

Queuing is an indication of delayed processing and increased service or response times. In the Oracle database, this analogy can be related to contention for resources due to concurrency, lack of system resources, lack of CPU processing power, slow network, network bandwidth, and so forth. Making system selections and the various resources that the system will contain should take into consideration the amount of processing, number of users accessing the system, and usage patterns.

Servers have a fixed amount of resources. Businesses are always on the positive note when gaining an increased user base. It becomes a need of utmost importance that focus and attention be given to determine the capacity of the servers and plan for these increases in workload to provided consistent response time for users.

Capacity Planning

A simple direct question probably arises as to why we should do capacity planning. Servers will let us know when they are out of resources, and user volumes are unpredictable. If we assume certain things, such as expected number of users, and we don't get the increased number of users, all of the investment could be wasted. On the contrary, if we did not plan, we would have surprises with overloaded servers and poor response times to users, thus affecting performance. Support for increased business is only one of the many benefits of capacity planning for the IT infrastructure. Other benefits include the following:

- Cost avoidance, cost savings, and competitive advantage. By predicting business growth through informed sources, organizations and management make informed decisions. This can be a considerable cost savings and advantage in the field. Because at the end of the day, slow systems and poor responses will drive customers/users to other similar businesses.

- Greater visibility into current and potential performance, and availability constraints that relate to

  - System and application resource constraints

  - Helping to understand design flaws. When applications cannot scale to increased workload, it indicates flaws in the overall architecture of the system. Stress testing and workload testing of the application would help determine such flaws.

- Ability to track and predict capacity consumption and related costs helps toward realistic future planning.

Similar to scalability, which is tomorrow's need (when the business grows and more users access the system), capacity planning is also for a future period; it is planning in infrastructure and resources required for the future. It involves estimating the space, computer hardware, technical expertise, and infrastructure resources that are required for a future period of time.

Based on the planned growth rate of the enterprise, the growth rate in terms of number of users as a result of increased business is determined. Based on these growth rates, the appropriate hardware configurations are selected.

Although capacity planning is for a future period, the planning is done based on current resources, workload, and system resources. The following factors influence the capacity of the servers:

- CPU utilization—CPU utilized over a specific period of time

- Transaction throughput—Transactions completed over a period of time

- Service time—Average time to complete a transaction

- Transaction capacity—Server capacity to handle number of transactions

- Queue length—Average number of transactions

- Response time—Average response time

Planning normally starts when the business requests increased user workload or product enhancements. After analyzing the business requirements, their current application, database configuration, and the growth requirements, careful analysis should be performed to quantify the benefits of switching to a RAC environment. In the case of a new application and database configuration, a similar analysis should also be performed to quantify if RAC would be necessary to meet the requirements of current and future business needs.

The first step in the quantification process is to analyze the current business requirements such as the following:

- Are there requirements that justify or require the systems to be up and running 24 hours a day, every day of the year?

- Are there sufficient businesses projections on the number of users that would be accessing the system and what the user growth rate will be?

- Will there be a steady growth rate that would indicate that the current system configurations might not be sufficient?

Once answers to these questions have been determined, a simulation model should be constructed to establish the scalability requirements for the planning or requirements team. While developing the simulation model, the architecture of the system and application should be taken into consideration.

The simulation should determine if any specific hardware architectures (symmetric multiprocessing [SMP], non-uniform memory access [NUMA], and so forth) would be required for the implementation of the system. During this initial hardware architecture evaluation, the question may arise as to whether a single instance configuration would be sufficient or a clustered solution would be required. If a single instance configuration is deemed sufficient, then whether the system would require protection from disasters would need to be determined. If disaster protection is a requirement, it may be implemented using the ODG feature.

Applications to run in a clustered configuration (e.g., clustered SMP, NUMA clusters) should be clusterizable such that the benefits could be measured in terms of global performance, availability (such as failover), and load balancing. (Availability basically refers to availability of systems to service users.) More important, the application should be scalable when additional resources are provided. From a performance aspect, the initial measurements would be to determine the required throughput of the application. Under normal scenarios, performance is measured by the number of transactions the system could process per second or the IOPS (input/output operations per second). Performance can also be measured by the throughput of the system, utilizing a simple formula such as the following:

$$\text{Throughput} = \text{the number of operations performed by the application} \div \text{the unit of time used for measurement}$$

There are two levels of throughput measurement: the minimum throughput expectation and the maximum throughput required. Tendencies are to justify the capacity with an average throughput (also called ideal throughput), which could be totally misleading. It's always in the best interest of the test to get the maximum possible throughput that causes the resources to be totally saturated.

Throughput can be determined by establishing the number of concurrent users or the maximum number of jobs that the system/servers can handle. This measurement could be based on the following:

- The interaction between the user and the application that has been mentioned in the business requirements.

- Length of this typical interaction to complete the request or job by the user measured as the acceptable response time, which is measured in units of time.

Based on the preceding criteria, the throughput measurement based on the number of users could be

$$\text{Throughput} = \text{the number of concurrent users (per requirements)}$$
$$\div \text{UART (the } user\ acceptable\ response\ time)$$

If this formula is applied to the current application or to the simulation model, then throughput of the system could be measured for the application (which is the inverse of the preceding formula):

$$\text{UART} = \text{throughput} \times \text{the number of concurrent users supported}$$

The throughput derived previously could be increased in several ways, such as the following:

- By making changes to the application; normally an expensive process because it may result in rewriting parts of or the entire application.

- Increasing the capacity of the hardware running the application; a situation of vertical scalability, which could also be an expensive process because hardware limitations could be experienced again after the current estimated users have been reached and the business grows.

- Clustering is probably the best opportunity in this situation due to the provision for horizontal scalability. Clustering enables the administrator to meet the increased demand of users as the business grows and requirements change (with higher numbers of concurrent users) by adding additional nodes to the cluster to help scale the application. This is done while providing the same amount of throughput and UART.

Once the clustering options have been decided, the next step is to determine how this will be done. It is imperative to consider or create a goal that this activity will accomplish before establishing the best method to incorporate it. It is often argued that maintenance should be simple; however, from an overall management perspective, the ultimate focus of the operation is geared toward performance.

Although maintenance is an important feature, performance plays a more important role in this process. Some options to consider during the clustering process are as follows:

- Multiplexed: Do multiple copies of the application run on each of the nodes in the cluster?

- Service oriented: Is the application designed in such a manner that it could be broken up into several pieces based on functionality and mode of operation? For example, users could be grouped based on functionality like accounts payable, accounts receivable, and payroll, all based on the departments that will be accessing these functionalities. The other alternative is to partition the application by the mode of operation like OLTP and batch or application behavior.

- Hybrid scenario: Is a combination of the previous two options a way to get the best result of both worlds? A possible combination would be to partition the application based on one of the criteria best suited for the application and business, then to multiplex the partitioned pieces.

The first two preceding items are true and feasible most of the time in the case of a business application. Because there are no specific protocols between clients, there is reliance on a central database server to serialize the transactions when maximizing the overall throughput and offering a consistent view of the database to all clients. This means that after the initial configuration, additional clients could be added without much difficulty, therefore providing increased linear throughput.

How to Measure Scaling

When the application is configured to run in a clustered configuration, the throughput, or global throughput, of an n-node clustered configuration could be measured using

$$T(n) = \text{SUM}t(i),$$

where $i = 1, ..., n$ and $t(i)$ is the throughput measured on one node in the clustered configuration.

Using the preceding formula, as we increase the number of nodes in the cluster, the value of n changes and so will the value of T. This will help in defining a throughput curve for the application configured to run on an n-node cluster.

Although computing the overall throughput of the application on an n-node cluster, the formula does not consider intangible factors such as performance of the servers, resource availability, network bandwidth, and so forth. Other factors that could hinder, improve, or contribute to the performance of the system must be considered. Ideally, a cluster should have all nodes with identical configuration for easy manageability and administration. However, if this is not the case, factors such as power of CPU, memory, and so forth should also be included in the computation. Adding these factors to the preceding formula would result in the following:

$$T(n) = n \times T \times S(n),$$

where $T(n)$ is the global throughput of the application running on n nodes and is measured by units of time; t, as we indicated previously, is the throughput for one node in the cluster; n is the number of nodes participating in the clustered configuration; and $S(n)$ is a coefficient that determines overall cluster throughput.

After considering the power and individual server details, factors outside the servers such as the network delays, network transfer delays, I/O latency of the storage array, and so forth should also be added to the formula. Although the previous measurements included factors that provide additional resources, this step would show any negative impact or overhead in the overall performance of the cluster.

Factors such as type of clustered hardware, topology, type of applications running on the clustered configuration, and so forth affect the scalability of the cluster and should also be considered as part of the equation. For example, massively parallel processing (MPP) architecture works well for a data warehouse implementation; however, for an OLTP implementation, a clustered SMP architecture would be better suited. With these factors added, the new formula would be

$$T(n) = nts(c,n,a,k),$$

where c is the type of clustered hardware, n is the node number, a is the type of application running on the clustered configuration, and k is the topology of the cluster.

Because all of these additional factors cannot be easily measured, only the previous formulas are used in the analysis.

The best-case scenario of scalability of an application would be when the application scales up with a constant factor of one, providing a consistent linear growth. However, this kind of scalability is not realistic.

Rather, it is typical for applications to have sub linear growth with the increase in nodes. The growth continues until a certain limit has been reached, after which adding additional nodes to the clustered configuration would not show any further advantage. This is demonstrated by the graph in Figure 2-1, which indicates that there is a linear scale-up with the addition of new nodes; however, after a certain percentage of scalability has been reached, a point of no return is reached on investment, and the scalability reduces with the addition of more nodes.

Capacity planning for an enterprise system takes many iterative steps. Every time there is a change in usage pattern, capacity planning has to be visited in some form or the other.

Estimating Size of Database Objects

Resource and performance capacity of the servers is one side of the puzzle. Equally important is to size/estimate the database for storage and the data growth. This would mean the database, the database objects, and the underlying storage subsystem would also have to be sized for today and tomorrow.

Oracle provides few packages and procedures that help determine the size of objects and indexes based on the estimated growth size. Even further, using the DBMS_SPACE.OBJECT_GROWTH_TREND function, a growth pattern for existing tables can be obtained.

The following query will list the object growth trend for an object; the data for the trend listed is gathered from Automatic Workload Repository (AWR). The growth trends for two of the tables are listed following. The OBJECT_GROWTH_TREND function returns four values:

- TIMEPOINT—Is a time stamp value indicating the time of the recording/reporting.

- SPACE_USAGE—Lists the amount of space used by the object at the given point in time.

- SPACE_ALLOCATED—Lists the amount of space allocated to the object in the table space at the given point in time.

- QUALITY—Indicates the quality of data reported; there are three possible values:

  - INTERPOLATED—The value did not meet the criteria of GOOD. As noted in the outputs following, the used and allocated are same. Basically, the values do not reflect any usage.

  - GOOD—The value whenever the value of TIME is based on recorded statistics. Value is marked good if at least 80% of the value is derived from GOOD instance values.

  - PROJECTED—The value of time is in the future as of the time the table was produced.

In a RAC environment, the output reflects the aggregation of values recorded across all instances in the cluster.

```
SELECT *
FROM    TABLE(dbms_space.object_growth_trend(object_owner => 'RAPUSR',
                object_name => 'HISTORY', object_type => 'TABLE'));


TIMEPOINT                      SPACE_USAGE SPACE_ALLOC QUALITY
------------------------------ ----------- ----------- --------------------
28-MAY-14 11.12.43.052162 AM     111082969   111082969 INTERPOLATED
29-MAY-14 11.12.43.052162 AM     111082969   111082969 INTERPOLATED
30-MAY-14 11.12.43.052162 AM     111082969   111082969 INTERPOLATED
31-MAY-14 11.12.43.052162 AM     111082969   111082969 INTERPOLATED
01-JUN-14 11.12.43.052162 AM     111082969   111082969 INTERPOLATED
02-JUN-14 11.12.43.052162 AM     111082969   111082969 INTERPOLATED
03-JUN-14 11.12.43.052162 AM     111082969   111082969 INTERPOLATED
04-JUN-14 11.12.43.052162 AM     131877793   134217728 GOOD
05-JUN-14 11.12.43.052162 AM     132003569   134369941 PROJECTED
06-JUN-14 11.12.43.052162 AM     132129344   134522153 PROJECTED
07-JUN-14 11.12.43.052162 AM     132255119   134674366 PROJECTED
08-JUN-14 11.12.43.052162 AM     132380894   134826579 PROJECTED
09-JUN-14 11.12.43.052162 AM     132506669   134978791 PROJECTED
```

Analysis of trend data from both the tables indicate that they are constant with no increase until June 4th, after which the growth is assumed, indicated by PROJECTED. The "QUALITY" column indicates an assumed future value. Using these growth trends, a projection is to be derived at to size the tables, indexes, and the database as a whole for future growth. These values also help drive the size of storage and distribution of data across spindles. Using the procedure DBMS_SPACE.CREATE_TABLE_COST, the estimated table size can be calculated:

```
DECLARE
 ub NUMBER;
 ab NUMBER;
BEGIN
DBMS_SPACE.CREATE_TABLE_COST('USERS',63,195006890,10,ub,ab);
DBMS_OUTPUT.PUT_LINE('Used Bytes      = ' || TO_CHAR(ub));
DBMS_OUTPUT.PUT_LINE('Allocated Bytes = ' || TO_CHAR(ab));
END;
/
Used Bytes      = 14522695680 (108GB)
Allocated Bytes = 14562623488 (108GB)

PL/SQL procedure successfully completed.
```

From the preceding output, with the current utilization, the table size should be set at 108 GB. This is probably a rough guess looking at the current workload conditions. However, if consulting with the business analysts of the organization a more realistic growth scenario could be determined after taking into account any future acquisitions, new marketing promotions, and so forth, that would drive additional business and growth of data. Once we have the storage size, user growth pattern, current workload of the system/servers, and so forth, the next step is to look at the sizing these servers for tomorrows need.

Architecture

Each application managed by each business unit in an enterprise is deployed on one database. This is because the database is designed and tuned to fit the application behavior, and such behavior may cause unfavorable results when other applications are run against them. Above this, for machine critical applications, the databases are configured on independent hardware platforms, isolating them from other databases within the enterprise. These multiple databases for each type of application managed and maintained by the various business units in isolation from other business units cause islands of data and databases. Such configurations results in several problems such as

- Underutilization of database resources

- High cost of database management

- High cost of information management

- Limited scalability and flexibility

In other words, there are no options to distribute workload based on availability of resources.

Oracle database basic architecture is centered around one server that will contain the memory structure containing data and user operations and the physical storage where data is persisted for future use. Such a configuration with one instance and one database is considered a single-instance configuration of the Oracle database. On the other hand, a more scalable version of the database would be many servers containing instances that access the same copy of the physical database and share data between instances via the cluster interconnect called a clustered database configuration. In this section, after a brief comparison, we discuss the Oracle RAC architecture.

Oracle Single-Instance vs. Clustered Configuration

Every Oracle configuration starts with a single instance, in the sense that even in the clustered Oracle configuration such as RAC, it starts with a single instance. From the basic level of database creation, database management, database performance tuning, and so forth, all operations start with a basic single-instance configuration and move to a clustered configuration. It is very important in every aspect of database administration and maintenance that each instance is considered as an individual unit before considering it as a combined cluster. Stand-alone, or single-instance, configuration in an enterprise system does not provide all the functionalities, such as availability and scalability. One way of providing for availability is by using some of the high-availability options accessible from Oracle, for example, the ODG. With this feature, data is migrated to a remote location by pushing data from the redo logs or archive logs to the remote location. The difficulty with such a configuration is that there could be loss of data when the node that contains the primary database fails, and the last set of redo logs are not copied over to the destination database. This creates an inconsistent environment.

Another high-availability option would be to use the Oracle Advanced Replication (OAR) or the Oracle Streams feature. This option is very similar to the ODG option; however, instead of copying the redo logs from the primary instance to the secondary, or target-replicated environment, data could be transferred more frequently like a record, or a group of records. This feature, when compared to the ODG option, provides a much closer level of data consistency. This is due to the fact that in the case of failure of the node that contains the primary database, only the last few rows, or sets, of data are not transferred.

From a disaster recovery or reporting solution, the ODG and OAR feature are high-availability options. Where data consistency is not an immediate concern, such as in the case of disasters basically due to an "act of God," where the primary database is not available, a remote database created by either of these options could help provide a backup opportunity to the enterprise system.

Oracle's clustered, or multi-instance configurations, comprise multiple nodes working as a cohesive unit, with each node in the cluster consisting of two or more instances talking to a common shared database. As has been discussed, this feature is the RAC configuration.

RAC Architecture

RAC is a clustered database solution that requires a two or more node hardware configuration capable of working together under a clustered software layer. A clustered hardware solution is managed by cluster management software that maintains cluster coherence between the various nodes in the cluster and manages common components such as the shared disk subsystem. Several vendors have provided cluster management software to manage their respective hardware platforms. For example, HP Tru64 manages HP platforms; Sun Cluster manages Sun platforms; and so forth; and there are others such as Veritas cluster manager that has cluster management software that supports more than one hardware vendor. In Oracle Database version 11g and above, the cluster management is provided using Oracle's ClusterWare.[1]

---

[1]Oracle Clusterware is part of Oracle Grid Infrastructure starting with Oracle Database 11g Release 2.

Figure 2-2 shows a high-level system stack and what is involved in a user request and system response overhead.

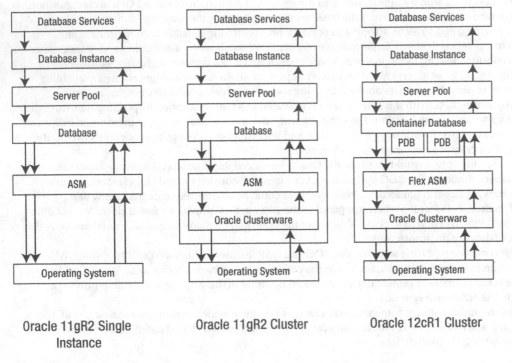

Figure 2-2. *Oracle single-instance and cluster stack (PDB = pluggable database)*

If you apply this to the database tier and expand the components of a server in a database stack, the stack would have a resemblance to Figure 2-2 for a single instance and an Oracle clustered configuration. This means there are several more measurements from various processes in a database stack that would need to be applied to our previous capacity planning equations. In other words, when a user makes a request for set of data, the request is not the only session or operation that will be on the server. There are other processes that manage the server and data that would be involved in the operation. Figure 2-2 compares the stack in a single-instance and clustered configuration.

To understand the stack and the overheads involved, it's important to understand the architecture of the stack and how data is processed and what kind of bottlenecks can affect the overall performance and capacity of these servers. In the next few sections and chapters ahead, we dissect many of these components and understand the overheads and optimization techniques. When deciding on the capacity of the servers, it would be good to take all this into consideration.

Figure 2-3 illustrates the various components of a clustered configuration.

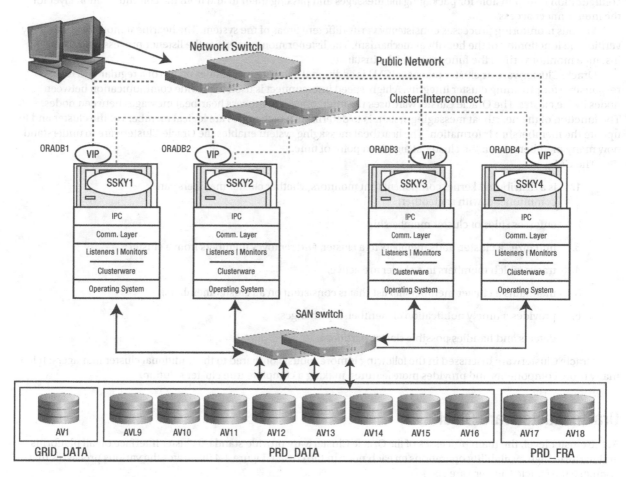

Figure 2-3. *Cluster components*

In Figure 2-3, the nodes are identified by a node name oradb1, oradb2, oradb3, and oradb4; and the database instances are identified by an instance name SSKY1, SSKY2, SSKY3, and SSKY4. The cluster components are

- Operating system
- Communication software layer
- Interprocess communication (IPC) protocol
- Oracle Clusterware or cluster manager

The communication software layer manages the communication between the nodes. It is also responsible for configuring and passing messages across the interconnect to the other nodes in the cluster. Although the Oracle Clusterware uses the messages returned by the heartbeat mechanism, it is the responsibility of the communication layer to ensure the transmission of the message to the Oracle Clusterware.

The network layer that consists of both the IPC and transmission control protocol (TCP) in a clustered configuration is responsible for packaging the messages and passing them to and from the communication layer for the interconnect access.

Various monitoring processes consistently verify different areas of the system. The heartbeat monitor continually verifies the functioning of the heartbeat mechanism. The listener monitor verifies the listener process, and the instance monitor verifies the functioning of the instance.

Oracle Clusterware or cluster manager (CM) is additional software that resides on top of a regular O/S that is responsible for providing cluster integrity. A high-speed interconnect is used to provide communication between nodes in the cluster. The Oracle Clusterware uses the interconnect to process heartbeat messages between nodes. The function of the heartbeat messaging system is to determine which nodes are logical members of the cluster and to update the membership information. The heartbeat messaging system enables the Oracle Clusterware to understand how many members are in the cluster at any given point of time.

The CM

1. is a distributed kernel component that monitors whether cluster members can communicate with each other;

2. enforces rules of cluster membership;

3. initializes a cluster, adds members to a cluster, and removes members from a cluster;

4. tracks which members in a cluster are active;

5. maintains a cluster membership list that is consistent on all cluster members;

6. provides a timely notification of membership changes;

7. detects and handles possible cluster partitions.

Oracle Clusterware discussed in the following is more robust compared to the traditional cluster managers: It has many more components and provides more features, making a complete true cluster solution.

Oracle Clusterware Stack

At the cluster level, the main processes of the Oracle Clusterware provide standard cluster interface on all platforms and perform high availability operations on each node in the cluster. Figure 2-4 illustrates the various processes that compose the Oracle Clusterware stack.

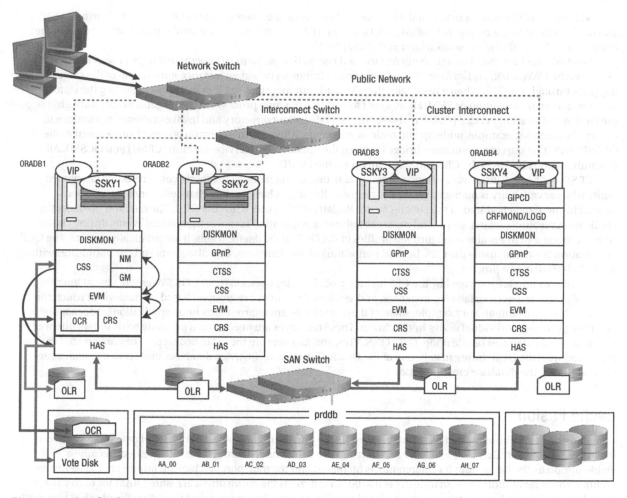

Figure 2-4. *Oracle Clusterware components*

Initiated by the Cluster Synchronization Services (CSS) process, the Oracle Cluster Synchronization Service Daemon or OCSSD is a process that performs the basic synchronization services between the various resources in the cluster. With the help of the voting disk (created as part of the Oracle Clusterware installation), it arbitrates ownership of the cluster among cluster nodes in the event of a complete private network failure. OCSSD is a critical daemon process, and a failure of this process causes the node (server) to reboot.

These services are performed by node membership (NM) service and the group membership (GM) services.

The NM checks the heartbeat across the various nodes in the cluster every second. It also alternates to check the heartbeat of the disk by performing a read/write operation every second. If the heartbeat/node members do not respond within 30 seconds, the node (among the surviving nodes) that was started first (master) will start evicting the other node(s) in the cluster.

NM also checks the voting disk to determine if there is a failure on any other nodes in the cluster. During this operation, NM will make an entry in the voting disk to inform its vote on availability. Similar operations are performed by other instances in the cluster. The three voting disks configured also provide a method to determine who in the cluster should survive. For example, if eviction of one of the nodes is necessitated by an unresponsive action, then the node that has two voting disks will start evicting the other node.

NM alternates its actions between the heartbeat check using the interconnect called Network Heartbeat (NHB) and the heartbeat to the voting disk called Disk Heartbeat (DHB) to determine the availability of other nodes in the cluster. (See the "Heartbeats" section later in this chapter.)

The GM provides group membership services. All clients that perform I/O operations register with the GM; for example, the LMON, DBWR, and so forth. Reconfiguration of instances (when an instance joins or leaves the cluster) happens through the GM. When a node fails, the GM sends out messages to other instances regarding the status.

Event manager daemon or EVMD is an event forwarding daemon process that propagates events through the Oracle Notification Service (ONS). It also scans the node callout directory and invokes callouts in reactions to detected events, for example, node up and node down events. Although this daemon is started subsequent to the OCSSD, EVMD is the communication bridge between the Cluster ready service daemon (CRSD) and OCSSD. All communications between the CRS and CSS happen via the EVMD.

CRSD or Oracle Clusterware daemon function is to define and manage the resources. A resource is a named entity whose availability is managed by the Clusterware. Resources have profiles that define metadata about them. This metadata is stored in the Oracle Cluster Registry (OCR). CRS reads the OCR. The daemon manages the application resources: starts, stops, and manages failover of application resources; generates events during cluster state changes; and maintains configuration profiles in the OCR. If the daemon fails, it automatically restarts. The OCR information is cached inside the CRS. Beyond performing all the functions, CRS also starts and communicates with the RACGIMON daemon process.

Resources that are managed by the CRS include global service daemon (GSD), ONS daemon, virtual Internet Protocol (VIP), listeners, databases, instances, and services. Resources are grouped based on the level at which they apply to the environment. For example, some of these resources are referred to as node applications (nodeapps), and they pertain to individual nodes in the cluster. These resources are needed on a per node basis independent of the number of databases on the node. GSD, ONS, VIPs, and listeners are the list of nodeapps. They are created and registered with the OCR during installation of the Oracle Clusterware. Listener, database, and service resources are created during the database creation process.

Cache Fusion

Cache fusion is a technology that uses a high-speed IPC to provide cache-to-cache transfer of data blocks between instances in a cluster. This technology for transferring data across nodes through the interconnect became a viable option as the bandwidth for interconnects increased and the transport mechanism improved. Cache fusion architecture is revolutionary in an industry sense because it treats the entire physical distinct RAM for each cluster node logically as one large database system global area (SGA), with the interconnect providing the physical transport among them.

The global cache service (GCS) and global enqueue service (GES) processes on each node manages the cache synchronization by using the cluster interconnect. Cache fusion addresses transaction concurrency between instances. The different scenarios of block sharing are broadly stated as the following:

- *Concurrent reads on multiple nodes*: This occurs when two or more instances participating in the clustered configuration are required to read the same data block. The block is shared between instances via the cluster interconnect. The first instance that reads the block would be the owning instance, and the subsequent instances that require access to the same block will request it via the cluster interconnect.

- *Concurrent reads and writes on different nodes*: This is a mixture of read/write operations against a single data block. A block available on any of the participating instances could be modified by a different instance while maintaining a copy/image that is different from the database. Such transactions use the interconnect. A block can be read as is, that is, in a current version, or a read consistent version could be built by applying required undo.

- *Concurrent writes on different nodes*: This is a situation in which multiple instances request modification of the same data block frequently.

During these block transfer requests between instances using the interconnect, the GCS process plays a significant role as the master/keeper of all requests between instances. GCS tracks the location and status of data blocks as well as the access privileges of various instances. Oracle uses the GCS for cache coherency when the current version of a data block is on one instance's buffer cache and another instance requests that block for modification.

When multiple instances require access to a block, and a different instance masters the block, the GCS resources track the movement of blocks through the master instance. Because of block transfer between instances, multiple copies of the same block could be on different instances. These blocks in different instances have different resource characteristics. These characteristics are identified by the following factors, which we discuss in the next two sections:

- Resource mode
- Resource role

Resource Mode

Resource mode is determined by various factors such as who is the original holder of the block, what operation is the block acquired to perform, what operation is the requesting holder intending to perform, what will be the outcome of the operation, and so forth. Table 2-1 lists the resource modes, its identifier, and a description of the resource mode.

Table 2-1. *Resource Modes*

Resource Mode	Identifier	Description
Null	N	Nodes holding blocks at this level convey no access rights.
Shared	S	This level indicates that the block is being held in protected read mode. That is, multiple instances have access to read this block but cannot modify it.
Exclusive	X	This indicates that the resource is held in Exclusive mode. Whereas consistent versions of the older blocks are available, other processes or nodes cannot write to the resource.

Resource Role

Role indicates if the mode is maintained local to the instance or if it's maintained across multiple instances, hence, at a global level. Table 2-2 illustrates the different roles and their descriptions.

Table 2-2. *Resource Roles*

Role	Description
Local	When the block, for the first time, is read into an instance's cache, and no other instance in the cluster has read the same block or is holding a copy of the block, then the block has a local role.
Global	If the block that was originally acquired has been modified by the holding instance, and based on a request from another instance, has copied the block, the block that was originally on one node is now present on multiple nodes and therefore has a global role.

Heartbeats

Heartbeat is a pooling mechanism in clustered platforms to verify if the other server participating in the cluster is alive. Oracle also uses the heartbeat mechanism to verify the health of the other nodes participating in the cluster. In a four-node cluster (Figure 2-4), every node will poll the other node in the cluster; ORADB1 will send a heartbeat message to ORADB2, ORADB3, and ORADB4. Similarly, ORADB2 will send a heartbeat message to ORADB1, ORADB3, and ORADB4. This helps each server in the cluster to understand the health of the other server in the cluster and take appropriate actions should polling fail. In RAC, the CSS performs polling in three different methods:

- Network Heartbeat (NHB)
- Disk Heartbeat (DHB)
- Local Heartbeat (LHB)

Network Heartbeat (NHB)

The NHB is sent over the private interconnect. CSS sends an NHB every second from one node to all the other nodes in a cluster and receives an NHB from the remote nodes similarly every second. The NHB contains timestamp information from the local node and is used by the remote. If an acknowledgment is not received from the other node in the cluster in 30 seconds (represented by the miscount value), CSS would request a cluster reconfiguration. The reconfiguration will not always be required. CSS will verify the health and state of the node through other methods before making a decision for reconfiguration.

Disk Heartbeat (DHB)

Apart from the NHB, we use the DHB, which is required for split-brain resolution. It contains a timestamp of the local time in Unix epoch seconds as well as a millisecond timer.

■ **Note**   The Unix epoch (or Unix time or POSIX time or Unix timestamp) is the number of seconds that have elapsed since January 1, 1970 (midnight Universal Time [UTC]/Greenwich Mean Time [GMT]), not counting leap seconds (in ISO 8601: 1970-01-01T00:00:00Z); "epoch" is often used as a synonym for "Unix time."

The DHB is the definitive mechanism to make a decision about whether a node is still alive. DHB is a mechanism where each server in the cluster will write a timestamp to the voting disk every second. In the case of NHB failure, CSS will verify the voting disk to check if the node in question has written any timestamp to the voting disk during the NHB missed timeframe to decide if cluster reconfiguration is required.

Unlike the NHB, there are two parameters that drive the DHB: a "long disk I/O" (LIOT) value and a "short disk I/O" (SIOT) value. When the DHB beats are missing for too long, the node is assumed to be dead. When connectivity to the disk is lost for too long, the disk is considered offline.

```
2014-01-14 20:08:08.467: [CSSD][1093892416]  misscount          30      reboot latency       3
2014-01-14 20:08:08.467: [CSSD][1093892416]  long I/O timeout  200      short I/O timeout    27
2014-01-14 20:08:08.467: [CSSD][1093892416]  rim hub timeout    30      grace period         0
2014-01-14 20:08:08.467: [CSSD][1093892416]  hub size           32  active version 12.1.0.1.0
2014-01-14 20:08:08.467: [CSSD][1093892416]  Listing unique IDs for 1 voting files:
2014-01-14 20:08:08.467: [CSSD][1093892416]    voting file 1: 8cccacc5-d4eb4ff7-bf541125-3ef008ae
```

As listed in the preceding, the LIOT is set to 200 seconds, and SIOT is set to 27 seconds. LIOT is used to determine the disk write latency, and SIOT is used by CSS during cluster reconfiguration. SIOT is similar to the misscount value used by the NHB; however, it is computed based on the reboot time (default reboot time is set to 3 seconds). The disktimeout, misscount, and reboottime can be determined using the following crsctl command:

```
[root@ssky1l4p1 orarootagent_root]# crsctl get css disktimeout
CRS-4678: Successful get disktimeout 200 for Cluster Synchronization Services.

[root@ssky1l4p1 orarootagent_root]# crsctl get css reboottime
CRS-4678: Successful get reboottime 3 for Cluster Synchronization Services.

[root@ssky1l4p1 orarootagent_root]# crsctl get css misscount
CRS-4678: Successful get misscount 30 for Cluster Synchronization Services.
```

Based on the default values listed in the preceding, the SIOT is 27 seconds (misscount less reboottime).

Local Heartbeat (LHB)

LHB is an internal heartbeat mechanism where the message is sent to the cssdmonitor and the cssdagent to keep them informed about the health of the CSS. LHB notifications also happen every second and use and share the same thread with the NHB and DHB.

System Change Number (SCN)

The SCN is required in a single instance configuration to serialize activities such as a block changes, redo entries, and replay of redo logs during a recovery operation. It has a more robust role in a RAC environment.

In a RAC configuration, more than one instance can make updates to the data blocks. These data blocks are transferred via the cluster interconnect between the instances. To track these successive generations of data blocks across instances, Oracle assigns (uses), to each data block that is generated, a unique logical timestamp or SCN. The SCN is used by Oracle to order the data block change events within each instance and across all instances.

In a RAC environment, separate SCNs are generated by each instance. However, in an effort to keep the transactions in a serial order, these instances have to resynchronize their SCNs to the highest SCN known in the cluster.

The method used by Oracle to synchronize its SCN to the highest SCN in the cluster is called *broadcast on commit*. Under this method, SCNs are propagated to other instances when a data is committed on an instance, meaning Oracle does not wait to piggyback the SCN change on to another message. Broadcast on commit is implemented by reducing the default value defined by the parameter MAX_COMMIT_PROPAGATION_DELAY. Reducing the value to less than 100 hundredths of a second increases the SCN propagation between instances.

Mastering of Resources

Based on the demand for resources on a specific file, the resource is maintained on the instance whose use of it is highest: for example, if instance SSKY1 was accessing an object A1 and data from that object was being processed for about 1,500 user requests all connected to instance SSKY1; and say instance SSKY2 also required access to the object A1 for 100 users. It's obvious that SSKY1 has more users accessing this object A1. Hence, instance SSKY1 would be allocated as the resource master for this file, and the global resource directory (GRD) for this object would be maintained on instance SSKY1. When instance SSKY2 requires information from this object, it must coordinate with the GCS and the GRD on instance SSKY1 to retrieve/transfer data across the cluster interconnect.

If the usage pattern changes—for example, the number of users on instance SSKY2 increases to 2,000 and on SSKY1 it drops to 500—the GCS and GES processes, in combination, would evaluate the current usage pattern and transfer the mastering of the resource via the interconnect to instance SSKY2. This entire process of re-mastering of resources is called *object affinity*. In other words, object affinity is *the use of dynamic resource re-mastering to move the location of the object masters for a database object to the instance where block operations are most frequently occurring.*

Object affinity optimizes the system in situations where update transactions are being executed on one instance. If activity is not localized, the resource ownership is distributed to the instances equitably.

Figure 2-5 illustrates object distribution in a four-node cluster. That is, instances SSKY1, SSKY2, SSKY3, and SSKY4 are mastering resources R1, R2, R3, R4, R5, R6, and R7, respectively.

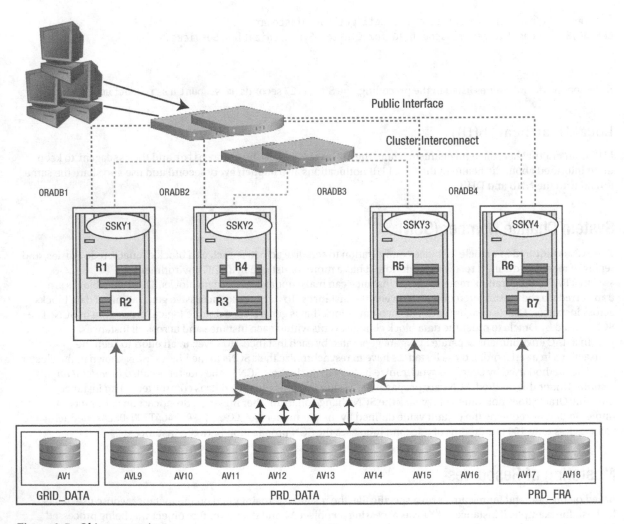

Figure 2-5. *Object mastering*

Mastering objects on the instance where the user activity is the highest enables optimization across the cluster and helps achieve workload distribution and quicker startup time. On a busy system, system performance could be affected if there is a constant change of workload on the instance causing resource utilization to change and in turn causing frequent re-mastering activity.

Re-mastering also happens when an instance joins or leaves the cluster. However, instead of re-mastering all locks/resources across all nodes, Oracle uses an algorithm called "lazy re-mastering." Basically, under this method, instead of load balancing the objects by removing all objects and re-mastering them evenly across instances, Oracle only re-masters the objects owned by the instance that crashed. Subsequently, during a future time GCS would consider placing the object master on an instance where the requests are the highest for the object.

Figure 2-6 illustrates the re-mastering of resources from instance SSKY4 to instances SSKY2 and SSKY3, respectively.

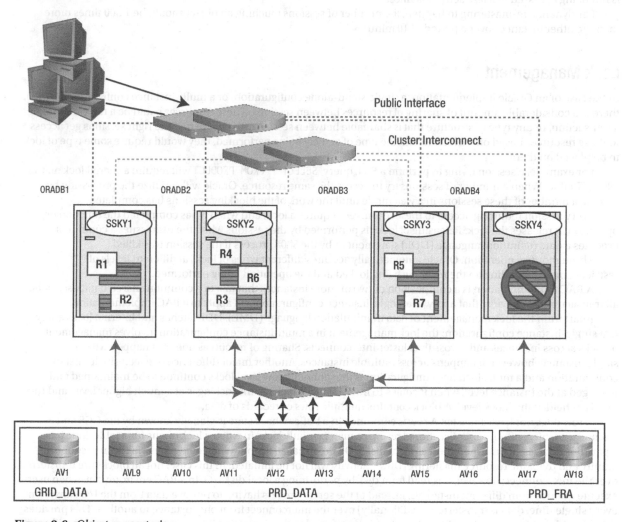

Figure 2-6. *Object re-mastering*

If instance SSKY4 crashes, instance SSKY1 and instance SSKY2 will continue to master their resources, namely, R1, R2, R3, and R4. As part of the recovery process, the resources mastered on the failed instance will now have to be mastered by one of the surviving instances. Oracle uses the lazy re-mastering concept and dynamically places the resource master on one of the surviving instances. Consequently, per our illustration in Figure 2-6, R6 is inherited by instance SSKY2 and R7 is inherited by instance SSKY3; instance SSKY1 is not affected.

At a later time when the user workload has stabilized (recovery is completed, users have failed over, etc.), GCS and GES will reassess the situation and perform a re-mastering operation to place the master on the instance where the demand is high.

A similar operation happens when an instance joins the cluster. Basically, a resource is removed from each of the available instances and moved to the instance that joined the cluster.

Re-mastering also happens when a master is located on an instance that is not active. Oracle requires additional resources to manage another resource master. Under these circumstances, Oracle will move the resource master that is not being accessed to a less active instance.

For dynamic re-mastering to happen, the number of sessions touching an object should be 1,500 times more than the other instances over a period of 10 minutes.[2]

Lock Management

In the case of an Oracle implementation, a single stand-alone configuration, or a multi-instance configuration (RAC), there is a considerable amount of sharing of resources between sessions. These resources could be a table definition, a transaction, or any type of structure that is shareable between sessions. To ensure that the right sessions get access to these resources based on their need and the type of activity being performed, they would require some type of lock to be placed on them.

For example, a session trying to perform a SQL query, SELECT * FROM PRODUCT will require a shared lock on the PRODUCT table. When a number of sessions try to access the same resource, Oracle will serialize the processing by placing a number of these sessions in a wait mode until the work of the blocking sessions has completed.

Every session requiring access to these resources acquires a lock; and when it has completed the function or operation, it releases the lock. Releasing of locks is performed by the sessions when the user issues a commit or executes a data definition language (DDL) statement or by the SMON process if the session was killed.

Throughout its operation, Oracle automatically acquires different types of locks at different levels of restrictiveness depending on the resource being locked and the operation being performed.

A RAC implementation is a composition of two or more instances that talk to a common shared database. Hence, all transactional behaviors that apply to a single-instance configuration will apply to a RAC implementation.

Apart from the lock management of data manipulation language (DML), DDL latches and internal locks apply to a single-instance configuration; the lock management in a multi-instance configuration involves management of locks across instances and across the cluster interconnects. Sharing of resources does not happen within a single instance; however, it happens across multiple instances. Another major difference between single-instance configuration and a multi-instance configuration is that although row level locks continue to be maintained and managed at the instance level, when it comes to inter-instance locking, the locking is at a much higher level, and the locks are held at the block level. A block contains multiple rows or records of data.

A row does not have a master. A row is contained in a buffer whose state is globally known by the GCS and the master. Object affinity and distributed resource manager only kicks in when a lock opens for a table, index, or a partition. This happens when there is lot of disk I/O and no cache fusion. When data pings via the interconnect, affinity and dynamic resource mastering (DRM) activity will not be initiated. In this case, not all blocks are transferred over the interconnect; however, it is read from disk by performing a local disk I/O. In a RAC environment, when users execute queries from different instances, instead of the server process having to retrieve data from the I/O subsystem every single time, data is transferred (traditionally) over the interconnect from one instance to another. This provides considerable performance benefits.[3] Once data is transferred to the requesting instance, the execution plan will then traverse through these rows to extract the actual result set requested by the user.

---

[2]These values are controlled by underscore parameters _GC_POLICY_MINIMUM and _GC_POLICY_TIME.

[3]This is because the latency of retrieving data from an I/O subsystem is much higher compared to transferring data over the network. Basically, network latency is much lower compared to I/O latency.

Multi-Instance Transaction Behavior

An instance reads a block from disk when either a user session or a process from another instance places a request. Although all instances participating in the cluster could access the block directly from disk (as in the previous versions of Oracle),[4] such an access would be expensive, especially when another instance in the cluster is already holding a copy of the block in its buffer and the same block could be accessed via the cluster interconnect. This operation maybe as simple as transferring the block via the cluster interconnect to the requesting instance. However, there are other factors involved during this process; for example, the block held by the original holder may have been modified, and the copy may not be placed on disk. It could very well be that the instance is holding only a copy of the block, whereas the block was initially modified by another instance and the block may have already undergone considerable changes. Yet, in another scenario, one of the instances requesting the block could be intending to delete a row from the block, while yet another instance is intending to make updates to the block.

How are these changes by multiple instances coordinated? How does Oracle ensure that these blocks are modified and tracked?

DBAs familiar with a single-instance configuration would know that Oracle is required to provide read consistency and ensure that multiple sessions do not see the in-flight transactions or rows that are being modified but not saved. RAC is no different; read consistency is provided at the cluster level across all instances. In a RAC configuration, while the data movement is at the block level, a single row from the block behaves similar to a regular single-instance configuration.

To cover all possible scenarios of cache fusion and sharing of blocks among the instances, the block behavior could be broadly classified into the following:

- Read/read behavior
- Read/write behavior
- Write/write behavior

Although these are just the high-level behaviors, there are quite a few possibilities that we discuss.

Read/Read Behavior

Under this behavior, there are basically two possibilities:

- The instance that first requested the block is the only instance holding the block for read purposes (read/read behavior with no transfer).
- The first instance is holding the block for read purposes; however, other instances also require access to the same block for read only purposes (read/read behavior with transfer).

Read/read Behavior with No Transfer

Figure 2-7 illustrates the steps involved when an instance acquires the block from disk and no other instance currently holds a copy of the same block. Instance SSKY3 will have to request a shared resource on the block for read-only purposes. (*For this discussion, we assume that* SSKY3 *is the first instance that requested this block, and it is not present in the shared areas of any other instances [*SSKY1, SSKY2, *and* SSKY4*]*).

---

[4]By enabling the `gc_files_to_lock` parameter, Oracle will disable the cache fusion functionality and instead would use the disks for the sharing of blocks. In other words, it would use the Oracle parallel server (OPS) behavior.

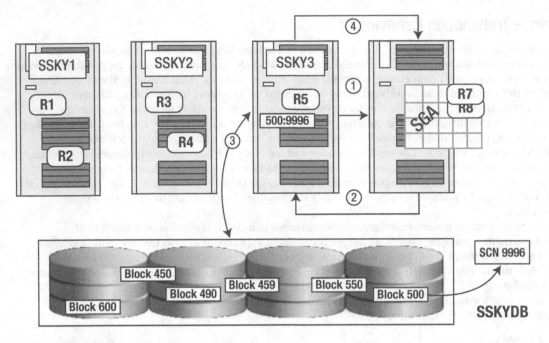

Figure 2-7. *Read/read behavior with no transfer*

The following steps are undertaken by SSKY3 to acquire the block from disk:

1. A user session or process attached to instance SSKY3 makes a request for a specific row of data. SSKY3 determines that the master for this specific resource is SSKY4. The request is directed to instance SSKY4 where the GRD for the object is maintained. *Oracle allocates a node to be the resource master based on the demand for the resource on a specific instance. If the object access increases on another node, Oracle performs a re-mastering operation to move the resource master for the object to the node.*

2. GCS, on verifying the GRD, determines that no other instance in the cluster has a copy of the block. GCS sends a message to SSKY3 requesting it to read the block from disk.

3. Instance SSKY3 initiates the I/O request to read the row from disk. The row is contained in block 500 and has SCN 9996. Because Oracle reads a block of data at a time, other rows are also retrieved as part of this read operation. The block is read into the buffer of instance SSKY3. Instance SSKY3 holds the block with SCN 9996 using a shared local mode.

4. SSKY3 now informs the GCS that the operation is successful. The GCS makes an entry in the GRD on instance SSKY4.

Read/Read Behavior with Transfer

We continue with the previous example/illustration. The Oracle process accessed the disk to retrieve a row contained in block 500 via instance SSKY3. The block is held in local shared mode, that is, no other instance has a copy of the block. We assume another user requires access to another row that is part of the same data block 500. This request is made by a user connected to instance SSKY2.

Figure 2-8 illustrates the steps involved when instance SSKY2 requires a block that is currently held by instance SSKY3. (To maintain clarity of the figure, Steps 1 to 4 are not repeated. Readers are advised to see Figure 2-7 in conjunction with Figure 2-8.)

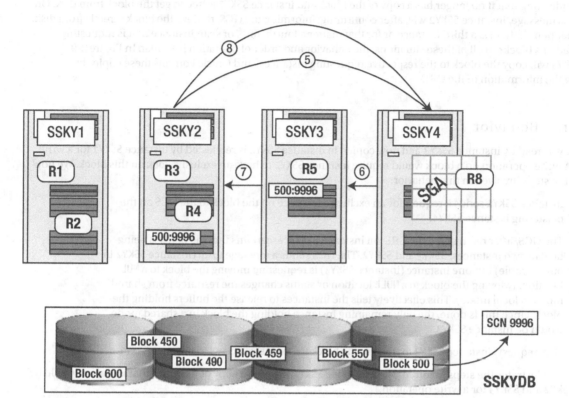

Figure 2-8. *Read/read behavior with transfer*

The steps in the figure include the following:

5. Instance SSKY2 sends a request for a read resource on the block to the GCS. Because the GRD for this resource is maintained on instance SSKY4, SSKY2 makes a request to SSKY4 requesting access to this block.

6. Instance SSKY4 checks against its GRD regarding the whereabouts of this block and determines that the block is currently held in instance SSKY3. GCS as the global cache manager for this resource sends a request to instance SSKY3 requesting it to transfer the block for shared access to instance SSKY2.

7. Instance SSKY3 ships a copy of the block to the requesting instance SSKY2. During this copy operation, SSKY3 indicates in the header of the message that instance SSKY3 is only sharing the block (which means SSKY3 is going to retain a copy of the block). It also informs SSKY2 that it is supposed to maintain the block at the same resource level.

8. Instance SSKY2 receives the block along with the shared resource level transferred via the message header from instance SSKY3. To complete the communication cycle, instance SSKY2 sends a message to the GCS that it has received a copy of the block. The GCS now updates the GRD.

The preceding discussion is making an optimistic assumption, namely, that everything is available as expected. Now what if this is not the case and instance SSKY3 did not have the block? In such a situation, instance SSKY3 would continue with the instruction received from the GCS. However, in the transfer operation, instance SSKY3 would send a message indicating that it no longer has a copy of the block and instance SSKY2 is free to get the block from disk. On receipt of this message, instance SSKY2 will, after confirming/informing the GCS, retrieve the block directly from disk.

What happens if there is a third instance or for that matter a fourth, fifth, or sixth instance that is requesting access to read this block? In all of these situations, the behavior and order of operation is similar. In Figure 2-9, instance SSKY3 will copy the block to the respective requesting instances; and Oracle controls these copies by maintaining the information in the GRD.

Read/Write Behavior

A block that was read by instance SSKY3 and now copied to instance SSKY2 is requested by instance SSKY1 for a write operation. A write operation on a block would require instance SSKY1 to have an exclusive lock on this block. We now go through the steps involved in this behavior:

9. Instance SSKY1 sends a request for an exclusive resource on the block to the GCS on the mastering instance SSKY4.

10. The GCS, after referring to the GRD on instance SSKY4, ascertains that the block is being held by two instances, SSKY3 and SSKY2. The GCS sends a message to all (instance SSKY2 in our example) but one instance (instance SSKY3) is requesting moving the block to a NULL location. (Moving the block to a NULL location or status changes the resource from shared mode to local mode). This effectively tells the instances to release the buffers holding the block. Once this is done, the only remaining instance holding the block in a shared mode would be instance SSKY3.

11. GCS requests instance SSKY3 to transfer the block for exclusive access to instance SSKY1.

Figure 2-9 illustrates the steps involved when instance SSKY1 requires a copy of the block that is currently held by instances SSKY2 and SSKY3 for a write operation.

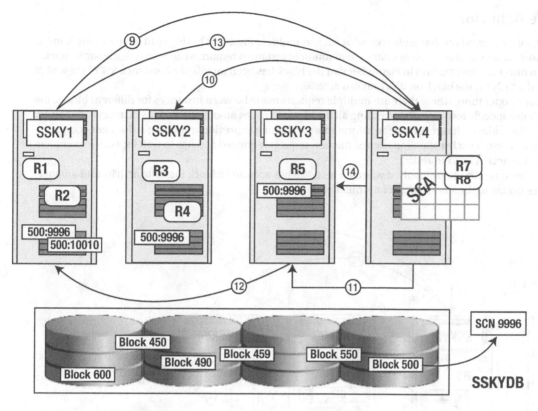

Figure 2-9. *Read/write behavior*

These are the steps shown in the figure:

12. Instance SSKY3, based on the request received from the GCS, will

    a. send the block to instance SSKY1 along with an indicator that it is closing its own resource and giving an exclusive resource for use to instance SSKY1;

    b. close its own resource, marking the buffer holding the block image as copy for consistent read (CR) and informing itself that the buffer area is available for reuse.

13. Instance SSKY1 converts its resource, makes the required updates to the block, and assigns it a new SCN number. SSKY1 then sends a message to the GCS indicating/confirming that it has an exclusive resource on the block. The message also piggybacks the message received from instance SSKY3 indicating that it has closed its own resource on this block. GCS now updates the GRD regarding the status of the block, and instance SSKY1 can now modify the block.

    Please note that at this stage, the copies of blocks on other instances would also be removed from the GRD.

As illustrated in Figure 2-9, instance SSKY1 has now modified the block and the new SCN is 10010.

14. The GCS confirms with instance SSKY3 that it has received notification regarding the status of the block in its buffer.

45

Write/Write Behavior

Previous discussions centered on shareable scenarios such as multiple instances having read copies of the same block. Now we look at how cache fusion operates when multiple instances require write access to the same block. Please note from our previous scenario in Figure 2-9 that the block has been modified by instance SSKY1 (new SCN value is 10010); the SCN for the block on disk remains at 9996.

In a continuous operation, where there are multiple requests made between instances for different blocks, the GCS is busy with the specific resource documenting all the block activities among the various instances. The GCS activity is sequential, unless it has recorded the information pertaining to previous requests; it does not accept or work on another request. If such a situation occurs, the new request is queued and has to wait for GCS to complete its current operation to accept this request.

Figure 2-10 illustrates the steps involved when an instance has acquired a block for write activity and another instance requires access to the same block for a similar write operation.

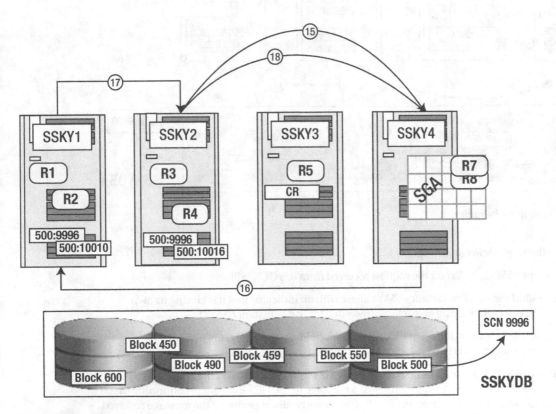

Figure 2-10. *Write/write behavior*

These are the steps:

15. Instance SSKY2, which originally had a read copy of the block, and based on the write request from instance SSKY1 received instructions from the GCS to clear the block buffer (marked as CR), now requires a copy of the block to make updates. Since the block is no longer in the local cache (local cache miss), instance SSKY2 makes a request to the GCS for an exclusive resource on the block.

16. If the GCS has completed all previous activities pertaining to other requests, the GCS makes a request to instance SSKY1 (the current holder of the block) to give exclusive resource on the block and to transfer the current image of the block to instance SSKY2.

17. Instance SSKY1 transfers the block to the requesting instance (SSKY2) after ensuring the following activities against this block have been completed:

- Logging any changes to the block and forcing a log flush if this has not already occurred.

  - LMS on SSKY1 posts the LGWR to write the redo for the dirty data buffer.

  - LGWR on SSKY1 performs a log I/O.

- Converting its resource to NULL with a past image (PI) status of 1, indicating that the buffer now contains a PI copy of the block.

- Sending an exclusive-keep copy of the block buffer to instance SSKY2. This indicates the block image has an SCN 10010, with an exclusive resource in global mode. SSKY1 also piggybacks a message indicating that the instance SSKY1 is holding a PI of the block.

GCS resource conversions and cache fusion block transfers occur completely outside the transaction boundaries. That is, an instance does not have to wait for a pending transaction to be completed before releasing an exclusive block resource.

18. After receipt of the message from instance SSKY1, instance SSKY2 will update the row in the block, assign it a new SCN number 10016, and send a message to the GCS. This message informs the GCS that instance SSKY2 now has the resource with an exclusive global status and that the previous holder instance SSKY1 now holds a PI version of the block with SCN 10010. The GCS will update the GRD with the latest status of the block.

Instance SSKY1 no longer has an exclusive resource on this block and hence cannot make any modifications to the block.

■ **Note** Despite multiple changes to the block made by the various instances, it should be noted that the block's SCN on disk remains at 9996.

Write/Read Behavior

We have looked at read/write behavior before; what would be the difference in the opposite situation? That is, what happens when a block is held by an instance after modification and another instance requires the latest copy of the block for a read operation? Unlike the previous read/write scenario, the block has undergone considerable modification, and the SCN held by the current holder of the block is different from what is found on disk.

In a single-instance configuration, a query looks for a read consistent image of the row, and the behavior in a clustered configuration is no different; Oracle has to provide a consistent read version of the block. In this example, the latest copy of the block is held by instance SSKY2 (based on our previous scenario as illustrated in Figure 2-10).

Figure 2-11 illustrates the steps involved when instance SSKY3 requires a block for read purposes. From our previous scenario, it is understood that the latest version of the block is currently held by instance SSKY2 in exclusive mode.

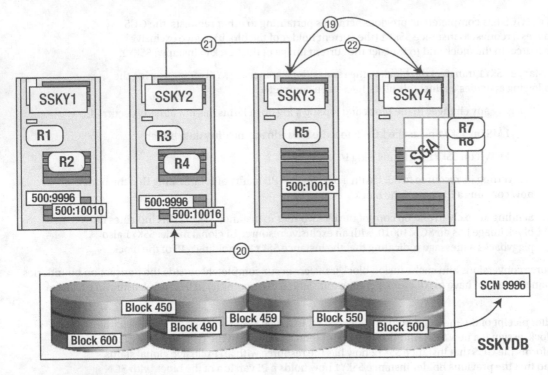

Figure 2-11. *Write/read behavior*

The following list describes the steps:

19. Instance SSKY3 once had a read copy of the block; however, based on a request from the GCS, it had converted it into a NULL resource (Step 10, Figure 2-9). Based on a new query request from a user, it now requires a read access to the block. To satisfy this request, instance SSKY3 makes a request to the GCS for the necessary shared resource.

20. Instance SSKY2 is the current holder of the block. To satisfy the request from instance SSKY3, the GCS requests instance SSKY2 to transfer the block.

21. Instance SSKY2, on receipt of the message request, completes all required work (instructs the LGWR to write redo changes to the redo log files, retains a PI image of the block) on the block and sends a copy of the block image to instance SSKY3. The block is to be transferred in a shared status with no exclusive rights; hence, instance SSKY2 has to downgrade its resources to shared mode before transferring the block across to instance SSKY3. While the transfer happens, instance SSKY2 retains the block's PI.

    Instance SSKY1 and instance SSKY2 have a PI of the block at their respective SCNs.

22. Instance SSKY3 now acknowledges receipt of the requested block by sending a message to the GCS. This includes the SCN of the PI currently retained by instance SSKY2. The GCS makes the required updates to the GRD.

    Instance SSKY3 now has the most recent copy of the block and it is now in a global shared mode.

Write to Disk Behavior

What happens when a block needs to be written to disk? Before we step into the mechanics of this, we recap the current state of the environment:

- Instance SSKY4 continues to be the master of the resource and holds the GRD for the block.

- Instance SSKY1 had once modified the block and currently holds the block with SCN 10010, having a global null resource and a PI.

- Instance SSKY2 also contains a modified copy of the block with SCN 10016. The current status of the block held by instance SSKY2 is in exclusive resource mode. This instance also holds a PI.

- Instance SSKY3 holds the latest consistent read image version of the block (in shared global mode) received from instance SSKY2, which means it is a copy of a block held by instance SSKY2.

- The disk contains the original block SCN 9996.

What could cause a write activity in a RAC environment? Transactional behavior in a RAC environment is no different when compared to a single-instance configuration. All normal rules of single instance, "flushing dirty blocks to disk," apply in this situation also. For example, writing to disk could happen under the following circumstances:

- *The number of dirty buffers reaches a threshold value.* This value is reached when there is not sufficient room in the database buffer cache for more data. In this situation, Oracle writes the dirty buffers to disk, freeing up space for new data.

- *A process is unable to find free buffers in the database buffer cache while scanning for blocks.* When a process reads data from the disk and does not find any free space in the buffer, it triggers the least recently used data in the buffer cache (dirty buffer) to be pushed down the stack and finally written to disk.

- *A timeout occurs.* A timeout is configured by setting the required timeout interval (LOG_CHECKPOINT_TIMEOUT) through a parameter defined in the parameter file. On every preset interval, the timeout is triggered to cause the database writer (DBWR) to write the dirty buffers to disk. In an ideal system, where the data is modified but not immediately written to disk (due to not having sufficient activity that would cause other mechanisms to trigger the write operation), this parameter is helpful.

- *The checkpoint process.* During a predefined interval defined by LOG_CHECKPOINT_INTERVAL or FAST_START_MTTR_TARGET parameter, when the CKPT process is triggered, it causes the DBWR and log writer (LGWR) processes to write the data from their respective buffer cache to disk. If neither of these parameters is defined, the automatic check pointing is enabled.

In a RAC environment, any participating instance could trigger a write request.

Figure 2-12 illustrates the various steps involved during a write to disk activity. In the current scenario, instances SSKY1 and SSKY2 have a modified version of the block and are different from the version on disk.

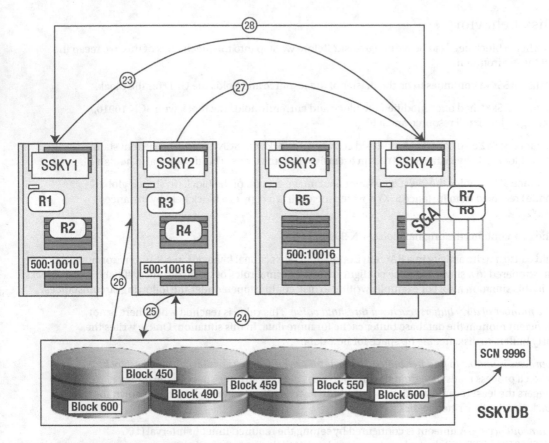

Figure 2-12. *Write to disk behavior*

We make the assumption in our scenario that instance SSKY1, due to a checkpoint request, is required to write the block to disk. Following are the steps taken to accomplish this activity:

23. Instance SSKY1 sends a write request to the GCS with the necessary SCN. The GCS, after determining from the GRD the list of instances that currently contain PI copies, marks them as requiring modification.

24. The GCS initiates the write operation by requesting instance SSKY2, which holds the latest modified block, to perform this operation. *During this process, while a write operation is outstanding, the GCS will not allow another write to be initiated until the current operation is completed.*

■ **Note** The GCS, as the controller of resources, determines which instance will actually perform the write operation; when an instance needs to write a block to disk upon a checkpoint request, the instance checks the role of the resource covering the block. If the role is global, the instance must inform the GCS of the write requirement. The GCS is responsible for finding the most current block image and informing the instance holding the image to perform the block write. In the scenario discussed, instance SSKY1 made the request; SSKY2 is holding a more recent version of the block.

---

25. Instance SSKY2 initiates the I/O with a write to disk request.

26. Once the I/O operation is complete, instance SSKY2 logs the fact that such an operation has been completed and a block written record (BWR) is placed in the redo log buffer. This activity advances the checkpoint, which in turn forces a log write and prevents redo prior to this point to be used for recovery purposes.

■ **Note** During a database recovery operation, the recovery process uses the BWR to validate if the redo information for the block prior to this point is needed.

---

27. Instance SSKY2 informs the GCS of the successful completion of the write operation. This notification also informs the GCS of the current resource status of the block and that the resource is going to a local role because the DBWR has written the current image to disk.

28. On receipt of the write notification, the GCS sends a message to all instances holding a PI instructing them to flush the PI. After completion of this process or if no PI remains, the instance holding the current exclusive resource is asked to switch to the local role. In the scenarios discussed previously, SSKY1 and SSKY2 are the two instances holding a PI. When instance SSKY2 receives a flush request from the GCS, it writes a BWR without flushing the log buffer. Once this completes, instance SSKY2 will hold the block with an exclusive local resource with no PIs, and all other PIs to this block held across various instances are purged.

After the dirty block has been written to disk, any subsequent operation will follow similar steps to complete any requests from users. For example, if an instance requires read access to a block after the block has been written to disk, the instance would check with the GCS and based on the instruction received from the GCS would retrieve the block from disk or will retrieve it from another instance that currently has a copy of the block.

The write/write behavior and write to disk behavior are possible during a DML operation.

In all the scenarios it should be noted that, unless necessary, no write activity to the disk happens. Every activity or state of the block was maintained as a resource in the instance where it was utilized last and reused a number of times from this location.

It should also be noted whereas in the preceding illustrations, we have discussed block sharing from various instances in the cluster, in a real world there could only be two possibilities.

Block Request Involving Two Instances or Two Hops

As discussed in the re-mastering section and subsequently in Step 1 (Figure 2-7), the resource master is maintained on the instance where the demand for the object is the highest, meaning usually the requested block should be on the instance that contains the resource master and the GRD for the resource.

1. In Figure 2-13, the instance SSKY3 requires a row from a block 500 and sends a request to the GCS of the resource.

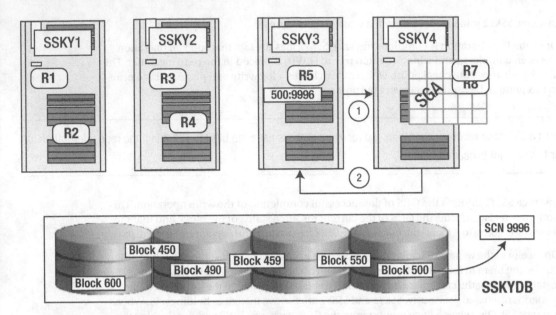

Figure 2-13. *Two-way block transfer*

2.   The block is found on instance SSKY4, and the GCS sends the block to instance SSKY3.

Block Request Involving Three Instances

In scenarios in which the block requested by another instance is not found on the instance that contains the master, the GCS will request the block to be retrieved from the disk; or if the block is found on another instance, it will send a message to the holding instance to send a copy of the block to the requesting instance (see Figure 2-14).

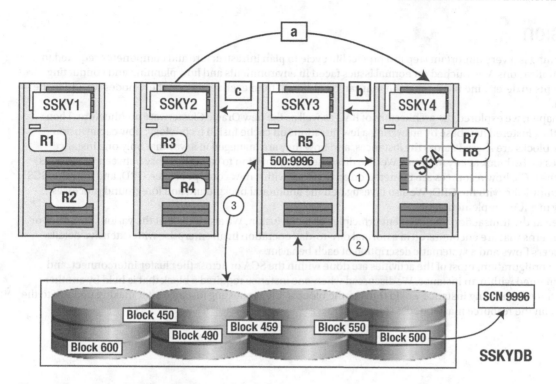

Figure 2-14. *Three-way block transfer*

As illustrated in Figure 2-14, there are two possibilities when the block is not found on the instance that is the master of the object (resource).

- Read the block from the disk.

  1. Instance SSKY1 requests for the block 500 from the GCS located on instance SSKY4.

  2. Instance SSKY4, after checking against the GRD, determines that neither Instance SSKY4 nor any other instance in the cluster has a copy of the block requested. Hence, it sends a message to the requesting instance to read the block from disk.

  3. Instance SSKY3 reads the block from disk.

- Request another instance to transfer the block.

  a. Instance SSKY2 requests block 500 from the GCS located on instance SSKY4.

  b. Instance SSKY4 verifies against its GRD and determines that the block is currently held by instance SSKY3. It sends a message to instance SSKY3 requesting it to send a copy of the block to instance SSKY2.

  c. Instance SSKY3 accepts the request and sends the block to instance SSKY2.

Conclusion

Capacity planning is a very important step in a project life cycle to plan infrastructure and components required to support the applications. We touched on normal issues faced in environments and how planning and conducting proof of concepts to determine the throughput that can be obtained from each server and the n-nodes we add to the configuration.

In this chapter, we explored the architecture of RAC as well as the new Oracle Clusterware architecture. Then we looked at the clustered database by answering a few questions on cache fusion technology: how cache fusion operates, how blocks are shared across the instances, and how they are managed in a way that only one instance makes changes to the block at any moment. We also discussed the provision to cache memory between the various instances by the GCS, how resources are mastered on an instance with a new concept of a the GRD, and how the GCS and GES communicate with the GRD. We also investigated the additional background and foreground processes available only in a RAC implementation.

We looked at the transaction management principles of cache fusion. We also looked at the various scenarios or behavioral patterns that are encountered in a normal day-to-day operation in an enterprise with extensive details, including process flows and a systematic description of each behavior.

In a RAC configuration, most of the activities are done within the SGA or across the cluster interconnect, and a copy is maintained within an instance. We discussed when one instance required a block that is held by another instance and how the holding instance would transfer the block to the requesting instance after making updates to the required GRD on the resource master node.

CHAPTER 3

■ ■ ■

Testing for Availability

RAC is a clustered database solution that provides two major functions, scalability and availability to business continuum. We discuss testing for scalability in Chapter 4.

Availability is the ability of the system to provide continuous service when one or more the components in the cluster fail. There are several components outside of the RAC software and database that are part of the cluster and are prone to failures. In this chapter, we discuss the basic failure points and the best practices that are to be followed to avoid such failures. Subsequently, we discuss the testing the hardware and application for availability.

Points of Failure (Gaps)

All application systems, including database systems, a can fail. The reasons for these failures range from natural disasters to human mistakes. Although most of these failures are beyond human control, it's important to consider why these failures occur.

RAC is a high availability solution. There are several points for potential failure in a RAC hardware configuration such as the interconnect, which is the primary backbone in a RAC configuration. Because RAC is comprised of several instances of Oracle, some of these failure scenarios could be found in the traditional stand-alone configuration, whereas others are specific to RAC.

Figure 3-1 illustrates the various areas of the system (O/S, hardware, and Oracle components) that could fail. The various failure scenarios in a six-node configuration as illustrated in Figure 3-1 are

1. Interconnect failure
2. Node failure
3. Instance failure
4. Media Failure
5. Oracle component failure

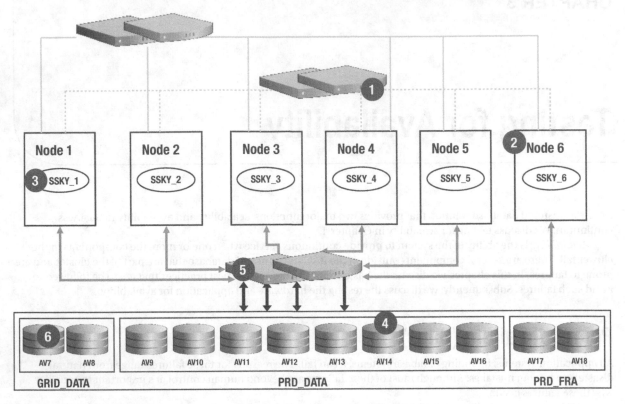

Figure 3-1. *Points of failure in a RAC hardware configuration*

We briefly examine each of these failure scenarios and discuss the various methods to protect them from these failures.

Interconnect Failure

If the interconnect between nodes fail, either because of a physical failure or a software failure in the communication or interprocess communication (IPC) layer, it appears to the Oracle Clusterware (OCW) at each end of the interconnect that the node at the other end has failed. The OCW should use an alternative method, such as checking for a quorum disk, to evaluate the status of the system. In the case of a complete communication link failure, a voting disk protocol is initiated. Whichever node grabs the most number of disks becomes the master. The master writes a kill block to the disk in case the communication link is down. Instance will then kill itself.

Eventually, it may shut down both the nodes involved in the operation or just one of the nodes at the end of the failed connection. It will evict the node by means of fencing to prevent any continued writes that could potentially corrupt the database.

Traditionally in a RAC environment, when a node or instance fails, an instance is elected to perform instance recovery. The Global Enqueue Service and the Global Cache Service are reconfigured after the failure; redo logs are merged and rolled forward. The transactions that have not been committed are rolled back.

This operation is performed by one of the surviving instances reading through the redo log files of the failed instance. Such recovery provides users immediate access to consistent data. However, in situations where the clusterware is deciding on which node(s) to shut down, access is denied and in turn the recovery operation is delayed; thus, data is not available for access. This is because recovery operations are not performed until the interconnect failure causes one of the instances or nodes to fail.

A typical situation under these circumstances would be when one or both of the instances lose communication with the other instance and waits until it receives a failure signal. The failure of the cluster interconnect could cause a communication failure between the two nodes. When the heartbeat mechanism between the two nodes is not successful, the OCW triggered by the heartbeat timeout parameter signals a node failure. However, because there was no physical failure of the instance and/or node, the Global Enqueue Service Monitor (LMON) process is unable to write to the disk regarding the status of the other instance.

Although there is no physical failure of the instance and/or node, every instance would wait to receive a communication from the other instance either that it's up and alive and communication could continue or that the other instance is down and is not communicating. If after a certain time period there is no response, one of the instances that is currently up will try to force shutdown of the instance that is not responding.

When the communication between the instances fail, the instances will slow down and hang eventually, with severe impact on performance. This is due to the fact that the Oracle kernel is repeatedly trying to shut down other unreachable instances to perform recovery. When this happens, it calls for a manual intervention (in extremely rare cases) where the DBA would be required to shutdown one of the instances to allow business to continue.

To avoid this single point of failure, business organizations should configure dual or multiple interconnects.

Methods of Implementing Redundant Interconnects

Oracle supports implementing redundant interconnects using one of the following methods.

CLUSTER_INTERCONNECT

One method of implementing this feature is to use the CLUSTER_INTERCONNECT parameter. By listing the IP addresses, Oracle is made aware of the additional interconnects and Oracle will use them for communication.

```
ALTER SYSTEM SET CLUSTER_INTERCONNECT= '192.30.0.96: 192.30.0.100: 192.30.0.98'
scope=SPFILE SID='SSKY_1';
Script: MVRACPDnTap_verifyic.sql
                          Impl
ADDR              Indx   Public   Type  Name    IP Address
----------------  -----  -------- ----- ------- -------------
00002B35D99D89A0  0      N        CI    eth23   192.30.0.96
00002B35D99D89A0  1      N        CI    eth21   192.30.0.100
00002B35D99D89A0  2      N        CI    eth22   192.30.0.98
Inst Name  IP Address     IS_PUBLIC Source
---- ----- -------------  --------- ------------------------------
1    eth21 192.30.0.100   NO        cluster_interconnects parameter
1    eth22 192.30.0.98    NO        cluster_interconnects parameter
1    eth23 192.30.0.96    NO        cluster_interconnects parameter
```

In this configuration, Instance 1 has three interconnects configured. The drawback to using the CLUSTER_INTERCONNECT parameter is that some of high availability (HA) features will be lost.

■ **Note**   Oracle does not recommend use of this parameter. This parameter does not guarantee HA on all platforms and in all releases of Oracle.

NIC Bonding

Using the parameter has benefits when there are multiple databases configured on the same cluster and when the desire is to route each database's interconnect traffic on a separate private network. However, considering the HA features, a better, more reliable method over the previous option would be to use the network interface card (NIC) pairing or bonding functionality available at the O/S level. Multiple NICs can be paired to act as a single logical entity.

NIC bonding or NIC pairing is a method of pairing multiple physical network connections into a single logical interface. This logical interface will be used to establish a connection with the database server. By allowing all network connections that are part of the logical interface to be used during communication, it provides load-balancing capabilities that would otherwise not be available. In addition, when one of the network connections fails, the other connection will continue to receive and transmit data, making it fault tolerant.

The first step in implementing the bonding functionality is to configure the bonding drivers. For example, in a Linux environment, this is done by adding the following to the /etc/modules.conf file:

```
alias bond0 bonding
options bond0 miimon=100 mode=0
```

The configuration consists of two lines for each logical interface. The value miimon (media independent interface monitor) is configured in milliseconds and represents the link monitoring frequency. Mode indicates the type of configuration that will be deployed between the interfaces that are bonded or paired together and how the physical interfaces that are part of the logical interface will be used. A value of 0 indicates that a round-robin policy will be used and all interfaces will take turns in transmitting; Mode 1 indicates that one of the interfaces will be configured as a backup device and Mode 2 indicates either of them would be used.

The next step is to configure the logical interfaces. Configuring the logical interface is to create the file ifcfg-bond0 for the private logical interfaces in the /etc/sysconfig/network-scripts directory:

```
[root@prddb3 network-scripts]# more ifcfg-bond2
# Linux NIC bonding between eth24 and eth25
# Murali Vallath
# December-21-2013
DEVICE=bond2
BOOTPROTO=none
BROADCAST=192.30.0.255
IPADDR=192.30.0.96
NETMASK=255.255.255.0
NETWORK=192.30.0.0
ONBOOT=yes
USERCTL=no
TYPE=Ethernet
```

■ **Note**   The /etc/sysconfig/network-scripts directory contains, by default, one configuration file per network interface and all the interface assigned credentials such as IP address, subnet details, and so forth. Users should have root privileges to complete this operation.

Modify the individual network interface configuration files to reflect the bonding details:

```
[root@prddb3 network-scripts]# more ifcfg-eth24
# Linux NIC bonding between eth24 and eth25
# Murali Vallath
# December-21-2013
DEVICE=eth24
BOOTPROTO=none
ONBOOT=yes
USERCTL=no
MASTER=bond2
SLAVE=yes
TYPE=Ethernet
HWADDR=00:D0:B7:6A:39:85
Modify ifcfg-eth25 to make similar updates
```

In the preceding file, the MASTER clause indicates which logical interface this specific NIC belongs to, and the SLAVE clause indicates that it's one among other NICs that are bonded to the master and is only a slave to its master.

■ **Note**   Similar changes should be made to all network configuration files on node prddb3 for bond2 logical interface described in this example.

The next step is to restart the network interfaces, and this can be done by using the following commands:

```
[root@prddb3 root]# service network stop
Shutting down interface eth0:              [ OK ]
Shutting down interface eth24:             [ OK ]
Shutting down interface eth25:             [ OK ]
Shutting down loopback interface:          [ OK ]
[root@prddb3 root]#
[root@prddb3 root]# service network start
Setting network parameters:                [ OK ]
Bringing up loopback interface:            [ OK ]
Bringing up interface bond2:               [ OK ]
[root@prddb3 root]#
```

The next step in the configuration process is to verify if the new logical interface is active. The following two options will help verify the configuration:

1. Verify from the messages generated during interface startup. This is found in the operating system specific log files.

```
[root@prddb3 root]# tail -15 /var/log/messages
network: Setting network parameters: succeeded
kernel: ip_tables: (C) 2000-2002 Netfilter core team
network: Bringing up loopback interface: succeeded
kernel: ip_tables: (C) 2000-2002 Netfilter core team
ifup: Enslaving eth25 to bond2
kernel: bonding: bond0: enslaving eth24 as an active interface with a down link.
```

```
ifup: Enslaving eth24 to bond2
kernel: eth24: link up.
kernel: eth24: Setting full-duplex based on negotiated link capability.
kernel: bonding: bond2: enslaving eth as an active interface with an up link.
network: Bringing up interface bond2: succeeded
kernel: ip_tables: (C) 2000-2002 Netfilter core team
kernel: e100: eth0 NIC Link is Up 100 Mbps Full duplex
kernel: bonding: bond0: link status definitely up for interface eth1.
network: Bringing up interface eth0: succeeded
sshd(pam_unix)[5066]: session opened for user root by (uid=0)
[root@prddb3 root]#
```

2. Verify the new active networks using the `ifconfig` command.

```
[root@prddb3 root]# ifconfig -a
bond2    Link encap:Ethernet HWaddr 00:D0:B7:6A:39:85
         inet addr:192.30.0.96 Bcast:192.30.0.255 Mask:255.255.255.0
         UP BROADCAST RUNNING MASTER MULTICAST MTU:1500 Metric:1
         RX packets:3162 errors:0 dropped:0 overruns:0 frame:0
         TX packets:1312 errors:0 dropped:0 overruns:0 carrier:0
         collisions:0 txqueuelen:0
         RX bytes:275327 (268.8 Kb) TX bytes:142369 (139.0 Kb)
eth24    Link encap:Ethernet HWaddr 00:D0:B7:6A:39:85
         inet addr:192.30.0.96 Bcast:192.30.0.255 Mask:255.255.255.0
         UP BROADCAST RUNNING SLAVE MULTICAST MTU:1500 Metric:1
         RX packets:804 errors:0 dropped:0 overruns:0 frame:0
         TX packets:1156 errors:0 dropped:0 overruns:0 carrier:0
         collisions:0 txqueuelen:1000
         RX bytes:83807 (81.8 Kb) TX bytes:120774 (117.9 Kb)
         Interrupt:11 Base address:0x2800 Memory:41500000-41500038
eth25    Link encap:Ethernet HWaddr 00:D0:B7:6A:39:85
         inet addr:192.30.0.96 Bcast:192.30.0.255 Mask:255.255.255.0
         UP BROADCAST RUNNING SLAVE MULTICAST MTU:1500 Metric:1
         RX packets:2358 errors:0 dropped:0 overruns:0 frame:0
         TX packets:156 errors:0 dropped:0 overruns:0 carrier:0
         collisions:0 txqueuelen:1000
         RX bytes:191520 (187.0 Kb) TX bytes:21933 (21.4 Kb)
         Interrupt:11 Base address:0x9000
eth2     Link encap:Ethernet HWaddr 00:09:5B:E0:45:94
....    .........    .........
```

■ **Note** The `ifconfig` output in the preceding displays all interfaces available on the node; however, once bonding has been configured, only the new logical IP address assigned to `bond2` will be accessible.

High Available IP (HAIP)

Starting with Oracle Database 11g Release 2 (11.2.0.2), there is a new paradigm shift to this entire configuration option implementation with the new HAIP feature. Using the HAIP feature, multiple NICs can be configured as private networks without any bonding or without the use of the CLUSTER_INTERCONNECTS parameter. Apart from providing continuous availability should an NIC in the configuration fail, Oracle load balances traffic across all the available NICs.

Starting with Oracle Database 11g Release 2 (11.2.0.2), HAIP is installed by default as part of the Grid infrastructure configuration. Figure 3-2 illustrates the Oracle Universal Installer (OUI) screen that allows configuration of one or more private interconnects. As part of the installation when root.sh script is executed, Oracle configures the HAIP resource. However, unlike the previous versions of RAC, the private network is not registered or managed directly in the Oracle Cluster Registry (OCR) file but added to the Grid Plug and Play (GPnP) profile on every server in the cluster. The OCR maintains information as to where the GPnP profile is located.

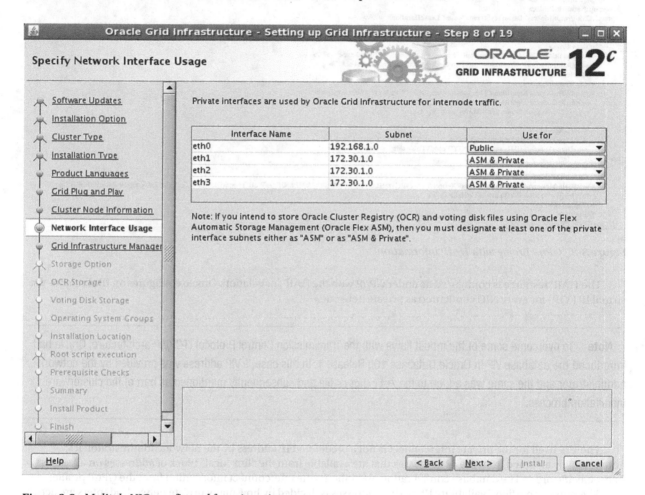

Figure 3-2. *Mulitple NICs configured for private interconnect*

GPnP Profile is an xml file located in $GRID_HOME/gpnp/<hostname>/profiles/peer directory. Figure 3-3 illustrates the output of the xml file viewed from a browser.

– <gpnp:GPnP-Profile Version="1.0" xsi:schemaLocation="http://www.grid-pnp.org/2005/11/gpnp-profile gpnp-profile.xsd" ProfileSequence="4"
    ClusterUId="e1dc4defa8b4ffbdbf7166965cba58b1" ClusterName="sskylc1-cluster" PALocation="">
  – <gpnp:Network-Profile>
    – <gpnp:HostNetwork id="gen" HostName="*">
        <gpnp:Network id="net1" IP="192.168.1.0" Adapter="eth0" Use="public"/>
        <gpnp:Network id="net2" IP="172.30.1.0" Adapter="eth1" Use="asm,cluster_interconnect"/>
        <gpnp:Network id="net3" IP="172.30.1.0" Adapter="eth2" Use="asm,cluster_interconnect"/>
        <gpnp:Network id="net4" IP="172.30.1.0" Adapter="eth3" Use="asm,cluster_interconnect"/>
      </gpnp:HostNetwork>
  </gpnp:Network-Profile>
  <orcl:CSS-Profile id="css" DiscoveryString="+asm" LeaseDuration="400"/>
  <orcl:ASM-Profile id="asm" DiscoveryString="/dev/oracleasm/disks" SPFile="+GRID_DATA/sskylc1-cluster/ASMPARAMETERFILE/registry.253.836491531" Mode="legacy"/>
  – <ds:Signature>
    – <ds:SignedInfo>
        <ds:CanonicalizationMethod Algorithm="http://www.w3.org/2001/10/xml-exc-c14n#"/>
        <ds:SignatureMethod Algorithm="http://www.w3.org/2000/09/xmldsig#rsa-sha1"/>
      – <ds:Reference URI="">
        – <ds:Transforms>
            <ds:Transform Algorithm="http://www.w3.org/2000/09/xmldsig#enveloped-signature"/>
          – <ds:Transform Algorithm="http://www.w3.org/2001/10/xml-exc-c14n#">
              <InclusiveNamespaces PrefixList="gpnp orcl xsi"/>
            </ds:Transform>
          </ds:Transforms>
          <ds:DigestMethod Algorithm="http://www.w3.org/2000/09/xmldsig#sha1"/>
          <ds:DigestValue>t6idM1s+m68pDslyXJYW6MdVGsU=</ds:DigestValue>
        </ds:Reference>
      </ds:SignedInfo>
    – <ds:SignatureValue>
        fjVyRE7HE64gWmYQconMwFDkSsc7+aRXk0gee/F1A/ZvBC1zzHLCV9YgqZol97jPl/gUcMBbNJEz+aWqB/YN8mkij4rCZat3gDLNxVPRx0Vdoj+Rew4cvrPlHtbRek1hkxFEfwg6
        /nzoWmyBL3VTNRwSN7QYc4N9RURHoQo2yjw=
      </ds:SignatureValue>
    </ds:Signature>
  </gpnp:GPnP-Profile>

Figure 3-3. *GPnP profile with HAIP information*

The HAIP resource is configured as under GPnP with the HAIP installation. Oracle configures an IP similar to the virtual IP (VIP) for every NIC configured as private network.

■ **Note**   To overcome some of the inbuilt flaws with the Transmission Control Protocol (TCP)/IP architecture, Oracle had introduced the database VIP in Oracle Database 10g Release 1. In this case, a VIP address was provided by the network administrator and the same was added to the /etc/hosts file and subsequently mentioned as part of the clusterware installation process.

The VIP used for the private interconnect is not a predefined IP address by the network administrator. It's automatically assigned from the IP addresses that are available from the "link local" block of addresses on all servers in no specific order. The database configuration also inherits the interconnect information from the GPnP profile.

The number of High Availability IP (HAIP) addresses is decided by how many private network adapters are active when OSW comes up on the first node in the cluster. If there's only one active private network, OSW will create one; if two, OSW will create two; and if more than two, OSW will create four HAIPs. The number of HAIPs won't change even if more private network adapters are activated later; a restart of clusterware on all nodes is required for new adapters to become effective.

OSW automatically picks link local addresses from reserved 169.254.*.* subnet for HAIP, and it will not attempt to use any 169.254.*.* address if it's already in use for another purpose. Using HAIP Interconnect traffic will be load balanced across all active interconnect interfaces, and the corresponding HAIP address will be failed over transparently to other adapters if one fails or becomes noncommunicative.[1]

---

[1]Metalink Note: 1210883.1, 11gR2 Grid Infrastructure Redundant Interconnect and ora.cluster_interconnect.haip

■ **Note** 169.254.0.0/16 is the "link local" block. It is allocated for communication between hosts on a single link. Hosts obtain these addresses by autoconfiguration, such as when a Dynamic Host Configuration Protocol (DHCP) server may not be found. This is a 16-bit address; class B subnet and can support up to 65,534 interfaces.

HAIP can be configured automatically when grid infrastructure is installed and configured directly from Oracle Database Release Version 11.2.0.2. In other cases, it can be configured manually using oifcfg utility.

```
[oracle@prddb1 ~]$ $GRID_HOME/bin/oifcfg getif
eth22 172.30.0.0 global cluster_interconnect
eth23 172.30.0.0 global cluster_interconnect
eth21 172.30.0.0 global cluster_interconnect
bond0 10.32.7.0 global public
```

Script: MVRACPDnTap_verifyic.sql

ADDR	Indx	Impl Public	Type	Name	IP Address
00002ABABE2F99D8	0	N	GPnP	eth22:1	169.254.38.59
00002ABABE2F99D8	1	N	GPnP	eth23:1	169.254.100.30
00002ABABE2F99D8	2	N	GPnP	eth21:1	169.254.141.217
00002ABABE2F99D8	3	N	GPnP	eth22:2	169.254.194.29
00002ABABE2F99D8	4	Y	GPnP	bond0	10.32.7.133
00002ABABE2F99D8	5	Y	GPnP	bond0:1	10.32.7.136
00002ABABE2F99D8	6	Y	GPnP	bond0:2	10.32.7.134

7 rows selected.

Interconnect Availability

Whereas both the bonding and HAIP features provide failover when a NIC in the configuration fails, HAIP provides load balancing between the NICs and a closer to linear scalability as additional NICs are added to the configuration.

■ **Note** In Chapter 14, we discuss the load balancing and scalability of this new feature in more detail.

The following node has three NICs configured for interconnects. For every NIC used for the interconnect Oracle assigns a HAIP (VIP). In the following, ifconfig -a output for the three NICs—eth21, eth22, and eth23—are illustrated:

```
eth21    Link encap:Ethernet HWaddr 00:23:7D:36:FE:F7
         inet addr:172.30.0.100 Bcast:172.30.0.255 Mask:255.255.255.0
         inet6 addr: fe80::223:7dff:fe36:fef7/64 Scope:Link
         UP BROADCAST RUNNING MULTICAST MTU:9000 Metric:1
         RX packets:2386967 errors:0 dropped:0 overruns:0 frame:0
         TX packets:297843 errors:0 dropped:0 overruns:0 carrier:0
         collisions:0 txqueuelen:1000
         RX bytes:447104612 (426.3 MiB) TX bytes:70895439 (67.6 MiB)
```

```
       Interrupt:98
eth21:1  Link encap:Ethernet HWaddr 00:23:7D:36:FE:F7
       inet addr:169.254.181.158 Bcast:169.254.191.255 Mask:255.255.192.0
       UP BROADCAST RUNNING MULTICAST MTU:9000 Metric:1
       Interrupt:98
eth22    Link encap:Ethernet HWaddr 00:23:7D:36:5B:90
       inet addr:172.30.0.98 Bcast:172.30.0.255 Mask:255.255.255.0
       inet6 addr: fe80::223:7dff:fe36:5b90/64 Scope:Link
       UP BROADCAST RUNNING MULTICAST MTU:9000 Metric:1
       RX packets:665462 errors:0 dropped:0 overruns:0 frame:0
       TX packets:168063 errors:0 dropped:0 overruns:0 carrier:0
       collisions:0 txqueuelen:1000
       RX bytes:217845225 (207.7 MiB) TX bytes:113734036 (108.4 MiB)
       Interrupt:169 Memory:f8000000-f8012800
eth22:1  Link encap:Ethernet HWaddr 00:23:7D:36:5B:90
       inet addr:169.254.3.23 Bcast:169.254.63.255 Mask:255.255.192.0
       UP BROADCAST RUNNING MULTICAST MTU:9000 Metric:1
       Interrupt:169 Memory:f8000000-f8012800
eth22:2  Link encap:Ethernet HWaddr 00:23:7D:36:5B:90
       inet addr:169.254.196.234 Bcast:169.254.255.255 Mask:255.255.192.0
       UP BROADCAST RUNNING MULTICAST MTU:9000 Metric:1
       Interrupt:169 Memory:f8000000-f8012800
eth23    Link encap:Ethernet HWaddr 00:23:7D:36:5B:94
       inet addr:172.30.0.96 Bcast:172.30.0.255 Mask:255.255.255.0
       inet6 addr: fe80::223:7dff:fe36:5b94/64 Scope:Link
       UP BROADCAST RUNNING MULTICAST MTU:9000 Metric:1
       RX packets:88927 errors:0 dropped:0 overruns:0 frame:0
       TX packets:81267 errors:0 dropped:0 overruns:0 carrier:0
       collisions:0 txqueuelen:1000
       RX bytes:88117506 (84.0 MiB) TX bytes:29941851 (28.5 MiB)
       Interrupt:177 Memory:fa000000-fa012800
eth23:1  Link encap:Ethernet HWaddr 00:23:7D:36:5B:94
       inet addr:169.254.110.128 Bcast:169.254.127.255 Mask:255.255.192.0
       UP BROADCAST RUNNING MULTICAST MTU:9000 Metric:1
       Interrupt:177 Memory:fa000000-fa012800
```

■ **Note**   In the preceding output, it should be noticed that there are two HAIPs assigned to eth22. This is because Oracle software assumes that NICs are assigned in pairs and only a max of 4 HAIPs will be assigned for the node.

The Oracle daemon process that manages the HA feature of the HAIP is called Grid IPC daemon (GIPCD). GIPCD maintains logs in the GRID_HOME/log/<node name>/gipcd directory and watches the availability of the NIC every 5 seconds, and the GIPCD monitor (GIPCDMON) checks on the load average of the NICs every 10 seconds.

If a NIC fails for any reason, the HAIP assigned to that NIC is assigned to one of the surviving NICs (similar to the database VIP feature that was introduced in Oracle Database 10g Release 2 except that the HAIP does not failover between servers. It remains on the same node when one or more NICs fail or are disabled when the entire node fails).

When a private NIC fails, the HAIP moves from the failed NIC to one of the surviving NICs on the server; and when both NICs in the preceding node configuration fails, the HAIP from all the failed private NICs failover to the surviving NICs. Illustrated in the example output following, the server has four private interconnects configured using the HAIP feature; three out of the four NICs fail, and the HAIP of all the failed NICs failover to the surviving NIC (eth21:1, eth21:2, eth21:3, and eth21:4).

```
eth21:1  Link encap:Ethernet  HWaddr 00:22:64:0E:8F:D3
        inet addr:169.254.21.103 Bcast:169.254.63.255 Mask:255.255.192.0
        UP BROADCAST RUNNING MULTICAST MTU:9000 Metric:1
        Interrupt:98
eth21:2  Link encap:Ethernet  HWaddr 00:22:64:0E:8F:D3
        inet addr:169.254.193.238 Bcast:169.254.255.255 Mask:255.255.192.0
        UP BROADCAST RUNNING MULTICAST MTU:9000 Metric:1
        Interrupt:98
eth21:3  Link encap:Ethernet  HWaddr 00:22:64:0E:8F:D3
        inet addr:169.254.91.154 Bcast:169.254.127.255 Mask:255.255.192.0
        UP BROADCAST RUNNING MULTICAST MTU:9000 Metric:1
        Interrupt:98
eth21:4  Link encap:Ethernet  HWaddr 00:22:64:0E:8F:D3
        inet addr:169.254.134.16 Bcast:169.254.191.255 Mask:255.255.192.0
        UP BROADCAST RUNNING MULTICAST MTU:9000 Metric:1
        Interrupt:98
```

What if the server had four of five NICs configured as private interconnects? In this case, when a NIC that has an assigned HAIP fails, the HAIP is assigned or moved to the new NIC on the node.

Node Failure

RAC comprises two or more instances sharing a single copy of a physical database. Prior to Oracle Database 11g Release 2, each instance is normally attached or configured to run on a specific node. This type of configuration where the instance is physically mapped to specific nodes in the cluster is called *admin managed configuration*. Starting with Oracle Database 11g Release 2, Oracle provides another method of database configuration where the instances can optionally not be mapped to any specific server in the cluster. This feature is called *pool-managed configuration*.

In a RAC configuration, if the node fails, the instance that includes Global Cache state (GCS) objects stored in the buffer cache and the shared pool, as well as the GCS processes on that node, will fail. Under such circumstances, the GCS must reconfigure itself to re-master the locks that were being managed by the failed node before instance recovery can occur. During reconfiguration process, the global buffer cache locks are replayed to produce a consistent state of the memory buffers.

Many cluster hardware vendors use a disk-based quorum system that allows each node to determine which other nodes are currently active members of the cluster. These systems also allow a node to remove itself from the cluster or to remove other nodes from the cluster. The latter is accomplished through a type of voting system, managed through the shared quorum disk, that allows nodes to determine which node will remain active if one or more of the nodes become disconnected from the cluster interconnect.

Using OCW places RAC in a more advantageous position because RAC uses both methods for failure detection. While the OCW maintains the heartbeat functions using the cluster interconnect (called *network heartbeat*—NHB), the OCW will also verify against the voting disk (called *disk heartbeat*—DHB) to check if the node has lost communication. Using the heartbeat mechanism, the OCW is able to verify the health of the other node members participating in the cluster. At each heartbeat, every member node gives its status to the other members. If they all agree, nothing further is done until the next heartbeat. If two or more nodes report a different configuration (e.g., the cluster interconnect is broken between a pair of nodes), then one member arbitrates among the different members in the cluster.

When a node, or the communication to a node, fails, the NHB between the two nodes in question is not successful. After waiting until the time-out period (defined by the `misscount` parameter), one of the remaining nodes detects the failure and attempts to reform the cluster. If the remaining nodes in the cluster are able to form a quorum, the OCW will reorganize the cluster membership.

■ **Note** We discuss NHB and DHB for node verification in much more detail in subsequent chapters.

CLUSTER PARAMETERS

The three parameters that control the node eviction rules and time out periods are

Misscount (MC)—defaults to 30 seconds. It's the maximum time in seconds that an NHB can be missed before entering into a cluster reconfiguration to evict the node. (The default value of this parameter when using vendor clusterware is 600 seconds to resolve any possible split-brain scenarios.)

Disktimeout (DTO)—defaults to 200 seconds. This is the time before an I/O operation against the voting disk should complete.

Reboottime (RBT)—defaults to 3 seconds. This is the time allowed for a node to complete a reboot after the Cluster Synchronization Services (CSS) daemon has been evicted.

This information can be obtained using the Oracle Clusterware Control (crsctl) utility:

```
$GRID_HOME/bin/crsctl get css
Usage:
  crsctl get css <parameter>
Displays the value of a Cluster Synchronization Services parameter
  clusterguid
  diagwait
  disktimeout
  misscount
  reboottime
  priority
  logfilesize
  leafmisscount
$GRID_HOME/bin/crsctl get css reboottime
CRS-4678: Successful get reboottime 3 for Cluster Synchronization Services.
```

The voting disk, on the other hand, is updated by each node in the cluster with a time stamp entry once every so many seconds. When a member arbitrates regarding the other members availability, the voting disk is consulted by the OCW to verify this arbitration. Once this configuration is tested, the arbitrating instance uses the shared disk to publish the proposed configuration to the other instances. All active instances then examine the published configuration, and, if necessary, terminate themselves.

The reconfiguration process regroups the nodes that are accessible and removes the nodes that have failed. For example, in a six-node cluster, if one node fails, the OCW will re-group among the remaining five nodes. The OCW performs the reorganization of the cluster membership when a node is added to or removed from a cluster. This information is exposed to the respective Oracle instances by the Global Enqueue Service Monitor (LMON) process on the participating instances.

Up to this point, the OCW did the failure detection. Because a node failure also involves an instance failure, there are further steps involved before one of the surviving instances perform recovery. Instance failure involves database crash recovery followed by instance recovery.

Instance Failure

RAC is comprised of several instances talking to a common shared physical database. Because several instances are involved in this configuration, one or multiple instance failures may occur. If all instances participating in the configuration fail, the database is in an unusable state and could be called a *crash* or *database crash*; and the recovery process associated with this failure is called a *crash recovery*.

If only one or more of these instances fail, there is only an instance failure; and the recovery process associated with this failure is called an *instance recovery*.

Instance failure could happen in several ways—the common reason for an instance failure is when the node fails due to reasons such as a power surge, operator error, and so forth, or because one of the components of the cluster—like the public NIC or the HBA device—failed. Other reasons for an instance failure could be when an operator issues a SHUTDOWN ABORT, causing an instance failure.

Recovery from an instance failure begins when one of the surviving nodes (whose heartbeat mechanism detected the failure first) informs the LMON process. The LMON process on each instance in the cluster communicates with the OCW on the respective nodes and initiates instance recovery. The recovering instance will acquire the locks for the redo thread of the other instance. The redo logs of the failed instance are read by the System Monitor (SMON) or recovery slaves during recovery.

Server Pools

Starting with Oracle Database 11g Release 2, Oracle has introduced a new feature for node and instance management called *Policy Managed*. This feature allows configuration of nodes into pools and prioritizes availability of nodes to the instances that are part of specific pools. As discussed in the previous sections, if there is a node crash and the pool does not have a sufficient number of instances required to be present in the pool, a server from another pool can automatically be provisioned to the pool where failure occurred and the instances automatically started. Using the pool management feature, rules can be defined based on criticality of the database and on workload patterns.

Oracle Component Failure

In Chapter 2, we discussed the various components of the RAC configuration. To keep the database up and running, the clusterware on the server should be functioning. Several components of the clusterware are configured to automatically restart (Cluster Ready Services Daemon [CRSD], Event Manager Daemon [EVMD], enable Oracle Notification Service [eONS], etc.) on failure; others are critical, and if they fail (Oracle High Availability Service Daemon [OHASD], Grid Naming Service Daemon [GNSD]) will cause the server or node to reboot automatically. There are other components, such as the OCR, Oracle Local Registry (OLR), and voting disks, that provide support for the clusterware to be functional and provide the HA services required. Starting with Oracle Database 11g Release 2, the voting disks and OCR files are managed by ASM.

Protecting the OCR

There are two methods in which redundancy for the OCR files can be provided.

Using ASM redundancy

There are three levels of redundancy supported by ASM:

1. Normal redundancy requires three diskgroups and maintains three mirrored copies of the OCR file.

2. High redundancy requires five diskgroups and maintains five mirrored copies of the OCR file.

3. External redundancy only requires one diskgroup and relies on the storage for external mirroring of the OCR file.

■ **Note**   The diskgroup requirements for the redundancy levels when configuring OCR files during Grid Infrastructure installation should not be confused with diskgroup requirements during database configuration. When configuring diskgroups for storing data and Fast Recovery Area (FRA), normal redundancy requires two disks/logical unit numbers (LUNs) to be part of the diskgroup. High redundancy requires three disks/LUNs or failure groups to be part of the diskgroup. External redundancy requires one disk/LUN to be part of the diskgroup.

Multiplexing

By configuring individual diskgroups and adding OCR files manually using the ocrconfig command, redundant copies of the OCR file can be maintained. With this file, two physical OCR files are maintained in parallel across two different diskgroups.

```
[root@prddb1 ~]# $GRID_HOME/bin/ocrcheck
Status of Oracle Cluster Registry is as follows :
     Version                  : 3
     Total space (kbytes)     : 262120
     Used space (kbytes)      : 2964
     Available space (kbytes) : 259156
     ID                       : 1549014030
     Device/File Name         : +PRDDB_GRID1
                                Device/File integrity check succeeded
     Device/File Name         : +PRDDB_GRID2
                                Device/File integrity check succeeded
                                Device/File not configured
                                Device/File not configured
                                Device/File not configured
     Cluster registry integrity check succeeded
```

Media Failure

Media failures comprise the failure of the various components of the database, such as data files, tablespaces, and the entire database itself. They occur when the Oracle file storage media is damaged and prevents Oracle from reading or writing data, resulting in the loss of one or more database files. These failures could affect one or all types of files necessary for the operation of an Oracle database, including online redo log files, archived redo log files, and control files.

The reasons for media failures could be a bad disk, controller failures, mirrored disk failures, block corruptions, or a power surge. Depending on the type of failure, a data file, tablespace, or the database could be affected. The extent of damage to the specific area will determine the amount of time that the media would be offline and access will be interrupted.

Database operation after a media failure of online redo log files or control files depends on whether the online redo log or control file has been set up with multiplexing. Storing the multiplexed files on separate diskgroups protects the copies from failures. For example, if a media failure damages one of the diskgroups of a multiplexed online redo log file, then database operation will continue from the other diskgroup without significant interruption. On the other hand, if the files were not multiplexed, damage to the single copy of the redo log file could cause the database operation to halt and may cause permanent loss of data.

All other types of media failures cause interruption of business if appropriate methods of business system protection are not provided. Oracle technology and maximum availability architecture solutions help protect business continuity during such media failures.

Protecting the Database

Maximum Availability Architecture (MAA) solutions from Oracle include RAC and Oracle data guard. Using these technologies, data is copied to a remote location to a close to identical hardware configuration and applied on a real-time basis. When failures (such as media failures) cause interruption of business, the database access locations can be switched over from the primary to the standby location providing continued availability. In Oracle Database 10g Release 2, a new feature was introduced called *fast-start failover* providing switchover of primary to standby location by allowing the original primary to act as standby, making failback operations seamless.

Recovery from media failures also depends on the type of media failure. Accordingly, either data file recovery, tablespace recovery, or database recovery is performed on the primary instance, returning it to a useable state.

Testing Hardware for Availability

As we have seen previously, RAC configuration has several components in its configuration. Whereas some of the components—such as the interconnect, nodes, storage, and so forth—are protected from failures by adding redundant infrastructure, other components such as the instance and database are protected by adding database features such as policy managed, data guard, and so forth.

Irrespective of the type of component and the type of failure that could occur in database configuration, it's important that all components are configured right and that they are validated before implementing them into production. To accomplish this, it's important that all components are tested for availability. In Chapter 1, we discussed very briefly the RAP methodology or procedure. If implemented, the methodology involves seven Phases (RAP) of testing. Among the seven phases, RAP Phase I, RAP Phase III, RAP Phase VI, and RAP Phase VII of the methodology focuses on availability testing.

RAP Phase I

During this step of testing, the various failure points will have to be tested to ensure that the RAC database will continue to function either as a single instance or as a cluster depending on where the failure has occurred. For example, from where the node failure occurred, the remaining nodes in the cluster should continue to function. Similarly, when a network switches to the storage array and fails, the redundant switch should continue to operate. Tests should be performed during load; meaning failures should be simulated considering they could happen in live production environments with user activity.

■ **Note** This is a critical test and should not be compromised. All failure points should be tested until the expected results are achieved. A detailed sample spreadsheet containing the failure points to be tested is provided in Appendix D.

Workshop

RAP Phase I checks for availability of the components and indirectly tests the stability of the cluster under load. In this workshop, we cover scenarios of testing a few components of the hardware.

This phase of the testing can be completed very early in the RAC migration process. Once the production hardware is ready and configured, this test should be completed. Under no circumstances should any of the RAP phases be ignored or compromised. The opportunity to identify and fix problems may not be available once the environment is in production; and it could become really late in the game when components start failing in production, defeating the entire goal of providing HA to the database.

Step 1

Gather all the required component information and create a test plan for those components that are prone to failures. List all components that can fail and interrupt the HA of the database environment. Examples of such components are

1. Interconnect or private NIC

2. HBA

3. Public NIC

4. Host/nodes

Table 3-1. RAP Phase 1—Test Results Recorder

Test #	Host Name	Interface	Test Method	Expected Behavior	Observation / Result	Status	Node1	Node2	Node3

The list should be created using a spreadsheet and all interfaces, including IP address (see Table 3-1).

> *Test #*: Because there will be a sequence of tests, this column contains the test number.
>
> *Host name*: This is the physical name assigned to the host. For example, if we are testing the private interconnect, the name here would be prddb1-priv.summersky.com or the short name prrddb1-priv.
>
> *Interface*: This is the name of the physical interface. For example, if the private interface is being tested, and the interface name assigned by the O/S is eth24, list eth24 in this column.
>
> *Test Method*: What kind of testing method do you plan to use to simulate failure of this interface?
>
> a. Physically pull the cable.
>
> b. Disable the port from the O/S: From the O/S prompt, disable the port.

The first method should be the preferred method for testing because when a failure happens, the entire interface is not reachable, which is best simulated by this option. With other methods, although they simulate a failure, the failure is not instantaneous.

■ **Note** Certain hardware implementations—for example, HP ProLiant BL680c (which is a blade)—if the servers are not distributed across multiple enclosures, could cause a concern to system administrators. Pulling a cable from one interface could affect the connection to all the servers in the enclosure. This is because uplinks are shared by all servers in the enclosure.

Expected Behavior: When this test is executed, what is the expected behavior? For example, when the cable from one of the NICs is pulled and there are dual interconnects configured either using the HAIP feature or bonding, the servers should not crash; however, if cable from both the private interfaces from one server are pulled, then a server should get evicted.

Observation/Result: The actual behavior is to be noted here: for example, even after pulling just one interface cable from the server if a server gets evicted. That is not a normal behavior. This should be noted and appropriate remedy tickets should be created with the network administration team to get this fixed.

Status: The status of this test is recorded. If the test was successful, that is, the results of the test were as expected, the status should indicate "SUCCESS"/OK. However, if a node crashed when one of the interfaces failed, it's an error and this column should contain "FAILURE"/FAIL. Also, if a remedy ticket is created, the ticket number should be noted here.

Node 1 through Node n: For each server or node defined in the cluster, note the status of that server for the test. For example, when cable from Node 1 was physically removed, a node was evicted by the clusterware. Note under the node name if the specific node crashed or not.

Step 2

Once the components to be tested have been identified, the next step is to start a load on the cluster. This does not require any application; we are just testing the stability of the cluster and any load testing tool available should be sufficient. Figure 3-4 illustrates a screen shot from a workload generated using Hammerora.

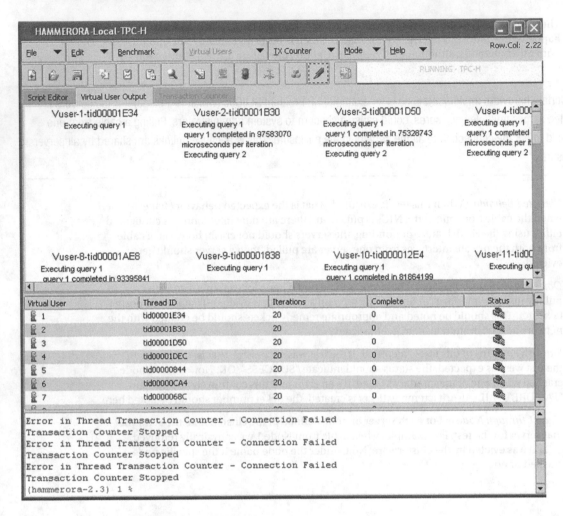

Figure 3-4. Hammerora workload generations

WORKLOAD-TESTING TOOLS

There are several standard workload-testing tools available as freeware or on a commercial basis. For example

- *Hammerora* is a load generation tool and provides standard Transaction Processing Performance Council Benchmark C (TPC-C) and Benchmark H (TPC-H) workloads.

- *Swingbench* is another free load testing tool available and written specifically for simulating workloads in a RAC environment.

- *Benchmark Factory* is commercial software and also used for a similar workload generation.

Please note that the idea here is not what type of transaction is being generated. The goal is to generate some workload on the cluster, preferably the type of workload that the cluster will support (OLTP, data warehouse, and so forth).

Step 3

Once there, the workload has stabilized and the connections can be seen against the database and the actual test can begin. For this step of the test, we would need the assistance of the system/network administrator who has access to the data center to physically pull cables from the interface.

```
Script: MVRACPDnTap_taftest.sql
INT  USERNAME  SERVICE_NA  FM     FT      FO    STATUS    COUNT(*)
---- --------  ----------  -----  ------  ----  --------  --------
  1  DBSNMP    SYS$USERS   NONE   NONE    NO    ACTIVE       1
     RAPDWH    PRDDB       BASIC  SELECT  NO    ACTIVE      385
. . . . . .
.. .. . .
  6  DBSNMP    SYS$USERS   NONE   NONE    NO    ACTIVE       2
     RAPDWH    PRDDB       BASIC  SELECT  NO    ACTIVE      386
```

The preceding output illustrates connections against six instances and all of them are connected using the transparent application failover (TAF) policy of BASIC and SELECT.

Step 4

Once the system administrator physically pulls the cable to the interface device, the results should be observed. In this test scenario, when one HBA cable was pulled, it did not affect the user connections to the database (see Table 3-2).

Table 3-2. *Test 1 Results Recorded*

Test #	Host Name	Interface	Test method	Expected Behavior	Observation / Result	Status	Node1	Node2	Node3
1	Db1	HBA1	Pull	Stable Server	Cluster Stable	OK	UP	UP	UP

```
Script: MVRACPDnTap_taftest.sql
INT  USERNAME  SERVICE_NA  FM     FT      FO    STATUS    COUNT(*)
---- --------  ----------  -----  ------  ----  --------  --------
  1  DBSNMP    SYS$USERS   NONE   NONE    NO    ACTIVE       1
     RAPDWH    PRDDB       BASIC  SELECT  NO    ACTIVE      385
. . . . . .
.. .. . .
  3  DBSNMP    SYS$USERS   NONE   NONE    NO    ACTIVE       2
     RAPDWH    PRDDB       BASIC  SELECT  NO    ACTIVE      286
. . . . . .
. . . . . .
  6  DBSNMP    SYS$USERS   NONE   NONE    NO    ACTIVE       2
     RAPDWH    PRDDB       BASIC  SELECT  NO    ACTIVE      386
```

Step 5

After *n* minutes, the HBA1 cable that was removed is plugged back into the interface and the cable from the second HBA2 device connected to Node db1 is removed. Similarly, the status of the test is recorded in the spreadsheet and one after the other, all HBA interfaces are tested.

Step 6

What if all the HBAs fail? What if there is a cascade effect on the HBA devices, that is, they start failing one after the other? What if more than one HBA fails? All possible scenarios should be tested using similar methods.

After the individual HBA devices have been tested, it's time to simultaneously pull cables from all HBA devices connected to Node db1: record the results (illustrated in Table 3-3).

Table 3-3. *Test 1 Results Recorded*

Test #	Host Name	Interface	Test method	Expected Behavior	Observation / Result	Status	Node1	Node2	Node3
1	prddb1	HBA1	Pull	Stable server	Cluster Stable	OK	UP	UP	UP
2	prddb1	HBA2	Pull	Stable Sever	Cluster Stable	OK	UP	UP	UP
3	prddb1	HBA1 and HBA2	Pull	Server panic & node eviction	prddbb1 Crashed	OK	CRASH	UP	UP

Please note that in Test 3 (illustrated in Table 3-3), when cable from both the HBA interfaces where pulled, the server crashed. Although the status indicated "OK," this was because the result was as expected. The Node db1 had two HBA devices, and when cable from both the devices where pulled, the clusterware panics, which then causes a node eviction.

Because the load testing tool uses tnsnames.ora file and the TAF policy has been set, it may be advantageous to also record if the users failed over from db1 to one or more of the other instances in the cluster. Along with the status, it's important to record the number of users who failed over and the time they took to failover.

For documentation and verification at a later stage, it's also a good practice to capture the log information from the database alert logs, CRS logs, CSS logs, and the system logs (/var/log/messages) file.

```
Output from/var/log/messages
Feb 11 19:01:57 prddb1 kernel: qla2xxx 0000:0a:00.0: LOOP DOWN detected (2 3 0).
Feb 11 19:02:13 prddb1 kernel: rport-2:0-0: blocked FC remote port time out: saving binding
Feb 11 19:02:13 prddb1 kernel: rport-2:0-1: blocked FC remote port time out: saving binding
Feb 11 19:02:13 prddb1 kernel: rport-2:0-2: blocked FC remote port time out: saving binding
Feb 11 19:02:13 prddb1 kernel: rport-2:0-3: blocked FC remote port time out: saving binding

      >>>>>SERVER CRASH

Feb 11 19:02:13 prddb1 kernel: Error:Mpx:Path Bus 2 Tgt 0 Lun 0 to OF278 is dead.
Feb 11 19:02:13 prddb1 kernel: Error:Mpx:Killing bus 2 to HP OPEN OF278 port 3A.
Feb 11 19:02:13 prddb1 kernel: Error:Mpx:Path Bus 2 Tgt 0 Lun 7 to OF278 is dead.
Feb 11 19:02:13 prddb1 kernel: Error:Mpx:Path Bus 2 Tgt 0 Lun 6 to OF278 is dead.
Feb 11 19:02:13 prddb1 kernel: Error:Mpx:Path Bus 2 Tgt 0 Lun 3 to OF278 is dead.
. . . . . . . . .
. . . . . . . .
```

```
Feb 11 19:02:13 prddb1 kernel: Error:Mpx:Path Bus 2 Tgt 0 Lun 2 to OF278 is dead.
Feb 11 19:02:13 prddb1 kernel: Error:Mpx:Path Bus 2 Tgt 1 Lun 0 to OF278 is dead.
Feb 11 19:02:13 prddb1 kernel: Error:Mpx:Killing bus 2 to HP OPEN  OF278 port 3B.
Feb 11 19:02:13 prddb1 kernel: Error:Mpx:Path Bus 2 Tgt 1 Lun 3 to OF278 is dead.
Feb 11 19:02:13 prddb1 kernel: Error:Mpx:Path Bus 2 Tgt 1 Lun 7 to OF278 is dead.
Feb 11 19:02:13 prddb1 kernel: Error:Mpx:Path Bus 2 Tgt 1 Lun 6 to OF278 is dead.
Feb 11 19:02:13 prddb1 kernel: Error:Mpx:Path Bus 2 Tgt 1 Lun 4 to OF278 is dead.
Feb 11 19:02:13 prddb1 kernel: Error:Mpx:Path Bus 2 Tgt 1 Lun 5 to OF278 is dead.
Feb 11 19:02:13 prddb1 kernel: Error:Mpx:Path Bus 2 Tgt 1 Lun 15 to OF278 is dead.
. . . . . .
. . . . . .
Feb 11 19:02:13 prddb1 kernel: Error:Mpx:Path Bus 2 Tgt 1 Lun 1 to OF278 is dead.
Feb 11 19:02:13 prddb1 kernel: Error:Mpx:Path Bus 2 Tgt 2 Lun 2 to OF278 is dead.
Feb 11 19:02:13 prddb1 kernel: Error:Mpx:Killing bus 2 to HP OPEN  OF278 port 3F.
Feb 11 19:02:13 prddb1 kernel: Error:Mpx:Path Bus 2 Tgt 2 Lun 13 to OF278 is dead.
Feb 11 19:02:13 prddb1 kernel: Error:Mpx:Path Bus 2 Tgt 2 Lun 3 to OF278 is dead.
Feb 11 19:02:13 prddb1 kernel: Error:Mpx:Path Bus 2 Tgt 2 Lun 7 to OF278 is dead.
Feb 11 19:02:13 prddb1 kernel: Error:Mpx:Path Bus 2 Tgt 2 Lun 6 to OF278 is dead.
Feb 11 19:02:13 prddb1 kernel: Error:Mpx:Path Bus 2 Tgt 2 Lun 4 to OF278 is dead.
. . . . . . .
Feb 11 19:02:13 prddb1 kernel: Error:Mpx:Path Bus 2 Tgt 3 Lun 15 to OF278 is dead.
Feb 11 19:02:35 prddb1 kernel: qla2xxx 0000:0a:00.0: LIP reset occured (f700).
Feb 11 19:02:35 prddb1 kernel: qla2xxx 0000:0a:00.0: LIP occured (f700).
Feb 11 19:02:35 prddb1 kernel: qla2xxx 0000:0a:00.0: LIP reset occured (f7f7).

      >>>>>>Interface restarts after failure.

Feb 11 19:02:35 prddb1 kernel: qla2xxx 0000:0a:00.0: LOOP UP detected (8 Gbps).
Feb 11 19:07:13 prddb1 kernel: Info:Mpx:Path Bus 2 Tgt 0 Lun 6 to OF278 is alive.
Feb 11 19:07:13 prddb1 kernel: Info:Mpx:Path Bus 2 Tgt 1 Lun 7 to OF278 is alive.
Feb 11 19:07:13 prddb1 kernel: Info:Mpx:Path Bus 2 Tgt 2 Lun 3 to OF278 is alive.
Feb 11 19:07:13 prddb1 kernel: Info:Mpx:Path Bus 2 Tgt 3 Lun 7 to OF278 is alive.
Feb 11 19:07:13 prddb1 kernel: Info:Mpx:Path Bus 2 Tgt 0 Lun 3 to OF278 is alive.
Feb 11 19:07:13 prddb1 kernel: Info:Mpx:Path Bus 2 Tgt 1 Lun 6 to OF278 is alive.
```

Step 7

Along with the load tests and user connections to the database, it's also a good practice to check the interconnect traffic for any errors. Early identification of problems will help in getting through subsequent phases of the tests sooner.

Testing Application for Availability

As pointed out several times throughout this book, the primary reasons why organizations prefer to implement their database on a RAC platform is to support the business requirements of availability and scalability. Both these features cannot be achieved just out of the box; complete availability requires incorporating some RAC-specific features into the application code, and scalability requires efficiently written interface between the application tier and the database tier.

When a server or node crashes, all database components configured on that server or node are also prone for failure. For example, in the previous discussions (Table 3-3), if Node prddb1 crashes because of the interface to the storage subsystem fails, this will cause ASM on that server to fail, which will trigger the database instance on that server to also fail. To take the real potential of the RAC's features, such failures should be made transparent to the user and should minimize transaction loss.

Such interruptions can be avoided by adopting and implementing fast application notification (FAN) and/ or transparent application failover (TAF) functionality. OCW has been architected with a built-in functionality that provides three levels of proactive failover and notification methods:

1. The OCW will automatically fail over any services registered with it to another node or instance based on the definitions in the OCR. Services and resources can be registered with the OCW using Oracle Enterprise Manager (OEM) and srvctl.

2. The OCW will use the Oracle notification services (ONS) to proactively notify the participating client machines of any state changes by sending DOWN and UP FAN events. The applications using Oracle call interface (OCI) calls interpret these events to proactively react to these situations by sending/routing new connections to the new destinations.

3. Using the policy managed configuration, rules can be defined across server pools. This is done by maintaining minimum/maximum number of instances in a pool. When a member in a pool fails and the pool is running short on the number of members required, members from another pool are automatically provisioned (provided all the pool management rules are met), and instances started, to support system availability and throughput requirements.

A service is an abstraction layer of a single system image executed against the same database with common functionality, quality expectations, and priority relative to other services. Examples of services could be payroll, accounts payable, order entry, and so on.

TAF allows client applications to continue working after the application loses its connection to the database. Although users may experience a brief pause during the time the database server fails over to a surviving cluster node, the session context is preserved. If configured using TAF, after the instance failover and database recovery completes, the application can automatically reconnect to one of the surviving instances and continue operations as if no failure had occurred.

■ **Note**   FAN, FCF, and TAF are discussed in detail in Chapter 15.

RAP Phase II—Availability and Load Balancing

Once the various components of the cluster are found to be stable from RAP Phase I testing, the project can go as planned for importing the database and data from the current production environment.

Once the database has been configured and the parameters set to match the current production, the next phase of RAP testing should be planned. The goal of this test is to verify the application behavior when one, more, or all instances crash within the cluster. How will the database tier provide business continuum when one or more components of the database fail? Is the application able to handle such failures? What happens to the user workload: did they notice the failure? What happens when there are media failures and the application is not able to retrieve or persist data into the database? All these questions are answered by business requirements. Phase III validates if these requirements are met.

■ **Note** This is a critical test and should not be compromised. All failure points should be tested until the expected results meet the business requirements and the SLAs for business continuum are achieved. A detailed sample spreadsheet containing the failure points to be tested is provided in Appendix D.

Workshop

Before beginning this phase of testing, the business rules and SLA requirements of the application should be reviewed. Based on the analysis, a test plan should be prepared covering all failure points. For verification and documentation purposes, test cases and results should be recorded and maintained.

Step 1

The initial step is to set up the tests: for example, create use cases for all test scenarios. Identify complex areas of the application and build test scripts to generate load for these areas. Tools such as LoadRunner or Real Application Testing (RAT) can be useful for this purpose. Once the test cases have been identified, design a spreadsheet with the appropriate columns; for example, the following template covers the basic level of testing (see Table 3-4).

Table 3-4. *RAP III—Testing the Application for Availability*

Test #	Description	# of Users	Test Case & Functionality	Description	Statistics	Status

Step 2

Using the LoadRunner scripts, generate user workload from the application once the required number of users is loaded. Monitor the database for workload distribution and user definitions.

Once the desired workloads are reached, shutdown abort one of the instances or crash one of the nodes in the cluster and observe the application behavior (see Table 3-5).

Table 3-5. *RAP III—Testing the Application for Availability*

Test #	Description	# of Users	Test Case & Functionality	Description	Statistics	Status
1	Baseline test	300	All app servers and & db servers accessible	No users fail over		Complete
2	Test 1	300	Shutdown abort instance 2	Users should fail over	No users failed over; instance recovery time = 12 seconds	Error

On verifying the user connections, it was noticed that the connect descriptor was not rightly defined on the application server. No failover policies or rules were defined. Second, the ONS server on the database server was not aware of the participating clients and could not notify the application server of an instance crash. The lack of these definitions caused connections to fail, and the user connections did not move/failover to one of the surviving instances.

Depending on the type of application and functionality being tested, users may not fail over. For example, in a highly insert-intensive application like concurrent manager (CM) in an E-Business Suite (EBS) system that is not designed to automatically rollback and re-execute the transaction, the CM manager is going to experience an error message.

Step 3

After making the required fixes to both the ONS and the application connect descriptors, the test was executed again. Querying the database for connections, it was found that the users were more evenly distributed (see also Table 3-6):

```
INT  USERNAME        SERVICE_NA  FM     FT      FO   STATUS     COUNT(*)
----  --------------  ----------  -----  ------  ---- ---------- --------
1    APPS            EBSPRD      BASIC  SELECT  NO   INACTIVE   20
     APPS            EBSWEB      BASIC  SELECT  NO   ACTIVE     113
     CORBIT          CORBIT      BASIC  SELECT  NO   ACTIVE     92
     DBSNMP          SYS$USERS   NONE   NONE    NO   ACTIVE     1
     SYS             SYS$USERS   NONE   NONE    NO   ACTIVE     3
2    APPS            EBSPRD      BASIC  SELECT  NO   INACTIVE   10
     APPS            EBSWEB      BASIC  SELECT  NO   ACTIVE     112
     BCIDBA          EBSPRD      BASIC  SELECT  NO   INACTIVE   3
     CORBIT          CORBIT      BASIC  SELECT  NO   ACTIVE     60
     DBSNMP          SYS$USERS   NONE   NONE    NO   ACTIVE     1
     SYS             SYS$USERS   NONE   NONE    NO   ACTIVE     1
. . . . . . . . . .
. . . . . . . . . .
6    APPS            EBSPRD      BASIC  SELECT  NO   INACTIVE   9
     APPS            EBSWEB      BASIC  SELECT  NO   INACTIVE   6
     APPS            EBSWEB      BASIC  SELECT  NO   ACTIVE     110
     BCIDBA          EBSPRD      BASIC  SELECT  NO   INACTIVE   4
     CORBIT          CORBIT      BASIC  SELECT  NO   ACTIVE     60
     DBSNMP          SYS$USERS   NONE   NONE    NO   ACTIVE     1
     SYS             SYS$USERS   NONE   NONE    NO   ACTIVE     1
```

Table 3-6. *RAP III—Testing the Application for Availability*

Test #	Description	#of Users	Test Case & Functionality	Description	Statistics	Status
1	Baseline test	300	All app servers and & db servers accessible			Complete
2	Test 1	300	Shutdown abort instance 2	Users should fail over	No users failed over; instance recovery time = 12 seconds	Error
2(a)	Test 1	300	Shutdown abort instance 2	Users should fail over	Users failed over; instance recovery time = 8 seconds	Complete

Step 4

Test all key functional areas of the application in a similar manner. Also test each instance and server for similar failures. Testing the application by functional areas can give a better control over what and where things need to be fixed.

RAP Phase III—HA

In machine-critical applications, failover of users due to instance or node failures is just one part of the puzzle. There is something beyond failure of instances, nodes, and services—for example, failure of the data center itself and media failures—that needs some additional attention and cannot be made transparent unless some customization and or implementation planning is done. There are several applications that require continuous availability with minimal or no downtime. Such as applications used by financial trading institutions cannot tolerate downtimes and for that matter have poor response times of over 6–7 seconds during critical business periods. Applications have expanded on some of the already available RAC features, which provide automatic failover between two different locations, synchronizing data using Oracle streams, or golden gate on a real-time basis. Applications such as these are affected by upgrades, power outages, natural disasters, and so forth. Business requirements for these types of applications require configuration of disaster recovery (DR) sites. It's important that before the production goes live, the application and database functionality for DR is also tested and the SLA requirements validated.

Workshop

In this workshop, two tests have to be completed: switchover (or planned failover) and failover from the primary site to the DR site.

■ **Note** The steps required to configure a DR site is beyond the scope of this book. In a RAC environment, where application downtime is critical, DR sites need to be configured with identical hardware, application, and database configurations.

Step 1—Switchover

Switchover operations are required when the primary database is required to be brought down for hardware and/or software maintenance. The DBA will perform a manual switchover of the environment from primary to standby/DR. Switchover is performed using data guard broker (DGB) using the SWITCHOVER TO "<database >" command. To start the switchover operations, all instances except one should be shut down using the SHUTDOWN IMMEDIATE option. The last instance should be kept available until such time when both the primary database and standby database have SYNCHRONIZED the activities. The failover status can be determined using the following query:

```
Script: MVRACPDnTap_dgsynchcheck.sql
INST INSTN FFS           FFCT    FFT FFOP OM         DUN    DBR
---- ------ ------------- ------- --- ----- ---------- ------ ----------
1    SSKY1  SYNCHRONIZED  SSKYDG  60  YES   READ WRITE SSKYDB PRIMARY
2    SSKY2  SYNCHRONIZED  SSKYDG  60  YES   READ WRITE SSKYDB PRIMARY
```

Shutdown all instances except one instance and verify the status

INST	INSTN	FFS	FFCT	FFT	FFOP	OM	DUN	DBR
1	SSKY1	SYNCHRONIZED	SSKYDG	60	YES	READ WRITE	SSKYDB	PRIMARY

Using the same query above, verify the standby database has the SYNCHRONIZED status also and once confirmed start the SWITCHOVER operation using DGMGRL utility.

INST	INSTN	FFS	FFCT	FFT	FFOP	OM	DUN	DBR
1	SSKYDG	SYNCHRONIZED	SSKYDG	60	YES	MOUNTED	SSKYDG	PHYSICAL STANDBY

```
DGMGRL> connect sys/oracle
Connected.
DGMGRL> switchover to 'SSKYDG';
Performing switchover NOW, please wait...
The above operation will start the shutdown of the only remaining RAC instance.
Operation requires shutdown of instance "SSKY1" on database "SSKYDB"
Shutting down instance "SSKY1"...
ORA-01109: database not open
Database dismounted.
ORACLE instance shut down.
```

The next steps in the SWITCHOVER operation is for the DGB to shutdown the standby database and change the state from STANDBY to PRIMARY.

```
Operation requires shutdown of instance "SSKYDG" on database "SSKYDG"
Shutting down instance "SSKYDG"...
ORA-01109: database not open
Database dismounted.
ORACLE instance shut down.
```

The DGB attempts to start the new primary and new standby instances. Unfortunately, because the listeners are not aware of these shutdown instances, Oracle returns an ORA-12514 error. At this time a manual intervention is required to start up the databases.

Operation requires startup of instance "SSKY1" on database "SSKYDB":

```
Starting instance "SSKY1"...
Unable to connect to database
ORA-12514: TNS:listener does not currently know of service requested in connect descriptor
Failed.
You are no longer connected to ORACLE
Please connect again.
Unable to start instance "SSKY1"
You must start instance "SSKY1" manually
Operation requires startup of instance "SSKYDG" on database "SSKYDG"
You must start instance "SSKYDG" manually
Switchover succeeded, new primary is "SSKYDG"
```

Once failover is complete, the query should be executed to verify the current state of both databases. Using the same query as previously, the new values are

```
New primary database - 'SSKYDG'
INST INSTN FFS            FFCT    FFT FFOP  OM         DUN     DBR
---- ------ ------------- ------- --- ------ ---------- ------ --------
1    SSKYDG SYNCHRONIZED  SSKYDB  60  YES    READ WRITE SSKYDG PRIMARY
The new standby database 'SSKYDB' and instances 'SSKY1' and 'SSKY2';
INST INSTN FFS            FFCT    FFT FFOP  OM         DUN     DBR
---- ------ ------------- ------- --- ------ --------- ------ ----------
1    SSKY1  SYNCHRONIZED  SSKYDB  60  YES    MOUNTED   SSKYDB PHYSICAL STANDBY
2    SSKY2  SYNCHRONIZED  SSKYDB  60  YES    MOUNTED   SSKYDB PHYSICAL STANDBY
```

This completes the SWITCHOVER operation; a similar operation is performed to change the databases back to their original states. Although the entire switchover activity is transparent, Oracle, behind the scene, will make the required parameter modifications to change the states of the respective databases before requesting a STARTUP operation.

Step 2—Failover

Unplanned failover occurs when the primary database environment is having problems due to either natural disasters or human errors and a temporary environment is required so the application can have access to the data and business can continue.

This specific issue has been resolved with Fast-Start Failover Observer (FSFO). When all instances in a RAC configuration (primary database) fail, the Observer will automatically perform required operations to make the standby database useable. The failover steps are as follows:

1. The data guard is in a steady state transmitting redo log from the primary to the standby locations.

2. The Observer is in a monitoring state of the configuration. During this period, the observer keeps track of both the standby and the primary databases.

3. We assume there was an act of nature causing the primary database, including all instances in the cluster, to crash.

4. The Observer detects that the primary database is not responding. The Observer repeatedly tries to make a connection; and after the number of seconds defined by the FastStartFailoverThreshold, the DGB property declares that the primary environment is not available.

5. The Observer at this point needs to verify with the standby database if it is ready to fail over and begins the failover process. The Observer initiates conversion of the standby database/instance from a "Standby" state to a "Primary" state. Whereas the Observer initiates this process, it is the remote file server (RFS) background process on the standby instance that performs the conversion. During this conversion process, depending on how active the primary database has been, it may take several minutes for the migration to complete.

   a. The standby database is taken into a NOMOUNT state after performing a dismount of the already mounted instance.

   b. A new control file is created with the required default parameters.

   c. Database recovery is performed.

    d.   Database is handed back over to the Observer and placed in a GUARD ALL status.

    e.   Database is opened.

    f.   All the required standby redo log files are added back to the configuration.

6.   The target standby database becomes the new primary database. Users can start accessing data as on any normal database. At this point it is very important to consider the configuration differences between the original primary and the new primary. If the configurations are not identical, the servers cannot process the same workload.

7.   At this stage, depending on how long it takes to repair the old primary, there could be a period where only one database is available. Once the old primary database is repaired, the Observer reestablishes connection.

8.   The Observer automatically reinstates the old primary database to be the new standby database. At this stage the redo transmission starts from the new primary database to the new standby database. The environment is back in a maximum availability mode.

In this specific scenario, because the primary database and the standby database environments are not of an identical configuration, it is important to switch the states back to their original state. That is, the new standby should be switched back as a primary database. This can be accomplished using the switchover operations discussed in the "planned failover" in "Step 1—Switchover" earlier in this workshop.

RAP Phase IV—Backup and Recovery

Backup and recovery is a critical area and part of everyday operation. However, because backup and recovery are operations for the future when a problem arises, seldom is any importance given to testing it with everyday operations. Backup operations are performed in case problems arise in the future and recovery of the database environment is required. Best practices warrant the use of Recovery Manager (RMAN) for backup and recovery of the RAC database.

    Part of the backup and recovery testing will also require the preparation of a backup and recovery strategy, or rules and guidelines around how often the database should be backed up. Where will the backup files be stored: on disk, in ASM, or directly on tape? If backup is retained on disk, how many days or weeks worth of backup files will be retained and will have to be documented? These rules and procedures will depend on the size of the database and mean time to repair (MTTR) policy.

Workshop

This workshop has two parts. Part 1 covers backup operations and Part 2 covers recovery operations.

Step 1

The first step in the backup testing is to define a backup strategy. The backup strategy is prepared based on the SLA requirements of the database. The MTBF and MTTF of the database should be considered when preparing the strategy. This strategy needs to be tested as part of RAP testing. For example, Table 3-7 gives a typical backup strategy for a clustered database configuration.

Table 3-7. *RAP Phase IV Database Backup Strategy*

Schedule	Level 0	Saturday at 1700 hours
	Level 1	Sunday thru Friday at 1700 Hours
	Archive log backup	Daily at 100, 400, 700, 1000, 1300, 1500, 2200 hours
Destination	Backup to ASM diskgroup +PRDDB_FRA	
Retention	Keep the most recent 7 days backup at +PRDDB_FRA	
	Keep the most recent 1 day's archive log backups in +PRDDB_FRA	
Size	RMAN backup : Average 1 TB	

Step 2

After the backup strategy is completed and reviewed with the team, the next step is to test the backup process. Either using scripts or using Oracle Grid Control, the database and other related components should be backed up. Along with the logs from the backup operations, the time taken to complete each stage of the backup should be recorded. Table 3-8 lists the various components to be backed up and the time taken for backing up these components.

Table 3-8. *RAP Phase IV Backup Components*

Backup Component		Location	Method	Time
Software			Tape backup	
	Grid Infrastructure	$GRID_HOME		
	RDBMS Binaries	$ORACLE_HOME		
ASM				
	SPFile		Disk/Tape backup	
	Metadata		Disk/Tape backup	
OCR		$GRID_HOME/cdata/PRDDBCW/	Disk/Tape backup	
OLR		$GRID_HOME/cdata/PRDDBCW/	Disk/Tape backup	
Database			Disk/Tape backup	
	Level 0	+PRDDB_FRA		
	Level 1	+PRDDB_FRA		
	Archive logs	+PRDDB_FRA		

Note: RDBMS = relational database management system; SPFile = server parameter file.

In addition to the time taken to back up the various components, it's also important to record the scalability of these backup operations. How many parallel slaves were used to back up the database? How many RAC instances participated in the backup operation? How many backup sets and how many backup sets per instance were used?

Step 3

After the backup operations are tested, the next step to test the recovery operation. Similar to the backup operation, the recovery of each of the components will have to be completed and recorded. In addition to the recovery of these components, other recovery scenarios—for example, datafile corruption, OCR corruption, and so forth—should also be tested. Table 3-9 lists the various recovery components and other recovery scenarios.

Table 3-9. RAP Phase IV Recovery Components

Recovery Components	Operation	Recovery Time
Software		
	Grid Infrastructure Binaries	
	RDBMS Binaries	
ASM		
	ASM SPFile	
	Metadata Recovery	
OCR	OCR Corruption recovery	
OLR	OLR Corruption recovery	
Database		
	Complete Recovery	
	Incomplete Recovery—Tablespace	
	Incomplete Recovery—Block Corruption	
	Incomplete Recovery—Datafile	
	Database SPFile Recovery	
	Control File Recovery	

Note: RDBMS = relational database management system; ASM = automatic storage management; SPFile = server parameter file; OCR = Oracle Cluster Registry; OLR = Oracle Local Registry.

In addition to the time taken to restore of the various components, it's also important to record the scalability of these restore operations. How many parallel slaves were used for the restore operation? How many RAC instances participated in the recovery operation? These and others should be tested and results recorded.

■ **Note**　Tuning the backup and recovery operations are discussed in Chapter 10.

Conclusion

RAC is an HA solution; however, it can only be HA when all the components that comprise the clustered configuration are HA.

Almost always when project timelines slip, it's the server-level tests that are comprised to meet the production go live dates. To ensure HA, these components have to be tested. Irrespective of how many clusters have been configured and how many times a RAC configuration has been deployed into production. We cannot stress enough on the fact of how important these tests are. None of these tests can be ignored. Moving from a single instance to a RAC configuration and a few days into production if RAC crashes due to a hardware failure or a component failure, RAC cannot be blamed: it's the lack of systematic testing that create such failures.

We discuss other tests around scalability and throughput in the next chapter. Availability testing has a final phase, which has not been discussed here. To maintain the flow of the various tests, we discuss the last phase of availability testing along with the scalability tests in the next chapter.

CHAPTER 4

■ ■ ■

Testing for Scalability

RAC is a clustered database solution that provides two major functions, namely, scalability and availability for business continuity. Chapter 3 discussed testing the hardware and application for availability. This chapter focuses on testing for scalability.

Depending on the context where it's applied, scalability is a relative term and can be defined in different ways. In our context, scalability is defined in terms of users: as the number of users accessing the system increases, the RAC configuration should be able to support the increase in demand in proportion to the number of users and without any degradation in service levels. It is important to understand that an application can scale in a clustered environment only if hardware that will host the application and database can scale. For an application to scale in a clustered environment it has to do so in a single-instance Oracle environment.

RAC is designed as a clustered database solution. To obtain the maximum scalability potential of the RAC environment, it's important that the hardware and application are scalable. In this chapter, we discuss testing the hardware for scalability and then how to test the application for scalability.

Scale-Up or Scale-Out

Database environments can be single-server, single-instance environments or multiserver, multi-instance environments (e.g., RAC). Based on business requirements and criticality of the application that is being supported, one type of configuration maybe preferred over the other. As the user base accessing the application increases, demand for resources on these servers also increases, causing scalability constraints. This causes reduced user response times. Servers can be scaled to accommodate these increased users in one of two ways.

Scale-Up

This is where adding additional CPU and memory providing additional resources for the increased user base increases the capacity of the servers. Figure 4-1 illustrates the scale-up (also called "vertical scalability") type of configuration. Scale-up or vertical scalability has the following limitations:

1. Every server is of a specific model or type of hardware and has physical limitations on how many total CPUs or memory banks it can have. For example, in DELL DL580, when the demand goes up, the machine can't just be augmented with additional CPUs because there maynot be any free slots available.

2. Although additional resources maybe added to the server, the server itself could be a single point of failure, meaning if the server fails, the connection to the application is lost. At this time, if a disaster recovery (DR) site has been configured, the application will be moved over there; or if there is no DR site, the users have to wait until the server is fixed and started again. Again, this could depend on the type of problem and the time it would take to fix the issue.

3. While scaling up on a single server can create a bottleneck causing a single point of failure. The scale-up option can also cause loss of processing power or limitations to scalability of the application when one or more servers in the configuration fail. For instance, if one out of the four servers in a four-node RAC cluster fails, availability is reduced by 25%. This is a substantial loss for most applications configured for prime time. Now consider that if two or more servers fail, the availability will reduce by 50% and 75%, respectively. Based on the workload and the active concurrent sessions, the cluster may not be useable.

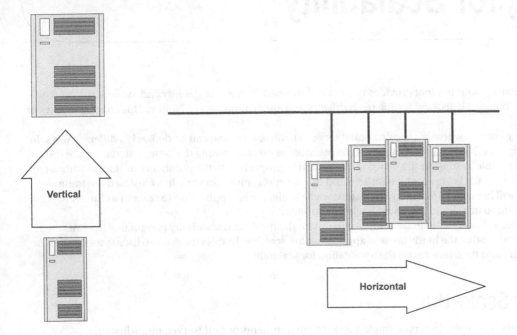

Figure 4-1. *Scale-in and scale-out*

Scale-Out

Whereas adding additional servers can increase the current resource capacity of the servers, each server within has the capacity to accommodate additional CPU and memory if required. Scale-out configurations are normally clustered configurations where servers are interconnected through a private dedicated network for cluster management. Figure 4-1 illustrates a scale-out configuration. Scale-out also has certain limitations:

1. Not all user applications can run on a clustered configuration. If the application and persistence layer (which contains all the SQL operations to the database) are not tuned and optimized efficiently, scale-out configurations may not bring the performance benefits expected. In many cases poorly running SQL statements could create negative impact when executed in a clustered configuration. A certain amount of testing is required to ensure that applications perform and scale per expectations.

2. Cost of implementing such a solution maybe much higher. The infrastructures, technical know-how, and the learning curve required implementing this solution maybe high.

Clustering provides great benefits of distributing workloads among the various servers participating in the cluster. RAC is a clustered database solution that is designed to help distribute workload among several servers. Added with some of the other features available with Oracle Database 11g Release 2 and higher, RAC provides scale-up and scale-out.

■ **Note**   Services and load-balancing features are covered in Chapter 15.

Scalable Components

Scalability of the RAC configuration depends on the scalability of components that comprise the RAC cluster. A RAC system effectively extends the local buffer cache and can therefore reduce the amount of physical I/O. Cache data transfers via the interconnect allow low latency access. This at the outset makes the interconnect as the primary component for scalability. As illustrated in Figure 4-2, RAC has seven components that can affect the overall performance of the database if not configured correctly.

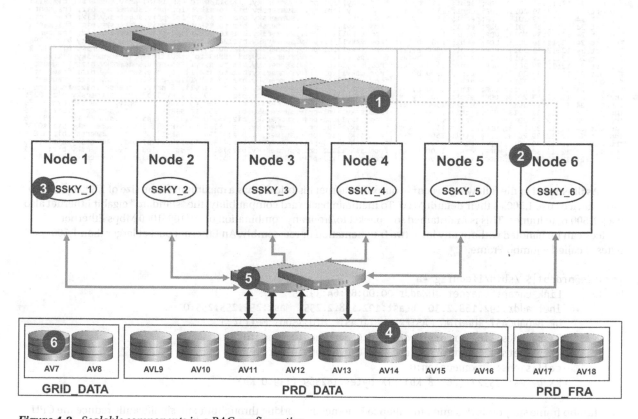

Figure 4-2. Scalable components in a RAC configuration

Interconnect

This is the backbone of the RAC architecture: data movement and sharing between instances in the cluster happen via the cluster interconnect.

Jumbo Frames

Ethernet traffic moves in units called frames. The maximum size of frames is called the maximum transmission unit (MTU) and is the largest packet a network device transmits. When a network device gets a frame larger than its MTU, the data is fragmented (broken into smaller frames) or dropped. The following output is from IPTraf (a network monitoring utility on Linux) and illustrates fragmentation of data transmitted on an Ethernet configuration without jumbo frames.

```
Thu Oct 24 12:12:38 2013; UDP; eth1; 1500 bytes; from ssky1l1p1-priv.summersky.biz to ssky1l1p4-priv.summersky.biz; fragment
Thu Oct 24 12:12:38 2013; UDP; eth1; 1500 bytes; from ssky1l1p1-priv.summersky.biz to ssky1l1p4-priv.summersky.biz; fragment
Thu Oct 24 12:12:38 2013; UDP; eth1; 1500 bytes; from ssky1l1p1-priv.summersky.biz to ssky1l1p4-priv.summersky.biz; fragment
Thu Oct 24 12:12:38 2013; UDP; eth1; 1500 bytes; from ssky1l1p1-priv.summersky.biz to ssky1l1p4-priv.summersky.biz; fragment
Thu Oct 24 12:12:38 2013; UDP; eth1; 1500 bytes; from ssky1l1p1-priv.summersky.biz to ssky1l1p4-priv.summersky.biz; fragment
Thu Oct 24 12:12:38 2013; UDP; eth1; 1500 bytes; from ssky1l1p1-priv.summersky.biz to ssky1l1p4-priv.summersky.biz; fragment
Thu Oct 24 12:12:39 2013; UDP; eth1; 1500 bytes; from ssky1l1p1-priv.summersky.biz:41853 to ssky1l1p3-priv.summersky.biz:47182
Thu Oct 24 12:12:39 2013; UDP; eth1; 1500 bytes; from ssky1l1p1-priv.summersky.biz:41853 to ssky1l1p3-priv.summersky.biz:47182
Thu Oct 24 12:12:39 2013; UDP; eth1; 1500 bytes; from ssky1l1p1-priv.summersky.biz:51180 to ssky1l1p3-priv.summersky.biz:9115
Thu Oct 24 12:12:39 2013; UDP; eth1; 1500 bytes; from ssky1l1p1-priv.summersky.biz to ssky1l1p2-priv.summersky.biz; fragment
Thu Oct 24 12:12:39 2013; UDP; eth1; 1500 bytes; from ssky1l1p1-priv.summersky.biz to ssky1l1p2-priv.summersky.biz; fragment
Thu Oct 24 12:12:39 2013; UDP; eth1; 1500 bytes; from ssky1l1p1-priv.summersky.biz to ssky1l1p2-priv.summersky.biz; fragment
Thu Oct 24 12:12:39 2013; UDP; eth1; 1500 bytes; from ssky1l1p1-priv.summersky.biz:9078 to ssky1l1p3-priv.summersky.biz:21299
Thu Oct 24 12:12:39 2013; UDP; eth1; 1500 bytes; from ssky1l1p1-priv.summersky.biz:9078 to ssky1l1p3-priv.summersky.biz:21299
Thu Oct 24 12:12:39 2013; UDP; eth1; 1500 bytes; from ssky1l1p1-priv.summersky.biz:9889 to ssky1l1p5-priv.summersky.biz:26081
Thu Oct 24 12:12:39 2013; UDP; eth1; 1500 bytes; from ssky1l1p1-priv.summersky.biz to ssky1l1p5-priv.summersky.biz; fragment
Thu Oct 24 12:12:39 2013; UDP; eth1; 1500 bytes; from ssky1l1p1-priv.summersky.biz to ssky1l1p5-priv.summersky.biz; fragment
Thu Oct 24 12:12:39 2013; UDP; eth1; 1500 bytes; from ssky1l1p1-priv.summersky.biz to ssky1l1p5-priv.summersky.biz; fragment
Thu Oct 24 12:12:39 2013; UDP; eth1; 1500 bytes; from ssky1l1p1-priv.summersky.biz:48390 to ssky1l1p5-priv.summersky.biz:40226
Thu Oct 24 12:12:39 2013; UDP; eth1; 1500 bytes; from ssky1l1p1-priv.summersky.biz:48390 to ssky1l1p5-priv.summersky.biz:52876
Thu Oct 24 12:12:39 2013; UDP; eth1; 1500 bytes; from ssky1l1p1-priv.summersky.biz:48390 to ssky1l1p5-priv.summersky.biz:40226
Thu Oct 24 12:12:39 2013; UDP; eth1; 1500 bytes; from ssky1l1p1-priv.summersky.biz:48390 to ssky1l1p5-priv.summersky.biz:52876
Thu Oct 24 12:12:39 2013; UDP; eth1; 1500 bytes; from ssky1l1p1-priv.summersky.biz:48390 to ssky1l1p5-priv.summersky.biz:40226
Thu Oct 24 12:12:39 2013; UDP; eth1; 1500 bytes; from ssky1l1p1-priv.summersky.biz:48390 to ssky1l1p5-priv.summersky.biz:52876
Thu Oct 24 12:12:39 2013; UDP; eth1; 1500 bytes; from ssky1l1p1-priv.summersky.biz:55436 to ssky1l1p3-priv.summersky.biz:38036
```

As illustrated in the following `ifconfig` output, Ethernet historically has a maximum frame size of 1,500 bytes,[1] so most devices use 1,500 as their default MTU. To maintain backward compatibility, the "standard" gigabit Ethernet also uses 1,500 byte frames. This is maintained so a packet to/from any combination of 10/100/1000 Mbps Ethernet devices can be handled without any layer two fragmentation or reassembly. An Ethernet packet larger than 1,500 bytes is called a Jumbo Frame.

```
[oracle@prddb1]$ /sbin/ifconfig -a
bond0     Link encap:Ethernet  HWaddr 00:D0:B7:6A:39:85
          inet addr:192.168.2.30  Bcast:192.168.2.255  Mask:255.255.255.0
          UP BROADCAST RUNNING MASTER MULTICAST  MTU:1500  Metric:1
          RX packets:3162 errors:0 dropped:0 overruns:0 frame:0
          TX packets:1312 errors:0 dropped:0 overruns:0 carrier:0
          collisions:0 txqueuelen:0
          RX bytes:275327 (268.8 Kb)  TX bytes:142369 (139.0 Kb)
```

Jumbo frame support is designed to enhance Ethernet networking throughput and significantly reduce the CPU utilization of large file transfers like large multimedia files or large data files by enabling more efficient larger payloads per packet. By sending larger payloads per packet, fewer packets need to be routed, reducing the overhead on CPU and potentially improving networking throughput. By using jumbo frames, the transfer frame sizes for Ethernet could be increased to 9,000 bytes.

Jumbo frames also reduce the impact of packet loss: to send and receive an 8k block, the entire data transfer needs to be fragmented into 5k to 6k smaller chunks and reassembled. If one of the frames is dropped, the block is lost.

---

[1]The Ethernet packet consists of a 1,500-byte payload + 14 bytes for header + virtual local area networks (VLAN) tag 4 bytes + cyclic redundancy check (CRC) 4 bytes.

■ **Note**   To obtain the complete benefit of the jumbo frames, all components of the hardware configuration must support jumbo frames (NICs, switches, and storage such as NetApps).

The steps to configure and enable jumbo frames are different based on the environments.

LINUX KERNEL 2.6

In Linux kernel Version 2.6, adding the MTU value to the /etc/sysconfig/network-scripts/ifcfg-eth<n> file (illustrated following) will enable jumbo frames.

```
[root@ssky1l3p3 network-scripts]# more ifcfg-eth0
# Linux NIC bonding between eth0 and eth1
# Murali Vallath
# JAN-29-2013
#
DEVICE=eth0
BOOTPROTO=none
ONBOOT=yes
USERCTL=no
MASTER=bond0
MTU=9000
SLAVE=yes
```

The output of the NIC should resemble the following after the network interfaces have been restarted:

```
bond0     Link encap:Ethernet  HWaddr 00:D0:B7:6A:39:85
          inet addr:192.168.2.30  Bcast:192.168.2.255  Mask:255.255.255.0
          UP BROADCAST RUNNING MASTER MULTICAST  MTU:9000  Metric:1
          RX packets:3162 errors:0 dropped:0 overruns:0 frame:0
          TX packets:1312 errors:0 dropped:0 overruns:0 carrier:0
          collisions:0 txqueuelen:0
          RX bytes:275327 (268.8 Kb)  TX bytes:142369 (139.0 Kb)
```

AIX

Using ifconfig and chdev,

```
chdev -P -l <interface> -a media_speed=Auto_Negotiation
ifconfig <interface> down detach
chdev -l <interface> -a jumbo_frames=yes
chdev -l <interface> -a mtu=9000
chdev -l <interface> -a state=up
```

Solaris

Bring the interface down (unplumb) and set the instance to accept jumbo frames:

```
# ifconfig <interface> down unplumb
# ndd -set /dev/<interface> instance 1
# ndd -set /dev/<interface> accept-jumbo 1
# ifconfig <interface> plumb <address> up
```

■ **Best Practice**   Jumbo frames provide overall performance improvements in a RAC environment and should be used.

Jumbo frames only help LAN performance; traffic leaving the LAN to the Internet is limited to packets of 1,500 bytes. Access to and from a RAC environment is mostly limited to the application server and local clients setting up jumbo frames should provide positive benefits. Large MTU sizes between the application server and database servers will allow increase of the session data unit (SDU) sizes. This allows for transfer of large volumes of data between the application server and database, such as when using array fetches.

More discussions on SDU and buffer sizing are forthcoming in Chapter 11.

ASM

The storage system is a shared component in the RAC architecture and although compared to a single instance configuration, its usage is of equal importance and performance is critical as a shared component of the cluster. Initial scalability testing of the storage system should be performed during capacity planning to determine the write storage allocation and best size and number of disk combinations. Scalability testing should be done taking into consideration the LUNs or individual disks (in case "just a bunch of disks" [JBOD] is used for storage), and I/O performance characteristics should be determined to ascertain performance. Tools such as Oracle Orion can be used to benchmark the I/O system without having to use an Oracle installation.

Instance

The scalability of an instance in the cluster depends largely on the quality of the executing SQL and how the memory pools are sized. The memory used by an Oracle instance is divided into shared pool, large pool, buffer cache, redo log buffer, and so forth. The sizing of these memory areas is influenced by parameters such as the degree of parallelism, multiblock read count, and so forth.

Almost always scalability limitations in clustered environments are caused by SQL statements that are not tested for memory efficiency and performance as well as memory caches that are not sized right.

With the dynamic provisioning of instances using the policy managed database option, scalability can be obtained by provision instances to the pool based on demand if the utilization of CPU and memory of a system cannot provide good service.

SQL*Net

System scalability also depends on the network and NIC between the application server and database tier. What is the packet rate that an interface supports? What packet sizes can be supported for best performance? The configuration and scalability of the application tier must be considered, too. However when testing the hardware for scalability, the application should not be included. These scalability tests only consider bare database servers.

Several features available from Oracle simply scale out of the box; however, when combined with the application, similar results maynot be obtained due to various reasons, for example, inefficiently written application code. To ensure optimal scalability of the code, systematic testing is required.

Testing Hardware for Scalability

In this phase of testing, the basic clustered hardware is tested with the Oracle RAC software to obtain scalability numbers, which will then become the baseline to other phases of testing.

Under no circumstances should any of the RAP phases be ignored or compromised because the luxury to identify and fix problems maynot be available once the environment is in production; and it could become really late in the game when components start failing in production, defeating the entire goal of providing HA to the database.

RAP Phase V Hardware Scalability

During this phase, a standard performance benchmarking software load will test the database environment, not including the application schemas and data. The purpose of this test is to verify the database and operating system performance characteristics. Based on the load tests and the statistics collected, the database and environment should be tuned. Once tuned, the testing should be repeated until a maximum or until such point when no or minimal scalability gains are noticed.

Workshop

Earlier in this chapter we discussed the various scalable components of a RAC cluster. RAP Phase V checks for scalability of these components and helps tune the configuration parameters to achieve the maximum throughput and response times that the server is capable of giving.

This phase of the testing can be completed very early in the RAC migration process. Once RAP Phase I is complete and it's determined that the various components are stable, the scalability of these components could be tested and tuned.

Step 1

Gather all information and settings from the various components, such as make, model, memory,and so forth. Collect information regarding configurations and settings from each component used in the cluster.

Along with this information regarding components, also collect the current operating system (O/S) level settings for the primary parameters for all of these components. For O/S parameters related to Oracle and network components, most implementations start with the basic parameters suggested by Oracle in the installation guides. This should be the initial baseline value before starting the tests.

Step 2

After the initial configuration information is collected, the next step is to start to load test the cluster. Compared to the Phase I tests where we used same of these tools to test the stability of the components, Phase V tests are more controlled and should be more organized and planned tests. The workloads used to test should be based on what type of application workload will use the cluster after it's deployed into production: OLTP, Data warehouse, or a mixed workload. Based on this, the appropriate testing tool and functionality should be used. For example, load-testing tools available in the market such as Hammerora support both TPC-C and TPC-H workloads. Whereas TPC-C gives you an OLTP type of workload TPC-H represents a data warehouse workload. Figure 4-3 illustrates a screenshot from a workload generated using Hammerora.

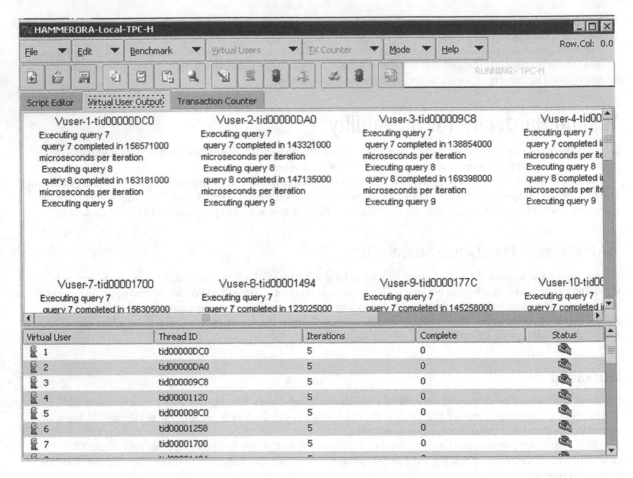

Figure 4-3. *Hammerora workload generator*

WORKLOAD TESTING TOOLS

There are several standard workload-testing tools available as freeware or on a commercial basis. For example

1. Hammerora is a load generation tool and provides standard TPC-C and TPC-H workloads.

2. Swingbench is another free load testing tool available and written specifically for simulating workloads in a RAC environment.

3. Benchmark Factory is commercial software and also used for a similar workload generation.

4. LoadRunner is a capture and execute simulation tool. It captures screens from application interfaces and executes the same screen as multiple users. It helps identify scalability features from various functional areas of the application.

There are probably several other load testing tools and products. It's not the product that's important; it's the features that support the type of tests and the statistics that is critical.

If industry standard test results are available, why perform another benchmark? Industry benchmarks are done on a specific set of hardware configuration and it's not necessary that all components used in the test are used in the cluster here. These tests are only to validate and tune the current configuration for scalability.

■ **Note** In this specific workshop example, we discuss a Datawarehouse implementation. The steps and procedures should be similar for an OLTP or a mixed workload configuration.

Step 3

As covered in the capacity planning discussion of Chapter 2, it's important to understand the ratio of user workload to the number of instances and the workload that can be handled per server. In Chapter 2, the tests focused on determining what kind of hardware is required; Phase II tests are to make sure the components configured are right and the parameters are sized and tuned well.

Scalability tests should start with a single node and other nodes should be added to the configuration through iterations. The first server becomes the initial baseline; and as new nodes are added to the configuration, bottlenecks identified and fixed, they become the new baseline for the test. Every time a baseline is determined, the new goal is set to improve the baseline in a subsequent test until there is a point of no return, meaning no improvements in scalability numbers.

Using the Hammerora tool (Figure 4-3), the initial testing goals are defined and listed in Table 4-1.

Table 4-1. *RAP Phase II—Hardware Scalability Load on One Server*

Test #	Scalability Factor	No. of Users	No. of Nodes	Iterations	Duration
1	1	20	1	5	1 hour

During the test, the CPU load average, the I/O load average, and the response times were acceptable. There was no indication on any component in the configuration that may require any changes.

Step 4

With a good satisfactory load average on the one instance of the database, the test can be repeated or workload can be increased after adding additional nodes to the cluster. So far it was a single instance configuration, and none of the RAC components were involved. In this test, as we move to a two-node configuration, the interconnects will be used and the storage system will be shared by more than one node. Table 4-2 illustrates tests with same scaling factor but with more user workload.

Table 4-2. *RAP Phase II—Scalability Load on Two Servers*

Test #	Scalability Factor	No. of Users	No. of Nodes	Iterations	Duration
2	1	30	2	5	1 hour

In Test 1, Hammerora was able to average about 12,000 queries per hour; and now with multiple servers and increased user workload, the queries per hour almost doubled. Figure 4-4 illustrates the transaction counter from the Hammerora tool illustrating an average workload of 22,680 queries per house.

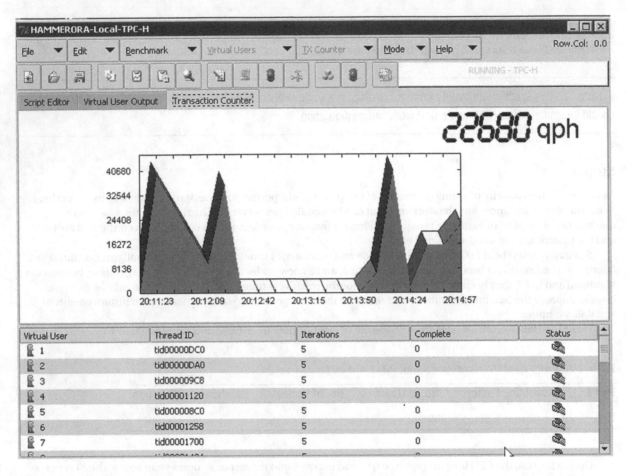

Figure 4-4. *Hammerora—Transactions counter 2-node cluster test*

The cluster-level statistics from OEM illustrated in Figure 4-5 also indicate that there are no bottlenecks from taking the tests to the next level. Response times are good, indicating further tests by adding additional users and increasing the number of servers in the cluster.

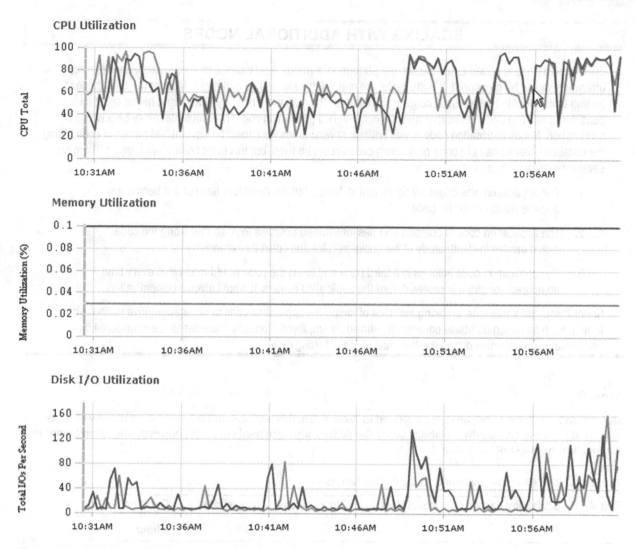

Figure 4-5. *OEM 11g—Cluster utilization and demand on 2-node RAC cluster*

SCALING WITH ADDITIONAL NODES

Every time a node is added to the cluster, the performance matrix, load balance characteristics, and resource utilization should be monitored. If bottlenecks are noticed, they should be optimized. Most of the time the load testing tools execute queries that are generic in nature. They are not efficiently written and hence could be considered as false bottlenecks that may not occur in real production code. This could definitely be a wrong assumption. Not all application code is well written; several times we encounter several bad pieces of code hitting the database. Ideally bad or poorly performing code should be fixed, but this does not always happen. There are several reasons for this:

1. The application was originally developed in-house, but the developer has not left behind any documentation to fix the code.

2. The application code is complex and has intertwined business logic so that fixing the code would involve in-depth study of the business rules and could be expensive.

3. The application code belongs to a third party and fixing the code would mean that every time an upgrade or patch is received from the application owners, it would involve customization.

Under these circumstances, breaking the rules of tuning the application code to other alternative methods of tuning, such as tuning database parameters, should be employed. Normally these areas are considered for performance optimization during the last phases of the testing cycle.

Step 5

Step 4 load testing was based on criteria defined in Table 4-2. In this test, seen in Table 4-3, the scalability factor is increased from 1 to 10. (Ideally scalability factor should have also increased gradually; however, due to limitations in the tool, this test has not been done.)

Table 4-3. *RAP Phase II—Scalability Load on Two Servers*

Test #	Scalability Factor	No. of Users	No. of Nodes	Iterations	Duration
3	10	40	4	5	1 hour

After 20 minutes into the run, there was high I/O contention and the latency numbers started tripling per the Cluster Health Monitor (CHM) illustrated in Figure 4-6. Combined with I/O waits was also high CPU utilization response times that were not acceptable.

emcpowerv	0.0	186.9	6	0	108	SYS
emcpowero	44600.4	44.4	96	10	105	SYS
emcpowere	45836.8	3.7	96	10	104	SYS
emcpowerf	43119.6	11.1	90	9	104	SYS
emcpoweri	47621.1	11.1	101	10	104	SYS
emcpowern	43112.2	55.5	96	9	102	SYS
emcpowerd	44307.9	25.9	95	10	101	SYS
emcpowerb	44511.5	7.4	93	9	101	SYS
emcpowerj	46629.1	0.0	96	9	99	SYS
emcpowerm	42705.0	22.2	88	9	99	SYS
emcpowera	44278.6	61.8	93	9	98	SYS

Figure 4-6. *11g CHM disk latency alarms*

The database had the parameter "PARALLEL_DEGREE_LIMIT" set to the CPU; however, because this was a datawarehouse workload, it would be appropriate to set the value of PARALLEL_DEGREE_LIMIT to I/O.

In a datawarehouse environment, where parallel operations are normal, the queries performed are I/O intensive and not CPU intensive. Changing this parameter to I/O was optimal based on statistics collected.

Before setting the value of this parameter to I/O, it's important to understand the I/O throughput of the storage subsystem. This can be understood using the DBMS_RESOURCE_MANAGER.CALIBRATE_IO procedure.

CALIBRATION

I/O calibration is useful to understand the performance of the storage subsystem. Oracle databases perform different types of I/O operations depending on the type of transaction or the number of blocks requested or persisted. It also depends on the type of workload the database will support. Getting a gauge over the I/O subsystem performance helps size and provisions the appropriate number and size of disks. The DBMS_RESOURCE_MANAGER.CALIBRATE_IO procedure calibrates the I/O subsystem using Oracle code stack; this gives a better understanding of the actual performance characteristics. Calibration is done using the following procedure:

```
SET SERVEROUTPUT ON
DECLARE
lat  INTEGER;
  iops INTEGER;
  mbps INTEGER;
BEGIN
-- DBMS_RESOURCE_MANAGER.CALIBRATE_IO (<DISKS>, <MAX_LATENCY>, iops, mbps, lat);
DBMS_RESOURCE_MANAGER.CALIBRATE_IO (8, 10, iops, mbps, lat);

  DBMS_OUTPUT.PUT_LINE ('max_iops = ' || iops);
  DBMS_OUTPUT.PUT_LINE ('latency  = ' || lat);
  DBMS_OUTPUT.PUT_LINE ('max_mbps = ' || mbps);

end;
/
```

In the preceding procedure, the two important parameters are

- DISKS or NUM_PHYSICAL_DISKS: Like the parameter clearly states, it's the physical disks not the number of LUN devices.

- MAX_LATENCY: This is the maximum latency for the disk access specified in milliseconds.

Once calibration is complete, the results of the calibration can be checked using the following script:

Script: MVRACPDnTap_iocalcheck1.sql

Last Calibration Date	Max IOPS	Max MBPS	Max PMBPS	Latency	Phy Disks
10-FEB-13 11.50	20738	1613	747	11	8

```
 INST_ID STATUS        Last Calibration Time
 -------- -------------  -------------------------------
        1 READY         10-FEB-13 11.50.38.279 AM
        2 READY         10-FEB-13 11.50.38.279 AM
        3 READY         10-FEB-13 11.50.38.279 AM
        4 READY         10-FEB-13 11.50.38.279 AM

 8 rows selected.
```

Running Test 3 again, there was no disk level I/O contention; however, after 30 minutes into the test, high CPU utilization and network issues were visible.

Latency numbers from the disks where normal and acceptable. However, the EM grid control, iptraf, and interactive verification against V$SYSSTAT indicated high latency on the interconnect.

```
INST_ID  Avg CR Blk Recv Time(ms)
-------- -------------------------
       1                      6.7
       2                     10.5
       3                     12.3
       4                     12.4
```

It was also observed that the interconnect had several packet losses and errors on checking the blocks lost statistics from V$SYSSTAT and O/S level statistics using netstat and ifconfig commands.

Checking the interconnect configuration indicated that jumbo frames were not configured. Datawarehouse workloads data is transferred in larger packet sizes, much larger than the database block size of 8k. Jumbo frames will help increase the transfer unit size from 1,500 to 9,000. This means the interconnect buffer sizes would be more comfortable for an Oracle datablock of 8k or higher.

After considerable deliberation and convincing the network team that jumbo frames are used only in a private network between the instances in the cluster and the fact that jumbo frames should not interfere with regular network traffic outside the cluster, jumbo frames were enabled.

MORE OF A MYTH FOR RAC CONFIGURATION

The reasons why Institute of Electrical and Electronics Engineers (IEEE[2]) has not certified that jumbo frames cannot be related to the configuration of jumbo frames in a closed RAC environment. In a RAC environment, jumbo frame implementation is in a private network closed configuration. Other networks should not be affected by this configuration. In fact, if it does, there is potentially an issue in the way it's configured.

Oracle supports and recommends the use of jumbo frames as a best practice for the private interconnect in a RAC configuration.

Step 6

After several iterations and testing of the cluster with different scalability factors, it was determined that the following test (Table 4-4) had the right scalability numbers that the cluster could handle. The tests showed response times above average and acceptable.

---

[2]See Ethernet Alliance (www.ethernetalliance.org) publication *Ethernet Jumbo Frames*, Version 0.1, November 12, 2009.

Table 4-4. *RAP Phase II—Scalability Load on Two Servers*

Test #	Scalability Factor	No. of Users	No. of Nodes	Iterations	Duration
6	10	60	8	5	1 hour

During the process of testing, the following network parameters were increased from their default values recommended by Oracle in the RAC installation and configuration guides:

```
fs.file-max = 6815744
fs.aio-max-nr = 3145728
vm.nr_hugepages=18433
net.core.wmem_max=12582912
net.core.rmem_max=12582912
net.ipv4.tcp_rmem= 10240 4194304 12582912
net.ipv4.tcp_wmem= 10240 4194304 12582912
net.core.netdev_max_backlog = 5000
net.ipv4.tcp_no_metrics_save = 1
net.ipv4.ip_local_port_range = 1024 65500
```

As illustrated in Figure 4-7, the overall throughput and workload on all eight nodes in the cluster are normal. The cluster components are scalable and the load average is recorded as the baseline for future comparisons.

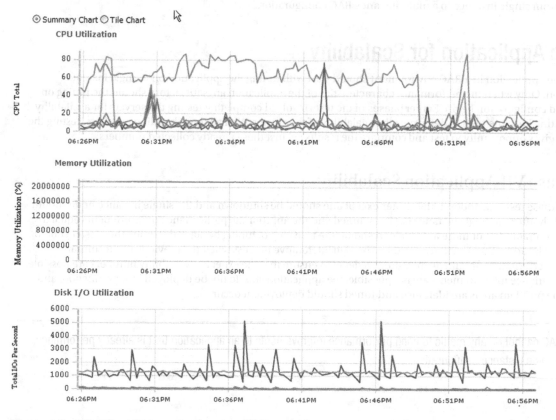

Figure 4-7. *OEM 11g: 8 Eight-node cluster scalability study*

■ **Note**   Testing storage to determine I/O throughputs can also be considered as part of the hardware scalability tests. However, storage-related tests should be performed earlier in the project life cycle—for example, when deciding on the type of storage required and what type of SAN configuration is required, how the disks should be sized, and so forth. Tools such as ORION available from Oracle are great for testing scalability of storage components. Usage and testing using ORION is included in Chapter 2.

Testing the Database for Scalability

The next phase in the process of testing is to ensure that the database is configured and tuned well. The application stack from top down consists of the application servers, the connection pool configuration, the network interface, the database, and the storage system.

While the stability of the cluster and the scalability components of the cluster have been verified using Phase I and Phase V, the next ideal step is to verify if the database scales as well. For this, it would be good to execute all of the SQL statements against the database without the overhead of the application. Phase VI of the testing can be optional provided there are no major issues identified in Phase VII, namely, testing the application for scalability.

Phase VI can use a new feature available within Oracle called "Database Replay" discussed in the next chapter. Database replay can help in migrations from single instance to RAC or to test scalability of the SQL queries and statements from single instance to a multi-instance RAC configuration.

Testing Application for Scalability

Testing of the application in a RAC environment should start with tuning the application on a single instance configuration. Only when the performance characteristics of the application are satisfactory should the tuning on the clustered configuration begin. Earlier phases of the tests involved completing testing the servers for availability and completing baseline tests to determine the scalability of the cluster. With all these baseline numbers, testing the application gives opportunity to test and compare the results against these already collected numbers.

RAP Phase VII Application Scalability

To perform these tests, all nodes in the cluster except one should be shutdown and the single instance node should be tested. Only after the single instance has been tuned and the appropriate performance measurements equal to the current configuration or more are obtained should the next step of tuning be started. Tuning the cluster should be performed by adding one instance at a time through an iterative process when the previous test results are satisfactory. Performance should be measured in detail to ensure that the expected scalability numbers are possible. If such performance measurements are not possible, the application should not be deployed into production, and only after the problem areas are identified and tuned should deployment occur.

■ **Note**   RAC cannot do any magic to bring performance improvements to an application that is already performing poorly on a single instance configuration.

Workshop

In this workshop, we walk through a testing scenario of scaling the application using LoadRunner. The idea here, like in most tests, is to achieve the optimal performance goal defined by business.

Step 1

This step is an information-gathering step. What is the goal of this test? What are the response time requirements for the critical areas of the application? What is the maximum number of concurrent users expected during go live, 3 months after go live, 6 months after go live, and 12 months after go live? These numbers will help testing the application for throughput and response times.

Step 2

When testing the application for scalability, the complete path of the transaction should be included in the test, meaning from the user interface, where the users request for data or enter orders, to the physical database, where data is persisted and or retrieved. This is unlike the Phase V test where only the database and the SQL statements were replayed.

To replay the front to back flow of data, tools such as LoadRunner should be used. LoadRunner can capture user screens with data being entered or retrieved and the exact screen can be repeated using multiple concurrent transactions.

Step 3

Using LoadRunner, the number of concurrent users and the ramp up time can be specified to create a user workload. Whereas in the various functional areas, the frequency of transactions, the think time, and so forth, should be consistent with real-life production environments.

Record the findings in a table (illustrated in Table 4-5) or spreadsheet for documentation, charting the comparisons as we go through other tests or when these operations are repeated at a later date.

Table 4-5. *RAP Phase VII—Data Collection Table*

Test #	Date	Time	# of Users	Duration	# of Db Servers	# of App Servers	Test	Description	Status

Table 4-5 is used for recording the findings from the test; the columns help us record the various matrixes that were used and collected from the test:

Test #: There will be a serious of tests, so this column will record the test number. It will help us reference this test by the number.

Date and Time: Record the date and time when the test was executed.

 # ofUsers: This lists how many users will be involved/simulated in the test. If you recall our earlier discussion, LoadRunner can be used to simulate workload patterns based on user navigation patterns captured from the current production users.

Duration: How long did the test run? Once again, using LoadRunner, the amount of time the test will be executed can be preset. Not always will or may the test run for the expected duration. It could fail because of various reasons, such as reaching the maximum capacity of the servers, wrong configuration of parameters, and so forth. If desired, the duration column can be expanded to list target duration and actual duration.

# of DB Servers: How many database servers were involved in the test? Remember, this is a scalability test, and it is important to understand the number of users to server ratio.

# of App Servers: Similar to the number of database servers, it's good to record the number of application servers involved in the test.

Test: What is the goal of this test? What should the expected resultsbe from this test?

Description: Details of the findings and or errors are noted in this column.

Status: The results noted in this column should be relative to the goal of the test listed in the "Test" Column. For example, the first test is to capture a baseline based on the performance numbers and business requirements. If the number of users could withstand the duration of the test and the test was able to provide the required response time, the result will be "Success."

Step 4

From our previous tests, we have several baselines; however, these baselines are not close in comparison to the baseline of the current production environments. Normally we would like to see performance and response times equal to or better from the new servers. If this is not the case, there should be sufficient justification for moving to the new configuration, such as cost saving, for example, migrating from a HP Superdome to a multinode Linux configuration.

As illustrated in Table 4-6, the test failed 10 minutes after start. Based on the number of users and the number of database servers used in this test, the results were as expected.

Table 4-6. RAP Phase VII—Load Test on One Server

Test #	Date & Time	# of Users	Test Duration	# of Db Servers	# of App Servers	Description	Status
1	10-Aug-xxxx 10:00 AM	40	60 minutes. Failed @ 10 minutes	1	6	Slow performance. Failed after 10 users. System saturated with overworked CPU.	FAILED

Step 5

The hardware configuration determined during capacity planning exercises for this production hardware was a 4-node, 4*4 servers to map to one HP superdome. Although it was a good idea to see how the one server will withstand the workload, should all the remaining servers in the new production server fail,in fact it may be worth testing with 1, 2, and 3 nodes to determine the business impact if this were to happen after implementing the new hardware into production.

Continuing with the scalability testing, the cluster was changed to a 4-node configuration. Table 4-7 illustrates the test and the results from the 4-node configuration test.

Table 4-7. *RAP Phase VII—Load Test on One Server*

Test #	Date & Time	# of Users	Test Duration	# of Db Servers	# of App Servers	Description	Status
2	10-Aug-xxxx 1 PM	40	60 minutes	4	6	Db server shows high CPU usage with 10 users. Identified a poorly performing SQL statement. Overall response times poor.	FAILED

Once again, the test illustrated in Table 4-7 failed. Similar to the previous tests, the failure of this test was due to lack of sufficient resources to complete the operation. However, the potential cause of the problem was focused on a bad SQL statement. The statement performed well in a single instance superdome environment. However, in a RAC environment, it had issues.

Step 6

It's important to tune the SQL statement to get the databases to scale.

Once the query was tuned and deployed back into the test environment, the test was repeated. This time the test succeeded and the response time expected was obtained. Although this could be improved, we looked at the internal RAC-related statistics and noticed high sequence number related waits.

Looking further identified high waits on sequences—PCT_SUCC_GETS< 50% and sequence UPDATES frequency high on Instance 1 and Instance 2:

```
INT  PARAMETER        GETS      MISSES    PCT_SUCC_GETS  UPDATES
----  --------------   --------  --------  -------------  ----------
   1  dc_sequences     24238     12205            49.6   24,238
   2  dc_sequences     20913     12203            41.6   20,911
   3  dc_sequences      2926       869            70.3    2,926
   4  dc_sequences      2621       886            66.2    2,621
```

All sequences were set to the default cache value of 20. In a RAC environment, sequences maybe requested from more than one session and from multiple instances in the cluster. Cache size of 20 may be minimal, and sequences that are frequently accessed should be set to a higher cache size.

Step 7

With the aforementioned fixes and repeating the tests, the overall response times for the database was normal: it was ready for testing beyond 4 nodes. We increased the DB servers to six instances (see Table 4-8).

Table 4-8. *RAP Phase VII—Load Test on Six Servers*

Test #	Date & Time	# of Users	Test Duration	# of Db Servers	# of App Servers	Description	Status
3	—	—	—	—	—	—	SUCCESS
4	12-Aug-xxxx	80	60 minutes	6	6	—	SUCCESS

With response times meeting the SLA requirements, the database servers are on the right track; they are scaling as expected.

Step 8

Now that the primary bottlenecks of the database and the application have been determined, the next series of tests (Table 4-9) is to determine the maximum number of users supported by the RAC cluster. In the next series of tests, the number of users, number of database servers, and also tests by increasing the number of application servers where performed based on demand for resources.

Table 4-9. *RAP Phase VII—Load Test on One Server*

Test #	Date & Time	# of Users	Test Duration	# of Db Servers	# of App Servers	Description	Status
9	20–Aug–xxxx	180	120 minutes	6	8	Db servers show normal CPU usage and workload is distributed across all db instances. Response times are slower compared to previous tests but within SLA requirements.	SUCCESS
10	25–Aug–xxxx	240	120 minutes	6	8	2 application servers and 2 database servers evicted because of high CPU usage and server overload.	FAILED

Test 10 failed due to server saturation; this means that the ideal configuration from the preceding tests is 90 users on a 6-node database cluster with 8 node application servers. Table 4-10 gives a snapshot of all the tests.

Table 4-10. *RAP Phase VII—Consolidated List of Tests*

Test #	# of Users	Duration	# of Db Servers	# of App Servers
1	40	2 hours	1	6
2	40	2 hours	4	6
3	40	2 hours	4	6
4	60	2 hours	4	6
5	80	2 hours	5	6
6	120	2 hours	5	6
7	140	2 hours	5	6
8	160	2 hours	5	7
9	180	2 hours	6	8
10	240	2 hours	6	8
11	240	2 hours	8	8
12	240	2 hours	8	8
13	180	2 hours	8	8

Data collected in Table 4-10 can be analyzed and interpreted in a graphic as illustrated in Figure 4-8. These graphs and charts compare the scalability numbers to the workload across various tests. What's the application server to database ratio required to accommodate the required number of users?

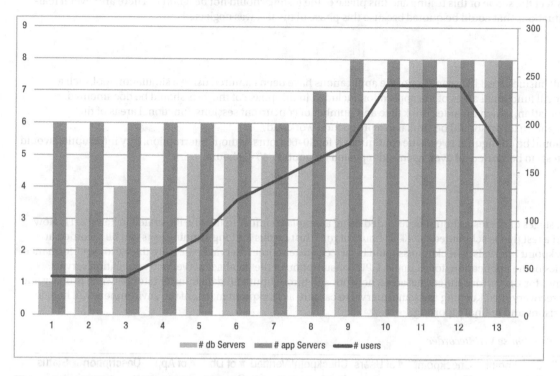

Figure 4-8. *RAP Phase VII—Application server's to db server's user workload*

End-to-End Testing

We have this far looked at testing several areas of the configuration through different phases. No matter how in-depth testing has been completed, the importance of the end-to-end testing of the entire application should not be skipped. In this test, the entire application stack along with the database tiers are tested with real-time realistic data loads streaming through the stack, simulating a real-life production workload. This would mean including redo log shipping to the standby database for disaster recovery, applying data, and verification for any archive log gaps. This test is to ensure all changes made to the various layers of the stack are now functional and do not cause any hidden issues when everything is working together. These tests are to be done on the production hardware before the hardware is made.

RAP Testing Phase VIII Burnout Tests

This phase of the testing is to verify the overall health of both the application and the databases when the database is constantly receiving transactions from the application. Using tools such as LoadRunner, a typical workload is generated against the database for a period of 40–60 hours and the stability of the environment is monitored. This phase of the testing is to verify any issues with application and database software components for memory leaks and other failures. The data and statistics collected from the tests can also help in the final tuning of the database and network parameters.

Workshop

In this workshop we discuss the various steps involved in the burnout testing of the application. Project time lines should not affect the scope of this testing and this phase of the testing should not be ignored. There are several real-life failure situations that could be quoted because this phase of the test was neglected.

Step 1

Ensure the all business real life scenarios of the applications have been captured using a simulation tool such as LoadRunner. All functional areas of the application included in this phase of the tests should be documented. The user simulation, which includes think time and number of concurrent sessions, functional areas of the applications, and so forth, should be similar to a production workload.

Tests should be configured to execute continuously for 40–60 hours without interruption. Any interruption would require the tests to be started all over again and repeated for another 40–60 hours.

Step 2

All tests and stages of the tests should be recorded using a template similar to the one illustrated in Table 4-11. How do we record a test that is scheduled for 40–60 hours of run? Test results for long-running tests can be recorded at various checkpoint intervals. Checkpointsshould be at a consistent time interval to measure the various performance characteristics of the application, for example, CPU consumption of the database server and application servers, response times for the various functional areas, network and throughput,and data transfer rates between primary and the disaster recovery sites.Keeping the same interval to capture a checkpoint matrix of the environment will help in easy comparisons and in final reporting.

Table 4-11. RAP Phase VIII Recorder

Checkpoint #	Checkpoint Date	Checkpoint Time	# of Users	Checkpoint/Verified Component	# of Db Servers	# of App Servers	Description	Status

Step 3

In our workshop, the total duration of the test is planned for 48 hours; and to have an even interval, we collect a snapshot of the environment every 4 hours (see Table 4-12).

Table 4-12. RAP Phase VIII Recording Initial Test

Checkpoint #	Checkpoint Date	Checkpoint Time	# of Users	Checkpoint/ Verified Component	# of Db Servers	# of App Servers	Description	Status
1	02/16/2011	8:00 AM	100	N/A	6	8	Start of RAP VIII	Success
2	02/16/2011	12:00 noon	100	Entire stack	6	8	Overall health of the environment	Good

Note: N/A = not applicable.

Along with the log being maintained in Table 4-12, screenshots and reports from the LoadRunner, Automatic Workload Repository (AWR), Automatic Database Diagnostic Monitor (ADDM), and other health check tools should also be collected and maintained.

Step 4

Similar to Step 3, continue the monitoring and recording of information every 4 hours. Record any kind of issues encountered. Table 4-13 illustrates an issue with the dataguard configuration. The DR site is not able to keep up with the redo log ship rates. The apply process is far behind and has created a large gap between the primary and standby environments. The primary site has switched from redo log shipping to archive log shipping. This is critical in a production environment and should be minimized.

Table 4-13. *RAP Phase VIII Recording Test Progress*

Checkpoint #	Checkpoint Date	Checkpoint Time	# of Users	Checkpoint/ Verified Component	# of Db Servers	# of App Servers	Description	Status
1	02/16/2011	8:00 AM	100	N/A	6	8	Start of RAP VIII	Success
2	02/16/2011	12:00 noon	100	Entire stack	6	8	Overall health of the environment	Good
3								
. . . .								
. . . .								
8	02/17/2011	12 :00 noon	100	Entire stack	6	8	Archive log gaps Apply process behind compared to the redo switch rates	Warning

Note: N/A = not available.

Step 5

On completion of the 48 hours of successful testing, the results should be recorded in the table (illustrated in Table 4-14) and should be documented. Final conclusions of the tests should be presented/reviewed with the DBA team and subsequently with the project team. The results of the tests should be the deciding factor to determine if the environment is ready for prime time production.

Table 4-14. *RAP VIII Recording Every 2 Hours*

Checkpoint #	Checkpoint Date	Checkpoint Time	# of Users	Checkpoint/ Verified Component	# of Db Servers	# of App Servers	Description	Status
1	02/16/2011	8:00 AM	100	N/A	6	8	Start of RAP VIII	Success
2	02/16/2011	12:00 noon	100	Entire stack	6	8	Overall health of the environment	Good
·········								
8	02/17/2011	12 :00 noon	100	Entire stack	6	8	Archive log gaps Apply process behind compared to the redo switch rates	Warning
·······								
16	02/18/2011	12:00noon	100	Entire stack	6	8		

Note: N/A = not available.

■ **Note** This report should be used for educational and reference purposes only. The report is not a complete report and the results indicated may vary from environment to environment based on the configuration such as O/S, application, and infrastructure being deployed.

Conclusion

Testing cannot be ignored under any circumstances. As we discussed earlier, scalability and availability are the primary benefits of moving to RAC configuration. What if these benefits cannot be achieved? What if the project is deployed into production and the performance is worse than it was on a single instance non-RAC database? Maybe the application cannot be made scalable and RAC maybe a bad choice or maybe RAC is not required to achieve scalability. It cannot be stressed enough how important it is to test the RAC cluster. On several occasions, RAC deployments have failed after moving into production because they have never been tested. RAP testing from Phase I thru Phase VIII are allcritical and should be completed for a smooth transition from single instance to a clustered scalable solution.

■ ■ ■

## CHAPTER 5

Real Application Testing

Today's Internet-based computing has created several challenges to the computing industry. The expansion of the global economy has increased workloads and user activities. Transactions can originate from any part of the world while the final persistence of the data into storage media happens in some unknown location millions of miles away. The expectations, irrespective of where the data is finally stored, either in the city or in some remote unknown location, require high response times.

In supporting increased user activities or increased number of users as the demand for Internet-based computing expands, more powerful infrastructure with high speed processors are being engineered. This means that the older systems that currently support production systems get replaced with newer technology.

Equally challenging to the increased workload and demand for Internet systems that provide higher response times, is the migration of systems from one technology to another.

In an *N*-tier computing model, there are several areas where bottlenecks can occur; and response times are measured taking into consideration the entire life cycle of a transaction. However, the primary area of concern is almost always found to be where the rubber meets the road, the database. Here the rubber is the SQL operations, and the road is the physical database. The performance of the persistence layer is extremely critical for the overall performance of any system, Internet, the old client server, the data warehouse, or even the space navigation systems.

Whereas performance of the persistence layer in any enterprise architecture is important, it's even more critical that this performance measurement is maintained or improved as systems are migrated to new technologies or when additional functionality is added to the systems.

The previous two chapters discussed various types of testing and how they all play an important role in the success of any RAC implementation. Testing performance and scalability of the application was discussed in Chapter 4. Scalability of the application is possible only if the persistence layer to the database also scales.

Testing the persistence layer without including the overhead of the application will help identify concurrency issues with SQL statements and DML operations. These queries can then be optimized and tested again before adding the overhead of the application and business logic. This also helps to create a baseline, which further helps to determine if the application interface to the database is slower and directing efforts to optimize the application. Oracle provides a tool called "database replay" to help understand impact to the overall performance of the environment when changes are made to the system and infrastructure. Whereas alternative methods can easily be developed using perl and other utilities, in this chapter, an attempt is being made to discuss the database replay tool from Oracle.

Persistence layer scalability tests should be performed against a copy of the production schema (on the new hardware platform) that contains the actual data from the current live production environment. The purpose of this test is to tune the instance and the database for application workloads not interfacing the business application. For such a test, an extract of the SQL queries from the application could be used; or tools available in the market, such as Real Application Testing (RAT), could be used.

Testing Methods

There are several methods of testing code. We discussed a few of the testing methods in the early chapters of this book. In this chapter, the focus is on testing the persistence layer, the layer that finally writes to the database. Testing the persistence layer can be done either by using a homegrown utility or the new software option available from Oracle called RAT.[1]

Method I—Using Homegrown Utilities

With this method, standard features available with Oracle database combined with some self-developed utilities can be used.

To get an acceptable user workload, this test will require data and user operations from a real production environment.

With this method, a load test should be performed against a copy of the production schema (on the new hardware platform) that contains the actual data from the current live production environment. The purpose of this test is to tune the instance and the database for application workloads not interfacing the business application.

Workshop

For this test, an extract of the SQL operations from the application is used. One method to extract these operations from a live system without user intervention is to trace them using Oracle event 10046 and then to parse the trace files through an application to extract the queries with their respective bind values.

Step 1

In a live production environment, enable Oracle event trace 10046 at Level 8 after connecting to the database as user 'sys'.

```
ALTER SESSION SET TRACEFILE_IDENTIFIER ='SSKY';
ALTER SYSTEM SET EVENTS '10046 TRACE NAME CONTEXT FOREVER, LEVEL 8';
```

Step 2

Setting the trace file identifier will help organize trace files that are started after the command was issued. The 10046 event generates the trace file in the directory identified by the parameter DIAGNOSTIC_DEST.

■ **Note**   Depending on the activity on the production servers, the number of trace files and their contents could be large and consume a considerable amount of disk space. Please ensure sufficient disk space is available before attempting this step.

Step 3

Concatenate all the trace files generated by the event in the user dump destination directory into one file or use the trcsess utility to combine the trace files into one.

```
cat *SSKY.trc  > SQLQueries.trc
```

---

[1]RAT requires an additional license.

Step 4

The TKPROF utility has a record switch that allows you to record the non-recursive SQL statements found in the trace file:

```
tkprof SQLQueries.trc SQLQueries.rpt record= SQLQueries.sql explain=rapusr/rapusr
table=rapusr.temp sys=no
```

tkprof should generate two outputs, the .rpt file that would contain the execution statistics for the trace collection and the .sql file that would contain the SQL statements found in the trace file.

■ **Note** A sample Perl script, MVRACPDnTap_extractsql.pl, which you can use to extract SQL statements from the trace file, is provided with the downloads for this book.

Step 5

Develop another perl or a java program that can read these SQL statements from the output file generated in Step 4 and execute them against the database in multiple sessions. The value of the number of sessions that each statement will execute can be a parameter to test increased workload.

Step 6

Using the queries extracted from Step 4 previously, perform a load test simulating the estimated user workload iterating the queries and measuring response times. This step is also an iterative process; the user load should be gradually increased through iterations. Through each iteration, statistics and other performance reports such as AWR should be collected. Then, based on the analysis, the instance and database parameters—and most important the SQL queries—should be tuned. This test could be performed either using a homegrown tool or third-party software such as Benchmark Factory (BMF).[2]

■ **Note** Performance should be monitored on all the tiers of the database server (O/S, instance, and database) during both load-testing phases using various performance-monitoring tools, which we discuss later in this chapter along with other performance tuning methods.

Method II—Using Real Application Testing

Although much of the work can be done manually using Method I, Oracle provides a product or feature, RAT[3] that is part of the database (can also be accessed using OEM/EM Cloud Control) and performs all the steps in Method I seamless to the DBA. Similar to other options that are part of OEM, RAT can also be used from the command line using PL/SQL packages and procedures. The RAT option includes two testing solutions: database replay and SQL performance analyzer.

Database replay allows testing of system and configuration changes to environments. It allows replaying a full production workload on the new system or servers that have configuration changes to help determine the overall impact of the change.

SQL analyzer, on the other hand, helps determine the impact of system and configuration changes on SQL statements by identifying any variation in SQL execution plans and performance statistics resulting from the change.

---

[2]Benchmark Factory is a software available from Quest Software (now Dell).
[3]RAT is available from EM or EM Cloud Control and requires additional licensing.

In a RAC environment, both these options allow testing the impact when moving from a single instance to a RAC configuration. It helps to determine the impact of moving from one instance to two or three instances and understanding the scalability and capacity requirements to execute the current production workload on the new configuration.

Database Replay

Like the feature's name, database replay helps to replay the current production workload in another environment. Such activity will help understand the application behavior on a new hardware or production environment.

Database replay (Figure 5-1) involves three major steps:

1. Capture, where the current workload is captured and collected for a user predefined time interval

2. Prepare, where the workload that is captured in the previous step is prepared for the next run

3. Run, where the workload captured from an existing production environment is executed on the new environment

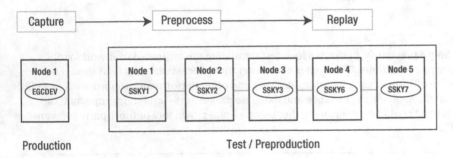

Figure 5-1. *Database replay steps*

Workshop

The workshop is to test workload in from a single instance environment on a 6-node RAC environment.

Workload Capture

In this phase, all external client requests directed to the Oracle database are tracked and stored in binary files called "capture files" on the system. These files contain all the relevant information, such as SQL statement, bind values, wall clock time, SCN numbers, and so forth, about the calls that are needed to replay the operation on the preproduction environment.

Step 1

Ensure that the new environment where the production workload will be executed is all ready for testing. Ensure that all RAP tests 1, 2, and 3 are completed and the required configuration changes or fixes have been made.

Before beginning the capture process, take a copy/snapshot of the current production database and restore it on a new test or preproduction environment. This is important because the database needs to be at a state before the capture begins so the replay on the new environment can have the same state of the rows before the collection begins.

Step 2

Identify the peak workload periods in the production environment to schedule the capture process. Database replay feature is part of the OEM and can be selected from the Software and Support tab (Figure 5-2) after selecting the current production database as the current target.

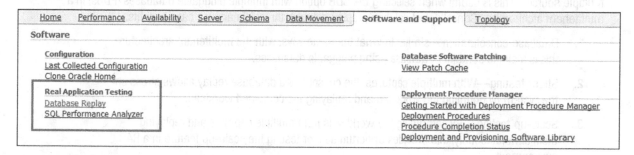

Figure 5-2. EM 11g, Real Application Testing options

■ **Note**   In EM12c cloud control, the Database Replay option is located under the Performance tab pull-down menu.

Step 3

From the two options available under EM 11g RAT, the database replay option should be selected to start scheduling the capture process.

The next screen provides the four stages of the database capture process. From this screen, select the Capture Production Workload option. This expands into three separates tasks (Figure 5-3). From the three tasks listed, select task 1, Capture Workload, by selecting the arrow on the Go to Task column on the right side.

Database Replay

Database Replay allows workloads to be captured from production systems and re-executed with high fidelity on test copies of production databases. This enables detailed analysis of how the proposed changes may affect production systems; for instance, patching or upgrading database software.

Page Refreshed **Mar 5, 2011 12:56:18 PM PST** (Refresh)

Task List

Expand All | Collapse All

Task Name	Description	Go to Task
▼ Capture Production Workload	Initiate or schedule a workload capture, export AWR data after capture, and copy captured files to the workload staging area.	
Capture Workload	Capture a workload from the production environment. This can be scheduled to accommodate a database restart if desired.	⇨
Export AWR Data	Export AWR data to provide a better performance comparison between captured and replayed workloads.	⇨
Copy to Workload Staging Area	Copy captured files away from production to the workload staging area for later preprocessing. For a cluster database, captured files from different database instances can be consolidated in the workload staging area.	⇨
▶ Prepare Test Database	Set up a test database from production, upgrade or otherwise modify the test database, and isolate the test database prior to replay.	
▶ Prepare for Replay	Prepare the workload capture files for replay (preprocess), copy the preprocessed workload files to the workload staging area, deploy the Replay Clients, and copy the preprocessed workload files to the Replay Client hosts.	
▶ Replay Workload on Test Database	Set up the workload replay on the test database, copy the replay results to the workload staging area, and analyze the results.	

Figure 5-3. OEM—Database Replay options

CONSOLIDATED DATABASE REPLAY

When migrating your current non-container database (non-CDB) into a CDB environment in Oracle Database 12c, the consolidated replay option comes in handy. It allows database replay at a single target of captures from multiple sources. This is useful when selecting the CDB option with multiple pluggable databases (PDBs) in a multitenant architecture. Consolidated database replay provides three primary use case benefits:

1. Database consolidation—similar to what the name says, with the multitenant architecture, this is a single container database using pluggable databases.

2. Stress testing—With multiple captures, the consolidated database replay allows stress on the system by doubling the workload and replaying the combined workload.

3. Scale-up testing—By combining the workloads from multiple captures and replaying them simultaneously, this provides opportunities for testing the scale-up feature in a RAC environment.

Steps to complete the consolidated replay are similar to the regular database replay option discussed in this chapter with a few additional steps:

- Locating captures into one directory—All captures from multiple sources should be placed into one directory (consolidated) for the consolidated replay option to work.

- Defining replay schedules—A replay schedule adds one or multiple workload captures into a consolidated replay and specifies the order in which the captures will start during replay.

- Remapping connections—Captured connection strings used to connect to the production system need to be remapped to the replay system.

- Remapping users——usernames of database users and schemas used to connect to the production system can be remapped during replay.

- Database replay—Once the mapping is complete, the database replay will execute exactly how the individual captures have completed. This is similar to the database replay in the older versions of RAT, with the exception that there are multiple database replays in place of one single database replay.

- Consolidated reporting—Whereas externally the replay would look like a single replay process, for all practical purposes they are replays of individual captures in a consolidated database environment. For comparison purposes, the reporting maintains these individual capture results and allows comparison with the replay results.

Step 4

The next screen (Figure 5-4) is the first step to scheduling the capture process. EM requests acknowledging the following:

1. Sufficient space to hold the capture files is available.

2. A clean backup copy of the database is available to restore to the preproduction database environment.

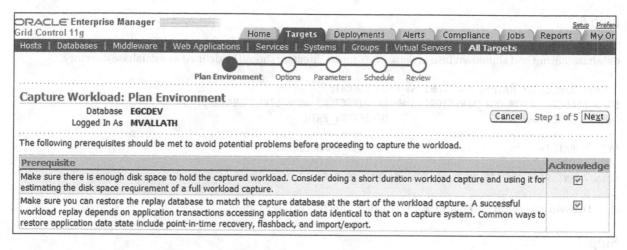

Figure 5-4. *OEM—Capture Workload environment*

If both tasks are completed, acknowledge the two prerequisites and click Next.

Step 5

The next screen (not shown) is the Options screen. Two primary options are available: to restart the database before beginning the capture and to provide rule-based filtering around the capture process to either exclude or include parts of the database activity (Figure 5-5). Once complete, click Next.

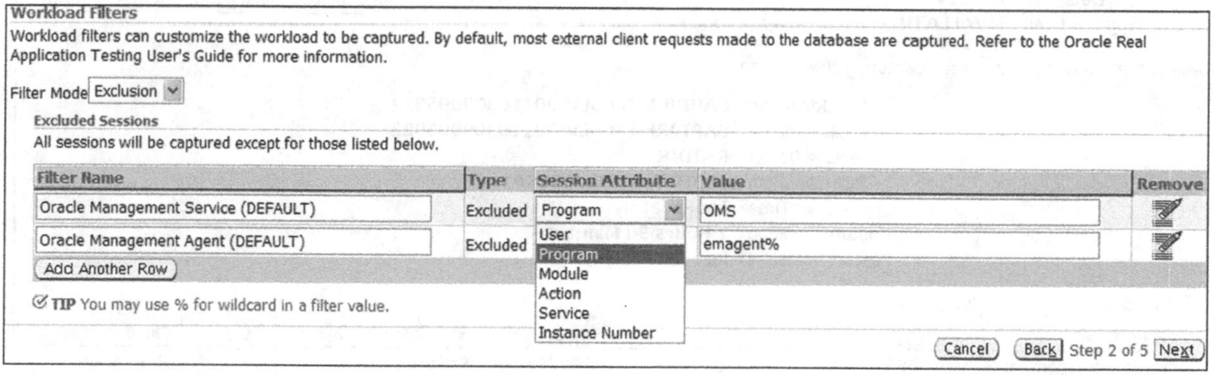

Figure 5-5. *OEM—Capture Exclusion Filter selection*

To capture a clean operation from the start to finish, it would be ideal to restart the database before starting the capture process. This will avoid starting the capture process in between an in-flight operation, which could adversely affect the replay. This may not be possible in certain situations, especially when a workload from a live production environment is being captured. Under such circumstances, it would be advised to start a capture when the database environment has minimal active sessions or activity. When this is required, the capture can be scheduled for a later period when the database activity is more realistic.

Step 6

The next screen (not shown) is to define workload capture parameters, such as capture name, capture directory, and database startup and shutdown instructions. The capture directory should be defined as a database directory.

```
CREATE DIRECTORY RATDIR AS '/OBITST_RMAN/EGCRAT/';
SQL> SELECT * FROM DBA_DIRECTORIES WHERE DIRECTORY_NAME LIKE '%RAT%';
OWNER  DIRECTORY_NAME                   DIRECTORY_PATH
------ -------------------------------- ----------------------------
SYS    RATDIR                           /OBITST_RMAN/EGCRAT

SQL> GRANT READ, WRITE ON DIRECTORY RATDIR TO RAPTEST;
```

This will allow Oracle to write the capture data directory to this location.

Step 7

The next screen (not shown) is the step to schedule the job for the capture process. Once the job is scheduled, the user has an option (Figure 5-6) to verify if all the capture details have been configured and ready for the capture. This screen provides a recap of the definitions from the previous screens and the job name. It also lists the directory where the capture will record the collection.

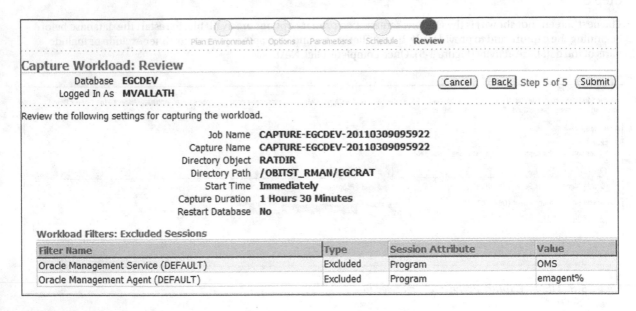

Figure 5-6. *OEM—Capture Workload Review*

Figure 5-6 also illustrates the filters selected (exclusion) and the other location information (directory and path) and schedule times. In this case, the capture is scheduled to start immediately. If everything is correct on the review screen, select Submit.

■ **Note** To make the movement of files from the current production to the new preproduction environment, it may be worth considering placing these files on a shared file system such as a network file system (NFS) mount. The advantage of placing them on NFS or shared mount locations is that it makes it easier to mount the volume on the new preproduction environment, which avoids copying the capture files across the network.

Step 8

Progress of the capture process (Figure 5-7) can be viewed by selecting the scheduled job from the jobs tab on OEM.

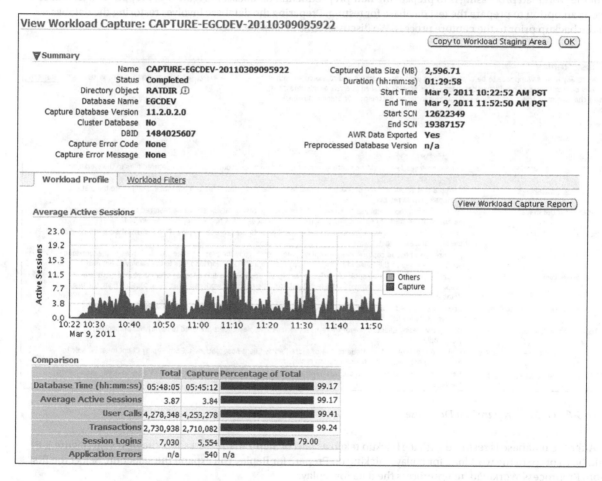

Figure 5-7. OEM—Workload Capture progress

Step 9

Once the capture job has completed successfully, the next step is to export the AWR data from the current capture environment, which you accomplish by selecting Export AWR Data (refer to Figure 5-3). Following the export of the AWR data, the capture data should be moved from the capture environment to a staging location for preprocessing using the Copy to Workload Staging Area task. This can also be accomplished from the screen illustrated in Figure 5-3.

The next step in the processing of the workload capture is to get the same ready for replay in the new preproduction environment.

Workload Processing

The information in the capture files located in a directory identified by RATDIR (see Figure 5-6) needs to be processed after the captured files are moved to the preproduction environment.

Step 10

Part of the workload processing is to prepare the new preproduction database. In Figure 5-8, Prepare Test Database contains an option to prepare the test database for testing. Preparing the database involves restoring the database from the backup prior to the capture process. We discussed this in Step 1 earlier.

Database Replay		Go to Task
Database Replay allows workloads to be captured from production systems and re-executed with high fidelity on test copies of production databases. This enables detailed analysis of how the proposed changes may affect production systems; for instance, patching or upgrading database software.	Page Refreshed **Mar 5, 2011 3:40:52 PM PST** (Refresh)	
Task List		
Expand All	Collapse All		
Task Name	**Description**	
▶ Capture Production Workload	Initiate or schedule a workload capture, export AWR data after capture, and copy captured files to the workload staging area.	
▼ Prepare Test Database	Set up a test database from production, upgrade or otherwise modify the test database, and isolate the test database prior to replay.	
Set Up Test Database	Clone the production database to a test environment. The test database should be restored to match the capture database at the start of capture. You may make any changes to the test environment as needed.	⮕
Isolate Test Database	Isolate the test system from production environment prior to the workload replay. This task must be performed on the test database target.	⮕
▼ Prepare for Replay	Prepare the workload capture files for replay (preprocess), copy the preprocessed workload files to the workload staging area, deploy the Replay Clients, and copy the preprocessed workload files to the Replay Client hosts.	
Preprocess Workload	Preprocessing prepares a captured workload for replay. You must do this once for every captured workload. Preprocessing is best performed in the test database. The captured workload must be accessible from the test database.	⮕
Copy to Workload Staging Area	Copy preprocessed workload files to the workload staging area. The preprocessed workload files must be accessible by the database server and the Replay Clients during replay.	⮕
Deploy Replay Clients	Deploy the Replay Client to one or more host machines. Replay Clients are used to replay the preprocessed workload.	⮕
Copy Workload to Replay Client Hosts	Copy the preprocessed workload to one or more Replay Client host machines. Each Replay Client must be able to access the preprocessed workload during replay.	⮕
▶ Replay Workload on Test Database	Set up the workload replay on the test database, copy the replay results to the workload staging area, and analyze the results.	

Figure 5-8. *OEM—Prepare Test Database*

After the database is restored with the backup taken as part of Step 1 in the workshop, the next step (Figure 5-8) would be to prepare the workload for replay. Clicking on Prepare for Replay will expand the selection. Select the first option, Preprocess Workload, to preprocess the data for replay.

Step 11

The first screen (Figure 5-9) under the Preprocess Captured Workload section is to identify or locate the workload directory. In this workshop, as discussed in Step 7, a shared NFS mount point is used to store the capture files. Due to this, the "Use an existing workload directory on this host" option is used.

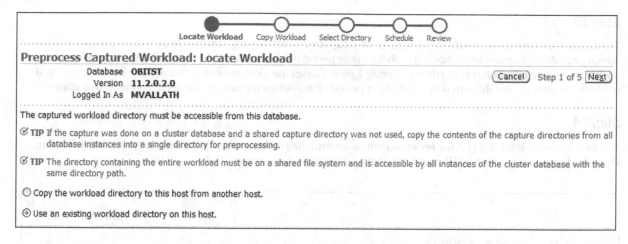

Figure 5-9. *OEM—Preprocess Captured Workload section*

Step 12

This third step in the preprocess section is to select the workload directory. Once again, similar to Step 6, a database directory needs to be created on the test/preproduction database. This directory also points to the same-shared NFS mount point that contains the capture files.

```
CREATE DIRECTORY RATDIR AS '/OBITST_RMAN/EGCRAT';
```

This will allow RAT to read the capture data to this location. As seen in Figure 5-10, once the directory is created and assigned to preprocess capture process, the capture information is located and details are displayed.

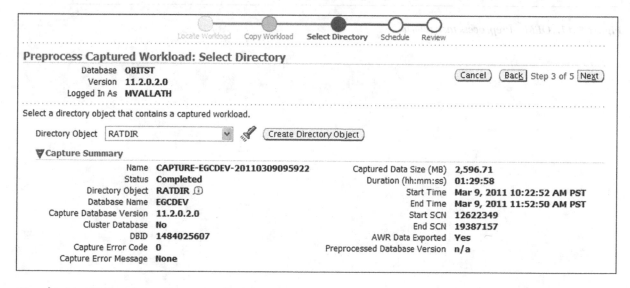

Figure 5-10. *OEM—Capture Directory selection*

Step 13

The next screen (not shown) is used to preprocess the captured workload step to schedule the job for execution. This screen provides the option to schedule the job for a later period or execute the job immediately. The capture process can be scheduled when the job is being defined during a period when the database activity is minimal; however, the ideal workload against the database may occur at a later period in time when the process cannot be monitored or started.

Step 14

The next screen (Figure 5-11) is the review screen to confirm the preprocess job definitions. If correct, click Submit. Once the job status is reviewed (Figure 5-12), it gives a status of the preprocess job.

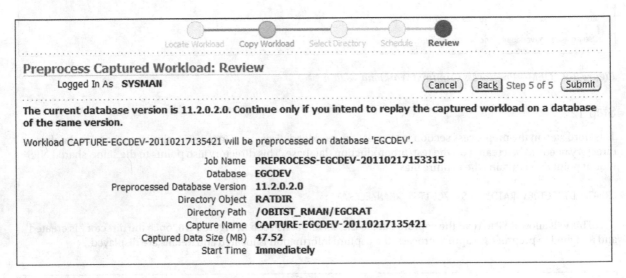

Figure 5-11. *OEM—Preprocess task review*

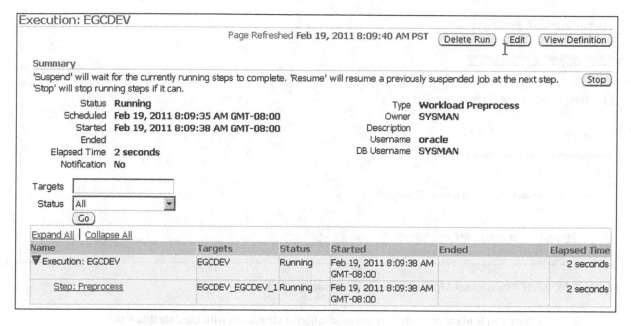

Figure 5-12. *OEM—Workload preprocess execution summary*

The following are performed during the preprocess activity:

1. Preprocess step in the database replay functionality creates a preprocess folder under the capture directory and analysis the capture workload. The directory contains the following files:

```
[oracle pp11.2.0.2.0]$ ls -ltr
total 93048
-rw-r--r-- 1 oracle dba    471200 Mar  9 15:54 wcr_login.pp
-rw-r----- 1 oracle dba  92590080 Mar  9 15:54 wcr_scn_order.extb
-rw-r----- 1 oracle dba    307200 Mar  9 15:54 wcr_seq_data.extb
-rw-r----- 1 oracle dba     12288 Mar  9 15:54 wcr_conn_data.extb
-rw-r----- 1 oracle dba     12288 Mar  9 15:54 wcr_data.extb
-rw-r----- 1 oracle dba   1634304 Mar  9 15:55 wcr_dep_graph.extb
-rw-r----- 1 oracle dba     12288 Mar  9 15:55 wcr_commits.extb
-rw-r----- 1 oracle dba    114688 Mar  9 15:55 wcr_references.extb
-rw-r--r-- 1 oracle dba        35 Mar  9 15:55 wcr_process.wmd
```

2. After the preprocess is complete, to understand what kind of workload to expect on the new preproduction server (workload captured on the existing production servers), run the following java routine:

```
/usr/java/jdk1.5.0_21/bin/java -classpath $ORACLE_HOME/jdbc/lib/ojdbc5.
jar:$ORACLE_HOME/rdbms/jlib/dbrparser.jar:$ORACLE_HOME/rdbms/jlib/dbranalyzer.
jar oracle.dbreplay.workload.checker.CaptureChecker /OBITST_RMAN/EGCRAT/ //
obitst-scan.summersky.biz:1521/obitst
```

The preceding process will produce an html file that contains an analysis of the workload and recommendations, illustrated in Figure 5-13, for the replay operation.

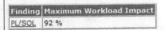

Summary of Findings

Finding	Maximum Workload Impact
PL/SQL	92 %

Findings and Recommendations

PL/SQL

Maximum Workload Impact: 92 % of DB Time

Rationale

If the replay is much slower than expected, try to run in unsynchronized mode.

Action

A significant part of your workload comes from PL/SQL.
If the PL/SQL blocks or functions have 'complicated' logic or multiple commits in them, they are hard to synchronize and they behavior might change during replay.
You might see a different workload profile during replay if this is the case.

Figure 5-13. OEM—Recommendations for the replay operations

3. The next step is to calibrate the test/preproduction environment with the data that was collected from the preprocessing of the capture workload. Calibration is done using the following command:

```
$ORACLE_HOME/bin/wrc mode=calibrate replaydir=/OBITST_RMAN/EGCRAT/
[oracle mvallath]$ $ORACLE_HOME/bin/wrc mode=calibrate replaydir=/OBITST_RMAN/EGCRAT/
Workload Replay Client: Release 11.2.0.2.0 - Production on Wed Mar 9 16:25:03 2011
Copyright (c) 1982, 2009, Oracle and/or its affiliates.  All rights reserved.
Report for Workload in: /OBITST_RMAN/EGCRAT/
-----------------------
Recommendation:
Consider using at least 4 clients divided among 1 CPU(s)
You will need at least 161 MB of memory per client process.
If your machine(s) cannot match that number, consider using more clients.

Workload Characteristics:
- max concurrency: 171 sessions
- total number of sessions: 5555

Assumptions:
- 1 client process per 50 concurrent sessions
- 4 client process per CPU
- 256 KB of memory cache per concurrent session
- think time scale = 100
- connect time scale = 100
- synchronization = TRUE
```

Workload Replay

After the capture data is made available to the target/test/preproduction servers, the next step is to replay the workload on this environment.

Similar to the other scalability tests discussed in the previous chapter, here again we start by testing one instance in the cluster; after we have an acceptable performance (similar to the current production), we can add additional instances to the cluster. For this purpose, all other instances should be shut down.

Step 15

To perform the replay process, expand "Replay Workload on Test Database" as illustrated in Figure 5-14. The expanded list contains several options and stages of the replay workload process, namely, replay workload and analyze results.

▼ Replay Workload on Test Database	Set up the workload replay on the test database, copy the replay results to the workload staging area, and analyze the results.	
Replay Workload	Replay the preprocessed workload on a test copy of the production database.	
Copy to Workload Staging Area	Copy replay results to the workload staging area for comparision analysis with future replays.	
Analyze Results	Analyze the effects of changes on workload performance.	

Figure 5-14. *OEM—Database replay options*

Select the Replay Workload option, which starts the replay setup process. The replay setup is an eight-step process. The first screen, illustrated in Figure 5-15, is to locate the workload that contains the preprocessed workload. At the bottom of the screen, there are two options. Select the "Use an existing workload directory on this host" option.

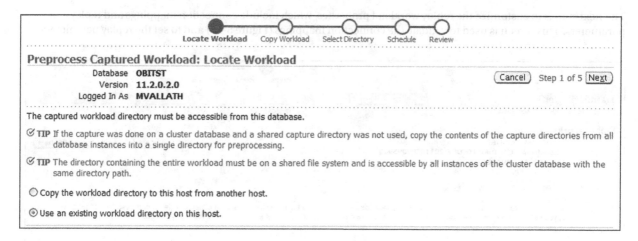

Figure 5-15. *OEM—Replay workload: Locate workload*

Please note, in this workshop, a common shared file system location is used, and mounting this volume on the test servers will allow the target test/preproduction servers to see this file.

Step 16

The next screen (Figure 5-16) is the screen to select the directory that contains the workload files to be replayed. In this screen, the database directory created on the target database in Step 12 is specified. Once the directory name is specified, OEM retrieves the capture workload information.

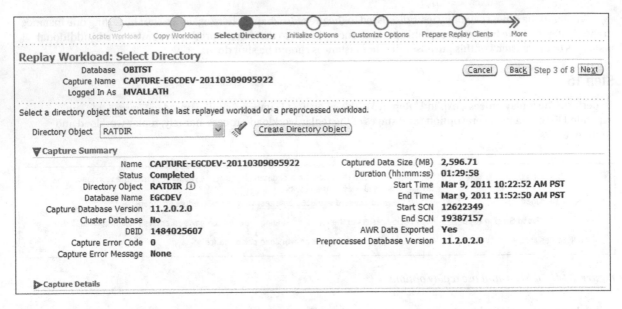

Figure 5-16. *OEM—Replay Workload: Directory identification*

Step 17

The next step is to customize the replay workload properties, which include connection mappings and replay parameters. This screen is used to validate the connection mappings (Figure 5-17) and to set the replay parameters.

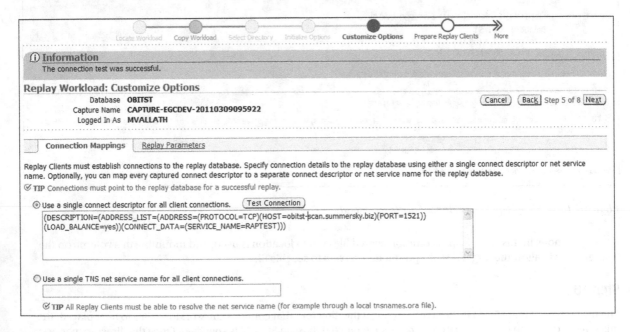

Figure 5-17. *OEM—Replay process connection verification*

Step 18

Once the connection string has been tested using the Test Connection button illustrated in Figure 5-17, the next step is to validate and change the default replay parameters. Click the Replay Parameters tab.

The screen illustrated in Figure 5-18 is a list of replay parameters with the default values. Most of the time defaults are sufficient. What is important is when replay parameters are selected, they are maintained through the various iterations of the replay tests to help baseline comparisons. For example, the synchronization value is set to SCN; from the capture process, results and summary of the SCN for the start and end of the capture are recorded. Keeping the parameters at the default will allow the same thresholds to be maintained between the current production and the new test/preproduction environment.

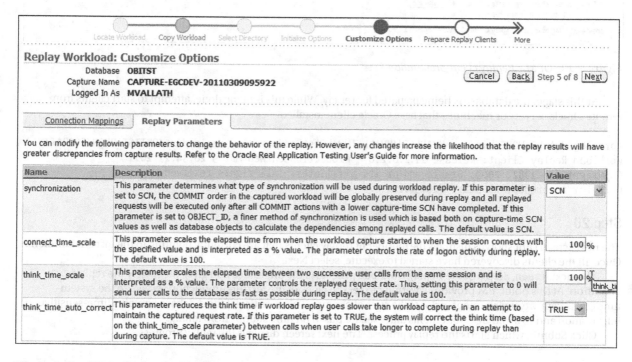

Figure 5-18. OEM—Replay Workload parameter settings

Step 19

The next screen (Figure 5-19) is a step to prepare the clients from where the tests will be executed. The replay driver uses a scalable, multithreaded architecture. The replay clients can be configured across multiple host machines if required. After estimating the number of clients required, click Next.

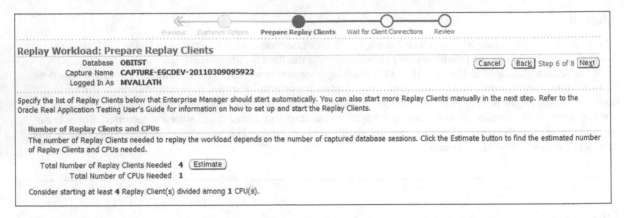

Figure 5-19. *OEM—Replay client preparation*

At this stage, the database is being prepared for replay. While this is being done, attempt to start clients from remote Oracle servers or machines that have Oracle client installed.

```
[oracle]$ORACLE_HOME/bin/wrc MVALLATH/MVALLATH@obitst mode=replay replaydir=/OBITST_RMAN/EGCRAT/
Workload Replay Client: Release 11.2.0.2.0 - Production on Wed Mar 9 20:34:27 2011
Copyright (c) 1982, 2009, Oracle and/or its affiliates.  All rights reserved.
Wait for the replay to start (20:34:27)
```

Step 20

The next screen (not shown) displays the number of replay clients that are currently pointing to the test environment. Once all the clients discovered have started to execute, select Next.

The next screen, Step 8 of the Replay Workload process is the final stage and gives the review the replay definition. At this point, EM provides a warning to set the clock of the test/preproduction servers to the system time of the capture environment, prior to the start of capture. This is critical if the database contains time-sensitive information and to avoid SQL statements that execute based on time stamps from failing.

Click Submit, which starts the replay process. The next screen displays the replay progress.

Step 21

Once the replay process is complete, compare the results with the primary production environment. In a migration project, when moving from single instance to RAC, the replay measurements on a single server should be equal to or better compared to the current production environment.

In the comparison output shown in Figure 5-20, there is a side-by-side comparison of the capture and replay process indicating that they are almost identical in performance and response time. The lower "Database Time" consumed by the entire workload indicates less consumption of resources; however, overall completion time has been the same.

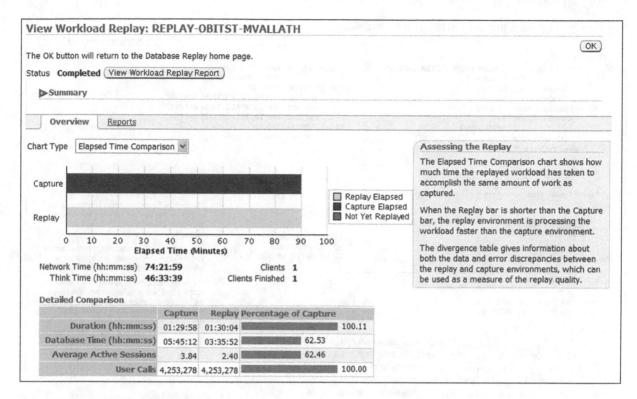

Figure 5-20. *OEM—Workload Replay status*

Apart from the summary illustrated in Figure 5-20, OEM also provides an analysis report. This can be obtained by selecting the Reports tab from the Summary screen that compares the capture and replay. It compares the AWR statistics between the capture and replay.

Step 22

Once a baseline comparison between the current production and the new production or test environment is completed, it's good practice to repeat the Workload Replay section (Steps 15 through 18) by adding one node at a time and comparing the results after every run with the previous baseline and with the capture baseline. Figure 5-21 illustrates the workload replay in a clustered environment. As one notices from the output, the replay time has increased significantly compared to the results illustrated in Step 21 with Figure 5-20.

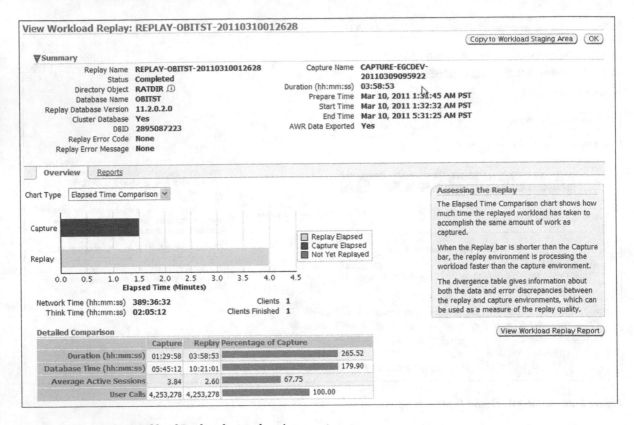

Figure 5-21. *OEM—Workload Replay clustered environment*

In Figure 5-21, the increase in replay time also shows an increase in the database time and also the network time. This entire matrix, along with the AWR statistics, should be used to tune the cluster and optimize performance. Every time a problem is identified and a solution is established to fix the problem, the results should be compared with the previous baseline. For example, the baseline at this time is the result from Step 21.

Between each iteration, it is important that the database is refreshed and the baseline version of the backup from the production server before the capture is restored. This will allow the same data sets to be added, modified, or deleted and the same number of rows to be returned by the SELECT statements.

RESET DATABASE USING TRANSPORTABLE TABLESPACE

When repeating the replay operations under different conditions, the test database needs to be reset to a period (point in time) before the original capture. This can become really time consuming. If the database replay only focuses on one schema, then the tablespace used by the schema can be refreshed using transportable tablespace.

1. Check if the tablespace to be transported is self-contained.

```
EXECUTE DBMS_TTS.TRANSPORT_SET_CHECK('RAPTEST', TRUE);
```

2. Verify against TRANSPORT_SET_VIOLATIONS if there are errors.

    ```
    SQL> SELECT * FROM TRANSPORT_SET_VIOLATIONS;
    ```

3. Convert the tablespace to be transported to read only.

    ```
    SQL> ALTER TABLESPACE RAPTEST READ ONLY;
    ```

4. Verify if the change made to the tablespace in the previous step has been completed successfully.

    ```
    SQL> SELECT TABLESPACE_NAME, STATUS, CONTENTS FROM DBA_TABLESPACES WHERE TABLESPACE_
    NAME ='RAPTEST';
    TABLESPACE_NAME                 STATUS    CONTENTS
    ------------------------------- --------- ---------
    RAPTEST                         READ ONLY PERMANENT
    ```

5. Create a directory where all data pump related files are stored. This step is optional; you could use the default DATA_PUMP_DIR instead.

    ```
    CREATE DIRECTORY TTS_DIR AS '+OBITST_DATA';
    ```

6. Verify the parameter change.

    ```
    SQL> COL OWNER FORMAT A10
    SQL> COL DIRECTORY_NAME FORMAT A12
    SQL> COL DIRECTORY_PATH FORMAT A35
    SQL> SELECT * FROM DBA_DIRECTORIES;
    ```

7. Invoke the Oracle Data Pump export utility as user system and specify the tablespaces in the transportable set.

    ```
    SQL>host bash-3.2$ expdp system dumpfile=expdat.dmp directory=TTS_DIR transport_
    tablespaces=raptest transport_full_check=y logfile=tts_export.log
    ```

8. Using RMAN, convert the datafile and store it into ASM. Although we don't have any real conversion required, this is the method to create a new datafile in the same database or a different database.

    ```
    bash-3.2$ rman target/
    RMAN> convert tablespace raptest format '+OBITST_DATA/obitst/datafile/raptest01.dbf';
    Starting conversion at source at 07-MAR-11
    using channel ORA_DISK_1
    channel ORA_DISK_1: starting datafile conversion
    input datafile file number=00038 name=+OBITST_DATA/obitst/datafile/
    raptest.321.70739082   7
    converted datafile=+OBITST_DATA/obitst/datafile/raptest01.dbf
    channel ORA_DISK_1: datafile conversion complete, elapsed time: 00:07:45
    Finished conversion at source at 07-MAR-11
    RMAN> exit
    bash-3.2$ exit (return to SQL plus)
    ```

9. Rename the current RAPTEST tablespace (give it a new name).

   ```
   SQL> ALTER TABLESPACE RAPTEST RENAME TO RAPTEST_COPY;
   ```

10. Verify rename of tablespace.

11. Import the transportable tablespace. Set the host from the SQL prompt to complete the operation.

    ```
    SQL> host bash-3.2$ impdp system dumpfile=expdat.dmp directory=data_pump_dir
    transport_datafiles ='+OBITST_DATA/obitst/datafile/raptest01.dbf' remap_
    schema=raptest:raptest1 logfile=tts_import.log
    ```

12. Change tablespace back to read write.

    ```
    SQL> ALTER TABLESPACE RAPTEST_COPY READ WRITE;
    ```

13. Change new tablespace to read write.

    ```
    SQL> ALTER TABLESPACE RAPTEST READ WRITE;
    ```

14. Assign the new tablespace as the default tablespace to owner schema.

    ```
    SQL> ALTER USER RAPTEST1 DEFAULT TABLESPACE RAPTEST;
    ```

■ **Note**   Another option to restore the database to an earlier state is to use flashback mode in the database and flash the database back to a point in time.

SQL Performance Analyzer

Similar to the Database Replay functionality, the SQL Performance Analyzer is focused on predicting and preventing performance problems for any environment changes that may affect SQL execution times. This functionality provides assessment of environment change on an SQL execution plan and statistics by running the SQL statements serially before change and after change on the different environments. Based on the reports generated from the Database Replay functionality when migrating from single instance to a RAC configuration, this functionality can help tune SQL statements to scale across multiple instances: for example, optimizing SQL statements to use parallelism on a single instance and then scaling the query across multiple instances. Apart from testing a single query or multiple queries for scalability, SQL Performance Analyzer (SPA) can also be used to test the effect of parameter changes or SQL structure changes or changes to Oracle database optimizer versions. Figure 5-22 illustrates the various options provided by SPA.

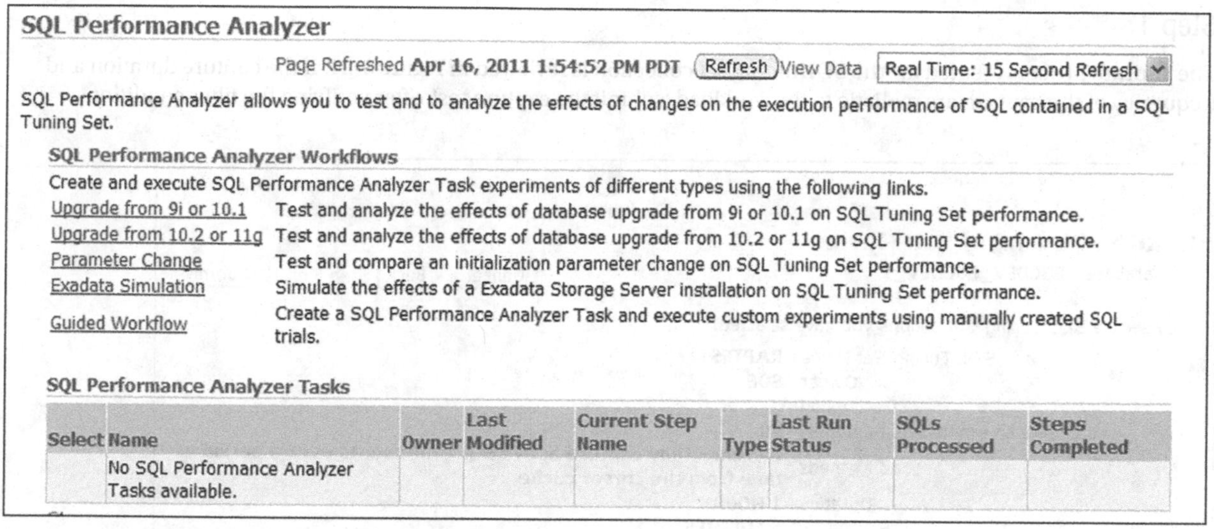

SQL Performance Analyzer

Page Refreshed **Apr 16, 2011 1:54:52 PM PDT** (Refresh)View Data | Real Time: 15 Second Refresh ▾ |

SQL Performance Analyzer allows you to test and to analyze the effects of changes on the execution performance of SQL contained in a SQL Tuning Set.

SQL Performance Analyzer Workflows

Create and execute SQL Performance Analyzer Task experiments of different types using the following links.

Upgrade from 9i or 10.1   Test and analyze the effects of database upgrade from 9i or 10.1 on SQL Tuning Set performance.
Upgrade from 10.2 or 11g   Test and analyze the effects of database upgrade from 10.2 or 11g on SQL Tuning Set performance.
Parameter Change   Test and compare an initialization parameter change on SQL Tuning Set performance.
Exadata Simulation   Simulate the effects of a Exadata Storage Server installation on SQL Tuning Set performance.
Guided Workflow   Create a SQL Performance Analyzer Task and execute custom experiments using manually created SQL trials.

SQL Performance Analyzer Tasks

Select	Name	Owner	Last Modified	Current Step Name	Type	Last Run Status	SQLs Processed	Steps Completed
	No SQL Performance Analyzer Tasks available.							

Figure 15-22. OEM—SQL Performance Analyzer options

■ **Note**   Although SPA is a similar testing tool to database replay, there is an important difference as well: SPA can be run in its own session, which allows you to run it against the actual database but under controlled conditions.

Workshop

To verify the performance of an SQL statement or a set of SQL statements, it's important to capture an SQL tuning set. The capture can be performed either from the current production environment or from the test/preproduction environment. Figure 5-23 illustrates the SQL set capture process.

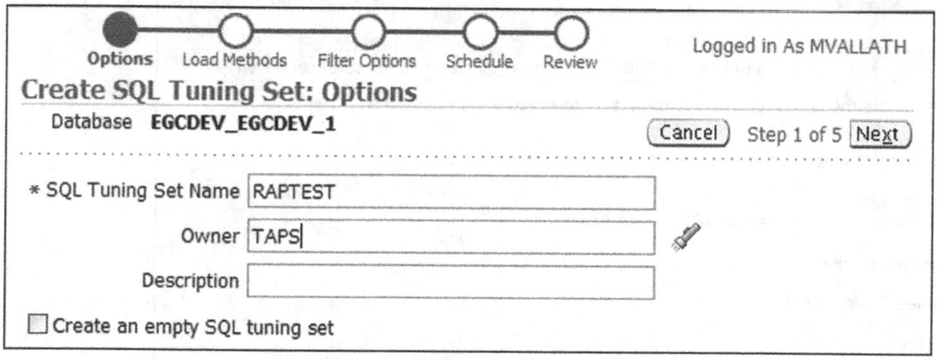

Options   Load Methods   Filter Options   Schedule   Review   Logged in As MVALLATH

Create SQL Tuning Set: Options

Database **EGCDEV_EGCDEV_1**   (Cancel) Step 1 of 5 (Next)

＊ SQL Tuning Set Name | RAPTEST |

Owner | TAPS |

Description | |

☐ Create an empty SQL tuning set

Figure 5-23. OEM—SQL Tuning Set creation

Step 1

The capture process created for the SQL tuning set collection is reviewed in Figure 5-24. If the capture duration and frequency of the capture are realistic to the workload, submit the capture task after verifying the filter conditions.

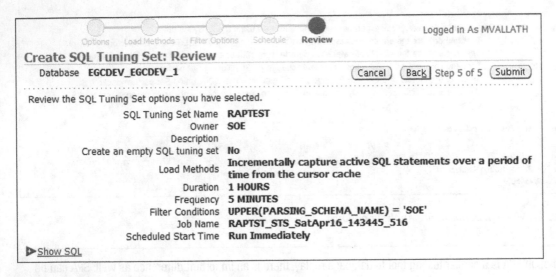

Figure 5-24. OEM—SQL Tuning Set capture task review

Step 2

SPA requires a single or a set of SQL statements to perform analysis. Once the SQL tuning set is created, the job illustrated in Figure 5-24 completes. The SQL Tuning Set is used as an input in the SPA process. Figure 5-25 illustrates a guided workflow process from OEM that helps perform analysis of SQL statements in two different execution environments.

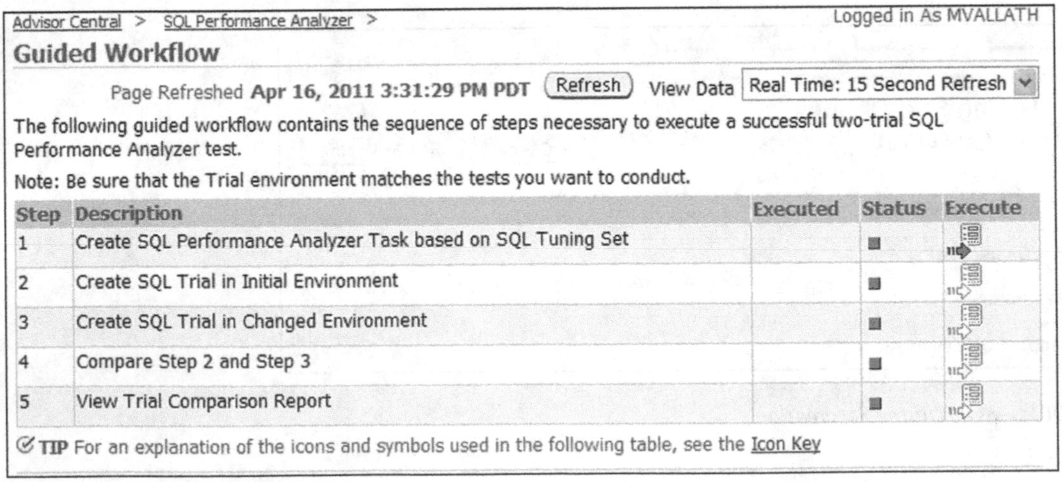

Figure 5-25. OEM—SPA Guided Workflow

Step 3

Once the task is created, the initial trail run (illustrated in Figure 5-26) of the SQL tuning statements is scheduled for execution.

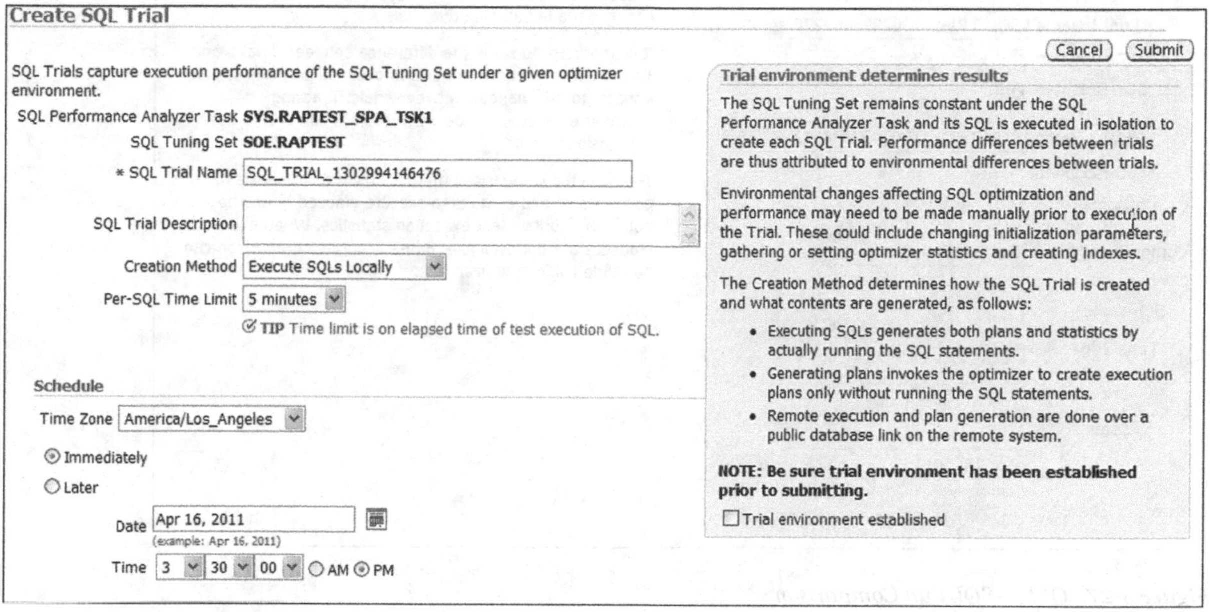

Create SQL Trial

Cancel   Submit

SQL Trials capture execution performance of the SQL Tuning Set under a given optimizer environment.

SQL Performance Analyzer Task **SYS.RAPTEST_SPA_TSK1**

SQL Tuning Set **SOE.RAPTEST**

* SQL Trial Name `SQL_TRIAL_1302994146476`

SQL Trial Description

Creation Method `Execute SQLs Locally`

Per-SQL Time Limit `5 minutes`

☞ **TIP** Time limit is on elapsed time of test execution of SQL.

Schedule

Time Zone `America/Los_Angeles`

⊙ Immediately

○ Later

Date `Apr 16, 2011`
(example: Apr 16, 2011)

Time `3` `30` `00` ○ AM ⊙ PM

Trial environment determines results

The SQL Tuning Set remains constant under the SQL Performance Analyzer Task and its SQL is executed in isolation to create each SQL Trial. Performance differences between trials are thus attributed to environmental differences between trials.

Environmental changes affecting SQL optimization and performance may need to be made manually prior to execution of the Trial. These could include changing initialization parameters, gathering or setting optimizer statistics and creating indexes.

The Creation Method determines how the SQL Trial is created and what contents are generated, as follows:

- Executing SQLs generates both plans and statistics by actually running the SQL statements.
- Generating plans invokes the optimizer to create execution plans only without running the SQL statements.
- Remote execution and plan generation are done over a public database link on the remote system.

NOTE: Be sure trial environment has been established prior to submitting.

☐ Trial environment established

Figure 5-26.   *OEM—SQL Trial run*

Step 4

The SPA task is executed in the new environment (see Figure 5-27, Run SQL Trial Comparison). Please note, new environments do not necessarily have to be RAC environments. The newness can be because of hardware platform change, client configuration change, SQL statement change, and so forth.

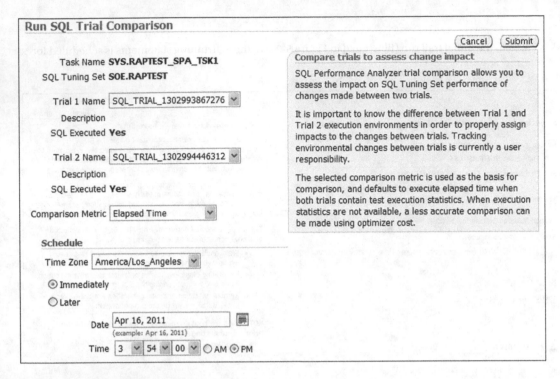

Figure 5-27. *OEM—SQL Run Comparison*

Step 5

Once the comparison task completes, it generates a SPA report, which illustrates the impact between the two runs. Illustrated in Figure 5-28, the tuning set has 17 queries and the over execution time was improved by about 5%.

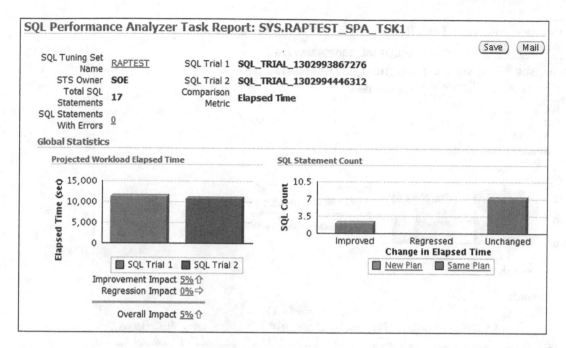

Figure 5-28. *OEM—SPA comparison report*

Step 6

If further tuning of the top SQL statements is desired, for example, the impact of a parameter change needs to be validated. The parameter change option illustrated in Figure 5-22 should be selected.

In this case, in Figure 5-29, the top SQL query is selected to verify the impact of a parameter change.

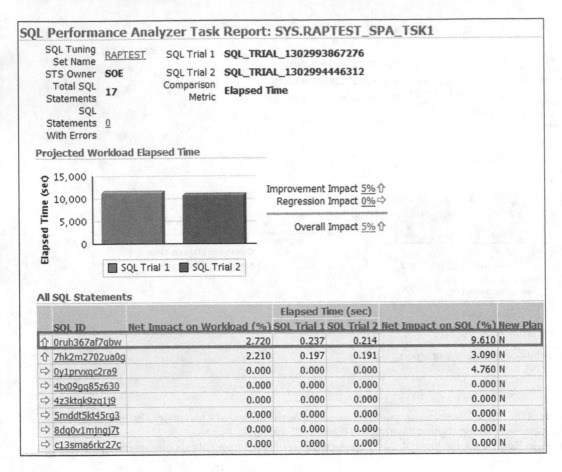

SQL Performance Analyzer Task Report: SYS.RAPTEST_SPA_TSK1

SQL Tuning Set Name	RAPTEST	SQL Trial 1	**SQL_TRIAL_1302993867276**
STS Owner	**SOE**	SQL Trial 2	**SQL_TRIAL_1302994446312**
Total SQL Statements	**17**	Comparison Metric	**Elapsed Time**
SQL Statements With Errors	0		

Projected Workload Elapsed Time

Improvement Impact 5% ⇧
Regression Impact 0% ⇨

Overall Impact 5% ⇧

All SQL Statements

SQL ID	Net Impact on Workload (%)	Elapsed Time (sec)		Net Impact on SQL (%)	New Plan
		SQL Trial 1	SQL Trial 2		
⇧ 0ruh367af7gbw	2.720	0.237	0.214	9.610	N
⇧ 7hk2m2702ua0g	2.210	0.197	0.191	3.090	N
⇨ 0y1prvxqc2ra9	0.000	0.000	0.000	4.760	N
⇨ 4tx09gq85z630	0.000	0.000	0.000	0.000	N
⇨ 4z3ktgk9zq1j9	0.000	0.000	0.000	0.000	N
⇨ 5mddt5kt45rg3	0.000	0.000	0.000	0.000	N
⇨ 8dq0v1mjngj7t	0.000	0.000	0.000	0.000	N
⇨ c13sma6rkr27c	0.000	0.000	0.000	0.000	N

Figure 5-29. *OEM—SPA–SQL statement impact*

The results of the execution can also be captured and saved in HTML format. The report based on the test run completed in Step 6 is illustrated in Figure 5-30.

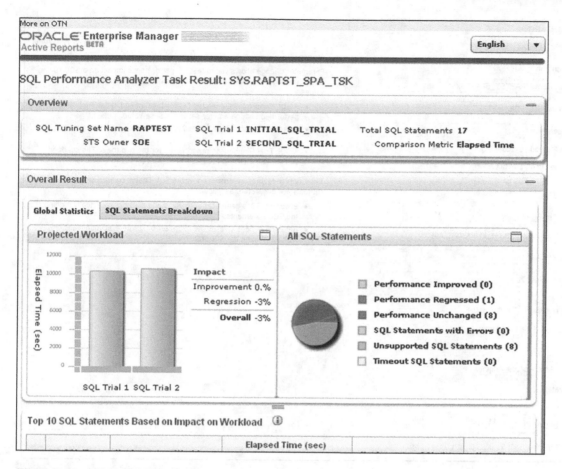

Figure 5-30. *OEM—SPA HTML comparison report*

Step 7

The OPTIMIZER_INDEX_COST_ADJ parameter is modified from its default value of 100 to 20 and executing the SQL statement using SPA validates the impact of this change as illustrated in Figure 5-31.

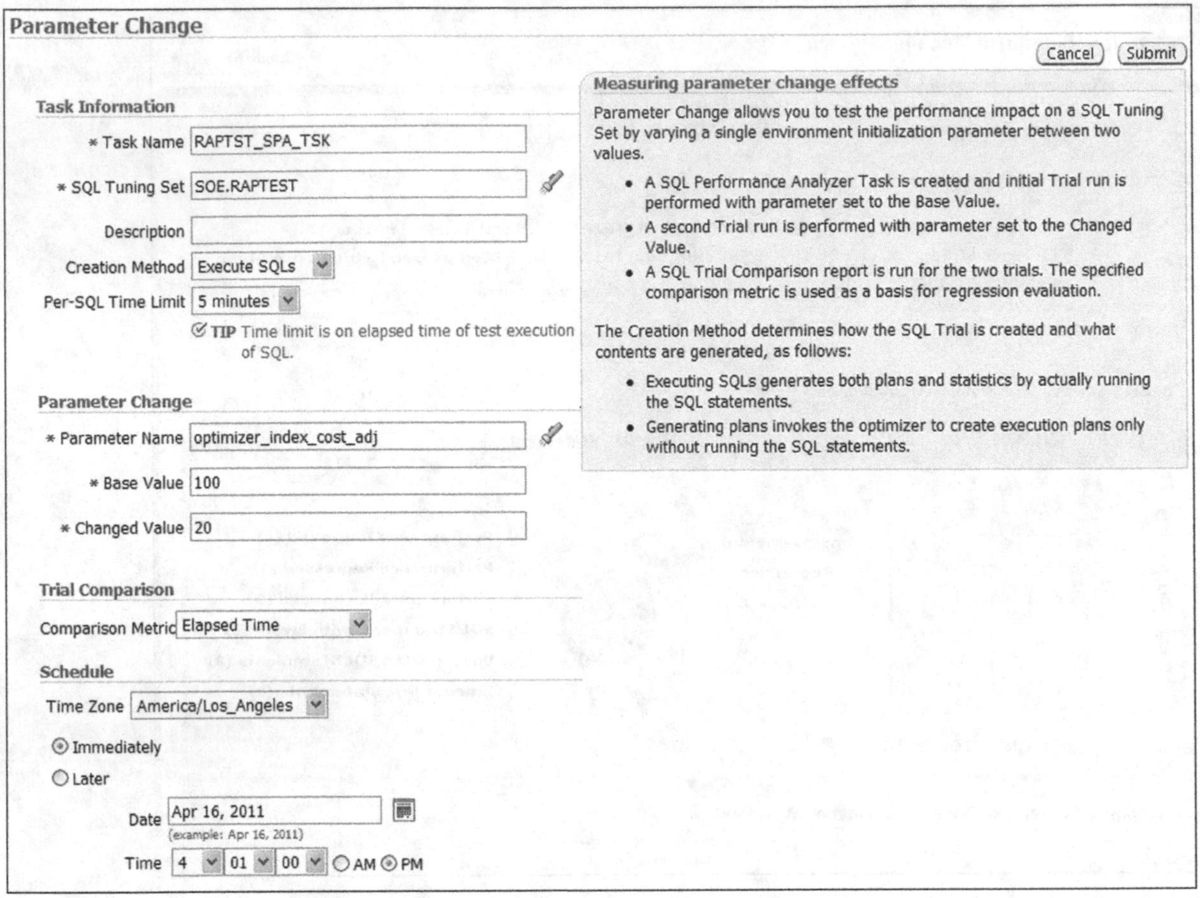

Parameter Change

Cancel   Submit

Task Information

* Task Name: RAPTST_SPA_TSK

* SQL Tuning Set: SOE.RAPTEST

Description:

Creation Method: Execute SQLs

Per-SQL Time Limit: 5 minutes

☑ **TIP** Time limit is on elapsed time of test execution of SQL.

Parameter Change

* Parameter Name: optimizer_index_cost_adj

* Base Value: 100

* Changed Value: 20

Trial Comparison

Comparison Metric: Elapsed Time

Schedule

Time Zone: America/Los_Angeles

⦿ Immediately

○ Later

Date: Apr 16, 2011
(example: Apr 16, 2011)

Time: 4 : 01 : 00 ○ AM ⦿ PM

Measuring parameter change effects

Parameter Change allows you to test the performance impact on a SQL Tuning Set by varying a single environment initialization parameter between two values.

- A SQL Performance Analyzer Task is created and initial Trial run is performed with parameter set to the Base Value.
- A second Trial run is performed with parameter set to the Changed Value.
- A SQL Trial Comparison report is run for the two trials. The specified comparison metric is used as a basis for regression evaluation.

The Creation Method determines how the SQL Trial is created and what contents are generated, as follows:

- Executing SQLs generates both plans and statistics by actually running the SQL statements.
- Generating plans invokes the optimizer to create execution plans only without running the SQL statements.

Figure 5-31. OEM—Effect of Parameter Change

Step 8

Once the SQL statement is executed with the new parameter value, the results of the tests are displayed in Figure 5-32.

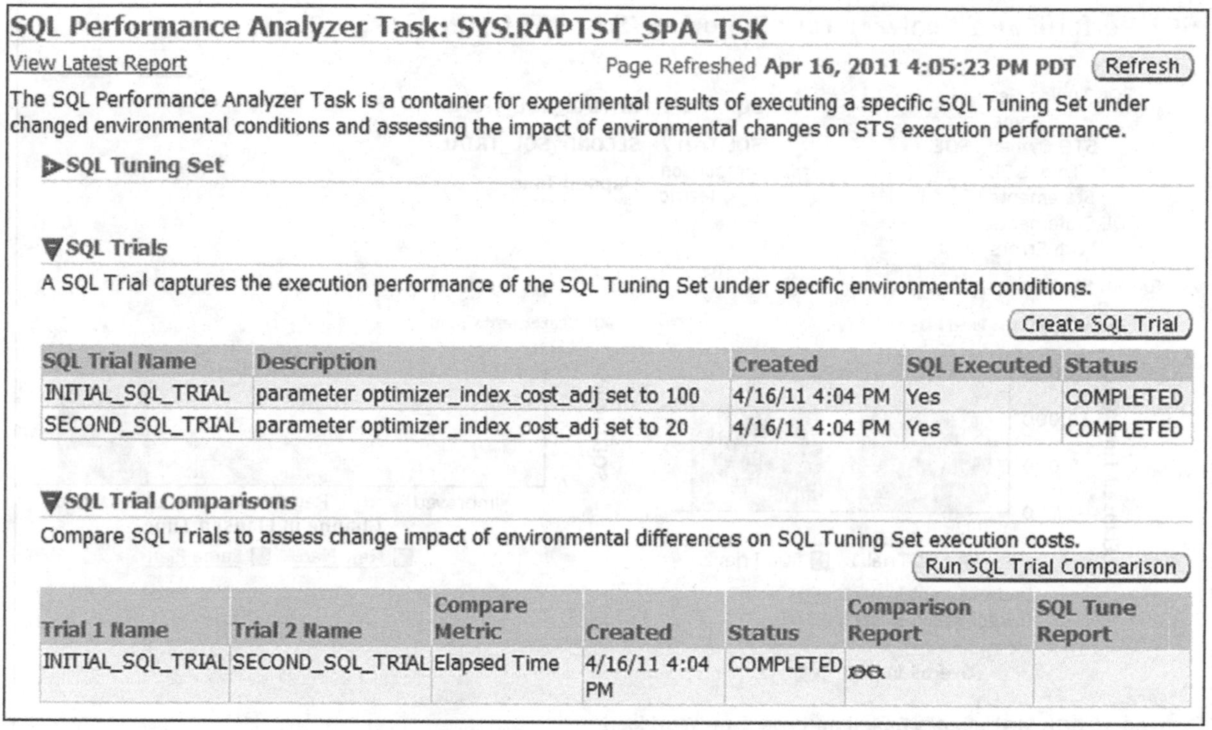

SQL Performance Analyzer Task: SYS.RAPTST_SPA_TSK

View Latest Report   Page Refreshed **Apr 16, 2011 4:05:23 PM PDT** (Refresh)

The SQL Performance Analyzer Task is a container for experimental results of executing a specific SQL Tuning Set under changed environmental conditions and assessing the impact of environmental changes on STS execution performance.

▷ **SQL Tuning Set**

▼ **SQL Trials**

A SQL Trial captures the execution performance of the SQL Tuning Set under specific environmental conditions.

(Create SQL Trial)

SQL Trial Name	Description	Created	SQL Executed	Status
INITIAL_SQL_TRIAL	parameter optimizer_index_cost_adj set to 100	4/16/11 4:04 PM	Yes	COMPLETED
SECOND_SQL_TRIAL	parameter optimizer_index_cost_adj set to 20	4/16/11 4:04 PM	Yes	COMPLETED

▼ **SQL Trial Comparisons**

Compare SQL Trials to assess change impact of environmental differences on SQL Tuning Set execution costs.

(Run SQL Trial Comparison)

Trial 1 Name	Trial 2 Name	Compare Metric	Created	Status	Comparison Report	SQL Tune Report
INITIAL_SQL_TRIAL	SECOND_SQL_TRIAL	Elapsed Time	4/16/11 4:04 PM	COMPLETED	⊖⊖	

Figure 5-32. *OEM—SPA SQL Trial Comparisons*

Step 9

From the 17 queries in the SQL tuning set, one of the queries has performed worse compared to executing the query before the parameter was modified. The query that performed worse is highlighted in Figure 5-33.

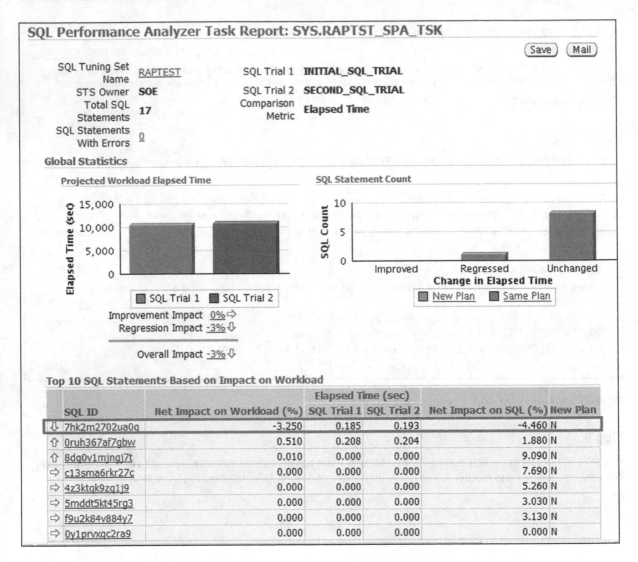

Figure 5-33. *OEM—Regression Impact*

Step 10

Activities of the SPA do not complete with the generation of the results set. The worst performing SQL statement identified in Figure 5-33 should be optimized. Figure 5-34 provides the opportunity to tune the SQL statement using the SQL Tuning Advisor.

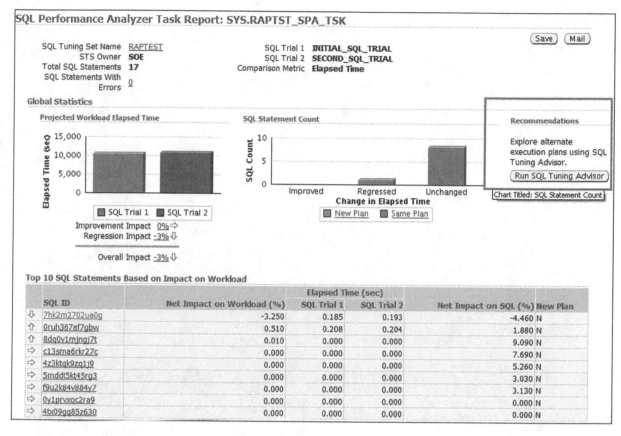

Figure 5-34. *OEM—SPA to SQL Tuning Advisor*

Once the query is tuned using the SQL tuning advisor or by rewriting the query after generating an xplan, the query should be deployed back into the test environment and testing performed. As discussed at several previous occasions, it's an iterative process. The goal of all this testing is to ensure that the migration from a single instance or after an application change has been made, the application and database perform.

Conclusion

In this chapter, we discussed RAP Testing Phase VI by testing the persistence layer of the application tier. We discussed and analyzed the use of the tools to complete this task and demonstrated the use of RAT for this purpose. Although RAT is pretty robust and provides a very high level out-of-the-box test to compare the current production to the new production or an application that has changes or between database software versions, it does not really provide the full potential to accelerate the load by scaling the number of users or sessions as additional nodes are being added to the cluster. Method I discussed in this chapter maybe the approach that will accomplish this task.

A combination of Methods I and II maybe required for a complete test of the database for scalability.

The focus of this chapter was to use RAT for scalability testing of the environment when moving from a single instance to a RAC environment or testing a specific query for scalability using SAP. However, RAT can also be used when performing upgrades, to test the effect of the database kernel changes, or to test the effect of database optimization in a newer version of the database: for example, when migrating from Oracle database 10g Release 2 or Oracle Database 11g Release 2 to Oracle Database 12c Release 1.

CHAPTER 6

■ ■ ■

Tools and Utilities

Performance tuning is a very wide subject; it can be approached artistically like someone trying to write music or paint a picture, which involves many discarded versions of the canvas or notes and bars by making changes to the system in an effort to improve the look or sound by trial and error. While ideally a more scientific approach to performance optimization is preferred, performance engineers start out with intuition before using scientific data. The performance engineer or DBA collects data or statistics from the following places:

- From areas of the application that are performing slowly
- During various times of the day when more users are using the system
- From heavily used functional areas of the application, etc.

When the appropriate statistics are collected, the database performance engineer can take a more methodical approach to tuning the system. A methodical approach based on data and evidence is a complete forensic approach for problem solving. In the information technology arena, the analysis is accomplished by understanding the reasons behind the slowness or poor performance, which again is based on statistics generated from tools and instrumentation provided by Oracle.

Performance analysis is an activity that must take multiple variables/circumstances into account; the causes for performance problems are complex so a thorough approach based on scientific principles must be adopted. All hypotheses and conclusions must be supported by data and need to be transparent. Performance analysis is not, as many people believe, an art form; it requires years of experience and intuition, but as an activity it can be likened to forensic reasoning. It requires rigorous data collection and the powers of deduction and inference. To aid in this method of data collection, Oracle provides several tools, utilities, and instrumentation that provide opportunities in statistics collection, analysis, and application of performance optimization to the Oracle environment.

Oracle Enterprise Manager

In this chapter, we will look at optimization features for the RAC database. The grid control supports all tiers of the application, which consist of the following:

- Database tier
- Web tier
- Application tier

At the database tier, apart from the traditional functionalities provided by Database Express, Cloud Control provides a holistic view of the RAC cluster.

Oracle Enterprise Manager (OEM) comes in two flavors: Database Express, which is installed during the database creation time with the database, and Cloud Control, which is a separate product that is installed and configured from a set of DVD or installer. Cloud Control can be installed on the same node as the database server or can be installed separately on another node (which is the preferred approach). EM Cloud Control is normally installed as two separate tiers: the repository and the EM console/client. While the client is accessed through a browser, the repository can be installed on most operating systems.

EM Cloud Control comprises a three-tier configuration: the target database that is controlled or monitored through an EM agent process installed on all database servers; the middle tier or the Oracle Management Server (OMS, also called the EM repository) where all the target database information is collected and stored; and the client or console tier used to display the information. The repository is used to capture and store information pertaining to the target tier.

■ **Note**　The functionalities offered by Database Express are a subset of the EM Cloud Control and contain most of the features with the exception of the OMS. Database Express also consists of an agent; however, the agent does not communicate with any OMS not configured.

The front tier is the console and is used to monitor the database (target tiers) via the management server. Storing the information in the management server provides additional functionality, such as sending a page to a DBA when any alert is encountered and collecting target tier statistics when the DBA is not monitoring the console for historical information.

The target tier consists of the instance, the database, and the intelligent agent that runs in the background and helps communicate database-related information back to the OMS. The intelligent agent also contains a data gatherer that is used to gather data on a continuous basis.

Figure 6-1 illustrates the EM Cloud Control component architecture. It represents the three-tier configuration consisting of the console or the user interface tier, the OMS tier or the middle tier, and the end tier or the target tier. The target tier can consist of multiple databases servers, application servers, and web servers across one or more locations that the EM Cloud Control will monitor and manage. A single EM Cloud Control configuration can administer and manage several targets across different operating systems, and with the recent Oracle acquisitions, it can administer and manage several types of applications using appropriate plug-ins.

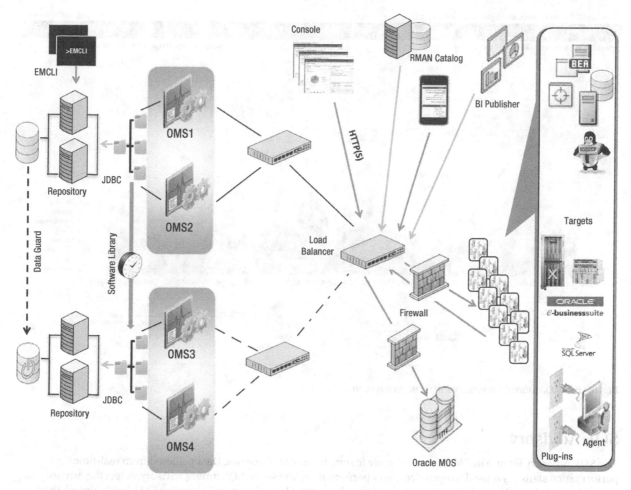

Figure 6-1. *Three-tier architecture*

Performance Manager

Apart from the database administration and maintenance functionality, the Database Express also contains the performance manager. This feature requires the Oracle Tuning Pack to be installed.

Figure 6-2 shows a Database Express 12c Summary health chart of the cluster and shows RAC-specific charts, overall workload, top SQL, etc. By highlighting specific items on the right side of each chart, additional details related to the specific highlighted item can be obtained by drilling down into them. For example, on the activity sessions chart for additional information on high CPU users, highlight the CPU tag and drill down to get additional information.

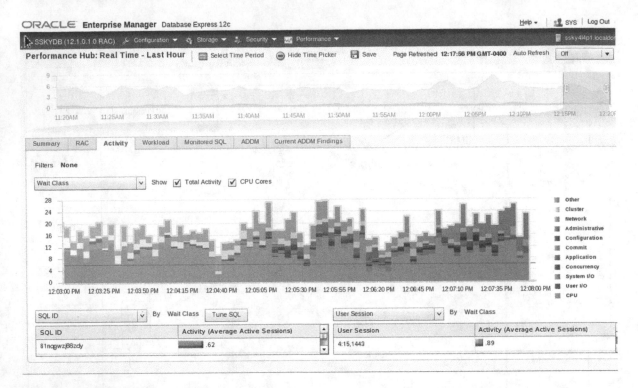

Figure 6-2. *Database Summary Performance screen*

SQL Advisory

The SQL Advisory feature in EM is a good, handy feature to tune SQL queries. Data gathered from real-time performance statistics is used to optimize query performance. To use the SQL tuning advisory, select the Advisory Central option from the performance page from the db express (12c)/Database Express or EM Cloud Control, then select the SQL Tuning Advisory option. This option provides the "Top Activity" (illustrated in Figure 6-3). Moving the scroll bar to a specific time frame on the top activity chart will list the "Top SQL" ordered by highest activity (illustrated in Figure 6-4).

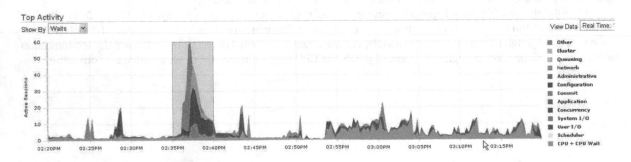

Figure 6-3. *EM- Oracle 11g Top Activity*

Drag the shaded box to change the time period for the details
Start Time May 20, 2014 3:03:00 PM

Top SQL: Cluster

Actions [Schedule SQL Tuning Advisor ▾] [Go]

Select All | Select None

Select	Activity (%) ▼		SQL ID	SQL Type
☐		14.29	19x1189chq3xd	SELECT
☐		14.29	1kz16yhs993h2	INSERT
☐		14.29	84ygtc6ucuafk	UPDATE
☐		14.29	9h2g2pguuh43a	DELETE
☐		14.29	byjkqqy2bfszt	UPDATE
☐		14.29	3vpa1s21sasn2	SELECT
☐		14.29	4zc1h0wxgqdds	SELECT

Figure 6-4. *Top SQL cluster*

Poor performance of queries could be due to several reasons, such as any of the following:

- *Stale optimizer statistics*: Oracle cost-based optimizer (CBO) uses the statistics collected to determine the best execution plan. Stale optimizer statistics that do not accurately represent the current status of the data in objects can easily mislead the optimizer to generate sub-optimal plans. There is no easy method to determine whether optimizer statistics are up-to-date or stale causing poor execution plans. Starting with Oracle Database 10g, the optimizer statistics collection has been automated. A new job called GATHER_STATS_JOB is created that runs the DBMS_STATS.GATHER_DATABASE_STATS_JOB_PROC procedure. The job is automatically scheduled to run every night.

- *Missing access structures*: The absence of appropriate access structures like indexes and materialized views is a common source of poor SQL performance.

- *Sub-optimal execution plan*: The CBO can sometimes choose a sub-optimal execution plan for a SQL statement. This is primarily because of incorrect estimates of some attributes of a SQL statement such as its cost, cardinality, or predicate selectivity.

- *Bad SQL*: Queries using Cartesian joins or UNION ALL clauses in a SQL query makes the execution plan really expensive and time consuming to retrieve the required rows.

As illustrated in Figure 6-4, the SELECT statement with SQL_ID 19x1189chq3xd has the highest activity. Once the queries to be tuned have been identified, click Schedule SQL Tuning Advisor and allow Oracle to tune the queries. The tuning process will perform statistics analysis, access path analysis, SQL profiling, and structure analysis before tuning the query. Oracle provides the modified query with a comparison of the execution plans before and after tuning. If the recommended changes are acceptable, the changes can be implemented.

■ **Note** A more detailed discussion on SQL tuning is forthcoming in Chapter 7.

Another option available under the SQL advisory section is the SQL access advisor. This complements the SQL tuning advisor functionality focusing on the identification of indexes, materialized views, and indexes on the materialized views to improve the performance of the entire SQL workload.

Automatic Workload Repository

The Automatic Workload Repository (AWR) is an enhanced version of the STATSPACK utility with a more user-friendly interface. Statistics and the entire workload information is collected (as a snapshot) automatically by the MMON background process every 60 minutes (default) and stored in the wrh$ and wri$ tables in the SYSAUX tablespace. The collected data is retained in the AWR for seven days (default) and then automatically purged. During the retention period, database performance and workload statistics can be generated into a report by comparing two snapshot periods. AWR collects data in two levels: TYPICAL (default) and ALL.

The following will change the default settings to 30-minute interval with a retention period of 30 days:

```
EXECUTE DBMS_WORKLOAD_REPOSITORY.MODIFY_SNAPSHOT_SETTINGS (interval =>30, retention => 43200);
```

AWR snapshots can also be captured manually using the DBMS_WORKLOAD_REPOSITORY.CREATE_SNAPSHOT() procedure. To capture a snapshot at the ALL level, a value of ALL is passed to the flush_level parameter of the CREATE_SNAPSHOT procedure. For example,

```
DBMS_WORKLOAD_REPOSITORY.CREATE_SNAPSHOT(flush_level=>ALL);
```

The number of top SQL queries reported by the AWR is also controlled by the STATISTICS_LEVEL parameter. When the value is TYPICAL, the top 30 queries are listed and when the value is ALL, the top 100 queries are list. This can be overridden using the following procedure:

```
DBMS_WORKLOAD_REPOSITORY.MODIFY_SNAPSHOT_SETTINGS (topnsql => 200);
```

During typical benchmarking cycles when a set of performance metrics needs to be saved as baseline for comparisons, the traditional methods used by DBAs have been to make an export of the performance data. AWR makes it more convenient using the following procedure:

```
DBMS_WORKLOAD_REPOSITORY.CREATE_BASELINE (<START SNAP ID>,<END SNAP ID>,<BASLINE NAME><DB ID>);
```

For example, the following procedure will create a baseline QAR1BLINE of the current database instance (default) represented by DB ID in the syntax above:

```
execute DBMS_WORKLOAD_REPOSITORY.CREATE_BASELINE (459,476,'QAR1BLINE');
```

Querying the DB_HIST_BASELINE table can validate the baseline definition.

```
COL BASELINE_NAME FORMAT A25
SELECT DBID,
       BASELINE_NAME,
       START_SNAP_ID,
       END_SNAP_ID
FROM   DBA_HIST_BASELINE;

    DBID BASELINE_NAME             START_SNAP_ID END_SNAP_ID
---------- ------------------------- ------------- -----------
4275027223 QAR1BLINE                           459         476
```

■ **Note** Creation of a baseline will override AWR automatic purging for the baseline snapshot range.

While AWR provides information concerning RAC, statistics are collected from all instances and stored by an instance number under a common SNAP_ID (SNAP_ID is the primary key for the AWR and is generated for every snapshot collection); in other words, statistics are collected by instance and not at the global level.

AWR reports or snapshot comparisons can be done either using a command line interface by executing an Oracle-provided SQL script ($ORACLE_HOME/rdbms/admin/awrrpt.sql) or using the EM interfaces. An HTML file can be generated and viewed using a browser by either method.

The script provides an option to pick a range of snapshots to generate comparison report. Once the range is selected, the report is generated in the default directory. In a RAC environment, starting with Oracle Database 11g Release 2, a cluster/group level summary report can be generated. Similar to the awrrpt.sql script, Oracle provides several scripts for data collection. These scripts and their purpose are listed in Table 6-1.

Table 6-1. *EM-Provided Scripts*

Script	Description
awrrpt.sql	Generates AWR reports for pairs of snapshot ids. The script defaults to the current database.
awrrpti.sql	Generates AWR reports for pairs of snapshot ids. Allows selection of a database.
awrddrpt.sql	Generates a comparison report between two snapshot periods. The reports being compared can be from the same database.
awrddrpi.sql	Generates a comparison report between two AWR reports. The reports being compared can be from the two different databases.
awrextr.sql	Performs a datapump export of the AWR data. This data can be moved to another environment or database.
awrloadsql	Performs a data pump imports/loads of the AWR data.
awrgrpti.sql	Generate RAC-related reports by choosing specific instances in the cluster.
awrgrpt.sql	Generate RAC-related reports for all available instances in the cluster.
awrgdrpt.sql	Generates RAC-related comparison reports between instances in the same database.
awrgdrpti.sql	Generates RAC-related comparison reports between different databases.
awrinfo.sql	Helps collect database-related general information. Information collected includes tablespace usage, schema/option usage, segment usage, retention policies, etc.
awrsqrpt.sql	Generates a report for a single SQL statement over multiple snapshots.
awrblmig.sql	Migrates the AWR baseline data from renamed BL tables back to the base tables.
addmrpt.sql	Generates ADDM analysis on a pair of AWR snapshots and generates a report.
ashrpt.sql	Generates an ASH report for the go live time.
ashrpti.sql	Apart from the basic database information, it shows major waits, top services/modules, top clients, etc.

Tuning, using the AWR, starts with identifying the top 10 foreground wait events reported in the first page of the report, illustrated in Figure 6-5.

Top 10 Foreground Events by Total Wait Time

Event	Waits	Total Wait Time (sec)	Wait Avg(ms)	% DB time	Wait Class
enq: TX - row lock contention	1,091	14.9K	13692	20.0	Application
enq: IV - contention	13,132	8802.6	670	11.8	Other
PX Deq: Slave Session Stats	6,771	5404.1	798	7.3	Other
DB CPU		4167.5		5.6	
library cache lock	3,762	3116.4	828	4.2	Concurrency
reliable message	1,063	2982.7	2806	4.0	Other
IPC send completion sync	20,202	2512.7	124	3.4	Other
row cache lock	10,056	2387.6	237	3.2	Concurrency
enq: PS - contention	6,484	1935.9	299	2.6	Other
JS kgl get object wait	2,045	1250	611	1.7	Administrative

Figure 6-5. *12c AWR – Top 10 Foreground Events*

Figure 6-5 provides the top 10 foreground wait events at the instance level and contains RAC-specific wait events. AWR also provides a global level cache load profile, illustrating the global cache activity between the various instances in the cluster. Figure 6-6 provides the overall workload characteristics on a RAC instance.

Global Cache and Enqueue Services - Workload Characteristics

Avg global enqueue get time (ms):	129.9
Avg global cache cr block receive time (ms):	187.0
Avg global cache current block receive time (ms):	204.7
Avg global cache cr block build time (ms):	0.0
Avg global cache cr block send time (ms):	0.0
Global cache log flushes for cr blocks served %:	1.9
Avg global cache cr block flush time (ms):	245.3
Avg global cache current block pin time (ms):	1.5
Avg global cache current block send time (ms):	0.0
Global cache log flushes for current blocks served %:	3.8
Avg global cache current block flush time (ms):	185.4

Global Cache and Enqueue Services - Messaging Statistics

Avg message sent queue time (ms):	32.8
Avg message sent queue time on ksxp (ms):	135.9
Avg message received queue time (ms):	9.9
Avg GCS message process time (ms):	16.5
Avg GES message process time (ms):	4.1
% of direct sent messages:	52.03
% of indirect sent messages:	43.18
% of flow controlled messages:	4.79

Figure 6-6. *12c AWR – RAC Workload Characteristics*

AWR is also organized into sections. When the AWR report is generated in a RAC environment, the second page of this report relates to RAC. Apart from the performance data illustrated in Figure 6-5 and 6-6, there is other important data discussed later in this section. The various profiles are calculated using the formulas described in Table 6-2.

Table 6-2. AWR – RAC- Global Cache Load Profile Formula

Profile	Formula
Global Cache blocks received	(gc current blocks received + gc cr blocks received)/elapsed time
Global Cache blocks served	(gc current blocks served + gc cr blocks served)/elapsed time
GCS/GES messages received	(gcs msgs received + ges msgs received)/elapsed time
GCS/GES messages sent	(gcs messages sent + ges messages sent)/elapsed time
DBWR Fusion writes	DBWR fusion writes/elapsed time
Estd. (Estimated) Interconnect traffic	(((gc cr blocks received + gc current blocks received + gc cr blocks served + gc current blocks served) * db_block_size) + ((gcs messages sent + ges messages sent + gcs msgs received + ges msgs received) * 200)/1024/elapsed time)

The formula in Table 6-2 is based on statistic values obtained from GV$SYSSTAT or GV$DLM_MISC views. The elapsed time is the time between the start and end of collection period. In the case of an AWR report, the elapsed time is the time between the two snapshots being compared. The load profile can be grouped by services using the GV$SERVICE_STATS view to obtain a more focused performance metric.

Figure 6-7 provides the overall performance of the instance with respect to global cache movement between instances.

Global Cache Transfer Stats

- Immediate (Immed) - Block Transfer NOT impacted by Remote Processing Delays
- Busy (Busy) - Block Transfer impacted by Remote Contention
- Congested (Congst) - Block Transfer impacted by Remote System Load
- ordered by CR + Current Blocks Received desc

Inst No	Block Class	CR				Current			
		Blocks Received	% Immed	% Busy	% Congst	Blocks Received	% Immed	% Busy	% Congst
3	data block	12,995	57.94	2.39	39.68	13,732	78.46	3.53	18.01
1	data block	5,306	53.98	15.79	30.23	6,133	73.39	4.92	21.69
3	Others	1,984	87.15	0.76	12.10	1,756	85.42	3.08	11.50
3	undo header	3,400	86.68	2.88	10.44	39	74.36	5.13	20.51
1	undo header	3,253	88.44	2.09	9.47	28	75.00	10.71	14.29
1	Others	1,267	83.43	0.16	16.42	895	85.59	1.01	13.41
1	undo block	77	75.32	18.18	6.49	0			
3	undo block	30	53.33	30.00	16.67	0			

Figure 6-7. 12c AWR – RAC- Global Cache Transfer Stats

The average values in Figure 6-6 are also based on statistic values from GV$SYSSTAT and GV$DLM_MISC views. Once the actual values are computed, the average is determined to provide an overall health of the cluster during the snapshot interval. Table 6-3 illustrates the statistic values used in some of the average workload characteristics listed in Figure 6-6.

Table 6-3. *AWR – RAC- Global Cache Load Profile Formula*

Statistic	Formula	Goal (ms)
Average Global Cache CR Block Receive Time	10 * gc cr block receive time / gc cr blocks received	1
Average Global Cache Current Block Receive Time	10 * gc current block receive time / gc current blocks received	1

AWR **Formula** provides other RAC-related performance statistics in the AWR report, such as

- RAC Report Summary
- Global Enqueue Statistics
- Global CR Served Stats
- Global CURRENT Served Statistics
- Global Cache Transfer Stats
- Global Cache Transfer Statistics aggregated per class

Among these the Global Cache Transfer Statistics is an informative section providing details of block transfers between various instances participating in the cluster. As illustrated in Figure 6-7, the transfer is broken down between CR and Current requests.

As mentioned earlier, in a RAC environment, a summary report can be generated using the script $ORACLE_HOME/rdbms/admin/awrgrpt.sql. This script will provide a consolidated summary of the RAC cluster grouping the report into sections. Figure 6-8 illustrates the top timed events across the various nodes in the cluster.

		Wait		Event		Wait Time			Summary Avg Wait Time (ms)				
	#	Class	Event	Waits	%Timeouts	Total(s)	Avg(ms)	%DB time	Avg	Min	Max	Std Dev	Cnt
*		DB CPU				59,366.29		40.58					3
	Commit	log file sync	9,223,465	3,147.00	36,866.20	4.00	25.20	4.25	3.52	4.69	0.64	3
	Configuration	log file switch completion	1,009,978	0.00	29,770.43	15.44	20.35	14.99	12.28	17.85	2.79	3
	System I/O	log file parallel write	3,951,528	0.00	6,411.28	1.62	4.38	1.61	1.52	1.69	0.09	3
	Other	gcs log flush sync	566,664	0.00	3,762.20	6.64	2.57	7.48	4.88	9.52	2.37	3
	User I/O	read by other session	935,588	0.00	2,369.44	2.53	1.62	2.33	1.25	3.03	0.94	3
	Cluster	gc buffer busy acquire	566,430	0.27	1,897.65	3.35	1.30	3.89	2.79	5.41	1.36	3
	Other	enq: CF - contention	25,322	7.14	1,890.56	74.66	1.29	74.35	71.98	76.56	2.29	3
	User I/O	direct path read temp	377,883	0.00	1,662.32	4.40	1.14	3.80	2.10	6.64	2.48	3
	System I/O	log file sequential read	381,748	0.00	1,295.74	3.39	0.89	3.54	2.83	3.96	0.62	3

Figure 6-8. *AWR - Cluster Top Timed Events Summary*

Similar to the Top Timed wait events illustrated in Figure 6-8, the AWR reports several summaries of areas that would otherwise have to be retrieved by generating individual reports from each instance in the cluster.

Automatic Workload Repository Warehouse

The default retention period for an AWR in Oracle Database 11g is eight days, and seven days for the previous releases. This minimal retention period is hardly sufficient for analyzing historical behavior or trend analysis related to specific issues around the database. As a best practice, the retention period is increased so historical information can be retained and analyzed if required; however, increasing the retention period for a considerably longer interval has some negative impact on the primary database, such as increased space usage, contention with read write operations, etc.

A new feature introduced in Oracle 12c allows the creation of an Automatic Workload Repository Warehouse (AWRW). Figure 6-9 illustrates the basic high-level process for creating the repository. AWR data is collected from various target databases and stored in a central repository or warehouse. From the warehouse additional reports can be generated.

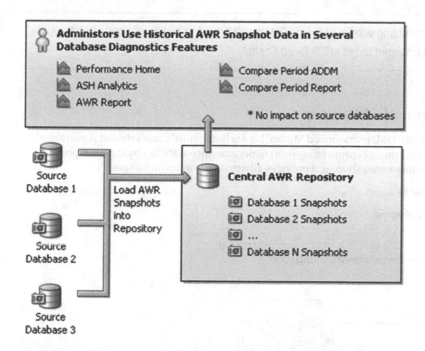

Figure 6-9. AWR warehouse

The following are the steps to create an AWRW.

1. Connect to the EM Cloud Control console with super administrator privileges.

2. From the Targets menu, select Databases.

3. On the Databases page, click the Performance tab, then select the AWR Warehouse option from the pull-down menu.

4. Click Configure. The first configuration page (Repository) appears.

5. Click the search icon to select the database to serve as the AWR warehouse.

6. Select the preferred or named credentials established for the target database and the target database host, and click Next.

7. In the AWR Snapshot Management screen, select the retention period. The default retention period for AWR data in the repository is indefinitely. However, this can be changed. Set the retention period to a number of years.

8. Set the snapshot upload interval. The default is 24 hours. The minimum interval is one hour. You can also upload snapshots on demand.

9. Select where on the warehouse database host to save exported dump files. For a cluster database, you have to specify a shared location that is accessible to all nodes.

10. Click Submit. This submits a job with the prefix CAW_LOAD_SETUP_. Upon successful job completion, the warehouse is ready for source databases to be added.

■ **Note**   The target database must be an existing version of Oracle Database 12.1.0.2 or higher, or Oracle Database 11.2.0.4 with the appropriate patch level managed target in EM Cloud Control.

Automatic Database Diagnostic Monitor

Automatic Database Diagnostic Monitor (ADDM, pronounced "Adam") is a self-diagnostic analysis and reporting tool. In an earlier section, we discussed the hourly capture (snapshot) of performance statistics by the AWR process. As illustrated in Figure 6-10, ADDM uses these snapshots and provides ádvice on the following issues:

- The problem and its potential location

- What areas of the system are affected

- Any performance issues

- Steps to improve the overall performance of the database

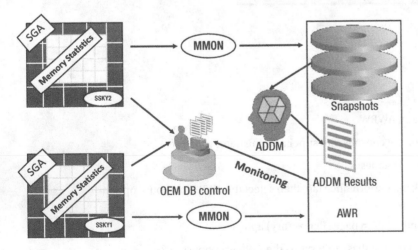

Figure 6-10. *AWR and ADDM process flow*

Like AWR, ADDM can also be generated using EM or using the `addmrpt.sql` script available in the `$ORACLE_HOME/rdbms/admin/` directory. These reports are stored by default for 30 days in the database before being purged. Reports are generated on predefined thresholds (which can be modified) for a predetermined set of areas. For example, the user I/O is defined by the parameter `DBIO_EXPECTED` and defaults to 1000 milliseconds. Another parameter that is used to calculate the amount of database time spent is the `DB_ELAPSED_TIME` parameter, which defaults to 0 milliseconds. Both these parameters can be modified using the `DBMS_ADVISOR.SET_DEFAULT_TASK_PARAMETER` PL/SQL procedure.

ADDM can be accessed by selecting the Advisor Central from either of the following pages:

- Clustered Database Performance page

- Database Instance Performance page

Once ADDM is selected using either of the options, EM automatically generates an ADDM analysis report on the latest AWR snapshot available and allows for regeneration of analysis based on a different snapshot period.

In Figure 6-11 ADDM provides an overall performance of the database and provides a list of findings based on the analysis of the snapshots selected. Apart from providing the findings, the analysis also reports on the percentage of impact. In this case, the impact is for Virtual Memory Paging and the percentage impact is 99.8%. The ADDM time scale shows considerable wait times from 5:30 PM thru about 10 AM the next day. This is the timeframe for the batch application execution.

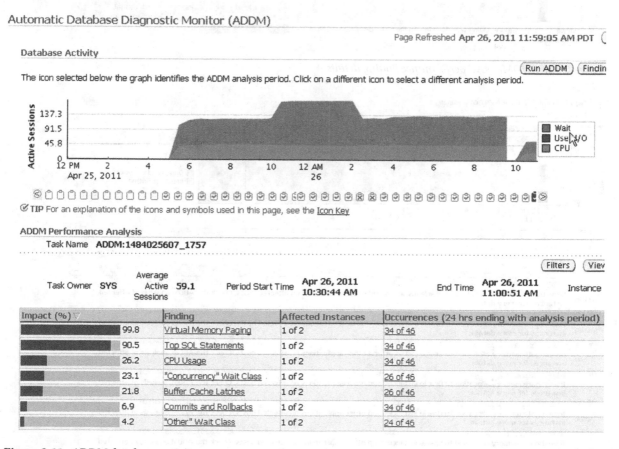

Figure 6-11. ADDM database activity

To understand the areas of impact and the recommendations for fixing this issue, click a specific finding. Once this is selected, EM provides the recommendations (illustrated in Figures 6-12 and 6-13).

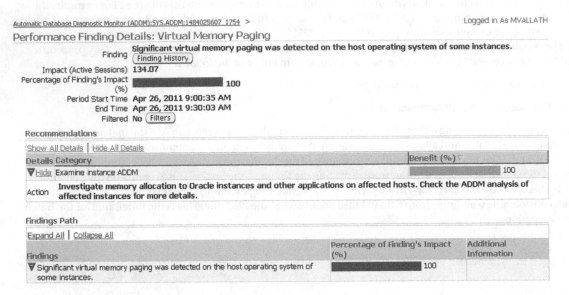

Figure 6-12. *ADDM – RAC performance finding details*

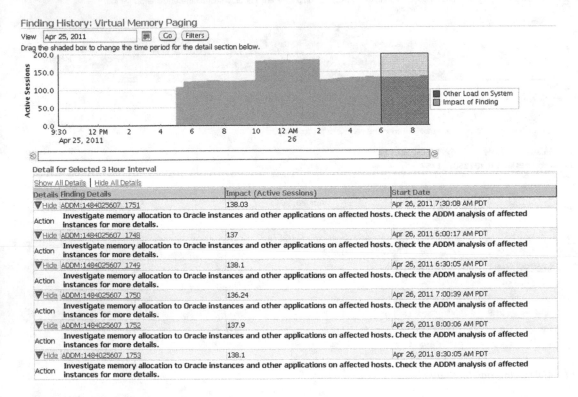

Figure 6-13. *ADDM – RAC, error impact over time*

The ADDM report in Figure 6-13 makes a recommendation to increase the memory of the Oracle instances. Before making any change it's always a good idea to explore the impact of the suggestion. For example, how many times has this error occurred? To determine if this occurred in the past, click the Finding History option. Figure 6-12 illustrates the impact of this error over the entire timeframe.

ADDM is also a good source to identify high-load SQL statements. For instance, in Figure 6-11 the second highest impact (90.5%) on the overall performance of the cluster are SQL statements, identified by Top SQL Statements. Every run of ADDM produces a report containing analysis and recommendations. These reports are stored by default for 30 days in the database before being purged. Apart from identifying high-load SQL statements, ADDM also recommends running SQL advisors on them to obtain optimal performance benefits.

Active Session History

AWR collects snapshots containing performance characteristics of the database; ADDM analyzes this information and provides recommendations on what changes could be made to improve efficiency of the database. A onetime occurrence of any issue is not a good indication of any specific performance problem. Similar to a situation where a bug is reported by a user in his or her application, the developer is interested in finding out if this bug is repeatable or if the error is reproducible. The developer may not spend time investigating it and could consider the situation a minor issue and prioritize it for further investigation at a later time. This is because a one-time occurrence of an issue does not really provide sufficient data to fix the problem. Repeated occurrences are when the data becomes consistent and tunable. Similarly, in a database environment, problems do arise, systems do slow down, occasional high spikes do occur. However, unless these spikes are reproducible or consistently happening over a length of time (past, present, and future), no real concern is given.

■ **Note** A methodical way to address frequently occurring or reproducible spikes is to consider ASH data for detailed analysis and have OSWatcher or the IPD/OS (CHM) always running.

Active session history (ASH, pronounced like the word "ash") tries to bridge this gap. ASH performs analysis of transient problems lasting for a few minutes or over various dimensions such as time, SQL_ID, module, action, etc. As mentioned, unlike the other reactive reporting issues, ASH is based on a sampled history of all events happening in the database. ASH data that is captured and stored for all active sessions is essentially a fact table (GV$ACTIVE_SESSION_HISTORY) in a data warehouse environment, with the columns as the dimensions of the fact table. In this view, there are about 13 important dimensions of data.

Similar to the AWR and ADDM features, ASH reports can also be generated from the EM console (Figure 6-14) or by using the ashrpt.sql script located in the $ORACLE_HOME/rdbms/admin directory on the database server. Figure 6-14 has two sections, the basic section illustrating the overall performance over a period of time, and the second section lists the load map of the wait event distribution categories under system I/O, CPU, cluster and commit.

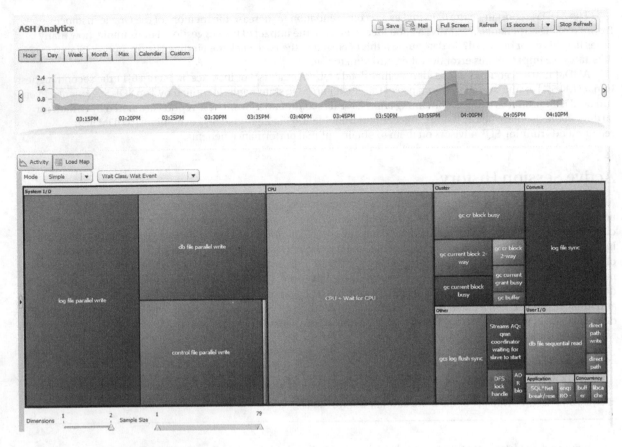

Figure 6-14. *12c EM - ASH Report*

Tools and Utilities from Oracle Support

The Oracle Metalink contains several tools and utilities. Let's walk through some of these tools. These tools, combined with the grid control, may make you wonder if you will need any additional third-party tools.

OSWATCHER

OSWATCHER (OSW) is an Oracle-provided set of collection scripts that collect various O/S-specific performance metrics using utilities such as mpstat, iostat, netstat, vmstat, etc. available at the O/S level. Control is passed from the main shell script (OSWatcher.sh) to individually spawned operating system data collector processes. These sub-data collector processes collect specific data, timestamp the data collected, and append the data to the collector output file. Depending on the O/S utility used and the type of data collected, data is stored in separate files in their respective directories.

The tool is flexible in that it can be configured to collect data at predefined intervals. This allows for uniform collection of data for various components of the server.

For the collection interval specified by the user, OSW captures about 60 data points before closing the file and opening another data collection set. While the interval can be defined, the number of data points is always fixed at 60. This means that each file will contain, at most, one hour of data. At the end of each hour, File Manager will wake up and copy the current file to an archive location and then create a new file.

Installing OSW is simple and straightforward. Download the tar file from Metalink[1] and untar the file at the appropriate location. For example, keeping a mount point for tools will help easy management.

```
tar xvf  osw.nnn.tar
```

Figure 6-15 illustrates the directory structure for OSW. All of the shell scripts are located under the OSW directory (OSW_HOME) and the outputs generated by oswatcher are located under the archive directory. Underneath this are subdirectories for each O/S metric. OSW is not cluster-aware, meaning that OSW will have to be configured on all nodes in the cluster and data collection enabled on all nodes.

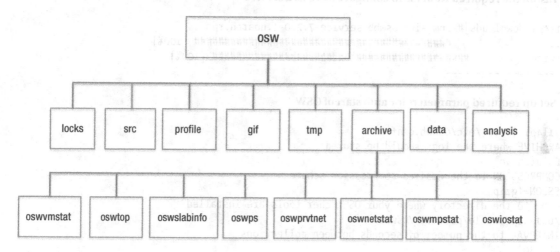

Figure 6-15. *OSW directory structure*

Since this is a shell script, collection can be done either as a foreground process or in the background. To enable data collection in the background, submit the primary script with the nohup option.

1. To start the OSW as a foreground process, use startOSW.sh.

2. To stop the OSW foreground process, use stopOSW.sh.

3. To submit the process in the background, use

    ```
    nohup ./startOSW.sh n1 n2 &
    ```

    where n1 is the interval for each snapshot and n2 is the retention period.

4. To generate graphs for the data collected using OSWg, use

    ```
    java -jar oswg.jar -I < complete path for the archive directory location>
    ```

OSWg requires a Windows type of server.

Data is collected to the archive folder under OSW_HOME. If this directory needs to be moved or copied to another location to retain specific data, OSW will create the archive folder and all subfolders automatically.

---

[1]Metalink Note #: 301137.1 - O/S Watcher User Guide.

■ **Note** In a RAC environment, OSWATCHER needs to be installed and run on all nodes in the cluster.

Configuring OSW to Start Automatically After a System Start

Systems issues don't appear after making appointments. To avoid surprises and to have most of the data available, OSW should be considered as a utility to run at regular intervals in the background.

Step 1: **Install the required RPM file to configure oswb as a service**

```
[root@ssky1l4p1 downloads]# rpm -ivh oswbb-service-7.2.0-1.noarch.rpm
Preparing...                ######################################### [100%]
1:oswbb-service            ######################################### [100%]
----------------------------
```

Step 2: **Set up required parameters for auto start of OSW**

```
 [root@ssky1l4p1 ]# vi /etc/oswbb.conf
# Set OSW_ARCHIVE where the logs should be stored
OSW_ARCHIVE='archive'
# Set OSW_COMPRESSION to the desired compression scheme
OSW_COMPRESSION='gzip'
# Set OSW_HOME to the directory where your OSWatcher tools are installed
OSW_HOME='/u01/app/oracle/product /oswbb'
# Set OSW_INTERVAL to the number of seconds between collections
OSW_INTERVAL='30'
# Set OSW_RETENTION to the number of hours logs are to be retained
OSW_RETENTION='48'
# Set OSW_USER to the owner of the OSW_HOME directory
OSW_USER='oracle'
----------------------------
```

Step 3: **Verify the chkconfig to ensure the OSW is enabled for auto start**

```
 [root@ssky1l4p1]# /sbin/chkconfig --list oswbb
oswbb          0:off   1:off   2:on   3:on   4:on   5:on   6:off
```

Step 4: **Start OSW as a service**

```
 [root@ssky1l4p1]#
 [root@ssky1l4p1]# /sbin/service oswbb start
Starting OSWatcher:                                    [  OK  ]
[root@ssky1l4p1]#
```

Step 5: **Stop OSW as a service**

```
[root@ssky1l4p1]# /sbin/service oswbb stop
Stopping OSWatcher:                                    [  OK  ]
```

As part of the startup process, the following lines are displayed on the default terminal output:

```
Info...You did not enter a value for snapshotInterval.
Info...Using default value = 30
Info...You did not enter a value for archiveInterval.
Info...Using default value = 48
Setting the archive log directory to /u01/app/oracle/product /oswbb/archive

Testing for discovery of OS Utilities...
VMSTAT found on your system.
IOSTAT found on your system.
MPSTAT found on your system.
IFCONFIG found on your system.
NETSTAT found on your system.
TOP found on your system.

Testing for discovery of OS CPU COUNT
oswbb is looking for the CPU COUNT on your system
CPU COUNT will be used by oswbba to automatically look for cpu problems

CPU COUNT found on your system.
CPU COUNT = 16

Discovery completed.

Starting OSWatcher Black Box v7.2  on Mon May 26 12:53:55 EDT 2014
With SnapshotInterval = 30
With ArchiveInterval = 48

OSWatcher Black Box - Written by Carl Davis, Center of Expertise,
Oracle Corporation
For questions on install/usage please go to MOS (Note:301137.1)
If you need further assistance or have comments or enhancement
requests you can email me Carl.Davis@Oracle.com

Data is stored in directory: /u01/app/oracle/product/oswbb/archive

Starting Data Collection...

oswbb heartbeat:Mon May 26 12:54:00 EDT 2014
```

Using the Collected Data

Data collected can be used as-is (raw) by transferring it to some external program/analyzer or it can be converted into graphs using the OSWg utility also provided by Oracle on Metalink. This uses the data collected by the OSW collector and generates graphs for the various snapshots and types of data collected.

Generally O/S level metrics are not sufficient to determine the root cause of a problem. However, they assist in determining why a certain situation occurred in the overall performance of the server. For example, why did something run very slow during a specific time of the day? The reason for this could be that the process or session in question consumed high CPU or the system was doing a huge amount of context switches (Figure 6-16).

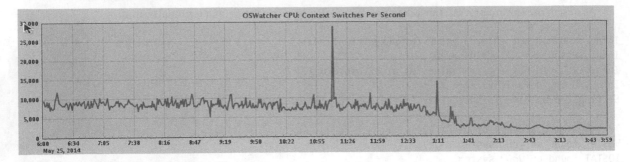

Figure 6-16. *OSW: CPU context switches*

The CPU usage maybe high because a process/session was engaged in traversing through large amounts of data in the buffer cache, which caused high requests for latches, or the O/S parameters were not correctly set, which caused a high context switch, which indirectly reflected on high CPU utilization (Figure 6-17) and this in turn made the user session considerably slower.

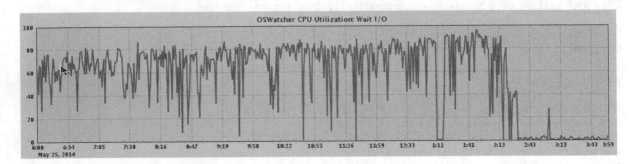

Figure 6-17. *OSW: CPU Utilization Chart*

In this particular situation, a SQL statement was using high CPU due to large logical I/O operations (Figure 6-18).

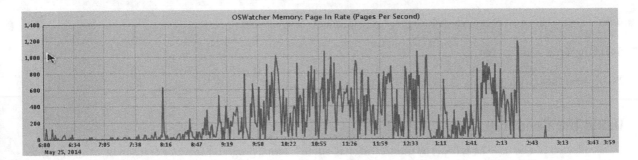

Figure 6-18. *OSW: CPU Interrupt Chart*

Below are the execution statistics for the SQL statement.

Buffer Gets	Executions	Gets per Exec	%Total	CPU Time (s)	Elapsed Time (s)	SQL Id
3,125,914,127	22,371	139,730.64	33.44	11873.44	24800.36	b8vsupuswn5mg

SQL Id	Query
b8vsupuswn5mg	SELECT SUM (RESRVD_QTY) FROM BCIINV_FG_AVAIL_RESRVS_V WHERE ORGANIZATION_ID =:B2 AND INVENTORY_ITEM_ID =:B1

The query accessed the data through a view. Once the underlying view was tuned, a few of the queries that accessed this view performed better, reducing CPU utilization.

In a RAC environment, if the background processes such as the LMS or LMD do not get sufficient CPU cycles or if there are scheduling delays at the O/S level, this could cause poor response times to the user. This could also be an indication that LMS is not configured to run in real time and is running at the default timeshare mode.

■ **Note**   Details on how to look through the data to understand the reasons behind such delay will be reviewed in the appropriate chapters.

Light Onboard Monitor (LTOM)

LTOM is a Java application designed to collect data based on a predefined set of rules. When conditions for these rules are met, the data pertaining to the request is captured. LTOM is considered more of a proactive tool vs. a reactive tool. An example of a reactive tool is EM, where the user has to be at the terminal to observe the problem, and based on the problem/alert reported by the EM, appropriate data needs to be collected and analyzed. LTOM is more proactive because data is collected as the problem occurs.

LTOM runs on most UNIX and Linux environments, is tightly integrated with the host operating system, and provides an integrated solution for detecting and collecting trace files for system performance issues as they occur. This is really beneficial since it is seldom possible to collect all relevant data when a problem actually occurs because the window is so minimal that such data may not exist for a considerable length of time. Frequently, the problem will have passed or the database will have shut down, which initializes the database, which means you must wait for the next occurrence of the problem and if everything is timed correctly, the data may be collected. LTOM does automatic problem detection and collects the necessary diagnostic traces in real time while the database/system performance problem is occurring.

LTOM can be downloaded from Metalink.[2] As suggested, when discussing OSW, it is in the best interest of the DBA to install all utilities into for example a tools mount point. Untar the file into this into the appropriate directory:

```
tar xvfp ltom.tar
```

LTOM is installed at a top directory, which is called the LTOM_HOME, and it's where all major utilities are located. Figure 6-19 illustrates the directory structure of LTOM, showing how it is configured and how its components and files are laid out.

---

[2]Metalink Note # 352363.1 LTOM - The On-Board Monitor User Guide.

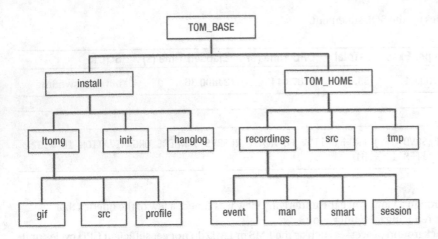

Figure 6-19. *LTOM directory structure*

Configuration of LTOM

The primary configuration of LTOM is performed by setting the parameters required to capture a matrix from the database servers. LTOM has several parameter files or properties file that are located under the init directory under $TOM_HOME, as illustrated in Figure 6-19. These parameter files include

- LTOM Deployment - tom_deploy.properties
- Hang Detection - hangDetect.properties
- Data Collector - dataCollect.properties
- Session Recorder - sessionRecorder.properties

Definitions and setting parameters in these files will be discussed under the appropriate sections later in this chapter.

Creating a Schema for LTOM to Collect Database Statistics

Perform the following steps for an LTOM schema for collecting statistics.

1. Create tablespace or identify tablespace for LTOM.

   ```
   SQL> CREATE TABLESPACE LTOM DATAFILE '+PRD_DATA';
   ```

2. Create a user that could be used by LTOM.

   ```
   SQL> CREATE USER TOM IDENTIFIED BY TOM DEFAULT TABLESPACE LTOM TEMPORARY TABLESPACE TEMP;
   ```

3. Grant required privileges.

   ```
   SQL> GRANT CONNECT, DBA, SYSDBA TO TOM;
   SQL> GRANT EXECUTE ON DBMS_SUPPORT TO TOM';
   ```

Configuring LTOM Properties

Once the scripts have been installed, LTOM needs to be configured for database connectivity and also for starting ltom in the background. The configuration parameters are stored in the tom_deploy.properties file located in the init directory under the $TOM_HOME location.

In this properties file the following are to be configured:

- Connection parameters:

    - The DB_CONNECT_STRING parameter defines the connection mode and type. The default type of connection uses the JDBC thin client. Because LTOM is configured to run on each node in the cluster, instance-specific connection information should be provided.

    - The INSTANCE parameter defines the instance to monitor and collect statistics.

    - The DB_USERID parameter defines the LTOM user id used by LTOM to make a connection to the database and collect appropriate statistics.

      ```
      DB_CONNECT_STRING=jdbc:oracle:thin:@prddb1:1521:PRD_1
        INSTANCE=PRD_1
      DB_USERID= tom
      ```

- System Profiler:

    - PROFILER= enables background collection of information required by the profiler.

    - PFREQ= is the frequency at which snapshots should be collected by the profiler.

    - SESSIONS= defines the type of sessions that should be monitored by the process.

    - LEVEL= determines the level of data to be captured. LTOM supports two levels for system profiling of data:

        - Level 1 is the basic bare minimum data collected and includes data from V$SESSION_WAIT view.

        - Level 2 provides a much more detailed output and includes data collected from V$SESSION_WAIT, V$SYSTEM_EVENT and V$SYSSTAT.

    - CPU= value is a Y/N value; when enabled, it profiles CPU-related statistics from the OS.

    - CSQL= is the parameter that will help profile SQL statements currently being executed. The values supported by this parameter include

        - I – Inline at every snapshot.

        - R – Generates a report at the end of profile collection.

        - N – Disables profiling of data.

    - PROFILE_TOP indicates if top process information should be profiled from the OS.

    - PROFILE_VMSAT indicates if VMSTAT data from the O/S should be profiled.

    - PROFILE_IOSTAT indicates if IOSTAT data from the O/S should be profiled.

```
PROFILER=TRUE
PFREQ=5
SESSIONS=W
LEVEL=2
CPU=Y
PROFILE_TOP=Y
PROFILE_VMSTAT =Y
PROFILE_IOSTAT=Y
```

Hang Detection

Similar to the high-level connection properties defined earlier, there are parameters for a specific collector. Hang detection properties are defined in the hangDetect.properties file.

- AUTO_HANG_DETECT = TRUE indicates if LTOM should capture statistics when the server goes into a hang state.

- HFREQ: < > indicates the frequency in which to collect hang related hang detection statistics.

The remaining three parameters in this section relate to the O/S-level matrix to be collected using OS provided utilities. They include VMSTAT, IOSTAT, and TOP.

Session Recorder

Session recorder properties are defined in the sessionRecorder.properties file.

- SESSION_RECORDER = when set to TRUE enables session recorder to collect session information.

- SFREQ= defines the frequency in which snapshots should be collected by LTOM for the session.

- TRACE= indicates, when collecting session information, where the data should be captured (in memory or file). Value of F indicates file and M indicates that trace data will be collected in memory.

- BUFFERS= specifies the number of bytes dedicated to trace an individual session.

- MAX_SESSIONS = indicates the maximum number of sessions that will be traced.

Executing LTOM

LTOM can be executed in three different ways:

- Interactively using the menu in Figure 6-20, where LTOM will prompt for the database user id and password

- Interactively where LTOM will not prompt for user id and password

- As a background process

```
Starting LTOM V4.1.2
LTOM written by Oracle Center of Expertise
Copyright (c)  2008 by Oracle Corporation


Enter 1  to Start Auto Hang Detection
Enter 2  to Stop  Auto Hang Detection
Enter 3  to Start System Profiling
Enter 4  to Stop  System Profiling
Enter 7  to Start Session Tracing
Enter 71 to Display Sessions Traced
Enter 72 to Dump All Trace Buffers
Enter 73 to Dump Specific Trace Buffer
Enter 74 to Stop Specific Session Tracing
Enter 8  to Stop All Session Tracing

Enter S  to Update status
Enter Q  to End Program
CURRENT STATUS: HangDetection=OFF Profiling=OFF AutoRec=OFF SessionRec=OFF
Please Select an Option:
```

Figure 6-20. LTOM Interactive Menu

The next parameter, XXRD, is a password encryption used when LTOM is executed in interactive and as a background process.

LTOM provides the following functionality:

- Automatic Hang Detection

- System Profiler

- Automatic Session Tracing

Automatic Hang Detection

This is a rules-based hang detection system. These rules are predefined by Oracle; however, the user has options to modify the rules or add additional rules to detect hangs. By default only non-idle wait events are considered for hang detection. These rules are saved in the hangDetect.properties file under $TOM_HOME/init directory.

The properties file is divided into three sections.

- *Event trigger rules section*: This section defines the various events that are required to capture hang statistics. The default parameters defined by Oracle in this section are sufficient most of the time. However, if additional events need to be configured, they can be added here using the following syntax:

  ```
  EVENT=A, VALUE=B
  Eg; EVENT=log file sync, VALUE=45
  ```

169

- *Sequencing rules*: In this section, the level of information that needs to be captured is defined. The primary parameters in this section are the following:

  - HANGANALYZE: This defines what level of analysis details should be collected when LTOM detects a hang on the database server. The various levels are defined in Table 6-4.

Table 6-4. HANGANALYZE Trace Levels

Level	Description
10	Dump all processes.
5	Dump all processes involved in wait chains.
4	Dump leaf nodes in wait chains.
3	Dump only processes thought to be in a hang.
2	Minimal output.
1	Very minimal output.

  - SYSTEMSTATE: This defines what level of SYSTEMSTATE dump should be collected. The default value of 266 (dump all the session history with process stack and current wait events) for this parameter should be sufficient. Other levels are listed in Table 6-5.

Table 6-5. SYSTEMSTATE Dump Levels

Level	Description
1	Very basic process information.
10	Most commonly used level and includes object trees for all processes. Includes RAC-related information in the trace files.
11	Includes dump of any resources not on the freelist. Information is added just after the "BUSY_GLOBAL_CACHE_ELEMENTS" section of the trace file.
256	Dumps out short stack information for each process.
266	Dump all the session history with process stack and current wait events.

- *Hang detection directives*: This section defines parameters that apply in a general nature to all scenarios. The important parameters in this section include:

  - LOOP_HANG_DETECT: TRUE or FALSE. If set to TRUE, LTOM will ignore the default behavior of detecting only a single hang and then exiting. When set to TRUE, LTOM will not exit after detecting the first hang but will continue indefinitely to look for other hangs. At each hang detection LTOM will collect diagnostic traces using the sequencing rules defined in this file. This parameter should be set with caution, as the automated continuous collection of diagnostic traces can severely degrade the performance of a system.

  - RAC_AWARE: It's a Boolean value of TRUE/FALSE and indicates that LTOM understand that this is a RAC cluster and all required cluster level information should be captured. LTOM will take all hang analyze and SYSTEMSTATE dumps with the -g flag.

When the hang detection mode is selected/enabled, automatic hang detection proceeds to run in the background in a silent mode, checking for hangs at predefined intervals set when this option is enabled.

The primary advantage for using this tool is that the tool is able to capture hangs and other issues within the environment when the support team is not available. E-mail notification can be configured to alert the user about the hang. To set up e-mail notification, edit the $TOM_HOME/src/ltommail.sh file. To prevent traces from constantly being generated once a hang is detected, only one set of diagnostic traces is collected and no further hangs will be detected until the mode has been turned off and re-enabled.

System Profiler

The System Profiler provides the ability to continually collect data from both the O/S and the database. It provides an integrated snapshot of the overall health of the OS together with the database. This data collection contains the output from O/S utilities (top, vmstat, and iostat) along with Oracle session data (V$SESSION, V$PROCESS, V$SESSION_WAIT, V$SYSTEM_EVENT, and V$SYSTEM_STATISTICS). The recording frequency and subsets of available data can also be configured when running the tool.

Automatic Session Tracing

How many times have DBAs received complaints from users that the system or a specific operation goes slow at different times of the day or a system in general is slow at various times of the day? When this occurs, most of the time we are not available, and if we are available, there is not sufficient time to capture all the required data. To understand what was going on in the environment, it would be helpful to capture the sessions and environment details at that point in time.

Automatic Session Tracing uses a set of rules defined in the properties file sessionRecorder.properties located in the init directory to determine when to turn on SQL Trace for individual Oracle sessions, using event 10046 at level 12 trace (discussed later in this chapter). Rules can be defined for database wait events, CPU, and specific users. For rules based on wait events, the automatic session recorder monitors certain V$ views at specified intervals and computes the average wait time between intervals for each event. This computed average wait time is compared to the rule definition for that event, if any. If a rule has been defined for that event and if the average wait time exceeds the rule threshold for that event, then LTOM turns on tracing for that session. Sessions are traced in a memory buffer or to a file. Tracing in memory has the advantage that it will not cause any additional IO to the disk system.

The rule definition for in memory tracing uses two thresholds, a minimum value and a maximum value, defined by the parameter EVENT=A, VALUE=B,C. The minimum value or minimum threshold defined by 'B' turns on the tracing for the session in memory and the maximum value or maximum threshold defined by 'C' forces the memory buffer to be written to disk to that session's respective trace file. For example,

```
EVENT=gc cr block lost, VALUE=1,100
```

The above parameter will capture all session related information when the session encounters wait event gc cr block lost.

Under this feature most of the tracing happens in memory and only allows the session to be continuously traced and written to disk when something significant occurs. The user can also manually force the memory buffer to be written to disk at any time by selecting the appropriate choice from the LTOM menu illustrated previously in Figure 6-19. The user specifies the amount of memory to dedicate to each session when starting LTOM along with the option to limit the number of sessions LTOM can trace

Cluster Health Monitor (CHM)

This is a monitoring and diagnostic tool available from Oracle and supported for Oracle database 10g, 11g, and 12c RAC environments. This tool is automatically installed with Oracle Grid Infrastructure (GI) in Oracle Database 11g Release 2 (11.2.0.2) and Oracle Database 12c Release 1. However, the methods of installation and configuration have changed through the various releases. For the earlier releases of Oracle, this tool can be downloaded from OTN and installed on either the Linux/UNIX environment or Windows environment or both.

There is a subtle difference between Oracle Database 11g Release 2 and Oracle Database 12c Release 1. In the earlier version, the repository used to store the diagnostic data was a Berkelydb compared to the Oracle Database 12c Release 1, called the management instance installed as part of the (GI) installation.

CHM provides real-time monitoring, continuously tracking O/S resource consumption at node, processes, and device levels to help diagnose degradation and failures of the various components in a RAC environment. In the versions 10g and 11g, the real-time data was available through a GUI interface or historical data could be replayed from the repository stored on individual nodes in the cluster to analyze issues such as high interconnect latency times, high CPU usage, runaway processes, high run queue lengths, and off course reasons and causes that lead to situations causing node evictions.

In Oracle Database 12c Version 1, only a command-line interface is available to analyze data.

Architecture

Similar to the Oracle clusterware, the CHM architecture is robust (as illustrated in Figure 6-21). CHM has several daemon processes that run on all servers to perform various tasks.

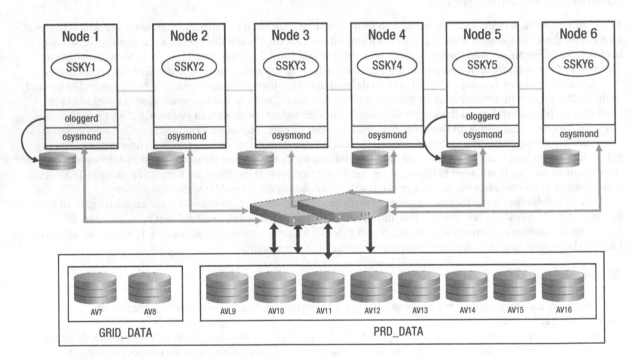

Figure 6-21. *CHM Oracle Database 12c architecture*

CHM consists of a database and three daemons:

- oproxyd is the proxy daemon that handles connections (prior to Oracle 12c). All connections are made via the public interface. If CHM is configured to use a dedicated private interface, then oproxyd listens on the public interface for external clients such as oclumon and crfgui (discussed later in this section). It is configured to run on all nodes in the cluster.

- osysmond is the primary daemon responsible for monitoring and O/S metric collection. It's responsible for metrics collection on all nodes in the cluster and sending the data to the ologgerd daemon process. osysmond is responsible for spawning/starting the ologgerd, and for some reason if the ologgerd dies, it will restart it.

- ologgerd, like the name says, is a logger daemon process. It receives data from the osysmond daemon and logs O/S metrics into a management db. One of the nodes in the cluster is the designated master node and a second node in the cluster is chosen as the standby for the master ologgerd. This ensures that statistics are collected on a continuous basis. Should the master node fail, the standby ologgerd becomes the master and designates another server to be the new standby.

- Berkeley DB (BDB)/Management DB: Data collected by the daemon process is retained in a database for a period of 24 hours (default). This retention period can be increased to a maximum period of 72 hours (259200 seconds) using the following command:

```
oclumon manage –bdb resize <size in number of seconds>
```

For example, oclumon manage –bdb resize 259200

As illustrated in Figure 6-21, appropriate daemons are started on all nodes in the cluster. A single instance of the database is created on the master node of the cluster. If the node fails, the database instance will be restarted on another node.

CHM has a command line interface called **oclumon**. This utility allows querying the BDB to get node-specific metrics for specific periods of time to view on a regular terminal. This is an interactive tool that can be used to get node level or full cluster level information. For example, to get a detailed output about all nodes in the cluster, use

```
oclumon dumpnodeview -v allnodes - last "00:30:00"
```

CHM Statistics

Once CHM is installed and enabled, the daemons will start collecting data and saving it to the database where the primary logger is currently residing. Statistics collected by CHM can be viewed using a command line interface with oclumon utility.

```
[oracle@ssky1l4p1 ~]$ oclumon manage -get alllogger -details

Logger = ssky1l4p2
Nodes = ssky1l4p2,ssky1l4p1
 [oracle@ssky1l4p1 ~]$ oclumon manage -get master

Master = ssky1l4p2

[oracle@ssky1l4p1 ~]$ oclumon manage -get repsize
CHM Repository Size = 136320

[oracle@ssky1l4p1 ~]$ oclumon manage -get reppath
CHM Repository Path = +GRID_DATA/_MGMTDB/DATAFILE/sysmgmtdata.260.846895815

[oracle@ssky1l4p1 ~]$ oclumon dumpnodeview -n ssky1l4p2
----------------------------------------

Node: ssky1l4p2 Clock: '14-05-24 23.32.53' SerialNo:11894

----------------------------------------
```

SYSTEM:

#pcpus: 12 #vcpus: 12 cpuht: N chipname: Intel(R) cpu: 23.85 cpuq: 1 physmemfree: 150304
physmemtotal: 4050928 mcache: 2640628 swapfree: 5455224 swaptotal: 6094840 hugepagetotal: 0
hugepagefree: 0 hugepagesize: 2048 ior: 94 iow: 579 ios: 66 swpin: 6 swpout: 0 pgin: 83 pgout: 948
netr: 465.167 netw: 426.277 procs: 339 rtprocs: 15 #fds: 27328 #sysfdlimit: 6815744 #disks: 10
#nics: 5 nicErrors: 0

TOP CONSUMERS:

topcpu: 'ora_lms0_sskydb(5719) 9.12' topprivmem: 'ocssd.bin(4772) 85572'
topshm: 'oracle_625_ssky(625) 640124' topfd: 'ocssd.bin(4772) 256' topthread: 'crsd.bin(4889) 40'

Node: ssky1l4p2 Clock: '14-05-24 23.32.58' SerialNo:11895

SYSTEM:

#pcpus: 12 #vcpus: 12 cpuht: N chipname: Intel(R) cpu: 24.22 cpuq: 6 physmemfree: 150552
physmemtotal: 4050928 mcache: 2640644 swapfree: 5455236 swaptotal: 6094840 hugepagetotal: 0
hugepagefree: 0 hugepagesize: 2048 ior: 89 iow: 1347 ios: 96 swpin: 0 swpout: 0 pgin: 92
pgout: 882 netr: 347.712 netw: 602.758 procs: 339 rtprocs: 15 #fds: 27360 #sysfdlimit: 6815744
#disks: 10 #nics: 5 nicErrors: 0

TOP CONSUMERS:

topcpu: 'ora_lms0_sskydb(5719) 5.88' topprivmem: 'ocssd.bin(4772) 85572'
topshm: 'oracle_625_ssky(625) 640124' topfd: 'ocssd.bin(4772) 256' topthread: 'crsd.bin(4889) 40'

Node: ssky1l4p2 Clock: '14-05-24 23.33.03' SerialNo:11896

SYSTEM:

#pcpus: 12 #vcpus: 12 cpuht: N chipname: Intel(R) cpu: 25.57 cpuq: 1 physmemfree: 150408
physmemtotal: 4050928 mcache: 2640664 swapfree: 5455236 swaptotal: 6094840 hugepagetotal: 0
hugepagefree: 0 hugepagesize: 2048 ior: 85 iow: 355 ios: 47 swpin: 0 swpout: 0 pgin: 85 pgout: 324
netr: 347.551 netw: 504.543 procs: 339 rtprocs: 15 #fds: 27360 #sysfdlimit: 6815744 #disks: 10
#nics: 5 nicErrors: 0

TOP CONSUMERS:

topcpu: 'ora_lms0_sskydb(5719) 7.29' topprivmem: 'ocssd.bin(4772) 85572'
topshm: 'oracle_625_ssky(625) 640132' topfd: 'ocssd.bin(4772) 256' topthread: 'crsd.bin(4889) 40'

Node ssky1l4p1 has received several alerts compared to many of the other servers in the cluster. All alerts indicate high I/O wait times, indicating that there is an I/O bottleneck on these devices from this specific node. Bottlenecks such as these indicate I/O problems on the device itself or the components that connect these servers to these disks. Since this is one of the few nodes reporting this problem, the I/O problem may not be with the physical device itself. Further investigation on the I/O paths to the SAN indicated that the system administrators configured only one HBA on node prddb1 while the other servers had four HBAs configured.

```
[root@ssky1l4p1 ~]# /sbin/powermt display
Symmetrix logical device count=0
CLARiiON logical device count=0
Hitachi logical device count=0
Invista logical device count=0
HP xp logical device count=21
Ess logical device count=0
HP HSx logical device count=0
==============================================================================
----- Host Bus Adapters ---------   ------ I/O Paths -----   ------ Stats ------
### HW Path                         Summary  Total  Dead  IO/Sec Q-IOs Errors
==============================================================================
   4 lpfc                           optimal   84     0      -      0     0
```

```
[root@ssky1l4p4 ~]# /sbin/powermt display
Symmetrix logical device count=0
CLARiiON logical device count=0
Hitachi logical device count=0
Invista logical device count=0
HP xp logical device count=21
Ess logical device count=0
HP HSx logical device count=0
==============================================================================
----- Host Bus Adapters ---------   ------ I/O Paths -----   ------ Stats ------
### HW Path                         Summary  Total  Dead  IO/Sec Q-IOs Errors
==============================================================================
   2 lpfc                           optimal   84     0      -      0     0
   3 lpfc                           optimal   84     0      -      0     0
   4 lpfc                           optimal   84     0      -      0     0
   5 lpfc                           optimal   84     0      -      0     0
```

HBA is the primary gateway between the node and the physical disks located on the SAN. Due to limitations on the hardware, it has been observed on several occasions that the number of slots for the host bus adapter (HBA) and the network interface card (NIC) are insufficient to provide a good I/O capacity. The number of ports on a switch and the number of controllers in a disk array should also be considered while tuning I/O capacity. Care should be provided to ensure that the number of HBAs is equal to the number of disk controllers. Using the disk controller slots to accommodate more disk arrays will have a negative impact on the total throughput.

For example, on a 16-port fiber channel switch, the ideal configuration would be to have 8 HBAs and 8 disk controllers, giving a total throughput of 8 * 200MB[3] = 1.6 GB/sec. Now, if the number of HBAs is reduced to 4 to provide room for additional storage, then the total throughput drops down by 50% (4 * 200 MB = 800MB/sec).

---

[3]Assuming the maximum theoretical payload of 2GB/s Fiber Channel is 200MB/sec.

EXPLAIN PLAN

Transactional activity in a system consists of SELECT, INSERT, UPDATE, and DELETE operations. When such an operation is performed, Oracle generates an execution plan for the statement. The execution plan is generated based on the statistics available and the underlying objects such as indexes, number of rows, filtering rules specified in the WHERE clause, etc. It is this execution plan that drives the manner in which data is retrieved from the database. If the performance or response time from the query is high, then based on the explain plan the query should be optimized. Such optimization may be by adding an index, or if the appropriate index is not being used, modifying the query to use the index, or rewriting the query to make it efficient.

An EXPLAIN PLAN for an SQL statement is generated using certain environmental settings such as enabling the AUTOTRACE feature and then executing the statement. The syntax to enable AUTOTRACE is

```
SET AUTOT[RACE] {OFF | ON TRACE[ONLY]} [EXP[LAIN]] [STAT[ISTICS]]
```

To set the AUTOTRACE feature, the user is required to have the PLUSTRACE role. In order to create the PLUSTRACE role, the plustrce.sql script needs to be executed as user sys. This script is located in ORACLE_HOME/sqlplus/admin directory.

The command used to generate the explain is

```
SQL> SET AUTOTRACE TRACEONLY;
SQL> SET TIMING ON;
```

This command sets the environment conditions and required variables. Subsequently, if the SQL statement is executed, the execution plan or explain plan for the statement is generated.

```
SELECT OL_W_ID,
       OL_D_ID,
       OL_NUMBER,
       SUM(OL_AMOUNT),
       SUM(OL_QUANTITY)
FROM   ORDER_LINE OL,
       ORDERS ORD
WHERE  OL.OL_O_ID = ORD.O_ID
  AND  OL.OL_W_ID = ORD.O_W_ID
  AND  OL.OL_D_ID = ORD.O_D_ID
GROUP BY OL_NUMBER,
         OL_W_ID,
         OL_D_ID;

300 rows selected.
Elapsed: 00:02:18.30
Execution Plan
-------------------------------
Plan hash value: 99144695
```

```
----------------------------------------------------------------------------
| Id  | Operation              | Name      |Rows  |Bytes |TempSpc|Cost (%CPU)| Time      |
----------------------------------------------------------------------------
|   0 | SELECT STATEMENT       |           | 150  | 4950 |       |  259K  (1)| 00:51:54 |
|   1 |  HASH GROUP BY         |           | 150  | 4950 |       |  259K  (1)| 00:51:54 |
|*  2 |   HASH JOIN            |           | 42M  |1340M |  94M  |  257K  (1)| 00:51:36 |
|   3 |    INDEX FAST FULL SCAN|ORDERS_I2  |4299K |  45M |       |  5458  (1)| 00:01:06 |
|   4 |    INDEX FAST FULL SCAN|IORDL      | 42M  | 902M |       |  178K  (1)| 00:35:42 |
----------------------------------------------------------------------------

Predicate Information (identified by operation id):
---------------------------------------------------

  2 - access("OL"."OL_O_ID"="ORD"."O_ID" AND "OL"."OL_W_ID"="ORD"."O_W_ID"  AND
            "OL"."OL_D_ID"="ORD"."O_D_ID")

Statistics
----------------------------------------------------------
        727  recursive calls
          0  db block gets
     455937  consistent gets
     455700  physical reads
          0  redo size
      11180  bytes sent via SQL*Net to client
        733  bytes received via SQL*Net from client
         21  SQL*Net roundtrips to/from client
         16  sorts (memory)
          0  sorts (disk)
        300  rows processed
```

■ **Note**   For an explanation on how to interpret the EXPLAIN PLAN for a SQL query, please refer to Metalink note number 46234.1.

DBMS_SQLTUNE

Similar to the explain plan output generated above, a new feature introduced in Oracle Database 11g Release 1 is the DBMS_SQLTUNE package, which contains several procedures providing more opportunities for generating explain plan outputs with more details and, in some cases, output in a graphical form using HTML.

- DBMS_SQLTUNE.REPORT_SQL_MONITOR

The report from this procedure is generated using the following commands:

```
SET LONG 1000000
SET LONGCHUNKSIZE 10000000
SET LINESIZE 200
SELECT DBMS_SQLTUNE.REPORT_SQL_MONITOR FROM DUAL;
```

The output generated from this procedure is similar to the one generated by the explain plan but with some additional information.

```
REPORT_SQL_MONITOR
-------------------------------------------------------------------------------
 Session          :  RAPTEST (642:3)
 SQL ID           :  cavwma8xnrv97
 SQL Execution ID :  16777216
 Execution Started:  04/25/2010 11:08:54
 First Refresh Time: 04/25/2010 11:09:04
 Last Refresh Time:  04/25/2010 11:10:33
 Duration         :  99s
 Module/Action    :  SQL*Plus/-
 Service          :  raptest
 Program          :  sqlplus@prddb1 (TNS V1-V3)
 Fetch Calls      :  21

REPORT_SQL_MONITOR
-------------------------------------------------------------------------------

Global Stats
=================================================================================
| Elapsed | Cpu     |   IO     | Cluster  | Fetch | Buffer | Read | Read  |
| Time(s) | Time(s) | Waits(s) | Waits(s) | Calls | Gets   | Reqs | Bytes |
=================================================================================
|     101 |      61 |       37 |     3.29 |    21 |   456K | 3824 |   3GB |
=================================================================================

SQL Plan Monitoring Details (Plan Hash Value=99144695)
=================================================================================

REPORT_SQL_MONITOR
_____
```

■ **Note**   Output is not shown due to its size.

- `DBMS_SQLTUNE.REPORT_SQL_MONITOR` in a graphical view

Using the same procedure available under `DBMS_SQLTUNE`, the above plan can be displayed in a graphical form (see Figure 6-22) using

```
SELECT  DBMS_SQLTUNE.REPORT_SQL_MONITOR(session_id=>sys_context('userenv','sid'),
report_level=>'ALL') AS report
FROM DUAL;
```

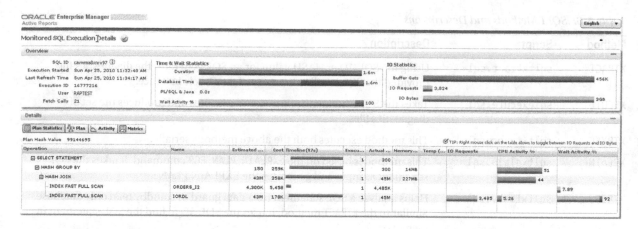

Figure 6-22. *Monitored SQL*

- SELECT DBMS_SQLTUNE.REPORT_SQL_MONITOR when a session is active

Another flavor of this report is to generate this when the session is active using

```
SELECT DBMS_SQLTUNE.REPORT_SQL_MONITOR(type=>'active') FROM DUAL;
```

SQLT

SQLT is a compressive tool/script that will help diagnose why a specific SQL statement may be performing poorly. It takes a single SQL statement (or SQL_ID) as input and outputs a set of diagnostics that can be used to improve the statement's performance.

SQLT provides large amounts of information on a wide range of topics pertinent to that SQL including execution plans, cost-based optimizer CBO statistics, schema objects metadata, performance statistics, configuration parameters, and other elements that influence the performance of the one SQL being analyzed.

The tool and the install guides can be downloaded from Metalink MOS #215187.1

SQLT provides several methods of information extraction. Table 6-6 lists the various methods, scripts, and their description.

Table 6-6. *SQLT Methods and Descriptions*

Method	Script	Description
XTRACT	sqltxtract.sql	Using the SQL_ID or HASH value for an SQL generates the diagnostics file, provided the SQL is still in memory of the Oracle instance.
XECUTE	sqlexecute.sql	Takes the SQL statement as input, and executes and produces the set of diagnostics files.
XTRXEC	sqltxtrxec.sql	This method executes both the above methods serially.
XPLAIN	sqltxplain.sql	This method is based on the EXPLAIN PLAN FOR command. It takes the SQL statement as input and generates the EXPLAIN PLAN.
XTRSBY	sqltxtrsby.sql	Helps analyze a SQL statement on a data guard or standby read only database. Similar to the XTRACT method, it uses the SQL_ID to find the SQL statement in memory.
XPREXT	sqltxperxt.sql	Generates a smaller subset of diagnostics compared to the XTRACT method listed above.
XPREXC	sqltxprexc.sql	Generates a smaller subset of diagnostics information compared to XECUTE method listed above.
COMPARE	sqltcompare.sql	This method helps compare the execution of SQL statements in two different environments. It compares plans, metadata, CBO statistics, and initialization parameters.
TRCANLZR	sqltrcanlzr.sql	It analyzes the trace file for a SQL statement and generates the diagnostics data.
TRCAXTR	sqltrcaxtr.sql	This method does the same as TRCANLZR but when the trace analysis completes, it continues with a XTRACT for the Top SQL found in the trace. Basically it consolidates all the generated reports by TRCANLZR and XTRACT on the Top SQL.
TRCASPLIT	sqltrcasplit.sql	It splits the data contained in 10046 and other trace files.
XTRSET	sqltxtrset.sql	This is a batch method that extracts from memory or AWR a list of SQL statements identified by SQL_ID and executes using the XTRACT method listed earlier each of the SQL statements.
SQLHC[4]	sqlhc.sql	SQLHC is used to check the environment in which a single SQL statement runs, checking CBO statistics, schema object metadata, configuration parameters, and other elements that may influence the performance of the one SQL being analyzed.

SQL Trace

SQL Trace is a utility that comes bundled with the Oracle database software. This utility is used to generate SQL trace information while the database is being used for a specific session. The output generated in the form of trace files from the process contains the execution plans used by the SQL queries.

---

[4]SQLHC is a standalone component of SQLT and can be downloaded from MOS note# 1366133.1.

SQL Trace is generated at the system level by setting the parameter SQL_TRACE = TRUE or at the session level with the following statement:

```
SQL>ALTER SESSION SET SQL_TRACE=TRUE;
```

Either method can be used; however, setting the parameter SQL_TRACE=TRUE will generate trace for all sessions. This can cause performance issues and should only be enabled when there are large numbers of statements having poor performance or when the bad statement cannot be identified. Enabling this parameter at the system level will also generate a significant amount of trace files in the user dump destination directory specified by the USER_DUMP_DEST parameter. The DBA should ensure that there is sufficient space in the user dump destination location before enabling this parameter.

Setting this parameter before executing SQL queries at the session level will generate trace for only queries executed in the session.

The trace files generated are basic raw files and are not easily readable. Oracle provides a utility called TKPROF, which can be used to format the trace files into a more readable form using the following command:

```
Usage: tkprof tracefile outputfile [explain= ] [table= ]
              [print= ] [insert= ] [sys= ] [sort= ]
  table=schema.tablename   Use 'schema.tablename' with 'explain=' option.
  explain=user/password    Connect to ORACLE and issue EXPLAIN PLAN.
  print=integer    List only the first 'integer' SQL statements.
  aggregate=yes|no
  insert=filename  List SQL statements and data inside INSERT statements.
  sys=no           TKPROF does not list SQL statements run as user SYS.
  record=filename  Record non-recursive statements found in the trace file.
  waits=yes|no     Record summary for any wait events found in the trace file.
  sort=option      Set of zero or more of the following sort options:
    prscnt  number of times parse was called
    prscpu  cpu time parsing
    prsela  elapsed time parsing
    prsdsk  number of disk reads during parse
    prsqry  number of buffers for consistent read during parse
    prscu   number of buffers for current read during parse
    prsmis  number of misses in library cache during parse
    execnt  number of execute was called
    execpu  cpu time spent executing
    exeela  elapsed time executing
    exedsk  number of disk reads during execute
    exeqry  number of buffers for consistent read during execute
    execu   number of buffers for current read during execute
    exerow  number of rows processed during execute
    exemis  number of library cache misses during execute
    fchcnt  number of times fetch was called
    fchcpu  cpu time spent fetching
    fchela  elapsed time fetching
    fchdsk  number of disk reads during fetch
    fchqry  number of buffers for consistent read during fetch
    fchcu   number of buffers for current read during fetch
    fchrow  number of rows fetched
    userid  userid of user that parsed the cursor
```

SQL Trace is a simple, straightforward approach to getting to the execution plan generated by Oracle for the various SQL queries. The information provided by these trace files is only minimal. While SQL_TRACE is a good start to getting to the basic execution behavior, it seldom provides any details on the actual reasons for the performance characteristics or the reasons why the optimizer showed a specific behavior during query execution.

Oracle provides certain events that can be enabled at the system or session level to capture information for all sessions or at the session level.

Event 10046

Enabling event 10046 at various levels provides varying details about the execution plans, performance characteristics, and other related information.

Level 1

This is enabled at the system level using

```
ALTER SYSTEM SET EVENTS '10046 TRACE NAME CONTEXT FOREVER, LEVEL 1';
```

or at the session level using

```
ALTER SESSION SET EVENTS '10046 TRACE NAME CONTEXT FOREVER, LEVEL 1';
```

Setting event 10046 at level 1 is equivalent to setting the SQL_TRACE parameter to TRUE in the init<SID>.ora file or turning on trace at a session level. The output produced by this event is generated in the user dump destination directory. The trace file can be interpreted in a more readable format using the TKPROF utility discussed earlier in the "SQL Trace" section.

The following is the output generated by using event 10046 at level 1 on the SQL query used earlier:

call	count	cpu	elapsed	disk	query	current	rows
Parse	1	0.06	0.15	14	170	0	0
Execute	1	0.00	0.00	0	0	0	0
Fetch	21	80.81	137.25	455687	455783	0	300
total	23	80.88	137.41	455701	455953	0	300

```
Misses in library cache during parse: 1
Optimizer mode: ALL_ROWS
Parsing user id: 99 (RAPTEST)
```

```
Rows      Row Source Operation
--------  ---------------------------------------------------
     300  HASH GROUP BY (cr=455783 pr=455687 pw=0 time=299 us cost=259483 size=4950 card=150)
44846573  HASH JOIN (cr=455783 pr=455687 pw=0 time=131297736 us cost=257957 size=1405564479
          card=42592863)
 4484793  INDEX FAST FULL SCAN ORDERS_I2 (cr=15100 pr=15080 pw=0 time=1345898 us cost=5458
          size=47299967 card=4299997)(object id 201148)
44846573  INDEX FAST FULL SCAN IORDL (cr=440683 pr=440607 pw=0 time=81889496 us cost=178429
          size=945961456 card=42998248)(object id 201090)
```

```
Rows       Execution Plan
--------   --------------------------------------------------
       0   SELECT STATEMENT    MODE: ALL_ROWS
     300   HASH (GROUP BY)
44846573   HASH JOIN
 4484793   INDEX    MODE: ANALYZED (FAST FULL SCAN) OF 'ORDERS_I2'
           (INDEX (UNIQUE))
44846573   INDEX    MODE: ANALYZED (FAST FULL SCAN) OF 'IORDL' (INDEX
           (UNIQUE))
```

Interpreting the trace output generated using tkprof:

- Call: Statistics for each cursor's activity are divided in to three areas:

  - Parse: Statistics from parsing the cursor. This includes information for plan generation, etc.

  - Execute: Statistics for the exaction phase of a cursor.

  - Fetch: Statistics for actually fetching the rows.

- Count: Number of times you have performed a particular activity on this particular cursor.

- CPU: CPU time used by this cursor.

- Elapsed: Elapsed time for this cursor.

- Disk: This indicates the number of blocks read from disk. Generally you want to see blocks being read from the buffer cache rather than disk.

- Query: This column is incremented if a buffer is read in consistent mode. A consistent mode buffer is one that has been generated to give a consistent read snapshot for a long running transaction. The buffer actually contains this status in its header.

- Current: This column is incremented if a buffer found in the buffer cache is new enough for the current transaction and is in current mode (and it is not a CR buffer). This applies to buffers that have been read in to the cache as well as buffers that already exist in the cache in current mode.

- Rows: Rows retrieved by this step.

Such detailed information is not found in a regular explain plan created from the AUTOTRACE feature.

Level 4

Level 1 tracing of event 10046 provides the basic SQL queries, sometimes to recreate the issue or to re-execute the query. These basic raw queries and their explain plans are not sufficient, especially if the query is using bind variables. While using bind variables is an excellent practice and should be in the best practices guide of the organization, for debugging and query tuning purposes, it would be helpful to determine the values used during the query execution that showed slower query execution. To determine the bind variables and the corresponding bind values, event 10046 at level 4 captures the information.

Similar to level 1, level 4 can be enabled at the system or session level using the following statements:

```
ALTER SYSTEM SET EVENTS '10046 TRACE NAME CONTEXT FOREVER, LEVEL 4';
ALTER SESSION SET EVENTS '10046 TRACE NAME CONTEXT FOREVER, LEVEL 4';
```

Level 8

Many times the query performs badly due to several reasons other than the way in which the query is written itself. For example, slow performance could be due to the way the table has been stored on disk, poor distribution of data on the disk, too many tables sharing the same data files, data heavily scattered or the query performing full table scans, waiting for resources. SQL could be efficient but due to contention for resources could increase response time. Under such circumstances, it is best to understand what type of resources the system is waiting on. This information can be obtained using level 8.

Similar to level 1 and level 4, level 8 can be enabled at the system or session levels through the following statements:

```
ALTER SYSTEM SET EVENTS '10046 TRACE NAME CONTEXT FOREVER, LEVEL 8';
ALTER SESSION SET EVENTS '10046 TRACE NAME CONTEXT FOREVER, LEVEL 8';
```

The following is the additional information generated by event 10046 at level 8:

```
Elapsed times include waiting on following events:
  Event waited on                      Times     Max. Wait  Total Waited
  ----------------------------------   Waited    ---------  ------------
  ges message buffer allocation        25636       0.00         0.08
  library cache lock                       2       0.00         0.00
  row cache lock                          18       0.00         0.00
  library cache pin                        1       0.00         0.00
  SQL*Net message to client               21       0.00         0.00
  Disk file operations I/O                 1       0.00         0.00
  gc cr grant 2-way                        2       0.00         0.00
  KSV master wait                          2       0.00         0.00
  ASM file metadata operation              2       0.00         0.00
  db file sequential read                  4       0.01         0.02
  gc cr multi block request            33403       0.00         1.73
  db file scattered read                3796       0.12        56.25
  asynch descriptor resize                 2       0.00         0.00
  db file parallel read                    1       0.00         0.00
  latch free                               1       0.00         0.00
  SQL*Net message from client             21       0.24         0.25
```

The above output lists the various wait events encountered during the query execution. Now from the above it is certain that there are several waits that could have caused a performance slowdown for the query and query itself may not be the problem. For example, the highest value in the Total Waited column is for a `gc cr multi-block request`.

Level 12

Level 12 provides a combined output of all the above levels. At this level, the execution plans, bind variables, bind values (generated with level 4), and the wait events (generated with level 8) are generated in the trace files. Most often, enabling event 10046 at level 12 will provide a comprehensive method of looking at the problem at hand. However, the output generated at this level can be large and may require considerable amount of disk space. Enabling trace at this level should be done only after ensuring sufficient space is available.

Similar to the other levels, level 12 can be enabled at the system or session levels through the following statements:

```
ALTER SYSTEM SET EVENTS '10046 TRACE NAME CONTEXT FOREVER, LEVEL 12';
ALTER SESSION SET EVENTS '10046 TRACE NAME CONTEXT FOREVER, LEVEL 12';
```

Event 10053

Sometimes, when a query is being tuned and after generating the explain plan and trace files, turning on event 10046, looking at wait statistics, and so forth, questions can arise. For example, why is the execution plan being generated in this fashion? Or why is the runtime performance different from executing this from a SQL*Plus session during query tuning?

Under these circumstances, turning on event 10053 will capture the actual steps that the CBO had taken to generate the execution plan.

Enabling event 10053 is similar to enabling any other event, such as using an ALTER SYSTEM or ALTER SESSION statement. However, unlike event 10046, which was discussed in the previous section, event 10053 can generate trace information only at two levels, level 1 and level 2.

```
ALTER SYSTEM SET EVENTS '10053 TRACE NAME CONTEXT FOREVER, LEVEL 1';
ALTER SESSION SET EVENTS '10053 TRACE NAME CONTEXT FOREVER, LEVEL 1';
```

The following is a partial output of the optimizer behavior generated from event 10053 at level 1:

```
.................................................
.................................................

OPTIMIZER STATISTICS AND COMPUTATIONS
**************************************
GENERAL PLANS
**************************************
Considering cardinality-based initial join order.
Permutations for Starting Table :0
Join order[1]:  ORDERS[ORD]#0  ORDER_LINE[OL]#1

***************
Now joining: ORDER_LINE[OL]#1
***************
NL Join
  Outer table: Card: 4299997.00  Cost: 5458.23  Resp: 5458.23  Degree: 1  Bytes: 11
Access path analysis for ORDER_LINE
  Access Path: index (index (FFS))
    Index: IORDL
    resc_io: 178117.88  resc_cpu: 9843318719
    ix_sel: 0.000000  ix_sel_with_filters: 1.000000
  Inner table: ORDER_LINE  Alias: OL
  Access Path: index (FFS)
    NL Join:  Cost: 767233834757.07  Resp: 767233834757.07  Degree: 1
      Cost_io: 765906333586.00  Cost_cpu: 42326241606806912
      Resp_io: 765906333586.00  Resp_cpu: 42326241606806912
OPTIMIZER PERCENT INDEX CACHING = 0
  ColGroup Usage:: PredCnt: 3  Matches Full:  Partial:
  ColGroup Usage:: PredCnt: 3  Matches Full:  Partial:
  Access Path: index (IndexOnly)
    Index: IORDL
    resc_io: 3.00  resc_cpu: 24214
```

```
      ix_sel: 0.000000  ix_sel_with_filters: 0.000000
      NL Join (ordered): Cost: 4950360.85  Resp: 4950360.85  Degree: 1
        Cost_io: 4947075.00  Cost_cpu: 104766394419
        Resp_io: 4947075.00  Resp_cpu: 104766394419


  Best NL cost: 4950360.85
          resc: 4950360.85  resc_io: 4947075.00  resc_cpu: 104766394419
          resp: 4950360.85  resp_io: 4947075.00  resc_cpu: 104766394419
Join selectivity using 1 ColGroups: 0.000000 (sel1 = 0.000000, sel2 = 0.000000)
Join Card:  42592862.717274 = = outer (4299997.000000) * inner (42998248.000000) * sel (0.000000)
Join Card - Rounded: 42592863 Computed: 42592862.72
Grouping column cardinality [ OL_NUMBER]    15
Grouping column cardinality [   OL_W_ID]     2
Grouping column cardinality [   OL_D_ID]    10
  Outer table:  ORDERS  Alias: ORD
    resc: 5458.23  card 4299997.00 bytes: 11  deg: 1  resp: 5458.23
  Inner table:  ORDER_LINE  Alias: OL
    resc: 178428.72 card: 42998248.00 bytes: 22 deg: 1 resp: 178428.72
    using dmeth: 2  #groups: 1
    SORT ressource        Sort statistics
      Sort width: 6142 Area size: 1048576 Max Area size:  1073741824
      Degree:              1
      Blocks to Sort: 12109 Row size:     23 Total Rows:      4299997
      Initial runs:   2 Merge passes:  1 IO Cost / pass:      6560
      Total IO sort cost: 18669    Total CPU sort cost: 4599195307
      Total Temp space used: 207234000
    SORT ressource        Sort statistics
      Sort width: 6142 Area size:  1048576 Max Area size: 1073741824
      Degree:                1
      Blocks to Sort: 184249 Row size: 35 Total Rows: 42998248
      Initial runs: 2 Merge passes: 1 IO Cost / pass: 99804
      Total IO sort cost: 284053  Total CPU sort cost: 53693990840
      Total Temp space used: 3453363000
  SM join: Resc: 488437.23  Resp: 488437.23  [multiMatchCost=0.00]
SM Join
  SM cost: 488437.23
    resc: 488437.23 resc_io: 486280.00 resc_cpu: 68781395928
    resp: 488437.23 resp_io: 486280.00 resp_cpu: 68781395928
  Outer table:  ORDERS  Alias: ORD
    resc: 5458.23  card 4299997.00 bytes: 11  deg: 1  resp: 5458.23
  Inner table:  ORDER_LINE  Alias: OL
    resc: 178428.72 card: 42998248.00 bytes: 22 deg: 1 resp: 178428.72
    using dmeth: 2  #groups: 1
    Cost per ptn: 74069.96  #ptns: 1
    hash_area: 256 (max=262144) buildfrag: 12073  probefrag: 178460  ppasses: 1
  Hash join: Resc: 257956.91  Resp: 257956.91  [multiMatchCost=0.00]
HA Join
  HA cost: 257956.91
    resc: 257956.91 resc_io: 257313.00 resc_cpu: 20530453418
    resp: 257956.91 resp_io: 257313.00 resp_cpu: 20530453418
```

```
GROUP BY sort
  ColGroup Usage:: PredCnt: 3  Matches Full:  Partial:
GROUP BY adjustment factor: 0.500000
GROUP BY cardinality:  150.000000, TABLE cardinality: 42592863.000000
    SORT ressource          Sort statistics
      Sort width: 6142 Area size: 1048576 Max Area size:  1073741824
      Degree:   1
      Blocks to Sort: 245087 Row size: 47 Total Rows: 42592863
      Initial runs:   1 Merge passes:  0 IO Cost / pass:    0
      Total IO sort cost: 0       Total CPU sort cost: 48667303854
      Total Temp space used: 0
Best:: JoinMethod: Hash
        Cost: 259483.29  Degree: 1 Resp: 259483.29  Card: 42592862.72 Bytes: 33
***********************
```

Best so far: Table#:0 cost:5458.2261 card: 4299997.0000 bytes: 47299967
**   Table#:1 cost:259483.2873 card: 42592862.7173 bytes: 1405564479**

```
***********************
Join order[2]:  ORDER_LINE[OL]#1  ORDERS[ORD]#0


***************
Now joining: ORDERS[ORD]#0
***************
NL Join
  Outer table: Card: 42998248.00  Cost: 178428.72  Resp: 178428.72  Degree: 1  Bytes: 22
Access path analysis for ORDERS
  Inner table: ORDERS Alias: ORD
  Access Path: TableScan
    NL Join:  Cost: 249713973874.97  Resp: 249713973874.97  Degree: 1
      Cost_io: 248407327395.00  Cost_cpu: 41661307584008368
      Resp_io: 248407327395.00  Resp_cpu: 41661307584008368
  Access Path: index (index (FFS))
    Index: ORDERS_I1
    resc_io: 9870.79  resc_cpu: 780458762
    ix_sel: 0.000000  ix_sel_with_filters: 1.000000
  Inner table: ORDERS Alias: ORD
  Access Path: index (FFS)
    NL Join:  Cost: 425479435734.14  Resp: 425479435734.14  Degree: 1
      Cost_io: 424426926161.00  Cost_cpu: 33558369255887276
      Resp_io: 424426926161.00  Resp_cpu: 33558369255887276
  Access Path: index (index (FFS))
    Index: ORDERS_I2
    resc_io: 5435.90  resc_cpu: 644891062
    ix_sel: 0.000000  ix_sel_with_filters: 1.000000
  Inner table: ORDERS  Alias: ORD
  Access Path: index (FFS)
    NL Join:  Cost: 234603861264.23  Resp: 234603861264.23  Degree: 1
      Cost_io: 233734175265.00  Cost_cpu: 27729195670497676
      Resp_io: 233734175265.00  Resp_cpu: 27729195670497676
  Access Path: index (UniqueScan)
    Index: ORDERS_I1
    resc_io: 1.00  resc_cpu: 9021
```

```
          ix_sel: 0.000000  ix_sel_with_filters: 0.000000
        NL Join (ordered): Cost: 43188842.83  Resp: 43188842.83  Degree: 1
          Cost_io: 43176368.00  Cost_cpu: 397749433156
          Resp_io: 43176368.00  Resp_cpu: 397749433156
kkofmx: index filter:"OL"."OL_O_ID"="ORD"."O_ID"

  ColGroup Usage:: PredCnt: 3  Matches Full:  Partial:
  ColGroup Usage:: PredCnt: 3  Matches Full:  Partial:
  Access Path: index (AllEqUnique)
    Index: ORDERS_I1
    resc_io: 1.00  resc_cpu: 9021
    ix_sel: 0.000000  ix_sel_with_filters: 0.000000
    NL Join (ordered): Cost: 43188842.83  Resp: 43188842.83  Degree: 1
      Cost_io: 43176368.00  Cost_cpu: 397749433156
      Resp_io: 43176368.00  Resp_cpu: 397749433156
  ColGroup Usage:: PredCnt: 2  Matches Full:  Partial:
  ColGroup Usage:: PredCnt: 3  Matches Full:  Partial:
  Access Path: index (IndexOnly)
    Index: ORDERS_I2
    resc_io: 1033.00  resc_cpu: 50357298
    ix_sel: 0.051399  ix_sel_with_filters: 0.000000
***** Logdef predicate Adjustment ******
Final IO cst 0.00 , CPU cst 0.00
***** End Logdef Adjustment ******
    NL Join (ordered): Cost: 44442301374.02  Resp: 44442301374.02  Degree: 1
      Cost_io: 44374390338.00  Cost_cpu: 2165285410693464
      Resp_io: 44374390338.00  Resp_cpu: 2165285410693464
****** trying bitmap/domain indexes ******
****** finished trying bitmap/domain indexes ******


  Best NL cost: 43188842.83
          resc: 43188842.83 resc_io: 43176368.00 resc_cpu: 397749433156
          resp: 43188842.83 resp_io: 43176368.00 resc_cpu: 397749433156
Join selectivity using 1 ColGroups: 0.000000 (sel1 = 0.000000, sel2 = 0.000000)
Join Card:  42592862.717274 = = outer (42998248.000000) * inner (4299997.000000) * sel (0.000000)
Join Card - Rounded: 42592863 Computed: 42592862.72
Grouping column cardinality [ OL_NUMBER]    15
Grouping column cardinality [   OL_W_ID]     2
Grouping column cardinality [   OL_D_ID]    10
  Outer table:  ORDER_LINE  Alias: OL
    resc: 178428.72 card 42998248.00 bytes: 22 deg: 1 resp: 178428.72
  Inner table:  ORDERS  Alias: ORD
    resc: 5458.23  card: 4299997.00  bytes: 11 deg: 1 resp: 5458.23
    using dmeth: 2  #groups: 1
    SORT ressource    Sort statistics
      Sort width: 6142 Area size: 1048576 Max Area size:  1073741824
      Degree:               1
      Blocks to Sort: 184249 Row size: 35 Total Rows: 42998248
      Initial runs: 2 Merge passes:  1 IO Cost / pass:  99804
      Total IO sort cost: 284053  Total CPU sort cost: 53693990840
      Total Temp space used: 3453363000
```

```
    SORT ressource    Sort statistics
      Sort width: 6142 Area size: 1048576 Max Area size: 1073741824
      Degree:              1
      Blocks to Sort: 12109 Row size: 23 Total Rows:  4299997
      Initial runs:    2 Merge passes:  1 IO Cost / pass: 6560
      Total IO sort cost: 18669        Total CPU sort cost: 4599195307
      Total Temp space used: 207234000
  SM join: Resc: 488437.23  Resp: 488437.23  [multiMatchCost=0.00]
SM Join
  SM cost: 488437.23
    resc: 488437.23 resc_io: 486280.00 resc_cpu: 68781395928
    resp: 488437.23 resp_io: 486280.00 resp_cpu: 68781395928
  Outer table:  ORDER_LINE  Alias: OL
    resc: 178428.72 card 42998248.00 bytes: 22 deg: 1 resp: 178428.72
  Inner table:  ORDERS  Alias: ORD
    resc: 5458.23  card: 4299997.00 bytes: 11 deg: 1 resp: 5458.23
    using dmeth: 2 #groups: 1
    Cost per ptn: 74009.27 #ptns: 1
    hash_area: 256 (max=262144) buildfrag: 178460  probefrag: 12073 ppasses: 1
  Hash join: Resc: 258016.32  Resp: 258016.32  [multiMatchCost=120.10]
  Outer table:  ORDERS  Alias: ORD
    resc: 5458.23  card 4299997.00  bytes: 11  deg: 1 resp: 5458.23
  Inner table:  ORDER_LINE  Alias: OL
    resc: 178428.72 card: 42998248.00 bytes: 22 deg: 1 resp: 178428.72
    using dmeth: 2 #groups: 1
    Cost per ptn: 74069.96 #ptns: 1
    hash_area: 256 (max=262144) buildfrag: 12073 probefrag: 178460  ppasses: 1
  Hash join: Resc: 257956.91  Resp: 257956.91  [multiMatchCost=0.00]
HA Join
  HA cost: 257956.91 swapped
    resc: 257956.91 resc_io: 257313.00 resc_cpu: 20530453418
    resp: 257956.91 resp_io: 257313.00 resp_cpu: 20530453418
GROUP BY sort
  ColGroup Usage:: PredCnt: 3  Matches Full:  Partial:
GROUP BY adjustment factor: 0.500000
GROUP BY cardinality:  150.000000, TABLE cardinality:  42592863.000000
    SORT ressource    Sort statistics
      Sort width: 6142 Area size: 1048576 Max Area size: 1073741824
      Degree:              1
      Blocks to Sort: 245087 Row size: 47 Total Rows: 42592863
      Initial runs:    1 Merge passes:  0 IO Cost / pass: 0
      Total IO sort cost: 0       Total CPU sort cost: 48667303854
      Total Temp space used: 0
Join order aborted: cost > best plan cost
***********************
(newjo-stop-1) k:0, spcnt:0, perm:2, maxperm:2000
```

```
*********************************
Number of join permutations tried: 2
*********************************
Consider using bloom filter between ORD[ORDERS] and OL[ORDER_LINE]
kkoBloomFilter: join ndv:0 reduction:1.000000 (limit:0.500000)  rejected because no single-tables
predicates
(newjo-save)    [0 1 ]
  ColGroup Usage:: PredCnt: 3  Matches Full:  Partial:
GROUP BY adjustment factor: 0.500000
GROUP BY cardinality:  150.000000, TABLE cardinality:  42592863.000000
    SORT ressource      Sort statistics
        Sort width: 6142 Area size: 1048576 Max Area size:  1073741824
        Degree:   1
        Blocks to Sort: 245087 Row size: 47 Total Rows:  42592863
        Initial runs:   1 Merge passes:  0 IO Cost / pass:  0
        Total IO sort cost: 0       Total CPU sort cost: 48667303854
        Total Temp space used: 0
Trying or-Expansion on query block SEL$1 (#1)
Transfer Optimizer annotations for query block SEL$1 (#1)
id=0 frofkksm[i] (sort-merge/hash) predicate="OL"."OL_O_ID"="ORD"."O_ID"
id=0 frofkksm[i] (sort-merge/hash) predicate="OL"."OL_W_ID"="ORD"."O_W_ID"
id=0 frofkksm[i] (sort-merge/hash) predicate="OL"."OL_D_ID"="ORD"."O_D_ID"
id=0 frosand (sort-merge/hash) predicate="OL"."OL_D_ID"="ORD"."O_D_ID" AND "OL"."OL_W_
ID"="ORD"."O_W_ID" AND "OL"."OL_O_ID"="ORD"."O_ID"
  ColGroup Usage:: PredCnt: 3  Matches Full:  Partial:
GROUP BY adjustment factor: 1.000000
Final cost for query block SEL$1 (#1) - All Rows Plan:
  Best join order: 1
  Cost: 259483.2873  Degree: 1  Card: 42592863.0000  Bytes: 1405564479
  Resc: 259483.2873  Resc_io: 257313.0000  Resc_cpu: 69197757272
  Resp: 259483.2873  Resp_io: 257313.0000  Resc_cpu: 69197757272
kkoqbc-subheap (delete addr=0x2b25e4dc7a40, in-use=55944, alloc=59112)
kkoqbc-end:
        :
    call(in-use=186432, alloc=259112), compile(in-use=322912, alloc=370520), execution(in-use=4104,
alloc=8088)

kkoqbc: finish optimizing query block SEL$1 (#1)
apadrv-end
```

The trace output from event 10053 illustrates how the CBO actually performs the cost computation process during the generation of an execution plan for a query.

For example, in the above illustration, the first join order is similar to what was specified in the SQL query.

```
Join order[1]:  ORDERS[ORD]#0  ORDER_LINE[OL]#1
```

Subsequently, Oracle creates a different join order and calculates its cost of its execution path.

```
Join order[2]:  ORDER_LINE[OL]#1  ORDERS[ORD]#0
```

For every join operation Oracle computes the cost of accessing the rows for a nested loop join (NL join), sort merge join (SM join), and hash join (HA join) operation. From these three access methods Oracle selects the operation that takes the least cost for execution. This is illustrated by the best so far after each join order cost computation.

```
***********************
Best so far: Table#:0 cost:5458.2261  card:4299997.0000  bytes:47299967
             Table#:1 cost:259483.2873 card:42592862.7173 bytes:1405564479
***********************
```

For the query used in this illustration, Oracle created 14 different join order checks (not all join orders have been illustrated for formatting and easy understanding purposes). However, if the best cost computed for a specific join order is not better than the next, Oracle does not calculate the best cost for the specific join order.

■ **Note**   In complex queries where there are several tables being joined, Oracle has to compute join orders for all possible table orders, which can be time-consuming. If queries are not being reused, which happens, for example, when literals instead of bind variables are used, Oracle will have to compute these join orders every single time and could create more severe performance problems.

Similarly to avoiding several join orders in a complex query with several table joins, the /*ORDERED*/ hint becomes very helpful. This hint will enforce the join order, and the optimizer, based on the hint, will use the user-specified join order for query execution.

Service-Module-Action

Oracle allows statistics collection at the following different levels:

- *At the system level*: Statistics from the time the instance was started can be collected and viewed from V$SYSSTAT or GV$SYSSTAT views.

- *At the session level*: Statistics for the active sessions can be collected and viewed from V$SESSTAT or GV$SESSSTAT views. Due to the volatile nature of the sessions, the life of statistics in these views is retained only for the life of the session. Statistics for the expired sessions can be viewed from V$ACTIVE_SESSION_HISTORY.

- *At the service level*: Sessions performing a similar kind of functionality can be grouped into database services. A service can be a subset of an application. This grouping provides a more granular instrumentation into the performance of these sessions when compared to the entire application. Statistics at the service level can be collected and viewed from the V$SERVICE_STATS view.

Oracle provides an additional level of data collection by defining modules within services or actions within modules. This helps in easy identification of performance areas within the application. Module and action level monitoring can be enabled using the following PL/SQL definition:

```
DBMS_MONITOR.SERV_MOD_ACT_STAT_ENABLE (<SERVICE_NAME>, <MODULE NAME>)
```

For example, to enable statistics collection for module Process Orders in service TAPS, the following should be executed on the database server on any one of the available instances:

```
SQL> EXEC  DBMS_MONITOR.SERV_MOD_ACT_STAT_ENABLE ('TAPS','Process Orders');
```

Once monitoring has been enabled, it remains active until such time as it is disabled using the following procedure:

```
EXEC DBMS_MONITOR.SERV_MOD_ACT_STAT_DISABLE (null,null);
```

These definitions can be verified by querying the DBA_ENABLED_AGGREGATIONS table.

```
Script:  MVRACPDnTap_enableAgg.sql
SELECT AGGREGATION_TYPE,
       QUALIFIER_ID1 MODULE,
       QUALIFIER_ID2 ACTION
FROM DBA_ENABLED_AGGREGATIONS;
AGGREGATION_TYPE       MODULE                  ACTION
--------------------   --------------------    ------
SERVICE_MODULE         Process Orders
```

Before monitoring the performance statistics, the application connecting to the database should connect to the SERVICE_NAME being monitored and the application should have the module identified in the code. The module name can be set in the application using the following procedure:

```
DBMS_APPLICATION_INFO.SET_MODULE (<MODULE NAME>, <ACTION TYPE>);
```

For example, to let the database know which module is being monitored, the following procedure should be executed from inside the application module:

```
EXEC DBMS_APPLICATION_INFO.SET_MODULE ('Process Orders');
```

Apart from monitoring individual modules, performance-related statistics can also be collected for any specific action. For example, to monitor the performance of various users executing update statements, you can execute the following procedure:

```
SQL> EXEC DBMS_MONITOR.SERV_MOD_ACT_STAT_ENABLE ('TAPS','Process Orders','UPDATE');
```

This feature of collecting a performance matrix for an action type within a module was not available until Oracle Database 10g and is a great feature that can be easily used. In a RAC environment where workload is distributed across multiple instances in the cluster, this helps collect statistics for a given module across the cluster.

Once the statistics collection has been enabled on the database server and on the client side, the performance metrics can be collected or monitored. For example, the output from the following script against the GV$SERVICE_STATS view provides a high level indication that lowercase "time" to match the other two uses? for TAPS on instance 1 is significantly high.

```
Script: MVRACPDnTap_ServiceStats.sql
SELECT INST_ID INT,
       SERVICE_NAME SERVICE,
       STAT_NAME,
       VALUE
FROM   GV$SERVICE_STATS
WHERE  VALUE > 0
AND    SERVICE_NAME ='TAPS'
ORDER  BY INST_ID,VALUE;
```

INT	SERVICE	STAT_NAME	VALUE
1	TAPS	gc current blocks received	416271
	TAPS	gc current block receive time	425438
	TAPS	gc cr block receive time	718109
	TAPS	user commits	809199
	TAPS	gc cr blocks received	1095112
	TAPS	parse count (total)	1200805
	TAPS	user calls	1204285
	TAPS	session cursor cache hits	3216342
	TAPS	execute count	4008106
	TAPS	application wait time	4256936
	TAPS	opened cursors cumulative	4864680
	TAPS	db block changes	5257103
	TAPS	parse time elapsed	77470767
	TAPS	user I/O wait time	221427713
	TAPS	redo size	749127052
	TAPS	session logical reads	2771428476
	TAPS	concurrency wait time	26596215043
	TAPS	cluster wait time	30073988481
	TAPS	DB CPU	53958463764
	TAPS	sql execute elapsed time	140380379249
	TAPS	DB time	151669575163

To identify the module and action type that caused the high DB time values, use the following script against the view GV$SERV_MOD_ACT_STATS:

```
Script: MVRACPDnTap_ServModActStats.sql
SELECT INST_ID INT,
       AGGREGATION_TYPE,
       SERVICE_NAME SERVICE,
       MODULE,
       ACTION,
       STAT_NAME,
       VALUE
FROM  GV$SERV_MOD_ACT_STATS
WHERE VALUE > 0
ORDER BY INST_ID,VALUE DESC;
```

Service, module, and action level statistics illustrated in Figure 6-23 can be viewed from the Enterprise Manager under the Top Consumers section.

Top Consumers

| Overview | Top Services | Top Modules | Top Actions | Top Clients | Top Sessions |

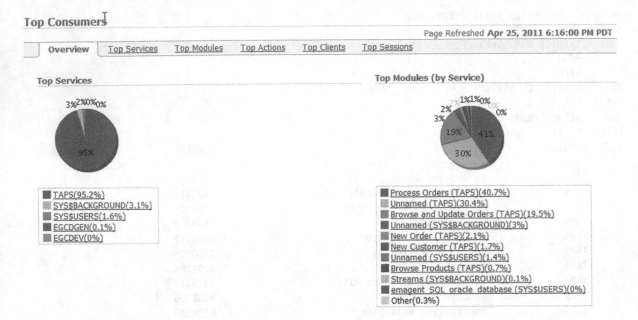

Figure 6-23. OEM - Top Consumers chart

The benefit provided for monitoring activity at the service level does not stop here. Tracing user operations is also available at the module and action level. Oracle generates one trace file per session connecting to the database using the SERVICE_NAME. Users connecting to the database may get attached to any one of the available instances supporting the service. The advantage of tracing at this level is when multiple trace files are generated from the current instance or across instances in the cluster. Data related to a specific action type can be grouped together. For example, the following procedure will enable tracing of a service at the module and action level:

```
DBMS_MONITOR.SERV_MOD_ACT_TRACE_ENABLE (<SERVICE_NAME>,<MODULE NAME>,<ACTION TYPE>);
SQL> EXEC DBMS_MONITOR.SERV_MOD_ACT_TRACE_ENABLE ('TAPS','Process Orders','UPDATE');
```

Apart from the basic SQL level trace information, additional information such as wait events encountered (collected by default), bind variables, and values used, etc. can also be collected. For example,

```
EXEC DBMS_MONITOR.SERV_MOD_ACT_TRACE_ENABLE (
  SERVICE_NAME => 'TAPS',
  MODULE_NAME  => 'Process Orders',
  ACTION_NAME  => DBMS_MONITOR.ALL_ACTIONS,
  WAITS        => TRUE,
  BINDS        => TRUE);
```

■ **Note**   The SERV_MOD_ACT_TRACE_ENABLE utility generates trace files similar to the trace files generated using event 10406 at level 1. Enabling wait events and binds will be similar to generating tracing using 10406 at level 12.

Once these procedures are executed on the database server, the trace files are generated in the USER_DUMP_DEST directory on the respective instances. Oracle generates one trace file for every session connecting to the database using the service TAPS. The trace files can then be consolidated based on different criteria.

The trcsess Utility

In a RAC environment, user sessions can connect to any one or more instances (through parallel slaves). When trace files are enabled at the service level, they can be generated in one or more instances where the database service is currently configured. Generating individual reports from these trace files and analyzing them one by one can be a cumbersome operation. Oracle provides a utility called trcsess (illustrated in Figure 6-24) that can be used to consolidate these trace files based on any one of the following criteria:

- Session ID
- Client ID
- Service Name
- Action Name
- Module Name

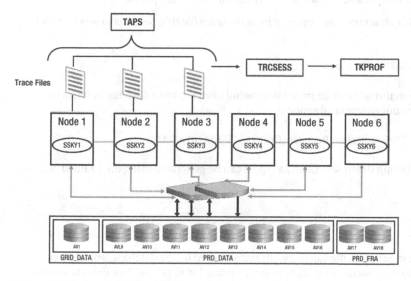

Figure 6-24. *trcsess Utility*

■ **Note**   Client ID, Service Name, Action Name, Module Name, etc. are set in the application using the DBMS_APPLICATION_INFO package.

Based on the example, the trace file will contain information (SQL statements, wait events encountered, bind variables, and bind values). This trace information can be scanned through and extracted by action type using the trcsess utility, and once extracted into a single file, it can be analyzed using the tkprof utility.

```
trcsess output=trcUPDATE.trc service=TAPS module='Process Orders' action=UPDATE  SSKY1_ora_*.trc
trcsess [output=<output file name >]  [session=<session ID>] [clientid=<clientid>]
[service=<service name>] [action=<action name>] [module=<module name>] <trace file names>
```

The parameters with a short description, used to generate the output using trcess, are listed below:

- <output file name> output destination default being standard output.
- <sessionID> session to be traced. Session id is a combination of session index and session serial number.
- <clientid> to be traced.
- <service name> service to be traced.
- <action name> action to be traced.
- <module name> module to be traced.
- <trace file names> is a space-separated list of trace files with wild card * supported.

The following trcsess command will extract trace information from the trace file that pertains to service SRV1 but contains all modules and actions:

```
trcsess output=trcTAPS.trc service=TAPS SSKY1_ora*.trc
```

Similarly, the following trcsess command will extract trace information from the trace files that pertains to service TAPS and module 'Process Orders' but contains all actions:

```
trcsess output=trcRead.trc service=TAPS module='Process Orders' SSKY1_ora*.trc
```

Once the trace files are consolidated using the trcsess utility, a report can be generated using the TKPROF utility discussed earlier.

Oracle's Wait Interface

In the AWR report discussions earlier, we mentioned the top five waits encountered by the database/application during a specific snapshot period. We also discussed collecting wait events using 10046 at level 8 earlier. These wait events are retrieved by the AWR process from certain data dictionary views and stored in AWR-specific tables.

Oracle's wait interface (OWI) helps to identify all wait events. This helps track the number of waits and the amount of time waited for each event throughout the life of a session.

The data dictionary views that comprise the wait interface include

- GV$SYSTEM_EVENT
- GV$SESSION_EVENT
- GV$SESSION_WAIT
- GV$EVENT_NAME

Unlike the AWR report that only reports information at the overall system level for the period of a snapshot, data dictionary views such as the GV$SESSION_EVENT and GV$SESSION_WAIT provide information at the session level.

■ **Note** The value of WAITING in the STATUS column in the GV$SESSION_WAIT view indicates that the session is currently waiting for resources. In all other cases, it indicates that the session in utilizing CPU.

Unlike the information in the GV$SYSTEM_EVENT, which is retained until the instance is bounced, the data available in session views is lost after the session has disconnected from the database. Due to the dynamic nature of these views and due to short span of a session's existence, collecting data from these views by querying them directly may be difficult. Starting with Oracle Database10g, the session history information can be retrieved from ASH views. The workaround to using this view is to capture the data in these views and store it in user-defined tables.

In order to retain the session statistics it is required that these statistics be written to a separate table before the session disconnects from the database. This can be implemented using the BEFORE LOGOFF ON DATABASE trigger. The BEFORE LOGOFF ON DATABASE trigger is created at the database level and is configured to capture all events from the session-related views and insert them into their respective tables.

```
COL EVENT# FORMAT 9999
COL NAME FORMAT A30
COL PARAMETER1 FORMAT A12
COL PARAMETER2 FORMAT A12
COL PARAMETER3 FORMAT A12
SELECT
EVENT#,
NAME,
PARAMETER1,
PARAMETER2,
PARAMETER3
FROM GV$EVENT_NAME
WHERE (NAME LIKE 'db%'
OR NAME LIKE '%parse%'
OR NAME LIKE '%cpu%'
OR NAME LIKE '%global%'
OR NAME LIKE 'gc%')
/
```

The next step is to identify the actual files and the tablespaces that map to these events. Once the tablespaces are identified, the next step is to identify which tables or indexes are contained in these tablespaces.

As illustrated below by querying the V$DATAFILE, V$TABLESPACE and DBA_TABLES view, the files are shared by more than one table:

```
COL FILE# FORMAT 9999
COL FNAME FORMAT A44
COL TNAME FORMAT A25
COL TABLE_NAME FORMAT A30
SELECT
        F.FILE#,
          F.NAME FNAME,
          T.NAME TNAME,
        TABLE_NAME
FROM  V$DATAFILE F,
      V$TABLESPACE T,
      DBA_TABLES
```

```
WHERE F.TS#=T.TS#
AND  (F.FILE#=??
OR   F.FILE#=??)
AND   T.NAME = TABLESPACE_NAME
```

FILE#	FNAME	TNAME	TABLE_NAME
11	+EGCDEV_DATA/egcdev/datafile/raptest.275.745061089	RAPTEST	CUSTOMER
11	+EGCDEV_DATA/egcdev/datafile/raptest.275.745061089	RAPTEST	CUSTOMER
13	+EGCDEV_DATA/egcdev/datafile/raptest.277.747755595	RAPTEST	CUSTOMER
13	+EGCDEV_DATA/egcdev/datafile/raptest.277.747755595	RAPTEST	CUSTOMER
14	+EGCDEV_DATA/egcdev/datafile/raptest.279.748210755	RAPTEST	CUSTOMER
14	+EGCDEV_DATA/egcdev/datafile/raptest.279.748210755	RAPTEST	CUSTOMER
13	+EGCDEV_DATA/egcdev/datafile/raptest.277.747755595	RAPTEST	CUSTOMERS
11	+EGCDEV_DATA/egcdev/datafile/raptest.275.745061089	RAPTEST	CUSTOMERS
14	+EGCDEV_DATA/egcdev/datafile/raptest.279.748210755	RAPTEST	CUSTOMERS
11	+EGCDEV_DATA/egcdev/datafile/raptest.275.745061089	RAPTEST	DISTRICT

Occasional contentions need not be of concern. However, if this contention is repeatable, the reasons need to be identified. From the above analysis there are two potential areas where the problem could be mapped. Either the contention is because the raw device partition is mapped to the same set of disks or it is because the tables are hot tables and need to be moved into their respective tablespaces to use different files to store the data.

So far we have discussed the OWI with respect to the database, in the sense that it concerns the information reported by GV$SESSION_EVENT, GV$SYSTEM_EVENT, and GV$SESSION_WAIT. These wait activities more or less relate to the database configuration or the behavior of SQL queries or the distribution of data in the database.

It is not just the database and the data that can report issues concerning bad performance; performance data from the operating system can also help in troubleshooting and problem solving. The OWI reports on system-level activities or waits at the system level such as CPU, memory, etc. Similar to the database statistics reported by the other three views, the wait activities for the CPU and memory can be obtained by querying the GV$SYSSTAT and GV$SESSTAT.

Similar to the GV$SYSTEM_EVENT that reports on the wait events at the instance level, GV$SYSSTAT also reports operating system statistics at the system level. This means that the statistics generated from this view only provide an overall health indication for the database in the cluster. Also, the data provided by this view covers the time since the instance was last bounced as indicated by the GV$INSTANCE view.

```
COL NAME FORMAT A40
SELECT
INST_ID,
      NAME,
      VALUE
FROM GV$SYSSTAT
WHERE (NAME LIKE 'db%'
OR     NAME LIKE '%prase%'
OR     NAME LIKE '%cpu%'
OR     NAME LIKE '%global%'
OR     NAME LIKE '%gc%')
```

The above output indicates the session statistics of the system. It indicates the amount of memory and CPU (not shown in the output) consumed by the session. Data from this output can be utilized for sizing the Oracle memory; if there is high CPU usage, you should consider tuning the query.

Conclusion

One of the main aspects of an application performing well is to ensure that the persistence layer, which comprises SQL statements accessing the database, performs well. While there are several products available from various vendors today, Oracle provides several options for tuning SQL queries. Under this category the EXPLAIN PLAN, SQL_TRACE, event 10046, and event 10053 were discussed with trace outputs.

The OWI, an internal mechanism that provides time-based wait statistics, was discussed in principle; the wait interface that comprises GV$SESSION_EVENT, GV$SYSTEM_EVENT, GV$SESSION_WAIT, GV$SYSSTAT, and GV$SESSTAT was discussed in length. The discussion also included a few examples regarding analyzing this data for improving the performance of the system. More details on the wait interface are forthcoming in Chapter 17.

RAC comprises many instances of Oracle with one common database. While the ultimate goal of the enterprise system is to have the clustered solution perform well, this cannot happen unless the individual instances perform well.

■ ■ ■

## CHAPTER 7

SQL Tuning

Every application, small or big, online or batch, OLTP or warehouse, all interact with the database using SQL. SQL could be either in the form of data manipulation language (DML) through INSERT, UPDATE, and DELETE operations; data definition language (DDL) in the form of CREATE, ALTER, and DROP; or in the form of queries where they SELECT and retrieve data from the database. SQL operations of any kind should be efficiently written to perform optimally and give good response times.

Performance of an SQL operation is driven by the optimizer behavior and the plan generated by the optimizer when the SQL is executed. The behavior of the optimizer is then driven by how well the SQL is written and the execution path that is available to perform the operation. The execution path determined by the optimizer can be altered in several ways, such as tuning the query to make it more efficient, by using optimizer hints that will force the exaction path in a specific way, changing database parameters that could give more resources to perform the operation, or change the structure of the object by adding features such as database partitions. In this chapter, we look at the execution paths and phases and identify methods of executing them and consider changing them to be more efficient. Efficient SQL operations provide good response times, which in turn reduce the total cost of operation and reduce database (DB)time. Along the way, we also explore some of the important parameters used for this process and those used by the optimizer.

Before we go into the steps of writing efficient SQL and optimizing the query for performance, we try to understand the basic SQL execution life cycle.

SQL Execution Life Cycle

Figure 7-1 illustrates the various stages or steps taken beginning with the time that a cursor is opened by the application. A similar operation (not illustrated) is also followed in a PL/SQL procedure and when the SQL statements are embedded inside the PL/SQL code. There are nine steps involved in an SQL statement execution. It should be noted that only the DML statements are required to perform all these steps. DDL statements such as CREATE, ALTER, and DROP operations are performed in two steps, namely, CREATE and PARSE.

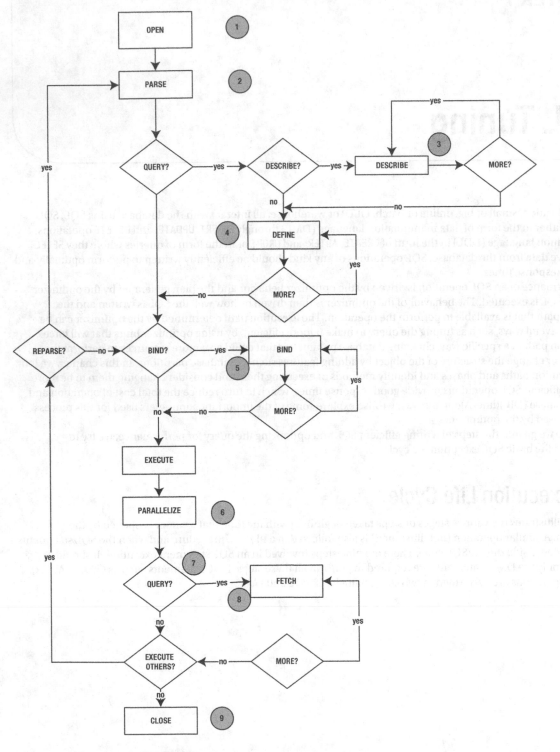

Figure 7-1. Parse operation flow diagram

Step 1: Create a Cursor

A cursor can be considered as an association between the data area in a client program and the Oracle server's data structures. When a program is required to process an SQL statement, it is required to open a cursor. In Oracle, the cursor contains a pointer to the current row; and, as the rows are fetched, the pointer moves to the next row until all the rows specified by the condition in the statement have been processed. Although the cursor is associated with the statement, it operates independently of the statement. The cursor is created by a program interface call (OPI) in expectation of an SQL statement.

SQL statement processing in general is complex in nature. It has to allocate and inspect various areas of the memory before the results are collected and returned to the user. The various physical components that the SQL statement has to iterate through are

- Client-side runtime memory
- Server-side runtime memory
- Server-side private SQL area
- Server side shared SQL area or the Library Cache

Step 2: Parse the Statement

This is the most complicated and expensive phase of the operation. During this phase, the statement is passed from the user's process to Oracle and is loaded into the shared SQL area. Before loading into the SQL shared area, the following steps have to be completed: the SQL statement is translated and verified, the table and columns checks are performed, and Oracle places a parse lock to prevent definitions from changing. While verifying the definitions, Oracle also checks the user privileges against the referenced objects. Oracle generates the query plan to determine the optimal execution path, followed by loading of the statement into the shared SQL area.

During this phase of operation, Oracle has to determine if the statement being executed is not identical to a previously executed statement. Based on the findings, Oracle will determine whether to use the previous parse information from a previous execution or if the statement has to be parsed before being executed. This is the advantage of the library cache feature. The library cache feature was introduced in version 7.0 of Oracle, which brought about the concept of sharing SQL statements.

There are two types of parses: soft parse and hard parse. Based on the repeated usage of the statement and Oracle finding the parse information in the library cache, it determines if this is a hard parse or a soft parse.

Hard Parse

When a statement is executed for the first time and Oracle does not find any information pertaining to this statement in the library cache, Oracle has to do a complete parse operation, which is also referred to as the hard parse. Hard parsing comprises of the following steps:

- Syntax checks on the statement
- Semantic checks on the statement
- Data dictionary validation for the objects and columns
- Name translation of the objects (with reference to synonyms)
- User privileges for the objects referenced in the SQL statement
- Generation of an execution plan, with the help of the Optimizer
- Loading of the statement into the library cache

Even after all of these steps have been completed and the statement has been loaded into the library cache/shareable area, it actually may not be in a shareable state. This is because Oracle has to place a lock on the cursor/statement header (cursors have two parts: the cursor header and the cursor body). The lock is placed on the header when the cursor is initially opened and released when the cursor is closed. Once the cursor is closed, the cursor obtains the shareable state (i.e., other sessions could see this statement in the library cache).

Before storing the statement in the library cache, Oracle computes a hash value and stores it on the hash table. Hash values are computed for every statement executed. These hash values are then compared against those in memory to find any matching values. If a matching value is found in memory, Oracle will use the execution plan already generated. If no matching values are found, it will start hard parsing the query.

Normally there is only one copy of the header that can be found in the library cache. However, there could be many copies of the cursor body. The reason why there could be many cursor bodies for the same cursor header is due to variations on the SQL statements. Variations in spacing, formatting, non-consistent usage of case, and so forth could cause variations because from Oracle's perspective, when it performs a comparison, it is going to compare character for character.

Versions of cursor body can be found by querying the V$SQLAREA view:

```
SELECT sql_id,
       version_count,
       loaded_versions,
       executions,
       hash_value
FROM   v$sqlarea
WHERE  version_count > 100;
```

SQL_ID	VERSION_COUNT	LOADED_VERSIONS	EXECUTIONS	HASH_VALUE
arx2rgss6k33m	104	104	42536	8.12E+08
0v6s91manuhz8	238	238	3272	3.58E+09
2nk2p4h18rbwf	110	110	2185	42708878
dbp7qgbgvmqgz	104	104	42536	3.75E+09

In an RAC environment, multiple versions of these SQL bodies could exist on every instance in the cluster where the queries are executed. In the illustration following, notice the SQL_ID across several instances:

```
SELECT inst_id,
       sql_id,
       version_count   vcnt,
       loaded_versions lver,
       executions      excs,
       hash_value      hval
FROM   gv$sqlarea
WHERE  version_count > 100
       AND executions > 1000
ORDER  BY sql_id;
```

INST_ID	SQL_ID	VCNT	LVER	EXCS	HVAL
4	4shbc31fv2jk7	141	61	4371	1571898951
5	4shbc31fv2jk7	123	61	4967	1571898951
5	a8q5m69h6npk6	125	52	4603	1617581638
4	a8q5m69h6npk6	152	57	5015	1617581638

Queries that have high version counts maintained on multiple instances also tend to show high CONCURRENCY_WAIT_TIME and CLUSTER_WAIT_TIME. When high version counts are maintained across multiple instances, the concurrency wait time (CONCURRENCY_WAIT_TIME) increases. Version counts also cause Oracle to perform a high degree of coordination among multiple instances; it increases the overall cluster wait time (CLUSTER_WAIT_TIME). The CLUSTER_WAIT_TIME column shows the total time spent waiting for all waits that are categorized under the "Cluster" class of wait events. The value is an accumulated wait time spent waiting for Oracle RAC cluster resources.

■ **Note** CONCURRENCY_WAIT_TIME and CLUSTER_WAIT_TIME statistics can be obtained from V$SQLSTATS.

The following query identifies queries that have high wait times:

```
SELECT inst_id                       inst,
       sql_id,
       cpu_time                      cputime,
       elapsed_time                  elpsdtime,
       px_servers_executions         pxsrvEx,
       application_wait_time         awt,
       concurrency_wait_time         conwt,
       cluster_wait_time             clwt,
       user_io_wait_time             uiwt
FROM   gv$sqlstats
WHERE  user_io_wait_time > 0
ORDER  BY user_io_wait_time;
```

INST	SQL_ID	CPUTIME	ELPSDTIME	PXSRVEX	AWT	CONWT	CLWT	UIWT
2	7u49y06aqxg1s	1280813	41663201	0	0	125214	15170669	22868319
3	2ns5gzz3fcpq2	7171914	30079286	0	0	29293	8539546	611029147
3	f47hz4fd4yyx8	3688442	272873315	0	0	196975	502986	23884755
3	0w26sk6t6gq98	5243202	99495596	0	1764954	1346243	693593	27981060
3	6q9zvynq8f0h0	1157818	38728380	0	995	45065	4157710	28085768
2	3waf8n8kvtntc	315952	31076715	0	0	21363	382094	30388177
3	7u49y06aqxg1s	1396798	48420345	0	0	16781	3554500	33859424
3	axq73su80h4wq	987849	60333409	0	0	43328	1108248	44998699
2	5k5207588w9ry	4778274	135105206	0	639018	1615341	1961831	45633987
2	fhf8upax5cxsz	7559852	154927182	0	713558	2151904	2413757	49989364
3	cvn54b7yz0s8u	934859	80678934	0	0	10912	7377111	52286936
3	fhf8upax5cxsz	10840350	220009195	0	2381637	12457716	3353428	61467176
4	0jzgrxvn2gag8	1451759	101130837	0	0	8391	12541211	603568199
4	4a0mfzwgqw5fq	60096857	220706621	0	0	194957	165022097	610027252

In Oracle 12.1.0 (12c), Oracle has added a few more delta columns related to cluster statistics. The "delta_" columns in the following query reflect time spent by the cursor (in microseconds) since the last AWR snapshot:

```
SELECT inst_id                       inst,
       sql_id,
       delta_cpu_time                dcputime,
       delta_elapsed_time            detime,
       delta_application_wait_time   dawt,
```

```
        delta_concurrency_time      dconwt,
        delta_cluster_wait_time     dclwt,
        delta_user_io_wait_time     duiwt
FROM    gv$sqlstats
WHERE   delta_user_io_wait_time > 0
ORDER   BY delta_user_io_wait_time;
```

Note that the SQL parsing and execution happens locally on each instance in a clustered environment. If the SQL or any dependencies change in one instance, it will invalidate in all the instances, and they have to be reparsed again locally on the respective instance.

After the initial header and body creation, subsequent bodies are created for the same header. Here are two reasons on why this could happen:

- The thresholds of the bind variables change because the string length of the contents of the bind variable has changed.

  For example, if the BOOK table is initially checked with "Oracle," and the next query checked the books table with "Testing and Tuning Oracle Real Application Clusters," Oracle notices that the length of the bind value has changed and cannot reuse the existing cursor body and therefore creates another one. The initial space allocation for a bind value is 50 bytes; anything over that requires a new body.

- SQL statements use literals instead of bind variables.

Hard parses are very costly for the Oracle's optimizer. The amount of validation that has to be performed during a parse consumes a significant amount of resources. When a user/session executes a query, the query is parsed and loaded in the library cache after Oracle has generated a hash value for the query. Subsequently, when another session or user executes the same query depending on the extent of similarity of the query that is already present in the library cache, it is reused and there is no parse operation involved. However, if it is a new query, it has to go through the Oracle parsing algorithm; this is considered a hard parse and is very costly. The total amount of hard parses can be determined using the following query:

```
SELECT pa.inst_id,
       pa.sid,
       pa.VALUE "Hard Parses",
       ex.VALUE "Execute Count"
FROM   gv$sesstat pa,
       gv$sesstat ex
WHERE  pa.sid = ex.sid
       AND pa.inst_id = ex.inst_id
       AND pa.statistic# = (SELECT statistic#
                            FROM   v$statname
                            WHERE  NAME = 'parse count (hard)')
       AND ex.statistic# = (SELECT statistic#
                            FROM   v$statname
                            WHERE  NAME = 'execute count')
       AND pa.VALUE > 0;
```

■ **Note** The preceding query collects hard parses on the active sessions; to get a complete count on the hard parses since the instance started, please use GV$SYSSTAT instead of GV$SESSTAT.

Soft Parse

As discussed earlier, before parsing the SQL statement, a hash value is generated for the SQL statement and the value is compared to the hash value with the statements already in the library cache. Once a matching statement is found, to ensure that nothing has changed between the previous executions and now, Oracle may have to do a simpler parse, depending on certain conditions. This parse is a soft parse and could be one of these kinds:

- If the user is accessing the SQL statement for the first time and finds it in memory, Oracle has to ensure that the statement is exactly the same as the one that the user has requested and ensure that the user has authentication to use the objects referenced in the SQL statement.

- If the user is accessing the SQL statement for the second time and finds it in the library cache, Oracle still has to validate to ensure that the grants for the objects referenced in the SQL statement have not changed.

The parse operation consumes memory and CPU cycles to complete the query; however, this reduces the response time considerably.

Step 3: Describe the Results

This step in the execution life cycle is required to determine the various objects, columns, and characteristics such as data type, length, and so forth. This step is more relevant when using dynamic queries.

Step 4: Define Query Output

Although the statement is executed and data is retrieved, appropriate memory variables are required to hold the output information. This step takes care of defining character type, length, and so forth for the variables where data will be retrieved and stored.

Step 5: Bind Any Variables

If bind variables are used, Oracle is required to bind them. This gives the Oracle server the location (binding by reference) where bind values will be stored in memory. Usage of bind variables is another important factor for efficient usage of memory and the overall performance of the system. Bind variables help in repeated execution of the same statement. Usage of literals (alternative to bind variables) causes statements to be unique and does not allow sharing of SQL statements. The nonshared statements consume memory and cause excessive parse operation.

Step 6: Parallelize the Statement

This step is performed only when parallelism is required and configured. When parallelism is chosen, the work of a query is divided among a number of slave processors. If this is required for parsing or if the query is eligible for parallel execution, it is determined during the parse step and the appropriate execution plan has to be defined.

■ **Note** Detailed discussion on parallel queries is in Chapter 9.

Step 7: Execute the Statement

This step executes the SQL statement and retrieves rows from disk or memory and places the values into the bind variables. If the statement is a query or an INSERT statement, no rows need to be locked because no data is being changed. If the statement is an UPDATE or DELETE statement, however, all rows that the statement affects are locked from use by other users of the database until the next COMMIT, ROLLBACK, or SAVEPOINT for the transaction. This protects the data from being changed by other sessions while it is being modified. This ensures data integrity.

When data is modified, before and after images describing the changes are written to the redo log buffer and the undo segments.

Step 8: Fetch Rows

From the bind variables defined in Step 5, the values that are obtained as a result of the statement execution, and the placement of values in the bind variables rows, are selected and ordered (if requested by the query), and each successive fetch retrieves another row of the result until the last row has been fetched. These results are returned into a table format to the calling interface.

Step 9: Close the Cursor

Once the data is returned to the calling interface, the cursor is closed.

Iteration of Steps 1 thru 6 will help generate the execution plan for the statement. The execution plan is then stored in the library cache and reused when another session executes the same statement.

When tuning an SQL statement, it's this process that we are trying to improve so response time to get the data back to the user is improved.

Capturing Execution Times

One of the first steps in looking at the performance of a query is to determine its execution time. During this analysis, it is important to understand where most of the time was spent by the session. What step in the query plan took the most time? An important parameter that drives keeping the time is the TIMED_STATISTICS and a few other parameters:

- TIMED_STATISTICS
- TIMED_OS_STATISTICS
- STATISTICS_LEVEL
- OPTIMIZER_USE_PENDING_STATISTICS (New in Oracle Database 12c, Version 1)

TIMED_STATISTICS

This is a very important parameter; turning this off will disable most of the time-based statistics gathering useful information for a scientific analysis. For example, when generating a 10046 trace, disabling this parameter will not show time statistics in the report. Check if the parameter has been enabled. If not, this needs to be turned on. Setting the STATISTICS_LEVEL parameter to TYPICAL, for example, automatically enables TIMED_STATISTICS to TRUE.

STATISTICS_LEVEL

This parameter sets the amount of statistics that will be collected. This parameter could be set to one of these three values: BASIC, TYPICAL, or ALL. TYPICAL is the default; when Oracle enables or sets the value to TYPICAL or ALL, it automatically enables the STATISTICS_LEVEL parameter.

Setting the STATISTICS_LEVEL to ALL will enable the collection of O/S-level statistics. This should be done only under controlled conditions because it could degrade performance to a great extent.

V$STATISTICS_LEVEL

The V$STATISTICS_LEVEL view provides the status of the statistics or advisories controlled by the STATISTICS_LEVEL initialization parameter. Most of the advice views will provide statistical advice when the STATISTICS_LEVEL is set to TYPICAL or ALL:

```
COL NAME FORMAT A38
SELECT statistics_name  NAME,
       session_status   ses_status,
       system_status    sys_status,
       activation_level alevel,
       session_settable sestable
FROM   v$statistics_level
/
```

NAME	SES_STAT	SYS_STAT	ALEVEL	SES
Buffer Cache Advice	ENABLED	ENABLED	TYPICAL	NO
MTTR Advice	ENABLED	ENABLED	TYPICAL	NO
Timed Statistics	ENABLED	ENABLED	TYPICAL	YES
Timed OS Statistics	DISABLED	DISABLED	ALL	YES
Segment Level Statistics	ENABLED	ENABLED	TYPICAL	NO
PGA Advice	ENABLED	ENABLED	TYPICAL	NO
Plan Execution Statistics	DISABLED	DISABLED	ALL	YES
Shared Pool Advice	ENABLED	ENABLED	TYPICAL	NO
Modification Monitoring	ENABLED	ENABLED	TYPICAL	NO
Longops Statistics	ENABLED	ENABLED	TYPICAL	NO
Bind Data Capture	ENABLED	ENABLED	TYPICAL	NO
Ultrafast Latch Statistics	ENABLED	ENABLED	TYPICAL	NO
Threshold-based Alerts	ENABLED	ENABLED	TYPICAL	NO
Global Cache Statistics	ENABLED	ENABLED	TYPICAL	NO
Global Cache CPU Statistics	DISABLED	DISABLED	ALL	NO
Active Session History	ENABLED	ENABLED	TYPICAL	NO
Undo Advisor, Alerts and Fast Ramp up	ENABLED	ENABLED	TYPICAL	NO
Streams Pool Advice	ENABLED	ENABLED	TYPICAL	NO
Time Model Events	ENABLED	ENABLED	TYPICAL	YES
Plan Execution Sampling	ENABLED	ENABLED	TYPICAL	YES
Automated Maintenance Tasks	ENABLED	ENABLED	TYPICAL	NO
Automatic DBOP Monitoring	ENABLED	ENABLED	TYPICAL	YES
SQL Monitoring	ENABLED	ENABLED	TYPICAL	YES
Adaptive Thresholds Enabled	ENABLED	ENABLED	TYPICAL	NO
V$IOSTAT_* statistics	ENABLED	ENABLED	TYPICAL	NO
OLAP row load time precision	ENABLED	ENABLED	TYPICAL	YES

TIMED_OS_STATISTICS

The TIMED_STATISTICS parameter discussed earlier will enable gathering of statistics at the database and instance level. The TIMED_OS_STATISTICS parameter will collect O/S-level statistics and is normally driven by the value of the STATISTICS_LEVEL parameter. When the STATISTICS_LEVEL parameter is set to ALL, TIMED_OS_STATISTICS is set to a value of 5, meaning that the servers should collect O/S statistics every 5 seconds.

The 10046 trace from the query following indicates the time metrics that were possible because the TIMED_STATISTICS parameter was enabled:

```
SELECT ol_w_id,
       ol_d_id,
       ol_number,
       SUM(ol_amount),
       SUM(ol_quantity)
FROM   order_line ol,
       orders ord
WHERE  ol.ol_o_id = ord.o_id
       AND ol.ol_w_id = ord.o_w_id
       AND ol.ol_d_id = ord.o_d_id
GROUP  BY ol_number,
         ol_w_id,
         ol_d_id
/
```

call	count	cpu	elapsed	disk	query	current	rows
Parse	1	0.01	0.02	0	0	0	0
Execute	1	0.00	0.00	0	0	0	0
Fetch	21	33.04	96.12	346671	347172	0	300
total	23	33.06	96.14	346671	347172	0	300

Misses in library cache during parse: 1
Optimizer mode: ALL_ROWS
Parsing user id: 89 (OBIPRD)

```
Rows     Row Source Operation
-------  ---------------------------------------------------------
    300  HASH GROUP BY (cr=347172 pr=346671 pw=0 time=299 us cost=126413 size=4950 card=150)
21541174   HASH JOIN  (cr=347172 pr=346671 pw=0 time=100269208 us cost=125703 size=680920944
card=20633968)
2153881    INDEX FAST FULL SCAN ORDERS_I2 (cr=12056 pr=11635 pw=0 time=629729 us cost=2743
size=22694870 card=2063170)(object id 86234)
21541174    INDEX FAST FULL SCAN IORDL (cr=335116 pr=335036 pw=0 time=79083112 us cost=87415
size=453947296 card=20633968)(object id 86202)
```

Elapsed times include waiting on following events:

Event waited on	Times Waited	Max. Wait	Total Waited
ges message buffer allocation	466	0.00	0.00
library cache lock	2	0.00	0.00
row cache lock	14	0.00	0.00

The time element in the row source operation column of the plan statistics will not be available if TIME_STATISTICS is not enabled. This is critical in determining the total time each execution step had taken to complete the operation.

Looking further at the statistics generated, the first question that probably arises is why there is 347,172 consistent gets (column query in the output) and almost an equal number of physical reads (column disk in the output) to get 300 rows. This tells us that Oracle had to filter through 347,172 rows of data to finally arrive at a 300 rows result set. During this process, Oracle also had to perform 346,671 disk reads, so almost every row read from the disk was loaded into the buffer before building the result set of 300 rows.

What Are Consistent Gets?

Blocks are retrieved from physical disks or from memory buffers. The blocks retrieved by Oracle are consistent with a given point in time or SCN (system change number). If such consistent blocks of data are not available in the buffer, Oracle will reconstruct the data block either by reading the block from disk or in the case of RAC instances, requesting the block from the current holder. Because these blocks are retrieved from buffer (logical), they are also called logical I/O's (LIO). Similarly, when blocks are retrieved from disk, they are called physical I/O (PIO). In the preceding example, blocks are retrieved from disk and then loaded into the buffer, so there are both PIOs and LIOs. The almost equal number of PIOs and LIOs are because the query is being executed for the first time; subsequent execution of the same query may only notice LIOs. Once again, because this is a GROUP BY operation, columns from these rows are summed on pivot column(s) (OL_W_ID, OL_D_ID, OL_NUMBER).

Consistent read statistics are incremented either

1. During a full table scan, where for every block read, the consistent read value is increased by 1, or

2. When data is accessed using indexes, in which case the consistent gets are incremented based on the index height.

This is because an index scan touches at least two blocks. Therefore, when a single row is accessed, the index scan takes more consistent gets. Although this is a true behavior, it does not occur all the time. In full table scan, logical I/O is higher in general. The increment is higher in the case of indexes because for every read there are two gets (index and the physical row). However, in the case of a full table scan that does not involve an index, it's only reading the row.

Different statistics counters are updated based on the type of operation performed. Any of the following types of statistics are LIOs:

• buffer gets

• consistent gets

• db block gets

• buffer pinned count

Similarly, db block gets statistic counters are used to get the most current copy of the block. Based on Oracle architecture, there could only be one current copy of a block in the buffer cache at any given time. The db block gets statistic is incremented when a block is read for update and when the segment header blocks are accessed. Because both consistent gets and db block gets are reading blocks from buffer, they are both logical reads. If both these statistics are present, then LIO is the sum of db block gets and consistent gets. Retrieving from the memory has always been less expensive compared to retrieving from disk. PIOs are generally more expensive because of the way the data is stored on disks and how the data has to be found (seek time) before they are actually read (read time). Comparing this behavior to an LIO operation, LIOs are less expensive because instead of scanning through various tracks on storage, memory buffers are scanned, and reading through logical memory structures is much cheaper compared to reading from storage.

Logical Reads

When data is read from physical storage (disk), it is placed into the buffer cache before filtering through the rows that match the criteria specified in the WHERE clause. Rows thus read are retained in the buffer, assuming other sessions executing similar queries may require the same data, reducing physical I/O. Queries not tuned to perform minimal I/O operations will retrieve a significantly larger number of rows, causing Oracle to traverse through the various rows, filtering what is not required instead of directly accessing rows that match. Such operations cause a significant amount of overhead and consume a large number of resources in the system.

Reading from buffer, or logical reads (or LIO operations), is cheaper compared to reading data from disk. However, in Oracle's architecture, high LIOs are not cheap enough that they can be ignored because when Oracle needs to read a row from buffer, it needs to place a shared lock on the row in buffer. To obtain a shared lock, Oracle has to request a latch on the buffer (cache buffers chains latch) from the O/S. Latches are not available in abundance. Often when a latch is requested, one is not immediately available because other processes are using them. When a latch is requested and the latch is not available, the requesting process will go into a sleep mode and after a few nanoseconds will wake up and request the latch again. This time it may or may not obtain the latch and may have to sleep again. Latch contention involves CPU spins and context switches and may cause high CPU consumption on the host if sessions access the same resource and data. When Oracle has to scan a large number of rows in the buffer to retrieve only a few rows that meet the search criteria, this can prove costly.

SQLs that issue high logical read rates in comparison to the actual number of database rows processed are possible candidates for SQL tuning efforts. Often the introduction of a new index or the creation of a more selective index will reduce the number of blocks that must be examined to find the rows required. For example, we examine the performance of the following query:

```
SELECT eusr_id,
       us.usec_total_logins,
       eu.eusr_role_cd,
       c.comp_scac_code,
       eu.eusr_login_name,
       ul.usrli_id
FROM   el_user eu,
       company c,
       user_login ul,
       user_security us
WHERE  ul.usrli_active_status_cd = 'Active'
       AND ul.usrli_logged_in_eusr_id = eu.eusr_id
       AND eu.eusr_comp_id = c.comp_id
       AND eu.eusr_id = us.usec_eusr_id
ORDER  BY c.comp_comp_type_cd,
          c.comp_name,
          eu.eusr_last_name;
```

call	count	cpu	elapsed	disk	query	current	rows
Parse	1	0.28	0.29	0	51	0	0
Execute	1	0.00	0.00	0	0	0	0
Fetch	4	26.31	40.35	12866	6556373	0	87
total	6	26.59	40.64	12866	6556424	0	87

```
Misses in library cache during parse: 1
Optimizer goal: ALL_ROWS
Parsing user id: 334 (MVALLATH)
```

```
Rows       Row Source Operation
-------    ----------------------------------------------------
     87    SORT ORDER BY (cr=3176 r=66 w=66 time=346886 us)
     87     TABLE ACCESS BY GLOBAL INDEX ROWID USER_SECURITY PARTITION: 1 1
           (cr=3176 r=66 w=66 time=338109 us)
     78      NESTED LOOPS  (cr=3088 r=66 w=66 time=334551 us)
     90       NESTED LOOPS  (cr=2596 r=66 w=66 time=322337 us)
     90        NESTED LOOPS  (cr=1614 r=66 w=66 time=309393 us)
     90         VIEW  (cr=632 r=66 w=66 time=293827 us)
  48390          HASH JOIN  (cr=632 r=66 w=66 time=292465 us)
6556373           TABLE ACCESS FULL USER_LOGIN (cr=190 r=0 w=0 time=38776 us)(object id 24891)
    970           TABLE ACCESS FULL EL_USER (cr=442 r=0 w=0 time=56947 us)(object id 24706)
     90          INDEX UNIQUE SCAN PK_EUSR PARTITION: 1 1 (cr=492 r=0 w=0 time=6055 us)
                 (object id 24741)
     90        TABLE ACCESS BY LOCAL INDEX ROWID COMPANY PARTITION: 1 1
              (cr=982 r=0 w=0 time=10135 us)
     90         INDEX UNIQUE SCAN PK_COMP PARTITION: 1 1 (cr=492 r=0 w=0 time=4905 us)
               (object id 24813)
     87      INDEX RANGE SCAN USEC_INDX1 (cr=492 r=0 w=0 time=9115 us)(object id 24694)


Rows       Execution Plan
-------    ----------------------------------------------------
      0    SELECT STATEMENT    GOAL: CHOOSE
     87     SORT (ORDER BY)
     87      TABLE ACCESS    GOAL: ANALYZED (BY GLOBAL INDEX ROWID) OF
                'USER_SECURITY' PARTITION: START=1 STOP=1
     78       NESTED LOOPS
     90        NESTED LOOPS
     90         NESTED LOOPS
     90          VIEW OF 'index$_join$_003'
     90           HASH JOIN
6556373            INDEX    GOAL: ANALYZED (FAST FULL SCAN) OF
                      'PK_USRLI' (UNIQUE) PARTITION: START=1 STOP=1
     90            INDEX    GOAL: ANALYZED (FAST FULL SCAN) OF
                      'USRLI_INDX1' (NON-UNIQUE)
     90          TABLE ACCESS    GOAL: ANALYZED (BY LOCAL INDEX ROWID)
                   OF 'ELOGEX_USER' PARTITION: START=1 STOP=1
     90           INDEX    GOAL: ANALYZED (UNIQUE SCAN) OF 'PK_EUSR'
                    (UNIQUE) PARTITION: START=1 STOP=1
     90         TABLE ACCESS    GOAL: ANALYZED (BY LOCAL INDEX ROWID) OF
                  'COMPANY' PARTITION: START=1 STOP=1
     90          INDEX    GOAL: ANALYZED (UNIQUE SCAN) OF 'PK_COMP'
                   (UNIQUE) PARTITION: START=1 STOP=1
     87        INDEX    GOAL: ANALYZED (RANGE SCAN) OF 'USEC_INDX1'
                (NON-UNIQUE)
```

In the tkprof (Transient Kernel Profiler utility) output from a 10046 event trace, which, it should be noted, retrieves just 87 rows from the database, the SQL is processing a large number (6556373) of rows from the USER_LOGIN table, and no index is being used to retrieve the data. Now, if an index is created on the USER_LOGIN table, the query performance improves:

```
SQL> CREATE INDEX USRLI_INDX1 ON USER_LOGIN(USRLI_ACTIVE_STATUS_CD);
Index created.
Rows     Row Source Operation
-------  -------------------------------------------------------
    487  SORT ORDER BY (cr=3176 r=66 w=66 time=346886 us)
    487   TABLE ACCESS BY GLOBAL INDEX ROWID USER_SECURITY PARTITION: 1 1
          (cr=3176 r=66 w=66 time=338109 us)
    978    NESTED LOOPS  (cr=3088 r=66 w=66 time=334551 us)
    490     NESTED LOOPS  (cr=2596 r=66 w=66 time=322337 us)
    490      NESTED LOOPS  (cr=1614 r=66 w=66 time=309393 us)
    490       VIEW  (cr=632 r=66 w=66 time=293827 us)
    490        HASH JOIN  (cr=632 r=66 w=66 time=292465 us)
  56373        INDEX FAST FULL SCAN PK_USRLI PARTITION: 1 1
               (cr=190 r=0 w=0 time=38776 us)(object id 24891)
    490         INDEX FAST FULL SCAN USRLI_INDX1 (cr=442 r=0 w=0 time=56947 us)
               (object id 24706)
    490       TABLE ACCESS BY LOCAL INDEX ROWID ELOGEX_USER PARTITION: 1 1
               (cr=982 r=0 w=0 time=12238 us)
    490        INDEX UNIQUE SCAN PK_EUSR PARTITION: 1 1 (cr=492 r=0 w=0 time=6055 us)
               (object id 24741)
    490      TABLE ACCESS BY LOCAL INDEX ROWID COMPANY PARTITION: 1 1
               (cr=982 r=0 w=0 time=10135 us)
    490       INDEX UNIQUE SCAN PK_COMP PARTITION: 1 1 (cr=492 r=0 w=0 time=4905 us)
               (object id 24813)
    487     INDEX RANGE SCAN USEC_INDX1 (cr=492 r=0 w=0 time=9115 us)(object id 24694)

Rows    Execution Plan
-------  -------------------------------------------------------
      0  SELECT STATEMENT    GOAL: CHOOSE
    487   SORT (ORDER BY)
    487    TABLE ACCESS   GOAL: ANALYZED (BY GLOBAL INDEX ROWID) OF
                 'USER_SECURITY' PARTITION: START=1 STOP=1
    978     NESTED LOOPS
    490      NESTED LOOPS
    490       NESTED LOOPS
    490        VIEW OF 'index$_join$_003'
    490         HASH JOIN
  56373         INDEX    GOAL: ANALYZED (FAST FULL SCAN) OF
                    'PK_USRLI' (UNIQUE) PARTITION: START=1 STOP=1
    490          INDEX    GOAL: ANALYZED (FAST FULL SCAN) OF
                    'USRLI_INDX1' (NON-UNIQUE)
    490        TABLE ACCESS   GOAL: ANALYZED (BY LOCAL INDEX ROWID)
                 OF 'ELOGEX_USER' PARTITION: START=1 STOP=1
    490         INDEX   GOAL: ANALYZED (UNIQUE SCAN) OF 'PK_EUSR'
                    (UNIQUE) PARTITION: START=1 STOP=1
    490       TABLE ACCESS   GOAL: ANALYZED (BY LOCAL INDEX ROWID) OF
                 'COMPANY' PARTITION: START=1 STOP=1
```

```
490        INDEX   GOAL: ANALYZED (UNIQUE SCAN) OF 'PK_COMP'
                   (UNIQUE) PARTITION: START=1 STOP=1
487    INDEX   GOAL: ANALYZED (RANGE SCAN) OF 'USEC_INDX1'(NON-UNIQUE)
```

The optimizer decides to use the new index USRL_INDX1 and reduces the number of rows retrieved. Now, if another index is added to the EL_USER table, further improvement in the query can be obtained. Indexes that are not selective do not improve query performance but can degrade DML performance. In RAC, unselective index blocks may be subject to interinstance contention, increasing the frequency of cache transfers for indexes belonging to INSERT-intensive tables.

Physical Reads

As illustrated in Figure 7-2, seeking of data occurs from the outside to the inside of the disk. The disk head seeks to find the data first. Once the sector and track where the data resides is found, the data is read. A typical disk drive today has a minimum seek time of approximately 1 ms for seeking the next track and a maximum seek time of approximately 11 ms for seeking the entire width of the disk.[1] A PIO involves all of these operations, making a PIO very expensive.

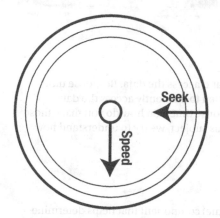

Figure 7-2. *Disk reads and seeks*

Oracle has to consult with the O/S to access data from the buffer. Every time Oracle needs to access a row in the buffer, there is a latch involved; a latch is a lock in memory. To obtain a latch, the session depends on the O/S. That means every time a row is read from the buffer (memory), Oracle needs to request a latch, and a request for a latch is a request for CPU. Getting a latch is not a straightforward task either. When an Oracle process needs a specific type of latch (e.g., cache buffers chains latch\), the latch may not be available, which means that after the process spins (for 2,000 times) trying to acquire the latch, it sleeps and tries again after x amount of seconds. This repeated activity of requesting a latch and CPU goes on until such time when it is able to successfully get a latch. If there are many rows in the buffer that need to be read, and every read requires a latch, which in turn requires CPU cycles, could mean high CPU activity. Such frequent requests for latches make the operation really expensive.

The other value that catches one's attention is the physical reads or PIOs. PIO, as we have discussed earlier, is even more expensive. PIOs can be tuned by examining the query and the underlying tables to ensure that there are indexes and if the optimizer is using the correct path when generating the execution plan. Event 10053, discussed in Chapter 6, could be helpful method to get this accomplished.

---

[1]Murali Vallath, Oracle 10g RAC – Grid, Services and Clustering, Digital Press, 2007.

Why Tune?

Irrespective of having high-performing hardware, a high-performing storage subsystem, or the abundance of resources on each of the nodes in the cluster, RAC cannot perform magic to fix poor performing queries. Actually, poor performing queries can be a serious issue when you move from a single instance configuration to a clustered configuration. In certain cases, a negative impact on the overall performance of the system could be noticed.

A top activity chart (illustrated in Figure 7-3) in EM could be a good starting point to determine high resource intensive queries and candidates for optimization.

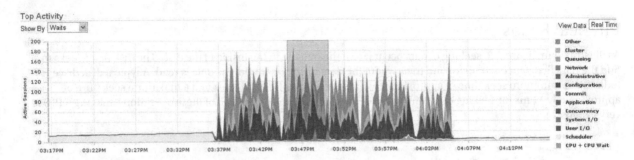

Figure 7-3. *EM—Top activity*

Efficiency of the system depends on the efficiency of the queries that run and access the data. Response time depends on how well the database is laid out and how well the queries are written to efficiently access the data. Efficient queries and well-managed database environments provide good response times. So how do you make those queries more efficient, or how do you tune the queries? Before stepping into this subject, we try to understand how the optimizer works.

Optimizer

Oracle's cost-based optimizer or CBO, or simply the optimizer, is an Oracle kernel component that helps determine the most efficient path to execute the SQL statement and access the data sets. The CBO determines the most efficient path of data excess based on statistics available and scientifically arrives at an access path by creating execution plans. Such plans are stored in the SGA for reuse by other users who execute the same SQL statement. The optimizer performs the following operations:

- Evaluates expressions and conditions contained in SQL statements

- Transforms SQL statements to make it more efficient

- Determines the goal of the optimization

- Generates a set of plans for the SQL statement based on the available access paths

- Determines the right join order

For every plan generated, the optimizer will estimate the cost based on statistics available in the data dictionary for the data distribution, number of rows, and storage characteristics such as the number of tables accessed, indexes available, and distribution of data into various data partitions.

The *cost* is an estimated value proportional to the expected resource needed to execute the statement with a particular plan. The optimizer calculates the cost of the access paths and the join order based on the estimated computer resources, which includes I/O, CPU, and memory.

The higher the cost, the longer the expected execution time will be.[2] Once the cost of each plan is determined, the optimizer will select the plan that has the lowest cost. This plan is then used during execution.

The various plans generated by the optimizer can be obtained using the 10053 event trace discussed in Chapter 6.

Optimizer Goals

Optimization of any task should have a goal and purpose. Normally computer-based optimization goals are targeted to provide high throughput or good response times. Oracle's optimizer is no exception; optimization is either for an OLTP workload where the quick response time is expected or a DSS (decision support system) workload where data is inserted or queried in larger volumes and where high throughput is expected. In certain cases in which the database has small organizations, the optimizer uses the same database to support both types of workload or a mixed workload.

By default the optimizer uses "throughput" as its optimizer goal; and by using different conditions, the goal could be changed. The factors that affect the optimizer goal are

- Database initialization parameter OPTIMIZER_MODE

- The manually forced Optimizer plan modification used in the query to change the execution path of the optimizer

- Optimizer statistics

OPTIMIZER_MODE

The OPTIMIZER_MODE initialization parameter establishes the default optimizer behavior of the instance when generating execution plans. The parameter accepts one of the three values:

ALL_ROWS: This is the default optimizer mode. When the database is created using DBCA (database configuration assistant), the OPTIMIZER_MODE defaults to ALL_ROWS. It attempts to optimize the query to get the very last row as fast as possible. Regardless of whether statistics are present, the statement is optimized for the best throughput, that is, to use the minimum amount of all available resources to complete the operation. For example, we take the following query:

```
SELECT  n_name,
        r_name,
        p_name,
        s_name,
        SUM(ps_supplycost)
FROM    rapdwh.region,
        rapdwh.nation,
        rapdwh.supplier,
        rapdwh.partsupp,
        rapdwh.part
WHERE   ps_partkey = p_partkey
        AND ps_suppkey = s_suppkey
        AND s_nationkey = n_nationkey
        AND n_regionkey = r_regionkey
```

---

[2]This does not apply to parallel operations where resource use is not directly related to the elapsed time.

```
GROUP  BY n_name,
          r_name,
          p_name,
          s_name;
```

The execution plan (not all columns shown, formatted for easy readability) for this
statement with the default mode of ALL_ROWS is the following:

```
------------------------------------------------------------
Plan hash value: 3952064199
------------------------------------------------------------
| Id  | Operation                       | Name     | Rows  |
------------------------------------------------------------
|   0 | SELECT STATEMENT                |          | 228M  |
|   1 |  PX COORDINATOR                 |          |       |
|   2 |   PX SEND QC (RANDOM)           | :TQ10007 | 228M  |
|   3 |    HASH GROUP BY                |          | 228M  |
|   4 |     PX RECEIVE                  |          | 228M  |
|   5 |      PX SEND HASH               | :TQ10006 | 228M  |
|*  6 |       HASH JOIN BUFFERED        |          | 228M  |
|   7 |        BUFFER SORT              |          |       |
|   8 |         PX RECEIVE              |          | 10    |
|   9 |          PX SEND BROADCAST      | :TQ10000 | 10    |
|  10 |           TABLE ACCESS FULL     | REGION   | 10    |
|* 11 |        HASH JOIN                |          | 114M  |
|  12 |         BUFFER SORT             |          |       |
|  13 |          PX RECEIVE             |          | 50    |
|  14 |           PX SEND BROADCAST     | :TQ10001 | 50    |
|  15 |            TABLE ACCESS FULL    | NATION   | 50    |
|* 16 |         HASH JOIN               |          | 57M   |
|  17 |          PX RECEIVE             |          | 2040K |
|  18 |           PX SEND HASH          | :TQ10004 | 2040K |
|  19 |            PX BLOCK ITERATOR    |          | 2040K |
|  20 |             TABLE ACCESS FULL   | SUPPLIER | 2040K |
|  21 |          PX RECEIVE             |          | 28M   |
|  22 |           PX SEND HASH          | :TQ10005 | 28M   |
|* 23 |            HASH JOIN BUFFERED   |          | 28M   |
|  24 |             PX RECEIVE          |          | 7204K |
|  25 |              PX SEND HASH       | :TQ10002 | 7204K |
|  26 |               PX BLOCK ITERATOR |          | 7204K |
|  27 |                TABLE ACCESS FULL| PART     | 7204K |
|  28 |             PX RECEIVE          |          | 28M   |
|  29 |              PX SEND HASH       | :TQ10003 | 28M   |
|  30 |               PX BLOCK ITERATOR |          | 28M   |
|  31 |                TABLE ACCESS FULL| PARTSUPP | 28M   |
------------------------------------------------------------
```

It should be noted that the optimizer executed the query in parallel, taking advantage of the
servers and the resources providing high throughput.

FIRST_ROWS_n: If the parameter is set to this value, the statement is optimized with a goal of best response time to return the first *n* number of rows; *n* can equal 1, 10, 100, or 1,000. The optimizer explores different plans and, for each one, computes the cost to produce the first *n* rows. It picks the plan that produces the first *n* rows with the lowest cost.

If the query discussed in the earlier example was executed with the parameter set to this value, there was no difference in the execution plan because the optimizer determined that irrespective of the goal or hint specified with the query, the best approach was to use parallel operation.

FIRST_ROWS: The optimizer uses a mix of costs and heuristics to find a best plan for fast delivery of the first few rows. The heuristic sometimes leads the optimizer to generate a plan whose cost is significantly larger than the cost of a plan without applying the heuristic. This mode or hint may be useful in a pure OLTP application where users are interested in seeing the first few rows on their browser soon and are seldom interested in seeing the entire query result, especially when the result size is large.

Manually Change Execution Paths

The execution plan generated by the optimizer may not be efficient enough; this could be due to several reasons. At such times, it may be required to force the optimizer to use a specific plan that has been tested and efficient. Common reasons when such methods would be required are

- Database upgrades
- Database initialization parameter changes
- Schema changes
- Optimizer statistics refresh or stale statistics
- Changes to the environment

Under these conditions, it may be required to change the optimizer behavior by using one of the available methods to force a specific execution plan. In this section, we look at some of these methods.

SQL Hints

A commonly practiced method to modify the behavior of the optimizer is to use SQL hints in the query. A hint will instruct the optimizer to follow a specific execution path. For example, in the query we discussed earlier, if the parallel option is not to be used, then the same query can be executed using the NOPARALLEL hint. This will force the optimizer to use a normal execution path.

```
SELECT /*+ NOPARALLEL */ n_name,
                    r_name,
                    p_name,
                    s_name,
                    SUM(ps_supplycost)
FROM    region,
        nation,
        supplier,
        partsupp,
        part
```

```
WHERE   ps_partkey = p_partkey
        AND ps_suppkey = s_suppkey
        AND s_nationkey = n_nationkey
        AND n_regionkey = r_regionkey
GROUP   BY n_name,
        r_name,
        p_name,
        s_name;
Plan hash value: 710495980
```

```
--------------------------------------------------------------------------------
| Id | Operation               | Name     | Rows | Bytes |TempSpc| Cost(%CPU)| Time     |
--------------------------------------------------------------------------------
|  0 | SELECT STATEMENT        |          | 228M |   29G |       | 7336K (1)| 24:27:18 |
|  1 |  HASH GROUP BY          |          | 228M |   29G |   31G | 7336K (1)| 24:27:18 |
|* 2 |   HASH JOIN             |          | 228M |   29G |       |  351K (1)| 01:10:19 |
|  3 |    TABLE ACCESS FULL    | REGION   |   10 |   270 |       |    3  (0)| 00:00:01 |
|* 4 |    HASH JOIN            |          | 114M |   11G |       |  350K (1)| 01:10:10 |
|  5 |     TABLE ACCESS FULL   | NATION   |   50 |  1450 |       |    3  (0)| 00:00:01 |
|* 6 |     HASH JOIN           |          |  57M | 4458M |   83M |  350K (1)| 01:10:06 |
|  7 |      TABLE ACCESS FULL  | SUPPLIER | 2040K|   60M |       | 10493 (1)| 00:02:06 |
|* 8 |      HASH JOIN          |          |  28M | 1372M |  343M |  251K (1)| 00:50:19 |
|  9 |       TABLE ACCESS FULL | PART     | 7204K|  261M |       | 37669 (1)| 00:07:33 |
| 10 |       TABLE ACCESS FULL | PARTSUPP |  28M |  354M |       |  162K (1)| 00:32:34 |
--------------------------------------------------------------------------------
```

There are different types of hints that could be applied based on the type of optimization path to be taken. Oracle supports over 60 different types of hints for the various types of operations. Multiple hints may also be used for the same SQL statement, for example, if you want to use the NOPARALLEL and the FIRST_ROWS hint at the same time. The statement block can only have a comment containing hints, and that comment must follow the SELECT, INSERT, UPDATE, and DELETE key words of the statement. Immediately following the comment, the "+" is used to tell the optimizer that there is a hint inside the comment. For example

```
SELECT /*+ NOPARALLEL, FIRST_ROWS */ ...
```

If the syntactically correct hint is not specified, the optimizer will not report any errors but will generate an execution path as if there was no hint specified.

Although Oracle does provide this method to change the optimizer behavior using hints, such a method should be avoided as much as possible. The disadvantage of using hints is the extra code that needs to be maintained, checked, and controlled every time there is change to the environment. Changes to the database and host environment can make hints obsolete or even have negative consequences. Due to these reasons, hints should only be used as a last resort to query optimization. Other more efficient methods should be used instead.

Hints help change the execution path for a given statement. What if all the statements in a session need to be changed? In this case, the execution paths can be changed for the entire session by modifying the Oracle initializing parameters.

Altering the Session

In an earlier section, we discussed that the optimizer mode is set at the system level when the database is started. The optimizer mode is defaulted to ALL_ROWS and can be changed at the system level, which means the parameter value will apply to the entire database (all user/sessions connecting to the database). The changes made in the init.ora file or the spfile applies to the entire database; the value can be modified to apply for just the session using an ALTER SESSION command before executing the statements in the session.

```
ALTER SESSION SET OPTIMIZER_MODE = FIRST_ROWS;
```

The preceding parameter can be embedded into the application; yet a better method would be to specifically execute this for a group of users accessing a schema using a logon trigger. Having this at the database level (as a database logon trigger) instead of hard coding such specific conditions in the application will reduce the application maintenance should the session-level parameter change.

```
CREATE OR REPLACE TRIGGER ALTER_SESSION_TRG
AFTER LOGON ON DATABASE
 BEGIN
    >>>  validate the user connected is eligible for the session level change
         >>> execute immediate ' ALTER SESSION SET  < PARAMETER NAME >> =  << VALUE>>;
END;
/
```

Similar to the OPTIMIZER_MODE parameter, there are several optimizer-related parameters that can be changed at the session level. Table 7-1 gives a list of optimizer parameters that can be changed at the session level.

Table 7-1. *Optimizer Parameters*

Parameter	Description
DB_FILE_MULTIBLOCK_READ_COUNT	Specifies the number of blocks that will be read in a single I/O. The optimizer uses the value to calculate the cost of full table scans and index fast full scans. The unit for this parameter is in blocks and is set to the maximum I/O size that the database can perform efficiently.
CURSOR_SHARING	Converts literals used in SQL statements to bind variables. This helps improve cursor sharing and reduce parsing.
RESULT_CACHE_MODE	Helps determine if all the queries will use the result cache feature or only queries that are hinted. If set to MANUAL, a hint is expected for the queries to cache the result.
RESULT_CACHE_REMOTE_EXPIRATION	Specifies the number of minutes for which a result that depends on remote database objects remains valid.
OPTIMIZER_MODE	Sets the optimizer mode at database instance startup.
STAR_TRANSFORMATION_ENABLED	Enables the optimizer to cost a start transformation for the star queries.
OPIMTIMIZER_INDEX_COST_ADJ	Adjusts the cost of index; the default value of this parameter is 100. When set to 100, optimizer evaluates indexes as an access path based on the normal cost model.
OPTIMIZER_INDEX_CACHING	Controls the cost analysis of an index with a nested loop.
OPTIMIZER_ADAPTIVE_REPORTING_ONLY	Controls the reporting mode for automatic reoptimization and adaptive plans.

SQL Automatic Tuning

In Oracle Database 10g, a new feature was introduced called automatic query tuning. With this feature, the query-tuning advisor will advise on what needs to be done with the query to improve performance. The tuning suggestions could be as simple as the optimizer statistics are stale and need to be generated again or as complex as the query needs to changed/rewritten.

These discovered suggestions are profiled in the database as corrections to poor performing queries. This information helps the optimizer improve selectivity estimates, and this helps the optimizer select better plans. The SQL profile provides the following benefits:

- Profiles prevent hard mapping of the optimizer to specific plans or subplans generated due to hard coded hints and stored outlines.

- Profiles help fix incorrect estimates while giving the optimizer the options to select the best plans based on the conditions posed.

No changes to the code are required when profiles are used. Oracle manages the changed plans for a query in the data dictionary and reuses the profile based on SQL_ID, keeping the use of the SQL profile transparent to the user. To understand this better, we take an example and discuss the process of generating an SQL profile.

Workshop—SQL Tuning Using SQL Tuning Advisor

In this workshop, we use the SQL tuning advisor option and try to optimize an SQL statement.

Step 1

The following SQL statement was executed in a production environment:

```
SELECT /*+ NOPARALLEL */ N_NAME, R_NAME, P_NAME, S_NAME, SUM(PS_SUPPLYCOST) FROM REGION, NATION,
SUPPLIER, PARTSUPP, PART WHERE PS_PARTKEY=P_PARTKEY AND PS_SUPPKEY = S_SUPPKEY AND S_NATIONKEY =
N_NATIONKEY AND N_REGIONKEY = R_REGIONKEY GROUP BY N_NAME,R_NAME,P_NAME,S_NAME;
Plan hash value: 710495980
```

Id	Operation	Name	Rows	Bytes	TempSpc	Cost(%CPU)	Time
0	SELECT STATEMENT		228M	29G		7336K (1)	24:27:18
1	HASH GROUP BY		228M	29G	31G	7336K (1)	24:27:18
* 2	HASH JOIN		228M	29G		351K (1)	01:10:19
3	TABLE ACCESS FULL	REGION	10	270		3 (0)	00:00:01
* 4	HASH JOIN		114M	11G		350K (1)	01:10:10
5	TABLE ACCESS FULL	NATION	50	1450		3 (0)	00:00:01
* 6	HASH JOIN		57M	4458M	83M	350K (1)	01:10:06
7	TABLE ACCESS FULL	SUPPLIER	2040K	60M		10493 (1)	00:02:06
* 8	HASH JOIN		28M	1372M	343M	251K (1)	00:50:19
9	TABLE ACCESS FULL	PART	7204K	261M		37669 (1)	00:07:33
10	TABLE ACCESS FULL	PARTSUPP	28M	354M		162K (1)	00:32:34

If the plan is analyzed, it should be clear that with the NOPARALLEL hint the query took over 24 minutes to complete execution. This is really expensive considering that the number of rows in the database is not very high. Now we try to use the SQL tuning advisor to help fix this query for better efficiency.

Step 2

If you examined the plan, you would notice that Oracle had performed a full scan on almost all the tables used in the statement. Full scans are normally expensive based on the number of rows that the table contains. If the number of rows are not high, probably a full scan would be more efficient compared to an indexed-based lookup. The first step for using the SQL tuning advisor is to identify the SQL_ID for the statement to be tuned:

```
SQL> SELECT sql_id,
       sql_text
FROM   v$sql
WHERE  sql_text LIKE '%SUM(PS_SUPPLYCOS%';
SQL_ID
-------------
SQL_TEXT
--------------------------------------------------------------------------------
gbybkujt0w0y6
SELECT /*+ NOPARALLEL */ N_NAME,R_NAME,P_NAME,S_NAME,SUM(PS_SUPPLYCOST) FROM region, NATION,
SUPPLIER, PARTSUPP, PART WHERE PS_PARTKEY=P_PARTKEY AND PS_SUPPKEY = S_SUPPKEY AND S_NATIONKEY =
N_NATIONKEY AND N_REGIONKEY = R_REGIONKEY GROUP BY N_NAME, R_NAME, P_NAME, S_NAME
```

Step 3

Using the SQL_ID from Step 2, we use the SQL advisor to create a tuning task:

```
SET SERVEROUTPUT ON
DECLARE
  mv_sql_tune_task_id  VARCHAR2(100);
BEGIN
  mv_sql_tune_task_id := DBMS_SQLTUNE.create_tuning_task (
                      sql_id      => ' gbybkujt0w0y6',
                      scope       => DBMS_SQLTUNE.scope_comprehensive,
                      time_limit  => 60,
                      task_name   => 'RACPTbook_workshop_chapter7',
                      description => 'Tuning task');
  DBMS_OUTPUT.put_line('mv_sql_tune_task_id: ' || mv_sql_tune_task_id);
END;
/
```

Step 4

Once the tuning task is created, the task needs to be executed using the EXECUTE_TUNING_TASK procedure following:

```
EXEC DBMS_SQLTUNE.execute_tuning_task(task_name => 'RACPTbook_workshop_chapter7');
```

Step 5

Verify the task status of the tuning task using the following query:

```
SQL> SELECT TASK_NAME, STATUS FROM DBA_ADVISOR_LOG WHERE TASK_NAME LIKE 'RAC%';
TASK_NAME                        STATUS
-------------------------------- ----------
RACPTbook_workshop_chapter7      COMPLETED
```

Step 6

Once the tuning task has completed, the recommendations can be generated using the following:

```
SET LONG 10000;
SET PAGESIZE 1000
SET LINESIZE 200
SELECT DBMS_SQLTUNE.report_tuning_task('RACPTbook_workshop_chapter7') AS recommendations FROM dual;
```

Based on the query and the current structure, the tuning optimizer can generate a very detailed list of recommendations or no recommendations at all if no changes are required. In this specific example, the tuning optimizer generated a list of recommendations.

```
RECOMMENDATIONS
-------------------------------------------------------------------------------
GENERAL INFORMATION SECTION
-------------------------------------------------------------------------------
Tuning Task Name     : RACPTbook_workshop_chapter7
Tuning Task Owner    : RAPDWH
Workload Type        : Single SQL Statement
Scope                : COMPREHENSIVE
Time Limit(seconds): 60
Completion Status    : COMPLETED
Started at           : 07/19/2010 18:32:07
Completed at         : 07/19/2010 18:33:38
-------------------------------------------------------------------------------
Schema Name: RAPDWH
SQL ID      : gbybkujt0w0y6
SQL Text    : SELECT /*+ NOPARALLEL */ N_NAME,R_NAME,P_NAME,S_NAME,SUM(PS_SUPPL
              YCOST) FROM REGION, NATION, SUPPLIER, PARTSUPP, PART WHERE
              PS_PARTKEY=P_PARTKEY AND PS_SUPPKEY = S_SUPPKEY AND S_NATIONKEY
              = N_NATIONKEY AND N_REGIONKEY = R_REGIONKEY GROUP BY
              N_NAME,R_NAME,P_NAME,S_NAME


-------------------------------------------------------------------------------
FINDINGS SECTION (1 finding)
-------------------------------------------------------------------------------

1- SQL Profile Finding (see explain plans section below)
--------------------------------------------------------
  A potentially better execution plan was found for this statement.
  Recommendation (estimated benefit: 90.15%)
  ------------------------------------------
  - Consider accepting the recommended SQL profile to use parallel execution for this statement.
    execute dbms_sqltune.accept_sql_profile(task_name =>
            'RACPTbook_workshop_chapter7', task_owner => 'RAPDWH', replace
            => TRUE, profile_type => DBMS_SQLTUNE.PX_PROFILE);
```

Executing this **query with (degree of parallelism) DOP 10** will improve its response time 90.16% over the original plan. However, there is some cost in enabling parallel execution. It will increase the statement's resource consumption by an estimated 1.58%, which may result in a reduction of system throughput.

Also, because these resources are consumed over a much smaller duration, the response time of concurrent statements might be negatively impacted if sufficient hardware capacity is not available.

The following data shows some sampled statistics for this SQL from the past week and projected weekly values when parallel execution is enabled:

```
                              Past week sampled statistics for this SQL
                              --------------------------------------------
Number of executions                                                 0
Percent of total activity                                            0
Percent of samples with #Active Sessions > 2*CPU                     0
Weekly DB time (in sec)                                              0
Projected statistics with Parallel Execution
                              --------------------------------------------
Weekly DB time (in sec)                                              0
```

The plan generated by the tuning optimizer using parallel threads follows. As noted in the preceding analysis, the execution time using the parallel query is just 2 minutes compared to 24 minutes when the NOPARALLEL hint was used:

```
Plan hash value: 2152260066

-------------------------------------------------------------------------------------
| Id | Operation                | Name     | Rows | Bytes |Cost(%CPU)| Time     |
-------------------------------------------------------------------------------------
|  0 | SELECT STATEMENT         |          | 228M |  29G  |  722K (1)| 02:24:25 |
|  1 |  PX COORDINATOR          |          |      |       |          |          |
|  2 |   PX SEND QC (RANDOM)    | :TQ10006 | 228M |  29G  |  722K (1)| 02:24:25 |
|  3 |    HASH GROUP BY         |          | 228M |  29G  |  722K (1)| 02:24:25 |
|  4 |     PX RECEIVE           |          | 228M |  29G  | 23574 (1)| 00:04:43 |
|  5 |      PX SEND HASH        | :TQ10005 | 228M |  29G  | 23574 (1)| 00:04:43 |
|* 6 |       HASH JOIN BUFFERED |          | 228M |  29G  | 23574 (1)| 00:04:43 |
|  7 |        PX RECEIVE        |          |   10 |  270  |     2 (0)| 00:00:01 |
|  8 |         PX SEND BROADCAST| :TQ10000 |   10 |  270  |     2 (0)| 00:00:01 |
|  9 |          PX BLOCK ITERATOR|         |   10 |  270  |     2 (0)| 00:00:01 |
| 10 |           TABLE ACCESS FULL| REGION |   10 |  270  |     2 (0)| 00:00:01 |
|* 11|        HASH JOIN         |          | 114M |  11G  | 23496 (1)| 00:04:42 |
| 12 |         PX RECEIVE       |          |   50 | 1450  |     2 (0)| 00:00:01 |
| 13 |          PX SEND BROADCAST| :TQ10001|   50 | 1450  |     2 (0)| 00:00:01 |
| 14 |           PX BLOCK ITERATOR|        |   50 | 1450  |     2 (0)| 00:00:01 |
| 15 |            TABLE ACCESS FULL| NATION |   50 | 1450  |     2 (0)| 00:00:01 |
|* 16|         HASH JOIN        |          |  57M | 4458M | 23455 (1)| 00:04:42 |
| 17 |          PX RECEIVE      |          | 2040K|  60M  |  1165 (1)| 00:00:14 |
| 18 |           PX SEND BROADCAST| :TQ10002| 2040K|  60M  |  1165 (1)| 00:00:14 |
| 19 |            PX BLOCK ITERATOR|       | 2040K|  60M  |  1165 (1)| 00:00:14 |
| 20 |             TABLE ACCESS FULL| SUPPLIER| 2040K| 60M | 1165 (1)| 00:00:14 |
|* 21|          HASH JOIN       |          |  28M | 1372M | 22270 (1)| 00:04:28 |
| 22 |           PX RECEIVE     |          | 7204K| 261M  |  4182 (1)| 00:00:51 |
| 23 |            PX SEND HASH  | :TQ10003 | 7204K| 261M  |  4182 (1)| 00:00:51 |
| 24 |             PX BLOCK ITERATOR|      | 7204K| 261M  |  4182 (1)| 00:00:51 |
| 25 |              TABLE ACCESS FULL| PART | 7204K| 261M  |  4182 (1)| 00:00:51 |
| 26 |           PX RECEIVE     |          |  28M | 354M  | 18075 (1)| 00:03:37 |
| 27 |            PX SEND HASH  | :TQ10004 |  28M | 354M  | 18075 (1)| 00:03:37 |
| 28 |             PX BLOCK ITERATOR|      |  28M | 354M  | 18075 (1)| 00:03:37 |
| 29 |              TABLE ACCESS FULL| PARTSUPP| 28M | 354M | 18075 (1)| 00:03:37 |
-------------------------------------------------------------------------------------
```

Once the change recommended by the optimizer has been validated, the profile can be saved without making any direct changes to the application code. So in spite of the query using a NOPARALLEL hint, the tuning optimizer will ignore this and use the execution plan saved as a query profile for future execution:

```
EXECUTE DBMS_SQLTUNE.ACCEPT_SQL_PROFILE(
        TASK_NAME => 'RACPTbook_workshop_chapter7',
        TASK_OWNER=> 'RAPDWH',
        REPLACE=> TRUE,
        PROFILE_TYPE => DBMS_SQLTUNE.PX_PROFILE);
```

Table 7-2 lists out the common type of access paths used by SQL statements and explains why such access paths are used by Oracle to get to the data sets.

Table 7-2. Access Paths[3]

Access Path	Explanation
Full table scan	Reads all rows from table and filters out those that do not meet the where clause predicates. Used when there are no indexes, DOP set, and so forth.
Table access by rowid	Rowid specifies the data file and data block containing the row and the location of the row in that block. Used if rowid is supplied by the index or in WHERE clause.
Index unique scan	Only one row will be returned. Used when the statement contains a unique or a primary key constraint that guarantees that only a single row is accessed.
Index range scan	Accesses adjacent index entries returns rowid values. Used with equality on nonunique indexes or range predicate on unique indexes.
Index skip scan	Skips the leading edge of the index and uses the rest. Advantageous if there are few distinct values in the leading column and many distinct values in the nonleading column.
Full index scan	Processes all leaf blocks of an index but only enough branch blocks to find the 1st leaf block. Used when all necessary columns are in an index and order by clause matches index structure or if sort merge join is done.
Fast full index scan	Scans all blocks in an index; used to replace a full table scan when all necessary columns are in the index.
Index joins	Hash joins of several indexes that together contain all the table columns that are referenced in the query.
Bitmap indexes	Uses a bitmap for key values and a mapping function that converts each bit position to a rowid. Can efficiently merge indexes that correspond to several conditions in a WHERE clause.

---

[3]Source: Oracle Corporation.

SQL Plan Management

An execution plan for a statement can change for a variety of reasons, such as optimizer version, optimizer statistics, optimizer parameter's schema changes, and SQL profile creation. SQL Plan Management (SPM) is a feature introduced in Oracle Database 11g that enables the system to automatically control the SQL plan by maintaining SQL plan baselines. With this feature enabled, a newly generated plan can be used only if the Oracle optimizer can determine that using the new plan will not impact the performance of the statement, in which case the optimizer will use the SQL plan stored from an earlier execution of the same statement. However, if the optimizer determines that the SQL plan is more efficient compared to the previous plan, it will use the new plan and will save this new plan as the new plan baseline for future use. Incorporating such a feature into the system provides performance stability of the system by avoiding plan regressions.

The SPM feature is enabled when the parameter OPTIMIZER_USE_SQL_PLAN_BASELINES is set to TRUE (default). OPTIMIZER_USE_SQL_PLAN_BASELINES controls the use of SQL plan baselines. When enabled, the optimizer looks for plans in SQL plan baselines for the SQL statement being complied. If any are found, then the optimizer will cost each plan in the SQL plan baseline and pick the one with the lowest cost.

■ **Note**   Plan baseline can also manually be created using DBMS_SQLTUNE.CREATE_SQL_PLAN_BASELINE.

For SQL statements that are executed frequently, the optimizer can maintain a history of its execution plans. To determine which of the statements are repeatable, the optimizer maintains a statement log. An SQL statement is considered repeatable when it is parsed or executed again after it has been logged. For these repeatable statements, the execution plans generated by the optimizer are maintained as a plan history containing information such as SQL text, outline, bind variables, and so forth, which is required by the optimizer to reproduce an execution plan if the statement is parsed or executed in the future.

As obviously noticeable, Figure 7-4 is history or a collection of execution plans for a given SQL statement generated over time. The first time a SQL statement is recognized as repeatable; the best cost plan generated by the optimizer will not be in the history and will be used. This first plan becomes the baseline. Subsequently, when a new plan is generated using the best-cost method, the plan is added to the plan history as an unaccepted plan. The optimizer then tries to find a matching plan in the SQL plan baseline and picks the plan with better performance (lowest cost), which is then integrated into the SQL plan baselines. When it is verified that an unaccepted plan does not cause any performance regression, the plan is changed to an accepted plan and integrated into the SQL plan baseline. Not all plans in the history are used; only plans that have been verified to not cause any performance regression would be used.

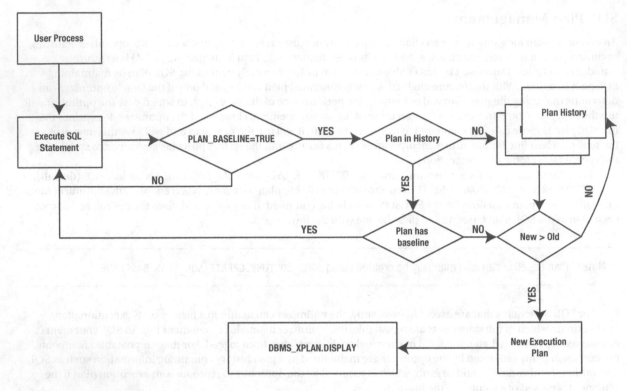

Figure 7-4. *SPM process flow*

The statement log, plan history, and plan baselines are stored in the SQL management base (SMB), which also contains SQL profiles. The SMB is part of the data dictionary and is stored in the SYSAUX tablespace. By default, the size allocated for plan management is 10% of the size of the SYSAUX tablespace. This can be changed using the DBMS_SPM.CONFIGURE procedure and can be set to a maximum space budget of 50%. The default unused plan retention period is 1 year and 1 week and will be automatically purged if it is not used for more than 1 year. The maximum retention period cannot be higher can 523 weeks.

The current setting of these parameters could be checked using the following query:

```
SQL> SELECT PARAMETER_NAME, PARAMETER_VALUE FROM DBA_SQL_MANAGEMENT_CONFIG;
PARAMETER_NAME                      PARAMETER_VALUE
----------------------------------- ----------------
SPACE_BUDGET_PERCENT                       10
PLAN_RETENTION_WEEKS                       53
```

If the default retention period needs to be increased to a higher value, the following procedure should help:

```
BEGIN DBMS_SPM.CONFIGURE('plan_retention_weeks',200); END;
```

Workshop—Plan Management

We use the SQL query example used in our previous discussions and discuss the process of SQL plan management.

Step 1

Execute the following query using SQL*Plus:

```
SELECT
/*+ NOPARALLEL */ n_name,
                  r_name,
                  p_name,
                  s_name,
                  SUM(ps_supplycost)
FROM    region,
        nation,
        supplier,
        partsupp,
        part
WHERE   ps_partkey = p_partkey
        AND ps_suppkey = s_suppkey
        AND s_nationkey = n_nationkey
        AND n_regionkey = r_regionkey
GROUP   BY n_name,
           r_name,
           p_name,
           s_name;
```

Step 2

We find the SQL_ID for this query from the V$SQL view:

```
SQL> SELECT SQL_ID,
        SQL_FULLTEXT
FROM    V$SQL
WHERE   SQL_TEXT LIKE 'SELECT /*+ NOPARALLEL */ N_NAME%';
SQL_ID          SQL_FULLTEXT
-------------   --------------------------------------
gbybkujt0w0y6   SELECT /*+ NOPARALLEL */ N_NAME,R_NAME,P
                _NAME,S_NAME,SUM(PS_SUPPLYCOST) FROM reg
```

Step 3

Using the SQL_ID, create a SQL plan baseline for the statement:

```
SQL> variable sqlid number;
SQL> EXECUTE :sqlid :=DBMS_SPM.LOAD_PLANS_FROM_CURSOR_CACHE(sql_id=>'gbybkujt0w0y6');
PL/SQL procedure successfully completed.
```

Step 4

This original query has a hint, and when the optimizer behavior changes due to improvements to the optimizer after a database upgrade, the execution plan changes. The suboptimal plan will need to be disabled. The SQL_HANDLE and PLAN_NAME required to disable the plan can be found from DBA_SQL_PLAN_BASELINES view:

```
SQL> SELECT SQL_HANDLE, PLAN_NAME, ENABLED FROM DBA_SQL_PLAN_BASELINES;

SQL_HANDLE                      PLAN_NAME                       ENA
------------------------------  ------------------------------  ---
SYS_SQL_26517e6bd220dc3c        SQL_PLAN_2cnbydg921r1w9dcc863f  YES
```

Step 5

Now that the PLAN_HANDLE and SQL_HANDLE have been obtained, it can be disabled using the ALTER_SQL_PLAN_BASELINE procedure:

```
SQL> variable sqlid number;
SQL> EXEC :sqlid :=DBMS_SPM.ALTER_SQL_PLAN_BASELINE (SQL_HANDLE => 'SYS_SQL_26517e6bd220dc3c',PLAN_
NAME => 'SQL_PLAN_2cnbydg921r1w9dcc863f',ATTRIBUTE_NAME=>'enabled',ATTRIBUTE_VALUE => 'NO');
PL/SQL procedure successfully completed.
```

Step 6

Check if the plan has been disabled by querying from DBA_SQL_PLAN_BASELINES:

```
SQL> SELECT SQL_HANDLE, PLAN_NAME, ENABLED FROM DBA_SQL_PLAN_BASELINES;

SQL_HANDLE                      PLAN_NAME                       ENA
------------------------------  ------------------------------  ---
SYS_SQL_26517e6bd220dc3c        SQL_PLAN_2cnbydg921r1w9dcc863f  NO
```

Step 7

Now that the optimizer has improved, execute the query without the hint:

```
SELECT  n_name,
        r_name,
        p_name,
        s_name,
        SUM(ps_supplycost)
FROM    region,
        nation,
        supplier,
        partsupp,
        part
WHERE   ps_partkey = p_partkey
        AND ps_suppkey = s_suppkey
        AND s_nationkey = n_nationkey
        AND n_regionkey = r_regionkey
```

```
GROUP  BY n_name,
          r_name,
          p_name,
          s_name;
```

Step 8

Find the SQL_ID and PLAN_HASH_VALUE for the new modified SQL statement from V$SQL view:

```
SQL> SELECT SQL_ID, PLAN_HASH_VALUE, SQL_FULLTEXT FROM V$SQL WHERE SQL_TEXT LIKE 'SELECT N_NAME,R_
NAME%';

SQL_ID        PLAN_HASH_VALUE SQL_FULLTEXT
------------- --------------- -------------------------------------------------------
5kzxaz6fbbncz      1879087708 SELECT N_NAME,R_NAME,P_NAME,S_NAME,SUM(P
                              S_SUPPLYCOST) FROM region,nation,supplie
```

Step 9

Using the values obtained from Step 8, create a new accepted plan for the original SQL statement by associating the modified plan to the original statements SQL_HANDLE:

```
SQL> EXEC :sqlid := DBMS_SPM.LOAD_PLANS_FROM_CURSOR_CACHE (SQL_ID=>'5kzxaz6fbbncz',PLAN_HASH_
VALUE=>1879087708, SQL_HANDLE => 'SYS_SQL_26517e6bd220dc3c');
PL/SQL procedure successfully completed.
```

Step 10

Verify from the DBA_SQL_PLAN_BASELINES to ensure the operation is successful:

```
SQL> SELECT SQL_HANDLE, PLAN_NAME, ENABLED FROM DBA_SQL_PLAN_BASELINES;

SQL_HANDLE                    PLAN_NAME                        ENA
----------------------------- -------------------------------- ---
SYS_SQL_26517e6bd220dc3c      SQL_PLAN_2cnbydg921r1w926d78b5   YES
SYS_SQL_26517e6bd220dc3c      SQL_PLAN_2cnbydg921r1w9dcc863f   NO
```

Once this new plan is proven to be the optimized plan, it can be made fixed until such time that a better optimizer plan is generated. The SQL plan baselines can be marked as fixed. Fixed SQL plan baselines indicate to the optimizer that they are preferred. Marking a plan as a fixed plan, the optimizer will only cost the fixed plan. If the fixed plan is not reproducible by the optimizer, it will generate a new plan and cost the remaining SQL plan baselines to select the plan with the lowest cost.

Optimizer Statistics

Statistics used by the optimizer when generating the execution plan are stored in the data dictionary. Statistics about physical storage characteristics and data distribution in the various schema objects are generated by using the DBMS_STATS package.

To get the right execution plans, statistics should be maintained not just when the database is created and after the initial load of data but on a regular basis based on the frequency in which the data volume changes. If no statistics are available or the statistics are stale, the execution plans generated by the optimizer may not be efficient enough. Under these conditions, the optimizer performs dynamic sampling depending on the setting of the OPTIMIZER_ DYNAMIC_SAMPLE parameter. This sampling may cause slower parse times; so for best performance, the optimizer should have representative optimizer statistics.

Statistics at the table level include number of rows, number of blocks, and row length column statistics such as number of distinct values, number of nulls in columns, data distribution, or histograms. Index statistics include number of leaf blocks, levels, and clustering factors. System statistics include I/O performance and CPU performance. All of these statistics are important and change with the volume of data changes or if the structure of the objects changes. The statistics collected are then maintained in the data dictionary tables of the database.

Starting with Oracle database 10g, Oracle automatically starts gathering statistics once every day. Although Oracle recommends using the automated process, in certain cases, it may be required to use homegrown procedures to collect statistics, either because such a frequent collection interval may not be required or the automated collection process maybe scheduled with conflicts with other processes.

The following procedure could be used to verify if the automatic gathering of statistics has been enabled:

```
SELECT  program_action,
        number_of_arguments  NOA,
        enabled
FROM    dba_scheduler_programs
WHERE   owner = 'SYS'
        AND program_name LIKE 'GATHER%';
PROGRAM_ACTION                                      NOA ENABL
-------------------------------------------- ---------- -----
dbms_stats.gather_database_stats_job_proc            0 TRUE
```

DBA_AUTOTASK_TASK displays all jobs that have been scheduled for automatic execution. As seen from the query output following, the GATHER_STATS_PROG is enabled for automatic statistics collection:

```
SQL> SELECT TASK_NAME, STATUS FROM DBA_AUTOTASK_TASK;

TASK_NAME                                       STATUS
----------------------------------------------- --------
AUTO_SQL_TUNING_PROG                            ENABLED
auto_space_advisor_prog                        ENABLED
gather_stats_prog                              ENABLED
```

The GATHER_DATABASE_STATS_JOB_PROC prioritizes database objects that require statistics so that objects that most need updated statistics are processed first, before the maintenance window closes.

Statistics can also be gathered manually using the DBMS_STATS package. It is used to gather statistics on tables and indexes and individual columns and partitions of tables. However, it does not gather cluster statistics. This is accomplished by collecting statistics on the individual tables instead of the whole cluster. DBMS_STATS collects statistics at the following levels:

```
GATHER_INDEX_STATS
GATHER_TABLE_STATS
GATHER_SCHEMA_STATS
GATHER_DICTIONARY_STATS
GATHER_DATABASE_STATS
```

When gathering statistics on a table, DBMS_STATS gathers information about the data distribution of the columns within the table. The most basic information about the data distribution, such as the maximum and minimum values for the column, may not be sufficient for the optimizer's needs if the data within the column is skewed. For skewed data distributions, histograms will have to be created as part of the column statistics to describe the data distribution of a given column. This is particularly helpful for data warehouse implementations where skewed data is normally present, and histograms help the optimizer to generate efficient execution plans. Histograms provide improved selectivity estimates in the presence of data skew, resulting in optimal execution plans with nonuniform data distributions.

Apart from the statistics, the optimizer also depends on the features of the Oracle database version that is available and the value of the version defined by the parameter OPTIMIZER_FEATURES_ENABLE. Using these parameters, specific versions of the optimizer features could be used by the database:

```
SELECT  NAME,
        VALUE
FROM    v$parameter
WHERE   NAME = 'optimizer_features_enable';

NAME                                             VALUE
---------------------------------------------    ----------------------
optimizer_features_enable                        12.1.0.1
```

Table 7-3 illustrates the various types of join types used by the optimizer when generating access plans.

Table 7-3. *Optimizer Join Types*[4]

Join Type	Explanation
Nested Loop Joins	For every row in the outer table, Oracle accesses all the rows in the inner table. Useful when joining small subsets of data and there is an efficient way to access the second table, for example, using index lookups.
Hash Joins	The smaller of the two tables is scanned and the resulting rows are used to build a hash table on the join key in memory. The larger table is then scanned, the join column of the resulting rows are hashed, and the values used to probe the hash table to finish the matching rows. Useful for larger tables and if equality predicates.
Sort Merge Joins	Consists of two steps. Both the inputs are sorted on the join key. The sorted lists are merged together. This is useful when the join condition between two tables is an inequality condition or one of the tables is already ordered, e.g., index access.
Cartesian Joins	Joins every row from one data source with every row from the other data source, creating the Cartesian Product of the two sets. Only good if tables are very small. The only choice if there is no join condition specified in the query.
Outer Joins	Returns all rows that satisfy the join condition and also returns all of the rows from the table without the (+) for which no rows from the other table satisfy the join condition.

[4]Source: Oracle Corporation.

Conclusion

In this chapter, we discussed the basic elements of tuning a SQL query. Query optimization is very critical for the optimal performance of the database. There was one incident when a customer decided to move his database to a RAC configuration because his single-instance Oracle database was maxed out on CPU every time. The customer expected that moving to a two-node RAC solution would buy him twice the amount of CPUs; unfortunately, it was a few SQL statements that were very poorly written that always caused the server to be consuming high CPU resources. In fact, moving to the RAC cluster made the situation even worse: all servers in his cluster maxed out on CPU resources. The end result was to tune the SQL queries to allow the application scale.

Writing efficient SQL statements and tuning the inefficient SQL statements using several of the methods discussed in this chapter is critical for the optimal performance of the RAC environment. No amount of resources can help do the magic to fix inefficient SQL statements.

CHAPTER 8

■ ■ ■

Parallel Query Tuning

A good analogy for parallel processing is to take an example from our everyday life. It's that time of the year: the holidays when people are anxiously waiting to exchange gifts. Several people need to be given gifts and to get the gifts ready, the package needs to be packed, glued, and labeled. Once finished it's either delivered in person or delivered to the post office for shipping. What if there was a method to break this entire processing into smaller pieces of work where a different person does each piece of work? One person cuts the paper, another assembles the gifts for one recipient, another cuts the adhesive tape, and finally one wraps up the gift and places the label. It would help in two aspects: first, if more than one person does the entire work, that person is not bored doing all the gifts all alone; second, when more people help in the process, the work will get done quicker. As the family network expands and more gifts have to be given in a subsequent year, this would mean increasing the number of people to complete the work sooner.

There is a limit to every activity; just increasing the number of people to help in the gift wrapping process may not help. These additional people should have a balanced distribution of work so there is even flow from one person to the other. If we have additional people to cut the adhesive tape, then one person may cut more than what can be used immediately or may have to wait for others to complete their work so the tape cutter could apply the tape. In other words, there could be bottlenecks in the process. Similarly, increasing the number of helpers through all stages could complete the work sooner; however, after a certain stage, the throughput of these helpers could be reduced. Because they could start talking and making stories in the process, their overall efficiency could be reduced.

What if one of the helpers took a restroom break, others will have to wait, and a backlog would be created. Ideally, the remaining people can divide the work of the missing person and complete the work but at a much slower speed.

We could apply this metaphor to information technology. If there were a large number of users making requests to the database simultaneously (or one user making a large request to retrieve a complex set of data) and there was only one CPU to process the request(s), the user(s) would have to wait several hours or possibly days for the results. (The length of the wait would be based on the complexity of the query, underlying database design, processing power of the computer, the volume of data being retrieved, etc.). If there were an opportunity for the user(s) to execute requests to the database in parallel, the request would speed up and complete much more quickly and efficiently.

Increasing the number of helpers for wrapping the gifts in our metaphor or processing of data across multiple processors is possible because of the work can be divided among the additional resources, for example, lanes and processors. This division of work into multiple, or asynchronous processing of a request is called a parallel activity or "parallel processing."

Parallel processing is the use of multiple processors to execute different parts of the same program simultaneously and provides the opportunity to divide the workload and obtain the results using available computer resources. The main goal of parallel processing is to reduce wall-clock time, that is, to "speed up" work. The scenarios discussed earlier are examples of parallel processing, and both the metaphor example and the one of a large number of users accessing data illustrate the goal of distributed processing.

In the example of the gift wrapping, the power and weakness of the parallel approach becomes visible by taking it to the extreme. In other words, as the number of people/helpers is increased, there will be a characteristic speedup curve, demonstrating how, up to a certain number of helpers, it is beneficial. However, anything over a certain point probably will give a reduced or negative benefit.

Figure 8-1 represents the increase in the number of helpers to the gift-wrapping process. It becomes evident that after a certain point, with a fifth person, more gifts are wrapped. The curve continues to show an upward growth until an eighth person is introduced, when the curve slowly starts to dip. This is because of skewing: the curve starts going down, indicating more time to complete the operation. This is an example of the law of diminishing returns. Too much of something may bring back a lesser satisfaction or benefit. A similar behavior will also be noticed in the example related to information technology.

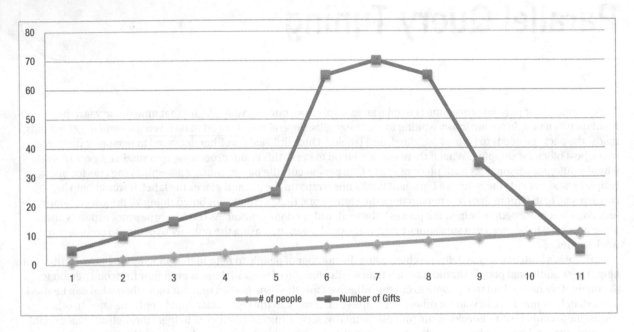

Figure 8-1. *Parallel processing example*

Parallel processing is the

- division of work into smaller tasks, that is, to divide and conquer
- assignment of many smaller tasks into multiple threads to execute simultaneously
- reduction of wall-clock time for execution of computer programs.

Why Parallel Processing?

There could be degraded performance of the system due to an increase in the number of users and contention for resources. When this occurs, one solution explored in Chapter 4 was to increase the processing power of the computer by adding additional resources such as CPU and memory, that is, vertically scaling the hardware. Although this is not ideal in most situations, it does potentially help provide a temporary solution toward supporting the increase in the number of users. Another solution was to add additional servers and scale the number of users in a linear or horizontal fashion. This would allow for distribution of users across multiple machines, thus providing linear scalability and availability.

If we had one large complex process and a computer with a single processor, this would take time to complete depending on many other factors. In this situation, one option is to increase the speed of the existing processor (like increasing the resources such as number of CPUs or CPU power or memory on the current hardware) to accept more workload. A given processor is made to specifications, it is made to perform at a certain speed; the same processor could not be increased in speed. However, the processor could be swapped with a higher-speed processor, provided that the hardware that uses it will support this new processor's architecture. This scenario is another flavor of vertical scalability. Instead of replacing the processor with another processor that is of a higher speed, an additional processor is added, providing twice the processing power and aiding in the distribution of work among the two processors.

This could be taken even further if you consider three or four processors or multiple computers or servers each with multiple processors. All these processors and servers could be put to use simultaneously to perform functions in parallel.

Coming back to our metaphor discussion, a person taking a restroom break could slow down packing, and if the break was a lunch break, the gift-wrapping process could be even slower, because it could cause serialization or queuing. Computer systems are no different; multiple processors don't always mean processing power is always there, and there could be one runaway process or one process that needs to retrieve a large volume of data using up all the power of these computers, which will cause other processes to queue or serialize.

Advantages of moving toward a parallel processing concept include the following:

- Adding one big server to handle the entire workload would be more expensive compared to adding many smaller servers, which help in providing the distribution of workload. One bigger server could indeed be faster compared to many smaller servers. However, the bigger server may be more costly (dollar wise) compared to the sum of all the smaller servers combined.

- Running a program in parallel on multiple processors or multiple processors across multiple servers is usually faster than running the same program on a single server processor.

- A system can be scaled or built up gradually. If, over time, a system becomes too small to handle these tasks, additional processors or servers can be added to meet the new requirements.

- On systems that are highly I/O intensive, a single process could do some work, wait for the I/O, get its turn to access the I/O subsystem, and do some work again, and so forth. If it's the monolithic process, all these become sequential. If multiple (parallel queries) PQs do it, they overlap, potentially utilizing additional I/O channels across one or multiple servers to the I/O subsystems and perform more efficiently.

Various types of hardware are available to support the parallel concepts, such as clustered SMP (symmetric multiprocessing), MPP (massively parallel processing), and clustered NUMA (non-uniform memory access). These clustered solutions provide linear scalability, help in distribution of workload, and provide availability. Due to the scalability factors built into these hardware architectures, they are all potential platforms for parallel processing.

Oracle and Parallel Processing

Oracle also supports parallel processing. Oracle's basic architecture (the background and foreground processes) demonstrates a parallel processing architecture if implemented on a hardware that supports multiple processors. Although Oracle supports most of the operating systems on most hardware platforms, its architecture may not scale on the smaller platforms that have only one processor but may cause high wait times because one processor has to be shared by the many background and foreground processes. Parallel processing is implemented on either a single stand-alone database configuration or on multi-instance database configurations, such as RAC.

When Oracle executes SQL statements in parallel, multiple processes work together to execute a single SQL statement. By dividing the work necessary to execute a statement among multiple processes, Oracle can execute the statement more quickly than if a single process executed it.

Parallel execution dramatically reduces response time for data-intensive operations on large databases such as those typically associated with decision support systems (DSS), operational data stores (ODS), data warehouses (DWH), certain types of online transaction processing (OLTP), and hybrid systems.

Parallel execution improves performance for the following:

- Queries that perform a full table scan
- Fast full index scans
- The creation of large indexes
- DML operations doing bulk inserts, updates, and deletes
- Aggregations and copying
- Partitioned index scans
- Database recovery

Parallel execution benefits systems have the following characteristics:

- Sufficient I/O bandwidth
- Underutilization (in the sense that the CPUs are mostly idle)
- Sufficient memory to handle multiple requests including sorting, hashing, and additional I/O buffers

Parallel processing requires additional resources to accommodate the additional processing requests. Lack of these additional resources to accommodate these requests could potentially cause serialization or queuing, causing slower performance. There are certain areas of the application where parallel execution will not be beneficial. For example

- Applications that have small singleton transactions, normally retrieving data from one table.
- Systems that have fewer resources available to take on this additional load of parallel operation. Basically, systems that are already heavy on CPU usage may not be suitable for parallel executions.

Whereas parallelism is used by the DBA for their DDL activity, larger benefits of parallelism in an everyday production environment comes from query execution. In the next section, we discuss the parallel query architecture.

Parallel Query Architecture

When a query is executed in parallel, the process that initiates the parallel query is called the query coordinator (QC). The QC is a server shadow process of the session running the PQ. The main function of the QC is to parse the query and partition the work between the *parallel server* (PX) processes.

During the parse operation, both serial and parallel plans are prepared based on the *degree of parallelism* (DOP). The QC then attempts to obtain the number of parallel server processes it wants to run. During these attempts, if it is unable to find sufficient parallel servers, the QC decides to run the query serially or puts the query in a queue; and when sufficient processes are available, they are released for processing.

If sufficient resources are available, and the QC is able to get the required number of parallel servers, the QC sends instructions to the PX. The coordination between the QC and PX is done by the mechanism of process queues. Process queues are also used for communication between two or more PX processes, and this is handled using queue references.

Queue references are a representation of a link between two process queues. They are always organized in pairs, one for the process at each end of the link. Each queue reference has four message buffers (three message buffers in the case of a single instance), which is used to communicate between the processes. Every parallel operation is given a unique serial number. All the processes involved as a sanity check on incoming messages use this serial number, as all messages carry this number.

PX, which is a background process, does most of the work for a PQ. PX is allocated in slave sets, which act as either producers or consumers. The number of slave sets required to complete the operation is determined based on the complex nature of the query, the amount of resources available, and parallel degree limit defined. For a simple query

```
SELECT /*+ PARALLEL (PRODUCT, 2) */ * FROM PRODUCT
```

Only one slave set can be used to scan the table (see Figure 8-2). These sets of slaves act as producers.

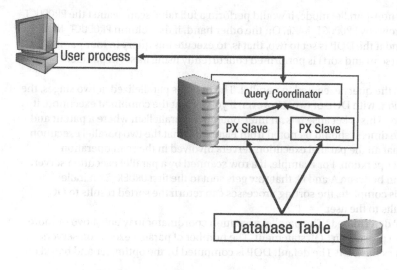

Figure 8-2. *Parallel query slaves*

However, if the query is of a more complex nature, such as a multi-table join or has a ORDER BY or GROUP BY operation, then probably more than one slave set (illustrated in Figure 8-3) would be used; and, in this scenario, the slaves act in both the producer and consumer roles. When acting as producers, slaves are making data available to the next step (using the table queues). When acting as consumers, slaves are taking data from a previous table queue and performing operations on it.

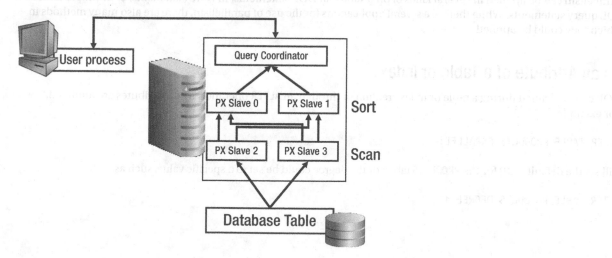

Figure 8-3. *Parallel processing with sort operation*

Only when there is a need for multiple slave sets (e.g., where statements have ORDER BY or GROUP BY conditions or statements that have multi-table joins) does the consumer come into operation.

We expand the previous query with an additional clause of ORDER BY operation:

```
SELECT *
FROM product
ORDER BY product_name;
```

If this query were executed in a regular non-parallel mode, it would perform a full table scan against the PRODUCT table, followed by a sorting of the retrieved rows by PRODUCT_NAME. On the other hand, if the column PRODUCT_NAME does not have an index associated with it, and if the DOP is set to two, that is, to execute this query in four parallel operations, then each of the two operations (scan and sort) is performed concurrently using its set of parallel execution servers.

Figure 8-3 represents a pictorial view of the query executed in parallel. The query is parallelized at two stages, the scan phase and the sort phase of the operation, with DOP of two. However, if you look at the combined execution, it is divided into four parallel execution servers. This is because it is an inter-operation parallelism where a parent and child operator can be performed at the same time. It should be noted from Figure 8-3 that the two parallel execution tiers are related to each other in the sense that all the parallel execution servers involved in the scan operation send rows to the servers performing the sort operation. For example, if a row scanned by a parallel execution server contains a value of the PRODUCT_NAME column between A and G, that row gets sent to the first ORDER BY parallel execution server. When the scan operation is complete, the sorting processes can return the sorted results to QC, which then returns the complete query results to the user.

How is the parallel degree limit or DOP determined? The parallel execution coordinator may enlist two or more of the instance's parallel execution servers to process an SQL statement. The number of parallel execution servers associated with a single operation is known as the DOP. The default DOP is computed by the optimizer and based on the system configuration; typically it's the

```
PARALLEL_THREADS_PER_CPU * CPU_COUNT (number of CPU cores) * ACTIVE_INSTANCE_COUNT (number of active
instances)
```

Methods of Applying Parallelism

Parallelism can be applied in several kinds of operations: in DDL statements, in DML statements, or in simple direct SQL query statements. While there are several applications for the use of parallelism, there are also many methods in which they could be applied.

As an Attribute of a Table or Index

DOP can be defined during a table or index creation or through an ALTER operation when attributes are modified. For example

```
ALTER TABLE PRODUCTS PARALLEL;
```

will set the default DOP for the PRODUCTS table; or the degree could be set to a specific value, such as

```
ALTER TABLE PRODUCTS DEGREE 12;
```

Setting the parallel attribute at the table or index level means defining a DOP that is applicable to all operations against the object:

```
SELECT owner,
       table_name,
       degree
FROM   dba_tables
WHERE  table_name = 'PRODUCTS';

OWNER      TABLE_NAME                      DEGREE
---------- ------------------------------- ----------
DWH        PRODUCTS                        12
```

Similarly, DOP can also be defined for other object types such as indexes. The attributes can be checked by querying DBA_INDEXES tables:

```
SELECT index_name,
       degree,
       instances
FROM   dba_indexes
WHERE  TRIM(degree) NOT IN ('1','0');
```

Also, a DOP can be specified when performing large operations such as creating a table with data based on the data available in one or more tables. A typical example of this is when moving large volumes of data, for example, in a decision support system to create summary tables. In this case, when data is moved from the original table to the new table, the SELECT part of the operation can be executed in parallel:

```
CREATE TABLE PRODUCT_SUMMARY PARALLEL NOLOGGING AS SELECT ... FROM
```

As a Default Value

The default DOP is computed by the optimizer and based on the system configuration and Oracle parameters; typically, DOP is calculated by

```
PARALLEL_THREADS_PER_CPU * CPU_COUNT (number of CPU cores) * ACTIVE_INSTANCE_COUNT (number of active
instances)
```

The following output is an extract from an Oracle trace during parallel query execution using event 43905 at level 124:

```
kxfplist
        Getting instance info for default group
kxfpGetTotalCpuCount
        kxfplist returned status: 2
kxfpGetTotalCpuCount
        Get cpu count from instance#1, status:Sucess, count:16
kxfpGetTotalCpuCount
        Get cpu count from instance#2, status:Sucess, count:16
kxfpGetTotalCpuCount
        Get cpu count from instance#3, status:Sucess, count:16
kxfrDefaultDOP
```

```
DOP Trace -- compute default DOP
    # CPU       = 16
    Threads/CPU = 2 ("parallel_threads_per_cpu")
    default DOP = 32 (# CPU * Threads/CPU)
    default DOP = 96 (DOP * # instance)
    Default DOP = 96
```

Although Oracle is intelligent enough to compute the DOP required for the operation, allowing the optimizer to calculate the default every single time for every session could hinder overall performance of the environment. It's true that with the advancement of technology, computer resources, such as CPU power, memory, and so forth are much cheaper compared to several years ago. However, while the computer resources have become cheaper so also has the data workload and size of the databases and the number of users increased in proportion. This means resources are not always available in abundance; there is always a limitation. All sessions using default DOP could hinder the performance of the database servers starving for resources. Oracle database has built-in limits and parameter settings that can help prevent such a behavior of system overload. Parameters such as PARALLEL_MAX_SERVERS, PARALLEL_MIN_PERCENT, PARALLEL_MIN_TIME_THRESHOLD, and so forth are examples of how the default DOP can be controlled from chewing up available resources.

■ **Note**   We discuss usage and definitions of these parameters later in this chapter.

At the Session Level

The DOP can also be set at the session level; this means the DOP set will apply to all queries executed within the session. For example

```
ALTER SESSION FORCE PARALLEL QUERY;

ALTER SESSION ENABLE PARALLEL DML ;
```

Setting parallelism at the session level maybe helpful when certain functional areas of the application require parallelism.

As a Hint in a Query

This is probably the common method of applying parallelism: using a hint as part of the statement. A hint can be added to a query to request the optimizer to generate an execution plan that requests parallel operations. For example, the following query has a hint to generate the default DOP:

```
SELECT /*+ PARALLEL */ ol_w_id,
                       ol_d_id,
                       ol_number,
                       SUM(ol_amount),
                       SUM(ol_quantity)
FROM   order_line ol,
       orders ord
```

```
WHERE   ol.ol_o_id = ord.o_id
        AND ol.ol_w_id = ord.o_w_id
        AND ol.ol_d_id = ord.o_d_id
GROUP   BY ol_number,
           ol_w_id,
           ol_d_id;
```

There are various kinds of hints that could help the parallel execution behavior such as the following:

- PARALLEL
- NOPARALLEL
- PQ_DISTRIBUTE

PARALLEL

The PARALLEL hint specifies the desired number of concurrent servers that can be used for parallel operation. The hint applies to the SELECT, INSERT, UPDATE, and DELETE portions of a statement, as well as to the table scan portion. When using this hint, the number of servers that can be used is twice the value in the PARALLEL hint clause, if sorting or grouping operations also take place.

Hints are also useful to control the DOP by specifically requesting the DOP in the hint. For example, the following query, if executed with default DOP, would execute 96 threads. However, if this needs to be controlled to say only 8 threads, the query could be hinted with DOP value of 8:

```
SELECT /*+ PARALLEL, 8 */ ol_w_id,
                          ol_d_id,
                          ol_number,
                          SUM(ol_amount),
                          SUM(ol_quantity)
FROM    order_line ol,
        orders ord
WHERE   ol.ol_o_id = ord.o_id
        AND ol.ol_w_id = ord.o_w_id
        AND ol.ol_d_id = ord.o_d_id
GROUP   BY ol_number,
           ol_w_id,
           ol_d_id
```

The following query[1] helps verify the requested DOP and what was actually allocated by the optimizer. As noticed from the output following, the DOP requested is 8 and the actual DOP allocated is also 8. There could be situations where the default DOP is used, but the actual DOP received is much lower. This could be because the optimizer was not able to find a sufficient amount of resources to allocate the requested DOP:

```
select
  px.inst_id INT,
  decode(px.qcinst_id,NULL,username,' - '||lower(substr(s.program,length(s.program)-4,4) ) )
"Username",
```

---

[1]Modified version of the SQL script found on Metalink Note #202219.1.

```
  decode(px.qcinst_id,NULL, 'QC', '(Slave)') "QC/Slave" ,
  to_char( px.server_set) "Slave Set",
  to_char(s.sid) "SID",
  decode(px.qcinst_id, NULL ,to_char(s.sid) ,px.qcsid) "QC SID",
  px.req_degree "Requested DOP",
  px.degree "Actual DOP",
  px.qcinst_id "QC Inst"
from
  gv$px_session px,
  gv$session s
where
  px.inst_id = s.inst_id
 and
  px.sid=s.sid (+)
 and
  px.serial#=s.serial#
 and
  username not in ('SYSTEM')
order by 6,2 desc
/
```

INT	Username	QC/Slave	QC SID	Requested DOP	Actual DOP
1	TPCC	QC	745		
3	- p004	(Slave)	745	8	8
2	- p002	(Slave)	745	8	8
1	- p004	(Slave)	745	8	8
2	- p000	(Slave)	745	8	8
3	- p005	(Slave)	745	8	8
2	- p003	(Slave)	745	8	8
3	- p000	(Slave)	745	8	8
1	- p005	(Slave)	745	8	8
2	- p001	(Slave)	745	8	8
2	- p004	(Slave)	745	8	8
1	- p000	(Slave)	745	8	8
3	- p001	(Slave)	745	8	8
3	- p002	(Slave)	745	8	8
2	- p005	(Slave)	745	8	8
1	- p001	(Slave)	745	8	8
3	- p003	(Slave)	745	8	8
1	- p002	(Slave)	745	8	8
1	- p003	(Slave)	745	8	8

The Oracle background processes are identified by the ora_p*nnn* where *n* indicates the number of the parallel execution servers started. The following output lists 8 parallel processes started on instance one (SSKYPRD_1) in a RAC environment:

```
oracle   22591   1 24 19:36 ?        00:00:07 ora_p000_SSKYPRD_1
oracle   22593   1 26 19:36 ?        00:00:07 ora_p001_SSKYPRD_1
oracle   22595   1 25 19:36 ?        00:00:07 ora_p002_SSKYPRD_1
oracle   22597   1 24 19:36 ?        00:00:07 ora_p003_SSKYPRD_1
```

```
oracle    22599    1 23 19:36 ?        00:00:06 ora_p004_SSKYPRD_1
oracle    22601    1 24 19:36 ?        00:00:07 ora_p005_SSKYPRD_1
oracle    22603    1 25 19:36 ?        00:00:07 ora_p006_SSKYPRD_1
oracle    22605    1 26 19:36 ?        00:00:07 ora_p007_SSKYPRD_1
```

NOPARALLEL

NOPARALLEL overrides the default DOP on the statement or the PARALLEL specification at the object level and disables parallel operation on the statement. For example

```
SELECT /*+ NOPARALLEL */ * FROM PRODUCT
```

PQ_DISTRIBUTE

This hint controls the distribution method for a specified join operation. The syntax of this hint is /*+ PQ_DISTRIBUTE (tablespace name, distribution) */ where *distribution* is the distribution method (e.g., "PARTITION" is a distribution method) to use between the producer and consumer slaves for the left and the right side of the join.

The hint applies to parallel INSERT... SELECT FROM... and parallel CREATE TABLE AS SELECT statements to specify how rows should be distributed between the producer (query) and the consumer (load) slaves.

In complex query statements where there are several tables/objects involved, it may be required to specify a full set of hints to ensure the optimal execution plan is obtained. If a full set of hints is not specified, then the optimizer will have to determine the remaining access paths to be used and the corresponding join methods. This means the partial hint definitions may not be used because the optimizer might have determined that the requested hint cannot be used due to the join methods and access paths selected by the optimizer.

Initialization Parameters

Like any feature in Oracle, apart from the hints and methods to enable, request, and optimize the feature, there are parameters that could set at the instance level. These parameters apply to all sessions that run on the instance.

PARALLEL_MIN_SERVERS

This parameter specifies the minimum number of parallel execution processes for the instance. The default value for this parameter is 0. If a value greater than 0 is defined, then Oracle starts the parallel execution processes at instance startup. The myth that this is a RAC-only parameter is wrong because it just defines the minimum parallel servers started during instance startup. This parameter applies to both a RAC and non-RAC environment. In a RAC environment, queries against the GV$ views occur in parallel, and setting this parameter to a higher number such as 2 or 4 would help in this operation.

PARALLEL_MAX_SERVERS

This parameter specifies the maximum number of parallel execution processes and parallel recovery processes that can be started for an instance. The default value is set to (10 * CPU_COUNT * PARALLEL_THREADS_PER_CPU). By defining a max value, processes are only added on an as-needed basis to the maximum defined by this parameter. Careful attention should be given to setting this value. If the value is set too high, this could cause degraded performance, especially when sufficient resources are not available.

PARALLEL_ADAPTIVE_MULTI_USER

This parameter enables the adaptive algorithm and helps improve performance in environments that use parallel executions. The algorithm automatically reduces the requested DOP based on the system load at query startup time. The effective DOP is based on the default DOP, or the degree from the table or hints, divided by a reduction factor.

Having `PARALLEL_ADAPTIVE_MULTI_USER` set to `TRUE` (default value) causes the DOP to be calculated as `PARALLEL_THREADS_PER_CPU * CPU_COUNT * (a reduction factor)`. The purpose of this parameter is to allow as many users as possible to concurrently run queries in parallel, taking into account the number of CPUs on the machine. As more parallel queries are issued, the number of slaves allocated to each will be reduced, thus preventing parallel queries from being forced to run serially or failing with the following error:

```
ORA-12827 insufficient parallel query slaves available
```

This parameter helps in the optimal utilization of resources; however, the response time of the operation maybe inconsistent. Reduced DOP could affect parallel operations that are time critical, providing inconsistent response times. Avoiding such inconsistent execution may require that a minimal DOP is guaranteed for the operation; this can be done by using the parameter `PARALLEL_MIN_PERCENT`.

PARALLEL_MIN_PERCENT

This helps specify the minimum percentage of parallel server processes required to start the parallel operation. This parameter defaults to 0, meaning that Oracle will always execute the statement, irrespective of the number of parallel server processes available. Once this parameter is set and there are insufficient parallel query servers available, error `ORA-12827` is generated and the statement will not execute.

PARALLEL_THREADS_PER_CPU

This parameter specifies the default DOP for the instance and determines the parallel adaptive and load-balancing algorithm. It describes the number of parallel execution threads that a CPU can handle during parallel execution. It is used to calculate the default DOP for the instance and determines the maximum number of parallel servers if `PARALLEL_MAX_SERVERS` parameter is not set. By setting this value, the parallel execution option is not enabled. Parallel execution can be enabled by defining the `PARALLEL` clause at the table level or by adding a `PARALLEL` hint to the SQL statement.

This parameter is OS dependent, and the default value of 2 is adequate in most cases. On systems that are I/O bound, increasing this value could help improve performance.

PARALLEL_EXECUTION_MESSAGE_SIZE

As discussed earlier, the parallel servers are started and managed by the QC. During this process, all communication between these processes happens by passing messages via memory buffers. In a RAC environment, these messages are passed across the private interconnect. The amount of messages that can be sent is determined by this parameter. On systems where parallel processing is significantly high, large amounts of such messages are sent. These message transfers could cause latency to the overall response time of the query. It's important to size this parameter appropriately to reduce parallel message latency.

■ **Note**   There are several new parameters introduced in Oracle Database 11g Release 2; we discuss these parameters later in the appropriate sections. A few of the new parameters are listed following.

```
NAME                                    TYPE          VALUE
------------------------------------    ----------    ----------------
fast_start_parallel_rollback            string        LOW
parallel_degree_limit                   string        CPU
parallel_degree_policy                  string        AUTO
parallel_force_local                    boolean       FALSE
parallel_io_cap_enabled                 boolean       FALSE
parallel_min_time_threshold             string        AUTO
parallel_servers_target                 integer       256
recovery_parallelism                    integer       2
```

Parallelization is dependent on the current data conditions such as volume and distribution, including data partitions, indexes, resources, number of instances, and so forth. Consequently, when data changes, if a more optimal execution plan or parallelization plan becomes available, Oracle will automatically adapt to the new situation. Passing of data back and forth between the various processes is done using table queues (TQ). TQ is an abstract communication mechanism that allows child data flow operations to send rows to its parents. Once the QC receives the results back, it passes them over to the user that made the original request.

Figure 8-4 represents basic PQ architecture. The slave set processes (P0 and P1) read data from disk, and, using the queue references and process queues, pass it to P3 and P2 for a sort and merge operation, if the query has a GROUP BY or ORDER BY clause. Once this operation is complete, slave sets pass through the queue reference layer TQ one last time before returning data back to the QC process. The QC then presents the results back to the client.

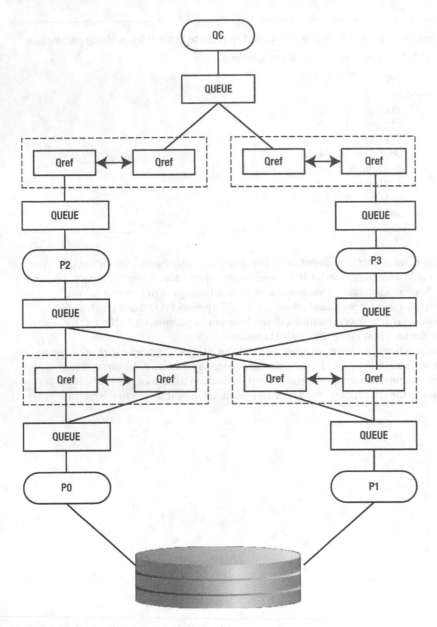

Figure 8-4. *Parallel query architecture*[2]

Beyond the parallel execution of the statement, in-between processes (e.g., sorting, ordering, joining, etc.) could also be executed in parallel. This kind of operation is called intra-operation parallelism and inter-operation parallelism.

---

[2]Source: Oracle Corporation

- Intra-operation parallelism is the parallelization of an individual operation, where the same operation is performed on smaller sets of rows by parallel execution servers.

- Inter-operation parallelism happens when two operations run concurrently on different sets of parallel execution servers with data flowing from one operation into the other.

The query (illustrated in Figure 8-5) is parallelized at two stages: the scan phase, also called the Producers (P0 and P1 operations illustrated in Figure 8-4), and the sort phase of the operation, also called the Consumers, with DOP of four resulting in eight parallel execution servers. This is because it is an inter-operation parallelism where a parent and child operator can be performed at the same time. As illustrated in Figure 8-5, each server in the producer set has a connection to each server in the consumer set.

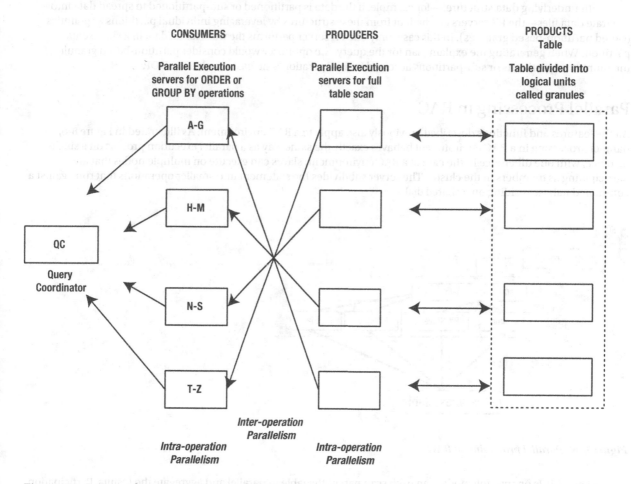

Figure 8-5. Intra- and inter-operation parallel processing

The producers who access the data divide the workload among the various parallel execution servers (determined by the DOP) to retrieve data from the tables. The amount of data sets each parallel execution server will retrieve is determined by the QC process and is in units called granules. *Granules are the smallest unit in which data is retrieved and managed in the memory structures of Oracle*. If the table or table partition being accessed is further dynamically partitioned into logical units (also called granules), these consist of a range of data blocks accessed by the PX processes. To get an even distribution of the work among the various PX processes, the number of granules is normally much higher than the requested DOP.

The QC process instructs the PX processes to retrieve data in granule units. PX processes execute the operation one granule at a time. When an execution server finishes reading the rows corresponding to a granule, and when there are more granules to be retrieved, it obtains another granule from the coordinator. This operation continues until the table has been completely read.

The two parallel execution tiers are related to each other; all the parallel execution servers involved in the scan operation send rows to the appropriate parallel execution server performing the sort operation. For example, if a row scanned by a parallel execution server contains a value of the PRODUCT_NAME column between A and G, that row gets sent to the first ORDER BY parallel execution server. When the scan operation is complete, the sorting processes can return the sorted results to QC. The QC then assembles the pieces into the desired full table scan and returns the results to the user.

With underlying data structures—for example, if the data is partitioned or sub-partitioned to spread data into separate data files—the PX servers can benefit from these structures by leveraging individual partitions as granules (called partition-based granules). In this case, only one PX server performs the work for all data in a single data partition. When generating the explain plan for the query, the optimizer would consider partition-based granules if the number of partitions or sub-partitions accessed in the operation is at least equal to the DOP.[3]

Parallel Processing in RAC

All the features and functions described previously also apply to a RAC environment. As illustrated in Figure 8-6, parallel processing in a RAC environment behaves exactly the same way as a parallel execution process on a single instance, with one difference in the case of a RAC environment: slaves can execute on multiple nodes that are participating as members in the cluster. The server subdivides the statement into smaller operations that run against a common database residing on a shared disk.

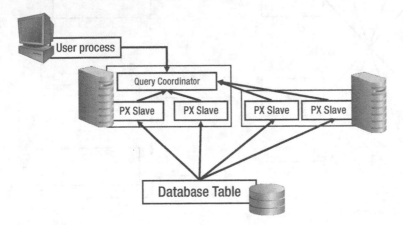

Figure 8-6. *Parallel processing in RAC*

Several CPUs on multiple nodes can each scan part of the table in parallel and aggregate the results. Participation of multiple nodes in a parallel execution task depends on the volume of work being handled by each of the servers. If the load on the system is minimal, the work will be spread across as many servers as determined by the optimizer when generating the DOP for the operation during execution plan generation. If the system is fully loaded, then a few local servers will be used to minimize any additional overhead required to coordinate local processes and to avoid any inter-instance overhead.

---

[3]"Parallel Execution Fundamentals in Oracle Database 11g Release 2," an Oracle White Paper, November 2009.

Prior to Oracle Database 11g Release 2, parallel query slaves bypassed the buffer cache and performed a direct path I/O to read data from disk into the PX server private workspace section. Starting with Oracle Database 11g Release 2, Oracle has enhanced the parallel query architecture significantly. Taking advantage of the advancement in memory management in servers and the large amount of memory available on the servers, parallel queries leverage the aggregated database buffer cache feature available in RAC to cache objects of very large sizes. Starting with Oracle Database 11g Release 2, with large amount of data stored in memory, Oracle now uses the in-memory PX feature.

With in-memory PX, when a SQL statement is issued in parallel, a check is conducted to determine if the objects accessed by the statement should be cached in the aggregated buffer cache of the system. The decision to use the aggregated buffer cache is based on the size of the object, the frequency at which the object changes, the frequency at which the object is accessed, and the size of the aggregated buffer cache. If these conditions are met, the object will be broken into smaller fragments and distributed to all participating nodes in the cluster and stored in their respective buffer caches. The size of the fragment depends on the type of data distribution strategy used to store the data. For example, if the database uses features such as hash partitioning, then each partition would be considered a fragment; if not, fragment sizes are based on the file number and extent number of the database object.[4]

Fragments mapped to a specific node in the cluster create instance affinity to the buffer cache of that instance. This means if data from these fragments are required, the PX servers on the nodes where the data resides will access the data in its buffer cache and return only the result to the instance where the statement was issued (where the QC is running) and not all the data required by the query. This new architecture reduces interconnect traffic significantly.

The output from event 43905 at level 124 also illustrates the slave distribution among the various instances in the RAC cluster. In the following output, there are three instances of Oracle and 96 slaves have to be distributed among the instances. As illustrated in the highlighted sections of the output, the optimizer decides to equally spread the slaves between the three instances in the cluster.

In the following output, the kxfpiinfo step illustrates that the optimizer has taken into consideration the number of CPUs available on each sever in the cluster and then the kxfpgsg step of the output allocates 32 slaves per instance (32*3), for a total of 96 slaves:

```
kxfrialo
        threads requested = 96 (from kxfrComputeThread())
kxfrialo
        adjusted no. threads = 96 (from kxfrAdjustDOP())
kxfrialo
        Start: allocating requested 96 slaves
kxfrAllocSlaves
        DOP trace -- call kxfpgsg to get 96 slaves
        num server requested = 96  load balancing:off adaptive:off
kxfplist
        Getting instance info for open group
kxfpiinfo
        inst[cpus:mxslv]
        1[16:320] 2[16:320] 3[16:320]
kxfpsori
        Sorted: 2(2:2) 1(1:1) 3(0:0)
kxfpgsg
        getting 2 sets of 96 threads, client parallel query execution flg=0x0
        Height=0, Affinity List Size=0, inst_total=3, coord=1
        Insts    2  1  3
        Threads  32 32 32
```

---

[4]"Parallel Execution Fundamentals in Oracle Database 11g Release 2," an Oracle White Paper, November 2009.

To further understand the parallel exaction architecture, we try to analyze the explain plan generated by optimizer to execute the query in parallel:

```
EXPLAIN PLAN FOR  SELECT n_name,
          r_name,
          p_name,
          s_name,
          SUM(ps_supplycost)
FROM      region,
          nation,
          supplier,
          partsupp,
          part
WHERE     ps_partkey = p_partkey
          AND ps_suppkey = s_suppkey
          AND s_nationkey = n_nationkey
          AND n_regionkey = r_regionkey
GROUP     BY n_name,
             r_name,
             p_name,
             s_name;
```

```
SQL> SELECT * FROM TABLE(DBMS_XPLAN.DISPLAY('PLAN_TABLE',NULL));

PLAN_TABLE_OUTPUT
--------------------------------------------------------------------------------
Plan hash value: 1879087708
```

Id	Operation	Name	Rows	Bytes	TempSpc	Cost (%CPU)	Time	TQ	IN-OUT	PQ Distrib
0	SELECT STATEMENT		228M	29G		722K (1)	02:24:25			
1	PX COORDINATOR									
2	PX SEND QC (RANDOM)	:TQ10006	228M	29G		722K (1)	02:24:25	Q1,06	P->S	QC (RAND)
3	HASH GROUP BY		228M	29G	31G	722K (1)	02:24:25	Q1,06	PCWP	
4	PX RECEIVE		228M	29G		23576 (1)	00:04:43	Q1,06	PCWP	
5	PX SEND HASH	:TQ10005	228M	29G		23576 (1)	00:04:43	Q1,05	P->P	HASH
* 6	HASH JOIN BUFFERED		228M	29G		23576 (1)	00:04:43	Q1,05	PCWP	
7	BUFFER SORT							Q1,05	PCWC	
8	PX RECEIVE		10	270		3 (0)	00:00:01	Q1,05	PCWP	
9	PX SEND BROADCAST	:TQ10000	10	270		3 (0)	00:00:01		S->P	BROADCAST
10	TABLE ACCESS FULL	REGION	10	270		3 (0)	00:00:01			
* 11	HASH JOIN		114M	11G		23497 (1)	00:04:42	Q1,05	PCWP	
12	BUFFER SORT							Q1,05	PCWC	
13	PX RECEIVE		50	1450		3 (0)	00:00:01	Q1,05	PCWP	
14	PX SEND BROADCAST	:TQ10001	50	1450		3 (0)	00:00:01		S->P	BROADCAST
15	TABLE ACCESS FULL	NATION	50	1450		3 (0)	00:00:01			
* 16	HASH JOIN		57M	4458M		23455 (1)	00:04:42	Q1,05	PCWP	
17	PX RECEIVE		2040K	60M		1165 (1)	00:00:14	Q1,05	PCWP	
18	PX SEND BROADCAST	:TQ10002	2040K	60M		1165 (1)	00:00:14	Q1,02	P->P	BROADCAST
19	PX BLOCK ITERATOR		2040K	60M		1165 (1)	00:00:14	Q1,02	PCWC	
20	TABLE ACCESS FULL	SUPPLIER	2040K	60M		1165 (1)	00:00:14	Q1,02	PCWP	
* 21	HASH JOIN		28M	1372M		22270 (1)	00:04:28	Q1,05	PCWP	
22	PX RECEIVE		7204K	261M		4182 (1)	00:00:51	Q1,05	PCWP	
23	PX SEND HASH	:TQ10003	7204K	261M		4182 (1)	00:00:51	Q1,03	P->P	HASH
24	PX BLOCK ITERATOR		7204K	261M		4182 (1)	00:00:51	Q1,03	PCWC	
25	TABLE ACCESS FULL	PART	7204K	261M		4182 (1)	00:00:51	Q1,03	PCWP	
26	PX RECEIVE		28M	354M		18075 (1)	00:03:37	Q1,05	PCWP	
27	PX SEND HASH	:TQ10004	28M	354M		18075 (1)	00:03:37	Q1,04	P->P	HASH
28	PX BLOCK ITERATOR		28M	354M		18075 (1)	00:03:37	Q1,04	PCWC	
29	TABLE ACCESS FULL	PARTSUPP	28M	354M		18075 (1)	00:03:37	Q1,04	PCWP	

```
Predicate Information (identified by operation id):

   6 - access("N_REGIONKEY"="R_REGIONKEY")
  11 - access("S_NATIONKEY"="N_NATIONKEY")
  16 - access("PS_SUPPKEY"="S_SUPPKEY")
  21 - access("PS_PARTKEY"="P_PARTKEY")
```

Table 8-1 illustrates the various columns in the preceding output and column description.

Table 8-1. *XPlan Column Description*

Column	Description
ID	A number assigned to each step in the execution plan.
Operation	Name of the internal operation performed. In the first row generated, the column contains SELECT STATEMENT. Other possible values in the first row include INSERT STATEMENT DELETE STATEMENT UPDATE STATEMENT
Name	Name of the object (TABLE, INDEX, PARTITION, etc.) on which the specific operation/action is performed.
Rows	Number of rows returned during the operation.
Bytes	Estimate by the query optimization approach of the number of bytes accessed by the operation.
TempSpc	Temporary space, in bytes, used by the operation as estimated by the query optimizer's approach.
Cost (%CPU)	Cost of the operation as estimated by the optimizers query approach. Cost is not determined for table access operations. The value of this column does not have any particular unit of measurement; it is merely a weighted value used to compare costs of execution plans. The value in parenthesis is the percentage of CPU utilized in the operation.
Time	Elapsed time in seconds of the operation as estimated by query optimization.
TQ, nn	The table queue number used in the operation to communicated between the slaves.
IN-OUT	This is the table queue type. Some of the important notations to understand in the previous output are P->P—Data is sent from one parallel operation to another. P->S—Data is sent from a parallel operation to a serial operation. S->P—Data is sent from a serial operation to a parallel operation.
PQ Distrib	Contains the method in which rows are mapped to the query servers. Some of the values of this column include HASH: Maps rows to individual PX servers using a hash function on the join key. This method helps to achieve an equal distribution of work for individual PX servers. Used for PARALLEL JOIN or PARALLEL GROUP BY. RANGE: Maps rows to query servers using ranges of the sort key. Individual PX servers work on a range of data so that the QC does not have to do any sorting, but only to present the individual parallel servers. Used when the statement contains an ORDER BY clause. BROADCAST: Broadcasts the rows of the entire table to each query server. This is normally used when there is a large range on the number of rows contained between the tables involved in the operation. Instead of redistributing rows from both result sets, the database sends the smaller result set to all PX servers to guarantee the individual servers are able to complete their join operation. The small result set may be produced in serial or parallel. QC(ORDER): The QC consumes the input in order, from the first to the last query server. Used when the statement contains an ORDER BY clause. QC(RANDOM): The QC consumes the input randomly. Used when the statement does not have an ORDER BY clause. KEY: Key redistribution ensures result sets for individual key values to be clumped together. This is an optimization that is primarily used for partial partition-wise joins to ensure only one side in the join has to be redistributed. ROUND ROBIN: This is normally the final redistribution before data is sent to the requesting process. Certain redistribution steps contain an additional suffix to the preceding verbs in RAC environments, called LOCAL. LOCAL redistribution is an optimization method used in RAC environments to minimize interconnects traffic for inter-node parallel queries (IPQ).

The column that is of real interest is the Operation column that explains the various steps taken by the optimizer to get the results sets together. Table 8-2 details out the description for the various operations.

Table 8-2. *Description of the XPLAN Operation Column*

Id	Operation	Description
0	SELECT STATEMENT	The statement being executed is a SELECT statement.
1	PX COORDINATOR	This is the query coordinator (QC) process.
2	PX SEND QC (RANDOM)	The PX server process sends the data back to the QC process and the QC process receives the data in a random order. Such an operation is normally noticed when the query has no ORDER BY clause as part of the statement. In the preceding example statement, we could also notice that the statement has a GROUP BY clause but no ORDER BY clause.
3	HASH GROUP BY	An aggregation operation based on calculation of hash value on the columns being grouped.
4	PX RECEIVE	The consumers receive the data collected by the producers, in this case to group them before transferring the data to the coordinator. As noticed, for every producer operation there is a consumer operation. The example involves a four table join, and there are four sets of producers and consumers.
5	PX SEND HASH	Maps rows to individual PX servers using a hash function on the join key access ("N_REGIONKEY"="R_REGIONKEY"). This method helps to achieve an equal distribution of work for individual PX servers. The optimizer uses this method of redistribution because of the GROUP BY clause in the statement.
6	HASH JOIN BUFFERED	This is a join operation between the REGION table and the NATION table using the REGIONKEY column in the respective tables. These columns are identified by R_REGIONKEY and N_REGIONKEY.
7	BUFFER SORT	The optimizer is using a buffering mechanism of a traditional sort operation; however, there is no sort operation involved (the query does not contain an ORDER BY operator). In this specific case, the optimizer is buffering the data to avoid multiple tabescans against real data blocks.[5]
8	PX RECEIVE	The consumers receive the data collected by the producer. The consumers receive the data collected by the producers in this case to group them before transferring the data to the coordinator. As noticed, for every producer operation there is a consumer operation. The example involves a four table join, and there are four sets of producers and consumers, in this case to group them before transferring the data to the coordinator. As noticed, for every producer operation there is a consumer operation.
9	PX SEND BROADCAST	Due to a larger variation in the number of the rows of the tables involved in the operation, the optimizer is using the broadcast method to redistribute data to the parallel execution servers. Instead of redistributing rows from both result sets, the database sends the smaller result set to all PX servers to guarantee the individual servers are able to complete their join operation.

(continued)

---

[5]Lewis, Jonathan. "Buffer Sorts." http://jonathanlewis.wordpress.com/2006/12/17/buffer-sorts/.

Table 8-2. (*continued*)

Id	Operation	Description
10	TABLE ACCESS FULL	Producer for the REGION table (illustrated in the Name column in XPLAN output previously).
11	HASH JOIN	This is a join operation between the SUPPLIER table and the NATION table using the NATIONKEY column in the respective tables. These columns are identified by S_NATIONKEY and N_NATIONKEY.
12	BUFFER SORT	The optimizer is using a buffering mechanism of a traditional sort operation; however, there is no sort operation involved (the query does not contain an ORDER BY operator). In this specific case, the optimizer is buffering the data to avoid multiple tabescans against real data blocks.[6]
13	PX RECEIVE	The consumers receive the data collected by the producers, in this case to group them before transferring the data to the coordinator. As noticed, for every producer operation there is a consumer operation. The example involves a four table join, and there are four sets of producers and consumers.
14	PX SEND BROADCAST	Due to a larger variation in the number of the rows of the tables involved in the operation, the optimizer is using the broadcast method to redistribute data to the parallel execution servers. Instead of redistributing rows from both result sets, the database sends the smaller result set to all PX servers to guarantee the individual servers are able to complete their join operation.
15	TABLE ACCESS FULL	Producer for the NATION table (illustrated in the Name column in XPLAN output previously).
16	HASH JOIN	This is a join operation between the PARTSUPP table and the SUPPLIER table using the SUPPKEY column in the respective tables. These columns are identified by PS_SUPPKEY and S_SUPPKEY.
17	PX RECEIVE	The consumers receive the data collected by the producers in this case to group them before transferring the data to the coordinator. As noticed for every producer operation there is a consumer operation. The example involves a four table join, and there are four sets of producers and consumers.
18	PX SEND BROADCAST	Due to a larger variation in the number of the rows of the tables involved in the operation, the optimizer is using the broadcast method to redistribute data to the parallel execution servers. Instead of redistributing rows from both result sets, the database sends the smaller result set to all PX servers to guarantee the individual servers are able to complete their join operation.
19	PX BLOCK ITERATOR	Oracle is accessing the blocks in granule units. In this case, the block range granule over partition granules are used. This step basically indicates that the tables have a large volume of data in the SUPPLIER table and the optimizer required several iterations to complete the operation.
20	TABLE ACCESS FULL	Producer for the SUPPLIER table (illustrated in the Name column in the XPLAN output previously).
21	HASH JOIN	This is a join operation between the PARTSUPP table and the PART table using the PARTKEY column in the respective tables. These columns are identified by PS_PARTKEY and P_PARTKEY.

(*continued*)

---

[6]Ibid.

Table 8-2. (*continued*)

Id	Operation	Description
22	PX RECEIVE	The consumers receive the data collected by the producers, in this case to group them before transferring the data to the coordinator. As noticed, for every producer operation there is a consumer operation. The example involves a four table join, and there are four sets of producers and consumers.
23	PX SEND BROADCAST	Due to a larger variation in the number of the rows of the tables involved in the operation, the optimizer is using the broadcast method to redistribute data to the parallel execution servers. Instead of redistributing rows from both result sets, the database sends the smaller result set to all PX servers to guarantee the individual servers are able to complete their join operation.
24	PX BLOCK ITERATOR	Oracle is accessing the blocks in granule units. In this case, the block range granule over partition granules are used. This step basically indicates that the tables have a large volume of data in the PART tables, and the optimizer required several iterations to complete the operation.
25	TABLE ACCESS FULL	Producer for the PART table (illustrated in the Name column in the XPLAN output previously).
26	PX RECEIVE	The consumers receive the data collected by the producers, in this case to group them before transferring the data to the coordinator. As noticed, for every producer operation there is a consumer operation. The example involves a four table join, and there are four sets of producers and consumers.
27	PX SEND HASH	Maps rows to individual PX servers using a hash function on the join key. This method helps to achieve an equal distribution of work for individual PX servers. The optimizer uses this method of redistribution because of the GROUP BY clause in the statement.
28	PX BLOCK ITERATOR	Oracle is accessing the blocks in granule units. This step basically indicates that the tables have a large volume of data in the PARTSUPP tables, and the optimizer required several iterations to complete the operation.
29	TABLE ACCESS FULL	Producer for the PARTSUPP table (illustrated in the Name e column in the XPLAN output previously).

Parallel Processing Parameters

Not every query or operation is ideal for a parallel operation. Parallelism could be set at the object level by setting DOP (threads) for the object or by using hints. Apart from this there are certain important parameters that have to be understood and used to take advantage of the full potential of the parallelism feature. A few of these parameters were discussed earlier in the "Initialization Parameters" section, and a few more are discussed in this section.

PARALLEL_DEGREE_POLICY

This parameter is new in Oracle Database 11g Release 2. It drives how parallelism is activated in the system. Whereas there are several methods to enable parallelism, this parameter basically helps implement them. The value for this parameter could be either AUTO when all statements are executed in parallel, or MANUAL when parallelism is only implemented when specific methods described under "methods of enabling parallelism" are used.

When the parameter is set to AUTO, this means that the auto DOP is active and the optimizer automatically decides if the statement should execute in parallel or not and what DOP should be used for the operation. While generating the DOP for the statement, the optimizer will take into consideration the resource requirements for the statement and if the estimated elapsed time for the statement is less than PARALLEL_MIN_TIME_THRESHOLD, the statement will run in a serial mode.

On the other hand, if the estimated elapsed time is higher than PARALLEL_MIN_TIME_THRESHOLD, the optimizer uses the costs to complete the operation and computes the DOP required to complete the operation. Once again, to avoid all the resources getting consumed by one operation, the optimizer further places a control based on parameter PARALLEL_DEGREE_LIMIT. The PARALLEL_DEGREE_LIMIT parameter drives the optimizer to take into consideration the number of CPUs available on the server or the capacity of the I/O subsystem.

Valid values for this parameter are

AUTO: Enables auto DOP, statement queuing, and in-memory parallel execution.

MANUAL: Disables auto DOP, statement queuing, and in-memory parallel execution. The optimizer reverts the behavior of parallel execution to what was available under older versions of Oracle.

LIMITED: Enables auto DOP; however, statement queuing and in-memory parallel execution features are disabled. Auto DOP is only applied to statements that access tables or indexes that have explicit PARALLEL attribute values.

PARALLEL_MIN_TIME_THRESHOLD

This parameter determines the minimum execution time a statement should have before the default auto DOP is applied to the statement. The default value for this parameter is 10 seconds and is derived from the underscore parameter _parallel_time_unit.[7] The optimizer first calculates a serial execution plan for the SQL statement, if the estimated execution elapse time is greater than PARALLEL_MIN_TIME_THRESHOLD; the statement becomes a candidate for automatic DOP discussed earlier.

PARALLEL_DEGREE_LIMIT

Not all systems have sufficient resources to support parallelism; in other words, resources are limited and what is available is shared between all that need them. Because of this, the optimizer automatically decides if parallelism is even an option and what DOP the statement should use. The limitations are enforced by the optimizer through the parameter PARALLEL_DEGREE_LIMIT.

The driving factor used when determining such limitations is either based on I/O or CPU. This is a new parameter introduced in Oracle Database 11g Release 2. This parameter drives if the parallel plan generated by the Oracle's cost-based optimizer should be driven by the I/O resources or the CPU resources available to the session, and thus the values for this parameter are I/O or CPU.

I/O

This value tells the optimizer that the maximum DOP is limited by the I/O capacity of the system. The values are calculated by dividing the total system throughput by the maximum I/O bandwidth per process. For the optimizer to obtain realistic I/O capacity, it is advised that the I/O system is calibrated using the Oracle provided package, DBMS_RESOURCE_MANAGER.CALIBRATE_IO.

---

[7]Underscore parameters are hidden parameters and should be modified only with prior guidance from Oracle support.

■ **Note**   In Oracle Database 11 Release 2, the MAX_PMBPS is required for the auto DOP to work. The MAX_PMBPS can be obtained in one of two ways, running the I/O calibration utility or manually setting this to a reasonable value.

The procedure is executed by providing the number of physical disks available for the database operation, and the maximum latency of these disks is determined through a benchmark operation using tools such as ORION or as provided by the manufacturer. On execution, the procedure will provide the maximum IOPS (input output per second) that can be sustained, maximum I/O throughput that can be sustained, expressed in megabytes per second, and the average latency of an I/O request in database block sizes.

> **NUM_DISKS**—To get the most accurate results, its best to provide the actual number of physical disks that are used for this database. The Storage Administrator can provide this value. Keep in mind that when ASM is used to manage the database files, say in the DATA diskgroup, then only physical disks that make up the DATA diskgroup should be used for the NUM_DISKS variable; that is, do not include the disks from the FRA diskgroup. In the example following; the DATA diskgroup is made up of 8 physicals (presented as 4 LUNs or ASM disks).[8]

> **LATENCY**—This should be set to the defined response time service level agreement(SLA)for your application, for example, your 95th percentile response time SLA is 10 seconds.

```
SET serveroutput ON
DECLARE
    lat  INTEGER;
    iops INTEGER;
    mbps INTEGER;
BEGIN
    -- DBMS_RESOURCE_MANAGER.CALIBRATE_IO (NUM_DISKS, LATENCY, iops, mbps, lat);
    dbms_resource_manager.calibrate_io (8, 10, iops, mbps, lat);

    dbms_output.put_line ('max_iops = ' || iops);

    dbms_output.put_line ('latency  = ' || lat);

    dbms_output.put_lint ('max_mbps = ' || mbps);
END;
/
max_iops = 42139
latency  = 1
max_mbps = 2541

PL/SQL procedure successfully completed.
```

The previous procedure will calibrate I/O for 8 disks with a latency of 10 per disk. Calibration progress can be verified from the GV$IO_CALIBRATION_STATUS view:

```
SQL> SELECT *
FROM   gv$io_calibration_status;
```

---

[8]Metalink Note # 1269321.1.

```
inst_id status        calibration_time
------- ------------- -------------------------
      2 IN PROGRESS   02-APR-10 09.54.07.105 PM
      1 IN PROGRESS   02-APR-10 09.54.07.105 PM
/
```

When the calibration is complete, calibration status changes to READY:

```
inst_id status        calibration_time
------- ------------- -------------------------
      2 READY         02-APR-10 10.14.12.846 PM
      1 READY         02-APR-10 10.14.12.846 PM
```

Once I/O calibration is complete, the calibration statistics can be viewed using the following:

```
SELECT MAX_IOPS,
       MAX_MBPS,
       MAX_PMBPS,
       LATENCY,
       NUM_PHYSICAL_DISKS
FROM   DBA_RSRC_IO_CALIBRATE;
```

MAX_IOPS	MAX_MBPS	MAX_PMBPS	LATENCY	NUM_PHYSICAL_DISKS
10735	1804	60	8	8

CPU

With this value set for the PARALLEL_DEGREE_LIMIT parameter, the maximum DOP is limited by the number of CPUs in the system. The formula used to compute the DOP in this situation is PARALLEL_THREADS_PER_CPU * CPU_COUNT * (*number of active instances*). If database services have been configured, the number of active instances is further confined by the number of preferred instances where the database service is active. This again depends on the type of database management method selected, that is, admin managed or policy managed, which we discuss later in this section.

Figure 8-7 illustrates the parallel execution process on a RAC environment. The QC process is on SSKY2 because SSKY2 is the query initiator. Notice that there are several parallel query slave (QP) processes spread across several instances in the cluster. This is because the query used the SALES service as its connect descriptor to execute this query. Parallel slaves are confined to the instances where the service is currently enabled, in other words, it has a service affinity when executing slaves. The number of nodes that can participate in the parallel execution depends on the DOP.

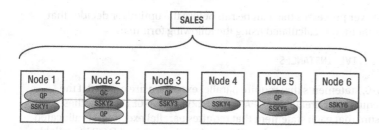

Figure 8-7. *Parallel servers (UNIFORM service) in a RAC environment*

In Oracle Database 11g Release 2, Oracle has changed the database services functionality. In the previous release of Oracle, database services could be defined on one or more instances in the cluster as preferred and available. This feature is only available if the admin managed option is selected when defining the database; if the policy managed option is selected, then database services can be either UNIFORM where the database service will be available on all instances in the cluster or SINGLETON where it will be available only on one instance in the cluster. In Figure 8-7, the database service is defined with the UNIFORM clause, and the parallel execution servers/slaves can start on all or any of the instances in the cluster.

Another method in which the database services and parallel queries could be controlled from running on all instances in the cluster is to use the policy managed option and grouping nodes into server pools. Figure 8-8 has two server pools; the database service SALES is defined as a UNIFORM service in sskypool1. This means that the parallel processes will also be confined to run within that sskypool1 pool.

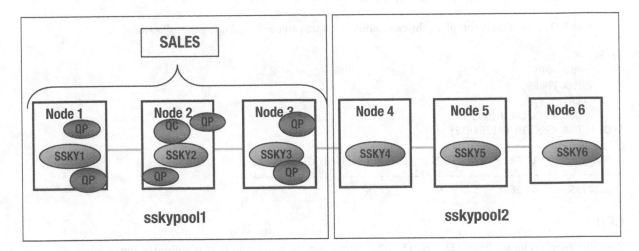

Figure 8-8. *UNIFORM distribution within a server pool*

PARALLEL_FORCE_LOCAL

This parameter is more geared toward a RAC environment where multiple instances can participate in a parallel operation. The parameter controls this behavior by confining the operation to the instance where the statement was initiated. The default value for this parameter is FALSE, meaning that the query can execute in any or all instances in the cluster based on the server pool configuration and the database service definitions.

PARALLEL_SERVERS_TARGET

This parameter controls the number of parallel server processes that can be run before the optimizer decides that there are none left and decides to queue the statement. It is calculated using the following formula:

```
4* CPU_COUNT * PARALLEL_TREADS_PER_CPU * ACTIVE_INSTANCES
```

When PARALLEL_DEGREE_POLICY is set to AUTO, statements that require parallel execution are queued if the number of parallel processes currently in use is equal to or greater than PARALLEL_SERVERS_TARGET. Under these circumstances, statement queuing is used to ensure that each statement that requires parallel execution is allocated the necessary parallel server resources. That is, statements are queued until such time the required DOP is available. Statements queued are dequeued for processing using the First In, First Out (FIFO) method.

There are two wait events associated with statement queuing during parallel execution. A statement that is ready to be selected (top of the queue) for execution waits on the event PX QUEUING: statement queue. All other statements in the queue are waiting on enq: JX - SQL statement queue.

Parallel DDL

All DDL operations, with the exception of tables with object or large objects (LOB) columns (data types), can use the parallel execution process. Examples of DDL statements are.

```
CREATE TABLE AS SELECT
CREATE INDEX
ALTER INDEX REBUILD (can be parallelized)
ALTER TABLE MOVE (or SPLIT in the case of partitioned tables)
```

The PARALLEL option can be set at table or index level by using the CREATE or ALTER operation as shown following:

```
CREATE TABLE PRODUCT PARALLEL (degree x instances y)
```

where x is the number of slaves to use per instance, per slave set, and y is the number of instances to be used to parallelize across. Each slave set gets x slaves per instance. If the IPQ is in use, there will be xy slaves per slave set. If the query being run is complex enough to require producer and consumer slave sets, the actual requirements are 2x, or, in the IPQ case, 2xy.

■ **Note**   Setting the DOP for a table or index will force the use of cost-based optimizer (CBO) even in the complete absence of statistics.

Parallel DML

Parallel DML (PDML) is most often used to speed up DML operations against large objects (e.g., overnight batch updates). The extra statement required to enable PDML is documented (in Oracle documentation) as being too much of an overhead for OLTP transactions. This feature was not intended to be used for small transactions, as the costs involved in calculating how data is to be partitioned amongst parallel execution slaves could actually decrease performance.

All DML operations (INSERT, UPDATE, and DELETE) could use the parallel execution process. PDML uses parallel execution mechanisms to speed up or scale up large DML operations against large database tables and indexes. INSERT INTO. . .SELECT FROM statements that operate against multiple tables as part of single DML operation can also use parallel operations.

Behavior of locks placed on the tables during DML operations is different between serial and PDML operations; therefore, it is required that PDML be explicitly enabled by issuing the following statement:

```
ALTER SESSION ENABLE PARALLEL DML;
```

Once this statement has been issued, any DML activity against a table with the parallel attribute will occur in parallel if no PDML restrictions are violated.

This statement must be the first statement of a transaction. If any transaction has not been rolled back or committed before enabling PDML, the following error will be raised:

```
ORA-12841: Cannot alter the session parallel DML state within a transaction
```

Once a PDML statement has been executed, a rollback or commit must be issued before the table can be modified again or queried within the same session. If the transaction is not committed or rolled back, subsequent DML or queries against the table will report

```
ORA-12838: cannot read/modify an object after modifying it in parallel
```

Each slave process is considered a separate transaction. Therefore, they cannot see any uncommitted data from other transactions, including the other slave processes currently working on the same parent transaction.

This is the reason that enabling PDML must be the first statement in a transaction. The coordinator processes (created when connecting to the database) will also create a separate transaction. These processes will not be able to see the data changed by the slave processes until it is committed; hence, the ORA-12838 error is raised when trying to view or modify the table.

Parallel Recovery

In the case of a database crash, instance failure, media failure, and so forth, Oracle performs a recovery operation against the respective files. Unless such recovery operation is complete, the database is not fully available to the user.

Parallel recovery divides the recovery operation by allocating different processes to different data blocks during the cache recovery phase of recovery. One example of where this could be used is when applying redo information from the redo logs. During recovery, the redo log is read and blocks that require application of redo log information are parsed out. These blocks are subsequently distributed evenly to all recovery processes to be read into the buffer cache.

Based on the type of recovery, there are two methods by which parallel recovery is enabled:

- Setting the RECOVERY_PARALLELISM parameter to the number of concurrent recovery processes for instance or crash recovery could enable parallel recovery. The value of this parameter should be greater than 1 and should not exceed the value of the PARALLEL_MAX_SERVERS initialization parameter. This parameter only supports recovery of instance or crash recovery.

- Setting the PARALLEL clause in the RECOVER DATABASE statement supports media recovery. Parallel media recovery is controlled by the RECOVER_PARALLEL command that selects a degree of parallelism equal to the number of CPUs available on all participating instances times the value of the PARALLEL_THREADS_PER_CPU initialization parameter. For example, if parallel recovery is performed with PARALLEL 4 and only one data file needs recovery, then four spawned processes read blocks from the data file to apply.

■ **Note**   Parallel recovery is discussed in detail in Chapter 10.

Optimizing Parallel Operations

Functionalities seldom do work out of the box; most functionalities have to be optimized for the type of operation based on several factors such as size of database, size of data being retrieved, availability of resources, concurrency of users, and so forth. Parallel operations are also not an exception to this. Some of the basic troubleshooting of the parallel query is explained following:

1. One of the first steps to determine if parallel query is doing any kind of parallel operation is to check the output of an explain plan. The PLAN_TABLE in the schema where the explain plan was performed contains a column called OTHER. Checking to determine whether this column contains the SQL generated for use by the slave processes indicates if the parallel query is executing as expected. For example, if this SQL contains hints such as /*+ ROWID(PRODUCT)*/, and these hints are clearly not in the original code, then it is likely that PQO (parallel query option) is being used. The ROWID hint is one of the internal methodologies used to process PQO queries.

2. Oracle provides two scripts to format the query on the PLAN_TABLE, utlxpls.sql and utlxplp.sql. One formats the output for a serial plan and the other can be used to format a parallel plan. Both of these scripts can be found in $ORACLE_HOME/rdbms/admin directory.

3. From the session that the query was executed, executing the following statement will, based on the statistics collected, provide an indication of whether the parallel query was executed:

    ```
    SELECT * FROM V$PQ_SESSTAT;
    ```

The output of this query will indicate if the last query that ran under this session was parallelized.

```
SQL> SELECT * FROM V$PQ_SESSTAT;

STATISTIC                        LAST_QUERY SESSION_TOTAL
-------------------------------- ---------- -------------
Queries Parallelized                      0             3
DML Parallelized                          0             0
DDL Parallelized                          0             0
DFO Trees                                 0             3
Server Threads                            0             0
Allocation Height                         0             0
Allocation Width                          0             0
Local Msgs Sent                           0         50578
Distr Msgs Sent                           0             0
Local Msgs Recv'd                         0         50570
Distr Msgs Recv'd                         0             0

11 rows selected.
```

From the preceding output, the LAST_QUERY column indicates the last query execution statistics and the SESSION_TOTAL column indicates the values that all queries executed in the current session.

The relevant statistics from the previous query are the following:

- `Queries Parallelized` indicates the number of `SELECT` statements that were executed in parallel. In the previous scenario, a total of three queries were executed in the current session.

- `DML Parallelized` indicates the number of DML statements that were executed in parallel. In the current session, there were no DML statements executed.

- `DFO Trees` (where DFO is data flow operator) indicates the number of times a serial execution plan was converted to a parallel plan. In the preceding scenario, a total of three queries were converted from a serial plan to a parallel plan.

- `Server Threads` indicates the number of parallel query slaves used.

- `Allocation Height` indicates the DOP for the instance.

- `Allocation Width` indicates the number of instances involved in this operation.

Yet another troubleshooting opportunity is to check the V$ views for slave activity. Executing the following statement will indicate if slaves are running:

```
SELECT SLAVE_NAME, STATUS, CPU_SECS_TOTAL
FROM V$PQ_SLAVE;
```

If the query returns no rows, this would indicate that there are no slaves running. If there were no difference in CPU usage between the two runs, this would indicate that there has been no CPU activity for the sampling period.

Running queries in parallel, as opposed to running them serially, can have benefits on performance. However, when defining parallel queries, the following should be taken into consideration:

- Parallel query has a significant startup cost.

- Multiple slave processes consume more CPU than single processes.

- Each slave process must have its own address space (memory allocation).

Parallel query was designed to reduce execution time for queries that had no option but to read large quantities of data. It maximizes the data throughput by spreading the read workload across multiple processes or slaves. Sort operations are also managed using the slaves' (TQ) structures.

This has the effect of increasing the CPU load on the system as a whole. If the system is running at maximum CPU utilization, parallel query will not get any more out of the query. If no more CPU is available, optimizer will, based on the resources available, make the decision to serialize the parallel operations.

The additional I/O requirements of the slave processes reading the data can also stress a heavily loaded I/O subsystem. Distributing data across multiple disk spindles may help alleviate situations where disk I/O may become a bottleneck. Additionally, queries may just run quicker serially. Typically, queries that use index lookups are not suited for PQO.

> **Nested Loops vs. Hash/Sort Merge Joins** Typically, parallel query tries to use full table scan (FTS) to access data, while lookups are divided between slaves on a `ROWID` range basis. Characteristically, nested loop joins are not really efficient with FTS. Hash joins and sort merge options are usually much more efficient at processing large amounts of data. However, there is a downside, as hash join and sort merge join do not allow row elimination based on data from a driving row source. This elimination can drastically reduce the data sets involved and could mean that a serial access path using index lookup is quicker than a parallel operation simply due to the volume of data eliminated.

> **Data Splitting:** Dividing the data up, passing it through multiple processes, and collating the results may make the cost of slave generation greater than retrieving the data serially.

Data Skew: Parallel queries divide data between reader slaves on a ROWID range basis. Although the same number of blocks is given to each slave, it does not mean that these blocks contain identical numbers of rows. In fact, some of the blocks could be completely empty. This can be especially problematic where large quantities of data are archived and deleted, as this results in many empty, or sparsely filled, blocks. The effect of this non-uniform data distribution is to cause queries to run slower than they might otherwise. This is because one slave does all the work. Under such situations, the only option that is available is to reorganize the data.

Data Dictionary Views to Monitor Parallel Operations

Oracle dynamic performance views provide a great insight into the performance statistics. These views provide great instrumentation into the functioning and behavior of parallel queries in a RAC or non-RAC environment.

GV$PX_BUFFER_ADVICE

Similar to most advice views available, the (G)V$PX_BUFFER_ADVICE view provides statistics on historical and projected maximum buffer usage by all parallel queries. This view is useful to monitor memory utilization and to size the system global area (SGA). The following output provides the current utilization across 8 instances of a RAC cluster (formatted for clarity). The following output indicates that there are sufficient buffers available and only a small percentage of this is used. The output also indicates that all instances in the cluster are balanced from a memory utilization perspective:

```
SELECT inst_id INT,
       statistic,
       value
FROM   gv$px_buffer_advice
ORDER  BY inst_id;

INT STATISTIC                    VALUE
---- -------------------------   ----------
   1 Servers Highwater              264
     Buffers HWM                   5349
     Estimated Buffers HWM        53064
     Servers Max                    256
     Estimated Buffers Max        49920
     Buffers Current Free           205
     Buffers Current Total         1125


 . . . . . . . . . . .   . . . . . .
 . . . . . . . . . . . . .  . . . . .
 . . . . . . . . . .   . . . . . . . .


   8 Servers Highwater              249
     Buffers HWM                   3030
     Estimated Buffers HWM        46872
     Servers Max                    256
     Estimated Buffers Max        49920
     Buffers Current Free           439
     Buffers Current Total          500
```

GV$PX_PROCESS_SYSSTAT

This view shows the status of query servers and provides buffer allocation statistics:

```
STATISTIC                      VALUE
------------------------------ ----------
Servers In Use                       0
Servers Available                   27
Servers Started                  12513
Servers Shutdown                 12486
Servers Highwater                  264
Servers Cleaned Up                   0
Server Sessions                 987699
Memory Chunks Allocated           3093
Memory Chunks Freed               3089
Memory Chunks Current                4
Memory Chunks HWM                   44
Buffers Allocated             36799839
Buffers Freed                 36799812
Buffers Current                     27
Buffers HWM                       5349
```

GV$PQ_SESSTAT

This view reflects the status of all current server groups in the system such as data about how queries allocated processes and how the multiuser and load balancing algorithms are affecting the default and hinted values:

```
STATISTIC                      LAST_QUERY SESSION_TOTAL
------------------------------ ---------- -------------
Queries Parallelized                    1             2
DML Parallelized                        0             0
DDL Parallelized                        0             0
DFO Trees                               1             2
Server Threads                          7             0
Allocation Height                       1             0
Allocation Width                        7             0
Local Msgs Sent                         3             6
Distr Msgs Sent                        18            36
Local Msgs Recv'd                       3             6
Distr Msgs Recv'd                      18            36
```

GV$PQ_TQSTAT

The view provides a detailed report of message traffic at the table queue level. The data in this view is valid only when queried from a session that is executing parallel SQL statements. A table queue is the pipeline between query server groups, between the parallel coordinator and a query server group, or between a query server group and the coordinator. The table queues are represented explicitly in the operation column by PX SEND and PX RECEIVE.

The view has a row for each query server process that reads from or writes to in each table queue. A table queue connecting 4 consumer processes to 4 producer processes has 8 rows in this view. Sum the bytes column and group by TQ_ID to obtain the total number of bytes sent through each table queue.

This view helps in determining any workload imbalances and helps to determine if the distribution is skewed. This would indicate that there is low cardinality or there are low numbers of distinct values.

```
SQL> DESC GV$PQ_TQSTAT
 Name                                      Null?     Type
 ---------------------------------------- -------- -------------
 DFO_NUMBER                                          NUMBER
 TQ_ID                                               NUMBER
 SERVER_TYPE                                         VARCHAR2(40)
 NUM_ROWS                                            NUMBER
 BYTES                                               NUMBER
 OPEN_TIME                                           NUMBER
 AVG_LATENCY                                         NUMBER
 WAITS                                               NUMBER
 TIMEOUTS                                            NUMBER
 PROCESS                                             VARCHAR2(40)
 INSTANCE                                            NUMBER

BREAK ON dfo_number ON tq_id
SELECT inst_id,
         dfo_number,
         tq_id,
         server_type,
         process,
         num_rows,
         bytes
FROM    gv$pq_tqstat
ORDER   BY dfo_number DESC,
           tq_id,
           server_type DESC,
           process
```

GV$PX_SESSION

This view shows data about query server sessions, groups, sets, and server numbers. It also displays real-time data about the processes working on behalf of parallel execution. It contains information such as requested DOP and the actual DOP granted to the operation:

```
SELECT qcsid,
       sid,
       inst_id       "INST",
       server_group  "GROUP",
       server_set    "SET",
       degree        "DEGREE",
       req_degree    "REQ DEGREE"
FROM   gv$px_session
ORDER  BY qcsid,
          qcinst_id,
          server_group,
          server_set;
```

QCSID	SID	INST	GROUP	SET	DEGREE	REQ DEGREE
208	158	1	1	1	7	7
208	167	4	1	1	7	7
208	704	7	1	1	7	7
208	649	6	1	1	7	7
208	454	5	1	1	7	7
208	63	2	1	1	7	7
208	168	8	1	1	7	7
208	208	1				
300	606	4	1	1	6	6
300	647	4	1	1	6	6
300	742	4	1	1	6	6
300	60	4	1	1	6	6
300	148	4	1	1	6	6
300	548	4	1	1	6	6

GV$PX_SESSTAT

This view is a join between the V$PX_SESSION and V$SESSTAT tables. All session statistics available to a normal session are available for all sessions performed using parallel execution.

```
SELECT qcsid,
       sid,
       inst_id       "INST",
       server_group  "GROUP",
       server_set    "SET",
       NAME          "STAT NAME",
       VALUE
FROM   gv$px_sesstat a,
       v$statname b
WHERE  a.statistic# = b.statistic#
       AND NAME LIKE 'physical reads'
       AND VALUE > 0
ORDER  BY qcsid,
          qcinst_id,
          server_group,
          server_set;
```

QCSID	SID	INST	GROUP	SET	STAT NAME	VALUE
208	208	1			physical reads	40
300	606	4	1	1	physical reads	636
300	548	4	1	1	physical reads	650
300	647	4	1	1	physical reads	595
300	742	4	1	1	physical reads	638
300	60	4	1	1	physical reads	632
300	148	4	1	1	physical reads	653
300	300	4			physical reads	7

8 rows selected

```
SELECT NAME,
       VALUE
FROM   v$sysstat
WHERE  UPPDER(NAME) LIKE '%PARALLEL OPERATIONS%'
       OR UPPER(NAME) LIKE '%PARALLELIZED%'
       OR UPPER(NAME) LIKE '%PX%';
```

```
NAME                                     VALUE
-----------------------------------      -----------
queries parallelized                        129681
DML statements parallelized                    110
DDL statements parallelized                   2372
DFO trees parallelized                      153353
Parallel operations not downgraded          151035
Parallel operations downgraded to s          34488
Parallel operations downgraded 75 t            156
Parallel operations downgraded 50 t            204
Parallel operations downgraded 25 t            116
Parallel operations downgraded 1 to           1842
PX local messages sent                    82452573
PX local messages recv'd                  82446792
PX remote messages sent                    1611916
PX remote messages recv'd                  1605765
```

```
SELECT px.inst_id                  INT,
       DECODE(px.qcinst_id, NULL, username,
                            ' - '
                      ||LOWER(Substr(s.program, LENGTH(s.program) - 4, 4))
       )
                                   "Username",
       DECODE(px.qcinst_id, NULL, 'QC',
                            '(Slave)') "QC/Slave",
       TO_CHAR(px.server_set)      "Slave Set",
       TO_CHAR(s.sid)              "SID",
       DECODE(px.qcinst_id, NULL, TO_CHAR(s.sid),
                            px.qcsid) "QC SID",
       px.req_degree               "Requested DOP",
       px.degree                   "Actual DOP",
       px.qcinst_id                "QC Inst",
       s.event                     "Wait Event"
FROM   gv$px_session px,
       gv$session s
WHERE  px.inst_id = s.inst_id
   AND px.sid = s.sid (+)
   AND px.serial# = s.serial#
   AND username NOT IN ('SYSTEM')
ORDER  BY 6,
         2 DESC
/
```

Output from the query illustrates that there are two parallel processing running, one on instance 1 and the other on instance 4. The parallel execution servers are confined to run only on one instance because the parameter PARALLEL_FORCE_LOCAL has been enabled. Most of the parallel execution servers are currently waiting on PX Deq: Execution Msg. Parallel execution servers transfer data back and forth between the QC using messages. The amount of message that could be transferred between instances is controlled using the parameter PARALLEL_EXECUTION_MESSAGE_SIZE. And the current size of this parameter in this specific example is 16. Based on the total time waited for the execution message, the value of this parameter may have to be increased.

```
01:54:37 SQL> show parameter parallel_execution
```

NAME	TYPE	VALUE
parallel_execution_message_size	integer	16384

INT	Username	QC/Slave	Slave Set	SID	QC SID	Req DOP	Actual DOP	QC Inst	Wait Event
1	DWH	QC		251	251				SQL*Net message from client
1	- p023	(Slave)	2	22	251	12	12	1	PX Deq: Execution Msg
1	- p022	(Slave)	2	743	251	12	12	1	PX Deq: Execution Msg
1	- p021	(Slave)	2	709	251	12	12	1	PX Deq: Execution Msg
1	- p020	(Slave)	2	658	251	12	12	1	PX Deq: Execution Msg
1	- p019	(Slave)	2	593	251	12	12	1	PX Deq: Execution Msg
1	- p018	(Slave)	2	557	251	12	12	1	PX Deq: Execution Msg
1	- p017	(Slave)	2	407	251	12	12	1	PX Deq: Execution Msg
1	- p016	(Slave)	2	353	251	12	12	1	PX Deq: Execution Msg
1	- p015	(Slave)	2	310	251	12	12	1	PX Deq: Execution Msg
1	- p014	(Slave)	2	258	251	12	12	1	PX Deq: Execution Msg
1	- p013	(Slave)	2	208	251	12	12	1	PX Deq: Execution Msg
1	- p012	(Slave)	2	163	251	12	12	1	PX Deq: Execution Msg
1	- p011	(Slave)	1	109	251	12	12	1	PX Deq Credit: send blkd
1	- p010	(Slave)	1	56	251	12	12	1	PX Deq Credit: send blkd
1	- p009	(Slave)	1	18	251	12	12	1	PX Deq Credit: send blkd
1	- p008	(Slave)	1	741	251	12	12	1	PX Deq Credit: send blkd
1	- p007	(Slave)	1	698	251	12	12	1	PX Deq: Execution Msg
1	- p006	(Slave)	1	655	251	12	12	1	PX Deq: Execution Msg
1	- p005	(Slave)	1	607	251	12	12	1	PX Deq: Execution Msg
1	- p004	(Slave)	1	548	251	12	12	1	PX Deq: Execution Msg
1	- p003	(Slave)	1	514	251	12	12	1	PX Deq: Execution Msg
1	- p002	(Slave)	1	465	251	12	12	1	PX Deq: Execution Msg
1	- p001	(Slave)	1	398	251	12	12	1	PX Deq: Execution Msg
1	- p000	(Slave)	1	348	251	12	12	1	PX Deq: Execution Msg
4	DWH	QC		300	300				SQL*Net message from client
4	- p007	(Slave)	1	148	300	6	6	4	PX Deq Credit: send blkd
4	- p005	(Slave)	1	60	300	6	6	4	PX Deq Credit: send blkd
4	- p003	(Slave)	1	742	300	6	6	4	PX Deq Credit: send blkd
4	- p002	(Slave)	1	647	300	6	6	4	PX Deq Credit: send blkd
4	- p001	(Slave)	1	606	300	6	6	4	PX Deq Credit: send blkd
4	- p000	(Slave)	1	548	300	6	6	4	PX Deq Credit: send blkd

GV$PX_PROCESS

This contains generic process-related information about parallel processes, including status, session ID, process ID, and other information.

```
SELECT pxp.inst_id INT,
       pxp.server_name,
       pxp.status,
       pid,
       spid,
       pxp.sid,
       pxp.serial#,
       username,
       service_name svcname
FROM   gv$px_process pxp,
       gv$session gvs
WHERE  gvs.inst_id = pxp.inst_id
  AND  gvs.sid = pxp.sid
  AND  gvs.serial# = pxp.serial#
  AND  username NOT IN ('SYS', 'SYSTEM');
```

The output from the query illustrates that there are two parallel jobs currently running with the QC on instance 8 and instance 5. The output has 24 parallel execution servers on instance 5 and 4 parallel execution servers on instance 8. The parallel servers are confined to single instance because in this specific example, the parameter PARALLEL_FORCE_LOCAL has been enabled.

INT	SERV	STATUS	PID	SPID	SID	SERIAL#	USERNAME	SVCNAME
8	P000	IN USE	49	8630	59	13633	MVALLATH	SSSVC1
8	P002	IN USE	51	8632	160	7979	MVALLATH	SSSVC1
8	P003	IN USE	54	8634	315	3890	MVALLATH	SSSVC1
8	P001	IN USE	56	30395	413	324	MVALLATH	SSSVC1
5	P005	IN USE	64	26015	17	842	DWH	SSSVC1
5	P006	IN USE	65	26017	53	4300	DWH	SSSVC1
5	P007	IN USE	66	26019	108	711	DWH	SSSVC1
5	P012	IN USE	34	24171	111	1139	DWH	SSSVC1
5	P008	IN USE	67	26021	163	8261	DWH	SSSVC1
5	P009	IN USE	68	26023	209	3222	DWH	SSSVC1
5	P014	IN USE	52	24175	219	1002	DWH	SSSVC1
5	P010	IN USE	69	26025	257	1442	DWH	SSSVC1
5	P015	IN USE	53	24177	263	1118	DWH	SSSVC1
5	P000	IN USE	54	26005	306	1045	DWH	SSSVC1
5	P011	IN USE	70	26027	319	1063	DWH	SSSVC1
5	P001	IN USE	55	26007	350	820	DWH	SSSVC1
5	P018	IN USE	71	24183	356	3612	DWH	SSSVC1
5	P019	IN USE	72	24185	400	2714	DWH	SSSVC1
5	P020	IN USE	73	24187	454	3617	DWH	SSSVC1
5	P021	IN USE	74	24189	502	1276	DWH	SSSVC1
5	P016	IN USE	58	24179	504	1404	DWH	SSSVC1

5	P022	IN USE	75	24191	549	739 DWH	SSSVC1
5	P017	IN USE	59	24181	562	22027 DWH	SSSVC1
5	P023	IN USE	76	24193	592	7108 DWH	SSSVC1
5	P013	IN USE	44	24173	605	210 DWH	SSSVC1
5	P002	IN USE	61	26009	648	4453 DWH	SSSVC1
5	P003	IN USE	62	26011	701	358 DWH	SSSVC1
5	P004	IN USE	63	26013	738	7416 DWH	SSSVC1

28 rows selected.

Wait Events Related to Parallel Operations

Resources are not available in abundance; there is always a hard limit on the amount of resources that are available for any operation. Parallel queries though can take advantage of utilizing resources across instances and can also encounter resources contention. Oracle provides instrumentation through its wait interface to understand resource waits. In this section, we discuss wait events that are related to parallel operations.[9]

PX Deq Credit: need buffer

The slaves and the QC use table queues for the communication. Each table queue uses buffer to send data between two slaves or a slave and the QC. At a given point in time, only a process can send data, and this is controlled by setting the credit bit on the table queue. A process needs the credit bit if it has to send data via a table queue. The credit bit is sent via a buffer from slave to slave or from a slave to the QC. This wait event indicates that the process is waiting for a buffer from the other slave/QC that sends the credit bit and so that it could send a block.

PX Deq Credit: send blkd[10]

The process wishes to send a message and does not have the flow control credit. Process must first dequeue a message to obtain the credit. This wait event indicates that the receiver has not dequeued and/or completely consumed the prior message yet.

PX Deq Credit: send blkd and **PX Deq Credit: need buffer** are nearly the same. Due to internal reason, you see PX Deq Credit: send blkd more on local systems and PX Deq Credit: need buffer more on RAC systems.

PX Deq: Msg Fragment

This is a non-idle wait normally noticed when several bits of the message are dequeued from a fragmented message. Fragmentation is an indication that the message buffer size may not be large enough. Increasing the size of PARALLEL_EXECUTION_MESSAGE_SIZE reduces the probability of message fragmentation. However, the contra effect of a considerable increase in the message size is an increase in memory overhead.

PX Deq: Execute Reply

This is an idle wait event. This wait is noticed when slaves have completed the execution of the SQL statement, and they send the results of the query back to the QC.

---

[9]Wait events in this section are limited to parallel operations; RAC-specific wait events are discussed in Chapter 17.
[10]Metalink Note # 271767.1.

PX qref latch

In an earlier section, "Parallel Query Architecture," we discussed how the producers, consumers, and the query coordinators are interconnected via queues to exchange data and messages. The PX qref latch helps protect these queues; and this latch usually indicates that the sender is faster than the receiver, indicating there is a communication overhead. Under such circumstances, Oracle recommends that increasing the PARALLEL_EXECUTION_MESSAGE_SIZE could ease the situation a bit. Also, if the system workload is really high, decreasing the DOP could also help.

PX Queuing: Statement Queue

This is a new event introduced in Oracle Database 11g Release 2 with the new parallel processing features. It indicates that there aren't sufficient parallel processes available to start execution servers, and the statement is queued until such time that parallel execution servers are available. This event also indicates that the statement is next in the queue to be selected for processing. Oracle follows the FIFO method when statements are placed into queue. The wait time indicates the time the statement is waiting since the statement was selected to be processed.

enq: JX SQL Statement Queue

Contrary to the PX queueing: statement queue event, this event indicates that the statement is in the queue; however, it has not been selected to be released yet. More statements in this queue indicate insufficient DOP or high allocation of DOP to other statements such that all statements do not get sufficient DOPs to start processing.

PX Deq: reap credit[11]

This wait event indicates that we are doing a non-blocking test to see if any channel has returned a message. We should see that although there are a high number of these events, the time accumulated to it should be zero (or really low).

Depending on which process is doing this, it could indicate that either the consumers are starved for data (IO bound perhaps) or the producers are waiting on the consumers to "return" the flow control credit (consumers may be compute or I/O bound). You should investigate query plans, check for data skew, I/O contention (table or tmp segment), and so forth, to get a deeper understanding of the symptoms.

PX Deq: Join ACK[12]

This is a non-idle wait. When a statement is executed in parallel, based on the DOP value, the QC has to build the required slave sets. In this process, the QC first sends join messages to each slave in the set being obtained and then waits for a join acknowledgement message to be returned from each slave in the set. This operation is repeated again if the parallel operation requires a second slave set. Memory is required for communication between 1.) Slave to slave and 2.) Slave to QC. The wait indicates that the QC sends a message to a slave and waits until memory is allocated and gets a message back from the slave.

---

[11]Metalink Note # 250947.1.
[12]Metalink Note # 250960.1.

Possible causes for this wait event are

1. The PQ slave OS process was killed or died. Until PMON has not cleaned up the internal structures, a new QC assumes they are still alive. When a new QC tries to get slaves, he sends a message to the slave to join the slave set; but we get no acknowledge message back. Check if someone killed an idle slave or a slave process has died. Compare the entries in V$PX_PROCESS and on OS level the name of the started PQ slaves.

2. Another possible cause is when SGA memory is so depleted that it is possible that the slave may not be able to establish its response channel to the QC to acknowledge the join message, force the slave to die so that the QC can be notified via PMON cleanup, and so forth.

PX Deq: Signal ACK

This is an idle wait event. It indicates that time waited by the QC to get acknowledgment receipts for the control messages sent by the QC to the slaves.

PX Deq: Parse Reply

This is a non-idle wait. This wait event indicates the time waited when the slaves parse their SQL statements. Only one slave will do the hard parse on an instance; which instance in the cluster is performing the hard parse cannot be determined from this wait event. Once the slaves have completed the hard parse operation, the processing starts. The reason for this wait event is due to library cache contention or improper sizing of library cache.

PX Deq: Execute Reply

This is an idle wait event. The QC is expecting a response and is expecting to dequeue data from the producer slave set. This occurs when the slaves have finished execution of the SQL statement and they send the results back to the QC.

Troubleshooting Using Oracle Event Interface

The event interface provided by Oracle helps look at the behavior of any specific operation within Oracle kernel. For example, as mentioned in Chapter 6, event 10053 will help you trace through the behavior of Oracle's optimizer. Event 10046 will help you analyze the execution plans generated by Oracle's optimizer. Similar to these events, there are those that could help debug the parallel query operations.

Event 10391 @ Level 128

Event 10391 will list the instantiation of slaves processes. It's useful to troubleshoot the distribution of slaves across multiple instances in a RAC cluster. Similar to other events, event 10391 can also be invoked at the system level or at the session level. The following will invoke the collection of this information at the session level:

```
alter session set events '10391 trace name context forever, level 128';
```

Once the event is invoked, the required SQL statement can be executed, and the trace file generated in the diag/trace directory will contain the following information:

```
*** SESSION ID:(150.5094) 2007-11-10 08:46:45.586
kxfrDmpSys
        dumping system information
          arch:255 ((unknown)
          sess:150 myiid:1 mynid:1 ninst:3 maxiid:3

          Instances running on that system:
            inum:0 iid:1
            inum:1 iid:2
            inum:2 iid:3
kxfrDmpUpdSys
        allocated slave set: nsset:1 nbslv:6
          Slave set 0: #nodes:3
          Min # slaves 2: Max # slaves:2
            List of Slaves:
              slv 0 nid:0
              slv 1 nid:0
              slv 2 nid:1
              slv 3 nid:1
              slv 4 nid:2
              slv 5 nid:2
            List of Nodes:
              node 0
              node 1
              node 2
```

The trace file is generated in two parts: the first part, titled **kxfrDmpSys,** contains system level details such as the number of nodes in the cluster indicated by maxiid. It also contains the information regarding the instance where the current session is currently present (indicated by mynid) and is currently node 1.

The second part of the trace file identified by **kxfrDmpUpdSys** contains the details of the execution.

Once the trace is complete, the event can be turned off using the following command:

```
alter session set events '10391 trace name context off';
```

Conclusion

In this chapter, we explored the details of parallel processing and the various options and features of parallel execution available under Oracle RDBMS. We demonstrated that parallel processing, with respect to RAC, is not much different from the traditional stand-alone implementation; it is just an extension to the functionality on a single stand-alone instance. The major difference, or advantage, in a RAC environment is that the parallel operation not only can be accomplished on the single instance but also can be processed on the other nodes that participated in the cluster configuration either by controlling it through parameters such as PARALLEL_FORCE_LOCAL or using server pools and database services to confine the parallel execution servers to specific instances in the cluster.

CHAPTER 9

∎ ∎ ∎

Tuning the Database

Business requirements like availability and scalability are some of the main features that are most often provided by the database vendor through some of their database products. For example, RAC, a feature that is available from Oracle Corporation, provides availability and scalability. With RAC, multiple instances can access a common shared database and, as the user base increases, additional instances can be added. Similarly, the requirement to provide high availability can be implemented using Oracle Data Guard (ODG). Certain business requirements can be implemented using certain database features, whereas other requirements such as throughput, recoverability, maintainability, manageability, security, and internationalization all come from good database design.

Designing a good system is essential, regardless of the software chosen for the layered products, including data and application management. Like the foundation of a building, if it is not laid out carefully, then there is potential for the entire structure to collapse. So it is of the utmost importance that the software foundation has a good architecture that is easy to maintain, perform, and scale, and also meets the business requirements of the enterprise for its short-term and long-term strategies.

A major step in the software development life cycle is to analyze the requirements, the various functions of the system, and also the system in its entirety. However, database and application designers approach their common goal from different perspectives. A good analogy is to imagine the application system as a house. The database design is the architectural plan that describes the house; it describes where different rooms are and how many doors or windows each room has. The application design, on the other hand, describes how the house will be used.

To continue this analogy, the database designer must know what rooms the occupants will need and the application designer will make sure that the occupants can get from one room to the next in the manner that they expect.

So careful consideration should be given when designing the house to make it very efficient, and this is possible only by analyzing all the requirements carefully. The requirements captured during the analysis phase have to be stored in some form for future use. In earlier days, this was done using plain flowcharts on paper. Today there are many tools available to help expedite this process in a more concise and precise manner.

Database design principles cannot be ignored when developing systems, despite having large, high performance servers such as Oracle's Exadata or the supercomputer that may be able to perform without tuning. The basic principles of database design cannot be ignored.

Good data modeling for efficient access paths and good distribution of data is the basis for performance persistence and retrieval of data. These are important principles that can help in the scalability of database servers.

When tuning systems using the traditional top-down approach, database and O/S tuning are normally the options of last resort.

However, there are features within the Oracle technology that should be taken advantage of to help applications to scale with ease. Some of the features, such as database partitioning, also help in the administration and maintenance of data. In this chapter, we will look at a few areas for database tuning:

- Distribution of data using data partitions
- Distribution of data access using database services

- Distribution of workload based on resource availability

- Accessing data from a database using indexes

- Tuning parameters to help improve performance

Data Partitioning

Partitioning of data objects not only provides opportunities for workload distribution and access optimization, but also increases isolation and may therefore have the advantage of reducing maintenance windows, recovery times, and the impact of failures.

Workload or I/O distribution improves query performance by allowing access to a subset of partitions, rather than the entire table. Instead of all users' requests being funneled into one segment containing all the data, they are now distributed or spread among the various data segments that contain this data.

Oracle provides different methods and criteria to partition the data. Based on the how data is stored (business rules), volume of data, data distribution, cardinality, and more importantly how the data will be retrieved back for analysis, etc., one or a combination of these methods can be used.

Partitioning is specified on a column or set of columns that becomes the partitioning key. This key will determine placement of data into the various partitions. During DML operations, data is directed to the appropriate partition based on the value of the partition key. A partition key

- Can consist of an ordered list of 1 to 16 columns.

- Can contain columns that are NULLABLE.

- Cannot contain a LEVEL, ROWID, or a column of type ROWID.

■ **Note**   Partitioning is an option that is included in the Enterprise Edition of the Oracle database product and is not licensed for the Standard Edition. In either case, installation and using this data requires an additional license.

Partitioning is useful for many different types of applications, particularly applications that manage large volumes of data. OLTP systems often benefit from improvements in manageability and availability, while data warehousing systems benefit from performance and manageability.

Oracle provides several partitioning methods:

- Range partitioning, where data is partitioned based on a range of column values. Each partition is defined by a value list for the partition key.

- Hash partitioning, where records are assigned to partitions using a hash function on values found in columns designated as the partitioning key.

- List partitioning, where each partition is defined with a predefined list of values from a specific column, which is the partitioning key. Each partition contains rows that contain the value contained in that column.

- Composite partitioning, which is the result of "subdividing" the range and hash or list partitioning. Under composite partitioning, a table is first partitioned using range, called the primary partition, and then each range partition is sub-partitioned using the hash or list value. A sub-partition of a partition has independent physical entities, which may reside in different tablespaces. Unlike range, list, and hash partitioning, with composite partitioning, sub-partitions, rather than partitions, are units for backup, recovery, Parallel DML (PDML), space management, etc. This means that a DBA can perform maintenance activities at the sub-partition level.

A partition is a segment of data with its own metadata. While logically a part of a table, partitions are actually segments that can be addressed directly with most of the internal characteristics of the parent objects (i.e. the table or index). This internal physical structure allows for independence and makes it a manageable target for backup, recovery, and other dataset-related operations.

Partitioned Indexes

Oracle provides various indexing methods that can be utilized based on the data or column being indexed and the access patterns on the columns. Selecting the right indexing strategy also depends on various factors, type of data being stored, uniqueness of data, cardinality of data, etc.

Based on how the data will be accessed from the different partitions, indexes on a partitioned table can be a local index and global index. While these are just types of indexes, they can be implemented using various indexing methods, such as bitmap indexes and B-tree indexes. So the challenge is not in the selection of the type of index, which is easier because it goes one-on-one with the type of implementation (e.g., partitioned indexes) but in the selection of the method used in indexing the tables. The various indexing methods are

- B-tree index
- Reverse key index
- Bitmap index
- Index-organized tables
- Function-based index

If no type of index is explicitly specified, Oracle creates a B-tree index by default. Figure 9-1 illustrates a B-tree index structure. Similar to Figure 9-1, an index structure contains several branches and steps in its structure. Initially, each index tree has one level. If the data in the table is very small, there may be only one index block. In that case, the leaf block is the same as the branch block. As the data grows, the level increases and then there is a branch block and a leaf block with a parent–child relationship. The maximum number of levels that the B-tree index can grow to is 24 (i.e., 0 to 23), which means that with two rows per index block it can hold approximately 18 billion leaf blocks. When the index look up is about 4-5 levels deep, it's worth considering partitioning the index.

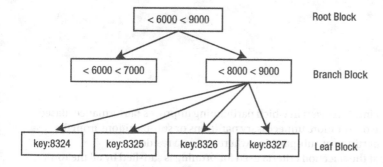

Figure 9-1. B-tree index structure

Once the type of index is identified, the type of implementation can be defined based on several factors such as data volume and access patterns. Similar to a data partition, an index partitioning will help improve manageability, availability, performance, and scalability. Partitioning of indexes can be done in one of two ways, either independent of the data partition, where the index is of a global nature (global indexes), or dependent on the data partition by directly linking to the partitioning method of tables where the indexing is of a local nature (local indexes).

Local Indexes

Each partition in a local index is associated with exactly one partition of the table. This enables Oracle to automatically keep the index partitions in sync with the table partitions. Database maintenance operations performed by the DBA on one partition, like rebuilding of a partition, reorganization of a partition, etc., only affect the partition where the maintenance is being performed.

Because of the one-to-one mapping between the index partition and the physical data partition, local indexes can be more efficient for a distributed workload when there is a clear access path based on the partition key. However, if the partition key is missing in the SQL statement, the optimizer will perform a full table scan across all the partitions.

Global Indexes

Global indexes are opposite to the locally partitioned indexes; a global index is associated with more than one partition of the table. For non-primary key/non-partitioned key based indexes that are created to optimize query performance, global indexes will be highly efficient for index lookups. However, if the index is used based on the partitioned key, it allows for partitioning elimination and only partitions containing the relevant index entry are accessed. The drawback of using the global index is the difficulty with managing individual partitions. Because a global index contains data across all partitions, dropping and rebuilding of partitions could be difficult.

Benefits of Partitioning

When multiple users access the data from multiple instances, while there is no guarantee that users will be accessing data that reside in different partitions, it provides the benefit of affinity of workloads to instances and partitions. This is more visible when using parallel queries. Parallel queries tend to use direct reads. The optimizer will generate parallel query execution plans to access data based on the partitions and submit slaves across instances. Efficiency of queries is improved because Oracle manages to lock information locally on the respective instances, eliminating the need to share them between clusters and thereby reducing interconnect traffic. Starting with Oracle Database 11g Release 2 (11.2.0.2) for buffered parallel queries, the parallel execution layer creates a partition to slave mapping.

Partitioning provides the following general performance benefits that are common to both a single instance configuration and a RAC configuration:

- Partition pruning
- Partition-wise joins
- Parallel DML

Partition Pruning

Partition pruning is one of the most effective and intuitive ways in which partitioning improves performance. Based on the queries optimization plan, it can eliminate one or more unnecessary partitions or sub-partitions from the queries execution plan, focusing directly on the partition or sub-partition where the data resides.

For example, if the optimizer determines that the selection criteria used for pruning is satisfied by all the rows in the accessed partition or sub-partition, it removes those criteria from the predicate list (WHERE clause) during evaluation in order to improve performance. However, there are certain limitations on using certain features; the optimizer cannot prune partitions if the SQL statement applies a function to the partitioning column. Similarly, the optimizer cannot use an index if the SQL statement applies a function to the indexed column, unless it is a function-based index.

Partition pruning occurs when there is an appropriate predicate on the partitioning key of a partitioned table. For range and list partitioning, partition pruning occurs for both equality/inequality predicates and range scan conditions. However, in the case of hash partitioning, partition pruning will occur only for equality predicates.

Partition-wise Joins

A partition-wise join is a join optimization that is used when joining two tables that are both partitioned along the join column(s). That is, if the tables and/or indexes have the same partition columns, the same number of partitions, and the same range values for range partitions, then the optimizer is able to perform joins partition by partition. By working with smaller sets, the number of rows that need to be joined is smaller, resulting in faster processing.

With partition-wise joins, the join operation is broken into smaller joins that are performed sequentially or in parallel. Partition-wise joins minimize the amount of data exchanged among parallel slaves during the execution of parallel joins by taking into account data distribution. It divides a large join into smaller joins between a pair of partitions from the two joined tables. To use this feature, you must equi-partition both tables on their join keys.

Sequence Numbers

Sequences (numbers) are used in many areas every day, from construction projects to kitchen projects to high-tech computer applications. The construction worker has to follow a sequence when he constructs a house or a building. In high-tech computer applications, sequence numbers are used to keep the transactional sequence. Oracle's architecture uses the system change number (SCN) to keep the transactional order and uses them during instance/database recovery operation.

Applications use sequences to generate a primary key for business entities. Applications that generate their own sequence (custom sequences) internally, and store the values in tables, can cause serious performance issues in a highly insert-intensive application. This is because each time a new number is required, the table has to be queried, the number changed, and the new value updated. In doing this, the database generates lot of log I/O and contention on the same block while the application updates the next sequence value. In a RAC environment, these high concurrency hot block issues will be extrapolated, causing severe performance issues.

Common problems that can be encountered when the application-generated custom sequences are used include the following:

- Row level locking causing high contention. Getting and maintaining sequences can cause enqueue contention on the sequence enqueue and latches.

- Due to the non-recursive nature of the transaction, in high INSERT intensive applications, updates to the table can be queued.

- There could be serious concurrency issues when this method is used.

- Additional GES traffic due to Global TX and TM enqueues for both transaction and the table involved in the operation.

The Oracle sequence generator reduces serialization where the statements of two transactions must generate sequential numbers at the same time. By avoiding the serialization when multiple users wait for each other to generate and use a sequence number, the sequence generator improves transaction throughput and, consequently, a user's wait will be considerably shorter. A sequence generator is useful for generating transaction-safe numbers for database transactions.

Sequences and Index Contention

Indexes, with key values generated using sequences, is subject to leaf block contention when the insert rate is high. This is because the index leaf block holding the highest key value is changed for every row inserted, as the values are monotonically ascending. In a RAC environment, this may lead to a high rate of current and CR blocks being transferred between nodes.

- Increasing the sequence cache size; the difference between sequence values generated by different instances increases successive index block splits and tends to create instance affinity to index leaf blocks.

- Increasing sequence cache also improves instance affinity to index keys deriving their values from sequences. This technique may result in significant performance gains for multi-instance INSERT intensive applications.

- Implementing the database partitioning option to physically distribute the data.

- Using Locally Managed Tablespaces (LMT) over dictionary-managed tablespaces.

- Using Automatic Segment Space Management (ASSM). ASSM can provide instance affinity to table blocks. Starting with Oracle Database 10g Release 2, ASSM is the default.

Another alternative to this solution is to use reverse key indexes, which will help distribute the data across several leaf blocks. While reverse key indexes can create performance issues with range scans, another alternative to avoid contention is to use locally partitioned indexes or hash partitioned indexes to avoid contention on leaf blocks.

Reverse Key Indexes

A reverse key index reverses the bytes of each column value indexed while keeping the column order. By reversing the keys of the index, the insertions become distributed across all leaf keys in the index. A reverse key index can be used in situations in which the user inserts ascending values and deletes lower values from the table, such as when using sequence-generated (surrogate keys) primary keys.

When using a surrogate key, especially in an insert-intensive application, the lowest level index leaf block will encounter extensive contention. For example, the key values 1324, 1325, 1326, etc., (illustrated in Figure 9-1) are sequentially written in ascending order. This will require a change to the leaf block, and when rows are inserted concurrently, it causes block splits to happen more frequently. The end result is a potential performance bottleneck. This overhead is even more significant in the RAC environment where multiple users insert data from different Oracle instances.

As the word "reverse" implies, the actual key value is reversed before being inserted into the index. For example, if the value of 4567 were reversed, its new value would be 7654. Compare the leaf block entries in Figure 9-2 with Figure 9-1; the leaf block entries are different between the two types of indexes.

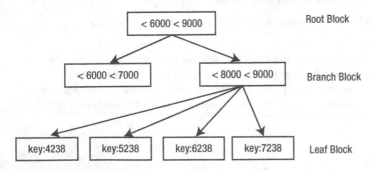

Figure 9-2. *Reverse key index structure*

When numbers are sequentially generated in ascending order, this has a significant effect in the distribution and scalability for an insert-intensive application. With the reverse option specified with the index creation statement, the potential issues described with the B-tree indexes (sequential indexes) can be avoided. Reverse key indexes are created using the following command:

```
CREATE INDEX PK_JBHIST ON JOB_HISTORY (JOBHIST_ID) REVERSE
```

A drawback of using reverse key indexes is that they requires more I/O due to loss of proximity. Also, range scans can cause significant full table scans due to wider spread of index leaf blocks. Local partitions and hash-partitioned indexes are preferred over reverse keys.

Workshop 1

AWR and SQL based queries against the enqueue statistics view indicate a high amount of requests for database sequences. Along with the number of requests, the wait times for this statistics also increase.

Step 1

Query the enqueue statistics view to determine the current performance average across the cluster. On noticing that the 'SQ' type of enqueue has high wait times, perform additional investigation.

The subset of the output generated from the query 'SQ' indicates a high number of requests and high cumulative wait times. Oracle raises the SQ enqueue when a lock is placed on the database sequence to ensure that only one process can replenish the sequence cache. This occurs when cache frequently keeps running out and the new cache has to be replenished more frequently.

Script: MVRACPDnTap_EnqStats.sql

```
SELECT inst_id       INT,
       eq_type       eq,
       eq_name,
       total_req#    tr,
       total_wait#   tw,
       succ_req#     sr,
       failed_req#   fr,
       cum_wait_time cwt
FROM   gv$enqueue_statistics
WHERE  total_req# > 1000
       AND cum_wait_time > 0
       AND eq_type IN ( 'TX', 'TM', 'SQ' )
ORDER  BY inst_id,
          total_req# DESC,
          total_wait# DESC,
          cum_wait_time DESC;
```

INT	EQ	EQ_NAME	TR	TW	SR	FR	CWT
1	TM	DML	62988023	2139	62978829	756	9350
	TX	Transaction	28637660	761	28641102	0	68020
	SQ	**Sequence Cache**	**57822**	**47278**	**57603**	**0**	**1917370**
	TX	Transaction	30156	13808	30156	0	224340
2	TM	DML	64071069	3368	64062637	941	8430
	TX	Transaction	29342805	727	29345321	0	79440
	TX	Transaction	75258	47680	75013	0	1949500
	SQ	**Sequence Cache**	**31992**	**15276**	**31992**	**0**	**204590**
	TX	Transaction	1720	177	1719	0	140
3	TM	DML	65880848	2390	65872229	983	8020
	TX	Transaction	30045006	765	30048075	0	71130
	TX	Transaction	57838	48805	57640	0	2013050
	SQ	Sequence Cache	31585	14806	31585	0	205760
4	TM	DML	33551829	5331	33548976	990	10980
	TX	Transaction	15844925	15836560	15852182	0	8912800
	TX	Transaction	538237	518908	538238	0	24403760
	SQ	Sequence Cache	510114	510094	510104	0	18639440
	TX	Transaction	44172	1619	44172	0	73730

Step 2

Based on the enqueue statistics collected, the next step is to check on the rowcache for the sequences. This is done by querying the GV$ROWCACHE view.

Script: MVRACPDnTap_rowcache.sql

```
SELECT inst_id int
     , parameter
     , sum(gets) gets
     , sum(getmisses) misses
     , 100*sum(gets - getmisses) / sum(gets) pct_succ_gets
     , sum(modifications)  updates
  FROM GV$ROWCACHE
 WHERE gets > 0
   AND 6 > 0
 GROUP BY INST_ID, parameter
 ORDER BY inst_id,
       6 desc;
```

INT	PARAMETER	GETS	MISSES	PCT_SUCC_GETS	UPDATES
1	dc_sequences	188898	85715	54.6	188,898
	dc_segments	44272	2602	94.1	618
	dc_rollback_segments	3148291	3842	99.9	211
	dc_tablespace_quotas	1427	907	36.4	198
	dc_objects	4108120	1686	100.0	78
	outstanding_alerts	6229	5348	14.1	68
2	dc_sequences	45823	35608	22.3	45,823
	dc_rollback_segments	7862462	3946	99.9	1,229
	dc_segments	201841	23098	88.6	1,036
	dc_tablespace_quotas	991	417	57.9	675
	dc_objects	260138	1304	99.5	56
	dc_object_ids	422596	1285	99.7	55
3	dc_sequences	248253	85714	65.5	248,252
	dc_segments	3418039	42533	98.8	1,357
	dc_rollback_segments	3105105	4643	99.9	219
	dc_tablespace_quotas	1343	911	32.2	191
	dc_objects	3853521	1577	100.0	151
	dc_object_ids	4978860	1938	100.0	55
4	dc_sequences	43384	34685	20.1	43,384
	dc_segments	215692	32954	84.7	1,141
	dc_rollback_segments	8011288	3294	100.0	1,099
	dc_tablespace_quotas	1107	417	62.3	577
	outstanding_alerts	6237	5338	14.4	68
	dc_objects	243894	1500	99.4	55

Apart from the columns displayed above, GV$ROWCACHE also contains columns to provide instruction on requests and contentions across various instances in the cluster. The output below illustrates the DLM (distributed lock manager) related columns. The DLM_* columns are populated only in a RAC environment.

Script: MVRACPDnTap_dlmrowcache.sql

```
SELECT inst_id int
    , parameter
    , sum(dlm_requests) requests,
    , sum(dlm_conflicts) conflicts
    , sum(dlm_releases)  releases
  FROM GV$ROWCACHE
 WHERE gets > 0
   AND 6 > 0
 GROUP BY INST_ID, parameter
 ORDER BY inst_id,
    6 desc;
```

INT	PARAMETER	DLM_REQUESTS	DLM_CONFLICTS	DLM_RELEASES
3	dc_sequences	377785	85705	177
	dc_histogram_defs	53829	426	20960
	outstanding_alerts	43966	21165	25
	dc_segments	33304	629	4952
	dc_objects	22247	794	8886
	dc_object_ids	14328	578	1646
	dc_rollback_segments	2679	211	0
	dc_tablespace_quotas	1175	64	2

The output above illustrates that the database sequences are used in more than one instance in the cluster and are distributed requests from other instances in the cluster. During these requests, the sessions faces conflicts.

Step 3

Output from Step 1 indicated high enqueue misses for sequence requests across all the instances in the cluster; the dc_sequence row cache statistics confirms this. The combination of gets, misses, updates, and the RAC-related requests against the dc_sequence row cache (Step 2) entry indicated contentions on the sequences generators.

Normally, high contention on database sequences are noticed when they are created with the ORDER clause or when the CACHE_SIZE is too small. Cache size usage can be monitored using the following query against the V$_SEQUENCES[1] view:

Script: MVRACPDnTap_seqcachebal.sql

```
SELECT inst_id              INT,
       sequence_owner       sowner,
       sequence_name        sname,
       cache_size,
       nextvalue,
       highwater,
       highwater - nextvalue  balancecache,
       background_instance_lock bil,
       instance_lock_flags  ilf,
       active_flag,
       order_flag
FROM  gv$_sequences
WHERE sequence_owner NOT IN ( 'SYS', 'SYSMAN', 'SYSTEM', 'DBSNMP' )
ORDER BY inst_id,
        sequence_owner;
```

From the output (not shown) of the above query, certain sequences were found to be defined with default cache value of 20 and with the ORDER clause, which causes the SQ enqueue wait event discussed in Step 1 to trigger every time the cache needs to be replenished. Apart from the SQ enqueue there are other lock-related events that are also triggered.

---

[1]V$_SEQUENCES is an undocumented view.

```
Username SERIAL#  SID Table Name          COMMAND  Lock Held     Lock Type
-------- -------  ---- ------------------  -------- ------------- ---------------------------------
RAPUSR      13   250 None                 INSERT   Exclusive     TX - Transaction enqueue lock
            13       RAPUSR.ORDERLN       INSERT   Row Exclusive TM - DML Enqueue Lock
            13       RAPUSR.ORDLN_SEQ     INSERT   Exclusive     SQ - Sequence number Enqueue lock
            13       RAPUSR.ORDLN_SEQ     INSERT   Exclusive     SV - Sequence number value lock
            13       SYS.ORA$BASE         INSERT   Share         AE - ????
RAPUSR     165    96 None                 INSERT   Exclusive     TX - Transaction enqueue lock
           165       RAPUSR.ORDER         INSERT   Row Exclusive TM - DML Enqueue Lock
           165       SYS.ORA$BASE         INSERT   Share         AE - ????
```

When sequences are defined with CACHE and ORDER clauses in RAC environment, and when multiple instances are inserting rows using the same SEQUENCE definition, the session requesting for the NEXTVAL of the sequence requires an exclusive access to the sequence. It requests a SV lock before inserting or making updates to the sequence value in the shared pool. Frequent requests from multiple instances for the NEXTVAL can cause severe contention and sessions may have to wait for an Enq: SV - contention event (Figure 9-3), followed by other wait events due to the repel effect such as gc current block busy and gc buffer busy acquire.

Top Timed Events

- Instance '*' - cluster wide summary
- '*' Waits, %Timeouts, Wait Time Total(s) : Cluster-wide total for the wait event
- '*' 'Wait Time Avg (ms)' : Cluster-wide average computed as (Wait Time Total / Event Waits) in ms
- '*' Summary 'Avg Wait Time (ms)' : Per-instance 'Wait Time Avg (ms)' used to compute the following statistics
- '*' [Avg/Min/Max/Std Dev] : average/minimum/maximum/standard deviation of per-instance 'Wait Time Avg(ms)'
- '*' Cnt : count of instances with wait times for the event

I#	Class	Event	Waits	%Timeouts	Total(s)	Avg(ms)	%DB time	Avg	Min	Max	Std Dev	Cnt
*	Other	enq: SV - contention	116,660	0.00	109,164.39	935.75	40.56	973.81	692.25	1139.57	245.12	3
	Cluster	gc current block busy	91,700	0.00	36,698.64	400.20	13.64	399.25	335.37	433.91	55.38	3
	System I/O	control file sequential read	351,073	0.00	23,800.03	67.79	8.84	66.43	46.10	99.01	28.50	3
	Cluster	gc buffer busy acquire	41,606	0.96	14,821.73	356.24	5.51	354.85	329.00	378.53	24.84	3
	Other	enq: IV - contention	23,011	2.79	12,525.24	544.32	4.65	541.91	524.29	556.67	16.38	3
	Other	PX Deq: reap credit	1,459,557	100.00	12,100.05	8.29	4.50	8.65	4.49	15.87	6.28	3
	Other	gcs log flush sync	297,270	65.64	12,072.32	40.61	4.49	39.58	36.91	43.47	3.45	3
	Other	enq: PS - contention	24,248	9.84	11,345.47	467.89	4.22	458.99	263.23	619.27	180.65	3
	Other	oracle thread bootstrap	6,208	0.00	10,422.91	1678.95	3.87	1684.42	1048.41	2789.06	960.30	3
		DB CPU			10,287.59		3.82					3

Figure 9-3. *AWR report: Top Timed Events*

While sequences can be defined with CACHE and ORDER clauses, performance impacts should be ascertained before implementing this option. In a RAC environment, unless absolutely required to satisfy business requirements, it's a good practice to use the CACHE and NOORDER clause when creating sequences.

Highly insert intensive tables that use sequences numbers for surrogate keys should have sufficiently high CACHE size. This will reduce the frequent updates to the dictionary cache. The dictionary cache will be updated only once with the new high watermark; in other words, when a NEXTVAL is requested, the row cache value of the sequence is changed in the dictionary cache and increased by the cache value.

Step 4

Modify the sequence definitions to increase the CACHE_SIZE for the demanding sequence definitions; setting them to NOORDER will reduce the contention and improve the overall response times.

Workshop 2

In this workshop, let's try to analyze the waits experienced during the INSERT operation in a RAC environment

Step 1

A good start to look at the overall SQL query performance is the V$SQLSTATS view. This view has considerable amount of information and provides instrumentation into the various resource layers of the database.

Script: MVRACPDnTap_clsqlstats.sql

```
SELECT inst_id          INT,
       sql_id,
       application_wait_time awt,
       concurrency_wait_time conwt,
       cluster_wait_time    clwt,
       io_interconnect_bytes ioicbytes
FROM   gv$sqlstats
WHERE  cluster_wait_time > 1000000
ORDER  BY inst_id,
       user_io_wait_time DESC;
```

INT	SQL_ID	AWT	CONWT	CLWT	IOICBYTES
1	4sk2z4rskuv4m	5333	1103230925	10615735924	48594944
	2ub6q6w9aa9pf	577	1961830	227813563	73883648
	ah2dbxq8w1d8h	2151	4856912	41917285	46096384
	fcxg48dtnwxqj	1479	307829	17081420	7299072
	0xta36p7ykq6g	0	358559	1658681	688128
	gbdcj3cn39mrm	8031	182480	1464970	5324800
2	4sk2z4rskuv4m	27978	1151084992	10582537422	51216384
	2ub6q6w9aa9pf	229	1705140	213407755	80986112
	ah2dbxq8w1d8h	3614	143960067	42598312	28966912
	fcxg48dtnwxqj	2654	250894	19748310	9322496
	0xta36p7ykq6g	0	162982	2758555	491520
	gbdcj3cn39mrm	429	112164	1854546	3538944
	9x7rfd9d7vcsg	523	158200	1400292	294912
4	3kvu10uhykg7y	29592274	6879477278	42519308702	14344192
	8436p6pb4j6pz	3.89E+08	2067177857	8736564233	6168576
	7g94kt7nkq1yt	612	672397897	8283446822	56672256
	2ub6q6w9aa9pf	1618	53981572	2026659828	51994624
	38kt82gam41ak	43108567	90322921	520242545	434176
	ast9xrxar0yx6	1309	11456019	273045708	4268032
	92ccq3p60gwz2	139	64122983	203911401	425984
	0h6tt5nw7kyad	1927	4306372	148356800	41164800

5	3kvu10uhykg7y	17437284	3266017235	34687603948	22257664
	8436p6pb4j6pz	1.84E+08	1039185500	7039642954	7233536
	7g94kt7nkq1yt	1086	444176496	6070377657	43016192
	2ub6q6w9aa9pf	4466	37937685	1578875870	38723584
	38kt82gam41ak	30676410	51508343	409237475	663552
	ast9xrxar0yx6	0	12114417	234604478	19947520
	92ccq3p60gwz2	0	36387561	185204879	1056768
	0h6tt5nw7kyad	987	1598312	129586820	32505856

In the output above, the statement with SQL_ID 3kvu10uhykg7y has the highest cluster wait times (CLWT column). The query also experienced high concurrency waits (CONWT column), and the average wait time (AWT column) was also high.

Step 2

With the help of the SQL_ID from Step 1, the actual sql text was determined.

```
SQL> SELECT SQL_ID, SQL_TEXT FROM GV$SQLSTATS WHERE SQL_ID='3kvu10uhykg7y';
SQL_ID
----------------
SQL_TEXT
--------------------------------------------------------------------------------------------
3kvu10uhykg7y
INSERT INTO RMQ_MESSAGE(MESSAGE_ID,RA_ID,RMQ_ID,REQUEST_ID,MESSAGE_TYPE,MESSAGE_TARGET_TYPE,
MESSAGE_VERSION,MESSAGE_PRIORITY,ACK_PROCESSING,REPLYTO_COMMAND_ID,MESSAGE_DATETIME)
VALUES (:1,:2,:3,:4,:5,:6,:7,:8,:9,:10,:11)
```

The statement is a DML operation, applying the understanding of the architecture discussed in Chapter 2. This could be a scenario where there is high block movement between instance 4 and instance 5. Step 1 also shows that the operation had a significantly high number of bytes transferred across the interconnect.

Step 3

In a RAC environment, with high insert operations where the operation includes a monotonously increasing sequence number based on primary keys, it is a good practice to isolate the transactions to one or few instances in the cluster.

The query was found only on instances 4 and 5. Drilling down further into the operation of this query and the current session information, the query is executed from an application connected to the database with a service name 'TAPS'. Checking the status of the service using the srvctl utility, it was determined that the service was running on instances 4 and 5 only.

```
SQL> !srvctl status service -db SSKYDB
Service FIPS is running on instance(s) SSKYDB_1,SSKYDB_2
Service SSKY is running on instance(s) SSKYDB_1,SSKYDB_2
Service GRUD is running on instance(s) SSKYDB_1,SSKYDB_2
Service TICKS is running on instance(s) SSKYDB_1,SSKYDB_2,SSKYDB_3,SSKYDB_4,SSKYDB_5
Service TAPS is running on instance(s) SSKYDB_4,SSKYDB_5
Service SRPT is running on instance(s) SSKYDB_5
```

Step 4

To understand the related wait events, it's important to understand the objects involved in the operation. The object name is visible in the output from Step 2 (RMQ_MESSAGE).

Step 5

Once the object name is obtained, the next step is to determine the blocks and the corresponding files involved in the operation. This information can be obtained either from GV$SESSION or GV$SESSION_WAIT views for any currently active sessions or from V$ACTIVE_SESSION_HISTORY for historical analysis of the query behavior.

Script: MVRACPDnTap_ashbysqlid.sql

```
SELECT inst_id,
       event,
       p1,
       p2,
       wait_class
FROM   gv$active_session_history
WHERE  sql_id = '3kvu1Ouhykg7y'
       AND event IS NOT NULL
ORDER  BY p2,
          p1;
```

INST_ID	EVENT	P1	P2	WAIT_CLASS
4	gc current block 3-way	143	49321	Cluster
5	db file sequential read	8	56097	User I/O
4	gc current block 3-way	149	78214	Cluster
5	buffer busy waits	149	78335	Concurrency
5	gc current grant busy	147	82459	Cluster
5	gc current grant busy	147	82467	Cluster
4	gc current block 2-way	145	89124	Cluster
4	gc current block 2-way	145	89483	Cluster
4	gc current block 2-way	140	90641	Cluster
4	gc current block congested	140	90834	Cluster
4	gc current block 2-way	140	90836	Cluster
4	gc current block 2-way	140	90879	Cluster
4	gc current block 2-way	140	90902	Cluster
4	gc current block 2-way	140	90918	Cluster
4	gc current block 2-way	140	90965	Cluster
5	gc current block 2-way	140	90969	Cluster
4	gc current block 2-way	140	90995	Cluster
4	gc current block 2-way	140	91079	Cluster
4	gc current block 2-way	140	91099	Cluster
5	gc current block 2-way	140	91115	Cluster
4	gc current block 2-way	140	91646	Cluster
4	buffer busy waits	147	92416	Concurrency
4	buffer busy waits	147	92419	Concurrency
4	buffer busy waits	147	92424	Concurrency

4	gc current block 2-way	147	92425	Cluster
4	buffer busy waits	147	92427	Concurrency
4	gc current grant 2-way	147	92428	Cluster
4	buffer busy waits	147	92431	Concurrency
4	buffer busy waits	147	92431	Concurrency
4	buffer busy waits	147	92431	Concurrency
4	buffer busy waits	147	92431	Concurrency
5	gc current block busy	147	92554	Cluster
4	gc current block busy	147	92556	Cluster
4	gc current block busy	147	92564	Cluster
5	gc current block busy	147	92596	Cluster
4	buffer busy waits	147	92839	Concurrency
4	buffer busy waits	147	92839	Concurrency
4	buffer busy waits	147	92839	Concurrency
4	buffer busy waits	147	92839	Concurrency
4	gc current block 2-way	147	93004	Cluster
4	gc current block busy	1	94673	Cluster
4	enq: TX - index contention	1.42E+09	29622275	Concurrency
4	enq: TX - index contention	1.42E+09	29753347	Concurrency
4	enq: TX - index contention	1.42E+09	31916054	Concurrency
5	enq: TX - index contention	1.42E+09	46596103	Concurrency
5	enq: TX - index contention	1.42E+09	46596103	Concurrency
5	enq: TX - index contention	1.42E+09	95354892	Concurrency
4	library cache lock	5.53E+10	5.52E+10	Concurrency
4	library cache: mutex X	2.18E+09	1.84E+13	Concurrency
4	library cache: mutex X	4.23E+09	2.38E+13	Concurrency
4	library cache: mutex X	4.23E+09	2.38E+13	Concurrency
4	library cache: mutex X	4.23E+09	2.38E+13	Concurrency

The output from the query above (output formatted for legibility) indicates data files 145, 146, 147, 148, 149, 150, and 151 are accessed several times and several blocks are repeatedly accessed between instances. Different file numbers indicate that there are several data files involved in the operation; verifying against V$DATAFILE, you see that all these files belong to the same tablespace.

```
SQL> SELECT ts#,
        file#,
        name
FROM  v$datafile
WHERE file# IN ( 145, 146, 147, 148,
                 149, 150, 151 );
```

TS#	FILE#	NAME
--------	--------	---
16	145	+SSKYDB__DATA/SSKYDB/datafile/data08.dbf
16	146	+SSKYDB__DATA/SSKYDB/datafile/data09.dbf
16	147	+SSKYDB__DATA/SSKYDB/datafile/data10.dbf
16	148	+SSKYDB__DATA/SSKYDB/datafile/data11.dbf
16	149	+SSKYDB__DATA/SSKYDB/datafile/data12.dbf
16	150	+SSKYDB__DATA/SSKYDB/datafile/data13.dbf
16	151	+SSKYDB__DATA/SSKYDB/datafile/data14.dbf

Step 6

What kind of waits did the query encounter that caused such high wait times? This information can be obtained either from GV$SESSION or GV$SESSION_WAIT views for any currently active sessions. However, to get the wait times for the operation over a period of time, you check against the GV$ACTIVE_SESSION_HISTORY view.

Inst	Event	Count	Total Time Waited
4	gc cr block 2-way	6705	130709999
4	gc buffer busy acquire	977	95153965
5	gc current grant busy	1553	94741345
5	gc cr grant 2-way	3878	77598705
4	gc current grant busy	5388	73536511
5	gc buffer busy acquire	897	65681455
5	gc cr block 2-way	5466	63163740
5	gc current block 3-way	4551	59585985
5	gc current block 2-way	5655	49691644
4	gc current block busy	1433	43599583
4	gc buffer busy release	588	38576658
4	gc cr grant 2-way	5098	33905067
5	gc current grant 2-way	959	59979554
4	gc current grant 2-way	999	55886144
5	gc cr multi block request	655	19934496
5	gc current block busy	355	11648503
5	gc cr disk read	1474	11501349
4	gc cr multi block request	651	9410566
4	gc current multi block request	103	9097616
5	gc cr block busy	730	9095815
4	gc cr failure	97	7045456
4	gc cr block congested	55	5563650
5	gc current multi block request	34	3456179
5	gc buffer busy release	54	3005641
5	gc cr block congested	13	5835114

Snapshots of the number of times the waits have been encountered and the total time waited by the events, for these data files indicate high inter-instance block activity. Concurrency related wait events (from the output of Step 5) are normally related to enqueues.

Step 7

Now that this information is obtained, the next step is to determine how to reduce this cluster-related overhead. There are several methods by which this could be addressed:

- Using database features such as partitioning. Is the current table/object already partitioned? If not, can it be partitioned and access to the various sets of data distributed across instances in the cluster since the idea of using a clustered environment is to distribute workload and use all the available resources? However, not always partitioning can be implemented without doing a complete profile of the application and understanding the access patterns of the queries. The execution plans and access criteria should match the partition keys for the optimizer to access the data efficiently.

- Yet another option available could be to isolate the operations of this object to a separate database service name and assign the service to only one instance in the cluster.

■ **Tip** In the data collected under Step 6, if `gc buffer busy waits` are higher, an option to optimize is to consider using indexing features such as reverse key indexes. This will spread the index leaf blocks, reducing concurrency wait times. Once again, while reverse key indexes are ideal for queries that have precise index-based retrieval, they can be extremely bad when used in range-based operations.

Undo Block Considerations

Excessive undo block shipment and contention for undo buffers usually happens when index blocks containing active transactions from multiple instances are read frequently.

When a SELECT statement needs to read a block with active transactions, it has to undo the changes to create a CR version. If the active transaction in the block belongs to more than one instance, there is a need to combine local and remote undo information for the CR operation. Depending on the amount of index blocks changed by multiple instances and the duration of transactions, the undo block shipment may become a bottleneck.

Usually this happens in applications that read recently inserted data very frequently and commit frequently. Techniques that can reduce such situations include the following:

- Shorter transactions reduce the likelihood that an index block in the cache contains uncommitted data, thereby reducing the need to access undo information for a consistent read.

- As explained earlier, increasing sequence cache sizes can reduce inter-instance concurrent access to index leaf blocks. A CR version of index blocks modified by only one instance can be fabricated without the need of remote undo information.

Similar to the INSERT operations, users can experience high waits due to cluster overheads even with SQL statements. Unlike the INSERT operation, SELECTs are less stressful when it comes to the locking and sharing of data blocks. However, the time taken to find the block due to lack of resources or when there is a larger amount of requests compared to what the system can handle can definitely be affected. Almost always, poor performance from SELECT operations is directly related to poorly written SQL statements.

Hard Parses

Hard parses are very costly for Oracle's optimizer. The amount of validation that has to be performed during a parse consumes a significant amount of resources. The primary reason for a repeated hard parse is the uniqueness of the queries present in the library cache/SGA. When a user/session executes a query, the query is parsed and loaded in the library cache after Oracle has generated a hash value for the query. Subsequently, when another session or user executes the same query depending on the extent of similarity of the query that is already present in the library cache, it is reused and there is no hard parse operation involved. However, if this query is not similar to the previous query or has values hard coded in the WHERE clause that make it different, it has to go through the Oracle parsing algorithm; this is considered as a hard parse and is very costly. The total amount of hard parses can be determined using the following query:

Script: MVRACPDnTap_hardparses.sql

```
SELECT  pa.inst_id,
        pa.sid,
        pa.VALUE "Hard Parses",
        ex.VALUE "Execute Count"
FROM    gv$sesstat pa,
        gv$sesstat ex
```

```
WHERE  pa.sid = ex.sid
       AND pa.inst_id = ex.inst_id
       AND pa.statistic# = (SELECT statistic#
                            FROM   v$statname
                            WHERE  NAME = 'parse count (hard)')
       AND ex.statistic# = (SELECT statistic#
                            FROM   v$statname
                            WHERE  NAME = 'execute count')
       AND pa.VALUE > 0;
```

When the query is executed for the very first time, it is parsed since the library cache needs to be "loaded," memory allocated, etc. It is considered normal behavior in Oracle's architecture to hardparse the statement. It is when repeated hard parses are made that it becomes a concern. Some of the reasons for hard parse operations are the following:

- Queries that use literals in the WHERE clause, making every query executed unique to the Oracle's optimizer because it will perform hard parse operations. The solution to these issues is to use bind variables instead of hard coded values in the queries.

- Bad or inefficient SQL is the cause for hard parses. In this inefficiency are included queries that do not use bind variables. Not using bind variables causes SQL queries to be parsed every single time because literals in queries make them different from a query that was executed previously.

Inefficient queries and using hard coded values/literals are within the control of the developer and can be rewritten so as to use bind variables. In the case of Java applications, the method is to use prepared statements.

In both these situations using bind variables and prepared statements, the query is by itself the same and will be reused every single time that a user executes this query and its present in the shared pool.

While using bind variables or prepared statements is an efficient practice, Oracle provides parameters that help improve efficiency of SQL queries.

To overcome the difficulties faced by most applications that use literals, Oracle has introduced a parameter called CURSOR_SHARING = FORCE. This parameter creates bind variables for all literals; thus, forcing cursor sharing.

- CURSOR_SHARING: To help with the bad SQL and to improve Oracle execution and reusability of the queries that use literals, Oracle introduced a parameter in Oracle database version 8 called CURSOR_SHARING. By enabling this parameter, Oracle will generate bind variables for all literals that it encounters, which means queries become reusable.

- SESSION_CACHED_CURSORS: This parameter specifies the number of session cursors to cache. When the cursors are cached, subsequent calls of the same SQL statement will move the cursor to the session cursor cache. Subsequently, when the same SQL statement is executed, the parse calls will find the cursor in the cache and use the already open cursor.

Another reason is the insufficient allocation of the SGA. When a large number of queries are executed, the queries have to be flushed out to give space for new ones. This repeated loading and unloading the SQL statements into the instance buffers can create high hard parse operations. The number reloads can be determined using the following query:

```
SELECT inst_id,
       sql_text,
       loads
FROM   gv$sqlstats
WHERE  loads > 100;
```

One way to reduce the hard parses that happen due to frequent loads is to increase the size of the shared pool using the parameter SHARED_POOL_SIZE. The ideal configuration of the shared pool can be determined by querying the V$SHARED_POOL_ADVICE view.

Like the shared pool algorithm, Oracle uses the LRU algorithm to remove entries in the session cursor cache.

As part of the features for optimizing the database, a feature that was introduced in Oracle 11g is not used for the right reasons. Let's discuss this feature, the result cache, in the next section.

Result Cache

In Oracle Database 11g Release 1, Oracle introduced the result cache feature. The name of the feature is self-explanatory. Cache the result (result cache), either on the client side using OCI calls or on the database server/instance level using an instance level cache area called result cache, part of the shared pool. The database result cache can be used by either a SQL statement/operation or using a database function. In this section, the two types of result cache operations at the database level are discussed.

The following parameters are used to manage the behavior of this feature:

```
NAME                             TYPE           VALUE
-------------------------------  -----------    ----------
client_result_cache_lag          big integer    3000
client_result_cache_size         big integer    0
result_cache_max_result          integer        5
result_cache_max_size            big integer    251680K
result_cache_mode                string         MANUAL
result_cache_remote_expiration   integer        0
```

The parameters client_result_cache_lag and client_result_cache_size are used to configure the result cache at the client side. The other parameters are used for configuring the result cache at the server side.

The size of the result cache on the server is determined by two parameters: result_cache_max_result and result_cache_max_size. By default, the result_cache_max_size parameter is about 0.25% of the memory_target parameter or 1% of the shared_pool parameter. This parameter can be modified to control how much is stored in the result cache. The result_cache_max_result parameter specifies what percentage of result_cache_max_size a single result cache can use. The default value is 5%.

Each result set is identified in the cache using a CACHE_ID, which is a 90-character-long string. The CACHE_ID for a query does not match the SQL_ID used to identify the query in the library cache and contained in V$SQL. Unlike the SQL_ID, which is generated for every SQL query executed against an Oracle database, the CACHE_ID is for an area or bucket in the result cache section of the shared pool that stores the end result of the query.

Query Result Cache

When a query is executed for the very first time, the user's process searches for the data in the database buffer cache. If data is there (because someone else retrieved this data before), it uses it; otherwise, it performs an I/O operation to retrieve data from the data file on disk into the buffer cache, and from this data, the final result set is built.

Subsequently, if another query requires the same data set, the process uses the data from the buffer cache to build the result set required by the user. Well, if the buffer cache contains data for reuse, then what's this new result cache? In simple terms, the result cache can be called a cache area within a cache, in this case, the shared pool. So, the result cache is an area in the shared pool and contains the end results of a query execution.

With the result cache feature, the final results of the query are stored in the result cache section of the shared pool and, subsequently, when a user executes the same query, instead of the process having to traverse through all the million rows in the buffer cache, the process bypasses this step and retrieves data from the result cache section of the shared pool.

In an Oracle RAC environment (Figure 9-4), this process is no different when the query is executed multiple times from one instance; results are retrieved from the result cache. So is there a difference? Actually, there is and there is not. The difference is when the second instance in the cluster executes the same query with the /*+ RESULT CACHE */ hint. Instead of getting all the rows from the I/O subsystem, only the results from the result cache are transferred.

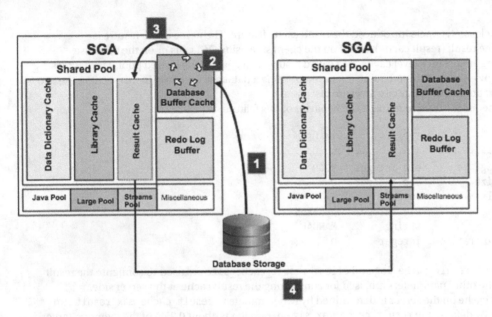

***Figure 9-4.** Result cache behavior in an Oracle RAC environment*

This is a great benefit in a data warehouse that uses RAC. In a data warehouse, large volumes of data are retrieved, filtered, sorted, and displayed to the user. When users from multiple instances execute the same query, there is the possibility that all of the rows will be transferred over the interconnect to the requesting instance. Using result cache helps reduce interconnect traffic or calls to the I/O subsystem. Then why does the documentation say the result cache is local to the instance? Because it is! In an Oracle RAC environment, the result cache is maintained locally within the shared pool of the instance. Figure 9-4 illustrates this through a four-step process.

1. Data is read from disk and populated into the buffer cache of the instance where the query was executed first.

2. Based on the WHERE condition of the query, the data is filtered in the buffer cache.

3. The final result set is populated into the result cache section of the shared pool.

4. Subsequently when another user executes the same query with the RESULT CACHE hint on another instance, the result set is moved from the result cache buffer of the holding instance to the requesting instance.

Workshop

Let's discuss this feature in an Oracle RAC environment step by step through a workshop.

Step 1

Let's check how much buffer has been allocated to the result cache section and how much is currently available. The current utilization of the result cache section of the shared pool can be determined using the following:

```
SQL>SET SERVEROUTPUT ON;
SQL>execute DBMS_RESULT_CACHE.MEMORY_REPORT(TRUE);

R e s u l t   C a c h e   M e m o r y   R e p o r t
[Parameters]
Block Size       = 1K bytes
Maximum Cache Size  = 251680K bytes (251680 blocks)
Maximum Result Size = 12584K bytes (12584 blocks)
[Memory]
Total Memory = 12784 bytes [0.000% of the Shared Pool]
... Fixed Memory = 12784 bytes [0.000% of the Shared Pool]
....... Memory Mgr = 200 bytes
....... Bloom Fltr = 2K bytes
.......  = 2088 bytes
....... Cache Mgr  = 5552 bytes
....... State Objs = 2896 bytes
... Dynamic Memory = 0 bytes [0.000% of the Shared Pool]
```

The result cache section of the shared pool can also be verified by querying against the v$sgastat view.

```
SELECT *
FROM  gv$sgastat
WHERE pool = 'shared pool'
      AND NAME LIKE 'Result%'
      AND inst_id = 1;
```

INST_ID	POOL	NAME	BYTES
1	shared pool	Result Cache: State Objs	2896
1	shared pool	Result Cache: Memory Mgr	200
1	shared pool	Result Cache:	2088
1	shared pool	Result Cache: Cache Mgr	5552
1	shared pool	Result Cache: Bloom Fltr	2048

The output above and the output generated by the memory report earlier indicate identical statistics.

From the output above, notice that no memory of the shared pool has been allocated to the result cache section (0.000% of the shared pool). The result cache is allocated from the dynamic memory section of the shared pool.

Indirectly, you can also verify whether there are any objects present in the result cache by using the following query. The following query lists of all the objects currently stored in the result cache:

Script: MVRACPDnTap_rcobjectcount.sql

```
COL INT format 999
SELECT inst_id       INT,
       id,
       TYPE,
       status,
       NAME,
       object_no     objno,
       cache_id,
       invalidations invals
FROM   gv$result_cache_objects
WHERE  inst_id = &&instnum;
```

Step 2

To get a better understanding of the result cache architecture, let's execute a normal query without any reference to the result cache feature. For comparison purposes, let's also trace the query using a 10046 trace and, using tkprof, generate a report.

```
SELECT OL_NUMBER, SUM (OL_AMOUNT), SUM (OL_QUANTITY)
FROM   ORDER_LINE OL, ORDERS ORD
WHERE  OL.OL_O_ID = ORD.O_ID AND
       OL.OL_W_ID = ORD.O_W_ID AND
       OL.OL_D_ID = ORD.O_D_ID
GROUP BY OL_NUMBER;
```

The output from the tkprof report indicates that about 347,000 rows were traversed to get the final result of 300 rows that is sent to user who executed query.

call	count	cpu	elapsed	disk	query	current	rows
Parse	1	0.01	0.02	0	0	0	0
Execute	1	0.00	0.00	0	0	0	0
Fetch	21	33.04	96.12	346671	347172	0	300
total	23	33.06	96.14	346671	347172	0	300

Step 3

If another user executes the query discussed in Step 1 and again by another set of users, the optimizer will generate the same plan and the server will have to do the same process of traversing through 347,000 rows to get the 300 rows back to the user.

Let's execute the query from Step 1 with the /*+ RESULT_CACHE */ hint on instance one (SSKY1) and examine the trace file generated from this execution.

```
SELECT /*+ RESULT_CACHE */ ol_w_id,
                           ol_d_id,
                           ol_number,
                           SUM(ol_amount),
                           SUM(ol_quantity)
FROM   order_line ol,
       orders ord
WHERE  ol.ol_o_id = ord.o_id
       AND ol.ol_w_id = ord.o_w_id
       AND ol.ol_d_id = ord.o_d_id
GROUP BY ol_number,
         ol_w_id,
         ol_d_id ;
```

call	count	cpu	elapsed	disk	query	current	rows
Parse	1	0.01	0.02	0	0	0	0
Execute	1	0.00	0.00	0	0	0	0
Fetch	21	33.85	97.00	346671	346755	0	300
total	23	33.86	97.03	346671	346755	0	300

```
Misses in library cache during parse: 1
Optimizer mode: ALL_ROWS
Parsing user id: 89  (TPCC)
```

```
Rows     Row Source Operation
-------  ---------------------------------------------------------
    300  RESULT CACHE 8fbjhchhd9zwh7uhn4mv7dhvga (cr=346755 pr=346671 pw=0 time=1046 us)
    300  HASH GROUP BY (cr=346755 pr=346671 pw=0 time=299 us cost=126413 size=4950 card=150)
21541174 HASH JOIN (cr=346755 pr=346671 pw=0 time=84263640 us cost=125703 size=680920944
                        card=20633968)
2153881  INDEX FAST FULL SCAN ORDERS_I2 (cr=11664 pr=11635 pw=0 time=566756 us cost=2743
                             size=22694870 card=2063170)(object id 86234)
21541174 INDEX FAST FULL SCAN IORDL (cr=335091 pr=335036 pw=0 time=62691616 us cost=87415
                             size=453947296 card=20633968)(object id 86202)
```

The first part of the statistics collected from the 10046-trace event is identical to the non-result cache operation. As illustrated in Figure 9-4,

1. Around 340,000 rows are read from the I/O subsystem.

2. They are traversed through the buffer cache to obtain a result of 300 summary rows.

3. The final set of 300 rows is then loaded into the result cache section of the shared pool.

Step 4

Let's check the result cache section and see what has changed.

```
SQL>SET SERVEROUTPUT ON;
SQL>execute DBMS_RESULT_CACHE.MEMORY_REPORT(TRUE);

R e s u l t   C a c h e   M e m o r y   R e p o r t
[Parameters]
Block Size          = 1K bytes
Maximum Cache Size  = 251680K bytes (251680 blocks)
Maximum Result Size = 12584K bytes (12584 blocks)
[Memory]
Total Memory = 207000 bytes [0.004% of the Shared Pool]
... Fixed Memory = 12784 bytes [0.000% of the Shared Pool]
....... Memory Mgr = 200 bytes
....... Bloom Fltr = 2K bytes
.......  = 2088 bytes
....... Cache Mgr  = 5552 bytes
....... State Objs = 2896 bytes
... Dynamic Memory = 194216 bytes [0.004% of the Shared Pool]
....... Overhead = 161448 bytes
.......... Hash Table    = 64K bytes (4K buckets)
.......... Chunk Ptrs    = 62920 bytes (7865 slots)
.......... Chunk Maps    = 31460 bytes
.......... Miscellaneous = 1532 bytes
....... Cache Memory = 32K bytes (32 blocks)
.......... Unused Memory = 23 blocks
.......... Used Memory = 9 blocks
.............. Dependencies = 2 blocks (2 count)
.............. Results = 7 blocks
.................. SQL = 7 blocks (1 count)
```

One execution of the query has changed the memory report. .004% of the dynamic memory section has been allocated to the result cache section to store 9 blocks of data. What's the math behind the 9 blocks of data? Two blocks are allocated to the dependent objects that are part of the query (ORDER_LINE and ORDERS) and 7 blocks are allocated to the result set of the query. There are 5 columns in the result set all having datatype NUMBER and the result has 300 rows. This amounts to about 5.5 blocks of data, which is rounded to 6 blocks; one additional block is used for the query metadata.

■ **Note**   The result cache block size should not be confused with the data block size. As indicated in the report, the result cache block size is 1K and the database block size is 8K.

A useful view to check on the objects stored in the result cache is the V$RESULT_CACHE_OBJECTS view. It provides most of the information contained in the result cache, including object dependency and invalidations when the underlying data or object changes.

The following subset of data from the V$RESULT_CACHE_OBJECTS view gives the basic information pertaining to the query and its results. The output lists two dependencies and one result. The result also contains information such as the number of columns and the total number of rows in the result set.

Script: MVRACPDnTap_rcobjectcount.sql

```
SELECT inst_id INT,
       id,
       TYPE,
       creation_timestamp,
       block_count,
       column_count,
       pin_count,
       row_count
FROM   gv$result_cache_objects
WHERE  inst_id =&& instnum;
```

INT	ID	TYPE	CREATION_	BLOCK_COUNT	COLUMN_COUNT	PIN_COUNT	ROW_COUNT
1	1	Dependency	20-APR-14	1	0	0	0
1	0	Dependency	20-APR-14	1	0	0	0
1	2	Result	20-APR-14	7	5	0	300

The following output lists all the objects used by the query (dependency) and the query itself stored as a result. Oracle generates the same CACHE_ID every single time for the exact same query, irrespective of how many times the query is executed and across how many instances in the cluster it is executed from.

Script: MVRACPDnTap_rcobjects.sql

```
SELECT inst_id       INT,
       id,
       TYPE,
       status,
       NAME,
       object_no     objno,
       cache_id,
       invalidations invals
FROM   gv$result_cache_objects
WHERE  inst_id = &&instnum;
```

INT	ID	TYPE	STATUS	NAME	OBJNO	CACHE_ID	INVALS
1	1	Dependency	Published	TPCC.ORDERS	86209	TPCC.ORDERS	0
1	0	Dependency	Published	TPCC.ORDER_LINE	86201	TPCC.ORDER_LINE	0
1	2	Result	Published	SELECT /*+ RESULT_CACHE */ OL_W_ID ,OL_D_ID,OL_NUMBER,sum(OL_AMOUNT), sum(OL_QUANTITY) FROM ORDER_LINE O L, ORDERS ORD WHERE OL.OL_	0	8fbjhchhd9zwh7uhn4mv7dhvga	0

■ **Note** The values found in column OBJECT_NO (OBJNO) correspond to the value of the OBJECT_ID column in the DBA_OBJECTS view.

Continuing our look at the subsets of data found in the V$RESULT_CACHE_OBJECTS, the following output lists the current space utilization of the results section for this operation:

Script: MVRACPDnTap_rcutil.sql

```
SELECT inst_id      INT,
       id,
       TYPE,
       block_count   blkcnt,
       column_count  clmcnt,
       scan_count,
       row_count     rcnt,
       row_size_max  rsm,
       row_size_avg  rsa,
       space_overhead soh,
       space_unused   sun
FROM   gv$result_cache_objects;
WHERE  inst_id =&& instnum;
```

INT	ID	TYPE	BLKCNT	CLMCNT	RCNT	RSM	RSA	SOH	SUN
1	1	Dependency	1	0	0	0	0	0	0
1	0	Dependency	1	0	0	0	0	0	0
1	2	Result	7	5	300	27	26	536	35

Step 5

From the previous output discussed in Step 2 of the workshop, you noticed that .004% of the dynamic memory section of the shared pool was utilized by this operation. The following query provides a detailed report:

```
SELECT *
FROM  gv$sgastat
WHERE pool = 'shared pool'
      AND NAME LIKE 'Result%'
      AND inst_id = 1;
```

INST_ID	POOL	NAME	BYTES
1	shared pool	Result Cache: State Objs	2896
1	shared pool	Result Cache	194216
1	shared pool	Result Cache: Memory Mgr	200
1	shared pool	Result Cache:	2088
1	shared pool	Result Cache: Cache Mgr	5552
1	shared pool	Result Cache: Bloom Fltr	2048

You now have an understanding of what happens with the result cache on instance one (SSKY1). As observed, this functionality has identical behavior as in the case of a single-instance implementation.

One of the great benefits of Oracle RAC is that multiple users can query against the same set of data from multiple instances in the cluster. If a user were to execute the exact same query from either instance 2 (SSKY2), instance 3 (SSKY3), or instance 4 (SSKY4), as discussed earlier, depending on the volume of data being retrieved, the data could be either transferred via the interconnect using cache fusion or, as in Oracle Database 11g Release 2, the data could be retrieved from storage. Again, not only does the process have to transfer all the data over the interconnect or load it from storage, the process has to traverse through all the rows available in the buffer cache before the result set is built.

Step 6

Cruising along with our workshop, let's execute the query on instance 3 (SSKY3) and observe the details. The great performance benefit of using the result cache feature in the Oracle RAC environment illustrated in Figure 9-4 is that only the final result set will be transferred between the instances, reducing considerable resources for both the CPU and network.

call	count	cpu	elapsed	disk	query	current	rows
Parse	1	0.01	0.02	0	0	0	0
Execute	1	0.00	0.00	0	0	0	0
Fetch	21	0.00	0.00	0	0	0	300
total	23	0.02	0.03	0	0	0	300

```
Misses in library cache during parse: 1
Optimizer mode: ALL_ROWS
Parsing user id: 89  (TPCC)

Rows     Row Source Operation
-------  ---------------------------------------------------
    300  RESULT CACHE  8fbjhchhd9zwh7uhn4mv7dhvga (cr=5 pr=0 pw=0 time=299 us)
      0  HASH GROUP BY (cr=0 pr=0 pw=0 time=0 us cost=126413 size=4950 card=150)
      0  HASH JOIN  (cr=0 pr=0 pw=0 time=0 us cost=125703 size=680920944 card=20633968)
      0  INDEX FAST FULL SCAN ORDERS_I2 (cr=0 pr=0 pw=0 time=0 us cost=2743 size=22694870
                              card=2063170)(object id 86234)
      0  INDEX FAST FULL SCAN IORDL (cr=0 pr=0 pw=0 time=0 us cost=87415 size=453947296
                              card=20633968)(object id 86202)
```

Based on the statistics collected using the 10046-trace event, there is no data being retrieved locally nor is there any traversing of rows in the buffer cache of the local instance. The execution plan indicates that there was fetch of just the final result set. How and where did this come from? Oracle Database was able to retrieve the result set from the result cache section of the shared pool in instance one and transfer the data over the interconnect. Isn't this neat? This really cuts down so much on data processing and improves resource utilization.

Step 7

The memory structure of the result cache section of the shared pool is also identical to the structure found on the instance where the query was executed for the first time. This proves two things: no additional memory or resource is utilized for the second instance, and each Oracle RAC instance maintains its own copy of the result set in its local result cache.

```
R e s u l t   C a c h e   M e m o r y   R e p o r t
[Parameters]
Block Size       = 1K bytes
Maximum Cache Size = 251680K bytes (251680 blocks)
Maximum Result Size = 12584K bytes (12584 blocks)
```

```
[Memory]
Total Memory = 208144 bytes [0.004% of the Shared Pool]
... Fixed Memory = 13928 bytes [0.000% of the Shared Pool]
....... Memory Mgr = 200 bytes
....... Bloom Fltr = 2K bytes
.......  = 3232 bytes
....... Cache Mgr  = 5552 bytes
....... State Objs = 2896 bytes
... Dynamic Memory = 194216 bytes [0.004% of the Shared Pool]
....... Overhead = 161448 bytes
........... Hash Table  = 64K bytes (4K buckets)
........... Chunk Ptrs  = 62920 bytes (7865 slots)
........... Chunk Maps  = 31460 bytes
........... Miscellaneous = 1532 bytes
....... Cache Memory = 32K bytes (32 blocks)
........... Unused Memory = 23 blocks
........... Used Memory = 9 blocks
............... Dependencies = 2 blocks (2 count)
............... Results = 7 blocks
.................. SQL = 7 blocks (1 count)

PL/SQL procedure successfully completed.
```

One execution of the query on instance 3 gives an identical memory structure to that on instance 1; .004% of the dynamic memory section has been allocated to the result cache section to store 9 blocks of data.

Step 8

Querying the GV$RESULT_CACHE_OBJECTS view, there are two result cache sections, one on instance 1 and another on instance 2, indicating that in an Oracle RAC environment, Oracle Database does not maintain a global result cache section. Rather, it manages the result cache locally on the respective instances.

Script: MVRACPDnTap_rcobjects.sql

```
INT ID TYPE       STATUS    NAME                              OBJNO CACHE_ID                      INVALS
--- -- ---------- --------- --------------------------------- ----- ----------------------------- ------
  3  1 Dependency Published TPCC.ORDERS                       86209 TPCC.ORDERS                        0
  3  0 Dependency Published TPCC.ORDER_LINE                   86201 TPCC.ORDER_LINE                    0
  3  2 Result     Published SELECT /*+ RESULT_CACHE */ OL_W_ID     0 8fbjhchhd9zwh7uhn4mv7dhvga         0
                            ,OL_D_ID,OL_NUMBER,sum(OL_AMOUNT),
                            sum(OL_QUANTITY) FROM ORDER_LINE O
                            L, ORDERS ORD WHERE OL.OL_

  1  1 Dependency Published TPCC.ORDERS                       86209 TPCC.ORDERS                        0
  1  0 Dependency Published TPCC.ORDER_LINE                   86201 TPCC.ORDER_LINE                    0
  1  2 Result     Published SELECT /*+ RESULT_CACHE */ OL_W_ID     0 8fbjhchhd9zwh7uhn4mv7dhvga         0
                            ,OL_D_ID,OL_NUMBER,sum(OL_AMOUNT),
                            sum(OL_QUANTITY) FROM ORDER_LINE O
                            L, ORDERS ORD WHERE OL.OL_
6 rows selected.
```

There are several factors to observe in the preceding output:

- The query has the same CACHE_ID on both instances.

- From the execution plan (Step 4), you observed that the number of rows in the result cache of instance 3 is identical to instance 1.

- The cluster has four instances; however, the view contains data only when the result cache for the instance has been utilized, meaning there are no entries in the result cache section for instance 2 and instance 4, respectively. However, when a user executes the identical query on either of these instances, the behavior observed on instance 3 will be duplicated on these instances.

Will the query keep returning the same result set all the time? What happens when data changes in the underlying objects? What happens to the result cache section that contains the results?

Good questions. Let's continue with the workshop and try to answer some of these questions.

When data changes in any of the underlying objects, Oracle Database invalidates the result set on all the instances in the cluster, indicating that subsequent execution of the same query will require fresh processing of data to rebuild the result set and store the result in the result cache section of the shared pool.

Script: MVRACPDnTap_rcobjects.sql

```
INT ID TYPE        STATUS     NAME                              OBJNO  CACHE_ID                    INVALS
--- -- ----------- ---------- --------------------------------- ------ --------------------------- ------
  1  1 Dependency  Published  TPCC.ORDERS                       86209  TPCC.ORDERS                      0
  1  0 Dependency  Published  TPCC.ORDER_LINE                   86201  TPCC.ORDER_LINE                  1
  1  2 Result      Invalid    SELECT /*+ RESULT_CACHE */ OL_W_ID     0  8fbjhchhd9zwh7uhn4mv7dhvga       0
                              ,OL_D_ID,OL_NUMBER,sum(OL_AMOUNT),
                              sum(OL_QUANTITY) FROM ORDER_LINE O
                              L, ORDERS ORD WHERE OL.OL_

  3  1 Dependency  Published  TPCC.ORDERS                       86209  TPCC.ORDERS                      0
  3  0 Dependency  Published  TPCC.ORDER_LINE                   86201  TPCC.ORDER_LINE                  1
  3  2 Result      Invalid    SELECT /*+ RESULT_CACHE */ OL_W_ID     0  8fbjhchhd9zwh7uhn4mv7dhvga       0
                              ,OL_D_ID,OL_NUMBER,sum(OL_AMOUNT),
                              sum(OL_QUANTITY) FROM ORDER_LINE O
                              L, ORDERS ORD WHERE OL.OL_
```

If the query is executed again to retrieve the new result set from the database, a new row (ID=9) is added to the result cache section. Oracle Database retains the invalid result set until the instance is bounced, the result cache is flushed, or the data in the result cache ages out of the buffer.

Script: MVRACPDnTap_rcobjects.sql

```
INT ID TYPE        STATUS     NAME                              OBJNO  CACHE_ID                    INVALS
--- -- ----------- ---------- --------------------------------- ------ --------------------------- ------
  1  1 Dependency  Published  TPCC.ORDERS                       86209  TPCC.ORDERS                      0
  1  0 Dependency  Published  TPCC.ORDER_LINE                   86201  TPCC.ORDER_LINE                  1
  1  9 Result      Published  SELECT /*+ RESULT_CACHE */ OL_W_ID     0  8fbjhchhd9zwh7uhn4mv7dhvga       0
                              ,OL_D_ID,OL_NUMBER,sum(OL_AMOUNT),
                              sum(OL_QUANTITY) FROM ORDER_LINE O
                              L, ORDERS ORD WHERE OL.OL_

  1  2 Result      Invalid    SELECT /*+ RESULT_CACHE */ OL_W_ID     0  8fbjhchhd9zwh7uhn4mv7dhvga       0
                              ,OL_D_ID,OL_NUMBER,sum(OL_AMOUNT),
                              sum(OL_QUANTITY) FROM ORDER_LINE O
                              L, ORDERS ORD WHERE OL.OL_

  3  1 Dependency  Published  TPCC.ORDERS                       86209  TPCC.ORDERS                      0
  3  0 Dependency  Published  TPCC.ORDER_LINE                   86201  TPCC.ORDER_LINE                  1
  3  2 Result      Invalid    SELECT /*+ RESULT_CACHE */ OL_W_ID     0  8fbjhchhd9zwh7uhn4mv7dhvga       0
                              ,OL_D_ID,OL_NUMBER,sum(OL_AMOUNT),
                              sum(OL_QUANTITY) FROM ORDER_LINE O
                              L, ORDERS ORD WHERE OL.OL_
```

In the output above, when a few rows are deleted from the ORDER_LINE table, the result row is marked as Invalid and the INVALIDATIONS (INVALS) counter of the GV$RESULT_CACHE_OBJECTS view is incremented. If, subsequently, there is another operation on the ORDER_LINE table, either by adding new rows or by deleting a few more rows, the counter will be incremented again. This indicates how many times the object was invalidated in the result cache.

How long does this remain invalid? Like other cache areas in an Oracle Database instance, the memory management of the result cache section is also the same; the invalid results will be moved to the dirty list and will be flushed out of the cache section as new data gets loaded to the cache section. When the query executes again, a new set of data is loaded into the result cache. The required result should always be the most current committed data to meet Read Consistency. Frequent invalidations and reloading can cause contention for the result cache and will trigger an 'enq: RC - Result Cache: Contention' wait event.

If the result cache for a query is invalidated on instance 1, the identical result caches, if they exist, on ALL instances will also be invalidated. Using the results cache feature only makes sense if the underlying tables/data do not change for long periods of time. As a best practice, the result cache feature is more suitable for a data warehouse environment.

Function Result Cache

Very similar to the behavior of the query result cache feature discussed earlier, the function result cache caches all the results returned by the user-defined function in the same result cache section of the shared pool. The result cache area is shared by both the results from the user-defined function and the query that uses /*+ RESULT CACHE */ hint.

Unlike the /*+ RESULT CACHE */ hint used in the query option earlier, the result cache is enabled at the function level by an attribute RESULT_CACHE with the function definition.

```
FUNCTION <name>    <INPUT PARAMETERS>
RESULT_CACHE
```

Apart from the result cache parameter, there is another optional parameter called RELIES_ON<object name> that is used to inform the optimizer regarding the base table that the function depends on. RELIES_ON will help invalidate any data in the result cache buffer should the base table referenced in the function change. Examples always help to explain concepts better, so let's do a workshop.

Workshop

In this workshop, the discussions will focus on defining and validating the function result cache feature.

Step 1

Create a function with the RESULT_CACHE and RELIES_ON attributes. The function below returns the balance on account for a customer:

```
CREATE OR REPLACE FUNCTION totalbalance(p_id IN NUMBER)
RETURN NUMBER
RESULT_CACHE RELIES_ON(CUSTOMER)
AS
  l_cust_total NUMBER := 0;
BEGIN -- get the total balance for the customer id passed in
    SELECT SUM(c_balance)
    INTO    l_cust_total
    FROM    customer
    WHERE   c_id = p_id;

    -- return the result
    RETURN l_cust_total;
END;
/
```

Step 2

Create the function in the respective schema by executing the definition from Step 1. After the function is created, execute the function

```
SELECT totalbalance(10) FROM DUAL;
```

Step 3

Validate the result cache section and see what has changed.

```
SQL> execute DBMS_RESULT_CACHE.MEMORY_REPORT(TRUE);
R e s u l t   C a c h e   M e m o r y   R e p o r t
[Parameters]
Block Size          = 1K bytes
Maximum Cache Size  = 14432K bytes (14432 blocks)
Maximum Result Size = 721K bytes (721 blocks)
[Memory]
Total Memory = 176312 bytes [0.039% of the Shared Pool]
... Fixed Memory = 12360 bytes [0.003% of the Shared Pool]
....... Memory Mgr = 208 bytes
....... Cache Mgr  = 256 bytes
.......  = 680 bytes
....... Bloom Fltr = 2K bytes
....... RAC Cbk    = 6240 bytes
....... State Objs = 2928 bytes
... Dynamic Memory = 163952 bytes [0.036% of the Shared Pool]
....... Overhead = 131184 bytes
.......... Hash Table   = 64K bytes (4K buckets)
.......... Chunk Ptrs   = 24K bytes (3K slots)
.......... Chunk Maps   = 12K bytes
.......... Miscellaneous = 131184 bytes
....... Cache Memory = 32K bytes (32 blocks)
.......... Unused Memory = 29 blocks
.......... Used Memory = 3 blocks
.............. Dependencies = 2 blocks (2 count)
.............. Results = 1 blocks
................. PLSQL = 1 blocks (1 count)
```

One execution of the query has changed the memory report. 0.036% of the dynamic memory section of the shared pool has been allocated to the result cache section to store three blocks of data. Similar to the discussion in the previous workshop on result cache, two blocks are allocated to the dependent object that is part of the query (CUSTOMER) and one block is allocated to the result set of the query. The PL/SQL block is identified in the result cache.

The V$RESULT_CACHE_OBJECTS view gives the basic information pertaining to the function and its results. The output lists one dependency and one result. The result also contains information such as the number of columns and the total number of rows in the result set.

Script: MVRACPDnTap_rcobjectcount.sql

```
SELECT  inst_id INT,
        id,
        TYPE,
        creation_timestamp,
        block_count,
        column_count,
        row_count
FROM    gv$result_cache_objects
WHERE   inst_id =&& instnum;
```

INT	ID	TYPE	STATUS	CREATION_	BLOCK_COUNT	COLUMN_COUNT	ROW_COUNT
2	2	Dependency	Published	05-AUG-14	1	0	0
2	0	Dependency	Published	05-AUG-14	1	0	0
2	1	Result	Published	05-AUG-14	1	1	1

The following output lists all the objects used by the query (dependency) and the function stored as a result. Oracle generates the same CACHE_ID every single time for the exact same function irrespective of how many times the function is executed and across how many instances in the cluster it is executed from.

Script: MVRACPDnTap_rcobjects.sql

```
SELECT  inst_id       INT,
        id,
        type,
        status,
        name,
        object_no     objno,
        cache_id,
        invalidations invals
FROM    gv$result_cache_objects
WHERE   inst_id = &&instnum;
```

INT	ID	TYPE	STATUS	NAME	OBJNO	CACHE_ID	INVALS
2	2	Dependency	Published	RAPUSR.CUSTOMER	91995	RAPUSR.CUSTOMER	0
2	0	Dependency	Published	RAPUSR.TOTALBALANCE	92922	RAPUSR.TOTALBALANCE	0
2	1	Result	Published	"RAPUSR"."TOTALBALANCE"::8."TOTALB ALANCE"#3048d2af80817a01 #1	0	cz680bz0arddp9gqgmk5ayr946	0

Continuing our look at the subsets of data found in the V$RESULT_CACHE_OBJECTS, the following output lists the current space utilization of the results section for this operation:

Script: MVRACPDnTap_rcutil.sql

```
SELECT  inst_id       INT,
        id,
        type,
        block_count   blkcnt,
        column_count  clmcnt,
        scan_count,
        row_count     rcnt,
```

```
            row_size_max   rsm,
            row_size_avg   rsa,
            space_overhead soh,
            space_unused   sun
FROM        gv$result_cache_objects;
WHERE       inst_id =&& instnum;
```

INT	ID	TYPE	BLKCNT	CLMCNT	SCAN_COUNT	RCNT	RSM	RSA	SOH	SUN
2	2	Dependency	1	0	0	0	0	0	0	0
2	0	Dependency	1	0	0	0	0	0	0	0
2	1	Result	1	1	0	1	5	5	373	646

Step 5

From the previous output discussed in Step 2 of the workshop, you noticed that .036% of the dynamic memory section of the shared pool was utilized by this operation. The following query provides a detailed report:

```
SELECT *
FROM    gv$sgastat
WHERE   pool = 'shared pool'
        AND name LIKE 'Result%';
```

INST_ID	POOL	NAME	BYTES	CON_ID
1	shared pool	Result Cache: Memory Mgr	208	0
1	shared pool	Result Cache: Cache Mgr	256	0
1	shared pool	Result Cache:	4088	0
1	shared pool	Result Cache: RAC Cbk	6240	0
1	shared pool	Result Cache: State Objs	2928	0
1	shared pool	Result Cache: Bloom Fltr	2048	0
2	shared pool	Result Cache: State Objs	2928	0
2	shared pool	Result Cache: Bloom Fltr	2048	0
2	shared pool	Result Cache	163952	0
2	shared pool	Result Cache: Memory Mgr	208	0
2	shared pool	Result Cache: Cache Mgr	256	0
2	shared pool	Result Cache: RAC Cbk	6240	0
2	shared pool	Result Cache:	680	0

As noticed from the discussions above, the behavior of result cache utilization and reusability of the results captured from executing a function or a SQL script (in the previous workshop) are very similar. This is also true when the PL/SQL function is executed on another instance in the RAC cluster. The results are transferred from the result cache of the first instance where it was executed to the new instance.

When data changes in any of the underlying objects, it invalidates the result set (output below ID=6) on all the instances in the cluster, indicating that subsequent execution of the same query will require fresh processing of data to rebuild the result set and store the result in the result cache section of the shared pool.

INT	ID	TYPE	STATUS	NAME	OBJNO	CACHE_ID	INVALS
2	2	Dependency	Published	RAPUSR.CUSTOMER	91995	RAPUSR.CUSTOMER	1
2	0	Dependency	Published	RAPUSR.TOTALBALANCE	92922	RAPUSR.TOTALBALANCE	0
2	1	Result	Invalid	"RAPUSR"."TOTALBALANCE"::8."TOTALB ALANCE"#3048d2af80817a01 #1	0	cz680bz0arddp9gqgmk5ayr946	0

If the PL/SQL function is executed again to retrieve the new result set from the database, a new row (ID=6) is added to the result cache section. Oracle Database retains the invalid result set (ID=1) until the instance is bounced, the result cache is flushed, or the data in the result cache ages out of the buffer. As noticed in the output below, other statements are also executed (for example ID=5).

```
INT  ID  TYPE         STATUS      NAME                            OBJNO  CACHE_ID                          INVALS
---- --- ----------   ----------  ------------------------------  -----  ------------------------------    ------
  2   4  Dependency   Published   RAPUSR.ORDER_LINE               92008  RAPUSR.ORDER_LINE                      0
  2   3  Dependency   Published   RAPUSR.ORDERS                   92003  RAPUSR.ORDERS                          0
  2   2  Dependency   Published   RAPUSR.CUSTOMER                 91995  RAPUSR.CUSTOMER                        1
  2   0  Dependency   Published   RAPUSR.TOTALBALANCE             92922  RAPUSR.TOTALBALANCE                    0
  2   6  Result       Published   "RAPUSR"."TOTALBALANCE"::8."TOTALB   0  cz680bz0arddp9gqgmk5ayr946            0
                                  ALANCE"#3048d2af80817a01 #1

  2   5  Result       Published   SELECT /*+ RESULT_CACHE */ OL_W_ID    0  5xh3hdqs0r6298wubzkunhpnfy            0
                                  ,OL_D_ID,OL_NUMBER,sum(OL_AMOUNT),
                                  sum(OL_QUANTITY) FROM ORDER_LINE O
                                  L, ORDERS ORD WHERE OL.OL_

  2   1  Result       Invalid     "RAPUSR"."TOTALBALANCE"::8."TOTALB    0  cz680bz0arddp9gqgmk5ayr946            0
                                  ALANCE"#3048d2af80817a01 #1
```

In the output above, the invalid result cache entry identified by ID=1 remains in buffer until such time the cache area is required by another operation. This is also reflected in the DBMS_RESULT_CACHE output below.

```
SQL> execute DBMS_RESULT_CACHE.MEMORY_REPORT(TRUE);
R e s u l t   C a c h e   M e m o r y   R e p o r t
[Parameters]
Block Size          = 1K bytes
Maximum Cache Size  = 14432K bytes (14432 blocks)
Maximum Result Size = 721K bytes (721 blocks)
[Memory]
Total Memory = 176312 bytes [0.035% of the Shared Pool]
... Fixed Memory = 12360 bytes [0.002% of the Shared Pool]
....... Memory Mgr = 208 bytes
....... Cache Mgr  = 256 bytes
.......  = 680 bytes
....... Bloom Fltr = 2K bytes
....... RAC Cbk    = 6240 bytes
....... State Objs = 2928 bytes
... Dynamic Memory = 163952 bytes [0.033% of the Shared Pool]
....... Overhead = 131184 bytes
.......... Hash Table    = 64K bytes (4K buckets)
.......... Chunk Ptrs    = 24K bytes (3K slots)
.......... Chunk Maps    = 12K bytes
.......... Miscellaneous = 131184 bytes
....... Cache Memory = 32K bytes (32 blocks)
.......... Unused Memory = 25 blocks
.......... Used Memory = 7 blocks
.............. Dependencies = 4 blocks (4 count)
.............. Results = 3 blocks
................. SQL     = 1 blocks (1 count)
................. PLSQL   = 1 blocks (1 count)
................. Invalid = 1 blocks (1 count)

PL/SQL procedure successfully completed.
```

In the output above, a section of the buffer is allocated to a SQL operation, a PL/SQL operation, and an invalid operation.

Limitations of the Result Cache

Not every feature will be able to do everything possible. Every feature has a few limitations in some of its operation. Result cache also has few limitations.

1. The primary limitation of the result cache is the fact that the results are stored in cache only. This means when the instance fails or is shut down for maintenance, the data is cleared. If it is highly critical that the result sets are permanently stored in the database, options such as materialized views should be used.

2. Result cache is a memory structure that does not contain any physical data that a materialized view would contain. Materialized views are database objects, and the result cache is a memory structure and data is not persistent.

3. If the data changes frequently or is volatile in nature, the caches will have to be invalidated and rebuilt frequently. This makes the use of result cache feature expensive and can increase memory management. These frequent invalidations can also create adverse inconsistent response times.

4. The result cache feature has to be manually used by using the HINT with specific queries. The AUTO option is available but is not supported.

5. There are a few types of operations that are not supported when using this feature. For example, queries cannot include or use SQL functions such as CURRENT_DATE, CURRENT_TIMESTAMP, LOCAL_TIMESTAMP, SYS_CONTEXT, SYS_GUID, SYS_TIMESTEMP, USERENV, and so on. If they are used, the following type of error occurs:

```
ERROR at line 1:
ORA-00904: "SYS_TIMESTAMP": invalid identifier
Tables in SYS and SYSTEM schema
Sequence CURRVAL and NEXTVAL pseudo columns
```

■ **Note**   When using the result cache feature, Oracle bypasses the buffer cache and transaction layer consistent reads, so queries will execute fast with less CPU. This makes buffer cache and other resources available for other operations.

In-Memory Cache

In Oracle Database 12c (12.1.0.2) a new feature is introduced, one that will allow self-optimization of a certain type of database queries that requires looking at several rows of data at the same time, such as in the case of a data warehouse operation. While OLTP operations are almost always row-based retrieval, where users requesting one or a few rows of data, data warehouse operations are range retrievals.

In-memory database cache is a new feature where Oracle will store data in two formats in the buffer: both the traditional row format (stored in the buffer cache) optimized for OLTP operations and a new columnar format optimized for analytical functions/data warehouse operations stored in a new cache area called *in-memory area*. This double format architecture is transparent to the application accessing the data, meaning no application level changes are required.

The in-memory area is a section of the SGA that has a fixed memory section (Figure 9-5) defined by the parameter INMEMORY_SIZE.

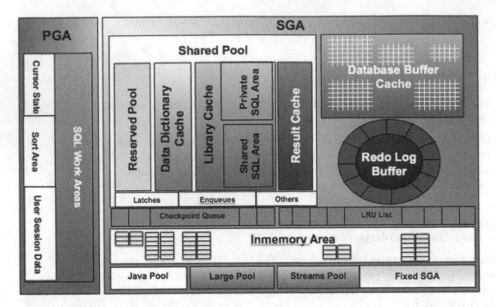

Figure 9-5. *SGA illustrating the in-memory area*

The optimizer in Oracle Database 12.1.0.2 has been enhanced to understand this new in-memory columnar format and the objects that are contained in it. If a query is looking for small number of rows, such as singleton select query or an index based retrieval, the optimizer will select the index access path after loading data into the buffer cache. On the other hand, if an analytical query is accessing few or smaller number of columns from a large number for rows, the optimizer will perform a full table or a partition scan via the in-memory column.

How Does This Work?

When rows are selected from the physical tables/storage media, the data is populated into the database buffer cache for index-based retrieval. In addition to this normal storage of data in the database buffer cache, data is also populated in the in-memory area of the SGA (illustrated in Figure 9-6). However, this only happens to those tables that have been defined with the INMEMORY attribute during table creation or through an ALTER TABLE statement.

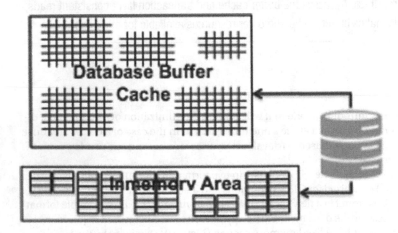

Figure 9-6. *Data population into in-memory area*

In addition to the INMEMORY attribute, two other attributes that could be helpful in the activity are PRIORITY and DISTRIBUTE. PRIORITY indicates the priority of populating the in-memory area with data from the tables that have the attribute INMEMORY, and DISTRIBUTE indicates the distribution of data in a RAC environment, should all the data be populated into all the instances in-memory area or should the data be split and distributed to the respective instances.

To better understand the behavior and utilization of the data in the in-memory area, let's sample the process via a workshop.

Workshop

In this workshop, let's discuss the creation of the in-memory area, its access, and how to monitor its functioning and memory utilization.

Step 1

The first step in a process of configuring the in-memory functionality is to identify tables that are good candidates for analytical operations and can benefit from the columnar format. Alter the table metadata and add the INMEMORY attributes.

```
ALTER TABLE STOCK INMEMORY PRIORITY LOW;
ALTER TABLE DISTRICT INMEMORY PRIORITY LOW;
```

Step 2

Allocate the fixed area in the SGA that will be used to store the data in a columnar format. With the PRIORITY LOW option, data is loaded after instance startup, but after all preliminary instance level startup functions including instance recovery are complete. The fixed area of the SGA for the in-memory area is defined by the parameter INMEMORY_SIZE. Set the area sufficiently large to accommodate all the columnar data identified in Step 1.

```
ALTER SYSTEM SET INMEMORY_SIZE = 10G SCOPE =SPFILE;
ALTER SYSTEM SET SGA_SIZE = 100G SCOPE=SPFILE;
```

■ **Note** The in-memory feature can also be invoked using the INMEMORY hint.

In the above change, when the in-memory area is allocated, the SGA area should also be increased proportionately. If sufficient memory is not allocated to store the columnar data, Oracle will report the following informational message in the alert log file:

```
Sun Aug 10 01:06:53 2014
Insufficient memory to populate table to inmemory area
Sun Aug 10 01:12:57 2014
Insufficient memory to populate table to inmemory area
Sun Aug 10 01:13:08 2014
```

Step 3

With the priority set to LOW, the tables identified in Step 1 will be auto-populated into the in-memory area of the SGA. This can be validated using the following script:

Script: MVRACPDnTap_impopcheck.sql

```
SELECT ims.inst_id              INT,
       ims.owner               OWNER,
       ims.segment_name        SEGNAME,
       ims.segment_type        SEGTYPE,
       ims.populate_status     STATUS,
       ims.inmemory_priority   PRIORITY,
       ims.inmemory_distribute DISTRIBUTE,
       ims.inmemory_duplicate  DUPLICATE,
       ims.inmemory_compression COMPRESSD,
       ims.bytes /ims.inmemory_size comp_ratio
FROM   gv$im_segments ims;
```

INT	OWNER	SEGNAME	SEGTYPE	STATUS	PRIORITY	DISTRIBUTE	DUPLICATE	COMPRESSD	COMP_RATIO
2	RAPUSR	STOCK	TABLE	STARTED	LOW	AUTO	NO DUPLICATE	FOR QUERY LOW	42.7565859
1	RAPUSR	STOCK	TABLE	STARTED	LOW	AUTO	NO DUPLICATE	FOR QUERY LOW	53.3368386
1	RAPUSR	DISTRICT	TABLE	STARTED	LOW	AUTO	NO DUPLICATE	FOR QUERY LOW	6.76013162
2	RAPUSR	DISTRICT	TABLE	STARTED	LOW	AUTO	NO DUPLICATE	FOR QUERY LOW	6.47506583

In the above output, the following are the column descriptions:

- **OWNER** is the owner of the object in the list.

- **SEGNAME** is the segment name/object name loaded into the in-memory area.

- **SEGTYPE** is the type of segment loaded into the in-memory area, such as a table, index partition, etc.

- **STATUS** is the current status of the operation. Valid values are STARTED and COMPLETED.

- **PRIORITY** specifies the priority to use when populating tables in the IM column store.

- **DISTRIBUTE** indicates how the data is distributed among the RAC instances in the cluster.

- **DUPLICATE** specifies how many copies of each In-Memory Compression Unit (IMCU) of the tables in the IM column store will be spread across all the Oracle RAC instances.

- **COMPRESSED** specifies that in-memory compression should be used for the instance.

- **COMP RATIO** is the current ratio of compression.

Most of the data are attributes or settings are assigned to the object through an ALTER statement.

The speed of data population depends on the number of in-memory server processes configured, which is controlled using the parameter INMEMORY_MAX_POPULATE_SERVERS. The server processes are identified by ora_wnnn_dbname, for example

```
SQL> !ps -ef | grep ora_w
oracle    11913    1  0 15:17 ?        00:00:00 ora_w001_SSKYDB_2
oracle    14199    1  0 15:22 ?        00:00:09 ora_w002_SSKYDB_2
oracle    31054    1  0 16:07 ?        00:00:00 ora_w003_SSKYDB_2
```

Data refresh/populate into the in-memory area can be monitored using the session level data from either the V$SESSION view or the V$SESSTAT view. The following query can be used to list the current stats for the in-memory load operation listed above. AWR also lists in-memory related statistics illustrated in Figure 9-7.

Statistic	Total	per Second	per Trans
IM populate CUs	7	0.00	0.02
IM populate CUs memcompress for query low	7	0.00	0.02
IM populate CUs requested	0	0.00	0.00
IM populate accumulated time (ms)	1,021,037	87.56	2,263.94
IM populate bytes from storage	1,346,183,168	115,436.98	2,984,885.07
IM populate bytes in-memory data	1,186,934,997	101,781.24	2,631,784.92
IM populate bytes uncompressed data	1,151,200,535	98,716.97	2,552,551.08
IM populate rows	3,754,976	321.99	8,325.89
IM populate segments requested	2	0.00	0.00
IM prepopulate CUs	0	0.00	0.00
IM prepopulate CUs memcompress for query low	0	0.00	0.00
IM prepopulate CUs requested	0	0.00	0.00
IM prepopulate accumulated time (ms)	0	0.00	0.00
IM prepopulate bytes from storage	0	0.00	0.00
IM prepopulate bytes in-memory data	0	0.00	0.00
IM prepopulate bytes uncompressed data	0	0.00	0.00
IM prepopulate rows	0	0.00	0.00
IM prepopulate segments	0	0.00	0.00
IM prepopulate segments requested	87	0.01	0.19
IM scan CUs columns accessed	40	0.00	0.09
IM scan CUs columns theoretical max	328	0.03	0.73
IM scan CUs invalid or missing revert to on disk extent	648	0.06	1.44
IM scan CUs memcompress for query low	20	0.00	0.04
IM scan CUs split pieces	94	0.01	0.21
IM scan bytes in-memory	2,812,210,742	241,150.78	6,235,500.54
IM scan bytes uncompressed	2,727,378,188	233,876.28	6,047,401.75
IM scan rows	8,901,958	763.35	19,738.27
IM scan rows projected	7,713,656	661.46	17,103.45
IM scan rows range excluded	1,188,302	101.90	2,634.82
IM scan rows valid	7,713,656	661.46	17,103.45
IM space CU bytes allocated	1,439,694,848	123,455.73	3,192,228.04
IM space CU creations initiated	25	0.00	0.06
IM space CU extents allocated	46	0.00	0.10
IM space SMU bytes allocated	458,752	39.34	1,017.19
IM space SMU creations initiated	7	0.00	0.02
IM space SMU extents allocated	7	0.00	0.02
IM space segments allocated	0	0.00	0.00

Figure 9-7. *AWR report with in-memory stats*

```
SELECT ss.inst_id INT,
       sn.name,
       sn.class,
       ss.value
FROM   gv$statname sn,
       gv$sesstat ss
WHERE  sn.inst_id = ss.inst_id
       AND sn.statistic# = ss.statistic#
       AND sn.name LIKE 'IM%'
       AND ss.value > 0;
```

Figure 9-7 has two highlighted sections. One show the stats generated while populating the in-memory area and the second section show stats while the SQL statements scan the in-memory area to get the required result sets.

■ **Note**   In-memory stats are captured under class 128.

Similar to the statistics, wait events related to the in-memory operation can also be checked from the V$SESSION_WAIT view.

Step 4

As illustrated in Figure 9-7, since data from the data files are populated into both the database buffer cache and in-memory area of the SGA, no specific query change is required to access the in-memory area of the SGA. Based on the type of query being executed, the optimizer will decide if data should be read from the database buffer cache or the in-memory columnar area.

The following query was executed after the data was loaded into the in-memory area (Step 3 above):

```
SELECT /*+ gather_plan_statistics */ d_name,
       SUM(s_quantity)
FROM   stock S,
       district D
WHERE  S.s_w_id = D.d_w_id
GROUP  BY d_name;
```

```
Plan hash value: 882718156
```

```
---------------------------------------------------------------
| Id  | Operation                     | Name     | Starts |
---------------------------------------------------------------
|   0 | SELECT STATEMENT              |          |      1 |
|   1 |  HASH GROUP BY                |          |      1 |
|*  2 |   HASH JOIN                   |          |      1 |
|   3 |    VIEW                       | VW_GBC_5 |      1 |
|   4 |     HASH GROUP BY             |          |      1 |
|   5 |      TABLE ACCESS INMEMORY FULL| STOCK   |      1 |
|   6 |    TABLE ACCESS INMEMORY FULL | DISTRICT |      1 |
---------------------------------------------------------------
```

In the plan output above, TABLE ACCESS INMEMORY FULL illustrates that the in-memory area was used for this operation.

IN-MEMORY AND RESULT CACHE

The introduction of the in-memory option in Oracle Database version 12.1.0.2 does have a corresponding effect in the behavior of the RESULT CACHE feature discussed in the previous section of this chapter. When the in-memory cache option is invoked and the in-memory area is populated, an analytical operation that uses the RESULT CACHE hint will populate the result cache buffer from the in-memory area instead of the database buffer cache. Figure 9-8 illustrates this through a four-step process.

1. Data is read from disk and populated into the in-memory area of the instance where the query was executed first.

2. Based on the WHERE condition of the query, the data is filtered in the buffer cache.

3. The final result set is populated into the result cache section of the shared pool.

4. Subsequently, when another user executes the same query with the RESULT CACHE hint on another instance, the result set is moved from the result cache buffer of the holding instance to the requesting instance.

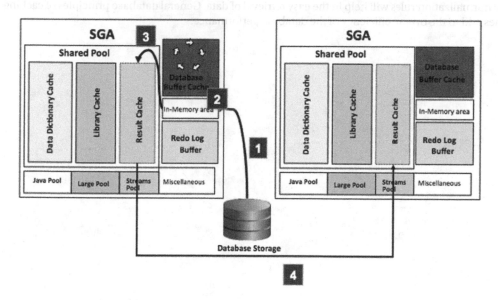

Figure 9-8. *Result cache from in-memory area*

The explain plan from executing the query discussed in the workshop earlier with the RESULT CACHE hint illustrates the usage of the in-memory area to filter the rows and to populate the result cache buffer.

```
SELECT /*+ RESULT_CACHE */ d_name,
                           SUM(s_quantity)
FROM   stock S,
       district D
WHERE S.s_w_id = D.d_w_id
GROUP BY d_name
```

Plan hash value: 882718156

Id	Operation	Name	Starts	E-Rows	A-Rows	A-Time
0	SELECT STATEMENT		1		3060	00:00:00.01
1	RESULT CACHE	g1cma4jnhvgc8354x98tjp702k	1		3060	00:00:00.01
2	HASH GROUP BY		0	3055	0	00:00:00.01
* 3	HASH JOIN		0	3055	0	00:00:00.01
4	VIEW	VW_GBC_5	0	306	0	00:00:00.01
5	HASH GROUP BY		0	306	0	00:00:00.01
6	TABLE ACCESS INMEMORY FULL	STOCK	0	29M	0	00:00:00.01
7	TABLE ACCESS INMEMORY FULL	DISTRICT	0	4024	0	00:00:00.01

Conclusion

Scalability of an application is critical to meet the needs of today's growing user economy. While scalability solutions such as RAC will perform and provide great benefits to this solution, it is important to configure and use some of the features that will help achieve this goal. Features such as partitioning and the result cache help in high-volume databases and provide easy scalability and response times. On the other hand, ensuring that the database is designed right by following the normalization rules will help in the easy retrieval of data. General database principles of caching and indexing strategies add to the overall efficiency of the database performance.

CHAPTER 10

■ ■ ■

Tuning Recovery

Every single system is prone to failure, be it natural, mechanical, or electronic; this could be the human system, automobiles, computer hardware, elevators, application servers, applications, database servers, databases, and network connectivity. Based on the critical nature of the item and its everyday use, these types of failures need an alternative way to provide the required service and or a method to keep the systems up and functioning. For example, human systems can fail due to sickness; and the sickness can be simple like a fever or complex like a heart attack. The immediate need in this situation is to visit a doctor and get treated. Treatments would help control the situation and get the body functioning again. An automobile can fail, which could be due to a simple failure like a flat tire. A backup option in this case would be a spare tire and some essential tools used to replace the tire. In some unavoidable conditions, an alternative method of transportation has to be used, for example, a bus or taxi. Electronic devices such as computer hardware are also prone to failures; these hardware come in many forms to comprise the entire enterprise configuration. Normally, protection against hardware failures is achieved by providing redundancy at all tiers of the configuration. This helps because when one component fails, the other will help continue operation.

On the database side, the storage system that physically stores the data needs to be protected. An example is mirroring the disk, where the data is copied to another disk to provide safety and failover when a disk in the array fails. This will provide the required redundancy against disk failures.

What happens when a privileged user accidently deletes rows from a table in a production database? What happens when this damage is only noticed a few days after the accident occurred? What happens when lightening hits the production center and the electric grid, causing a short circuit that damages the entire storage subsystem? In all these situations, an alternative method over and beyond the redundant hardware architecture is required to get to the bottom of the problem for resolution, namely, a process to retrieve and recover the lost data.

The answer is that a copy of the data needs to be saved regularly to another media and stored in a remote location. Such a method of data storage will protect the enterprise from losing its valuable data. The method of copying data from a live system for storage in a remote location is called a *backup process*.

Backing up the database and related datafiles are just not sufficient; when issues arise, they should be able to restore and recover the database with easy and quick measures. As database sizes grow larger and larger, simple backup techniques or media to store them may not be sufficient to meet the SLA requirements of the business. Recovery of a database should be efficient and optimized for performance to make the environment highly available. After all, if recovery was never a concern and databases are always secure from data loss, why would we need to make a backup of the data? So the end result is to ensure recovery of the database.

In a RAC environment, multiple instances provide access to data, giving availability to the environment. However, servers or instances in a RAC environment are also prone to failures; and recovery of instances is critical to make changes made by users available to other instances in the cluster.

Commonly, in a RAC environment, there are primarily two types of recovery scenarios: instance recovery and media recovery. However, when all instances in a RAC environment crash while the underlying method to recover still continues to be instance-level recovery, the terminology is *crash recovery*.

Instance Recovery

Instance recovery is to recover the database when an instance crashes midstream during user activity. Unlike in a traditional single instance database scenario, recovery of an instance in a RAC environment is dynamic and happens while the database is up and active. It is probably the most important aspect of recovery that applies to RAC. The idea of having multiple nodes in a clustered configuration is to provide availability with the assumption that if one or more instances in the cluster where to fail, the remaining instance would provide business continuum. For this reason, instance recovery becomes more critical.

One of the primary requirements of a RAC configuration is to have the redo logs of all instances participating in the cluster on the shared storage. The primary reason for such a requirement is to provide visibility of the redo logs of any instance in the cluster to all other instances. This allows for any instance in the cluster to perform an instance recovery operation during an instance failure.

Instance failure could happen in several ways; the common reason for an instance failure is when the node itself fails. The node failure could be due to several reasons including power surge, operator error, and so forth. Other reasons for an instance failure could be because a certain background process fails or dies or when there is a kernel-level exception encountered by the instance, causing an ORA-0600 or ORA-07445 error. Issuing a SHUTDOWN ABORT command could also cause an instance failure.

Instance failures could be of different kinds:

- The instance is totally down and the users do not have any access to the instance.

- The instance is up; however, when connecting to it, there is a hang situation or the user gets no response.

In the case in which an instance is not available, users could continue accessing the database via one of the other surviving instances in an active-active configuration provided the failover option has been enabled in the application.

Recovery from an instance failure happens from another instance that is up and running that is part of the cluster configuration and whose heartbeat mechanism detected the failure first and informed the LMON process on the node. The LMON process on each cluster node communicates with the CM on the respective node and exposes that information to the respective instances.

LMON provides the monitoring function by continually sending messages from the node on which it runs and often by writing to the shared disk. When the node fails to perform these functions, the other nodes consider that node as no longer a member of the cluster. Such a failure causes a change in a node's membership status within the cluster.

The LMON process controls the recovery of the failed instance by taking over its redo log files and performing instance recovery.

How Does Oracle Know That Recovery Is Required for a Given Data File?

The system change number (SCN) is a logical clock inside the database kernel that increments with each and every change made to the database. The SCN describes a "version" or a committed version of the database. When a database performs a checkpoint operation, an SCN (called the checkpoint SCN) is written to the data file headers. This is called the start SCN. There is also an SCN value in the control file for every data file, which is called the stop SCN. There is another data structure called the checkpoint counter in each data file header and also in the control file for each data file entry. The checkpoint counter increments every time a checkpoint happens on a data file and the start SCN value is updated. When a data file is in hot backup mode, the checkpoint information in the file header is frozen; but the checkpoint counter still gets updated.

When the database is shut down gracefully, with the SHUTDOWN NORMAL or SHUTDOWN IMMEDIATE command, Oracle performs a checkpoint and copies the start SCN value of each data file to its corresponding stop SCN value in the control file before the actual shutdown of the database.

When the database is started, Oracle performs two checks (among other consistency checks):

- To see if the start SCN value in every data file header matches with its corresponding stop SCN value in the control file.

- To see if the checkpoint counter values match.

If both these checks are successful, then Oracle determines that recovery is not required for that data file. These two checks are done for all data files that are online.

If the start SCN of a specific data file doesn't match the stop SCN value in the control file, then at least a recovery is required. This can happen when the database is shut down with the SHUTDOWN ABORT statement or if the instance crashes. Oracle performs a check on the data files by checking the checkpoint counters. If the checkpoint counter check fails, then Oracle knows that the data file has been replaced with a backup copy (while the instance was down) and therefore, media recovery is required.

■ **Note** Applying the redo records in the online log files to the data files performs instance recovery. However, media recovery may require applying the archived redo log files as well.

The Instance Recovery Process

After one or more nodes in a cluster fail, the recovery process would consist of several steps to restore the data contained in the redo log and database buffers at the instance (cache) level and blocks at the database level:

1. During the first phase of recovery, GES remasters the enqueues and GCS remasters its resources from the failed instance among the surviving instances.

2. The first step in the GCS remastering process is for Oracle to assign a new incarnation number.

3. Oracle determines how many more nodes are remaining in the cluster. (Nodes are identified by a numeric number starting with 0 and incremented by 1 for every additional node in the cluster). In our example, there are three nodes remaining in the cluster.

4. Subsequently, in an attempt to recreate the resource master of the failed instance, all GCS resource requests and write requests are temporarily suspended (the global resource directory, or global resource directory (GRD), is frozen).

5. All the dead shadow processes related to the GCS are cleaned from the failed instance.

6. After enqueues are reconfigured, one of the surviving instances can grab the instance recovery enqueue.

7. At the same time as GCS resources are remastered, SMON determines the set of blocks that need recovery. This set is called the recovery set. As we discussed in Chapter 2, with cache fusion, an instance ships the contents of its block to the requesting instance without writing the block to the disk, that is, the on-disk version of the blocks may not contain the changes that are made by either instance. Because of this behavior, SMON needs to merge the content of all the online redo logs of each failed instance to determine the recovery set and the order of recovery.

8. At this stage, buffer space for recovery is allocated, and the resources that were identified in the previous reading of the redo logs are claimed as recovery resources. This is done to avoid other instances from accessing those resources.

9. A new master node for the cluster is created (assigning a new master node is only performed if the failed node was the previous master node in the cluster). All GCS shadow processes are now traversed (redistributed between all of the remaining instances), GCS is removed from a frozen state, and this completes the reconfiguration process.

■ **Note**   GCS shadows to be traversed could be estimated from V$GES_ENQUEUE. For example,

```
SELECT COUNT(*) FROM v$ges_enqueue WHERE resource_name1 LIKE '%BL%';
```

would help determine the blocks to be traversed.

The following extract is from the alert log file of an Oracle Database version 11.2.0.2 recovering instance; it displays the steps that Oracle has to perform during instance recovery:

```
Thu Apr 10 09:00:29 2014
Reconfiguration started (old inc 4, new inc 6)
List of instances:
 1 (myinst: 1)
Global Resource Directory frozen
* dead instance detected - domain 0 invalid = TRUE
Communication channels reestablished
Master broadcasted resource hash value bitmaps
Non-local Process blocks cleaned out
Thu Apr 10 09:00:29 2014
LMS 0: 1 GCS shadows cancelled, 1 closed, 0 Xw survived
Set master node info
Submitted all remote-enqueue requests
Dwn-cvts replayed, VALBLKs dubious
All grantable enqueues granted
Post SMON to start 1st pass IR
Thu Apr 10 09:00:29 2014
Instance recovery: looking for dead threads
Beginning instance recovery of 1 threads
 Submitted all GCS remote-cache requests
 Post SMON to start 1st pass IR
 Fix write in gcs resources
Reconfiguration complete
parallel recovery started with 2 processes
Started redo scan
Thu Apr 10 09:00:50 2014
Completed redo scan
 read 34017 KB redo, 8416 data blocks need recovery
Thu Apr 10 09:01:25 2014
Started redo application at
 Thread 2: logseq 4, block 418
```

```
Recovery of Online Redo Log: Thread 2 Group 4 Seq 4 Reading mem 0
  Mem# 0: +DATA/rac/onlinelog/group_4.267.781699385
Thu Apr 10 09:01:36 2014
minact-scn: master found reconf/inst-rec before recscn scan old-inc#:6 new-inc#:6
Thu Apr 10 09:01:42 2014
Completed redo application of 25.25MB
Thu Apr 10 09:03:14 2014
LMON (ospid: 5187) waits for latch 'enqueue hash chains' for 80 secs.
Thu Apr 10 09:07:04 2014
.......
Thu Apr 10 09:13:44 2014
GES: System Load is HIGH.
GES: Current load is 31.70 and high load threshold is 10.00
Thu Apr 10 09:13:48 2014
Completed instance recovery at
 Thread 2: logseq 4, block 68453, scn 1495515
 3745 data blocks read, 12020 data blocks written, 34017 redo k-bytes read
Thread 2 advanced to log sequence 5 (thread recovery)
Thu Apr 10 09:14:00 2014
minact-scn: master continuing after IR
minact-scn: Master considers inst:2 dead
Thu Apr 10 09:14:20 2014
```

10. During remastering of GRD resources and when the GCS services managed on the failed instance get relocated, instance recovery is paused.

11. Oracle performs recovery by traversing through the redo logs in two passes. It's called the rollforward and rollback phases of recovery. During rollforward recovery, all dirty blocks affected by committed transactions are written to the datafile; and during rollback recovery, all blocks updated on the disk as a result of transactions that have not been committed are rolled back.

12. Oracle starts the database recovery process and begins the cache recovery process, that is, rolling forward committed transactions. This is made possible by reading the redo log files of the failed instance. Because of the shared storage subsystem, redo log files of all instances participating in the cluster are visible to other instances. This makes any one instance (nodes remaining in the cluster and were started first) that detected the failure to read the redo log files of the failed instance and start the recovery process.

- Cache recovery is the first pass of reading the redo logs by SMON on the active instance. The redo logs files are read and applied to the active instance performing the recovery operation through a parallel execution.

- During this process, SMON will merge the redo thread ordered by the SCN to ensure that changes are applied in an orderly manner. It will also find the block written record (BWR) in the redo stream and remove entries that are no longer needed for recovery because they were PIs of blocks already written to disk. SMON recovers blocks found during this first pass and acquires the required locks needed for this operation. The final product of the first pass log read is a recovery set that only contains blocks modified by the failed instance, with no subsequent BWR to indicate that the blocks were later written. The recovering SMON process will then inform each lock element's master node for each block in the recovery list that it will be taking ownership of the block and lock for recovery. Other instances will not be able to acquire these locks until the recovery operation is completed. At this point, full access to the database is available.

13. While cache recovery takes place, work occurs at a slower pace. Once this stage of the recovery operation is complete, it is considered full database availability, now all data is accessible including that which resided on the failed instance.

14. After completion of the cache recovery process, Oracle starts the transaction recovery operation, that is, rolling back of all uncommitted transactions.

- Compared to cache recovery where the recovery is of a forward nature, that is, rolling forward of the transactions from the redo logs, the transaction recovery handles uncommitted transactions; hence, operation is to roll back all uncommitted transactions of a failed instance. In addition, during this pass, the redo threads for the failed instances are merged by SCN, and the redo is applied to the data files.

- During this process of rolling back uncommitted transactions, Oracle uses a technology called *fast-start fault recovery* in which it performs the transaction recovery as a deferred process as a background activity. Oracle uses a multi-version and consistency method to provide on-demand rollback of only those rows blocked by expired transactions. This feature prevents new transactions from waiting for the rollback activity to complete.

- Depending on how the transaction failed, the recovery is performed either by the SMON process or by the server process that initiated the transaction. The following output illustrates the various steps from the time the redo log is scanned to the activity performed by the SMON process completing the recovery.

```
Wed Aug 27 10:07:59 2014
Completed redo scan
 read 3298 KB redo, 589 data blocks need recovery
* validated domain 0, flags = 0x0

Wed Aug 27 10:08:00 2014
Started redo application at
 Thread 2: logseq 353, block 1930

Wed Aug 27 10:08:03 2014
Recovery of Online Redo Log: Thread 2 Group 3 Seq 353 Reading mem 0
  Mem# 0: +SSKY_DATA/SSKYDB/ONLINELOG/group_3.266.854233685
  Mem# 1: +SSKY_FRA/SSKYDB/ONLINELOG/group_3.259.854233687

Wed Aug 27 10:08:04 2014
Completed redo application of 1.93MB
Wed Aug 27 10:08:10 2014
Completed instance recovery at
 Thread 2: logseq 353, block 8527, scn 36904445
 498 data blocks read, 765 data blocks written, 3298 redo k-bytes read

Wed Aug 27 10:08:13 2014
Thread 2 advanced to log sequence 354 (thread recovery)
SMON[INST-TXN-RECO]:about to recover undo segment 1 status:3 inst:1
SMON[INST-TXN-RECO]:about to recover undo segment 2 status:3 inst:1
SMON[INST-TXN-RECO]:about to recover undo segment 3 status:3 inst:1
SMON[INST-TXN-RECO]:about to recover undo segment 4 status:3 inst:1
SMON[INST-TXN-RECO]:about to recover undo segment 5 status:3 inst:1
SMON[INST-TXN-RECO]:about to recover undo segment 6 status:3 inst:1
```

```
SMON[INST-TXN-RECO]:about to recover undo segment 7 status:3 inst:1
SMON[INST-TXN-RECO]:about to recover undo segment 8 status:3 inst:1
SMON[INST-TXN-RECO]:about to recover undo segment 9 status:3 inst:1
SMON[INST-TXN-RECO]:about to recover undo segment 10 status:3 inst:1
Wed Aug 27 10:08:15 2014
```

FAST-START PARALLEL ROLLBACK

Fast-start parallel rollback is performed by SMON, which acts as a coordinator and rolls back transactions using parallel processing across multiple server processes. The parallel execution option is useful when transactions run for a longer duration before committing. When using this feature, each node spawns a recovery coordinator and recovery process to assist with parallel rollback operations.

Setting the parameter FAST_START_PARALLEL_ROLLBACK enables the fast-start parallel rollback feature. This setting indicates the number of processes to be involved in the rollback operation. The valid values are FALSE, LOW, and HIGH. The default value is LOW.

- LOW—DOP is set to 2 * CPU_COUNT

- HIGH—DOP is set to 4 * CPU_COUNT

In most cases, transaction recovery can be monitored by querying the V$FAST_START_TRANSACTIONS view. However, if the recovery data is less than 10 undo blocks, Oracle fails to report data through this view, in which case querying the X$KTUXE view could be helpful:

```
SELECT usn,
       state,
       undoblockstotal                  "Total",
       undoblocksdone                   "Done",
       undoblockstotal - undoblocksdone "ToDo",
       decode(cputime, 0, 'unknown',
                       SYSDATE + ( ( ( undoblockstotal - undoblocksdone ) / (
                                       undoblocksdone / cputime ) ) /
                                                              86400 ))
                               "Estimated time to complete"
FROM   v$fast_start_transactions;
```

■ **Note**   In Oracle Database Release 12.1.0, there are improvements in the overall performance of the RAC environment. If in a RAC environment, multiple nodes in the cluster fail and only one surviving node remains, the RDBMS kernel module will shut down all LMS background processes and treat the cluster database as a single instance. The alert log shows **"Decreasing number of real time LMS from 1 to 0"** illustrating this.

Tuning Instance Recovery

One of the primary reasons for implementing a RAC solution is continued availability. When one server or instance fails, there are other servers and instances in the configuration that will support and continue to provide data availability to the application and users. This means that when one instance or server fails, one of the surviving instances should be able to read the changes made by the failed instance and perform any data recovery. This is the reason why it's a requirement that redo log files are located on shared storage and accessible by all instances in the cluster.

When a server or instance fails, users connected to the instance can failover or get reconnected transparently to one of the other instances depending on the type of connection implementation. As discussed in the previous section, instance recovery is performed in two phases: cache recovery followed by transaction recovery. Until instance recovery is completed, data changes made on instance 1 are not available or written to the datafiles.

What is being recovered? Data blocks changed by committed transactions (and hence written to redo log files) but not yet written to datafiles will need to be written to datafiles. This would mean the size and content of the redo log files would have an impact on the instance recovery. The first step would be to tune the redo log activity, what size of redo and how frequently the redo log files should switch, and how to size the redo logs.

Like most performance optimization situations, there is a positive and negative side to optimizing the redo log activity. Keeping the redo log files small and switching the redo log files more frequently (frequent checkpoint) would help reduce the recovery time; however, the I/O activity on the database files would increase.

Depending on the number of datafiles in a database, a checkpoint can be a highly resource intensive operation because all datafile headers are frozen during the checkpoint. The idea is to balance or have a performance trade-off when it comes to tuning frequency of log switches. Ideally, it would be a good practice to have about four to five redo log switches per hour. Using the query following, the hourly redo log switches could be determined for a week:

Script: MVRACPDnTap_redologswitches.sql

```
select
    substr(to_char(first_time,'MM/DD-Day'),1,9) day,
    to_char(sum(decode(to_char(first_time,'HH24'),'00',1,0)),'99') "00",
    to_char(sum(decode(to_char(first_time,'HH24'),'01',1,0)),'99') "01",
    to_char(sum(decode(to_char(first_time,'HH24'),'02',1,0)),'99') "02",
    to_char(sum(decode(to_char(first_time,'HH24'),'03',1,0)),'99') "03",
    to_char(sum(decode(to_char(first_time,'HH24'),'04',1,0)),'99') "04",
    to_char(sum(decode(to_char(first_time,'HH24'),'05',1,0)),'99') "05",
    to_char(sum(decode(to_char(first_time,'HH24'),'06',1,0)),'99') "06",
    to_char(sum(decode(to_char(first_time,'HH24'),'07',1,0)),'99') "07",
    to_char(sum(decode(to_char(first_time,'HH24'),'08',1,0)),'99') "08",
    to_char(sum(decode(to_char(first_time,'HH24'),'09',1,0)),'99') "09",
    to_char(sum(decode(to_char(first_time,'HH24'),'10',1,0)),'99') "10",
    to_char(sum(decode(to_char(first_time,'HH24'),'11',1,0)),'99') "11",
    to_char(sum(decode(to_char(first_time,'HH24'),'12',1,0)),'99') "12",
    to_char(sum(decode(to_char(first_time,'HH24'),'13',1,0)),'99') "13",
    to_char(sum(decode(to_char(first_time,'HH24'),'14',1,0)),'99') "14",
    to_char(sum(decode(to_char(first_time,'HH24'),'15',1,0)),'99') "15",
    to_char(sum(decode(to_char(first_time,'HH24'),'16',1,0)),'99') "16",
    to_char(sum(decode(to_char(first_time,'HH24'),'17',1,0)),'99') "17",
    to_char(sum(decode(to_char(first_time,'HH24'),'18',1,0)),'99') "18",
    to_char(sum(decode(to_char(first_time,'HH24'),'19',1,0)),'99') "19",
    to_char(sum(decode(to_char(first_time,'HH24'),'20',1,0)),'99') "20",
    to_char(sum(decode(to_char(first_time,'HH24'),'21',1,0)),'99') "21",
    to_char(sum(decode(to_char(first_time,'HH24'),'22',1,0)),'99') "22",
    to_char(sum(decode(to_char(first_time,'HH24'),'23',1,0)),'99') "23",
```

```
to_char((sum(decode(to_char(first_time,'HH24'),'00',1,0))+
sum(decode(to_char(first_time,'HH24'),'01',1,0))+
sum(decode(to_char(first_time,'HH24'),'02',1,0))+
sum(decode(to_char(first_time,'HH24'),'03',1,0))+
sum(decode(to_char(first_time,'HH24'),'04',1,0))+
sum(decode(to_char(first_time,'HH24'),'05',1,0))+
sum(decode(to_char(first_time,'HH24'),'06',1,0))+
sum(decode(to_char(first_time,'HH24'),'07',1,0))+
sum(decode(to_char(first_time,'HH24'),'08',1,0))+
sum(decode(to_char(first_time,'HH24'),'09',1,0))+
sum(decode(to_char(first_time,'HH24'),'10',1,0))+
sum(decode(to_char(first_time,'HH24'),'11',1,0))+
sum(decode(to_char(first_time,'HH24'),'12',1,0))+
sum(decode(to_char(first_time,'HH24'),'13',1,0))+
sum(decode(to_char(first_time,'HH24'),'14',1,0))+
sum(decode(to_char(first_time,'HH24'),'15',1,0))+
sum(decode(to_char(first_time,'HH24'),'16',1,0))+
sum(decode(to_char(first_time,'HH24'),'17',1,0))+
sum(decode(to_char(first_time,'HH24'),'18',1,0))+
sum(decode(to_char(first_time,'HH24'),'19',1,0))+
sum(decode(to_char(first_time,'HH24'),'20',1,0))+
sum(decode(to_char(first_time,'HH24'),'21',1,0))+
sum(decode(to_char(first_time,'HH24'),'22',1,0))+
sum(decode(to_char(first_time,'HH24'),'23',1,0))),'999') total
from v$log
where trunc(first_time) > (trunc(sysdate) - 7)
group by substr(to_char(first_time,'MM/DD-Day'),1,9)
order by 1 ;
```

Day /LSW	0	1	2	3	4	5	6	7	8	9	10	11	12	13	14	15	16	17	18	19	20	21	22	23	Total
01/08-Wed	42	22	316	213	141	119	73	82	96	107	321	11	11	58	21	3	15	14	47	24	16	0	20	30	1802
01/09-Thu	15	20	294	221	241	110	94	94	112	112	233	10	15	51	4	0	3	41	40	0	10	0	21	0	1741
01/10-Fri	15	18	284	223	230	118	90	92	8	13	323	30	29	76	58	0	5	11	17	20	27	10	16	24	1737
01/11-Sat	13	20	274	221	270	114	80	110	6	0	310	0	0	0	0	0	0	0	0	0	2	0	0	0	1420
01/12-Sun	12	20	274	231	260	110	80	92	4	2	10	0	0	0	0	0	0	0	0	0	2	0	0	1	1098
01/13-Mon	15	21	274	221	294	119	90	93	11	14	322	80	22	94	13	81	10	20	18	23	27	17	40	22	1941
01/14-Tue	15	20	295	241	144	110	91	82	14	16	301	70	0	86	23	80	14	21	15	26	29	27	16	25	1761

It is noticed in the output and the graphical view of the data (Figure 10-1) that there are high redo log switch rates throughout the day. However, it's extremely high between 2 AM and 10 AM every day. Further analysis of the data revealed that during this period, the application has high batch load activity. Comparing this to the ideal switch rates of four or five per hour, the current redo log switch intervals are significantly high.

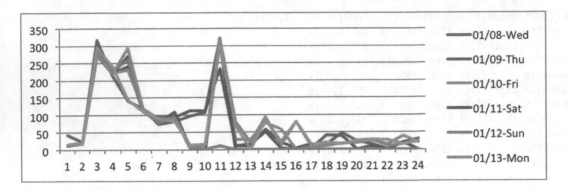

Figure 10-1. *Redo log switches*

For performance reasons, redo log switches should be kept to as low a value as possible when considering the recovery times involved. Large redo log files with few switches per hour would help reduce I/O contention and wait times. However, smaller sized redo log files with more frequent switches will ensure data is moved from the log files to the data files, keeping the recovery required to a minimal size should an instance crash. However, more controlled methods such as using the parameter FAST_START_MTTR_TARGET (discussed later in this chapter) using the related advisory should be adhered to to improve recovery times.

Parallelism

This would mean instance recovery should be made efficient, which means it needs to be tuned. Instance recovery can be tuned using the parameter RECOVERY_PARALLELISM.

RECOVERY_PARALLELISM specifies the number of processes to participate in instance or crash recovery. To force a serial crash recovery, this parameter should be set to 0 or 1. Along with the RECOVERY_PARALLELISM parameter, increasing the PARALLEL_EXECUTION_MESSAGE SIZE value to a higher number would help improve recovery slave session performance. In the same context, increasing the PARALLEL_MIN_SERVER value from its default value of 0 would help pre-spawn recovery slaves at startup, thus avoiding the need to spawn them when recovery is required and improving recovery performance.

```
Thu Aug 28 15:51:41 2014
 Post SMON to start 1st pass IR
Thu Aug 28 15:51:41 2014
minact-scn: Inst 2 is now the master inc#:4 mmon proc-id:5372 status:0x7
minact-scn status: grec-scn:0x0000.00000000 gmin-scn:0x0000.023bc527 gcalc-scn:0x0000.023bdc42
minact-scn: master found reconf/inst-rec before recscn scan old-inc#:4 new-inc#:4
Thu Aug 28 15:51:41 2014
Instance recovery: looking for dead threads
Thu Aug 28 15:51:43 2014
 Submitted all GCS remote-cache requests
 Fix write in gcs resources
Thu Aug 28 15:51:43 2014
Reconfiguration complete (total time 9.4 secs)
Thu Aug 28 15:51:45 2014
Beginning instance recovery of 1 threads
 parallel recovery started with 4 processes
```

```
Thu Aug 28 15:51:46 2014
Started redo scan
Thu Aug 28 15:51:52 2014
Completed redo scan
 read 2492 KB redo, 422 data blocks need recovery
* validated domain 0, flags = 0x0
Thu Aug 28 15:51:53 2014
```

Checkpoint

Another parameter that could help in improving instance recovery time is setting the FAST_START_MTTR_TARGET value to a higher number from its default value of zero. This parameter helps reduce the recovery time by increasing the incremental checkpoint interval and reducing the amount of blocks to be recovered during instance recovery. Setting this parameter to a high value could help reduce the overall instance recovery time; however, it would add additional overhead on the performance of the database. Frequent checkpointing will increase the activity of the DBWR process and cause increasing overall I/O. The ideal value of the parameter could be determined by using the advisory view V$MTTR_TARGET_ADVICE:

```
SELECT inst_id,
       mttr_target_for_estimate MTFE,
       dirty_limit              DL,
       advice_status            Advice,
       estd_cache_writes        ECW,
       estd_total_ios           ETIO
FROM   gv$mttr_target_advice;
```

INST_ID	MTFE	DL	ADVIC	ECW	ETIO
1	372	9609	ON	7079	21369
1	39	1000	ON	19306	33596
1	122	3151	ON	8902	23192
1	205	5295	ON	7079	21369
1	288	7440	ON	7079	21369

In the output, there is a great fluctuation in the estimated I/O operations (ETIO) as a result of setting the value of the parameter FAST_START_MTTR_TARGET to the max (3,600 seconds) supported. Reducing the value of this parameter would mean higher frequency of incremental checkpointing, reducing instance recovery time; however, there could be a significant increase in DBWR activity. It's important that a balance is obtained between performance during normal activity vs. recovery time during instance and database crash.

Setting a value for the FAST_START_MTTR_TARGET would mean the other recovery-related parameters (FAST_START_IO_TARGET, LOG_CHECKPOINT_INTERVAL, and LOG_CHECKPOINT_TIMEOUT) should be disabled.

■ **Note**   In Oracle Database 12c (12.1.0), the default value for PARALLEL_MIN_SERVERS is computed by CPU_COUNT * PARALLEL_THREADS_PER_CPU *2, and the default value of PARALLEL_EXECUTION_MESSAGE_SIZE is set to 16,384.

Redo Log Sizing Advisory

Earlier, we discussed the various factors that influence the recovery times. Among these various factors one item that stands apart from the rest is the redo log file size. The DBWR and the LGWR activity depend on the redo log file sizes. Whereas larger redo log files provide better performance, undersized redo log files increase checkpoint activity, thus increasing workload contentions and higher CPU utilization. There should be an ideal value that will help maintain performance while at the same time try to reduce the time required to perform instance/crash recovery.

Using the data provided in the OPTIMAL_LOGFILE_SIZE column in V$INSTANCE_RECOVERY view, the redo log file sizes can be tuned. However, the column is not populated by default by the advisory; it requires setting the parameter FAST_START_MTTR_TARGET. We now try to understand the effect of setting the right sizes and the suggestions by the advisor.

1. Determine the current size of the redo log files using the following query:

```
SELECT  group#,
        thread#,
        sequence#,
        bytes,
        blocksize,
        members,
        archived,
        status
FROM    v$log;
```

GROUP#	THREAD#	SEQUENCE#	BYTES	BLOCKSIZE	MEMBERS	ARC	STATUS
1	1	393	52428800	512	2	NO	CURRENT
2	1	392	52428800	512	2	NO	INACTIVE
3	1	392	52428800	512	2	NO	INACTIVE
4	2	355	52428800	512	2	NO	CURRENT
5	2	354	52428800	512	2	NO	INACTIVE
6	2	354	52428800	512	2	NO	INACTIVE

From the output generated by executing the query, its understood that the current size of the redo log file is 50 MB.

2. As discussed earlier, to determine the optimal size of the redo log file size, the FAST_START_MTTR_TARGET parameter should be set. We check the current value of this parameter:

```
SQL> show parameter fast_start
```

NAME	TYPE	VALUE
fast_start_io_target	integer	0
fast_start_mttr_target	integer	70
fast_start_parallel_rollback	string	LOW

From the preceding output, the current FAST_START_MTTR_TARGET value is set much higher than the default value.

3. Check if the advisory has updated the OPTIMAL_REDOLOG_FILE SIZE column. Executing the following query against the V$INSTANCE_RECOVERY view will help understand the current value for the redo log file size:

```
SELECT actual_redo_blks    ARB,
       target_redo_blks    TRB,
       target_mttr         TMTTR,
       estimated_mttr      EMTTR,
       optimal_logfile_size OLS,
       ckpt_block_writes   CBW
FROM   v$instance_recovery;
```

ARB	TRB	TMTTR	EMTTR	OLS	CBW
2089	7309	15	2	367	1040

Based on the current activity of the database, the suggested MTTR value is 15, and the recommended size for the redo log file size is 367. Making changes to the database would help reduce the actual redo blocks to be recovered.

These measurements and tuning of the redo log file size are only guidelines to help improve/optimize instance/crash recovery times. Instance recovery times can vary depending on if the instance crash was due to node failure or instance failure (without node failure). In the case of a node failure, additional activity, for example, reconfiguring the group membership of the cluster, has to be completed before instance recovery begins. Once the clusterware completes the cluster-level reconfiguration, LMON process takes over to complete its activity related to the cluster level. Oracle records this in the LMON trace file of the instance that performs recovery. (The output following is from a Oracle Database version 12.1.0 instance recovery and contains more details compared to the prior versions of Oracle).

```
*** 2014-04-02 22:23:22.077
kjxgmrcfg: Reconfiguration started, type 1
CGS/IMR TIMEOUTS:
  CSS recovery timeout = 31 sec (Total CSS waittime = 65)
  IMR Reconfig timeout = 75 sec
  CGS rcfg timeout = 85 sec
kjxgmcs: Setting state to 4 0.

*** 2014-04-02 22:23:22.239
    Name Service frozen
kjxgmcs: Setting state to 4 1.
kjxgrdecidever: No old version members in the cluster
kjxgrssvote: reconfig bitmap chksum 0x19a68269 cnt 1 master 1 ret 0
kjxgrpropmsg: SSMEMI: inst 1 - no disk vote
kjxgrpropmsg: SSVOTE: Master indicates no Disk Voting
2014-04-02 22:23:22.253464 : kjxgrDiskVote: nonblocking method is chosen
kjxgrDiskVote: Only one inst in the cluster - no disk vote
2014-04-02 22:23:22.468535 : kjxgrDiskVote: Obtained RR update lock for sequence 5, RR seq 4
*** 2014-04-02 22:23:22.589
2014-04-02 22:23:22.589726 : kjxgrDiskVote: derive membership from CSS (no disk votes)
2014-04-02 22:23:22.589788 : proposed membership: 1
2014-04-02 22:23:22.833840 : kjxgrDiskVote: new membership is updated by inst 1, seq 6
2014-04-02 22:23:22.833913 : kjxgrDiskVote: bitmap: 1
```

```
CGS/IMR TIMEOUTS:
   CSS recovery timeout = 31 sec (Total CSS waittime = 65)
   IMR Reconfig timeout = 75 sec
   CGS rcfg timeout = 85 sec
kjxgmmeminfo: can not invalidate inst 3


.....
.....
.....
2014-04-02 22:23:22.939618 :
Reconfiguration started (old inc 4, new inc 6)
TIMEOUTS:
   Local health check timeout: 70 sec
   Rcfg process freeze timeout: 70 sec
   Remote health check timeout: 140 sec
   Defer Queue timeout: 163 secs
   CGS rcfg timeout: 85 sec
   Synchronization timeout: 248 sec
   DLM rcfg timeout: 744 sec
List of instances:
 1 (myinst: 1)
OMF 1
2014-04-02 22:23:22.943798 : * Begin lmon rcfg step KJGA_RCFG_FREEZE
* kjfc_pub_bigns: previous MM mode, no change unless there is a rora requester (MM->SM)
.....
.....
* dead instance detected - domain 0 invalid = TRUE
.....
2014-04-02 22:23:23.026708 :
2014-04-02 22:23:23.026750 :   Post SMON to start 1st pass IR
2014-04-02 22:23:23.043695 :   Submitted all GCS cache requests
2014-04-02 22:23:23.043950 : * Begin lmon rcfg step KJGA_RCFG_FIXWRITES
.....
.....
.....


2014-04-02 22:23:23.066174 :
Reconfiguration complete (total time 0.1 secs)

* DOMAIN MAPPINGS after Reconfiguration :
*    DOMAIN 0 (valid 0): 1
* End of domain mappings
.....
.....
.....
*** 2014-04-02 22:24:23.130
kjfmPriCheckAllowed: this is the only instance of this DB
kjfmPriCheckAllowed: instance must lower LMS priorities
kjfmPriCheck: # of real time LMS decreasing from 1 to 0
```

```
kjfmPriCheck: cannot make further changes to LMS priorities - single-inst mode
.....
.....
.....
*** 2014-04-02 22:27:21.439
global enqueue service detaching from CM:pid=22953
2014-04-02 22:27:21.479573 : kjxgrdisable: IMR recording device closed, terminating IMR
```

Crash Recovery

Crash recovery is the failure of all instances in a RAC environment or one instance in a single-instance environment. Operations are identical to an instance recovery; however, recovery is performed by the first instance that is started following a crash.

Thread Recovery

Thread recovery is used in both the crash recovery and instance recovery situations. The aim of a thread recovery is to restore the data block images that were in the cache of the failed instance but had not been checkpointed back to disk.

One redo thread is processed at a time, beginning from the last checkpoint and continuing to the end of the thread. All redo is applied from each thread before the next thread is started.

Online Block Level Recovery

Online block recovery is unique to the RAC implementation. Online block recovery occurs when a data buffer becomes corrupt in an instance's cache. Block recovery will occur if either a foreground process dies while applying changes or if an error is generated during redo application. If the block recovery is to be performed because of the foreground process dying, then PMON initiates online block recovery. However, if this is not the case, then the foreground process attempts to make an online recovery of the block.

Under normal circumstances, this involves finding the block's predecessor and applying redo records to this predecessor from the online logs of the local instance. However, under the cache fusion architecture, copies of blocks are available in the cache of other instances, and therefore, the predecessor is the most recent past image (PI) for that buffer that exists in the cache of another instance. If, under certain circumstances, there is no PI for the corrupted buffer, the block image from the disk data is used as the predecessor image.

Media Recovery

Any database is prone to failures; and during such failures, there could be situations when there is loss of data either due to data corruption or human error or unforeseen disaster. In the case of the initial two situations, the database is normally restored either completely, for example, when a disk goes bad or partially (point in time) when a specific object needs to be restored. In the third situation, "unforeseen disaster," a new database will need to be configured and the data restored to it (if the external media is available); or a disaster recovery strategy will need to be implemented. This strategy will require using tools such as Data Guard or Oracle Streams that will allow users to connect to this disaster recovery location when the primary database is down.

Performance tuning strategies that apply to taking data of disk (backup) to a backup media would also apply to taking data from backup media and reapplying it back to the disk (restore). Tuning backup would require looking at various layers of the hardware stack. Some of the key tuning principles include the following:

1. Determine throughput: It's important to determine the maximum input disk, output media, and network throughput. Throughput of the various devices should be determined to understand how fast I/O could be done. For example, to test the maximum throughput of the disk I/O subsystem, tools such as ORION can help. Network throughput will depend on the type of configuration; for example, in a RAC environment, multiple instances could be used to perform backup in parallel, which means interconnect would be used to some extent. If the backup sets are being written to external media, it may be good idea to have dedicated backup networks and when tuning the network, checking the network buffer sizes, media management client/server buffer size, client/socket timeout parameter settings, and so forth.

2. Configure disk for optimal performance: Using ASM for storage of archive logs and backup sets would help improve overall performance and would also improve recovery time.

3. Optimize throughput to the backup destination: To get maximum potential of the bandwidth between the backup process and the I/O subsystem (disk or tape), utilize asynchronous I/O.

   - For disk backup: On systems where native asynchronous I/O is not supported, set DBWR_IO_SLAVES parameter to a 4 per session.

   - For tape backup: Set BACKUP_TAPE_IO_SLAVES parameter to 1 per channel process.

4. Optimize Backup methods: Utilizing tools such as RMAN to backup data and restore data would help maintain a balanced backup strategy. When using RMAN backup, optimize the various RMAN parameters:

   - Number of channels

   - Parallelism

   - Number of backup sets defined by FILESPERSET parameter

   - Maximum size of backup set

5. Tuning RMAN: Apart from configuration parameters we discussed in the previous step, there are a few other parameters that may help to tune the backup and restore operations:

   - _BACKUP_FILE_BUFCNT

     - Defaults to 16, normally matches the number of disks

     - Number of input buffers per channel allocated: When the number of disks is large and a higher number of channels need to be allocated, then this value can be increased to improve overall performance.

   - Achieve balance between memory usage and I/O

     - _BACKUP_FILE_BUFSZ

     - Defaults to 1048576 and normally matches the stripe size of the I/O subsystem. When larger stripe sizes are used when configuring ASM diskgroups, the value of this parameter needs to be adjusted or sized to match the stripe size.

■ **Caution**   Underscore parameters are undocumented and should be set or modified only with prior approval from Oracle support. Prior to Oracle Database 11g Release 2, _BACKUP_FILE_BUFCNT was called _BACKUP_KSFQ_BUFCNT, and _BACKUP_FILE_BUFSZ was called _BACKUP_KSFQ_BUFSZ.[1]

Fast Recovery Area

The fast recovery area (called flash recovery area in earlier versions of Oracle) is an Oracle-managed directory, file system, or ASM diskgroup that provides a centralized disk location for backup and recovery files. All the files you need to completely recover a database from a media failure are part of the fast recovery area.

Some of the recovery-related files stored in the fast recovery area include the following:

- Current control file

- Online redo logs

- Archived redo logs

- Flashback logs

- Control file autobackups

- Datafile and control file copies

- Backup pieces

Implementing the FRA (flash recovery area) feature involves configuring two important parameters.

- DB_RECOVERY_FILE_DEST_SIZE specifies the maximum storage in bytes of data to be used by the FRA for this database. Note, however, that this value does not include certain kinds of disk overhead: Block 0 or the OS block header of each Oracle file is not included in this size. Allow an extra 10% for this data when computing the actual disk usage required for the FRA.

- DB_RECOVERY_FILE_DEST_SIZE does not indicate the real size occupied on disk when the underlying file system is mirrored, compressed, or in some other way affected by overhead not known to Oracle. For example, if you can configure the fast recovery area on a normal redundancy (two-way mirrored) ASM disk group, each file of X bytes occupies 2X bytes on the ASM disk group. In such a case, DB_RECOVERY_FILE_DEST_SIZE must be set to no more than 1/2 the size of the disks for the ASM diskgroup. Likewise, when using a high redundancy (three-way mirrored) ASM diskgroup, DB_RECOVERY_FILE_DEST_SIZE must be no more than 1/3 the size of the disks in the disk group, and so on.

As with any feature that requires storage space, the first step in the process is to size the storage area that would contain the FRA data. Sizing should be based on what kind of files and to what retention level the files will be saved in

---

[1]Chien, Timothy and Greg Green, "Recovery Manager (RMAN) Configuration and Performance Tuning Best Practices." Oracle Open World, 2010.

this location. The recovery area should be able to contain a copy of all datafiles in the database and the incremental backups per the backup strategy. Oracle has provided a formula to calculate space required for FRA location:

$$space\ required = size\ of\ a\ copy\ of\ database + size\ of\ an\ incremental\ backup$$
$$+ size\ of\ (n + 1)\ days\ of\ archived\ redo\ logs$$
$$+ size\ of\ (y + 1)\ days\ of\ foreign\ archived\ redo\ logs$$
$$(for\ logical\ standby) + size\ of\ control\ file +$$
$$size\ of\ an\ online\ redo\ log\ member \times number\ of\ log\ groups$$
$$+ size\ of\ flashback\ logs\ (based\ on$$
$$DB\_FLASHBACK\_RETENTION\_TARGET\ value),$$

where n is the interval in days between incremental updates, and y is the delay in applying the foreign archived redo logs on a logical standby database.

Once the size is determined, the physical configuration of the FRA could be initiated. Assuming that the database is already configured for archiving, and the database is currently in ARCHIVELOG mode, the first step to this process is to connect to the target database using RMAN:

1. Specify the size of the FRA using the following command:

   ALTER SYSTEM SET DB_RECOVERY_FILE_DEST_SIZE = <> SCOPE = SPFILE;

2. Specify the location of the FRA using the following command:

   ALTER SYSTEM SET DB_RECOVERY_FILE_DEST ='+SSKY_FRA' SCOPE = SPFILE;

   The preceding steps will configure the FRA, and the area will be managed by RMAN during its routine backup operations based on predefined retention policies. It's important that the destination file location specified by the parameter is on shared storage. Configuring this area to reside on ASM storage provides good performance benefits.

3. FRA is automatically managed for space utilization based on the retention policies defined in RMAN. The space utilization could be verified using the following scripts:

```
14:04:01 SQL> SELECT * FROM V$RECOVERY_FILE_DEST;
```

NAME	SPACE_LIMIT	SPACE_USED	SPACE_RECLAIMABLE	NUMBER_OF_FILES	CON_ID
+SSKY_FRA	5368709120	235929600	0	117	0

```
Elapsed: 00:00:02.23
14:04:13 SQL> SELECT * FROM V$FLASH_RECOVERY_AREA_USAGE;
```

FILE_TYPE	PERCENT_SPACE_USED	PERCENT_SPACE_RECLAIMABLE	NUMBER_OF_FILES	CON_ID
CONTROL FILE	.37	0	1	0
REDO LOG	3.98	0	4	0
ARCHIVED LOG	4.05	2.01	28	0
BACKUP PIECE	3.94	3.86	8	0
IMAGE COPY	15.94	10.43	76	0
FLASHBACK LOG	0	0	0	0
FOREIGN ARCHIVED LOG	0	0	0	0
AUXILIARY DATAFILE COPY	0	0	0	0

```
8 rows selected.
```

4. Time to time errors could be generated due to various reasons. A common reason is when the FRA is not purged and is reaching its maximum limits. Space utilization could be checked using the following scripts:

```
SELECT object_type,
       message_type,
       message_level,
       reason,
       suggested_action
FROM   dba_outstanding_alerts;
```

■ **Note** If the FRA is not large enough to hold the flashback logs, then the database will overwrite flashback logs from the earliest SCNs. Consequently, the flashback database window can be shorter than the value specified by the flashback retention target.

Configuring FRA is a good practice for the overall recovery operations using RMAN. It helps to have one holistic location for your backup and recovery process and helps in easy restore and instance/crash/media recovery operation.

Conclusion

As discussed in the early chapters of the book, the primary reason for moving to a RAC environment is availability and then scalability. For business continuum after an instance or server or database crashes, it's important that the data is available for users. This could be achieved by optimizing data recovery. In the case of crash or instance recovery, after the first pass (cache recovery) is completed, users can start accessing the data. The second phase of recovery (transaction recovery) can or could take longer and completes in the background. Depending on the business and SLA requirements, using some of the parameters discussed could help reduce the time required to complete recovery; however, the optimization should be measured against overall performance of the environment.

Although backup is important, equally important is the restore operation and the recovery of the database from failures. However, not much attention is given to this area to optimize the restore operation. There are very few parameters or areas of the system that need to be superficially tuned just to improve efficiency of the backup and restore operations. Most of the tuning completed from other areas of the hardware infrastructure and the database should also help improve backup and restore performance, for example, tuning the I/O subsystem, tuning the network, tuning the database, and so forth.

CHAPTER 11

■ ■ ■

Tuning Oracle Net

In an *n*-tier architecture solution, each tier connects to the other via a network component. An Oracle database that normally resides on the database tier provides connectivity via a network layer.

Oracle application systems use an SQL Net interface between the Oracle application software and the underlying network protocol layer. By using these interface layers, users accessing the database are able to access, modify, share, and store data.

There are two phases when the user accesses the database to retrieve or store the data: the connect phase and the query phase. The connect phase is where the application server makes a connection on behalf of the user to the physical database. The query phase involves retrieving or storing the data into the physical database.

The user makes a connection to the database for one of several operations

- To insert rows into the database; data is sent from the client application to the database server via a network layer

- To select data sets from the database, which involves sending data from the database and servers to the application servers, again using the network layer

- A mixture of the preceding two operations where data is selected, modified, and loaded back into the database

Both of these phases play an important role in the overall response time of the user operation. Whereas the query phase can be tuned using database-related parameters and layout structures, the connect phase depends on several factors. Some of these factors include the type of network interface, network bandwidth, availability of the listener, the availability of the instance, number of sessions permitted on the instance, and so forth.

Making the Connection

In a typical implementation, a database request starts when a client (SQL plus client or an application server) makes a connection to the database application. This request for connection, at a very high level, is received by the listener on the database server; and if the requested database service through the connect descriptor is registered with the listener, the listener parses the connection request to the database instance on the server.

The connection initiation client can be one or more of these types: SQL Plus or application server that uses a Java Database Connectivity (JDBC) thick client or thin client. Once the connection is initiated, as illustrated in Figure 11-1, it has to traverse through the stages and layers of network stack before making a physical connection to the database.

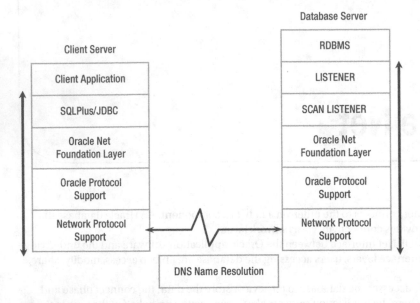

Figure 11-1. *User connection*

Figure 11-1 illustrates two sides of the configuration: the client server that initiates the configuration and the database server where the connection is targeted. On both sides of the configuration there are," several network layers, which include the "Oracle Net foundation layer (ONFL," "Oracle protocol support layer," and the "Transport Protocol layer." In the Oracle Net architecture, the connectivity drivers, the ONFL, the protocol layers, and the listeners on the database server are of primary importance.

Connectivity Drivers

Oracle supports various types of connection methods. The common types of connection interfaces found in the implementations are the SQL Plus and JDBC (Type 2 and Type 4) drivers.

Oracle Net Foundation Layer (ONFL)

This layer is responsible for establishing and maintaining connection between the client application and the database server. This layer exists on both the client side and the database server side and performs identical functions on both ends. Apart from this primary activity, it's also responsible for exchanging messages between the two ends of the communication channel: the client application, which is the source, and the database server, which is the target. ONFL performs these tasks using the transparent network substrate (TNS) technology. TNS is a common type of interface that incorporates the Open Systems Interconnect (OSI) transport and network layer protocols. It enables peer-to-peer application connectivity. TNS technology is responsible for the following:

- Locating the database server based on the host entries used in the connect descriptor; it uses the DNS server for name resolution or the DNS/GNS combination if GNS is implemented in a RAC environment

- How many protocols involved in the connection

- How many interrupt handles that exist between client and database server based on the capabilities of each

Both SQL Plus and the JDBC Type 4 connection methods use the TNS technology to establish connection to the database. JDBC Type 2 driver, primarily used in Java applications, converts the JDBC invocations to call the OCI driver, which is then sent over Oracle Net to the Oracle database. Type 2 drivers do not use the TNS technology.

Oracle Protocol Support Layer

This layer acts as an interface between the ONFL and the industry standard network protocols such as the TCP/IP, named pipes, and so forth.

Listeners

There are two types of listeners in an Oracle Database 11g Release 2 RAC configuration.

SCAN Listeners

Single Client Access Name (SCAN) is a new feature introduced in Oracle Database 11g that provides a single name for clients to access Oracle databases running on the cluster. Similar to the single level cluster alias that existed in the virtual memory system (VMS) and Tru64 clustered environments, the SCAN provides a single address reference to the entire cluster. Similar to the cluster alias, the SCAN also has intelligence built into it for load balancing and failover from client connections to the database.

To configure a SCAN reference to the cluster, the network administrator maps one host reference that maps to three physical IPs definitions in the domain name system (DNS).

During cluster configuration, for each of the three IP addresses that the SCAN resolves to, a SCAN VIP resource is created and a SCAN listener is created. The SCAN listener is dependent on the)SCAN VIP and the three SCAN VIPs will be dispersed across the cluster. Assuming that a cluster consists of three or more nodes, each pair of resources is started on a different server in the cluster:

```
[mvallath@prddb1 mysql]$ nslookup prddb-scan
Server:        10.62.85.12
Address:       10.62.85.12#53
Name:   prddb-scan.summersky.biz
Address: 10.62.70.13
Name:   prddb-scan.summersky.biz
Address: 10.62.70.14
Name:   prddb-scan.summersky.biz
Address: 10.62.70.15
```

In Figure 11-1, when the connection request is received from the client via the network interface to the database server, the SCAN listener receives (illustrated in Figure 11-2) the request and redirects the connection to the local listener on the node where the least loaded instance is running. In a RAC configuration, a node needs at least one network adapter that provides the interface (e.g., an Ethernet adapter) to the local area network (LAN) that allows users/applications to connect and query data from the database. This is normally considered as the public network interface. Public network adapters are visible to users external to the node participating in the cluster. Network adapters are identified by an Internet static IP address, which is assigned during O/S configuration.

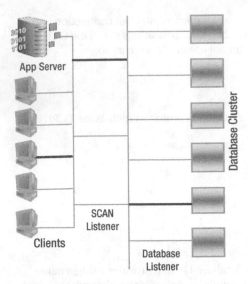

Figure 11-2. *SCAN and database listeners*

IP ADDRESS

An IP address is a four-part number with each part represented by a number between 0 and 255. Part of that IP address represents the network the computer exists on, whereas the remainder identifies the specific host on that network. The four-part number is selected based on the size of the network in the organization. Network sizes are classified into three classes based on the size. Class A has a number between 0 and 127, Class B has a number between 128 and 191, and Class C has a number between 192 and 223. An example of an IP address is 192.168.200.60.

Database Listeners

The database listener, also called Oracle Net Listener, is responsible for making routing requests received from clients to the right databases by mapping the service request handle from the client connection to the services that are registered with the listener.

When a database instance starts, the instance establishes a communication path with the listener using a new background process in Oracle 12c "listener registration process" (LREG). The LREG process provides the listener with the instance name, database service name, and the type and addresses of service handlers. This information is used by the listener to route client requests to the respective database instances.

Load Balancing

One primary feature of a clustered environment is to distribute workload across the various nodes/instances in the cluster. To achieve this distribution, it would be advantageous to place new connections on systems that have a higher number of resources in the cluster.

Load balancing can be configured on the database service using Server Control (SRVCTL), Enterprise Manager (EM), or Oracle provided Procedural Language (PL)/SQL packages. Load balancing is based on number of sessions or the number of resources available on the various instances. The following illustrates the current load balancing definition for database service RAPTEST:

```
[oracle@prddb1 ~]$ srvctl config service -d PRDDB -s RAPTEST
Service name: RAPTEST
Service is enabled
Server pool: prddbpool1
Cardinality: UNIFORM
Disconnect: false
Service role: PRIMARY
Management policy: AUTOMATIC
DTP transaction: false
AQ HA notifications: true
Failover type: SELECT
Failover method: BASIC
TAF failover retries: 135
TAF failover delay: 25
Connection Load Balancing Goal: SHORT
Runtime Load Balancing Goal: THROUGHPUT
TAF policy specification: NONE
```

Unlike the previous releases of RAC, starting with Oracle Database 11g Release 2, load balancing occurs out of the box when SCAN is implemented, provided the connections are initiated from an Oracle Database 11g Release 2 client. How do you verify if the load-balancing feature is working? The Manageability Monitor (MMON) background process generates load advices. The advices are stored in GV$SERVICEMETRIC view and is used to communicate with the SCAN listeners regarding the current load average. For example, the following query displays the load characteristics as updated by MMON in GV$SERVICEMETRIC view. The view is joined with GV$INSTANCE and GV$ACTIVE_SERVICES to obtain additional information:

Script Name: MVRACPDnTap_svcloadstats.sql

Service	Instance	Service Time Elapsed mSec/Call	CPU Time mSec/Call	DB Time mSec/Call	Calls/sec
PRDDB	PRDDB_1	0	0	0	.00
	PRDDB_2	0	0	0	.00
RAPTEST	PRDDB_1	18800	2829	18800	134.93
	PRDDB_2	19143	2929	19143	164.47
SYS$USERS	PRDDB_1	1212	1100	1212	5.99
	PRDDB_2	3959	4761	3959	4.19

In the preceding output, database service RAPTESTs are balanced across both the instances in the cluster. When a message is received by the SCAN listener regarding the current state of the instance, it redirects connections to the local listener on the node where the least loaded instance is running.

GV$SERVICEMETRIC

GV$SERVICEMETRIC contains metric values measured for all the services defined in the database. These values are updated by the MMON process as it captures load and other service-related information from the system global area (SGA). Updates to this view happen in 5-second and 1-minute intervals.

Apart from making updates to the GV$SERVICEMETRIC view, MMON also updates the operating system statistics and uses this information to determine the load characteristics on the various nodes in the cluster. The following query output from GV$OSSTAT provides the operating system statistics:

```
SQL> SELECT * FROM GV$OSSTAT WHERE INST_ID=1;
   INST_ID STAT_NAME                              VALUE  OSSTAT_ID
---------- ------------------------------------ ---------- ----------
         1 NUM_CPUS                                   2          0
         1 IDLE_TIME                             134867          1
         1 BUSY_TIME                              82151          2
         1 USER_TIME                              66198          3
         1 SYS_TIME                               15953          4
         1 NICE_TIME                                  0          6
         1 RSRC_MGR_CPU_WAIT_TIME                     0         14
         1 LOAD                              6.65917969         15
         1 PHYSICAL_MEMORY_BYTES              433270784       1008
```

GV$OSSTAT

GV$OSSTAT contains O/S statistics updated by the MMON process and is used to determine the load on the nodes/servers. The value updated by the MMON process is then processed and sent to the participating clients by the MMON Lite (MMNL) process. The values are in hundredths of a second, as a processor has been busy executing code, and is averaged over all processors.

Tracing the Load Metric Capture

Load balancing can be verified by enabling tracing at the database level using event 10735 at Level 3. Tracing can be enabled using the following statement:

```
SQL> ALTER SYSTEM SET EVENTS '10735 TRACE NAME CONTEXT FOREVER, LEVEL 3';
```

When the trace is enabled, the MMNL process writes additional load average information into its trace file stored in the user dump destination directory of the instance. The user dump destination directory can be determined after connecting to the database and verifying the parameter USER_DUMP_DEST.

The MMNL trace file contains the activities involving the cluster and or services that are being monitored. This provides the insight into how the client machines using this metric will react. The output following is an extract of the trace for the database service RAPTEST. The output indicates the various load matrixes and the call function that helps determine the local server threshold:

```
[oracle@prddb1 trace]$ cat PRDDB_1_mmnl_23263.trc | grep RAPTEST
kswsgfntpt : Metrics for svc : RAPTEST
kswsgfntpt : svc / fgval / clbdelta / scount : RAPTEST / 0.0000/ 100.0000 0
kswsgthr: calling kelr_get_local_threshold() svc:RAPTEST
kswsgfntpt : Metrics for svc : RAPTEST
kswsgfntpt : svc / fgval / clbdelta / scount : RAPTEST / 4.1667/ 5050.0000 2
kswsgthr: calling kelr_get_local_threshold() svc:RAPTEST
kswsgfntpt : Metrics for svc : RAPTEST
kswsgfntpt : svc / fgval / clbdelta / scount : RAPTEST / 14.5833/ 2541.6113 7
kswsgthr: calling kelr_get_local_threshold() svc:RAPTEST
```

```
kswsgfntpt : Metrics for svc : RAPTEST
kswsgfntpt : svc / fgval / clbdelta / scount : RAPTEST / 14.5833/ 1277.6327 7
kswsgthr: calling kelr_get_local_threshold() svc:RAPTEST
kswsgfntpt : Metrics for svc : RAPTEST
kswsgfntpt : svc / fgval / clbdelta / scount : RAPTEST / 18.7500/ 643.0413 9
kswsgthr: calling kelr_get_local_threshold() svc:RAPTEST
kswsgfntpt : Metrics for svc : RAPTEST
kswsgfntpt : svc / fgval / clbdelta / scount : RAPTEST / 27.0833/ 324.2762 13
kswsgthr: calling kelr_get_local_threshold() svc:RAPTEST
kswsgfntpt : Metrics for svc : RAPTEST
kswsgfntpt : svc / fgval / clbdelta / scount : RAPTEST / 33.3333/ 163.8512 16
kswsgthr: calling kelr_get_local_threshold() svc:RAPTEST
kswsgfntpt : Metrics for svc : RAPTEST
kswsgfntpt : svc / fgval / clbdelta / scount : RAPTEST / 100.0000/ 82.8510 20
kswsgthr: calling kelr_get_local_threshold() svc:RAPTEST
kswsgfntpt : Metrics for svc : RAPTEST
kswsgfntpt : svc / fgval / clbdelta / scount : RAPTEST / 100.0000/ 50.0000 25
kswsgthr: calling kelr_get_local_threshold() svc:RAPTEST
kswsgfntpt : Metrics for svc : RAPTEST
kswsgfntpt : svc / fgval / clbdelta / scount : RAPTEST / 100.0000/ 50.0000 28
kswsgthr: calling kelr_get_local_threshold() svc:RAPTEST
kswsgfntpt : Metrics for svc : RAPTEST
kswsgfntpt : svc / fgval / clbdelta / scount : RAPTEST / 100.0000/ 50.0000 31
kswsgthr: calling kelr_get_local_threshold() svc:RAPTEST
```

There are two parts to the preceding output. The Oracle kernel makes the call to determine the threshold definitions using "kelr_get_local_threshold" and is identified by "kswsgthr." The line starting with "kswsgfntpt" displays the value for the various stats.

The "svc" indicates the service name. In the trace output just shown, "RAPTEST" is the service name.

The "clbdelta" indicates the connection load balance percentage value currently utilized by the service RAPTEST on that instance.

The "scount" indicates the number of sessions that have made connections using that service on the instance.

The output should be read using the following format for better understanding:

```
kswsgfntpt : svc      / fgval   / clbdelta / scount :
             RAPTEST / 100.0000/ 50.0000 /  25
```

In the preceding output, there is 50 percent load balance, and 25 sessions are connected to the service RAPTEST.

Connection Throughput

All clients connect to the database to do one of two things: either to write (INSERT) or modify (UPDATE) data into the database or to read (SELECT) data from the database. As discussed earlier, speed at which data is written to the database or retrieved from the database is normally measured by response time. Apart from the speed at which data can be retrieved from the database or written to the database, response time also depends on the speed and volume of the data transmission between the client machines and the database servers. This situation becomes more obvious when large volumes or blocks of data need to be transmitted between the client and the database. Applications request data from the database in number of rows. This is driven by the settings on the application browser on the number of rows that it would like to view and display. The actual number of rows that can be received by the application is controlled by the array size or buffer size that can hold these rows. Tuning the array size or buffer size is required to improve the overall response times of the operation.

■ **Note**   The non-TCP related parameters are discussed in detail in Chapter 14.

Workshop

In the previous section, we discussed the buffer size of the application to request higher volumes of data. The buffer sizes are controlled using various parameters. At the O/S level, the network buffer sizes are driven by TCP parameter and the transport unit sizes.

Step 1

As part of the RAP testing discussed in Chapters 3 thru 5, we discussed that while tuning the servers for scalability, the network-related parameters needed to be verified and tuned if possible. The common buffer-related parameters and default values required to configure Oracle Database 11g Release 2 RAC on Linux are the following:

```
net.ipv4.tcp_rmem=4096 4194304 4194304
net.ipv4.tcp_wmem=98304 4194304 4194304
net.ipv4.tcp_window_scaling=1
```

The `tcp_rmem` is used to set the amount of memory reserved for TCP receive buffers. The first value 4096 of the parameter `tcp_rmem` just shown is the minimum receive buffer for each TCP connection; and this buffer is always allocated to a TCP socket, even when there is a high demand on the system. The second value specified tells the kernel the default receive buffer allocated for each TCP socket. The third value specifies the maximum receive buffer that can be allocated for a TCP socket.

The `tcp_wmem` is used to set the amount of memory reserved for TCP send buffers. Similar to the receive buffer, this variable also takes three different values, which hold information on how much TCP send buffer memory space each TCP socket has to use. The first value in this variable tells the minimum TCP send buffer space available for a single TCP socket. The second value in the variable tells us the default buffer space allowed for a single TCP socket to use. The third value tells the kernel the maximum TCP send buffer.

Step 2

Oracle relies on the volume of data that each Oracle session can transmit, called the session data unit (SDU). Prior to Oracle Database Version 11g, the SDU defaulted to 2K; the new default value is 8K. Because the Oracle database block size in typical applications defaults to 8K, this size is sufficient in most cases. However, when larger volumes of data are being handled between two destinations—for instance, in the case of a dataguard implementation, when redo data is sent from the primary database to the standby database—higher SDU sizes of up to 32K are recommended.

Every time a packet or buffer of data is transmitted to a destination, if the buffer size is not sufficiently large enough to hold this data, the packet is broken down into smaller sizes. This means it could take several round-trips for the enter packet/buffer to reach the destination. Apart from the multiple network trips to complete the transmission, every time a packet reaches a destination, TCP needs to send an ACK (acknowledgment) signal back to the sender. Increasing the SDU size would reduce the number of round-trips and the number of ACKs that need to be transmitted.

To get the best results from setting the SDU sizes, the values should be set for both the client and the database server, for example, to increase the size from 8K to 16K.

The parameters should then be added to the connection descriptor on the client system or to the SQL*Net file. For example, the following SDU settings in the TNS connection descriptor will set the value of the SDU to 16K:

```
SSKYDB =
  (DESCRIPTION =
     (SDU = 16384)
     (FAILOVER = ON)
     (ADDRESS = (PROTOCOL = TCP)(HOST = oradb-scan.sumsky.net)(PORT = 1521))
     (LOAD_BALANCE = YES)
   (CONNECT_DATA =
     (SERVER = DEDICATED)
     (SERVICE_NAME = SSKYDB)
     (FAILOVER_MODE =
        (TYPE = SELECT)(METHOD = BASIC)(RETRIES = 10)(DELAY = 3)
   )
  )
 )
```

Similar settings should also be made to the listener to ensure that the bytes received by the server are also of a similar size. For example, the following SDU settings to the listener will set the receive value to 16K:

```
SID_LIST_LISTENER =
(SID_DESC =
     (SDU=16384)
     (SID_NAME = SSKY1)
))
```

Network delays in receiving user requests and sending data back to the users affect the overall performance of the application/environment. This also adds to the transmit time. Such delays translate themselves into SQL*Net related wait events (wait events are discussed later).

Similar to the MTU settings we tuned for the private interconnect (discussed in Chapter 4), the SDU settings for the SQL*Net connect descriptor can also be tuned. Optimal SDU settings can be determined by the repeated data/buffer requests by enabling SQL*Net and listener trace at both the client and server levels.

SQL*Net tracing can be enabled by adding the following parameters to the SQLNET.ora file on the client machines located in $GRID_HOME/network/admin directory:

```
trace_level_client=16
trace_file_client=client
trace_timestamp_client=ON
```

Listener tracing on the servers can be enabled by adding the following parameters to the listener.ora file to trace connections made to a specific listener or the sqlnet.ora file to trace connections to all listeners. These files are on the server side in the $GRID_HOME/network/admin directory:

```
trace_level_server=16
trace_file_server=server
trace_timestamp_server=ON
```

Trace files are generated in $GRID_HOME/network/trace directories on the respective servers.

Step 3

Increasing the buffer sizes only helps in the transmission of data to and from the client machines. However, if the client is not able to receive these increased buffer sizes, the client is going to wait until the buffer is exhausted and is reloaded with new content; and the database server is going to wait to send this data because the network has not delivered the previous content.

To improve receive and send times, the local buffer sizes on the application servers need to be increased. Depending on the type of connection used by the client, there are two parameters that could be sized appropriately:

1. The . arraysize is used in applications that use the SQL*Plus and the TNS technology for making connections to the database; the default value for this parameter is 15.

2. The . FetchSize is used in JDBC applications that use the Type 2 or Type 4 type of connection; typically this parameter defaults to 10 rows.

Step 3(a)

Verify the current array size of the environment using the following command:

```
SHOW ARRAYSIZE
arraysize 15
```

Step 3(b)

To capture the current activity and performance statistics of the query executed from the client session against a data warehouse application, set the event 10046 at Level 12 to execute the query.

```
alter session set events '10046 trace name context forever, level 12';
SELECT ol_number,
       ol_amount,
       ol_quantity
FROM   order_line ol,
       orders ord
WHERE  ol.ol_o_id = ord.o_id
       AND ol.ol_w_id = ord.o_w_id
       AND ol.ol_d_id = ord.o_d_id;
alter session set events '10046 trace name context off';
```

Step 3(c)

Using Oracle Trace Analyzer,[1] analyze the trace file to generate the required analysis reports. The trace file can be found in the user dump destination directory of the instance where the query was executed. In the output following, the trace file EGCDEV_1_ora_24536_MVEGCDEV_1_Mar30_0321.trc is passed to the trace analyzer:

```
SQL> connect TRCANLZR/TRCANLZR
Connected.
SQL> @$TOOLS_HOME/trca/run/trcanlzr.sql PRDDB_1_ora_24536_MVEGCDEV_1_Mar30_0321.trc
Parameter 1:
Trace Filename or control_file.txt (required)
```

---

[1]Trace Analyzer—Metalink Note 224270.1: *TRCANLZR—Interpreting Raw SQL Traces with Binds and/or Waits generated by EVENT 10046.*

```
Value passed to trcanlzr.sql:
~~~~~~~~~~~~~~~~~~~~~~~~~~~~~~

TRACE_FILENAME: PRDDB_1_ora_24536_MVEGCDEV_1_Mar30_0321.trc
Analyzing PRDDB_1_ora_24536_MVEGCDEV_1_Mar30_0321.trc
To monitor progress, login as TRCANLZR into another session and execute:
SQL> SELECT * FROM trca$_log_v;
... analyzing trace(s) ...
Trace Analyzer completed.
Review first trcanlzr_error.log file for possible fatal errors.
Review next trca_e77025.log for parsing messages and totals.
Copying now generated files into local directory
TKPROF: Release 11.2.0.2.0 - Development on Thu Mar 31 11:42:14 2011
Copyright (c) 1982, 2009, Oracle and/or its affiliates.  All rights reserved.
  adding: trca_e77025.html
File trca_e77025.zip has been created
TRCANLZR completed.
```

Step 3(d)

From the zip file generated in the previous step, extract the contents and review the trace analyzer report using a browser. Figure 11-3 illustrates a snapshot of the report and the high-level details from the query execution with the array size of 15 (default).

In Figure 11-3, the query takes a significant amount of time to complete the request, the total response time (Response Time Summary section) is 17,308 seconds, and the number of calls to the database to physically get the rows indicated by the "Fetch, call count" is also high. The database experienced high waits on SQL Net message from and to client, indicating that although the database itself was idle, it could not transmit the data to the client due to limitations in the client configuration to receive these data transfers.

Step 3(e)

To check and validate the appropriate array size that would help improve the overall response time, test with various array sizes. Check the network traffic during this analysis and ensure setting the array size to a higher number, for example, 200:

```
SET ARRAYSIZE 200
SHOW ARRAYSIZE
arraysize 200
```

Response Time Summary

Response Time Component	Time (in secs)	pct of total resp time	Time (in secs)	pct of total resp time	Time (in secs)	pct of total resp time
CPU Time:	50.137	0.3%				
Non-idle Wait Time:	73.142	0.4%				
ET Unaccounted-for Time:	-0.994	0.0%				
Total Elapsed Time[1]:			122.285	0.7%		
Idle Wait Time:			17126.017	98.9%		
RT Unaccounted-for Time:			60.044	0.3%		
Total Response Time[2]:					17308.347	100.0%

(1) Total Elapsed Time = "CPU Time" + "Non-Idle Wait Time" + "ET Unaccounted-for Time".
(2) Total Response Time = "Total Elapsed Time" + "Idle Wait Time" + "RT Unaccounted-for Time".
Total Accounted-for Time = "CPU Time" + "Non-Idle Wait Time" + "Idle Wait Time" = 17248.302 secs.
Total Uncounted-for Time = "ET Unaccounted-for Time" + "RT Unaccounted-for Time" = 59.050 secs.
Go to Top

Overall Time and Totals (Non-Recursive and Recursive)

Call	Total Response Time[3]	Response Time Accounted-for[2]	Elapsed Time[1]	CPU Time	Non-Idle Wait Time	Elapsed Time Unaccounted-for	Idle Wait Time	Response Time Unaccounted-for
Parse:		0.321	0.019	0.017	0.001	0.001	0.301	
Execute:		0.026	0.026	0.028	0.000	-0.002	0.000	
Fetch:		17247.956	122.240	50.092	73.141	-0.993	17125.716	
Total:	17308.347	17248.302	122.285	50.137	73.142	-0.994	17126.017	60.044

(1) Elapsed Time = "CPU Time" + "Non-Idle Wait Time" + "Elapsed Time Unaccounted-for".
(2) Response Time Accounted-for = "Elapsed Time" + "Idle Wait Time".
(3) Total Response Time = "Response Time Accounted-for" + "Response Time Unaccounted-for".

Call	Call Count	OS Buffer Gets (disk)	BG Consistent Read Mode (query)	BG Current Mode (current)	Rows Processed or Returned	Library Cache Misses	Times Waited Non-Idle	Times Waited Idle
Parse:	21	6	154	0	0	19	18	2
Execute:	47	0	49	0	2	18	2	0
Fetch:	1168056	288265	1438733	0	17519613	0	1170354	1167972
Total:	1168124	288271	1438936	0	17519615	37	1170374	1167974

Event Name	Wait Class	Non-Idle Wait Time	Times Waited Non-Idle	Idle Wait Time	Times Waited Idle	Average Wait Time	Max Wait Time	Blocks	Average Blocks
SQL*Net message from client:	Idle			17126.016	1167972	0.014663	1.978495	0	
db file scattered read:	User I/O	72.325	2355			0.030711	0.316468	288261	122.4
SQL*Net message to client:	Network	0.729	1167973			0.000001	0.003104	0	
db file sequential read:	User I/O	0.087	10			0.008709	0.026429	10	1
KSV master wait:	Idle			0.001	2	0.000656	0.001195	0	
row cache lock:	Concurrency	0.001	18			0.000069	0.000089	0	
ASM file metadata operation:	Other	0.000	1			0.000067	0.000067	0	
asynch descriptor resize:	Other	0.000	16			0.000002	0.000003	0	
Disk file operations I/O:	User I/O	0.000	1			0.000007	0.000007	0	
Total:		73.142	1170374	17126.017	1167974				

Figure 11-3. Trace analyzer report—Array size 15

Step 3(f)

After the array size is set to 200, execute the query from Step 3(b) once again and analyze the trace file using the Oracle trace analyzer .(illustrated in Step 3(c)). A subset of the report is illustrated in Figure 11-4.

As seen in Figure 11-4, the overall response time has improved several folds. The total response time is 1,076 seconds compared to 17,308 seconds (array size of 15). Whereas the total number of rows processed remains the same, the number of fetches performed on the database server has dropped significantly. The SQL Net related wait times were also reduced, indicating that increasing the array size helps in the overall response time of the operation.

Wait Events related to SQL*Net

The following are the list of wait events related to SQL Net. Depending on the type of operation, some of the events are treated as idle events and can be ignored.

SQL*Net Message to Client

This event occurs when the database needs to send a message to the participating client and the client is busy processing its requests and is not ready to accept new data or messages from the database server. This indicates that the database is waiting for the client to be ready and is not able to complete its operation. This event does not indicate that the database is busy. Because the operation cannot be completed, it affects the response time of the operation.

In Figure 11-3 and in Figure 11-4, this is indicated as a network related wait event. The overall wait time changed when the array size was increased from the default value of 15 to 200.

SQL*Net Message from Client

This is the contrary to the previous wait event. This event is triggered when the database is waiting to receive messages from the client. The client has initiated a session and has started to send data and/or messages to the database server but has paused. This paused time is measured in seconds is recorded (SECONDS_IN_WAIT column in V$SESSION) as wait times in the database. Oracle records these wait events as idle wait events because the database does not perform any operation during this time. High waits on this event could indicate poor response time to the end user and cannot be ignored. High waits on this event normally trigger some kind of network problem that needs to be investigated further.

Response Time Summary

Response Time Component	Time (in secs)	pct of total resp time	Time (in secs)	pct of total resp time	Time (in secs)	pct of total resp time
CPU Time:	22.480	2.1%				
Non-idle Wait Time:	55.729	5.2%				
ET Unaccounted-for Time:	-0.342	0.0%				
Total Elapsed Time[1]:			77.867	7.2%		
Idle Wait Time:			994.112	92.3%		
RT Unaccounted-for Time:			4.506	0.4%		
Total Response Time[2]:					1076.484	100.0%

(1) Total Elapsed Time = "CPU Time" + "Non-Idle Wait Time" + "ET Unaccounted-for Time".
(2) Total Response Time = "Total Elapsed Time" + "Idle Wait Time" + "RT Unaccounted-for Time".
Total Accounted-for Time = "CPU Time" + "Non-Idle Wait Time" + "Idle Wait Time" = 1071.979 secs.
Total Unccounted-for Time = "ET Unaccounted-for Time" + "RT Unaccounted-for Time" = 4.164 secs.

Go to Top

Overall Time and Totals (Non-Recursive and Recursive)

Call	Total Response Time[3]	Response Time Accounted-for[2]	Elapsed Time[1]	CPU Time	Non-Idle Wait Time	Elapsed Time Unaccounted-for	Idle Wait Time	Response Time Unaccounted-for
Parse:		0.020	0.019	0.018	0.001	0.000	0.001	
Execute:		0.026	0.026	0.026	0.000	0.000	0.000	
Fetch:		1071.933	77.822	22.436	55.728	-0.341	994.111	
Total:	1076.484	1071.979	77.867	22.480	55.729	-0.342	994.112	4.506

(1) Elapsed Time = "CPU Time" + "Non-Idle Wait Time" + "Elapsed Time Unaccounted-for".
(2) Response Time Accounted-for = "Elapsed Time" + "Idle Wait Time".
(3) Total Response Time = "Response Time Accounted-for" + "Response Time Unaccounted-for".

Call	Call Count	OS Buffer Gets (disk)	BG Consistent Read Mode (query)	BG Current Mode (current)	Rows Processed or Returned	Library Cache Misses	Times Waited Non-Idle	Times Waited Idle
Parse:	21	7	154	0	0	19	18	2
Execute:	47	0	46	0	2	18	2	0
Fetch:	87684	288265	374641	0	17519613	0	89983	87600
Total:	87752	288272	374841	0	17519615	37	90003	87602

Event Name	Wait Class	Non-Idle Wait Time	Times Waited Non-Idle	Idle Wait Time	Times Waited Idle	Average Wait Time	Max Wait Time	Blocks	Average Blocks
SQL*Net message from client:	Idle			994.111	87600	0.011348	3.771431	0	
db file scattered read:	User I/O	55.597	2355			0.023608	0.302264	288261	122.4
db file sequential read:	User I/O	0.078	11			0.007047	0.022888	11	1
SQL*Net message to client:	Network	0.053	87601			0.000001	0.000108	0	
row cache lock:	Concurrency	0.001	18			0.000065	0.000083	0	
KSV master wait:	Idle			0.001	2	0.000552	0.000986	0	
ASM file metadata operation:	Other	0.000	1			0.000060	0.000060	0	
asynch descriptor resize:	Other	0.000	16			0.000002	0.000004	0	
Disk file operations I/O:	User I/O	0.000	1			0.000008	0.000008	0	
Total:		55.729	90003	994.112	87602				

Go to Top

Figure 11-4. Trace analyzer report—Array size 200

SQL*Net More Data to Client

Oracle is attempting to send more data or messages to the client over and above the SDU limit. This event indicates tuning the SDU parameter at the SQL Net layer. Please note that starting with Oracle Database 11g, the SDU defaults to 8K.

SQL*Net More Data From Client

This is similar to the previous event; however, in this case, the event is triggered when the client is attempting to send packets larger than the SDU size. This event normally occurs in batch application performing high-volume inserts. Increasing the SDU size can help improve this wait event.

Conclusion

Response times for the end user are just not confined to tuning the database and SQL queries. If the buffer or pipe that carries the data back and forth between the client or application server and the database server is not sufficiently sized, the overall response time maybe affected. Similarly, if the application server or the client is not tuned or has network buffers sized well, the database will spend time waiting to send data to the client; and only when the client buffer is freed up will new data be sent to the client application.

Tuning the network layers using the SDU parameters and where possible using network technologies such as jumbo frames and setting the array sizes inside the application code to a large size should be considered in tuning the application to give good response times.

CHAPTER 12

■ ■ ■

Tuning the Storage Subsystem

Decisions about how to design or configure storage hardware and software should be centered on what kind of performance is required from the I/O subsystem. This depends on the type of application, supported workload characteristics, service level agreements (SLA), and so forth. However, due to factors such as cost, reliability, availability, power, and ease of use, performance is often neglected and does not meet expectations. Trade-offs are often made between cost and performance, ease-of-use and performance, and consolidation and performance. Trade-offs at the cost of performance are made in all tiers of the storage layer (not to mention in other areas of the infrastructure, such as network and processor speeds). File-cache management, file-system architecture, and volume management translate application calls into individual storage access requests. These requests traverse the storage driver stack and generate streams of commands that are presented to the disk subsystem. The sequence, type, and number of calls and the subsequent translation can improve or degrade overall performance of the I/O subsystem.

Good planning of the storage topology and data layout for throughput or response times can make the difference between excellent workload and application performance and having poor workload with high response times that result in poor application performance.

Choosing Storage

The basic function of storage systems is to provide storage resources to the servers for primary datastore, for mirrored datastore, or for backup datastore. A wide variety of storage systems are available in the marketplace and serve different purposes, with varied performance characteristics and features. The storage devices include RAID disk arrays, Just a Bunch of Disks (JBOD), tape systems, and so on. The types of interfaces provided on these devices include SCSI, fiber channel, and Ethernet.

The most important considerations in choosing storage systems include the following:

- Understanding business needs for high availability of data, data protection, performance, and data recovery

- Understanding the characteristics of current and future storage workloads

- Understanding the application behavior and access patterns for planning and performance requirements

- Understanding necessary storage space, bandwidth, and latency requirements for the current and future growth of business

- Understanding business needs for data layout, such as striping, redundancy, and backup strategy

Regarding the storage considerations we have just discussed, the workload characteristics are probably the most important. Workload in this context is defined as the total amount of work that is performed at the storage subsystem. To better understand the I/O workloads on the system, the following should also be understood with respect to the application:

- Read:write ratio

- Sequential vs. random access

- Data access patterns, arrival patterns, and size of data being requested and/or written with each request

- Inter-arrival rates and concurrency (patterns of request arrival rates)

A workload characterized by the number of transactions is called a **transaction-based workload** and is measured in I/O per second (IOPS). A workload characterized by large I/O is called **throughput-based workload** and is measured in megabytes per second (MBps). Both these workloads are conflicting in nature and consequently they work best with a wide range of configuration settings across all pieces of the storage subsystem.

Transaction-Based Workload

High-performance-based transaction environments cannot be created on low-cost storage subsystems. These low-cost storage systems have a very small cache and cause flushing in and flushing out of the data from cache, thus causing the frequent retrieval of data from disks. On the other hand, modern storage arrays have larger caches—for example a 6780 array has 64GB cache and is perhaps more effective for an OLTP-based workload, where I/O requests are randomly distributed over a large database.

Environments that require many distributed random I/O requests depend heavily on the number of back-end drives that are available for parallel processing of the host's workload. When data is confined to few disk drives, it can result in high queuing, which would cause long response times.

In such implementations, the IOPS acceptable is an important factor in deciding how large a storage subsystem is required. While willingness to have higher response times can help in reducing the cost, this may not be acceptable to the user community.

Because these are slow random I/O operations and because workload content can be continually changing throughout the course of the day, these bottlenecks can be very mysterious in nature and can appear and disappear or move from one location to another over time.

Throughput-Based Workload

This kind of workload is typically seen with applications that require massive amounts of data to be sent or received and frequently use large sequential blocks to reduce disk latency. Throughput rates for these types of operations are dependent on the internal bandwidth of the storage subsystem. In such systems fewer drives are needed to reach maximum throughput rates. In this environment, read operations make use of cache to stage greater chunks of data at a time in order to improve the overall performance.

Typically a data warehouse or data mart falls into this category. Users query large amounts of data which are normally bulk reads; however, read caches may not always help as it is rare that several users look at the same data sets simultaneously, or, for that matter, that the same user looks at the same set of data again.

Mixed Workload

Most business environments tend to define the storage system so it is able to meet both types of workloads, or mixed workloads. Mixed workloads introduce additional challenges around the sizing and configuration of the storage systems. While the combination of workloads may be difficult due the uniqueness of the data set and the access methods required (for both transaction-based workloads and throughput-based workloads) in larger environments, it is common to implement them as a mixed workload in smaller organizations to save on hardware and administration costs.

When implementing mixed workloads in large database environments, the bandwidth of the storage arrays, the disk controllers, and the HBA cards on all the servers must be taken into account. Read and write cache at the storage level could be advantageous only for write operations due to the frequent changes in the database patterns. Server configurations such as Oracle Database Machine have been designed for such environments.

Choosing the Storage Array

There are several factors to be taken into consideration when choosing one's storage array and adapters. A storage array's internal architecture can vary between vendors and even between models. Choice of which storage array normally depends on the type of storage communication protocol that is currently used in the organization, and could be one of the following:

- Fiber Channel (FC) or SCSI

- SAS or SATA

- Support of hardware RAID

- Maximum storage bandwidth

Storage arrays typically have several front-end adapters. These front-end adapters have two sides. One side has ports, which connect into the Fiber Channel switch. The other side connects into the cache contoller located inside of the storage array.

The cache controller manages the storage-array cache. The storage arrays have a read and write cache area. Read cache is used to store recently accessed data, and the write cache is used to buffer writes (write-back cache). The read/write cache can range from 128GB to 2TB[1] for high-end arrays. In cases where the cache is mirrored, the capacity would be half that.

When a read request for a block is received by the cache controller via the front-end port, the cache controller checks for the buffer block in the cache. If the data buffer is found in the cache, the block is returned back up through the fiber channel/network and eventually to the application.

The cache controller can also prefetch sequentially-accessed data blocks. If the cache controller determines that the application is accessing contiguous disk blocks, the prefetch algorithms will be triggered (set with thresholds) to prefetch the data to be stored in the read cache, providing significant improvement in access time.

Similar to the read-request operation discussed earlier, the write request is also received by the cache controller via the front-end port; however, to the write-cache area, and later to the back-end disks. Most storage arrays have a non-volatile random access memory (NVRAM) battery system that protects in-flight operations from the loss of power.

Storage-Wide Considerations for Performance

The primary reason for performance issues is almost always poorly written SQL queries. Making the queries efficient by optimizing the access paths could fix performance problems to a great extent. Similarly, on the storage subsystem side of things, there could be high I/O activity, which could cause slower performance. The reasons for the slower performance could be one of the following:

- The throughput of the disks is low.

- The SAN has not been optimally configured.

---

[1]Configuration- EMC VMAX20K 2 Engines—128GB shared global cache, mirrored 64GB usable per engine.

- There is high contention on the storage subsystem due to unproportional access paths.

- There is a faulty or congested I/O channel due to unproportional access paths.

- There are high queue lengths due to one or more of the issues previously discussed.

To overcome any I/O-related issues, the following components would need to be examined:

- Host server (number of servers)

- Volume manager or storage subsystem configuration

Servers and storage subsystems should be tuned for the type of workload that would be accessing the data from these disks.

Disk Drive Performance

Figure 12-1 illustrates the seek time vs. disk access speed. It is based on the head movement from the outside of the disk to the inside of the disk. This shows that the speed to get a data block would be quicker from the outside than from reading the data from the inside sectors of the disk platter. Performance of the disk drives is dictated by the following factors:

- Rotation (spindle) speed – the speed at which the disk or platters rotate, allowing the read/write heads to retrieve or store the data. This is measured in revolutions per minute (RPM).

- Seek time – the average time it takes to find the data on the platters; does not include the read time.

- Speed and size of the disk buffer memory.

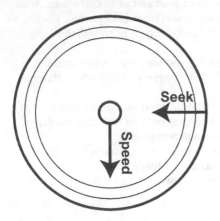

Figure 12-1. Seek time and seek speed[2, 3]

The access time can be illustrated as:

$$Access\ Time = Command\ Overhead\ Time + Seek\ Time + Settle\ Time + Rotational\ Latency$$

[2]Oracle 10g RAC – *Grid, Services, and Clustering*, Murali Vallath, Digital Press, 2007.
[3]Oracle Automatic Storage Management – *Under-the-Hood & Practical Deployment Guide,* Nitin Vengurlekar, Murali Vallath, Rich Long, Oracle Press, 2008.

As seen in this formula, the access time is affected by the seek time and by the rotational delay (measured as latency) of the disks. This means the access time is the sum of the seek time and rotational latency. So, for a disk with 4 millisecond (ms) seek time and 4ms rotational latency, it could take about 8ms from the moment the disk initiates the read request (seeks to find the data) to the moment when it actually starts reading it. The advent of faster disks, which essentially means disks spin faster (or have a higher RPM), translates into a reduced rotational delay.

However, by the same measure, the seek time has not reduced very significantly over the years. Let's delve a little deeper into this seek time.

The *seek time* of a hard disk measures the amount of time required for the read/write heads to move between tracks over the surfaces of the platters. Seek time *is* one of the most important metrics when discussing performance specifications. Switching between tracks requires the head actuator to move the head arms physically. Head arm movement between tracks is a mechanical operation and takes a specific amount of time. This time required depends on the distance between the tracks. As in most mechanical operations, there is certain overhead involved in track switching.

Seek time is normally expressed in milliseconds, with average seek times for most drives today ranging from 5ms to 7ms. When computing the overall response time for a user request or disk operation, a millisecond is an *enormous* amount of time. Considering that the speed of the system bus is measured in nanoseconds, even small reductions in seek times can result in improvements in overall system performance.

There are three different seek-time specifications defined by disk drive manufacturers:

- **Average seek time:** It is the average time to seek the data from one random track (cylinder) to any other.

- **Track-to-track:** This is the time required to seek between adjacent tracks, is usually around .4ms.

- **Full stroke:** This is the amount of time to seek the entire width of the disk, from the innermost track to the outermost. The typical range is between 10.2ms and 12ms.

Compare seeking from adjacent tracks (track-to-track) with seeking end to end (full stroke). At first glance it is obvious that it takes longer for the head to move to the next track as compared to the head moving across several tracks. However, when examined closely, the difference is only 3%. Where is all the time taken? A significant portion of the seek time is really settling time, which is a pre-determined delay programmed in the drive electronics.

The database applications have always favored several disks of smaller capacity, because the number of disks, and not the overall storage capacity of those disks, determines the limit on I/O operations. More disks meant more read/write heads, which in turn meant higher number of I/O operations, which helped in the overall performance of the database. Despite the I/O advantages obtained by using many disks of small capacity, unfortunately manufacturers these days only make large-capacity disks. To complicate matters, these days there are choices within and across drive families; for example, 73GB 15k RPM, 73GB 10K RPM, 146GB 15K RPM, 300GB 10K RPM, or 750GB 10K RPM.

Based on the above observation, it makes sense to have fewer expensive 10K disks or even 7200RPM disks as compared to a few expensive 15K RPM disks. One should size for the number of disk read/write heads as opposed to capacity or even rotational speed.

Moreover, as the drive capacity increases within a particular family of drives, the performance per physical drive may not increase. For example, when comparing a 146GB 10K RPM drive with a 300GB drive, though the *capacity* doubles, the *access density*, or the number of I/Os per gigabyte that the drive can perform, is cut in half. Thus, it is important to strike a balance between performance and cost by configuring the system based on the number of drives required for performance rather than to configure them for the required capacity.

Storage Contention

The path that the host server uses to access the data, the host volume manager, HBA, SAN fabric, and the storage subsystem controller used in accessing the logical drives should all be configured for optimal performance. In an Oracle RAC environment the number of nodes and servers accessing the storage subsystem should be taken into consideration when configuring these access paths. Figure 12-2 illustrates the storage stack and the related software access paths in a typical storage configuration.

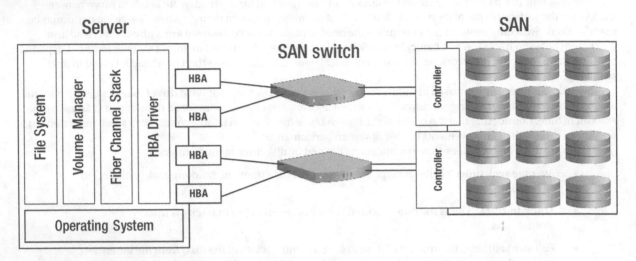

Figure 12-2. *Storage access paths*

In Figure 12-2 the server has a file system and a volume manger that interface to the storage SAN through the Fiber Channel and HBA drivers using the HBA cards, SAN switch, and the disk controllers. On the SAN end of the configuration, the switch will interface with the disk controllers through the various ports. These ports are assigned to those of the HBA device. The ratio of number of ports mapped to the HBA device depends on the criticality of the application, the throughput, and the performance requirements. Figure 12-3 illustrates a configuration in which an HBA is mapped to 16 ports. This is normally not the case in a production environment, where the ratio between the HBA device to the number of ports is about half. For example, in an Oracle Business Intelligence Enterprise Edition (OBIEE) production environment configured on an 8-node RAC cluster, each with a dual-port HBA, the HBAs were mapped to 8 ports on the disk controller.

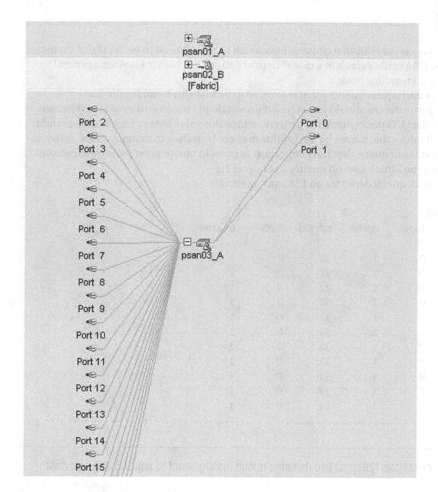

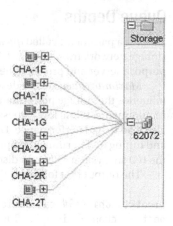

Figure 12-3. *HBA-to-port mappings*

When increasing the number of nodes and servers accessing the storage subsystem, seldom is any consideration given to the number of interfaces to the storage subsystem and the capacity of the I/O path. Care should be given to ensuring that the number of HBAs is equal to the number of disk controllers. Using the disk controller slots to accommodate more disk arrays could have a negative impact on the total throughput of the I/O subsystem.

For example, on a 16-port Fiber Channel switch, the ideal configuration would be to have 8 HBAs and 8 disk controller ports, giving a total throughput of $8 \times 200MB$[4] $= 1.6$ GB/sec. However, if the number of HBAs is reduced to 4 to provide room for additional storage; then the total throughput drops down by 50% (4×200 MB $= 800MB$/sec).

The number of controllers that is mapped to an HBA device determines the speed of the write operation. How many controllers an HBA device can map also depends on the queue depth of the HBA devices.

---

[4]Assuming the maximum theoretical payload of 2GB/sec, Fiber Channel is 200MB/sec. Source: Oracle Corporation.

Queue Depths

There is a parameter called *queue depth* on the HBA that controls how much data is allowed to be "in flight" on the storage network from that card. Most HBA cards default to a queue depth of 30 or 32, which is ideal for a general purpose server and prevents the SAN from getting busy.

Maximum queue depth describes the request quantity that is allowed to be in flight; it can significantly influence the storage performance. Queue depths should be set based on workload characteristics and performance requirements. While low values can affect I/O performance negatively, setting this value to very high number could also lead to bad performance. Default values that are set by the vendor may not be sufficient in many cases. Analysis and tuning to determine the optimal value of queue depths is important in order to obtain good performance from the I/O subsystem. (Refer to discussion on Little's Law on queues in Chapter 2.)

The output that follows is the default queue depth for an EMC storage array:

```
[root@tstdb1 sg]# cat device_hdr
host    chan    id    lun    type    opens    qdepth    busy    online
[root@tstdb1 sg]# cat devices
0       0       0     0      0       1        32        0       1
0       0       0     1      0       1        32        0       1
0       0       0     2      0       1        32        0       1
0       0       0     3      0       1        32        0       1
0       0       0     4      0       1        32        0       1
0       0       0     5      0       1        32        0       1
1       0       0     0      0       1        32        0       1
0       0       0     6      0       1        32        0       1
1       0       0     1      0       1        32        0       1
1       0       0     2      0       1        32        0       1
0       0       0     7      0       1        32        0       1
```

■ **Note** Certain storage vendors (for example, Netapps) use dynamic queue management to adjust the queue depth sizes based on workload.

As we discussed in the previous section, the number of controllers on the storage array should be proportional to the number of servers and their combined HBAs. If this is not the case, there could be queuing problems and delayed I/O activity to the database. The number of hosts an array can adequately support depends on the available queues per physical storage port, the number of storage ports, and the array's available bandwidth.

The iostat utility on Linux and Unix OS servers can be used to determine the queue lengths of the various devices, as follows:

```
iostat -d -x interval count
```

- **-d**: Display the device utilization report (d = disk)
- **-x**: Display extended statistics including disk utilization
- **interval**: The time period in seconds between two samples. **iostat 5** will give data at each 5-second interval
- **count**: The number of times the data is needed. **iostat 5** will give data 5 times in 5-second intervals

```
[root@prddb1 ~]# iostat -d -x 10 | grep 'emcpower.1'
Device:    rrqm/s wrqm/s r/s  w/s  rsec/s wsec/s avgrq  avgqu await svctm %util
emcpoweri1  3.81   0.03  6.51 0.09 1569.01 14.28  239.79 0.07  10.21 3.88  2.56
emcpowerj1  3.84   0.03  6.53 0.09 1581.08 14.27  240.71 0.07  10.23 3.87  2.57
emcpowerk1  3.83   0.03  6.64 0.10 1578.72 14.14  236.53 0.07   9.99 3.76  2.53
emcpowerl1  3.81   0.03  6.47 0.09 1568.73 13.96  241.12 0.07  10.26 3.86  2.53
emcpowerm1  3.86   0.03  6.61 0.10 1588.03 13.86  238.75 0.07   9.98 3.79  2.54
emcpowern1  3.82   0.03  6.50 0.10 1571.59 14.54  240.04 0.07  10.13 3.85  2.54
emcpowero1  3.81   0.03  7.99 0.13 1617.88 16.13  201.09 0.07   8.52 3.37  2.74
emcpowerp1  3.86   0.03  9.17 0.46 1670.98 26.49  176.18 0.07   7.49 3.09  2.98
emcpowera1  3.84   0.03  6.63 0.11 1581.65 14.48  236.65 0.07  10.23 3.83  2.58
emcpowerb1  3.85   0.03  6.55 0.10 1583.33 15.78  240.19 0.07  10.27 3.78  2.51
emcpowerc1  3.82   0.03  6.52 0.10 1572.85 15.02  240.10 0.07  10.42 3.88  2.56
emcpowerd1  3.85   0.03  6.52 0.10 1583.59 14.52  241.22 0.07  10.49 3.89  2.58
emcpowere1  3.83   0.03  6.51 0.09 1574.33 13.99  240.73 0.07  10.31 3.79  2.50
emcpowerf1  3.85   0.03  6.55 0.09 1585.99 13.95  240.70 0.07  10.32 3.84  2.55
emcpowerg1  3.86   0.03  6.52 0.09 1584.81 14.00  241.68 0.07  10.36 3.85  2.55
emcpowerh1  3.83   0.03  6.56 0.09 1577.65 14.83  239.39 0.07  10.26 3.84  2.56
```

Where,

- **rrqm/s**: The number of read requests merged per second that were queued to the hard disk

- **wrqm/s**: The number of write requests merged per second that were queued to the hard disk

- **r/s**: The number of read requests per second

- **w/s**: The number of write requests per second

- **rsec/s**: The number of sectors read from the hard disk per second

- **wsec/s**: The number of sectors written to the hard disk per second

- **avgrq**: The average size (in sectors) of the requests that were issued to the device

- **avgqu**: The average queue length of the requests that were issued to the device

- **await**: The average time (in milliseconds) for I/O requests issued to the device to be served. This includes the time spent by the requests in the queue and the time spent servicing them

- **svctm**: The average service time (in milliseconds) for I/O requests that were issued to the device

- **%util**: Percentage of CPU time during which I/O requests were issued to the device (bandwidth utilization for the device). Device saturation occurs when this value is close to 100%

The columns that are important for measuring the queue depth utilization are rrqm/s, wrqm/s, avgrq-sz (avgrq), avgqu-sz (avgqu), and svctm.

HBAs with larger queue depths help SQL queries that are highly I/O intensive—for example, in a data warehouse—and also help increase the number of I/O requests allowed to be in flight. However this may not be true for other kinds of applications like online transaction processing (OLTP) or, for that matter, clustered environments. In the case of RAC implementation where there is the potential transfer of uncommitted blocks between instances, this may not be useful unless there is service available to instance affinity. This is due to requests for blocks that have not been committed.

As we saw earlier in Figure 12-2, the controllers receive data from the HBA devices via the SAN switches, which is then written to the logical disks. Similar to the queue depth setting on the HBA cards, there is a *cache size* defined on the controllers that increases performance and improves scalability. The cache tier helps buffer I/O requests to the disks and prevents data loss during power outages; it is configured with an internal power backup mechanism. Certain storage devices, for example, Oracle's ZFS Storage, perform the write to disk activity in parallel while the cache is being populated, thus protecting the data during power outages.

There are two types of cache that can be managed at the disk/storage level: read cache and write cache.

Read Cache

Controllers attempt to "read ahead" (read-ahead policy), anticipating future read requests from the OS and buffering from sequential sectors of the logical drive when seeking data. There are benefits of using the read-ahead policy, as data is written sequentially. Read cache holds data that has been previously read, making subsequent reads of the same data sets faster by eliminating the need for the controller to go back to the disk for the data.

Write Cache

Write cache can be implemented in one of two ways:

- **Write-Back.** With this option, the controller sends a write-request completion signal as soon as the data is in the controller cache; it does not wait for the data to be written to disk. Write-back caching may provide improved performance since subsequent read requests can retrieve data from the controller cache more quickly than when reading it from the disk. The greater the size of the cache, the more data is buffered, thus improving throughput and IOPS of data written.

- **Write-Through.** With this option, the controller sends a write-request completion signal only after the data has been successfully written to disk. Write-through caching provides better data security compared to write-back caching, since the system assumes the data is available only after it has been safely written to the disk.

Apart from the configuration and sizing of parameters, performance of the I/O system also depends on the following:

- How the LUNs have been carved

- What type of RAID has been configured

- Whether the logical drives reside on the same array

- How the data spread across all the members of the array, including the number of drives being used as well as the size and speed of these devices or disks

All of these variables can have a great impact on the overall performance of the I/O subsystem.

ZFS DISK CACHE

ZFS (Zettabyte File System) guarantees that the data is written on disk before the write system call completes, even if write cache is enabled. When a synchronized write I/O operation is performed, the write transaction will be written to the ZFS intent log (ZIL) first. Once the transaction is saved to the ZIL on the physical disk platter (not on write cache), ZFS can replay the I/O, even if a sudden power outage happens before the data is updated to the file system. Therefore, even if write cache is enabled on disk, ZFS can guarantee the data is written by synchronized I/O in case of a power outage. However, if synchronized I/O is not enabled, the data will be written to disk several (or more) seconds after the write system call returns. In this case, an unexpected power failure may cause data loss.[5]

---

[5]MOS Note: 1122223.1 How ZFS Manages Write Cache on Disk.

Oracle Files and RAID

There are several types of RAID, each of which has its positives and negatives when it comes to its usage. Based on the type of data stored and retrieved, a specific type of RAID implementation is used. In this section, a few of the RAID implementations and their corresponding usage with respect to Oracle database files are discussed.

Different types of files in Oracle have different types of access behavioral patterns. TEMP tablespace/datafile is temporary; sort data that does not fit into the sort area of the buffer are written to this file for a temporary period of time and then flushed when the sort operation is completed. This means there are frequent writes and deletes. A datafile used by an OLTP database application has frequent small INSERT/DELETE/UPDATE operations compared to a datafile used for a data warehouse application. In a data warehouse the inserts are batch/bulk (large numbers of rows are inserted via a batch-load process) and seldom are there any updates or deletes. Figure 12-4 illustrates the various types of database files and the kinds of operations they do in the database.

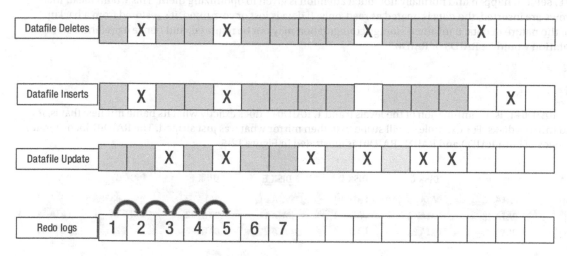

Figure 12-4. *Database file operation*

Datafiles

Figure 12-4 illustrates two different file types: datafile and redolog file. Datafile operations (INSERT/UPDATE/DELETE) indicated by X illustrate that the operations are random and occur at different locations of the physical file. Deleting data from the database could occur at different locations of the datafile, depending on the type of data being deleted and based on the business criteria (for example, an employee leaves the organization). Similarly, INSERT operations can also occur at different locations of the physical datafile. In Figure 12-4, when rows are deleted the space becomes available, and the DBWR process may decide to use that space for inserting a new row into an existing block if the space is sufficient, otherwise it would write to the end of the file, depending on the amount of contiguous space available. The third scenario illustrated for a datafile in Figure 12-4 is an UPDATE operation. In the case of updates, the row already exists at a specific location, but the values of certain columns are changed or populated. In certain cases, the row update may fit back into the same location provided if there is no significant row-length increase; that is, the column values don't change significantly or existing NULL columns have not been populated with data. Most of the time, depending on the how well the PCTFREE is sized, the existing space may be sufficient. However, if this is not the case the updated row may not fit back into the same location, and so part of the row would be moved into a different segment location, which causes either row movement or row chaining.

■ **Note** 70% (the default) of the space in the block is used to insert new rows. The remaining space is maintained for growth of existing rows.

When data is scattered at different locations and is retrieved from different locations, as in the case of the datafile illustrated in Figure 12-4, the storage subsystem would benefit if it were efficient enough to handle the widely distributed data. In such situations, RAID01 (Figure 12-5) or RAID10 (Figure 12-6) could be preferred storage solutions.

While database operations in an OLTP environment follow a pattern of random access, the pattern may be different in a data warehouse (DWH) operation. In the case of DWH, there are large inserts followed by reading in a larger number of rows (range retrieval). Other data manipulation language (DML) operations, such as UPDATE and DELETE, seldom happen and normally not much attention is given to optimizing them. This would mean that once the rows are inserted, the data is treated as read-only. If data is lost or corrupted, it's restored from a backup. Because of the nature of data, a mirrored storage configuration may not be required, and hence a preferred storage implementation would be RAID5 or RAID6.

RAID01

RAID01, or RAID0+1, is a combination of the levels 0 and 1. RAID0+1 does exactly what its name implies; that is, it stripes and mirrors disks. For example, it will stripe first, then mirror what was just striped. The RAID01 incorporates the advantages of both RAID0 and RAID1. RAID01 is illustrated in Figure 12-5.

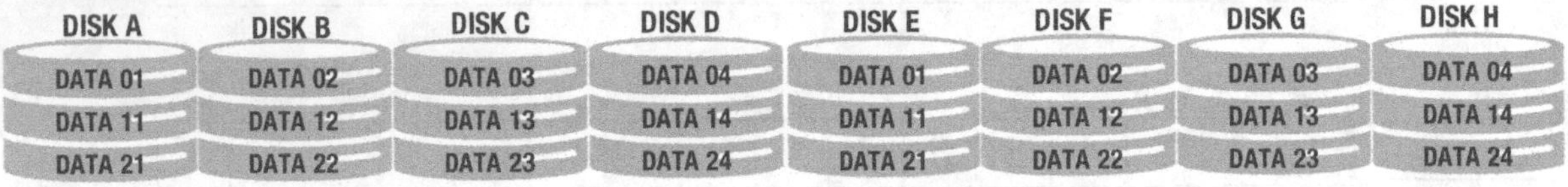

Figure 12-5. *RAID01*

Figure 12-5 illustrates a four-way striped, mirrored volume with eight disks (A–H). A given set of data in a file is split or striped across the disks (A–D) with the stripe first and then mirrored across disks (E–H, in this case). Due to the method by which these disks are grouped and striped, if one of the pieces becomes unavailable due to a disk failure, the entire mirror member becomes unavailable. This means the loss of an entire mirror reduces the I/O servicing capacity of the storage device by 50%.[6]

RAID 10

RAID1+0, or RAID10, is also a combination of RAID0 and RAID1. In RAID10, the disks are mirrored and then striped, i.e., mirror first then stripe what was mirrored. All the advantages (mirroring and striping) that apply to the RAID01 configuration apply to this RAID configuration as well. However, the organization of mirrored sets is different from the previous configuration.

In Figure 12-6, DATA 01 is mirrored on the adjoining disks (DISK A and DISK B) and DATA 02 is mirrored on the subsequent two disks (DISK C and DISK D). This illustration contains eight mirrored and striped disks. Unlike RAID01 (illustrated in Figure 12-5), the loss of one disk in a mirror member does not disable the entire mirrored volume, which means it does not reduce the I/O servicing capacity of the volume by 50%.

---

[6]HP OpenVMS Programming Concepts Manual, June 2002 http://h71000.www7.hp.com/doc/731final/5841/5841pro.html.

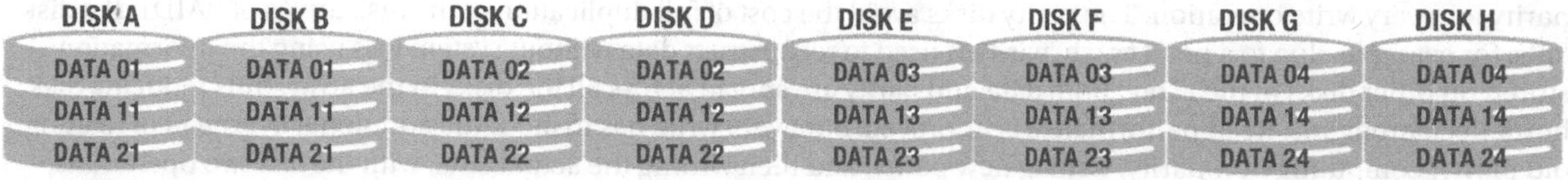

DISK A	DISK B	DISK C	DISK D	DISK E	DISK F	DISK G	DISK H
DATA 01	DATA 01	DATA 02	DATA 02	DATA 03	DATA 03	DATA 04	DATA 04
DATA 11	DATA 11	DATA 12	DATA 12	DATA 13	DATA 13	DATA 14	DATA 14
DATA 21	DATA 21	DATA 22	DATA 22	DATA 23	DATA 23	DATA 24	DATA 24

Figure 12-6. RAID10

■ **Note**   RAID configurations can be implemented at the software level or at the hardware level. Software-level RAIDs mean multiple writes at the same time. However, in the case of hardware-level RAIDs, writes happen to one of the mirrored volumes and are copied to the other mirrored volumes at the controller level.

RAID10 is the most common type of RAID solution deployed for Oracle databases. The mirroring feature of RAID that can be implemented at the hardware level, called a hardware RAID, is available with RAID10.

RAID5

Under RAID5, parity calculations provide data redundancy, and the parity is stored with the data. This means that the parity is distributed across the number of drives configured in the volume. (*Parity* is a term for error checking). Parity algorithms contain error correction code (ECC) capabilities, which calculate parity for a given stripe or chunk of data within a RAID volume. If a single drive fails, the RAID5 array can reconstruct that data from the parity information held on other disks.

Figure 12-7 illustrates the physical placement of stripes (DATA 01 through DATA 04) with their corresponding parities distributed across the five disks in the volume:

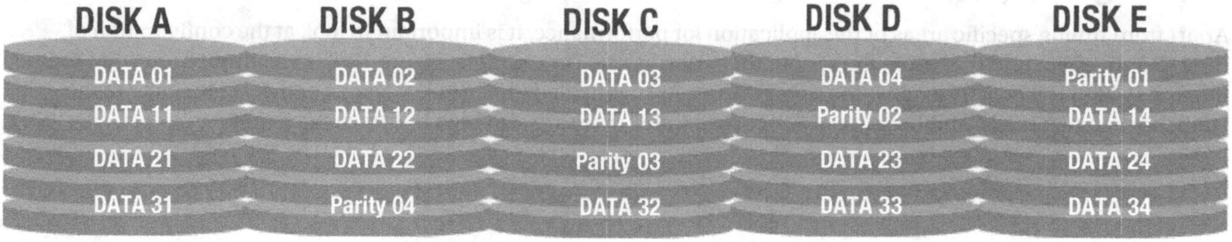

DISK A	DISK B	DISK C	DISK D	DISK E
DATA 01	DATA 02	DATA 03	DATA 04	Parity 01
DATA 11	DATA 12	DATA 13	Parity 02	DATA 14
DATA 21	DATA 22	Parity 03	DATA 23	DATA 24
DATA 31	Parity 04	DATA 32	DATA 33	DATA 34

Figure 12-7. RAID5

Figure 12-7 is a four-way striped RAID5 illustration of where data and parity are distributed.

RAID5 is not recommended for OLTP because of its extremely poor performance doing small writes at high concurrency levels. This is because the continuous processes of reading a stripe, calculating the new parity, and writing the stripe back to the disk (with new parity) make write-time significantly longer. RAID5 computes and writes parity for every write operation. The parity disks avoid the cost of full duplication of the disk drives of RAID1. If a disk fails, for example, due to a head crash, parity is used to reconstruct data without system loss using the information stored on other disks in the array. Both data and parity are spread across all the disks in the array, thus reducing disk bottleneck problems. Read performance is improved, but every write has to incur the additional overhead of reading old parity, computing new parity, writing new parity, and then writing the actual data, with the last two operations happening while two disk drives are locked.

Redolog Files

In the various discussions around datafiles, the operations performed on them are of a mixed-operations nature, as there are writes and reads from the datafiles. Redolog files write often and read rarely (for example, in case a recovery may be required). Since the type of operation is writing, no gains can be obtained by striping the storage array. Figure 12-4 illustrates that redolog rows are written sequentially, one after the other. Due to the sequential nature of writes, I/O is also sequential, so a RAID1 storage-array configuration would provide performance benefits for redolog implementation.

RAID1

RAID1 is known as mirroring and is used when all the writes issued to a given disk are duplicated to another disk. This provides a high-availability solution; if there is a failure of the first disk, the second disk or mirror can take over without any data loss. Apart from providing redundancy for data on the disks, mirroring also helps reduce read contention by directing reads to disks volumes that are less busy.

Similar to redolog files, backup sets generated by the recovery manager (RMAN) and archive logs generated during redolog switch activity are all mostly write configurations and are good candidates to be configured on RAID1.

Testing to Determine Performance

Apart from tuning specific areas of the application for performance, it is important to look at the configuration of the I/O subsystem and then tune the system for performance. For example, Figure 12-8 is an output from OEM that illustrates high I/O activity against the storage array. As highlighted, the primary type of activity at the time of the snapshot is direct reads, and because of direct-read waits, there are also high buffer-cache reads.

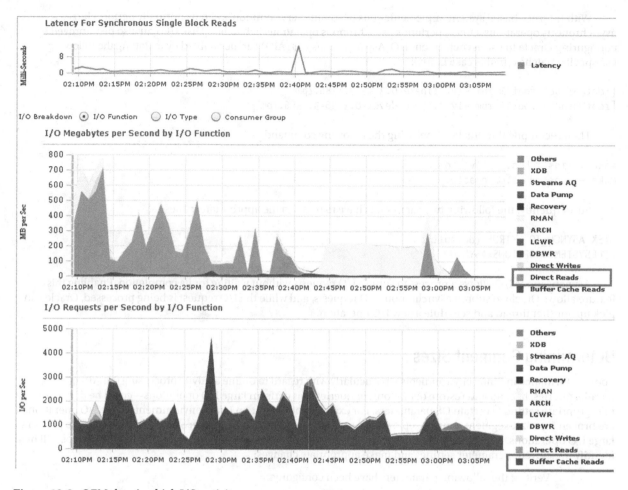

Figure 12-8. *OEM showing high I/O activity*

The storage system should be verified to ensure that all disks in the storage array are of high-performing (tier one) storage. While it may be difficult to have the entire storage array contain disks of the same performance characteristics, care should be taken to ensure that disks within a disk group have identical capacity and performance characteristics. A poor-performing disk in a disk group can create inconsistent I/O activity. When using Automatic Storage Management (ASM), performance characteristics of the individual disks within a diskgroup can be monitored using EM (see section "Enterprise Manager to Monitor Storage").

Types of I/O Operations

Depending on the measurements we are trying to capture and the statistics we are trying to analyze, I/O can be categorized as belonging to one of the following:

- Read vs. write
- Single-block vs. multi-block
- Random vs. sequential
- Synchronous vs. asynchronous

With Internet-based system implementations becoming very common, systems normally perform large, asynchronous operations. Oracle performs asynchronous operations in batches. Disk I/O can also be improved by configuring Oracle to use asynchronous I/O. Asynchronous I/O (AIO) can be enabled by installing the following OS-specific patches (in this case Linux):

```
[root@oradb3 root]$ rpm -ivf libaio-0.3.96-3.i386.rpm
[root@oradb3 root]$ rpm -ivf libaio-devel-0.3.96-3.i386.rpm
```

Then recompile the Oracle kernel using the following command:

```
make -f ins_rdbms.mk async_on
make -f ins_rdbms.mk oracle
```

Subsequently, the following two parameters have to be set to the appropriate values:

```
DISK_ASYNCH_IO = TRUE (default)
FILESYSTEMIO_OPTIONS=ASYNCH
```

Asynchronous I/O allows a process to submit I/O requests without waiting for its completion. Enabling this feature allows Oracle to submit asynchronous I/O requests, and while the I/O request is being processed, Oracle can pick up another thread and schedule a new I/O operation.

Determining Segment Sizes

Poor performance in Linux environments—particularly with regard to online analytic processing (OLAP) queries, parallel queries, backup and restore operations, or queries that perform large I/O operations—could be due to the inappropriate setting of certain OS parameters. For example, by default on Linux environments, large I/O operations are broken into 32K-segment chunks, separating system I/O operations into smaller sizes. To allow Oracle to perform large I/O operations, certain default values at the OS should be configured appropriately. The following steps will help identify the current parameter settings and make appropriate changes:

1. Verify if the following parameters have been configured:

```
# cat /proc/sys/fs/superbh-behavior
# cat /proc/sys/fs/aio-max-size
# cat /proc/sys/fs/aio-max-nr
# cat /proc/sys/fs/aio-nr
```

- **aio-max-size**. The aio-max-size parameter specifies the maximum block size that one single AIO write/read operation can do.

- **aio-nr** and **aio-max-nr**. aio-nr is the running total of the number of events specified on the io_setup system call for all currently active AIO contexts. If aio-nr reaches aio-max-nr, then io_setup will fail. aio-nr shows the current system-wide number of asynchronous I/O requests. aio-max-nr allows you to change the maximum value that aio-nr can increase to.

Increasing the value of the aio-max-size and aio_max_ns parameters to 1048576 and 56K, respectively, helps the performance of the ASM disks, because ASM performs I/O in 1MB-sized chunks.

2. Update the parameters by adding the following lines to /etc/sysctl.conf file:

```
fs.superbh-behavior = 2
fs.aio-max-size = 1048576
fs.aio-max-nr = 512
```

Setting these values in the sysctl.conf file will retain these kernel parameters across reboots. To change them dynamically on a running system, issue the following commands as user "root":

```
# echo 2 > /proc/sys/fs/superbh-behavior
# echo 1048576 > /proc/sys/fs/aio-max-size
# echo 512 > /proc/sys/fs/aio-max-nr
```

Disk Performance Characteristics

When configuring diskgroups or volume groups, care should be taken in identifying disks of the same performance characteristics. Such verification could be done using either the simple dd command or any disk calibration tool such as Orion.[7] For example:

```
dd bs=1048576 count=200 if=/dev/sdc of=/dev/null
```

This command will copy 200 blocks by reading one block at a time (up to a maximum of 1048576 bytes) from an input device and writing it to an output device. When testing disks for Oracle database, the block size should represent the Oracle block size times the value defined using the parameter MULTI_BLOCK_READ_COUNT to obtain optimal disk performance.

The following is the description of the various options used with the dd command:

- bs=bytes — reads that many bytes of data at a time
- count=blocks — copies number of blocks specified by the count parameter
- if=file — specifies the input file to read data from, for example a disk
- of=file — specifies the output device of file where the data will be written to

When testing disk performance characteristics, user concurrency should be considered from multiple nodes in an RAC environment. Running multiple dd commands could also simulate user concurrency. By using standard OS commands such as vmstat, the concurrency level could be increased gradually to determine the highest throughput rate and beyond, where there is a point of zero increase.

Oracle and I/O Characteristics

Oracle RDBMS has several data file types to store various kinds of data elements, such as table data, index data, redo data, and so forth, and uses several types of operations, such as INSERT, UPDATE, DELETE, and SELECT, to manipulate this data. Depending on the nature of the application, these operations can affect a very small or a very large amount of data. For example, in an OLTP application, normal operations are queries, which return only a single row and are efficiently satisfied by an index lookup.

---

[7]Starting with Oracle Database 11g Release 2, Orion is installed as part of the Grid Infrastructure installation.

In a data warehouse application, the operations are normally range retrievals and the data is normally retrieved through expensive scan operations. In both cases, based on the configuration, the data may be retrieved using Oracle's parallel query technology. In certain cases, this could be a complex operation in which multiple tables are joined, which is done after sorting the data in a specific order. When data is retrieved it could be possible that an appropriate index is available and Oracle performs index retrieval, but if the optimizer decides that a scan operation is more efficient, the process steps through all the rows in the table to retrieve the appropriate data.

Besides the DML operations and SELECT statements, Oracle's methods of operation when managing redo and undo are also different. For example, SQL operations involve different amounts of data, and DML operations generate a variable amount of redo (open-ended write) and undo, which will at some point be written to disk (redo to the online logs, undo to the undo tablespaces) or read from disk (undo for large, consistent reads).

Oracle databases have to support a wide range of data access operations, some of which are relatively simple, while others maybe complicated. The challenge for Oracle Corporation and Oracle DBAs is to establish a storage subsystem that is easy to manage yet capable of handling a wide range of data access requests.

The characteristics of an application are:

- I/O access patterns
- Variables affecting I/O performance

I/O Access Patterns

Business data needs to be persisted for future processing, needs to be able to be modified, and needs to be able to be removed from the database in many cases. Apart from modifications and deletions, data is queriered several times for analysis and processing. Methods of accessing this data could vary depending on the purpose for which it's retrieved. This section discusses various methods of data access.

Sequential Data Access

Sequential data access is typically observed in a data warehouse operation where data is retrieved using range-scan or full-table-scan operations. During such operations, physically contiguous blocks are retrieved, causing large I/O requests. Normally when there is contention for resources during sequential access, Oracle reflects this resource contention using the "db file scattered read" wait event.

- Synchronous scattered vector reads (corresponds to full-table scans)
- Asynchronous sequential reads (corresponds to direct-path reads). Direct-path reads are performed based on the DISK_ASYNC_IO parameter
- Synchronous sequential writes (corresponds to direct-path writes). Direct-path writes are performed based on the DISK_ASYNC_IO parameter
- Synchronous gather writes (corresponds to LGWR writes)
- Typically noticed in:
  - Data warehouses
  - Queries with table or index scans
  - Direct data loads
  - Backup, restore, and archiving

> ■ **Note**   In a database operation full-scan operations are treated as a direct-path read. A direct-path read is a physical I/O from a data file that bypasses the buffer cache and reads the data block directly into process-private memory. However, in environments that support asynchronous I/O, Oracle can submit I/O requests and continue processing. Oracle can then later pick up the results of the I/O request and wait on "direct-path read" until the required I/O completes.

Random Data Access

Random data access is typically observed in an OLTP environment or an environment that has high transaction-based workloads. In such environments, a smaller volume of data is retrieved from different locations of the I/O system, causing frequent movement of the disk headers. Appropriate tuning or optimization of objects using data partitioning, as well as creating appropriate data-retrieval indexes, could minimize contention in such environments. Oracle reports resource contention during such operations using a "db file sequential read" wait event.

- I/Os are the size of the database block, e.g., 8 KB

- Synchronous single reads (corresponds to single block or singleton select operations)

- Asynchronous non-contiguous writes, i.e., scattered in buffer and on disk (corresponds to DBWR writes)

- Typically noticed in OLTP databases

Variables Affecting I/O Performance

The basic variables that affect I/O performance are the I/O size, stripe size, stripe width, concurrency, and alignment.

- I/O size — the unit size in bytes of the single I/O operation; typically dictated by the block size and or the MULTI_BLOCK_READ_COUNT parameter value

- Stripe size — the size of an allocation unit on each disk device in an array unit. Each disk device will have the same stripe size. In an ASM environment, apart from the strip size defined at the LUN level, the graininess of the file (coarse grain or fine grain)

- Stripe width —the product of the stripe size and number of disks in that stripe array

- Concurrency — the number of distinct concurrent I/O operations against the disk array

> ■ **Note**   ASM supports two types of file-extent distributions: coarse and fine. In a coarse-grain distribution, each file extent is mapped to a single allocation unit. In the case of fine-grain distribution, each grain is interleaved 128K across groups of 8 AUs. Fine distribution breaks up large-sized I/O operations into multiple 128K I/O operations that can execute in parallel, which benefits sequential I/Os. Coarse- and fine-grain attributes are pre-defined as part of system templates for all system-related files; e.g., redo and archive log files are defined as fine grain, whereas datafiles are coarse.

Oracle-Supported Access Types

Starting with Oracle Database 11g Release 2, Oracle RAC supports two types of storage for database files:

- Clustered file system (CFS)
- Automatic Storage Management (ASM)

■ **Note** The ASM clustered file system is available as a shared storage solution; however, it's not supported for database files at this time.

Clustered File System

A file system is a hierarchical tree of directories containing files implemented on raw device partitions. In a file system, there is a cache buffer over the raw devices that optimizes the number of times the OS must access the disk. This releases the process that actually writes to disk, freeing the process to perform its next write-to-cache operation. Buffering helps retain data until such time as the buffer is full before performing a bulk write to the disk. This can have the effect of enhancing system performance.

System failures before writing the data from the cache can result in the loss of file system integrity. Additionally, the file system adds overhead to any operation that reads or writes data in direct accordance to its physical layout.

Clustered file systems (CFS), illustrated earlier in Figure 12-2, allow access from multiple hosts to the same file system data. This reduces the number of copies of the same data while distributing the load across those hosts going to the same data.

When an application operates against a file, that action brings into play various pieces of file system metadata that map a file to blocks of storage, which are typically accessed and managed using a file system cache.

CFS overcomes the administrative drawbacks of using a collection of raw devices and provides an easier storage management solution. Oracle supports several types of file systems; for example, Oracle clustered file system (OCFS), Veritas clustered file system (VCFS), Tru64 file system, and so on. These file systems have been popularly used on their respective supported platforms—for example, VCFS is used on Sun clusters and more recently on AIX platforms; OCFS is developed by Oracle Corporation and supports both the Windows and Linux environments.

Oracle also supports another file system maintaining the underlying ASM diskgroups—the ASM clustered file system (ACFS). ACFS is discussed later in this section.

Automatic Storage Management

Oracle Automatic Storage Management (ASM) is a combined volume manager and cluster-capable file system. Disks are allocated to ASM for management and control in the same way that a volume manager manages volumes. ASM is highly integrated with, and highly optimized for, Oracle Database. It has become the best-practice standard for Oracle Database storage.

Combining volume management functions with a file system (illustrated in Figure 12-9 Configuration type A) allows a level of integration and efficiency that would not otherwise be possible. For example, ASM is able to avoid the overhead associated with a conventional file system and achieve native raw disk performance for the files it supports.

ASM also supports the use of just a bunch of disks (JBOD) for the creation of a diskgroup. When individual disks are used, multiple disks are combined together to form a diskgroup, as illustrated in Figure 12-9 Configuration type B.

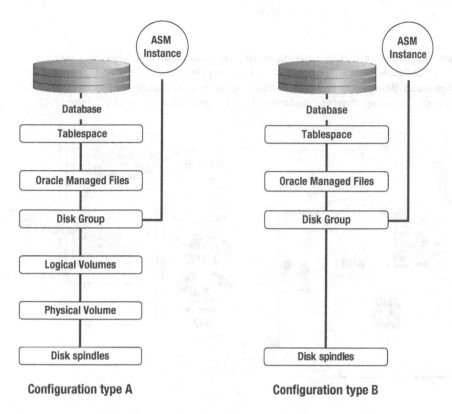

Figure 12-9. *ASM disk structure*

ASM Clustered File System

The ACFS architecture introduces a new ASM file type, known as a dynamic volume. A dynamic volume is essentially an ASM file that can be presented as a volume to a file system rather than as a data file to the Oracle database. The ASM Dynamic Volume Manager (ADVM), along with the associated device driver, provides the interface between dynamic volumes and the ACFS. You can even run other file systems, such as ext3, over an ASM dynamic volume.

The ADVM is an enabler of ACFS. It provides volume-management services and a standard disk device driver interface, thus enabling ACFS to utilize the space allocated to an ASM dynamic volume inside an ASM disk group. An ASM dynamic volume is a new type of ASM file that can be used to house a file system. Like other ASM files, an ASM volume file must be wholly contained within a diskgroup, and there can be many volume files in one diskgroup.

ASM dynamic volumes are created using SQL or by means of the ASMCMD command-line tool or the ASMCA graphical management tool. After a volume is created, it needs to be enabled in order to generate an operating system device node under /dev/asm. An ACFS is created over the ASM volume device. Alternatively, an ASM volume device can be used to support other file systems, such as ext3.

An ADVM driver maps I/O requests against an ASM volume device to the underlying dynamic volume file contained inside an ASM diskgroup.

ASM Architecture

ASM is the storage-management solution from Oracle. Like a database instance, ASM has an instance of its own. Starting with Oracle Database Version 12c Release 1, with the flex-ASM option, only three instances of ASM are required to support a multi-node RAC configuration. Being an instance itself, ASM also has a set of background and foreground processes. To understand how all the various components related to ASM work together, let us examine Figure 12-10.

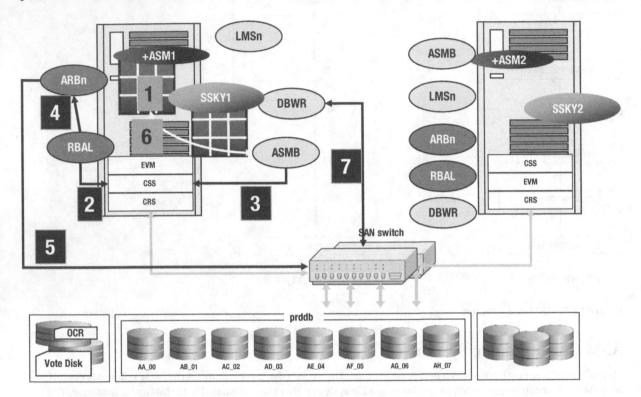

Figure 12-10. *ASM process flow*

1. When the diskgroup is created, the ASM instance loads this information into the SGA of the ASM instance; it is stored on each disk header within the diskgroup.

2. At the start of the ASM instance, the ASM Rebalance Master Process (RBAL) is a background process that will discover, open, and mount all ASM diskgroups on the respective nodes. After the diskgroup is mounted (on instance startup) ASM registers the diskgroup name, the instance name, and the corresponding Oracle Home path with Cluster Synchronization Service (CSS).

3. The ASM Background Process (ASMB) on the RDBMS instance will verify with the CSS if any diskgroups are assigned to it and then obtain the connect string to the ASM instance. During the RDBMS instance startup process, this information is used by the RDBMS instance to retrieve all diskgroup information from the ASM instance.

4. When a user adds a new disk to an existing diskgroup, the RBAL background process will create a map to reorganize the extents in the diskgroup. The RBAL process will then send a message to the ARBn background process to reorganize the extents. The number of ARBn background processes started is based on the parameter ASM_POWER_LIMIT.

5. The ARBn background process will perform datafile reorganization. The time taken to complete the reorganization is directly dependent on the number of ARBn processes started and, as discussed earlier, it depends on the value of the parameter ASM_POWER_LIMIT.

6. When the RDBMS instance opens a file or when a new file is created by the database administrator (DBA), the RDBMS instance interacts with the ASM instance as a client to obtain the file layout from the ASM instance. It then performs the following actions:[8]

    a. The DBA issues a statement to create a tablespace or add a datafile; the database requests ASM for file creation.

    b. An ASM foreground process creates a Continuing Operation Directory (COD) entry and allocates space for the new file across the diskgroup.

    c. The ASMB background process on the database instance receives an extent map for the new file from the ASM instance.

    d. The file is now open and the database process initializes the file.

7. After initialization, the database process requests that the file creation is committed. This causes the ASM foreground process to clear the COD entry and mark the file as created.

8. Acknowledgment of the file commit implicitly closes the file. The database instance will need to reopen the file for future I/O.

9. Based on user activity on the database instance, any updates to the data on the ASM devices are performed by the DBWR process on the RDBMS instance. Such activity is performed using the layout obtained by the RDBMS instance from the ASM instance (illustrated in Step 6 above).

Allocation Units

Within an ASM disk, space on a diskgroup is divided into allocation units (AU). The default AU size is one megabyte and can be set to a different value during diskgroup creation. However, once the diskgroup is created, changing the AU size would mean creating a new diskgroup with the new AU size and moving data from the existing diskgroup to the new diskgroup. Larger AU sizes may be useful in very large database (VLDB) scenarios or when using specialized storage hardware.

Space is allocated to ASM files in units known as file extents. The relationship between file extents and allocation units is as follows. An extent contains:

- One AU for each of the first 20,000 extents

- Four AUs for each of the next 20,000 extents

- 16 AUs for extents above 40,000

For the first 20,000 extents within a file, each extent contains one allocation unit. Extents are allocated on different disks in a round robin fashion in order to spread the file and distribute I/O during read/write operations. Beyond the first 20,000 extents, space is allocated in groups of eight extents at a time. Each extent contains four allocation units for the second 20,000 extents, or 16 allocation units for all extents beyond 40,000. Extents are still allocated on different disks to spread the file out, but, in addition, each allocation unit is written in turn to a different extent until each set of eight extents is filled. The result is that consecutive allocation units will always be in different extents.

---

[8]*Oracle Automatic Storage Management – Under-the-Hood & Practical Deployment Guide* – Nitin Vengurlekar, Murali Vallath, Rich Long., Oracle Press, 2008.

The following query output gives the total extents across various diskgroups from the ASM instance:

```
SQL> SELECT group_kfdat          dg#,
            COUNT(number_kfdat) "# of AU's"
     FROM   x$kfdat
     GROUP  BY group_kfdat;

       DG#   # of AU's
     ---------- ----------
         1     4945920
         2      133504
         3        5376
         4      617792
         5      824320
```

ASM keeps track of a file's layout with metadata called an extent map. An extent map is a name-value-pair table that maps file extents to AUs on disk. Extent maps are primarily used by database instances to map the location of data on disk.

The following query will help determine the total number of AUs allocated and how many free AUs are available:

```
SELECT group_kfdat               group#,
       number_kfdat              disk#,
       decode(v_kfdat, 'V', 'Used',
                      'Free') "Used",
       COUNT(*)                  "# of AUs"
FROM   x$kfdat
GROUP  BY group_kfdat,
          number_kfdat,
          v_kfdat
ORDER  BY group_kfdat,
          number_kfdat,
          v_kfdat;

   GROUP#     DISK# Used         # of AUs
  ---------- ---------- ------------ ----------
          3          0 Free           616469
          3          0 Used             1323
          4          0 Free             4491
          4          0 Used              885
          5          0 Free            73318
          5          0 Used            29722
          5          1 Free            73317
          5          1 Used            29723
          5          2 Free            73313
          5          2 Used            29727
          5          3 Free            73317
          5          3 Used            29723
          5          4 Free            73314
          5          4 Used            29726
          5          5 Free            73318
```

5	5 Used	29722
5	6 Free	73311
5	6 Used	29729
5	7 Free	73317
5	7 Used	29723

How Many Diskgroups?

Quite often these question are asked: How many disks are required for an RAC database? What is the best practice for creating diskgroups? While the best practice is to isolate the clusterware data and real data from recoverable data and backup files, there are no fixed rules for how many diskgroups are ideal.

The number of diskgroups should depend on the type of implementation, the criticality of the data, and the storage performance characteristics. For a small database with less I/O activity, the configuration could consist of three diskgroups:

- GRID_DATA — to store OCR and voting disk

- SSKY_DATA — to store database files

- SSKY_FRA — to have the multiplex copies of redolog files and fast recovery area files

For a more critical database with high I/O, and when the decision to keep redolog files on RAID1 compared to the other files, it would be good practice to have five diskgroups:

- GRID_DATA — to store OCR and voting files

- SSKY_DATA — to store database data files

- SSKY_REDO1 — to have the redolog files

- SSKY_REDO2 — to multiplex the redolog files

- SSKY_FRA — to store backup sets, fast recovery area files, and so on

In the above configuration, SSKY_REDO1, SSKY_REDO2, and SSKY_FRA will be on RAID1. GRID_DATA and SSKY_DATA could be RAID10/RAID01 or RAID5 disk arrays.

Monitoring ASM

In an earlier section we discussed how an ASM instance and an RDBMS instance would communicate to complete specific steps during instance startup. During this process of communication, and during the various administrative functions performed by ASM on the diskgroups, ASM would require resources. As in a RDBMS instance, in spite of ASM being a lightweight instance, it also contains an SGA. Similar to an RAC environment, ASM instances also have cache fusion activity over the interconnect. For example, the default SGA is:

```
SQL> show sga
Total System Global Area 283930624 bytes
Fixed Size                  2212656 bytes
Variable Size             256552144 bytes
ASM Cache                  25165824 bytes
SQL>
```

The SGA is broken into the shared pool, large pool, and shared pool reserved sizes. Default values for these parameters are:

```
NAME                                 TYPE           VALUE
------------------------------------ -----------    ------------
large_pool_size                      big integer    12M
max_dump_file_size                   string         unlimited
sga_max_size                         big integer    272M
shared_pool_reserved_size            big integer    9646899
shared_pool_size                     big integer    0
sort_area_size                       integer        65536
workarea_size_policy                 string         AUTO
memory_max_target                    big integer    272M
memory_target                        big integer    272M
sga_target                           big integer    0
```

By default the SGA for the ASM instance is sized very small. In the majority of these situations, the default SGA size is sufficient. However, when the application performs high I/O activity or when the ASM instance supports more than six clients, adding additional resources to the ASM instance may be required to improve performance. For example, increasing the LARGE_POOL_SIZE of the ASM instance helps in the communications between ASM and its clients:

```
SELECT  p.number_kfdpartner,
        d.failgroup
FROM    x$kfdpartner p,
        v$asm_disk d
WHERE   p.disk = 0
        AND p.grp = 1
        AND p.grp = group_number
        AND p.number_kfdpartner = d.disk_number;
```

Data Dictionary Views to Monitor Storage

Oracle's method of providing visibility for the underlying metadata of the various features and database functionality is to provide database views. ASM is no exception. In this section, two of the important views related to performance are discussed.

V$ASM_OPERATION

In everyday business activity, additional storage space is required to persist data and to find additional storage space; more disks need to be added to the existing diskgroups. One of the features of ASM is to balance I/O among all disks in the diskgroup. This is possible because of the way ASM distributes data across the underlying disks in a diskgroup. When disks are added or removed from an existing diskgroup, data is rebalanced or distributed across all the disks equally. The V$ASM_OPERATION view helps monitor the rebalance operation.

While the redistribution of data across the available disks is an excellent feature, it's not without additional overhead. The number of RAC instances impacts the diskgroup rebalance operation scalability. The speed of the rebalance operation can be improved by increasing the number of ARBx processes with the init.ora parameter ASM_POWER_LIMIT or with the POWER clause. Valid values for the ASM_POWER_LIMIT parameter and the POWER clause are 1-11. Due to the global cache inter-instance activity and the coordination required for rebalancing, additional RAC instances could cause a linear degradation in performance. One of the methods to force a quicker rebalance operation is to dismount the diskgroup and mount the group in restricted mode; however, this would potentially cause the database to be unable to access disks, thus causing outage. Like most features, a correct balance between the number of processes and time is required in order to manage resources and allow business to continue without downtime.

V$IOSTAT_FILE

This view displays information regarding the disk I/O statistics of database files. Statistics are listed for each data file and temp file; however, for other types of files, such as archive logs and backup sets, statistics are consolidated into one entry. The output illustrates that the operations have been small, quick-read options, indicated by the small_read_megabytes column, with multi-block reads indicated by the large_read_megabytes column. The last column, large_read_servicetime, lists the service time for multi-block read requests.

Script: MVRACPDnTap_iostat.sql

```
SELECT file_no,
       filetype_name,
       small_read_megabytes,
       large_read_megabytes,
       large_read_servicetime
FROM   v$iostat_file;
```

File #	File Type	Small Read (Megabytes)	Large Read (Megabytes)	Large Read Service Time
0	Other	35	2349	44279
0	Control File	20219	284	2822
0	Log File	1	42546	0
0	Archive Log	0	27962	184702
0	Data File Backup	0	0	0
0	Data File Incrementa	0	0	0
0	Archive Log Backup	0	0	0
0	Data File Copy	0	0	0
0	Flashback Log	0	0	0
0	Data Pump Dump File	0	0	0
1	Data File	144	275	3606
1	Temp File	388	364	0
2	Data File	287	3	154
2	Temp File	3271	2884	95
3	Data File	0	0	0
3	Temp File	2969	3102	40
4	Data File	3	0	0
4	Temp File	973	2089	15
5	Data File	0	0	0
5	Temp File	1091	1020	104
6	Temp File	540	1690	62
7	Temp File	1118	1574	107
8	Temp File	1130	1068	14
9	Temp File	549	1207	43

Figure 12-11 illustrates performance statistics for this view through OEM. Historical I/O statistics from this view are captured in three separate views:

- DBA_HIST_IOSTAT_DETAIL — This view displays I/O statistics aggregated by combination of file type and function.

- DBA_HIST_IOSTAT_FILETYPE — This view displays I/O statistics by file type. Statistics from file types like flashback log, control file, temp file, data file, and so on are contained in this view.

- DBA_HIST_IOSTAT_FUNCTION — This view displays I/O statistics by function. Statistics from functions like Recovery, Buffer Cache Reads, RMAN, Data Pump, LGWR, DBWR, and so forth are contained in this view.

Member Disks	Average Response Time (ms)	Average Throughput (MB per second)	Total I/O Calls	Reads Total	Hot	Cold	Errors	Writes Total	Hot	Cold	Errors
Disk Group - OBIPRD_DATA	35.56	5.86	2975635414	2548525491	0	2548469635	0	427109923	0	426476024	0
ASM_EPA_CL1024	36.25	5.84	183975238	156791199	0	156789031	0	27184039	0	26468639	0
ASM_EPB_CL1036	36.62	5.86	182367093	156152562	0	156149758	0	26214531	0	26236232	0
ASM_EPC_CL1048	36.12	5.86	181978906	156018995	0	155990884	0	25959911	0	25980574	0
ASM_EPD_CL105A	35.85	5.81	181830386	155415922	0	155415157	0	26414464	0	26415675	0
ASM_EPE_CL1524	36.74	5.83	181515965	155572328	0	155569419	0	25943637	0	25943442	0
ASM_EPF_CL1536	36.76	5.84	182329712	156069531	0	156067303	0	26260181	0	26259756	0
ASM_EPG_CL1548	35.92	5.81	181232451	155138256	0	155136188	0	26094195	0	26094303	0
ASM_EPH_CL155A	36.1	5.79	181575126	155442657	0	155440311	0	26132469	0	26152346	0
ASM_EPI_CL0A7E	36.42	5.81	180972237	155042030	0	155040403	0	25930207	0	25931218	0
ASM_EPJ_CL0A90	36.01	5.81	181278437	155192385	0	155190193	0	26086052	0	26084771	0
ASM_EPK_CL0AA2	36.5	5.83	182936978	156507706	0	156505835	0	26429272	0	26429598	0
ASM_EPL_CL0AB4	36.83	5.83	181601316	155065394	0	155063486	0	26535922	0	26535604	0
ASM_EPM_CL0C24	35.55	5.85	182139804	156170775	0	156172821	0	25969029	0	25967981	0
ASM_EPN_CL0C36	36.27	5.8	181421469	155112732	0	155109894	0	26308737	0	26308293	0
ASM_EPO_CL0C48	33.2	5.95	200841389	171678551	0	171676623	0	29162838	0	29162164	0
ASM_EPP_CL0C5A	29.51	6.18	227638907	197154468	0	197152329	0	30484439	0	30505428	0

Figure 12-11. *OEM – I/O statistics for all disks in the diskgroup*

Enterprise Manager to Monitor Storage

Enterprise Manager is a good way to look at the performance of disks and diskgroups in ASM. Once the ASM targets are discovered, OEM provides performance charts at the diskgroup level; those charts can be drilled down to the disk level. Figure 12-12 displays I/O performance statistics for the various diskgroups used by ASM-supported databases (clients) on the server.

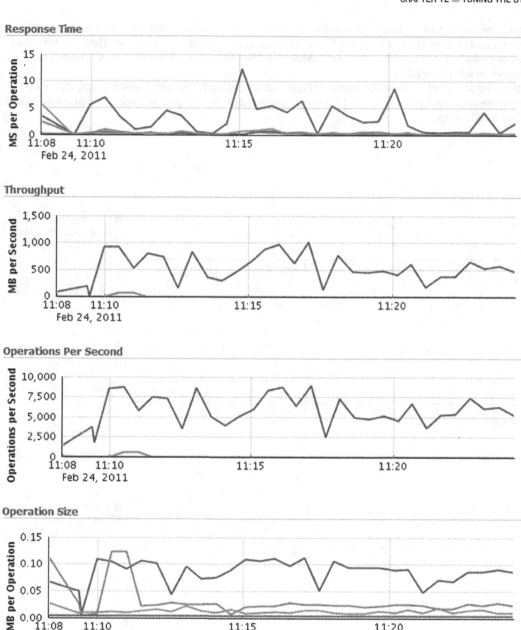

Figure 12-12. OEM – Diskgroup-level performance statistics

In Figure 12-12, the response-time chart displays I/O responses in milliseconds per operation. The throughput chart, which is the second chart in Figure 12-12, displays I/O throughput in megabits per second. There are two other charts: operations per second list the number of I/O operations performed by second and the operation size chart graphs the I/O operation size in megabits.

Similar to the diskgroup-level statistics illustrated in Figure 12-12 and the I/O statistics displayed in Figure 12-11, statistics can also be viewed from OEM. Figure 12-13 shows response time, throughput, and operation-size statistics at the disk level within a diskgroup.

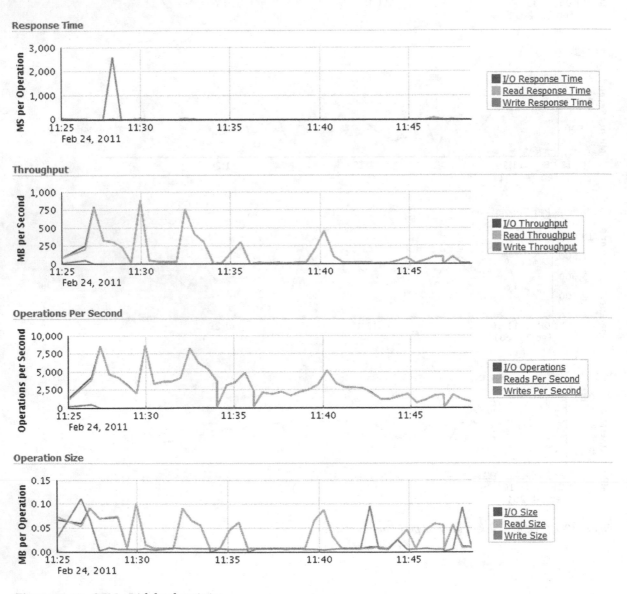

Figure 12-13. *OEM – Disk-level statistics*

Conclusion

In this chapter we discussed some basics about disk management and optimizing storage for high-end computing. We discussed RAID types and the corresponding database files that are suitable to be stored on them. You should take away the fact that most of the performance optimization for ASM should be completed during the disk selection and configuration process and during RAP testing. ASM is a high-performing storage-management solution. Using correct configurations and best practices will provide optimal I/O performance.

CHAPTER 13

■ ■ ■

Tuning Global Cache

Real Application Cluster (RAC) can be considered as an extension to the single instance configuration. As a concept, this is true, because RAC is a composition of several instances of Oracle. However, there are quite a few differences in the management of these components, the additional background process, the additional files, and the sharing of resources between instances, not to mention the additional layered components present at the operating system level to support a clustered hardware environment. All of these additional components in a RAC system make it different from a single-instance configuration. It is also in a RAC configuration that the real difference between a database and an instance is noticed. Although this difference does exist in a regular single-instance configuration, this is seldom noticed because the database and an instance are not distinguished from each other as they are in a RAC configuration (e.g., in a single-instance configuration, the instance and the database are identified by the same name).

When multiple instances access the same database, data retrieved by the user sessions on the various instances are maintained in the local instance. Subsequently, if another user in another instance requires the same data, the data is transferred over the interconnect to the requesting instance through "Cache Fusion," that is, provided the data has not been modified or the data has not been flushed out of the local cache buffer: when data is pushed out of the buffer cache due to cache replacement and the data is re-read from disk, or if cached in another RAC instance, read via the private interconnect. When data is transferred from one instance to the other, the sending instance sends copies of the blocks to the requesting instance. Depending on whether the request is for write or read and on internal policies of Cache Fusion, the sending instance changes the status of the locally cached data and may retain a current or past version of the data in its buffer cache before sending. This means multiple instances can potentially have the same blocks of data, or versions of the same data at different times (i.e., current as of a certain SCN) Whereas regular instance management rules apply to data copies within the instance, data access and data sharing across instances needs to be managed from a global level across the cluster within the boundaries of server pools and across one or more instances through the use of database services. Modifications to data need to be globally consistent and guarantee coherence. The global cache and Cache Fusion implements a state machine via message passing to guarantee global cache coherence. Cache Fusion does not use locks in the traditional sense; it maintains and passes state via messages.

Global Cache

When reading or modifying data across instances, it's all about locating the data blocks, making a request to the object master, and allowing the data to be transferred from the holding instance to the requesting instance. These services are performed by two processes: global cache service (GCS) and global enqueue services (GES).

When a user session requires a data block to satisfy its operation, the GCS uses the global resource directory (GRD) to look up the whether the data is located in the cache of another instance or on disk and requests the desired read or write access to the block. The GCS processes are using the GRD to maintain the status of each object and each cached block on the respective instances. Contents of the GRD are distributed across all the active instances, and its entries require a small amount of memory per buffer, which effectively increases the memory requirements for the buffer cache of an Oracle RAC instance by a small percentage. Cache Fusion (illustrated in Figure 13-1) moves current and consistent data buffers from an instance that contains the block to other instances. This saves an I/O operation to re-read the blocks from disk and is faster than a disk access. When a consistent image of the block is needed or a changed block is required on another instance, Cache Fusion transfers the block image directly between the affected instances using the private interconnect.

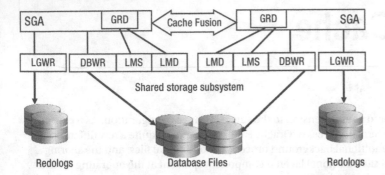

Figure 13-1. *Cache Fusion*

The GCS processes on each node manage the cache synchronization by using cluster interconnect. RAC addresses correct transactional concurrency between instances. The different scenarios of block sharing are broadly stated as the following:

- *Concurrent reads on multiple nodes:* This occurs when two or more instances participating in the clustered configuration are required to read the same data block. The block is shared between instances via the cluster interconnect. Initially, the first instance that reads the block from disk and the subsequent instances that require access to the same block will request it via the cluster interconnect. Access rights and ownership of the block are transferred with the data.

- *Concurrent reads and writes on different nodes:* This is a mixture of read/write operations on data. A data block available on any of the participating instances could be modified by multiple instances, whereas the version of the data block in the physical database may be an earlier copy until such time that the DBWR on one of the instances decides to write the block to database. Transactions where blocks are requested from another instance either for a read or for a write operation use the interconnect. A block can be read as is, that is, in a current version, or a read consistent version could be built by applying undo.

- *Concurrent writes on different nodes:* This is a situation where multiple instances make requests for modification to the same data block frequently. In these two situations where modifications are involved, global consistency of data blocks are maintained by assigning access modes and versioning.

RAC Specific Background Processes

A RAC system comprises two or more nodes (instances) accessing a common shared database (i.e., one database is mounted and open by multiple instances concurrently). In this case, each instance will have all the background process used in a stand-alone configuration plus the additional background processes required specifically for RAC.

Each instance has its own SGA, several background processes, and each instance runs on a separate machine in the cluster having its own CPU and physical memory. Keeping the configurations identical across all nodes in the cluster would be beneficial for easy maintenance and load balancing. In the following sections, we discuss the various RAC related background processes.

LMSn

The Global cache service' is multithreaded and includes block server processes (LMS*n*) that copy data blocks directly from the holding instance's buffer cache to the foreground process on the requesting instance. The LMS processes produce read consistent copies (versions) for any blocks that are being requested for consistent read by the remote instance. They maintain the global state of each buffer in the global cache. The initial number of LMS*n* processes is driven by the parameter GCS_SERVER_PROCESSES.

The number of LMS processes (Table 13-1) to allocate to an instance is based on the number of CPUs on the server and is driven by the following algorithm:

> If the server has between 1 to 3 CPUs, Oracle sets this parameter to value 1; and if the server has between 4 to 15 CPUs, Oracle sets this parameter to value 2.

Table 13-1. *LMS Processes*[1]

Oracle RAC 10g (10.2.0.4)		Oracle RAC 11g and 12c	
# of CPUs	# of LMS	# of CPUs	# of LMS
<= 2	1	<= 4	1
<= 12	2	<= 16	2
>= 12	#cpu/4	>= 16	#cpu/4
		Additional LMS for every 32 CPUs	

However, the method of calculating the value for this parameter changes when the number of CPUs is more than 16. The value is computed using the formula 2 + (CPUs/32). If the result includes a fraction, then the fraction is disregarded. That is, if you had 20 CPUs, then 2 + (20/32) would equal 2 LMS processes. A more specific example, on a ProLiant DL370 G6 server with 16 cores (2 physical × 8 core), the number of LMS processes will be 2 + 16/32 = 2.5. Because the fraction part of this value is ignored, the value is set to 2.

In an ASM instance (clustered environment), where the Cache Fusion activity is confined to the transfer of metadata information when disks are added or removed, the value of this parameter is set to 1.

Prior to Oracle Database 11g Release 2, the value of this parameter was also based on the number of CPUs; however, Oracle used a standard formula of allocating and starting one LMS process for every pair of CPUs. For example, for the ProLiant DL370 G6 server with 16 cores, Oracle will set the value of this parameter to 4 (4 LMS processes).

Oracle supports up to 36 LMS processes (0–9 and a–z).

LMON

The global enqueue service monitor (LMON) is a background process that monitors the state and health of the RDBMS instances in the cluster. It communicates with the cluster monitor and initiates reconfiguration when the state of a node or instance changes. When a node joins or leaves the cluster, it coordinates the reconfiguration of locks and resources. In particular, LMON performs reconfiguration of GES and GCS resources.

---

[1]Source: Oracle Corporation.

LMD*n*

The global enqueue service deamon (LMD*n*) is a background process that manages enqueue requests. It processes incoming enqueue message requests and controls access to global enqueues. The LMD process also handles global deadlock detection and remote resource requests (remote resource requests are requests originating from another instance). Examples of enqueues encountered in a RAC environment are the following:

- TX—Transaction lock: will be acquired for the following reasons:

  - When a row is locked. TX Transaction lock is acquired when a transaction initiates its first change and is held until the transaction does a COMMIT or ROLLBACK. It is used mainly as a queuing mechanism so that other sessions can wait for the transaction to complete.

  - Every transaction that needs to modify a block requires a slot in the ITL (interested transaction list) of the block. If there are no slots in the ITL of the block, then the requesting session will wait on one of the active transaction locks.

- IS—Instance State: can be encountered during enqueue operations to synchronize instances.

LCK0

The lock process (LCK0) manages global requests for the row cache and library cache and is responsible for cross-instance broadcasts. Its major use is for the row cache and library cache and for some cross-instance calls (which are basically remote function invocations on all instances in the cluster). With LMD and LCK, the responsibility for global enqueues is shared between the two. None of them is managing the buffer cache. This handles all requests for resources other than data blocks.

LMHB

Global Cache/Enqueue Service Heartbeat Monitor (LMHB) was introduced in Oracle Database 11g Release 2 and monitors the heartbeat of LMON, LMD, and LMS*n* processes to ensure they are running normally without blocking or spinning.

ACMS

Atomic Control File to Memory Service (ACMS) introduced in Oracle Database 11g Release 2 is an agent that contributes to ensuring distributed SGA memory updates. It is globally committed across SGAs on success or globally aborted/rolled back if a failure occurs. This coordinates consistent updates to a control file resource with its SGA counterpart on all instances in an Oracle RAC environment.

The ACMS process works with a coordinating caller to ensure that an operation is executed on every instance in Oracle RAC despite failures. ACMS is the process in which a distributed operation is called. As a result, this process can exhibit a variety of behaviors. In general, ACMS is limited to small, non-blocking state changes for a limited set of cross-instance operations.

RMS*n*

Oracle RAC Management Processes (RMS*n*) introduced in Oracle Database 11g Release 2 performs manageability tasks for RAC tasks accomplished by an RMS*n* process when instances are added to the cluster.

RSMN

Remote Slave Monitor (RSMN) introduced in Oracle Database 11g Release 2 manages background slave process creation and communication on remote instances. This background process manages the creation of slave processes and the communication with their coordinators and peers. These background slave processes perform tasks on behalf of a coordinating process running in another cluster instance.

PING

Interconnect Latency Measurement Process (PING) assesses the latencies associated with any two instances in the cluster. Every few seconds, the process in one instance sends two messages to the target instance. One message is of size 500 bytes and the second message if of size 8KB. Once the message is received by the target instance, it's acknowledged indicating the health of the interconnect.

IPC0

IPC service background process (IPC0) is a new background process introduced in Oracle Database 12c Release 1. It handles very high rates of incoming connect requests as well as completing reconfigurations to support basic messaging and RDMA (remote direct memory access) primitives over several transports such as UDP (User Datagram Protocol), RDS (Reliable Datagram Sockets), Infiniband, and RC (reliable connection).

LDDn

Global Enqueue Service Daemon Helper Slave (LDDn) introduced in Oracle Database 12c Release 1, are slave processes spawned on demand by the LMDn process. These slaves help perform certain tasks when certain workloads start creating performance bottlenecks.

Resource Availability

To manage the request for data blocks, Oracle needs buffers in its memory where requests and locks related to these requests could be maintained. Such resources are global cache resources and maintained in the SGA of every instance in the cluster. Figure 13-2 illustrates both global cache and global enqueue resource buffers maintained in the shared pool and SGA.

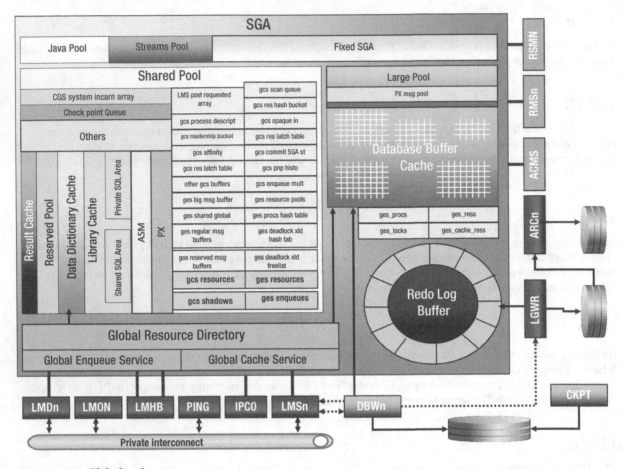

Figure 13-2. *Global cache*

■ **Note**   Figure 13-2 does not illustrate all of the global cache and global enqueue buffers; those that could not be illustrated have been grouped under the `other gcs buffers` category.

Resources available on any machine or to an Oracle instance are limited, meaning resources are not available in abundance and that if a process on the system would need them, they may not be immediately available. There is a physical limit on the amount of resources available on any system. For example, the processor resources is limited by the number of CPUs available on the system; the amount of memory or cache area is limited by the amount of physical memory available on the system and its availability depends on how busy the system is. Now for an Oracle process, this is further limited by the actual amount of memory allocated to the SGA. Within the SGA, the shared pool, the buffer cache, and so forth, are again preallocated from the total SGA (defined by the SGA_TARGET_SIZE parameter). These are memory allocations used by a regular single-instance configuration.

In a RAC environment, there are no parameters to allocate any global-specific resources such as global cache size or global shared pool area. Oracle allocates a certain portion of the available resources from the shared pool or SGA for global activity. The availability of global resources can be monitored using the view GV$RESOURCE_LIMIT. For example, the workshop in the next section illustrates a small example on how the global cache section can be monitored.

RAC memory resource usage of the shared pool can be monitored by querying the V$SGASTAT view for GCS, GES, and KCL (kernel cache layer) related entries. Similarly, the current and maximum number of GCS resources/shadows (resource names gcs_resources and gcs_shadows) and GES resources/enqueues (resource names ges_ress and ges_locks) can be obtained by querying the V$RESOURCE_LIMIT views. In case there is a shortage of memory for the GCS/GES related components, Oracle will dynamically allocate memory from the free memory pool in the shared pool. It is recommended to carefully calculate the resources and enqueues as needed because dynamic memory allocation from the shared pool is an expensive operation.

```
SQL> oradebug setmypid
        SQL> oradebug call kjcsdmp
```

Workshop

In this workshop, we try to understand the sizing of the resources and state objects used by the GCS and GES in the SGA.

Step 1

The following query generates the output showing the current utilization of global resources:

Script: MVRACPDnTap_reslimit.sql

```
SELECT inst_id              INT,
       resource_name,
       current_utilization CU,
       max_utilization      MU,
       initial_allocation   IA,
       limit_value          LV
FROM   gv$resource_limit
WHERE  max_utilization > 0
       AND resource_name LIKE 'g%'
ORDER  BY inst_id,
          resource_name
```

```
/
INT RESOURCE_NAME             CU         MU         IA         LV
---- -------------------- ---------- ---------- ---------- ----------
   4 gcs_resources           267451     902764    2933330    2933330
     gcs_shadows             370593    1201829    2933330    2933330
     ges_big_msgs                15        177       1730  UNLIMITED
     ges_cache_ress            1935      10779          0  UNLIMITED
     ges_locks               117376     122591      30568  UNLIMITED
     ges_procs                   52        250        507        507
     ges_reg_msgs               112        423       1730  UNLIMITED
     ges_ress                207337     214851      23093  UNLIMITED
     ges_rsv_msgs                 0          2       1000       1000

   5 gcs_resources           733332    1225463     733332     733332
     gcs_shadows             666100    1108372     733332     733332
     ges_big_msgs                19        665       1730  UNLIMITED
     ges_cache_ress           65694      66002          0  UNLIMITED
     ges_locks               116840     122653      30568  UNLIMITED
     ges_procs                   50        361        507        507
     ges_reg_msgs               112       2327       1730  UNLIMITED
     ges_ress                290784     296283      23093  UNLIMITED
     ges_rsv_msgs                 0          1       1000       1000

   6 gcs_resources           434030    1539482    3666663    3666663
     gcs_shadows             412483    1465106    3666663    3666663
     ges_big_msgs                19       1136       1730  UNLIMITED
     ges_cache_ress           48859      49008          0  UNLIMITED
     ges_locks               162986     167576      30568  UNLIMITED
     ges_procs                   57        275        507        507
     ges_reg_msgs               148       2933       1730  UNLIMITED
     ges_ress                211414     292337      23093  UNLIMITED
     ges_rsv_msgs                 0          1       1000       1000

   8 gcs_resources           346997    1154116    3666663    3666663
     gcs_shadows             428505    1504463    3666663    3666663
     ges_big_msgs                21        558       1730  UNLIMITED
     ges_cache_ress           1935      14602          0  UNLIMITED
     ges_locks               178960     183777      30568  UNLIMITED
     ges_procs                   75        337        507        507
     ges_reg_msgs               123        475       1730  UNLIMITED
     ges_ress                208104     276539      23093  UNLIMITED
     ges_rsv_msgs                 0          2       1000       1000
```

Step 2

Instance 5 could be low on global resources; the MU (MAXIMUM_UTILIZATION) has increased and is significantly high (1225463), whereas the IA (INITIAL_ALLOCATION) and the CU (CURRENT_UTILIZATION) are identical and low, indicating at times instance 5 was low on shared pool resources or there was significant utilization of global resources.

The memory allocated for GES resources and communications buffers is part of the SGA and shared pool. It is not used by the library cache and also cannot be configured via the server parameter file.

Step 3

As discussed earlier, most of the shared pool related resources, specifically those showing high resource sizes, are part of the shared pool. It's in the best interest to check the shared pool utilization for instance 5. Shared pool for all instances has been set to a size of 20G.

```
SQL> SELECT inst_id,
        NAME,
        VALUE
FROM    gv$parameter
WHERE   NAME LIKE 'shared_pool_size%'
ORDER   BY inst_id;

   INST_ID NAME                             VALUE
---------- -------------------------------- --------------
         1 shared_pool_size                 21474836480
         2 shared_pool_size                 21474836480
         3 shared_pool_size                 21474836480
         4 shared_pool_size                 21474836480
         5 shared_pool_size                 21474836480
         6 shared_pool_size                 21474836480
         7 shared_pool_size                 21474836480
         8 shared_pool_size                 21474836480

8 rows selected.
```

Step 4

Further investigation of the instances indicated that automatic memory management has been enabled. This would mean that the 20G allocated to the shared pool is just a startup value and should grow or shrink based on demand.

```
SQL> show parameter sga_

NAME                                         TYPE        VALUE
------------------------------------------   ----------- ----------
sga_max_size                                 big integer 70G
sga_target                                   big integer 0
```

Step 5

Checking the GV$SHARED_POOL_ADVICE indicated that the server is low on the shared pool. Based on the frequent need for a higher shared pool, increasing the start value to 30G provided improved performances.

The chain effect of having a low-shared pool size can also be causing issues with performance of SQL statements. If the SGA or shared pool needs to grow or shrink, it could result in library cache invalidation, reparses, and therefore a slowdown in SQL execution.

■ **Note**   The rule should be, when the MAX_UTILIZATION (MU) gets close to the LIMIT_VALUE (LV) or the INITIAL_ALLOCATION (IA) and remains the same at this value for a considerable amount of time, consider increasing the SHARED_POOL.

Script Name: MVRACPDnTap_sharedpooladvice.sql

```
SELECT inst_id INT, SHARED_POOL_SIZE_FOR_ESTIMATE "SP SIZE ESTD",
       SHARED_POOL_SIZE_FACTOR "SP SIZE FCTR",
       ESTD_LC_SIZE "ESTD LC SIZE",
       ESTD_LC_MEMORY_OBJECTS "ESTD MEM OBJ",
       ESTD_LC_TIME_SAVED  "ESTD TM SAVED",
       ESTD_LC_MEMORY_OBJECT_HITS  "EST. HITS"
FROM GV$SHARED_POOL_ADVICE
/
```

INT	SP SIZE ESTD	SP SIZE FCTR	ESTD LC SIZE	ESTD MEM OBJ	ESTD TM SAVED	EST. HITS
7	6144	.30	771	32105	10803523	50664998
	8192	.40	2837	119280	10803646	136808228
	10240	.50	4877	201844	10803858	136827511
	12288	.60	6489	261305	10803862	13682811
	14336	.70	7039	283925	10803862	136828120
	16384	.80	7039	283925	10803862	136828120
	18432	.90	7039	283925	10803862	136828120
	20480	**1.00**	**7039**	**283925**	**10803862**	**136828120**
	22528	1.10	7039	283925	10803862	136828120
	24576	1.20	7039	283925	10803862	136828120
	26624	1.30	7039	283925	10803862	136828120
	28672	1.40	7039	283925	10803862	136828120
	30720	1.50	7039	283925	10803862	136828120
	32768	1.60	7039	283925	10803862	136828120
	34816	1.70	7039	283925	10803862	136828120
	36864	1.80	7039	283925	10803862	136828120
	38912	1.90	7039	283925	10803862	136828120
	40960	2.00	7039	283925	10803862	136828120
8	10240	.50	872	57422	20207181	101328865
	12288	.60	2936	168828	20207597	241279737
	14336	.70	4982	237870	20208268	241339690
	16384	.80	7029	300921	20208435	241355506
	18432	.90	9076	364428	20208494	241360401
	20480	**1.00**	**11122**	**421755**	**20208512**	**241361402**
	22528	1.10	13170	485945	20208520	241361981
	24576	1.20	15010	553094	20208525	241362371
	26624	1.30	16088	595282	20208525	241362430
	28672	1.40	16332	604192	20208525	241362434
	30720	1.50	16332	604192	20208525	241362434
	32768	1.60	16332	604192	20208525	241362434
	34816	1.70	16332	604192	20208525	241362434
	36864	1.80	16332	604192	20208525	241362434
	38912	1.90	16332	604192	20208525	241362434
	40960	2.00	16332	604192	20208525	241362434

> ■ **Note** From the earlier output from GV$RESOURCE_LIMIT, it should be noted that whereas gcs_resources and gcs_shadows (illustrated in Figure 13-2) are maintained in the shared pool, other parameters are maintained in other sections of the SGA, for example, the fixed SGA.

Step 6

Why are only two instances in the cluster starving for shared pool sizes compared to the other instances? This could be an indication to look at the processes or application configured to run on these instances. The following query lists the current service-to-instance distribution:

```
SQL>!srvctl status service -d PRDDB
Service BCKUP: prddb7, prddb8
Service BIAPPS: prddb1, prddb2, prddb3, prddb4, prddb5,
Service BIETL: prddb6,prddb7, prddb8
Service DBAUSER: prddb1, prddb2, prddb3, prddb4, prddb5, prddb6
Service ENDUSER: prddb7, prddb8
```

Step 7

The RAC cluster has workload distributed using database services. And the average services times for these services indicate that the workload has not been distributed evenly across all the instances in the cluster.

Script: MVRACPDnTap_SvcStats.sql

```
break on SERVICE_NAME skip 1
SELECT SERVICE_NAME,
       INSTANCE_NAME,
       ELAPSEDPERCALL SERVICE_TIME,
       CPUPERCALL      CPU_TIME,
       DBTIMEPERCALL  DB_TIME,
       CALLSPERSEC    THROUGHPUT
FROM   GV$INSTANCE       GVI,
       GV$ACTIVE_SERVICES GVAS,
       GV$SERVICEMETRIC   GVSM
WHERE  GVAS.INST_ID   = GVSM.INST_ID
AND    GVAS.NAME_HASH = GVSM.SERVICE_NAME_HASH
AND    GVI.INST_ID    = GVSM.INST_ID
AND    GVSM.GROUP_ID  = 10
AND    GVSM.SERVICE_NAME NOT IN ('SYS$BACKGROUND')
ORDER BY
   SERVICE_NAME,
   GVI.INST_ID;
```

Service Name	Instance Name	Service Time Elapsed mSec/Call	CPU Time mSec/Call	DB Time mSec/Call	Calls/sec
DBAUSER	PRDDB1	4118982	268000	4118982	.19
	PRDDB2	0	0	0	.00
	PRDDB3	54175	54500	54175	.39
	PRDDB4	0	0	0	.00
	PRDDB5	0	0	0	.00
	PRDDB6	0	0	0	.00
ENDUSER	PRDDB7	7487921	168000	7487921	.00
	PRDDB8	756606	60286	756606	3.24
BIAPPS	PRDDB1	5683365	287000	5683365	.17
	PRDDB2	4879139	358000	4879139	.00
	PRDDB3	7232351	287000	7232351	.19
	PRDDB4	4280285	161000	4280285	.00
	PRDDB5	2176095	174000	2176095	.00
BIETL	PRDDB6	1313075	65600	1313075	1.20
	PRDDB7	10113853	190000	10113853	.00
	PRDDB8	21474104	197176	1474104	3.28
BCKUP	PRDDB7	0	0	0	.00
	PRDDB8	0	0	0	.00

Step 8

From the output, it can be noticed that instances 7 and 8 are both running services BIETL; that is probably why these servers are consuming higher resources. BIETL is a highly insert-intensive data loading application. Because this is an INSERT mostly application, data sharing between other instances is much lower. This was noticed from the extremely low activity across the interconnect on other nodes in the cluster. If there are a sufficient number of servers and data can be further distributed, the additional resources required could be obtained by adding additional nodes during the time of peak load and balance resource utilization.

Think Outside the Interconnect

When a user process retrieves data from the database connecting to one instance in the cluster, the data is usually cached locally on the instance. Subsequently, when another user process on another instance requires the same block of data and is not able to find a buffered copy in its local cache, it can acquire the block image from the holding instance over the interconnect faster than reading the block from disk. Cache Fusion moves current blocks between instances (illustrated in Figure 13-1) rather than re-reading the blocks from disk. When a consistent block is needed or a changed block is required on another instance, Cache Fusion transfers the block image directly between the affected instances.

Why is that so? Why is reading blocks from disk unfavorable to reading over the interconnect? This is because the latency of performing a single physical disk I/O is much higher compared to the latency of reading or transferring a block of data over the network. On the contrary, if the latency of the interconnect is higher compared to the latency of the disk system, it defeats the purpose of implementing a RAC solution. Argument against this could be that with recent developments with improved high-speed storage, this may not be true anymore. However, although there have been considerable improvements in the performance of the storage subsystems, equally there have been improvements with high speed, high throughput interconnects (10GigE). For a full table scan, disk access achieves higher throughput than global cache, because the global cache does not do large I/Os very well and is CPU intensive. The trade-off is multidimensional: Interconnect latency is traded off for disk access when the disks are not very fast and therefore inexpensive. This is more true in OTLP systems that predominantly have single random block access.

We look at a two scenarios to better understand the RAC behavior.

Scenario 1: Block Request Involving Two Instances

Figure 13-3 is a four-node RAC cluster. All instances maintain masters for various objects represented by R1 thru R8. In our discussions, we assume that the data blocks for the object discussed are mastered on instance 4 (SSKY4).

1. The user session requests for a block of data and the GCS process checks the local cache for the data block; when data is not found, GCS makes a request to the object master. In Figure 13-3, the instance SSKY3 requires a row from a block at data block address file#100, block# 500 (100/500) and makes a request to the GCS of the resource.

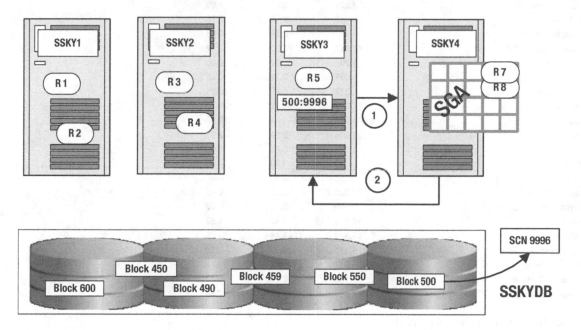

Figure 13-3. *Cache Fusion 2-way*

2. GCS on SSKY4 after checking with the GRD determines that the block is currently in its local cache. The block is found on instance SSKY4, and the GCS sends the block to the requesting instance SSKY3.

This instrumentation required to determine the time taken for each of these steps is available within the Oracle Database in the GV$SYSSTAT or the GV$SESSTAT views. RAC-specific statistics are in class 8, 32, and 40 (see Figure 13-4) and are grouped under "Other Instance Activity Stats" in an AWR report.

Statistic	Total	per Second	per Trans
Batched IO (bound) vector count	1,403	0.13	0.03
file io service time	0	0.00	0.00
free buffer inspected	1,709,146	157.57	37.76
free buffer requested	3,323,764	306.42	73.44
gc blocks compressed	1,341,849	123.71	29.65
gc blocks lost	12,103	1.12	0.27
gc cleanout applied	0	0.00	0.00
gc cleanout saved	30	0.00	0.00
gc cr block flush time	1,120,917	103.34	24.77
gc cr block receive time	1,131,895	104.35	25.01
gc cr blocks flushed	634,032	58.45	14.01
gc cr blocks received	1,224,174	112.86	27.05
gc cr blocks served	1,457,956	134.41	32.21
gc current block flush time	103,964	9.58	2.30
gc current block pin time	14,101	1.30	0.31
gc current block receive time	113,325	10.45	2.50
gc current blocks flushed	16,087	1.48	0.36
gc current blocks pinned	3,717	0.34	0.08
gc current blocks received	141,047	13.00	3.12
gc current blocks served	129,298	11.92	2.86
gc force cr read cr	4,097	0.38	0.09
gc force cr read current	377	0.03	0.01
gc kbytes saved	5,737,095	528.91	126.76
gc kbytes sent	6,960,954	641.74	153.80
gc local grants	132,815	12.24	2.93
gc read time waited	2	0.00	0.00
gc read wait timeouts	30	0.00	0.00
gc read waits	38	0.00	0.00
gc reader bypass grants	22,225	2.05	0.49
gc reader bypass waits	10	0.00	0.00
gc remote grants	82,676	7.62	1.83
gcs messages sent	2,705,948	249.46	59.79
ges messages sent	151,510	13.97	3.35
global enqueue get time	1,609,917	148.42	35.57
global enqueue gets async	7,905	0.73	0.17
global enqueue gets sync	809,069	74.59	17.88

Figure 13-4. *AWR—Instance activity statistics*

In this scenario, the following statistics are updated by Oracle. Considering this was a read-only block request, only the `cr` (consistent read) statistics are updated.

`gc cr blocks served`: Number of consistent read blocks served. It indicates the total number of blocks the current instance has sent to the requesting instances. In a multinode RAC environment, multiple instances may request for the same block; the value displayed by these statistics provides the total blocks served. In the example discussed previously, these statistics would be incremented in the instance SSKY4.

`gc cr blocks received`: When a consistent read version of the block is not found in the local buffer cache of the requesting instance, an attempt is made to get the block from the remote instance. This is the total number of consistent read blocks received by the current instance from other instances. When blocks are not found in the local cache, the block is requested from other instances. In the previous example, this statistics would be incremented in the instance SSKY3. Building a consistent read version of the block may involve several operations, for example, reading the data or undo block from disk or requesting a portion of the block from another instance. Due to this activity, occasionally there could be delays in building the requested CR block. In these situations, an incomplete copy of the block is sent. If a partial copy of the block is received, it may be rolled back when the full version of the block is received at a later stage.

`gc cr block receive time`: The total time taken to receive the block from the holder of the block. The activity is timed from the point when the request is made until it completes. The matric is stored in centiseconds. The following formula helps determine the average time per CR block in milliseconds.

10 * gc cr block receive time ÷ gc cr blocks received

`gc cr block send time`: When the block is requested by another instance, the value represents the total time taken to send the blocks. The value is influenced by conditions such as locks and time taken to downgrade the lock, and so forth.

`gc cr block read wait time`: Represents the time taken waiting to read the consistent read block from buffer or into the buffer from disk.

`gc current block send time`: The value collected by this counter indicates the time taken to send the "current" block requests that are held by the current instance to the requesting instances in the cluster.

`gc current block served`: The data collected by this counter indicates the total number of current blocks served by the current instance.

`gc current block received`: The data collected by this counter indicates the total number of requests for modification of a current block received from other instances in the cluster. Once the block is received, the counter is incremented.

`gc current block receive time`: This statistic indicates the time taken for receiving the block from the current holding instance. It's the total time from the moment a request was made by a session on the instance until the block is received. The unit of measurement is centiseconds. The following formula gives the average roundtrip time for a request in milliseconds:

10 × gc current block receive time ÷ gc current blocks received gc current block pin time: Once the block is received, it needs to be pinned into the buffer before the block is modified. This statistic means that a buffer is pinned, that is, a user is making a change in it when a BAST[2] (the signal from another instance to send the data) arrives. This counter indicates the time taken by the current instance to process BAST. The value is influenced by the current state of the buffer: if the buffer is currently available, does the DBWR need to flush the dirty buffers to disk before space is found in the buffer to pin the block? The counter provides the total time taken. A pinned buffer cannot be sent immediately and will wait on a down convert queue until the user has finished modifying the buffer. The user will notify LMS when it releases the pin on the buffer. The value is stored in centiseconds. The following formula determines the average pin time in milliseconds:

$$10 \times gc\ current\ block\ pin\ time \div gc\ current\ blocks\ served$$

gc current block flush time: When blocks are modified and commit the change, Oracle needs to flush the blocks from the buffer cache to the redo logs by the LGWR background process on the instance holding the block. If BAST (the signal from another instance to send the data) arrives and the redo for a modification has not been written to the redo log yet, the block cannot be sent immediately. It will be placed on a log flush queue until the LGWR has completed writing to the redo logs. When the redo is written, the LMS can send the block. The value in this statistic provides the time taken for the redo sync before the data block could be sent.

Depending on the type of data block requests, the following wait events could also be updated:

- gc current block 2 way
- gc current grant busy
- gc current grant congested
- gc cr block 2 way

■ **Note** Wait events are discussed in Chapter 17.

Scenario 2: Block Request Involving Three Instances

In scenarios where the block requested by another instance is not found on the instance that masters the resource, the GCS will grant permission to read the block from disk; or if the block is found on another instance, it will send a message to the holding instance to send a copy of the block to the requesting instance.

As illustrated in Figure 13-5, there are two possibilities when the block is not found on the instance that is the master of the object (resource). Figure 13-5 is a four-node RAC cluster. All instances maintain masters for various objects represented by R1 thru R8. In our discussions, we refer to data blocks that are mastered on instance 4 (SSKY4).

---

[2]BAST (Blocking asynchronous system trap), a notification mechanism to release a block used by the global cache service.

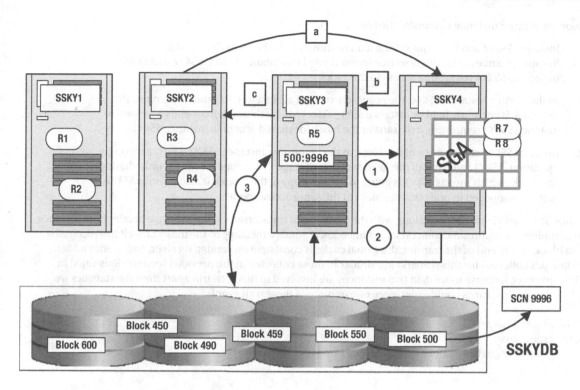

Figure 13-5. *Cache Fusion 3 way*

i) Read the block from the disk.

1. A user session or process attached to instance SSKY3 makes a request for a block at DBA file# 100, block# 500 (100/500). SSKY3 determines the master for this specific block that contains the row is SSKY4. The request is directed to instance SSKY4 where the GRD for the object is maintained. *Oracle allocates a node to be the resource master based on the demand for the resource on a specific instance. If the object access increases on another node, Oracle performs a remastering operation to move the resource master for the object to the node.*

2. Instance SSKY4 after checking against the GRD determines that neither instance SSKY4 nor any other instance in the cluster has a copy of the block (100/500), so the data must be on disk. Hence, a grant message is sent to the requesting instance to read the block from disk. The grant gives the reader on instance SSKY3 the permission to read the block from disk.

3. Instance SSKY3 reads the block from disk. The foreground process in instance SSKY3 initiates the I/O request to read the block 100/500 from disk. The row is contained in block 500 and has SCN 9996. Because Oracle reads a block of data at a time, other rows are also retrieved as part of this read operation. The block is read into the buffer of instance SSKY3. Instance SSKY3 holds the block with SCN 9996 using a shared local (SL) mode.

ii) Request another instance to transfer the block.

a. Instance SSKY2 sends a request for a read resource on the block to the GCS master. Because the master for this resource is maintained on instance SSKY4, SSKY2 makes a request to SSKY4 requesting access to this block.

b. At the master, instance SSKY4, the request is verified against its GRD and determines that the block is currently held by instance SSKY3. The LMS for this resources ends a request to instance SSKY3 requesting it to transfer the block for shared access to instance SSKY2.

c. Instance SSKY3 ships a copy of the block to the requesting instance SSKY2. During this copy operation, SSKY3 indicates in the header of the message that instance SSKY3 is only sharing the block (which means SSKY3 is going to retain a copy of the block). It also informs SSKY2 that it is supposed to maintain the block at the same access mode.

Instance SSKY2 receives the block along with the access right transferred via the message header from instance SSKY3. To complete the communication cycle, instance SSKY2 sends a message to the master that it has received a copy of the block. At the end of the transfer, the global cache is consistent on sender, receiver, and master nodes.

The statistics collected for this scenario are similar to those collected in the previous scenario illustrated in Figure 13-3. However, because more than two instances are involved in this scenario apart from the statistics we discussed earlier, the instances could experience one or more of these wait events:

```
gc current block 3 way
gc current grant busy
gc current grant congested
gc cr block 3 way
```

■ **Note**   Wait events are discussed in Chapter 17.

From the RAC architecture discussed previously, the cluster interconnect is the backbone and primary component in a RAC configuration. For obvious reasons and because the way the RAC is architected, one tends to blame the interconnect latency or bandwidth for performance issues on the interconnect versus looking at the root cause of the problem.

In a RAC environment, illustrated in Figure 13-3 and Figure 13-5, when a session on one instance requests for a block, if the block is not found on the local buffer of the requesting instance, the block is requested from the holding instance and transferred to the requesting instance. During this process, instead of rereading the block of data from disk, the data is transferred from the holding instance to the requesting instance. When a request for a block is received, the GCS processes get involved, locating the block with the help of the GRD; and based on the type of operation, the user is granted appropriate rights before the data is physically transferred across the interconnect to the requesting instance. At the block serving instance, this entire process can be grouped under two primary phases: the prepare phase and the transfer phase. As obviously noted, the transfer phase involves shipping or sending the block of data from the holding instance to the requesting instance and it involves the interconnect. However, the point to be noted is that unless the block is prepared and ready to be shipped, it cannot be transferred. So the first step is to prepare the block.

Prepare Phase

Irrespective of the type of block being transferred (current block or consistent read block), the average time required to prepare the block for transmission to the requestor is computed using the following formula:

Prepare latency = Blocks served time ÷ number of blocks served

How do you compute the time required to serve data blocks? This is the primary part of the preparation phase, and the steps depend on the type of block being served (current—DML block or CR—consistent read block). The steps involved include the time required to

1. Build the block

2. Flush the block to redo logs, if the redo is pending at the time of the BAST

3. Send the block

4. Pin the block to the buffer

This instrumentation required to determine the time taken for each of these steps is available within the Oracle database in the GV$SYSSTAT or the GV$SESSTAT views. Using the matrix available in these views, the blocks served time can be calculated using

Blocks served time = (gc cr block flush time ÷ gc cur blocks flushed

+ gc current block flush time ÷ gc current blocks flushed + gc current block pin time)

× 10

Similarly, using the statistics available in the V$SYSSTAT views, the blocks served can also be calculated:

Blocks served = (gc current blocks served + gc cr blocks served)

Performance Impact of the Prepare Phase

The primary function of finding and processing the requested data block in the prepare phase belongs to the GCS performed by the LMS background process. Most of the functions that the LMS performs, such as granting rights to data blocks, finding the block, placing the block on flush, down convert or defer queues, and so forth, all require CPU resources. Every request performed by the LMS background process requires eight O/S latches (controlled by the underscore parameter _GC_LATCHES = 8).

LATCH

A latch[3] is a type of a lock that can be very quickly acquired and freed. Latches are typically used to prevent more than one process from executing the same piece of code at a given time. Associated with each latch is a cleanup procedure that will be called if a process dies while holding the latch. Latches have an associated level that is used to prevent deadlocks. Once a process acquires a latch at a certain level, it cannot subsequently acquire a latch at a level that is equal to or less than that level (unless it acquires it nowait).

---

[3]Metalink Note # 22908.1.

Lack of CPU resources, or when there are several high consumers for CPU resources on the servers, could directly impact GCS and GES activities including allocation of latches to complete these activities.

LMS processes request one operation at a time. Only after completing one request will it attempt the next request. This means if LMS functions are delayed, there could be queuing on requests, causing overall slow response times on the RAC database. However, multiple LMSs can operate in parallel.

High latency numbers experienced during the prepare phase discussed previously could have several reasons, such as CPU starvation, scheduling delays, and high run queue lengths affecting the LMS processes and the foregrounds waiting for response from an LMS. Starting with Oracle Database Version 10.2.0.3, Oracle has changed the priority of the LMS processes. In the process output following, the LMS is running at the RR (round robin) class and at a higher priority compared to the time-sharing (TS) class that the other background processes use.

```
[oracle@prddb1 ~]$ ps -flcae | egrep "TTY|_l"
F S UID         PID  PPID CLS PRI ADDR SZ WCHAN  STIME TTY      TIME CMD
0 S oracle     5104  2346 TS   21 - 15290 pipe_w 13:21 pts/0 00:00:00 egrep TTY|_l
0 S oracle    15763     1 TS   24 - 120911 -     Nov13 ?    00:00:21 asm_lmon_+ASM7
0 S oracle    15765     1 TS   24 - 123040 624857 Nov13 ?   00:01:06 asm_lmd0_+ASM7
0 S oracle    16713     1 RR   41 - 122912 624857 Nov13 ?   00:00:01 asm_lms0_+ASM7
0 S oracle    16719     1 TS   21 - 119072 -     Nov13 ?    00:00:00 asm_lmhb_+ASM7
0 S oracle    16736     1 TS   24 - 119935 -     Nov13 ?    00:00:00 asm_lgwr_+ASM7
0 S oracle    16779     1 TS   24 - 119338 624840 Nov13 ?   00:00:00 asm_lck0_+ASM7
0 S oracle    19810     1 TS   24 - 18537705 156203 Nov13 ? 00:03:44 ora_lmon_PRD_1
0 S oracle    19812     1 TS   24 - 18538806 624857 Nov13 ? 00:05:44 ora_lmd0_PRD_1
0 S oracle    19817     1 RR   41 - 18540918 -    Nov13 ?   00:04:27 ora_lms0_PRD_1
0 S oracle    19821     1 RR   41 - 18541434 -    Nov13 ?   00:04:31 ora_lms1_PRD_1
0 S oracle    19827     1 TS   24 - 18534262 -    Nov13 ?   00:00:00 ora_lmhb_PRD_1
0 S oracle    19835     1 TS   24 - 18540697 -    Nov13 ?   00:00:44 ora_lgwr_PRD_1
0 S oracle    19892     1 TS   24 - 18537087 969103 Nov13 ? 00:05:24 ora_lck0_PRD_1
```

Starting with Oracle Database 11g Release 2, the LMS and VKTM (virtual keeper of time) background processes are set internally[4] to run at high priority.

Almost always, a good step to look at the reasons for resource contention is to look at the Oracle wait interface using GV$SYSTEM_EVENT, GV$SESSION_EVENT, GV$SESSION_WAIT, GV$SESSION_WAIT_HISTOGRAMS, and GV$EVENT_NAME; Any wait event that ends with the word "congestion" implies that the LMS is very busy or starving for CPU. Scheduling delays and CPU starvation for shadow processes can be recognized statistically.

Transfer Phase

Similar to the prepare latency, we also need to compute the transfer latency to determine what part of the round trip is slowing down the system. The transfer latency is computed as follows:

$$Transfer\ latency = Interconnect\ latency - prepare\ latency$$

---

[4]Setting of the LMS to run at this priority class is driven by the underscore parameter _HIGH_PRIORITY_PROCESSES, and the values are set to LMS|VKTM. VKTM (Virtual Time Keeper) is a new background process introduced in Oracle Database 11g Release 2 and manages the time across the RAC cluster.

We have found the components involved in prepare latency. What about interconnect latency? The average interconnect (roundtrip) latency depends on the number of data blocks received and the time required to receive these data blocks. Average interconnect latency can be computed using the following:

$$Average\ interconnect\ latency = Blocks\ receive\ time \div blocks\ received$$

Data blocks received is the sum of both the current blocks received and the CR blocks received. Similarly, the time taken to receive these blocks is also the time taken to receive a current block and the CR block.

Once again, all the instrumentation required to compute the transfer latency is also available with the Oracle database in the GV$SYSSTAT and GV$SESSTAT views. Data required to compute the transfer latency could be arrived at using the following two equations:

$$Blocks\ receive\ time = (gc\ cr\ block\ receive\ time + gc\ current\ block\ receive\ time) \times 10$$

$$Blocks\ received = (gc\ cr\ blocks\ received + gc\ current\ blocks\ received)$$

The statistics would point to either the prepare phase or the transfer phase. If the statistics on the transfer phase are significantly on the higher side, causing concern, for obvious reasons, the interconnect configuration and setup may have to be looked at. However, if the prepare phase is of concern, the root cause of the problem should be identified by looking at what is causing these high numbers. The reasons could be resource contention, lack of resources, or the process is simply waiting or hung.

■ **Note** Detailed discussions on the transfer phase with respect to the interconnect and the components involved in the transfer phase are forthcoming in Chapter 14.

Workshop

We now try to understand the environment illustrated in Figure 13-6. The eight-node cluster is configured into two server pools: Server Pool 1 (SSKYPOOL1), which is configured with BIAPPS uniform service, and Server Pool 2 (SSKYPOOL2) are configured with BIETL uniform service.

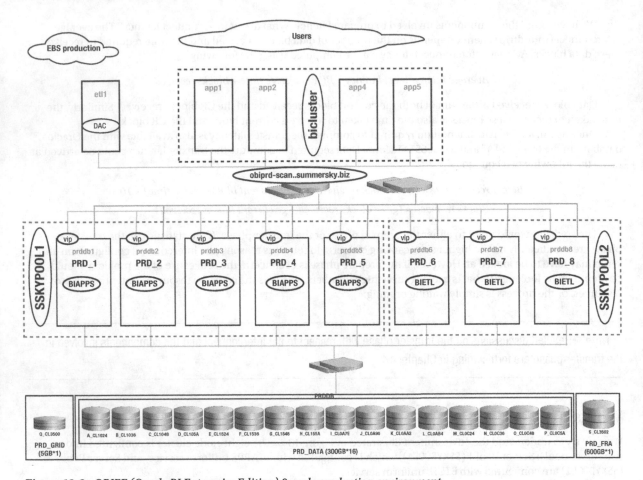

Figure 13-6. *OBIEE (Oracle BI Enterprise Edition) 8-node production environment*

The following output illustrates the instance to host to service mapping, giving us a better understanding of the environment:

Instance	Instance Name	Host Name	Instance Startup Time	Up Days	Service Name
1	PRD_1	prddb3	01-OCT-10 01:01:59	36	PRDDB
	PRD_1	prddb3	01-OCT-10 01:01:59	36	BIAPPS
2	PRD_2	prddb4	01-OCT-10 01:03:51	36	BIAPPS
	PRD_2	prddb4	01-OCT-10 01:03:51	36	PRDDB
3	PRD_3	prddb5	01-OCT-10 01:02:53	36	PRDDB
	PRD_3	prddb5	01-OCT-10 01:02:53	36	BIAPPS
4	PRD_4	prddb6	01-OCT-10 01:02:55	36	BIAPPS
	PRD_4	prddb6	01-OCT-10 01:02:55	36	PRDDB

5	PRD_5	prddb7	01-OCT-10 01:07:05	36	BIAPPS
	PRD_5	prddb7	01-OCT-10 01:07:05	36	PRDDB
6	PRD_6	prddb8	19-OCT-10 08:55:45	17	BIETL
	PRD_6	prddb8	19-OCT-10 08:55:45	17	PRDDB
7	PRD_7	prddb1	19-OCT-10 07:31:26	18	BIETL
	PRD_7	prddb1	19-OCT-10 07:31:26	18	PRDDB
8	PRD_8	prddb2	08-OCT-10 05:17:47	29	BIETL
	PRD_8	prddb2	08-OCT-10 05:17:47	29	PRDDB

Based on the discussions in the previous two sections, let's start to look at a production environment to determine which phase of the global cache service is causing a system to slow down.

Step 1

Using the following query, determine the average time for the prepare phase of the operation:

Script: MVRACPDnTap_ blkpreptime11g.sql

```
SELECT b1.INST_ID INT,
((b1.VALUE + b2.VALUE + b3.VALUE + b4.value + b5.value + b6.value)*10) "BLK SRV TIME",
   (b7.VALUE + b8.VALUE) "BLK SRVD",
   ((b7.VALUE + b8.VALUE)/((b1.VALUE + b2.VALUE + b3.VALUE + b4.value + b5.value + b6.value)*10))
   "PREP TIME"
FROM GV$SYSSTAT b1,
     GV$SYSSTAT b2,
     GV$SYSSTAT b3,
     GV$SYSSTAT b4,
     GV$SYSSTAT b5,
     GV$SYSSTAT b6,
     GV$SYSSTAT b7,
     GV$SYSSTAT b8
WHERE b1.NAME = 'gc cr block build time'
AND    b2.NAME = 'gc cr block flush time'
AND    b3.NAME = 'gc current block flush time'
AND    b4.NAME = 'gc cr block send time'
AND    b5.NAME = 'gc current block send time'
AND    b6.NAME = 'gc current block pin time'
AND    b7.NAME = 'gc cr blocks served'
AND    b8.NAME = 'gc current blocks served'
AND    b1.INST_ID = b2.INST_ID
AND    b1.INST_ID = b3.INST_ID
AND    b1.INST_ID = b4.INST_ID
AND    b1.INST_ID = b5.INST_ID
AND    b1.INST_ID = b6.INST_ID
AND    b1.INST_ID = b7.INST_ID
AND    b1.INST_ID = b8.INST_ID
ORDER BY 1;
```

INT	BLK SRV TIME	BLK SRVD	PREP TIME
1	1447970	7271960	5.02
2	936210	9382593	10.02
3	1252730	5337366	4.26
4	900880	4810821	5.34
5	90650	636710	7.02
6	2435470	23721688	9.74
7	453510	1347489	2.97
8	1085640	9456850	8.71

8 rows selected.

From the preceding output, the prepare time is significantly high on all the instances in the cluster. Before we analyze the situation further, let's look at the transfer time on these servers.

Step 2

The following queries help us compute these values to determine what is slowing down the process:

Script: MVRACPDnTap_ blksndtime.sql

```
SELECT
    B1.INST_ID INT,
((B1.VALUE/B2.VALUE ) *10) "Avg CR BRT(ms)",
    ((B3.VALUE/B4.VALUE ) *10) "Avg CUR BRT(ms)"
FROM GV$SYSSTAT B1,
    GV$SYSSTAT B2,
    GV$SYSSTAT B3,
    GV$SYSSTAT B4
WHERE B1.NAME = 'gc cr block receive time'
AND    B2.NAME = 'gc cr blocks received'
AND    B3.NAME = 'gc current block receive time'
AND    B4.NAME = 'gc current blocks received'
AND    B1.INST_ID = B2.INST_ID
AND    B1.INST_ID = B3.INST_ID
AND    B1.INST_ID = B4.INST_ID
ORDER BY 1
/
```

INT	Avg CR BRT(ms)	Avg CUR BRT(ms)
1	1.75	1.71
2	1.11	.67
3	1.24	.52
4	1.42	.47
5	1.28	.66
6	.91	.52
7	.87	.50
8	.82	.51

8 rows selected.

The average transfer times (latency) for both the consistent read blocks and current blocks on all servers are normal. Instance 1 does show an exception over the other instances; however, such exceptions are normal in any environment and can be safely ignored. Why is the prepare latency high? Or can this be reduced? Let's try to explore some of the configurations and monitor other areas of the database to determine what can be done to improve on the prepare time latency of the cluster.

Step 3

A good starting point to look at what could be causing the high latency numbers is to look at Oracle wait interface. Figure 13-6 illustrates two server pools with two primary application areas. We can generate cluster level AWR summary reports for these pools. As discussed in Chapter 6, AWR has several command line scripts that can be used to generate a variety of reports from the AWR. Using the awrgrpti.sql script, generate the following two reports:

1. Report 1 will collect summary for the instance configured in SSKYPOOL1:

```
SQL> @$ORACLE_HOME/rdbms/admin/awrgrpti.sql
Specify the Report Type
~~~~~~~~~~~~~~~~~~~~~~~~~
Would you like an HTML report, or a plain text report?
Enter 'html' for an HTML report, or 'text' for plain text
Defaults to 'html'
Enter value for report_type:
Type Specified:  html

Instances in this Workload Repository schema
~~~~~~~~~~~~~~~~~~~~~~~~~~~~~~~~~~~~~~~~~~~~~~

  DB Id     INSTT_NUM DB Name     INSTT_NAME       Host
------------ ---------- ------------ ---------------- -----------
· · · · · · · · · · · · · · · ·
· · · · · · · · · · · · · · · ·
Enter value for dbid: 2952283821
Using 2952283821 for database Id
Enter value for instance_numbers_or_all: 1,2,3,4,5
Using instances 1,2,3,4,5 (default 'ALL')

Specify the number of days of snapshots to choose from
~~~~~~~~~~~~~~~~~~~~~~~~~~~~~~~~~~~~~~~~~~~~~~~~~~~~~~~~~
Entering the number of days (n) will result in the most recent
(n) days of snapshots being listed.  Pressing <return> without
specifying a number lists all completed snapshots.
Enter value for num_days:  2
Specify the Begin and End Snapshot Ids
~~~~~~~~~~~~~~~~~~~~~~~~~~~~~~~~~~~~~~~~
Enter value for begin_snap: 9265
Begin Snapshot Id specified: 9265
Enter value forend_snap: 9279
```

This generates a summary report for the range of snap (snapshot) id specified for instance 1 through 5. Figure 13-7 illustrates the "Top Timed Events" for these instances.

I#	Wait		Event		Wait Time			Summary Avg Wait Time (ms)				
	Class	Event	Waits	%Timeouts	Total(s)	Avg(ms)	%DB time	Avg	Min	Max	Std Dev	Cnt
*	User I/O	db file sequential read	799,936	0.00	21,025.34	26.28	37.05	26.72	23.22	29.99	2.40	5
		DB CPU			13,604.89		23.97					5
	Cluster	qc buffer busy acquire	4,491,554	0.00	10,599.81	2.36	18.68	2.79	1.83	3.90	0.88	5
	Cluster	qc current grant 2-way	1,786,319	0.00	3,293.15	1.84	5.80	3.92	1.51	5.99	2.15	5
	Scheduler	resmgr:cpu quantum	26,634	0.00	2,006.94	75.35	3.54	74.01	53.55	86.97	12.42	5
	Cluster	qc remaster	2,617	57.02	44,887	17.15	3.23	17.15	10.45	24.86	1.39	5
	User I/O	db file parallel read	51,055	0.00	1,336.48	26.18	2.36	22.69	16.79	29.06	4.67	5
	Other	name-service call wait	11,957	0.00	1,006.28	84.16	1.77	84.22	81.46	88.39	2.69	5
	System I/O	control file sequential read	483,897	0.02	955.60	1.97	1.68	1.98	1.78	2.58	0.34	5
	Cluster	gc current grant busy	131	86.26	693.00	5290.08	1.22	5794.38	5282.27	6306.50	724.24	5

Figure 13-7. Top timed events for instance in SSKYPOOL1

From the output illustrated in Figure 13-7, approximately 29% of the waits are related to cluster. Amount of time spent on "DB CPU" is about 24%. All cluster-related wait events and the resmgr: cpu quantum wait event indicate that the resource manager has been enabled and that it is throttling to get CPU. With all gc events (gc buffer busy acquire, gc current grant 2-way, gc remaster, gc current grant busy, and so forth) is an indication of contention. DB CPU is not a reflection of the overall CPU usage, and the overall CPU usage should be investigated. One way to look at the overall CPU usage is to look at top five wait events on the respective instances in the cluster.

How many CPUs do these servers have? The number of CPUs can be determined either by checking with the system administrators or using the command grep processor /proc/cpuinfo. These servers are configured with 16 CPUs each; this indicates that the lack of CPUs could not be the reason for the high cluster-related waits.

2. Check the top waits from the SSKYPOOL2, which hosts the BIETL service. Using the similar steps discussed in the previous step, generate the AWR cluster summary report for instances 6, 7, and 8. Figure 13-8 illustrates the "Top Timed Events."

I#	Wait		Event		Wait Time			Summary Avg Wait Time (ms)				
	Class	Event	Waits	%Timeouts	Total(s)	Avg(ms)	%DB time	Avg	Min	Max	Std Dev	Cnt
*		DB CPU			59,366.29		40.58					3
	Commit	log file sync	9,223,465	3,147.00	36,866.20	4.00	25.20	4.25	3.52	4.69	0.64	3
	Configuration	log file switch completion	1,009,978	0.00	29,770.43	15.44	20.35	14.99	12.28	17.85	2.79	3
	System I/O	log file parallel write	3,951,528	0.00	6,411.28	1.62	4.38	1.61	1.52	1.69	0.09	3
	Other	gcs log flush sync	566,664	0.00	3,762.20	6.64	2.57	7.48	4.88	9.52	2.37	3
	User I/O	read by other session	935,588	0.00	2,369.44	2.53	1.62	2.33	1.25	3.03	0.94	3
	Cluster	gc buffer busy acquire	566,430	0.27	1,897.65	3.35	1.30	3.89	2.79	5.41	1.36	3
	Other	enq: CF - contention	25,322	7.14	1,890.56	74.66	1.29	74.35	71.98	76.56	2.29	3
	User I/O	direct path read temp	377,883	0.00	1,662.32	4.40	1.14	3.80	2.10	6.64	2.48	3
	System I/O	log file sequential read	381,748	0.00	1,295.74	3.39	0.89	3.54	2.83	3.96	0.62	3

Figure 13-8. Top timed events for instances in SSKYPOOL2

Instances in SSKYPOOL2 show a totally different view of the current condition; the cluster-related wait times are not as high as in Figure 13-7. However, SSKYPOOL2 shows high log file related wait times.

Out of the box, Figure 13-8 indicates high wait times for log file sync, log file parallel writes, and the log file switch completion. The reason could be one or all of the following:

- Excessive number of logs files being generated.

- LGWR performance is poor due to a bad I/O subsystem. The I/O throughput of the disks is not good enough for such high write activity.

- Servers starving for CPU resources.

- The LMS process in the RAC environment initiates log file synchronization when flushing blocks to disk prior to transferring modified blocks with redo that has not been written to the log to a requester on another instance (this is indicated by gcs log flush sync wait event). This would mean looking at the LGWR activity and disk-related I/O. Slowness of the LGWR could be an indication of bottleneck at the disk I/O level. This could impact on all block transfers (Cache Fusion) that require a log flush before sending the block to the requestor.

The output following shows the number of redo log switches every hour. There are over 700 log switches per day, which average about 29 switches per hour and is significantly high. It's a good rule of thumb to follow about one log switch every 20 minutes, which averages about 3–4 log switches per hour and 96–100 log switches per day:

```
IID Day   Lsw  00  01  02  03  04  05  06  07  08  09  10  11  12  13  14  15  16  17  18  19  20  21  22  23  Total
--- --------- --- --- --- --- --- --- --- --- --- --- --- --- --- --- --- --- --- --- --- --- --- --- --- --- ------
  7 11/19-Fri  54  41  72  71  52  10  34  18  11  14  21  38  14  35  22  36  49  32  12  56  33  58  52  55   890
    11/20-Sat  62  25  26  72  29  32  10  18  11  16  21  38  14  35  22  36  45  32   5  13  42  48  38  51   741
```

■ **Note** In Oracle Database 12c Release 1, a new background process, "Log Writer Slave (LGn)" is introduced. LGn are slave processes created by the LGWR to improve the performance of writing to the redo log files.

Step 4

High log switch activity could be due to either smaller sized redo log files or the FAST_START_MTTR_TARGET value has been configured low to reduce the recovery time. Tuning this parameter could be helpful in sizing the right MTTR (mean time to recovery) size. Querying the GV$INSTANCE_RECOVERY view may be helpful to determine the right size of this parameter.

■ **Note** Please refer to Chapter 10 for additional information on tuning recovery.

In this specific scenario, increasing the FAST_START_MTTR_TARGET value to 1,800 reduced the redo log switch interval and reduced the log file related wait times.

■ **Note** If LGWR-related waits continue to be an issue, increasing the priority of the LGWR process maybe worth considering; or locating the redo log files on RAID 1 type of storage may also be useful.

Step 5

Checking back at Figure 13-7 that shows high wait times on most of the RAC activities, this was a serialization issue. When the problem with the log file sync on instances 6, 7, and 8 was fixed, the contention experienced by the online users was resolved.

However, during the process of analyzing the root cause of the problem, O/S level statistics collected using tools such as OSWATCHER and collectl provided great insight into high CPU usage that was actually a false indication of the root cause of the problem. Due to the high log file activity and disk I/O contention, the delay was noticed as high

CPU usage. Monitoring the priority setting of the LMS background processes indicated they are running at the correct priority levels.

The LMS does not wait for a log flush unless there is nothing else to do and a log flush is pending. The LMS keeps processing arriving messages, and each time it completes a request, it checks if the log flush queue for any completed operations. In the scenario discussed previously, the log flush by LGWR took a long time delaying the sending of data that was on the log flush queue. These delays are usually in the order of magnitude of an I/O while an immediate block send would complete in a few microseconds.

Mastering and Remastering

Based on the access to the data of a specific object, the global state of the object is maintained (aka mastered) on the instance that uses it more than other instances. For example, if instance SSKY1 was accessing an object A1, and data from the object was read in about 1,500 user requests all connected to instance SSKY1, and say instance SSKY2 also required access to object A1 for 100 users. It's obvious that SSKY1 has more users accessing this object A1. Hence, instance SSKY1 would be elected as the resource master for this object. When another instance, for example, SSKY2, needs to access data in an object mastered on SSKY1, it will coordinate with the GCS and the GRD on instance SSKY1. If the usage pattern changes, for example, the number of logical reads on instance SSKY2 increases due to 2,000 user requests and on SSKY1 it drops to 500 causing reads from disk. The global cache would monitor and detect the current usage pattern and transfer the mastering of the object via the interconnect to instance SSKY2. This entire process of remastering serves the purpose of supporting *object affinity*. In other words, object affinity implies *the use of dynamic resource remastering to move the location of the resource masters for the database object (e.g., table, index, partition) to the instance where block operations are most frequently occurring.*

■ **Note**   If blocks from an object move around frequently between instances, but most accesses are on SSKY2, affinity will not kick in. It will only kick in when most of the OPENS are from SSKY2 (i.e., reads from disk).

Object affinity optimizes the system in situations where update transactions are being executed on one instance. If activity is not localized, the resource ownership is distributed to the instances equitably on the basis of data block addresses. Whereas remastering is based on the number of times the object is touched in a particular instance, the requirement is that it has read 1,500 times more than the other instance in a period of approximately 10 minutes. The touch count logic for remastering and the maximum period before remastering occurs is tunable using the underscore parameters[5] _GC_POLICY_MINIMUM and _GC_POLICY_TIME.[6]

Figure 13-9 illustrates resource distribution in a four-node cluster. That is, instances SSKY1, SSKY2, SSKY3, and SSKY4 are mastering resources R1, R2, R3, R4, R5, R6, and R7, respectively.

---

[5]Underscore parameters should be modified only after consultation with Oracle support.
[6]In previous versions of Oracle, this was based on parameters _GC_AFFINITY_MINIMUM and _GC_AFFINITY_TIME.

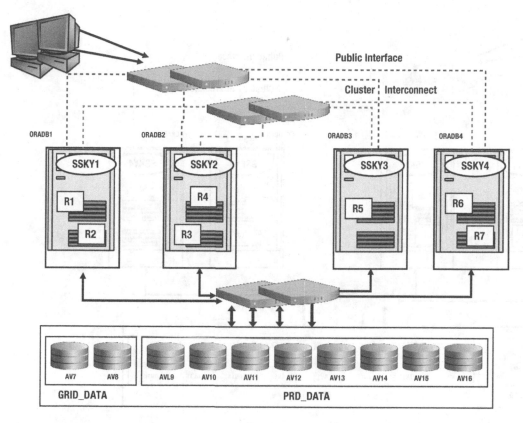

Figure 13-9. *Resource mastering*

Mastering resources on the instance that has affinity to most of the data in a segment increases locality of access and reduces message transfers. On a busy system, system performance could be affected if there is a constant change of workload on the instance, causing resource utilization to change and in turn causing the object master to get relocated to the instance where the access for the object is the highest.

Remastering also happens when an instance joins or leaves the cluster. This is different from the process of dynamic remastering described earlier. However, instead of remastering all locks/resources across all nodes, Oracle uses an algorithm called "lazy remastering." Basically, under this method, instead of load balancing the resources by removing all resources and remastering them evenly across instances (this was how resources got distributed in prior versions of Oracle such as Oracle Parallel Server), Oracle only remastering the resources owned by the instance that crashed. If the crashed instance had an affinity to an object, the object affinity is dissolved and the data blocks belonging to the object are mastered according to the default distribution algorithm.

Figure 13-10 illustrates the remastering of resources from instance SSKY4 to instances SSKY2 and SSKY3, respectively, when instance SSKY4 crashes.

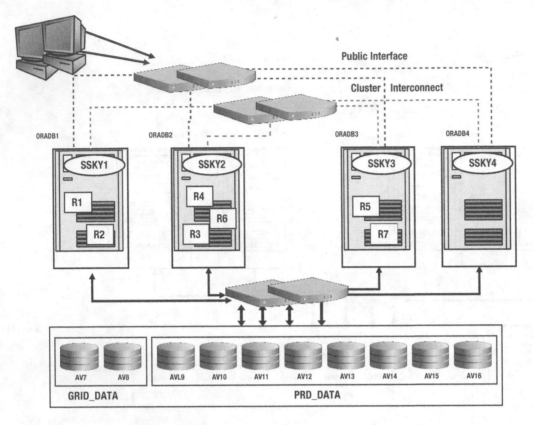

Figure 13-10. *Resource re-mastering*

Instance SSKY1 and instance SSKY2 will continue to master their resources, namely, R1, R2, R3, and R4. As part of the recovery process, the resources mastered on the failed instance will now have to be mastered by one of the surviving instances. Oracle uses the lazy remastering concept and hashes the data blocks previously mastered by the failed instance to one of the surviving instances during recovery. Consequently, per our illustration in Figure 13-9, R6 is inherited by instance SSKY2 and R7 is inherited by instance SSKY3; instance SSKY1 is not affected.

At a later time when the user workload has stabilized (recovery is completed, users have failed over, etc.), the global cache process may revalidate the affinity statistics and perform a remastering operation to place the master on the instance where the demand is high.

A similar operation happens when a crashed instance joins, or a new instance is added to, the cluster. Basically, resources are redistributed and removed from each of the available instances and moved to the instance that joined the cluster.

Monitoring Remastering

One of the primary scalability factors for Oracle is balancing resource demands on each instance by satisfying requests on local nodes where demand for the resource is high. As discussed earlier, when the number of opens for the object increases on another instance to number on the current instance, the master moves from the instance that is currently mastering the instance to the new instance where the demand for the object is higher. This is called resource remastering for a database object. Affinity is established when most data blocks for a segment are read into one instance and never ping out. They may be pushed out of the cache and later read back in from disk, but always by the same instance. The following query against the GV$DYNAMIC_REMASTER_STATS[7] view gives the current remaster activity:

```
SELECT INST_ID INT, REMASTER_OPS OPS,
       REMASTER_TIME RT,
       REMASTERED_OBJECTS RO,
       CURRENT_OBJECTS CO,
       SYNC_TIME ST
FROM   GV$DYNAMIC_REMASTER_STATS
ORDER BY INST_ID;

       INT        OPS         RT         RO         CO         ST
---------- ---------- ---------- ---------- ---------- ----------
         1       1152      97023       1870        232      47257
         2       1151      97191       1869          1      55836
         3       1151      97114       1869          2      54963
         4       1152      97146       1870          2      58169
         5       1151      97182       1869          3      57783
         6       1151      97150       1869         21      31957
         7       1151      97528       1869         21      70858
         8       1151      97148       1869         36      34547

8 rows selected.
```

In the preceding output, REMASTER_OPS indicates the number of remaster operations completed this far; REMASTER_TIME indicates the time spent on remaster activities; REMASTERED_OBJECTS indicates the number of objects remastered; CURRENT_OBJECTS column indicates the number of objects mastered on the current instance and has not been remastered; and SYNC_TIME indicates the amount of time spent in cache synchronization activities during the remaster operation.

■ **Note** All values in this view are cumulative, meaning they reflect the remastering activity since the instance started.

On a clustered configuration with more than two nodes, if there is significantly high number of three-way wait events (numbers greater than two-way wait events), it would indicate there is a significant amount of data sharing across all nodes in the cluster. In such cases, there is a high amount of gc cr/current two-way grants and the remastering algorithm may not occur.

The statistics gc local/remote grants would also indicate whether locality of masters is effective or not. The goal is to maximize local grants. Remastering statistics can also be viewed from the AWR report (illustrated in Figure 13-11).

---

[7]GV$DYNAMIC_REMASTER_STATS is based on X$KJDRMAFNSTATS.

Name	Total	per Remaster Op	Begin Snap	End Snap
remaster ops	115	1.00		
remastered objects	219	1.90		
replayed locks received	358,418	3,116.68		
replayed locks sent	864,600	7,518.26		
resources cleaned	0	0.00		
remaster time (s)	109.9	0.96		
quiesce time (s)	24.1	0.21		
freeze time (s)	1.6	0.01		
cleanup time (s)	10.6	0.09		
replay time (s)	12.8	0.11		
fixwrite time (s)	21.1	0.18		
sync time (s)	39.3	0.34		
affinity objects			18	19

Figure 13-11. *Dynamic re-mastering statistics*

Objects that have been mastered and remastered on the various instances can be determined from the GV$GCSPFMASTER_INFO view. The following output illustrates the current master (identified by CM column) and previous master (identified by PM column) instances for a few of the objects. The output has been sorted on the objects that have been remastered the highest number of times (identified by the CNT column) since the instances were started.

Script Name: MVRACPDnTap_findhotobjmasters.sql

```
SELECT inst_id                          INT,
       owner,
       GCSPF.data_object_id             OBJID,
       object_name                      ONAME,
       subobject_name                   SONAME,
       Decode(object_type, 'TABLE PARTITION', 'TP',
                           'TABLE SUBPARTITION', 'TSP',
                           'TABLE', 'T',
                           'INDEX SUBPARTITION', 'ISP',
                           'INDEX PARTITION', 'IP',
                           'CLUSTER', 'C',
                           'SEQUENCE', 'S',
                           'INDEX', 'I')  OT,
       gc_mastering_policy              GC_MP,
decode(CURRENT_MASTER,'0','1','1','2','2','3','3','4','4','5','5','6','6','7','7','8','8',
'9','9','10') CM,

decode(PREVIOUS_MASTER,'0','1','1','2','2','3','3','4','4','5','5','6','6','7','7','8','8',
'9','9','10','32767','NO') PM,
       remaster_cnt                     CNT
FROM   gv$gcspfmaster_info GCSPF,
       dba_objects DO
```

```
WHERE  GCSPF.data_object_id = DO.data_object_id
       AND remaster_cnt > 1
ORDER  BY inst_id,
          10 DESC;
```

OBJID	ONAME/SONAME	OT	GC_MP	CM	PM	CNT
470215	X_SRV_REQ_CHARGES_D	T	Affinity	5	8	11
469833	W_PRODUCT_XACT_A	T	Affinity	7	8	10
492984	W_INV_DY_BAL_F_20101231	IP	Affinity	7	8	8
501323	W_INV_MTHBAL_F_U1	I	Affinity	6	7	6
470136	X_SRV_INSTALL_BASE_AUDIT_F	T	Affinity	6	8	6
613934	W_GL_REVN_F1_20101131	TP	Affinity	8	7	5
492704	BCI_W_PROD_XACT_F_N2	I	Affinity	8	6	5
469945	W_SALES_SCHEDULE_LINE_F	T	Affinity	6	8	5
468803	W_SLS_ORDR_LIN_F_20080331	TP	Affinity	6	8	4
501319	X_SRV_REQ_CHARGES_F_U1	I	Affinity	6	8	4
493462	W_EMP_DAYSNP_F_U1	I	Affinity	7	6	4
1092087	X_SRV_REQ_F_U1	I	Affinity	6	8	4
489597	X_SRV_REQ_CHARGES_D_U1	I	Affinity	8	7	3
469403	W_AR_AGING_INVOICE_A	T	Affinity	8	7	3

From the preceding output, most of the objects are currently being mastered by instances 6, 7, and 8. The output also illustrates objects at the partition level (IP = index partition and TP = table partition). Recollecting from Figure 13-6, instances 6, 7, and 8 are from SSKYPOOL2 and run the BIETL database service.

From Figure 13-7 discussed in the previous workshop, one of the primary wait events experienced by the instance in SSKYPOOL1 is the gc remaster. It amounted to about 3.23% of the wait time and also experienced several timeouts during remaster operations. Contentions experienced during remastering operations are primarily due to a high level of modifications to blocks within an object. As illustrated in the previous output, BIETL is a load process and data is being loaded through instances 6, 7, and 8 (SSKYPOOL2), causing frequent opens on the objects. This in turn causes frequent DRM or also could indicate the DRM is taking a long time to complete. Starting with Oracle Database 11g Release 2, dynamic remastering is the default configuration and can be disabled by setting _GC_POLICY_TIME[8] parameter to 0. (In prior releases of RAC, dynamic remastering could be disabled using the parameter _LM_DYNAMIC_REMASTERING or by setting the parameter _GC_AFFINITY_TIME=0. Mastering and remastering of objects is based on policies, illustrated in column GC_MP in the preceding output.

Polices for the object can also be obtained by querying the V$POLICY_HISTORY view as illustrated in the following output.

Script: MVRACPDnTap_policyhistory.sql

```
SELECT inst_id,
       policy_event,
       data_object_id,
       target_instance_number,
       event_date
```

---

[8]Underscore parameters should be changed only with prior approval and discussion with Oracle support.

```
FROM    gv$policy_history
WHERE   data_object_id IN (SELECT data_object_id
                           FROM    gv$policy_history
                           GROUP   BY data_object_id
                           HAVING Count(*) > 19)
ORDER   BY data_object_id,
           inst_id;
```

Inst	Policy Event	Data Object ID	Target Inst #	Event Date
2	push_affinity	468751	4	02/04/2014 09:24:34
2	push_affinity	468751	5	02/03/2014 21:33:53
2	push_affinity	468751	3	02/01/2014 07:39:58
3	dissolve_affinity	468751	3	02/02/2014 11:31:43
3	push_affinity	468751	1	02/08/2014 02:30:00
3	push_affinity	468751	5	02/04/2014 16:45:01
3	push_affinity	468751	5	02/01/2014 12:40:16
3	push_affinity	468751	2	02/02/2014 19:02:15
4	push_affinity	468751	1	01/31/2014 15:08:57
4	push_affinity	468751	3	02/02/2014 01:21:01
4	push_affinity	468751	5	02/01/2014 03:09:40
4	push_affinity	468751	1	02/04/2014 11:24:40
4	push_affinity	468751	2	02/04/2014 20:15:13
5	dissolve_affinity	468751	5	02/08/2014 14:20:46
5	push_affinity	468751	4	02/04/2014 16:55:02
5	push_affinity	468751	2	02/04/2014 08:44:32
5	push_affinity	468751	2	02/01/2014 07:29:57
5	push_affinity	468751	4	02/01/2014 18:50:39

Based on the type of transactions (shared, exclusive), the objects are mastered in the respective instances, providing different access rights to the sessions accessing these objects. The following output from X$OBJECT_POLICY_STATISTICS gives current statistics on the type of access the objects have on the instances that are currently being mastered. The SOPENS column indicates the number of times the object has been master on the instance in shared mode. XOPENS indicates exclusive mode, and XREFS indicates exclusive reference:

Script: MVRACPDnTap_objpolicystats.sql

```
SELECT object                          OBJID,
       object_name                     ONAME,
       Decode(object_type, 'TABLE PARTITION', 'TP',
                           'TABLE SUBPARTITION', 'TSP',
                           'TABLE', 'T',
                           'INDEX SUBPARTITION', 'ISP',
                           'INDEX PARTITION', 'IP',
                           'CLUSTER', 'C',
                           'SEQUENCE', 'S',
                           'INDEX', 'I') OT,
       node,
       sopens,
       xopens,
       xfers,
       dirty
```

```
FROM    x$object_policy_statistics,
        dba_objects DO
WHERE   object = DO.data_object_id;
```

OBJID	ONAME	OT	NODE	SOPENS	XOPENS	XFERS	DIRTY
267	SMON_SCN_TO_TIME_AUX	C	2	4	0	0	0
267	SMON_SCN_TO_TIME_AUX	C	1	2	0	2	0
267	SMON_SCN_TIME	T	1	2	0	2	0
12871	SYS_IOT_TOP_12870	I	6	0	1	22	5
12873	SYS_IOT_TOP_12872	I	8	0	2	18	5
12873	SYS_IOT_TOP_12872	I	7	1	2	21	6
12873	SYS_IOT_TOP_12872	I	3	0	1	19	2
12873	SYS_IOT_TOP_12872	I	1	1	32	15	12
1224829	AQ$_SYS$SERVICE_METRICS_TAB_L	T	6	2	0	14	0
1224829	AQ$_SYS$SERVICE_METRICS_TAB_L	T	2	2	0	4	0
12879	SYS_IOT_TOP_12878	I	6	1	1	23	1
615325	W_GL_REVN_F1_20100731	IP	2	348	0	0	0
615532	W_GL_REVN_F1_20100731	IP	2	692	0	0	0
1253333	BCI$COGS_MTH_A_MV01	T	1	149	1	0	1
469503	W_CUSTOMER_LOC_D	T	4	135	0	0	0
469503	W_CUSTOMER_LOC_D	T	1	108	0	0	0
613930	W_GL_REVN_F1_20100731	TP	2	7313	6	0	0
613929	W_GL_REVN_F1_20100631	TP	2	182159	52	0	73
616636	W_GL_REVN_F1_20100731	IP	2	1309	0	0	0

Similar to the "remaster" wait event illustrated in Figure 13-7, remastering activities can also be seen via Enterprise Manager as illustrated in Figure 13-12.

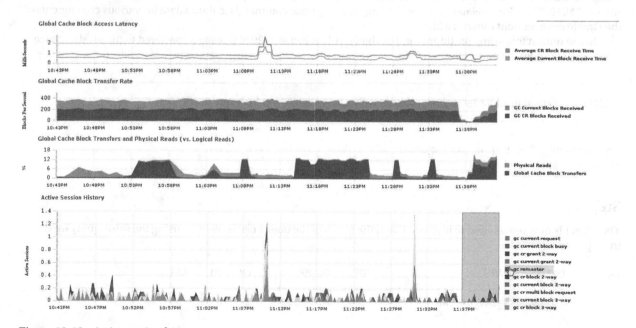

Figure 13-12. *Active session history*

Manual Remastering

As discussed earlier, mastering and remastering of objects based on usage is a default behavior starting with Oracle Database 11g Release 2. However, in situations when we need to decide the location of the master irrespective of the usage to control performance, it can be done manually.

Workshop—Manual Remastering of Objects

Manual remastering of objects is done using the ORADEBUG utility that is not documented by Oracle. Use of this feature should be done in a test environment only to understand and test the GCS behavior. However, if such a change is required in the production environment, prior consent from the Oracle Support team is suggested.

Step 1

Determine the current masters of the various objects using the GV$GCSPFMASTER_INFO view. From the output following, XW_INV_DAYBAL_F_U1 is an object of type index partition and is currently managed on instance 8. It is probably stuck on that instance while all the access related to that object is currently on instance 1. The reason the remaster operation is taking a longer time than expected is due to several things such as intensive CPU usage, lack of memory, paging, and swapping. The GCS processes are really busy and not able to keep up with requests.

```
INT      OBJID  ONAME                     OT    GC_MP        CM  PM  CNT
----     ------ ----------------------    ----  ----------   --- --- ----
  1      492984 XW_INV_DAYBAL_F_U1        IP    Affinity      8   6   6
```

Step 2

Using the ORADEBUG utility, several of Oracle diagnostic operations can be performed either using the built in functions such as LKDEBUG (for RAC-related troubleshooting) or using trace commands to dump data for various components of the Oracle environment into trace files.

In the output following, partitioned index object with object id 492984 is being remastered to the local instance where the command is now being executed.

■ **Note**   Object id used for remastering objects is the DATA_OBJECT_ID from DBA_OBJECTS.

```
SQL> oradebug lkdebug -m pkey 492984
Statement processed.
```

Step 3

The object is now remastered to instance 1, and the status of the object can be verified using the same query used in Step 1:

```
INT      OBJID  ONAME                     OT    GC_MP        CM  PM  CNT
----     ------ ----------------------    ----  ----------   --- --- ----
  1      492984 XW_INV_DAYBAL_F_U1        IP    Affinity      1   8   7
```

REMASTERING

Remaster activity is performed by the LMD process, and the activity is recorded in the trace files of the LMD process on the respective nodes.

On the holder node (prddb8) / instance (prd_8)

Once the remaster operation is issued on instance 1 (prd_1), the GCS and GES process on the requesting instance locates the current object master using the local GRD and sends the remaster request via the cluster interconnect as a message to the current holder of the object master, instance 8.

On the holder instance, the following activity is captured:

```
*** 2013-11-27 13:17:55.687
* received DRM start msg from 1 (cnt 1, last 1, rmno 431)
Rcvd DRM(431) AFFINITY Transfer pkey 492984.0 from 8 to 1 oscan 0.1
ftd (30) received from node 4 (12/0.30.0)
ftd (30) received from node 2 (12/0.30.0)
ftd (30) received from node 3 (12/0.30.0)
. . . . . . . . . . .
. . . . . . . . . . . .
td (37) received from node 4 (12/0.38.0)
ftd (37) received from node 6 (12/0.38.0)
ftd (37) received from node 7 (12/0.38.0)
ftd (37) received from node 1 (12/0.38.0)
all ftds received
2013-11-27 13:17:58.130186 :
End DRM(431) for pkey transfer request(s) from 1
```

On the requestor node (prddb1) / instance (prd_1)

The LMD process receives a request for a new RM (remaster) operation. This is the instance that is making the remaster request, so the message should be interpreted as master received. The request is sent by instance 1 to the current holder of the object (instance 8). Once instance 8 receives the request, it starts sending the transfer operation. As noted from the time stamp of when the request is received, the transfer process begins immediately.

```
*** 2013-11-27 13:17:55.686
* kjdrchkdrm: found a new RM request
*** 2013-11-27 13:17:55.687
Begin DRM(431) (swin 0) - AFFINITY transfer pkey 492984.0 to 1 oscan 1.1
kjiobjscn 1
ftd (30) received from node 4 (12/0.30.0)
ftd (30) received from node 2 (12/0.30.0)
ftd (30) received from node 3 (12/0.30.0)
ftd (30) received from node 7 (12/0.30.0)
ftd (30) received from node 5 (12/0.30.0)
ftd (30) received from node 6 (12/0.30.0)
ftd (30) received from node 8 (12/0.31.0)
all ftds received
```

```
. . . . . . . . . . .   . . . .
. . . . . . . . . . .   . . . .
. . . . . . . . . . .   . . . .
. . . . . . . . . . .   . . . .
td (35) received from node 8 (12/0.36.0)
future ftd (37) received from node 5 (12/0.36.0)
future ftd (37) received from node 8 (12/0.36.0)
future ftd (37) received from node 4 (12/0.36.0)
future ftd (37) received from node 3 (12/0.36.0)
future ftd (37) received from node 6 (12/0.36.0)
future ftd (37) received from node 2 (12/0.36.0)
ftd (37) received from node 7 (12/0.36.0)
all ftds received
* kjxftdn: break from kjxftdn, post lmon later
ftd (30) received from node 4 (12/0.30.0)
ftd (30) received from node 3 (12/0.30.0)
. . . . . . . . . . .
. . . . . . . . . . .

* kjxftdn: break from kjxftdn, post lmon later
2013-11-27 13:17:58.131929 :
* End DRM for pkey remastering request(s) (locally requested)
```

Global Cache Optimization

When a user queries data from the database, data is retrieved from the storage subsystem, loaded into the buffer cache, and data is traversed until the final result set is extracted. The final data set is then sent to the user. Subsequently, if another user executes the same query, data is read from the buffer cache and data result sets are returned back to the user. Not always is the data readily available; in situations such as insufficient buffer space that holds the data or when data is modified by another session, data in the buffer needs to be refreshed and reloaded.

In a RAC environment, when users execute queries from different instances, instead of the having to retrieve data from the I/O subsystem every single time, data is transferred over the interconnect from one instance to another. This provides considerable performance benefits. Once data is transferred to the requesting instance, the execution plan will then traverse through these rows to extract the actual result set requested by the user.

In certain situations, for example, when the segment is large and would not fit into the buffer cache, causing the optimizer to choose a full table scan, it becomes more efficient to flush all dirty buffers and read directly from disk (serial direct read, same as direct read for PQ [parallel query]) or it is read-mostly.

There are several types of data access patterns that can be implemented in a RAC environment based on the type of application and database. For example, (1) if the query is going against a small subset of data like in an OLTP implementation, data is accessed locally from storage; (2) if the query was going against a larger set of data such as in a data warehouse implementation, you may consider using the parallel execution and taking advantage of the resources available across multiple instances; and (3) if the query performs analytical functions and or is a summary table, you could consider using the result cache feature in Oracle Database 11g where the final results are stored in the results cache, making it available for other users in the system. In Oracle Database 11g Release 2, each of these options follow different methods by which data is retrieved; and in some cases, these methods have changed compared to the previous releases of Oracle RDBMS.

In a four-node cluster (Figure 13-12), when the query is executed in instance 1 (SSKY1), as illustrated in the 10046[9] trace output, the query performs in index fast full scan of the two database tables ORDERS and ORDER_LINE. This operation reads 345,361 blocks of data from disk (physical I/O) and performs another 345,447 logical I/O operations. The final result set is 300 rows that are then sent back to the user:

```
SELECT  ol_w_id,
        ol_d_id,
        ol_number,
        SUM(ol_amount),
        SUM(ol_quantity)
FROM    order_line ol,
        orders ord
WHERE   ol.ol_o_id = ord.o_id
        AND ol.ol_w_id = ord.o_w_id
        AND ol.ol_d_id = ord.o_d_id
GROUP   BY ol_number,
           ol_w_id,
           ol_d_id
```

call	count	cpu	elapsed	disk	query	current	rows
Parse	1	0.00	0.01	0	0	0	0
Execute	1	0.00	0.00	0	0	0	0
Fetch	21	18.42	77.41	345361	345447	0	300
total	23	18.43	77.42	345361	345447	0	300

```
Misses in library cache during parse: 1
Optimizer mode: ALL_ROWS
Parsing user id: 89  (schema name)
```

Rows	Row Source Operation

```
    300  HASH GROUP BY (cr=345447 pr=345361 pw=0 time=149 us cost=126413 size=4950 card=150)
21349787 HASH JOIN  (cr=345447 pr=345361 pw=0 time=59061480 us cost=125703 size=680920944
card=20633968)
2134685  INDEX FAST FULL SCAN ORDERS_I2 (cr=11248 pr=11219 pw=0 time=258291 us cost=2743
size=22694870 card=2063170)(object id 86234)
21349787 INDEX FAST FULL SCAN IORDL (cr=334199 pr=334142 pw=0 time=47799580 us cost=87415
size=453947296 card=20633968)(object id 86202)
```

---

[9]10046 trace can be enabled using `alter session set events "10046 trace name context forever, level 12"` and can be disabled using `alter session set events "10046 trace name context off."` The trace output will be generated in the location defined by the parameter `user_dump_dest`.

If this query was executed on instance 2 (SSKY2), the complete operation is performed all over again (the execution plan looks identical), including the physical I/O and the logical operations before getting the full results of 300 rows:

```
call     count       cpu    elapsed       disk      query    current      rows
-------  ------  --------  ----------  ---------  ---------  ---------   -------
Parse         1      0.01        0.01          0          0          0         0
Execute       1      0.00        0.00          0          0          0         0
Fetch        21     31.74       74.34     345361     345447          0       300
-------  ------  --------  ----------  ---------  ---------  ---------   -------
total        23     31.76       74.36     345361     345447          0       300
```

```
Misses in library cache during parse: 1
Optimizer mode: ALL_ROWS
Parsing user id: 89  (schema name)
```

```
Rows     Row Source Operation
-------  -------------------------------------------------------
    300  HASH GROUP BY (cr=345447 pr=345361 pw=0 time=299 us cost=126413 size=4950 card=150)
21349787 HASH JOIN  (cr=345447 pr=345361 pw=0 time=62985040 us cost=125703 size=680920944
card=20633968)
 2134685  INDEX FAST FULL SCAN ORDERS_I2 (cr=11248 pr=11219 pw=0 time=490345 us cost=2743
size=22694870 card=2063170)(object id 86234)
21349787 INDEX FAST FULL SCAN IORDL (cr=334199 pr=334142 pw=0 time=42913972 us cost=87415
size=453947296 card=20633968)(object id 86202)
```

Analyzing the trace outputs from the two instances and the following listed wait events, we notice that there was no cache synchronization of data. As discussed earlier, this is a new observation with Oracle Database 11g Release 2 RAC (unlike in Oracle 10g) when Oracle finds it more efficient that a local I/O operation would be more beneficial to avoid transferring data across the interconnect.

Instance 1 (SSKY1)		Instance 2 (SSKY2)	
Event waited on	Times Waited	Event waited on	Times Waited
row cache lock	14	row cache lock	18
SQL*Net message to client	21	SQL*Net message to client	21
db file sequential read	6	db file sequential read	6
db file parallel read	1	db file parallel read	96
db file scattered read	2762	db file scattered read	2667
gc current grant busy	206		
gc cr block 2-way	50	gc cr block 2-way	21
SQL*Net message from client	21	SQL*Net message from client	21
		gc cr multi block request	112
		gc cr block 3-way	22

> ■ **Note**   "gc current block 2-way" wait event occurs when the block is currently not in the buffer cache of the local instance but is available on another instance (holder), and the block needs to be transferred over the interconnect to the requesting instance, performing a two-hop operation.

Applying this to the previous discussion, the block was not in the buffer cache of instance 2 (requestor); however, because a previous user executed this query on instance 1 (holder), the blocks had to be transferred via the interconnect to instance 2.

> ■ **Note**   "gc current block 3-way" wait event occurs when the block is currently not in the buffer cache of the local instance (requestor) but is available on another instance (holder); however, the block was mastered on a third instance, and the request for the block (message) had to perform 3 hops before the requesting instance received the block. Irrespective of the number of instances in the cluster, this is the maximum number of hops that can occur before the requestor receives the block.

Comparing the logical I/O operations between Oracle Database 11g Release 2 and Oracle Database 10g Release 2, it is obvious that there is a higher amount of logical I/O in Oracle Database 10g Release 2 compared to Oracle Database 11g Release 2. This is the result of the improvements that have been incorporated into the Oracle Database 11g Release 2 optimizer.

Queries with High Cluster Overhead

Queries not tuned can also be an overhead to the performance across the cluster, causing high delays. In Oracle Database 10g, four new columns were introduced to help identify queries that are performing poorly in general and specifically in a RAC environment.

Using the CLUSTER_WAIT_TIME column in GV$SQLSTATS view, queries that are experiencing cluster-related waits can be identified and tuned. For example, the following query lists the SQL queries giving the wait times experienced at various stages of the operation:

Script: MVRACPDnTap_sqlstats.sql

```
SELECT  inst_id           -    INT,
        sql_id,
        application_wait_time awt,
        concurrency_wait_time conwt,
        cluster_wait_time     clwt,
        user_io_wait_time     uiwt
FROM    gv$sqlstats
WHERE   cluster_wait_time > 10000
ORDER   BY inst_id,
           user_io_wait_time desc;
```

SQL_ID	Appl Wait (ms)	Con Wait (ms)	Cluster Wait (ms)	User I/O wait (ms)
akb0u6dfpbcqn	12458.69	50881.92	68022.46	1049989.45
1dq43tb564dmb	26041.02	55622.92	71508.33	371585.91
4vtan8phkg4d0	.88	17.39	76868.96	336453.90
7npc1vbn2qwga	18004.79	52477.85	78335.88	1482720.46
6vd3bn115g0h7	6.13	1510.75	85650.27	651101.40
6v9fbpz6tpjhy	.80	127.32	86482.62	2243458.18
3aycbjhvzgrk0	1.86	167.34	88968.07	4079031.46
argkfb1k5m1zu	.00	104.20	90153.16	5070781.66
0308r77fnfdzx	.54	553.85	105665.74	176199.54
4dra31bj7pqvr	2.03	106.54	160539.64	2738713.70
aka36ggk0gjpa	6.17	23143.29	223482.02	5718669.42
0kkhhb2w93cx0	2.13	33484.57	235952.26	6912.19
c4vucwab0u7ht	.00	694.43	263394.35	171307.56
b8h7a9cy1tz81	8.31	485.29	267919.84	3606626.98
3p777gjzf6zhj	7.85	219.88	441139.22	6095130.74
c3h445x17v910	2.33	504.53	472236.90	4719911.04
g7mt7ptq286u7	34228.53	99153.58	487576.19	6971.50
6zyv4k3b8c9f0	2.16	114.17	551468.72	25795599.91
d47vn4kg3ksyv	.00	33301.52	972390.02	2206026.51

Once the queries with high cluster wait time have been identified, the specific query can be retrieved using the SQL_ID.

```
SQL> SELECT SQL_FULLTEXT FROM GV$SQLSTATS WHERE SQL_ID='d47vn4kg3ksyv';
SQL_FULLTEXT
--------------------------------------------------------------------
SELECT   SCHEDULES.SUPPLIER_WID, SCHEDULES.PRODUCT_WID, SCHEDULES.PLANT_LOC_WID, SCHEDULES.
INVENTORY_ORG_WID, SCHEDULES.PURCH_OR
G_WID, SCHEDULES.STORAGE_LOC_WID, SCHEDULES.RCPT_LOC_WID, SCHEDULES.PURCH_GROUP_ORG_WID, SCHEDULES.
COMPANY_ORG_WID, SCHEDULES.X
ACT_TYPE_WID, SCHEDULES.LINE_TYPE_WID, SCHEDULES.CREATED_BY_WID, SCHEDULES.CHANGED_BY_WID,
SCHEDULES.INVENTORY_PROD_WID, SCHEDU
```

SQL_FULLTEXT is of datatype BLOB. To retrieve the complete information from this column, PL/SQL packages such as DBMS_LOB.READ should be used.

In Oracle Database 11g Release 2, a few more columns have been added to V$SQLSTATS view, providing even closer instrumentation into cluster-level statistics:

```
IO_CELL_OFFLOAD_ELIGIBLE_BYTES              NUMBER
IO_INTERCONNECT_BYTES                       NUMBER
PHYSICAL_READ_REQUESTS                      NUMBER
PHYSICAL_READ_BYTES                         NUMBER
PHYSICAL_WRITE_REQUESTS                     NUMBER
PHYSICAL_WRITE_BYTES                        NUMBER
EXACT_MATCHING_SIGNATURE                    NUMBER
FORCE_MATCHING_SIGNATURE                    NUMBER
IO_CELL_UNCOMPRESSED_BYTES                  NUMBER
IO_CELL_OFFLOAD_RETURNED_BYTES              NUMBER
```

Blockers and Deadlocks

When two users request access to same row of data for update, all users except the first will remain in wait mode until the first user has committed or rolled back the change. This is true irrespective of whether it is a single-instance configuration or a clustered RAC configuration. In the RAC configuration, apart from users on the same instance, users from other instances can also request the same row at the same time. The following query helps identify a blocking session in a RAC environment:

Script: MVRACPDnTap_blockers.sql

```
SELECT DECODE(G.INST_ID,1,'SSKY1',2,'SSKY2') INSTANCE,
       S.SID,
       G.TYPE,
       S.USERNAME,
       S.SERIAL#,
       S.PROCESS,
       DECODE(LMODE,0,'None',1,'Null',2,'Row-S',3,'Row-X',4,'Share',5,'S/ROW', 6,'Exclusive') LMODE,
       DECODE(REQUEST,0,'None',1,'Null',2,'Row-S',3,'Row-X',4,'Share', 5,'S/ROW',6,'Exclusive')
        REQUEST,
       DECODE(REQUEST,0,'BLOCKER','WAITER') STATE
FROM   GV$GLOBAL_BLOCKED_LOCKS G,
       GV$SESSION S
WHERE  G.SID = S.SID
AND    G.INST_ID = S.INST_ID
ORDER BY STATE
INSTANCE      SID TY USERN   SERIAL# PROCESS       LMODE     REQUEST    STATE
----------    ---- -- -----  ----------  ------------  ---------  ---------  -------
SSKY2         132 TX OE          519 2576:820      Exclusive None       BLOCKER
SSKY2         148 TX OE           78 980:3388      None      Exclusive  WAITER
SSKY1         139 TX OE          114 3192:2972     None      Exclusive  WAITER
```

In the preceding output, the session with SID# 132 on instance SSKY2 is the BLOCKER because this session accessed this row first in an exclusive mode and has not either committed or rolled back the transaction. Subsequently, the session with SID# 148 also on instance SSKY2 requested for this same row for update, followed by SID# 139 from instance SSKY1. Both these SIDs (Session IDs) will remain, as WAITER(s), until such time the row is available to the session to complete its update operation.

Blockers can also be determined from the EM by selecting the "Blocking Sessions" option from the database performance page.

Identifying Hot Blocks

When the same sets of blocks are requested back and forth between the various instances in the cluster, the sessions requesting for the block may have to wait until the holding instance has released it. Similarly, the frequent changes of blocks may require the copies of blocks currently in the buffer of the respective instances to be refreshed, increasing high interconnect traffic. Although all of this is normal behavior in a RAC cluster, excessive access of a few blocks of data from multiple instances can cause I/O contention and become segment-level hot spots for tuning.

What Causes Hot Blocks?

When data is acquired from the buffer cache of the instance, Oracle requires it to acquire a latch, which is the "Cache Buffers Chains" latch. This means Oracle will acquire a latch every time it searches for a data block cached in the buffer cache. The database buffer cache is a linked list chain of data blocks and needs to be scanned when a data block needs to be accessed. Every time Oracle tries to acquire a block from the buffer, it needs to acquire a latch from the O/S; and when the latch is not available, the process goes to sleep (waits). The more times it sleeps, either the CPU as a resource is not available or the child buffer is busy and not able to access the blocks.

Yet another but common reason is the buffer busy situation. When data in the buffer needs to be accessed for several reasons (replacing with new data block, for data block modifications, for flushing the data block, etc.), and the buffer is currently being accessed or locked by another session, the Oracle session wanting to access the block from buffer has to wait until such time that the buffer becomes available. High buffer busy waits can lead to a slowdown of the overall response time for users.

Following some of the best practices with index and data file creation would help reduce some of these contentions:

1. Using ASM will help distribute extents across disks distributing I/O.

2. Using locally managed tablespaces reduces updates to the data dictionary, thus reducing I/O contentions.

3. Using ASSM (Automatic Segment Storage Management) when creating tablespaces will help space management contention at the segment level. Insert-intensive applications can gain when multiple sessions because with ASSM, there is no need to manage FREELISTS and FREELIST GROUPS.

4. Using database-partitioning features to distribute data across different partitions can reduce contention.

■ **Note** Please refer to Chapter 9 for more discussions on these best practices.

Workshop—Identifying Hot Blocks

Hot blocks are normally experienced when sessions frequently access data from the buffer cache or request data held in the buffer of another instance. To determine the hot objects, we could use one of two methods.

Method 1
Step 1

Because cache buffers chain latch is a child latch querying GV$LATCH_CHILDREN view, it will give a list of latch addresses that have the highest sleeps.

Script: MVRACPDnTap_ latch_childrencbc.sql

```
SELECT inst_id INT,
       child#  "Child",
       addr    "Address",
       gets    "Gets",
       misses  "Misses",
       sleeps  "Sleeps"
```

```
FROM    gv$latch_children
WHERE   NAME = 'cache buffers chains'
        AND sleeps > 100
ORDER   BY 1,
           6,
           2,
           3;
```

INT	Child	Address	Gets	Misses	Sleeps
1	175974	00000011244E9830	9385329	2858981	12759
	25761	0000001123684E48	5943627	2576659	125958
	13962	0000001123570C50	11049054	7048742	394381
	251077	**0000001124C02A68**	**1.32E+08**	**72061090**	**2760136**
2	227816	0000001124198588	28054003	2488138	14060
	25761	00000010E3726B58	4713115	2018104	103497
	13962	00000010E3612960	11301142	8143583	477962
	251077	00000010E4CA4778	1.17E+08	69463081	3243099
3	43955	00000010E30BB9E8	1542331	913767	11602
	13962	0000001123570C50	11098333	7682783	559700
	251077	0000001124C02A68	1.31E+08	67702851	2046647
4	160316	0000001123B2A728	21587857	1659464	12831
	25761	00000010E3726B58	8824900	3082195	118113
	13962	00000010E3612960	45018900	31817473	2199646
	251077	00000010E4CA4778	1.36E+08	74955924	3107749

Step 2

From Step 1, determine the LATCH_ID or address that has the highest sleep counts. For that address, determine the objects and the number of times that the object has been touched using the following query:

Script: MVRACPDnTap_seglatchstats.sql

```
SELECT e.owner
                ||'.'
                || e.segment_name        segment_name,
                e.extent_id              extent#,
                x.dbablk - e.block_id + 1 block#,
                x.tch,
                l.child#
FROM    sys.v$latch_children l,
        sys.x$bh x,
        sys.dba_extents e
WHERE   x.hladdr = '0000001123570C50'
        AND e.file_id = x.file#
        AND x.hladdr = l.addr
        AND x.dbablk BETWEEN e.block_id AND e.block_id + e.blocks - 1
ORDER   BY x.tch DESC;
```

SEGMENT_NAME	EXTENT#	BLOCK#	TCH	CHILD#
DWH.W_ORG_D	70	44	260	251077
DWH.W_GL_BALANCE_F	48	7	6	251077
DWH.X_SRV_DEMAND_F_M9	18	24	5	251077
DWH.W_GL_BALANCE_F	125	853	40	251077
DWH.X_SRV_DEMAND_F	177	326	4	251077
DWH.X_SRV_INSTALL_BASE_SUM	71	17	2	251077
DWH.X_SRV_NOTES_F	233	83	1	251077
DWH.X_SRV_INSTALL_BASE_SUM	146	88	1	251077
DWH.X_SRV_REQ_F_M12	0	4	10	251077

Method 2

This method is not quite as straightforward as Method 1; however, it gives more precise details regarding the hot blocks and the underlying segments.

Step 1

Oracle introduced a new X$ table to collect the hot blocks in Oracle Database 10g Release 2 called X$KSLHOT. However, this table is not normally populated. To get data into this view, the _DB_HOT_BLOCK_TRACKING parameter has to be enabled.[10]

```
ALTER SYSTEM SET "_db_hot_block_tracking"=TRUE SCOPE=BOTH;
```

In a RAC environment, depending on what service is used to access the various instances and what tables or schema the specific instance is mapped to access, blocks can be accessed by any instance in the cluster. It is advisable to enable this parameter across all instances in the cluster.

INT	NAME	VALUE
1	_db_hot_block_tracking	TRUE
2	_db_hot_block_tracking	TRUE
3	_db_hot_block_tracking	TRUE
4	_db_hot_block_tracking	TRUE

Step 2

Once the parameter is enabled, Oracle will start populating this view with the current access statistics. Here is the output for the view:

```
SQL> SELECT * FROM X$KSLHOT;
```

ADDR	INDX	INST_ID	KSLHOT_ID	KSLHOT_REF
0000001101C02200	0	1	8896745	680
0000001101C02210	1	1	3.69E+08	1
0000001101C02220	2	1	8769114	2

---

[10]Underscore parameters should be enabled only with prior consultation with Oracle Support.

0000001101C02230	3	1	8764874	200
0000001101C02240	4	1	8769044	1
0000001101C02250	5	1	3.69E+08	1
0000001101C02260	6	1	3.69E+08	1
0000001101C02270	7	1	3.73E+08	0
0000001101C02280	8	1	8764893	0
0000001101C02290	9	1	8468694	0

Step 3

The previous output includes the following information. ADDR (address) is a buffer used by Oracle to track the hot blocks. INDX (index) is used internally to search the buffer inside the array. INST_ID is the instance where the data is being collected, KSLHOT_ID is the RDBA (relative data block address), and KSLHOT_REF is the count of the relative number of times the block was accessed and contention was encountered.

Once we have the RDBA number, the next step in the process is to get the segment details using the information we have.

The DBMS_UTILITY package has two procedures, DATA_BLOCK_ADDRESS_FILE and DATA_BLOCK_ADDRESS_BLOCK, that can help convert the RDBA into a file number and block number, respectively.

```
SELECT  DBMS_UTILITY.DATA_BLOCK_ADDRESS_FILE( TO_NUMBER('8896745', 'XXXXXXXX') ) FILE#,
        DBMS_UTILITY.DATA_BLOCK_ADDRESS_BLOCK( TO_NUMBER('8896749', 'XXXXXXXX') ) BLOCK#
FROM    DUAL;

    FILE#     BLOCK#
---------- ----------
       34     616261
```

Step 4

Using the FILE# and BLOCK# from the preceding output, the segment details for the hot block can be determined from DBA_EXTENTS.

```
SELECT  OWNER       ,
        SEGMENT_NAME,
        SEGMENT_TYPE,
        TABLESPACE_NAME
FROM    DBA_EXTENTS
WHERE   FILE_ID = 34
        AND 616261 BETWEEN BLOCK_ID AND BLOCK_ID+BLOCKS-1;

OWNER  SEGMENT_NAME                     SEGMENT_TYPE        TABLESPACE_NAME
------ -------------------------------- ------------------- ---------------
DWH    X_SRV_REQ_DEBRIEF_LINE_F_M6      INDEX PARTITION     DWH_DATA
```

The datafile associated with the FILE# can be obtained from V$DATAFILE using the following query:

```
SQL>  SELECT NAME, TS# FROM V$DATAFILE WHERE FILE#=34;

NAME                                                       TS#
--------------------------------------------------------- ----------
+PRD_DATA/PRD/datafile/dwh_data3.464.718185229             32
```

Data Dictionary Views to Monitor Global Cache

Oracle dynamic performance views provide a great insight into the performance statistics. These views provide great instrumentation into the functioning and behavior of global cache in a RAC environment.

GV$INSTANCE_CACHE_TRANSFER

This view displays statistics for blocks transferred among instances in the cluster, the view captures data based on where the data is originated; for example, in the outputs following, data is sent from instance 1 to other instances in the cluster. The current block (CUR_BLOCK) is the most up-to-date copy containing all recent modifications, and the consistent read block (CR_BLOCK) contains consistent read copy of the block prior to modifications. Cache transfer statistics are collected for the classes listed in Table 13-2 for both CR blocks and CUR blocks.

Table 13-2. Cache Transfer Classes

Class	Description
Data block	Data blocks
Unused	
Undo header	Undo header information
Save undo header	Undo header information
Bitmap index block	Bitmap index block information
File header block	File header block information
Free list	Free list information if ASSM is not used for segment management
Undo block	Undo block information
Segment header	Segment header of data segment
Extent map	Extent maps of the data files
Sort block	Sort blocks
Save undo block	Undo blocks saved
Bitmap block	Bitmap blocks when local managed tablespace is used

Script: MVRACPDnTap_instCacheTrans.sql

```
SELECT  INST_ID INT   ,
        INSTANCE TRG_INST,
        CLASS        ,
        CR_BLOCK     ,
        CR_BLOCK_TIME/1000 CR_BLK_TIM,
        CR_2HOP      ,
        CR_3HOP      ,
```

```
        CR_BUSY          ,
        CR_CONGESTED
FROM    GV$INSTANCE_CACHE_TRANSFER
WHERE   INSTANCE       < 9
        AND CR_BLOCK > 0
ORDER BY INST_ID,
        INSTANCE;
```

| | Trg | | | CR | | | | |
In	Int	CLASS	CR_BLOCK	Blk Time	CR_2HOP	CR_3HOP	CR_BUSY	Cong
1	7	extent map	42	15.792	13	29	0	0
	7	segment header	1958	2284.246	614	1344	4	2
	7	data block	1119390	89956062	433015	686375	5195	277729
	7	1st level bmb	13659	1140596	6007	7652	5	292
	7	undo block	3699	1693.6	3699	0	78	0
	7	undo header	2055	5886.439	2055	0	102	5
	7	2nd level bmb	789	1560.292	146	643	9	1
	8	data block	1051046	94099141	368066	682980	1170	59377
	8	segment header	1944	2417.038	480	1464	3	4
	8	extent map	95	50.67	30	65	0	0
	8	1st level bmb	12298	1073348	6105	6193	60	386
	8	undo header	1673	5168.873	1672	1	73	3
	8	3rd level bmb	6	1.654	2	4	0	0
	8	2nd level bmb	734	2088.574	114	620	4	0
	8	undo block	5244	2392.223	5244	0	62	3

Similar to the CR block transfer statistics, current block statistics are also visible from GV$INSTANCE_CACHE_TRANSFER view (MVRACPDnTap_instCacheTrans.sql script includes queries for both CR and CUR data block transfers). In Oracle Database 11g Release 2, the scope of data displayed has been increased with additional columns.

Historical data for this view is stored in DBA_HIST_INST_CACHE_TRANSFER.

GV$GES_ENQUEUE

This view describes all locks currently maintained by the Global Enqueue Service and helps in identifying global lockers and waiters across the cluster.

Script: MVRACPDnTap_gesLockBlockers.sql

```
SELECT dl.inst_id                                      INT,
       ' '
       ||To_char(s.sid)
       ||',',
       || To_char(s.serial#)                           "SID_SER",
       p.spid                                          SPID,
       dl.resource_name1                               RNAME,
       Decode (Substr (dl.grant_level, 1, 8), 'KJUSERNL', 'Null',
                                      'KJUSERCR', 'Row-S (SS)',
                                      'KJUSERCW', 'Row-X (SX)',
                                      'KJUSERPR', 'Share',
                                      'KJUSERPW', 'S/Row-X (SSX)',
```

```
                                          'KJUSEREX', 'Exclusive',
                                          request_level)      AS GRANT_LVL,
        Decode (Substr(dl.request_level, 1, 8), 'KJUSERNL', 'Null',
                                          'KJUSERCR', 'Row-S (SS)',
                                          'KJUSERCW', 'Row-X (SX)',
                                          'KJUSERPR', 'Share',
                                          'KJUSERPW', 'S/Row-X (SSX)',
                                          'KJUSEREX', 'Exclusive',
                                          request_level)      AS REQ_LVL,
        Decode (Substr(dl.state, 1, 8), 'KJUSERGR', 'Granted',
                                    'KJUSEROP', 'Opening',
                                    'KJUSERCA', 'Cancelling',
                                    'KJUSERCV', 'Converting') AS LOCK_STATE,
        sw.event                                      EVENT,
        sw.seconds_in_wait                            WTs
FROM    gv$ges_enqueue dl,
        gv$process p,
        gv$session s,
        gv$session_wait sw
WHERE   blocker = 1
        AND ( dl.inst_id = p.inst_id
            AND dl.pid = p.spid )
        AND ( p.inst_id = s.inst_id
            AND p.addr = s.paddr )
        AND ( s.inst_id = sw.inst_id
            AND s.sid = sw.sid )
ORDER  BY sw.seconds_in_wait DESC; = s.paddr)
AND (s.inst_id = sw.inst_id and s.sid=sw.sid)
ORDER BY sw.seconds_in_wait  DESC;


INT   SesID,Ser#    SPID    RNAME               GRANT_LVL    REQ_LVL
----  -----------   ------  ------------------  ----------   ----------
   1  247,1         18994   [0x19][0x2],[RS]    Exclusive    Exclusive
   3  100,1         6713    [0x1][0x0],[PW]     Row-X (SX)   Row-X (SX)
   2  100,1         31778   [0x1][0x0],[PW]     Row-X (SX)   Row-X (SX)
```

GV$CR_BLOCK_SERVER

The view provides statistics on the global cache activity (GCS) between instances in the cluster. The view is also extremely useful to determine LMS activity and could be useful to determine prepare time issues during global cache management. If the overall cluster activity and response time is slow, it should be directly mapped to the prepare time of the LMS process.

This view is heavily loaded, meaning it has a significant amount of information and provides leads into further investigations into specific areas if required.

DISK_READ_RESULTS indicates the number of times the instance had to read the requested block from disk because the block was not found in the local buffer, nor was it found in the buffer of another instance. Significantly high numbers in this column could indicate insufficient sizing of the buffer cache and the shared pool.

This means that the master sent a cr request to an instance in which it believes the requested data is cached. However, when the message arrives at that instance, the data block is no longer in the cache. The LMS returns a disk read status. Such a scenario is a rare case and mostly caused by a race condition. This could also be due to an undersized buffer cache.

CR_REQUESTS and **CURRENT_REQUESTS** together amount to the total number of requests that the instance had received. It helps to determine the overall load of the instances.

DATA_REQUESTS, **UNDO_REQUESTS**, and **TX_REQUEST** together indicate the amount of blocks processed by the LMS process; it gives pointers on how busy the LMS is and if the number of LMS processes should be increased or not. DATA stands for data or index blocks, UNDO indicates undo blocks, and TX indicates undo segment headers.

FAIRNESS_DOWN_CONVERTS indicates the number of times a data block was requested for modifications and the LMS had granted an exclusive lock. However, if the block was not modified, the lock had to be down-converted.

The number of times a block that was modified in the past received a consistent read request before it is down-converted to S to avoid frequent block reads via the interconnect. The idea is that there a more reads than writes, and therefore the block should not be held in X mode for too long.

LIGHT_WORKS is the number of times the light-work rule was evoked. This rule prevents the LMS processes from going to disk or forwarding messages to another instance while responding to CR requests for data, undo, or undo segment header blocks.

The LMS could not find the block that was requested in the local cache nor could it be constructed (in the case of cr copies) from local information. That is, when serving blocks, LMS must not be slowed down by reading from disk or requesting data from another instance, which would be too complex and suboptimal. In such a case, the LMS would return an appropriate status to the requester. The requester then reads the data from disk and rolls back.

```
SQL> desc GV$CR_BLOCK_SERVER
Name                     Null?    Type
------------------------ -------- ------------
INST_ID                           NUMBER
CR_REQUESTS                       NUMBER
CURRENT_REQUESTS                  NUMBER
DATA_REQUESTS                     NUMBER
UNDO_REQUESTS                     NUMBER
TX_REQUESTS                       NUMBER
OTHER_REQUESTS                    NUMBER
CURRENT_RESULTS                   NUMBER
PRIVATE_RESULTS                   NUMBER
ZERO_RESULTS                      NUMBER
DISK_READ_RESULTS                 NUMBER
FAIL_RESULTS                      NUMBER
STALE                             NUMBER
FAIRNESS_DOWN_CONVERTS            NUMBER
```

```
FAIRNESS_CLEARS                    NUMBER
FREE_GC_ELEMENTS                   NUMBER
FLUSHES                            NUMBER
FLUSHES_QUEUED                     NUMBER
FLUSH_QUEUE_FULL                   NUMBER
FLUSH_MAX_TIME                     NUMBER
LIGHT_WORKS                        NUMBER
ERRORS                             NUMBER
```

Script: *MVRACPDnTap_crblksrvr.sql*

```
SELECT inst_id                                          INT,
       ( cr_requests + current_requests )               "BR",
       ( data_requests + undo_requests + tx_requests )  "HBLMS",
       disk_read_results                                "DR",
       fail_results                                     "FR",
       fairness_down_converts                           "FDC",
       flushes,
       flush_max_time                                   "FMT",
       light_works                                      "LW",
       errors                                           "ERR"
FROM   gv$cr_block_server
ORDER  BY inst_id;
```

In	Blocks Received	Reqsts Handled By LMS	Disk Reads	Failures	Down Converts	Flushes	Flush Time	LW	Errors
1	47331	45948	2	5	14386	4789	198633	1098	0
2	83893	80222	720	16	34915	2776	253516	2134	0
3	60262	56767	373	24	18598	2963	126301	1999	0
4	65914	62605	484	5	19511	3013	100035	1932	0
5	81390	67136	340	14	36161	2392	117637	1154	0
6	1848995	1831623	860	610	1081569	99468	535471	32224	0
7	1690931	1677306	918	193	994073	140368	1468958	8544	0
8	2626341	2609583	701	229	1616399	107090	152438	11218	0

The preceding output gives the total consistent read requests received by the respective instances, the number of consistent read blocks served by the LMS background process, and the number of failures during the activity. However, the counts in the "failure" column are not due to lost blocks but exceptions created during the "prepare" phase. In the preceding output, instances 6, 7, and 8 have significantly high activity because these instances run the ETL (extract, transform, load) batch loads.

■ **Note**   When there is high number of "failures," it's important to follow up with Oracle support to ensure there are no known bugs. When creating service requests, the LMS trace files should be provided for analysis.

Historical data for this view is maintained in DBA_HIST_CR_BLOCK_SERVER.

GV$CURRENT_BLOCK_SERVER

This displays wait statistics encountered during the various stages of the GCS processes during a Cache Fusion operation involving current blocks. When a current block is requested, the block needs to be pinned to the buffer of the requesting instance; changes to the blocks need to be flushed to the redo log files; and finally, the data blocks need to be written to the datafiles. This view shows the wait statistics encountered during these stages:

```
SQL> DESC GV$CURRENT_BLOCK_SERVER
 Name                    Null?     Type
 --------------- -------- ------------
 INST_ID                   NUMBER
 PIN1                      NUMBER
 PIN10                     NUMBER
 PIN100                    NUMBER
 PIN1000                   NUMBER
 PIN10000                  NUMBER
 FLUSH1                    NUMBER
 FLUSH10                   NUMBER
 FLUSH100                  NUMBER
 FLUSH1000                 NUMBER
 FLUSH10000                NUMBER
 WRITE1                    NUMBER
 WRITE10                   NUMBER
 WRITE100                  NUMBER
 WRITE1000                 NUMBER
 WRITE10000                NUMBER
 CLEANDC                   NUMBER
 RCVDC                     NUMBER
 QUEUEDC                   NUMBER
 EVICTDC                   NUMBER
 WRITEDC                   NUMBER
```

Script: MVRACPDnTap_curblksrvr.sql

```
SELECT inst_id INT,
       pin100,
       pin1000,
       pin10000,
       flush100,
       flush1000,
       write100,
       write1000,
       write10000,
       evictdc,
       writedc
FROM   gv$current_block_server
ORDER  BY inst_id;
```

Here is a sample output (formatted for inclusion in the book):

In	Pin 100-1000 ms	Flush 10-100 ms	**Flush 100-1000 ms**	**Write 10-100 ms**	**Write 100-1000 ms**	EVICTDC	WRITEDC
1	0	9	207	932	82	484071	11802
2	1	5	189	1551	150	353875	8552
3	0	7	204	6469	396	420054	16367
4	0	9	161	2704	126	840889	10347
5	0	6	272	1991	204	256154	18344
6	0	1	651	35092	12378	227796	903243
7	1	2	843	62992	8090	450609	413363
8	0	1	589	30706	3096	236854	280688

Historical data for this view is maintained in DBA_HIST_CURRENT_BLOCK_SERVER.

GV$GES_CONVERT_LOCAL

This view displays statistics for local GES enqueue operations and records average convert times, count information, and timed statistics for global enqueue requests for consistent read requests/operations. It is a useful view to determine the type of locks conversions (listed in Table 13-3) that happen locally on the instance or on the remote servers.

Table 13-3. Lock Conversion Types

Conversion Type	Description
NULL -> SS	NULL mode to subshared mode.
NULL -> SX	NULL mode to shared exclusive mode.
NULL -> S	NULL mode to shared mode occurs when a block is selected by a query. The block may or may not be present in the buffer cache. If a current copy of the block is in the cache, then only a lock conversation takes place, and the lock is not read from disk again.
NULL -> SSX	NULL mode to subshared exclusive mode.
NULL -> X	NULL mode to exclusive mode. This conversion occurs when reading a block into the SGA for DML operation (INSERT, UPDATE, DELETE).
SS -> SX	Subshared mode to shared exclusive mode.
SS -> S	Subshared mode to shared mode.
SS -> SSX	Subshared mode to subshared exclusive mode.
SS -> X	Subshared mode to exclusive mode.
SX -> S	Shared exclusive mode to shared mode.
SX -> SSX	Shared exclusive mode to subshared exclusive mode.
SX -> X	Shared exclusive mode to exclusive mode.
S -> SX	Shared mode to shared exclusive mode.
S -> X	Shared mode to exclusive mode occurs when a block is read into the SGA by a SELECT statement, and then a DML statement is issued against the same block.
SSX -> X	Subshared exclusive to exclusive mode.

Script: MVRACPDnTap_convert_local.sql

```
SELECT inst_id          INT,
       convert_type     CT,
       average_convert_time ACT,
       convert_count    CC
FROM   gv$ges_convert_local
WHERE  average_convert_time > 0
ORDER  BY inst_id;

Cur                   Average
Inst Convert Type    Convert Time Convert Count
---- --------------- ------------ -------------
   1 NULL -> SS            1           187
     NULL -> SX            1             8
     NULL -> S             1         83295
     NULL -> SSX           9         28359
     NULL -> X             4          7155
     S    -> X             1          3453
     SSX  -> X             3          2198
```

GV$GES_CONVERT_REMOTE

These are display values for remote GES enqueue operations. This view records average convert times, count information, and timed statistics for global enqueue requests for CURRENT blocks. It is a useful view to determine the type of locks conversions that did not occur locally on the instance and had happened on one of the remote instances in the cluster. This view is also useful to determine the amount of cluster overhead from moving from a single-instance configuration to a clustered RAC database configuration.

■ **Note** The various types of conversions are illustrated in Table 13-3.

Script: MVRACPDnTap_convert_remote.sql

```
SELECT inst_id          INT,
       convert_type     CT,
       average_convert_time ACT,
       convert_count    CC
FROM   gv$ges_convert_remote
WHERE  average_convert_time > 0
ORDER  BY inst_id;

Cur                   Average
Inst Convert Type    Convert Time Convert Count
---- --------------- ------------ -------------
   1 NULL -> SS            1          4715
     NULL -> SX            2           181
     NULL -> S             1        756076
     NULL -> SSX           6           606
     NULL -> X             5         29425
     S    -> X             1          2990
     SSX  -> X             9           695
```

GV$LIBRARYCACHE

The view contains statistics showing library cache performance and activities. When looking at RAC from each individual instance in the cluster, the RELOADS and INVALIDATIONS columns should be monitored. RELOADS indicates the number of times the objects had to be reloaded into the library cache due to one or more of the following reasons:

- Objects aging out of the library cache.

- Objects being flushed out of library cache because there is insufficient memory to hold the objects for long periods of time.

Because reloads are due to objects being flushed out, increasing the size of the shared pool should help.

INVALIDATIONS occur when the objects become invalid because the underlying dependent objects may have been modified. Invalidations cause the objects to be reparsed once the underlying dependent objects have become valid.

In a RAC environment, the columns of importance are DLM_LOCK_REQUESTS, DLM_PIN_REQUESTS, DLM_PIN_RELEASES, and DLM_INVALIDATIONS. These columns are populated due to activity across instances in the cluster when access to library cache objects must be synchronized with other instances in the cluster. The distributed lock manager (DLM) in a RAC environment:

```
SQL> DESC V$LIBRARYCACHE
 Name                             Null?    Type
 -------------------------------- -------- ----------------
 NAMESPACE                                 VARCHAR2(64)
 GETS                                      NUMBER
 GETHITS                                   NUMBER
 GETHITRATIO                               NUMBER
 PINS                                      NUMBER
 PINHITS                                   NUMBER
 PINHITRATIO                               NUMBER
 RELOADS                                   NUMBER
 INVALIDATIONS                             NUMBER
 DLM_LOCK_REQUESTS                         NUMBER
 DLM_PIN_REQUESTS                          NUMBER
 DLM_PIN_RELEASES                          NUMBER
 DLM_INVALIDATION_REQUESTS                 NUMBER
 DLM_INVALIDATIONS                         NUMBER
```

Script: MVRACPDnTap_dlmlibcache.sql

```
    SELECT inst_id                  INT,
           namespace,
           dlm_lock_requests        DLREQ,
           dlm_pin_requests         DPREQ,
           dlm_pin_releases         DPREL,
           dlm_invalidation_requests DINVREQ,
           dlm_invalidations        DINV
    FROM   gv$librarycache
    ORDER  BY inst_id;
```

Inst	NAMESPACE	Lock Requests	Pin Requests	Pin Releases	Inval Requests	Invals
1	SQL AREA	0	0	0	0	0
	TABLE/PROCEDURE	122724	1469838	1469838	0	0
	BODY	0	1181194	1181194	0	0
	TRIGGER	0	3697	3697	0	0
	INDEX	76331	79864	79864	0	0
	CLUSTER	987	1011	1011	0	0
	DIRECTORY	0	2	2	0	0
	QUEUE	19751	61177	61177	0	0
	SUMMARY	8177	8177	8177	96	96
	APP CONTEXT	0	0	0	0	0
	RULESET	0	88	88	0	0
	XML SCHEMA	20	20	20	0	0
	SUBSCRIPTION	19669	19684	19684	0	0
	LOCATION	1	216430	216430	0	0
	XDB CONFIG	0	0	0	0	0
	USER AGENT	9834	9834	9834	0	0
	SECURITY CLASS	17	17	17	0	0
	XDB ACL	2	2	2	0	0
	EDITION	11870	11870	11870	0	0
	DBLINK	22770	0	0	0	0
	OBJECT ID	0	0	0	0	0
	SCHEMA	11149	0	0	0	0
	DBINSTANCE	0	0	0	0	0

History for the library cache statistics is maintained in DBA_HIST_LIBRARYCACHE.

GV$ROWCACHE

This dynamic view is used to measure the caching behavior of the dictionary cache. The dictionary cache is part of the shared pool and does not have any tunable parameters other than the SHARED_POOL initialization parameter itself. This means that if the shared pool has not been sized correctly, there is a direct impact on the dictionary cache.

Applications not using locally managed tablespaces (LMT) could experience high dc_used_extents, dc_segments, and dc_free_extents counts. This is due to frequent access to the dictionary to update the latest extent information. Using LMT reduces this activity because all tablespace management is performed locally at the tablespace level.

```
SQL> desc v$rowcache
 Name                 Null?    Type
 -------------------- -------- ----------------
 CACHE#                        NUMBER
 TYPE                          VARCHAR2(11)
 SUBORDINATE#                  NUMBER
 PARAMETER                     VARCHAR2(32)
 COUNT                         NUMBER
 USAGE                         NUMBER
 FIXED                         NUMBER
 GETS                          NUMBER
 GETMISSES                     NUMBER
 SCANS                         NUMBER
```

```
SCANMISSES                     NUMBER
SCANCOMPLETES                  NUMBER
MODIFICATIONS                  NUMBER
FLUSHES                        NUMBER
DLM_REQUESTS                   NUMBER
DLM_CONFLICTS                  NUMBER
DLM_RELEASES                   NUMBER
```

A common parameter that should be of concern in a RAC environment is the dc_sequences. This indicates that there are not enough cache sizes defined for the various sequences used by the application. Tuning or increasing the cache sizes for the commonly used database sequences should help reduce the contention.

Similar to the GV$LIBRARYCACHE view discussed earlier, Oracle maintains statistics from the DLM for the parameters available in GV$ROWCACHE view. These columns give indications on global level requests, conflicts, or contention and how frequently the objects managed by the parameter are released:

Script: MVRACPDnTap_rowcache.sql

```
SELECT inst_id                             INT,
       parameter,
       SUM(gets)                           gets,
       SUM(getmisses)                      misses,
       100 * SUM(gets - getmisses) / SUM(gets) pct_succ_gets,
       SUM(modifications)                  updates
FROM   gv$rowcache
WHERE  gets > 0
GROUP  BY inst_id,
          parameter
ORDER  BY inst_id;
```

INT	PARAMETER	GETS	MISSES	PCT_SUCC_GETS	UPDATES
1	dc_awr_control	2419	133	94.5	14
	dc_files	504	84	83.3	0
	dc_global_oids	1671	37	97.8	0
	dc_histogram_data	854110	6643	99.2	0
	dc_histogram_defs	332053	12613	96.2	2,766
	dc_object_grants	179	43	76.0	0
	dc_objects	19529704	11766	99.9	6,174
	dc_profiles	9304	2	100.0	0
	dc_rollback_segments	1350573	2216	99.8	69
	dc_segments	**2526359**	**36460**	**98.6**	**1,275**
	dc_sequences	**437**	**113**	**74.1**	**437**
	dc_table_scns	92	31	66.3	0
	dc_tablespaces	2466261	30	100.0	0
	dc_users	3546497	2098	99.9	0
	global database name	119406	1	100.0	0
	kqlsubheap_object	280915	89	100.0	0
	outstanding_alerts	5345	4953	7.3	363
	sch_lj_objs	4	4	.0	0
	sch_lj_oids	197	14	92.9	0

History of this data is maintained in DBA_HIST_ROWCACHE_SUMMARY.

Enterprise Manager to Monitor Global Cache

Oracle enterprise manager (OEM) cloud control has several enhancements in Oracle EM 12c and in the database (DB) express version of OEM that is installed as part of the database install. Global cache access statistics are displayed in Figure 13-15. This chart can be viewed from the performance-monitoring tab after selecting the database from the targets tab of the DB console.

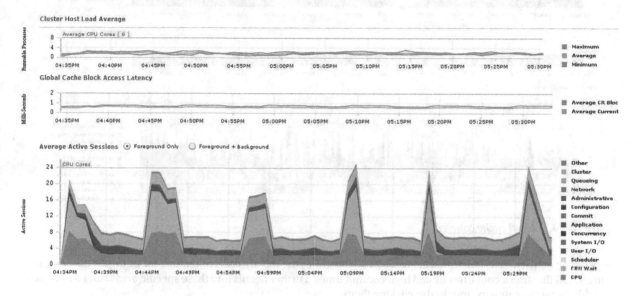

Figure 13-13. *Cluster host load average*

Similar to Figure 13-13, EM cloud control provides a number of other performance matrixes similar to Figure 13-14, which provides a view of the current global cache, block access latency, and block transfers between instances. Apart from this, Figure 13-14 lists the latest sessions and the global wait statistics.

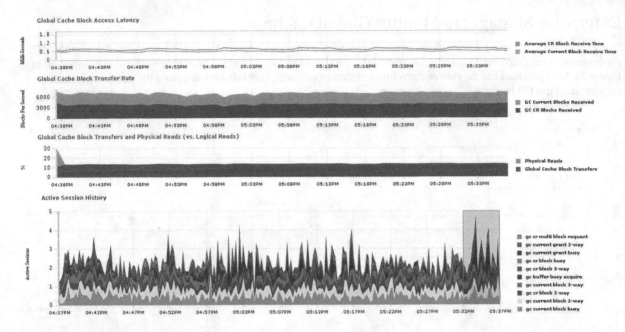

Figure 13-14. *Global cache coherency*

The top activity chart illustrated in Figure 13-15 illustrates the top areas of contention, for example, the chart in Figure 13-15 illustrates concurrency and high commit times. Further details into these specific areas can be obtained by highlighting the category and double clicking them.

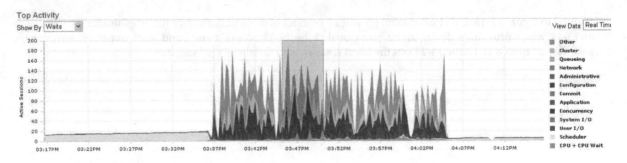

Figure 13-15. *Top activity*

■ **Note**   Discussions on RAC-related wait events can be found in Chapter 17.

Troubleshooting Using Oracle Event Interface

The event interface provided by Oracle helps look at the behavior of a specific operation within the Oracle kernel. For example, as mentioned in Chapter 6, "Tools and Utilities," event 10053 will help you trace through the behavior of Oracle's optimizer. Event 10046 will help you analyze the execution plans generated by Oracle's optimizer. Similar to these events there are those that could help debug the parallel query operations.

Event 10708 @ Level 1—Trace RAC Buffer Cache

This event is used to trace the current RAC buffer cache to understand what is contained in the global cache and the details. Setting this event helps look deeper into the global block content.

```
SQL> alter system set events '10708 trace name context forever, level 1';
System altered.
KCL: A99: anti-lock: share downconvert
GLOBAL CACHE ELEMENT DUMP (address: 0x6ffce3b20):
  id1: 0x701 id2: 0x3e pkey: OBJ#513436 block: (62/1793)
  lock: S rls: 0x0 acq: 0x3 latch: 0
  flags: 0x20 fair: 0 recovery: 0 fpin: 'kclwh1'
  bscn: 0x0.0 bctx: (nil) write: 0 scan: 0x0
  lcp: 0x11c8007540 lnk: [0x11c8007598,0x11c8007598] lch: [0xabe6a3898,0xabe6a3898]
  seq: 4 hist: 340 143:0 354 32
  LIST OF BUFFERS LINKED TO THIS GLOBAL CACHE ELEMENT:
    flg: 0x00000000 state: SCURRENT tsn: 32 tsh: 0 mode: SHR foq: 0
      pin: 'kdiwh15: kdifxs' pinwait: 'gc current request'
      addr: 0xabe6a3768 obj: 513436 cls: DATA bscn: 0x8e5.b1fe4cad
 GCS CLIENT 0x6ffce3b98,1 resp[(nil),0x701.3e] pkey 513436.0
   grant 1 cvt 2 mdrole 0x809 st 0x101 lst 0x20 GRANTQ rl LOCAL
   master 5 owner 1 sid 0 remote[0x1118ea0bd8,3] hist 0x9212385
   history 0x5.0x47.0x4.0x49.0x0.0x0.0x0.0x0.0x0.0x0.
   cflag 0x0 sender 0 flags 0x0 replay# 0 abast (nil).x0.1
   disk: 0x0000.00000000 write request: 0x0000.00000000
   pi scn: 0x0000.00000000 sq[(nil),(nil)]
   msgseq 0x2 updseq 0x0 reqids[2,0,0] infop (nil)
   pkey 513436.0 undo 0 stat 0 masters[32768, 1->1] reminc 12 RM# 13
 flg x0 type x1 afftime x8f085144
   hv 69 [stat 0x0, 5->5, wm 32768, RMno 0, reminc 10, dom 0]
   kjga st 0x4, step 0.0.0, cinc 12, rmno 69, flags 0x0
   lb 0, hb 0, myb 8416, drmb 8416, apifrz 0
GCS CLIENT END

SQL> alter system set events '10708 trace name context off';
```

The preceding output is the global cache element dump. The dissection of the dump will help understand the current contents and contains the following information:

- OBJ# is the object being mastered.
- block is the data block being managed in the global cache.
- bscn—Block SCN.
- pin—Pin buffer number identified by "kdiwh15: kdifxs."

- pinwait—The block currently experienced wait while pinning block to buffer. Wait time currently captured in "gc current request."

- Number of grants to the current object in global cache is identified by grant.

- GRANTQ rl LOCAL—There was a local grant of resource to the block.

- Master of the object identified by master 5 is contained in instance 5.

```
SQL> SELECT OWNER, OBJECT_ID, OBJECT_TYPE FROM dba_objects where object_id=513436;

OWNER                        OBJECT_ID OBJECT_TYPE
---------------------------- ---------- --------------------
DWH                             513436 INDEX
```

Event 10430 @ Level 1—Trace Dynamic Remastering

This trace event will capture the remaster requests and transfers on the respective nodes. The trace is recorded in the LMD trace file.

```
SQL> ALTER SYSTEM SET EVENTS '10430 trace name context forever, level 1';
System altered.

SQL> ALTER SYSTEM SET EVENTS '10430 trace name context off';
System altered.
```

Event 10432 @ Level 1—Trace GCS Cache Fusion Calls

This trace event will capture the global cache service fusion calls. The trace files are recorded in the diagnostic trace directory.

```
SQL> ALTER SYSTEM SET EVENTS '10432 trace name context forever, level 1';
*** 2010-11-29 15:01:02.000
stale cvak fr 3:0x1122331d98([0x53594e43][0x10],[IV])[h=KJUSERNL,n=KJUSEREX,b=KJUSERNL,ls=KJUSERST
  AT_NOVALUE]:0x20004 < 0x0
2010-11-29 15:06:10.319979*: * kjmdm: msgs to be sent for ha phase1 found! (snd_for_p1 1)

*** 2010-11-29 15:06:10.320
2010-11-29 15:06:10.319979*: * kjmsp1 called, msgs to send, p2ack dump at beginning:
2010-11-29 15:06:10.319979*:
* Begin dump saved p2ack info:
* p2id 67.8, ack count 1, valid 1, ready 1
*   to 2, subt 1, cvt lvl 5, is_cvt_b 0, maxs 784
2010-11-29 15:06:10.319979*:
* End dump saved p2ack info
2010-11-29 15:06:10.319979*: * kjmsp1: p2ack p2id 67.8 ready for sending
2010-11-29 15:06:10.319979*: * kjmsp1: will send KJX_HA_P2 msg to 3
2010-11-29 15:06:10.319979*: * subtype 1, p2id 67.8, cvt lvl x5, is cvt blkr 0, maxsessions 784
2010-11-29 15:06:10.319979*:
*          kjurn[0] = x4c4f434b
```

```
2010-11-29 15:06:10.319979*:
*           kjurn[1] = x10
2010-11-29 15:06:10.319979*:
*           kjurn[2] = x5f015649

SQL> ALTER SYSTEM SET EVENTS '10432 trace name context off';
```

Conclusion

In this chapter, we looked at the global cache architecture and global cache management parts of the RAC environment. We also discussed the various hot spots and areas that should be monitored and looked at in detail when performance becomes a concern in a RAC environment. It's a common myth between the DBAs and management to credit the entire reason behind slow performance in a RAC environment to the cluster interconnect, which is not the usual reason. Interconnect is not always the problem, but the primary reasons are poorly written SQL statements and using servers that are not sized correctly for the workload. To understand the root cause of the performance issue, it is important to break the entire process into prepare and transfer phases.

We also looked at other common issues faced by users in a RAC environment and how to monitor and troubleshoot.

Global cache is a primary focus area in a RAC environment. This chapter is not complete because of the relationship of global cache to other components of the cluster. This is discussed in the appropriate chapters of this book.

CHAPTER 14

■ ■ ■

Tuning the Cluster Interconnect

In the previous chapter, we discussed that RAC was a configuration of multiple instances clustered together to provide a scalable, high availability environment for information exchange. These servers communicate with each other using a private network called the cluster interconnect.

The interconnect provides performance critical direct memory access and message passing between instances on different servers for transparent consistent access to user data and metadata. The function of the interconnect is to transport or transfer application (RDBMS and cluster) specific data between instances on different servers. This suggestion also implies that the interconnect must have a specific configuration to perform its functions well. An alternative formulation would be applications; middleware communicate with database instances via the public interconnect, and instances in a tightly coupled RAC cluster communicate with each other via the private interconnect.

Verification and monitoring of the performance of the interconnect is of primary importance. There are several important factors that should be considered when configuring the interconnect, and such factors should be verified.

The first and foremost requirement is that it should be a dedicated network connection. The network should at a minimum be a 1 GigE configuration. The network buffer sizes should be set to the maximum supported by the O/S.

■ **Note** The reader is requested to consult Chapter 13 before attempting to read this chapter.

Cluster Interconnect

The cluster interconnect must be a high-bandwidth, low-latency communication facility that connects each node to other nodes in the cluster and routes messages among the nodes. In a RAC environment, the primary transport mechanism to sharing data blocks between instances is the private interconnect. As illustrated in Figure 14-1, if a user on instance one makes a request for a data block, and the block is not available on the local cache of the instance, then a request is sent to the master of the object. Based on the entries in the GRD, the master will send a request to the current holder. The entire block is transferred to the requestor. However, if there are a few rows of the blocks that are locked by the holder in exclusive mode because the user is making a DML operation, the user on the other instance will see row locks. In certain situations, for example, when the buffer is pinned by the user, the block may not be sent immediately. We illustrate this using a sequence diagram (see Figure 14-1).

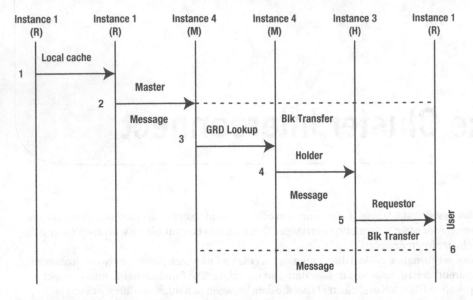

Figure 14-1. *Sequence diagram for a block request*

Figure 14-1 illustrates the sequence of steps to get a data block to the requestor:

1. A user accesses data and the server process tries to find the data in the local buffer cache of the instance to see if the block is present. If the block is found in the local cache (not illustrated), the data is fetched and there is no inter-instance communication involved.

2. If the block is not found in the local buffer cache, the GCS makes a request to determine whether another instance has the data cached. To make this request, GCS sends a message to the instance, which "masters" the block: in this case, Instance 4. The message containing the request is sent from Instance 1 to Instance 4 across the interconnect.

3. Instance 4 determines the current global state to find the current holder (holding instance) of the block.

4. Instance 4 sends a message to the current holder of the block (Instance 3), authorizing it to send the block to the requestor.

5. Instance 3 receives the request from the master and prepares the process to transfer the block to the requestor. Instance 3 transfers the block to the requestor Instance 1 via the interconnect.

6. Instance 1, on receipt of the block, sends an acknowledgement message to the master (not illustrated).

In the entire process, there are two types of operations that involve the interconnect: sending/receiving messages and block transfer.

When more than two instances are participating in the clustered configuration, the block transfer may require 3 hops to complete the operation. Also, if the master or the block is located in the local cache of the instance where the user session had originally made the request, messaging and data transfer requests are reduced.

Block Transfer

When a block is not found in the local cache, the current location of the physical block is identified and transferred from the current holder to the requestor (illustrated in Step 5 in Figure 14-1). As discussed in the previous chapter, block transfer involves several steps, including finding the block, changing permissions of the block, flushing the blocks to redo logs files (if the block was modified), pinning the block, and so forth.

ASYNCHRONOUS SYSTEM TRAP AND BLOCKING ASYNCHRONOUS SYSTEM TRAP

When a block is requested and is available for transfer, the block is sent immediately. However, on the contrary, if the block requested is held by the holding instance in an exclusive mode, the requestor remains in wait mode (if the buffer is not pinned) until such time the data requested is released by the holder and is ready for transfer to the requestor. Oracle uses the concept of an Asynchronous System Trap (AST) and Blocking Asynchronous System Trap (BAST) to notify processes of events concerning the state of a block.

ASTs are interrupts that occur asynchronously (out of sequence) with respect to the process's execution. An AST provides a transfer of control to a user-specified procedure that handles the event. For example, you can use ASTs to signal a program to execute a routine whenever a certain condition occurs.[1]

In RAC, the lock-related operations are handled by the GES. ASTs are generic interrupt service routines. There are two types of ASTs in a RAC implementation. One is called the Acquisition Asynchronous System Trap or AAST and the other is called the Blocking Asynchronous System Trap or BAST.

When a process wants to access a resource in a RAC environment, it needs to acquire a lock and this will be given by the GES. Before granting the lock to the process, the GES will send the global AST to the holder of that resource, and the holder may grant access to the requesting process. Once the required locks on that resource are obtained, the GES will send another AST (AAST) to tell that you have acquired the lock.

When a process tries to acquire a block, and the holding instance has a lock on the block, this conflicts with the request being made. If the lock on the block is in a conflicting mode, the holder will receive a BAST signal to release the lock. Once the release has been processed, the lock can be granted, and the event notifying the requestor of the grant is the AST.

GES will have the queue of requests/converts and will be delivering AST when the requested grant has completed. BAST is the special kind of interrupt or notifier that will be sent for a lock/buffer held/pinned in a different mode by the process holding the resource to initiate the correct action to handle the request consistently. AAST and BAST statistics can be viewed by querying the V$DLM_MISC view.

---

[1] *HP OpenVMS Programming Concepts Manual*, June 2002. http://h71000.www7.hp.com/doc/731final/5841/5841pro.html.

Types of Interconnects

There are different types of interconnects available; some are proprietary, such as the LLT (low latency transport) available from Veritas, or generic, such as the 10GigE and 1GigE interconnect. There are others that are high-speed, top-of-line interconnects, such as the InfiniBand, or those that help keep latency low in long distance data transfer, such as the blackfiber.

In this section, we discuss two of the common types of interconnects used in Oracle RAC implementations.

10 Gigabit Ethernet

Gigabit Ethernet has evolved from the original 10 Mbps Ethernet; 10 BASE-T; and the 100 Mbps Fast Ethernet standards, 100BASE-TX and 100BASE-FX. The IEEE (Institute of Electrical and Electronics Engineers) and the Gigabit Ethernet Alliance support a 10-Gigabit Ethernet (10GigE). 10GigE is the latest evolution in networking options providing excellent high-speed communication between devices. Almost always, a GigE or 10GigE network is sufficient for most types of workload computing, other technologies such as Infiniband (discussed later) may not be required and could be an expensive solution.

Benefits of using Gigabit Ethernet over its predecessors include the following:

- 10GigE is 10 times faster than GigE and 100 times faster than 100Mbps Fast Ethernet

- Increased bandwidth for higher performance and elimination of bottlenecks

- Full-duplex capacity, allowing for increased bandwidth

- Full compatibility with the large installed base of Ethernet and Fast Ethernet nodes

- Transfer of large amounts of data quickly across networks

Oracle supports and recommends the use of user datagram protocol (UDP) for Linux/Unix environments and TCP for Windows environments as the communication layer for the interconnect.

UDP is defined to make available a datagram mode of packet-switched computer communication in the environment of an interconnected set of computer networks. The protocol is transaction oriented, and delivery and duplicate protection are not guaranteed.[2] This protocol assumes that the Internet Protocol (IP) is used as the underlying protocol.

TCP is a set of rules used along with the Internet Protocol (IP) to send data in the form of message units between computers over the Internet. Whereas IP takes care of handling the actual delivery of the data, TCP takes care of keeping track of the individual units of data (called packets) that a message is divided into for efficient routing through the Internet.

InfiniBand Technology

The demands of the Internet and distributed computing are challenging the scalability, reliability, availability, and performance of servers. InfiniBand™ architecture represents a new approach to I/O technology and is based on the collective research, knowledge, and experience of the industry's leaders and computer vendors.

InfiniBand architecture specifies channels that are created by attaching host channel adapters (HCA) within a server chassis to host channel adapters in other server chassis. This is done for high-performance IPC and to target channel adapters connecting Infiniband-enabled servers to remote storage and communication networks through InfiniBand switches. InfiniBand links transfer data at 2.5 Gbits/second, utilizing both copper wire and fiber optics for transmission. It can carry any combination of I/O, network, and IPC messages.

---

[2]Tierney, Brian L., Jason R. Lee, Dan Gunter, and Martin Stoufer. "Improving Distributed Application Performance Using TCP Instrumentation," May 2003. Lawrence Berkeley National Laboratory—Tom Dunigan, Oak Ridge National Laboratory.

InfiniBand architecture has the following communication characteristics:

- User-level access to message passing

- Remote Direct Memory Access (RDMA) in read and write mode

- Up to a maximum of 2Gb message in a single transfer

The memory protection mechanism defined by the InfiniBand architecture allows an InfiniBand HCA to transfer data directly into or out of an application buffer. To protect these buffers from unauthorized access, a process called memory registration is employed. Memory registration allows data transfers to be initiated directly from user mode, eliminating costly context switches to the kernel. Another benefit of allowing the InfiniBand, RDMA allows direct memory access, bypassing the memory in the O/S. This eliminates the context switches to the kernel and eliminates the need to copy data to or from system buffers on a send or receive operation, respectively.

InfiniBand architecture also has another unique feature called a memory window. The memory window provides a way for the application to grant remote read and/or write to a specified buffer at a byte-level granularity to another application. Memory windows are used in conjunction with RDMA read or RDMA write to control remote access to the application buffers. Data could be transferred either by the push or pull method, that is, either the sending node would send (push) the data over to the requester or the requester could get to the holder and get (pull) the data.

Table 14-1 lists the throughput differences between the two types of interconnect protocols.

Table 14-1. *Interconnect Throughput*

Interconnect Type	Throughput
Gigabit Ethernet	80 Megabits per second
InfiniBand	160 Megabits per second

Oracle supports InfiniBand using the reliable datagram socket (RDS) protocol. This protocol multiplexes UDP packets over InfiniBand connection, improving performance in an Oracle RAC environment.

RDS is a reliable-socket off-load driver and inter-processor communication (IPC) protocol with low overhead, low latency, and high bandwidth. RDS enables enhanced application performance and cluster scalability. RDS over InfiniBand uses approximately 50% less CPU per operation than IPoIB (Internet Protocol over InfiniBand) and operates with approximately half the latency of UDP over Ethernet.

Network Throughput and Bandwidth

Bandwidth refers to the amount of bandwidth *currently available* on the network, whereas available throughput is the throughput actually possible, given the end-system hardware (CPU speed and load, network interface card [NIC], I/O bus speed, disk speed), O/S, TCP stack, TCP parameters, and so on. We now look at some network-related tuning options.

Tuning Network Buffer Sizes

As a basic installation and configuration requirement, network buffer sizes discussed in the Oracle installation documents are the bare minimum required for RAC functioning. Monitoring and measuring network latencies can help increase these buffer sizes even further provided the O/S supports such an increase.

TCP protocol uses a congestion window scheme to determine how many packets can be transmitted at any one time. The maximum congestion window size is determined by how much buffer space the kernel has allocated for each socket. If the buffers are too small, the TCP congestion window will never completely open; and on the other hand, if the buffers are too large, the sender can overrun the receiver, causing the TCP window to shut down. The common buffer-related parameters and default values required to configure Oracle Database 11g Release 2 RAC or higher on Linux are the following:

```
net.core.rmem_default = 262144
net.core.wmem_default = 262144
net.core.rmem_max = 4194304
net.core.wmem_max = 4194304
net.ipv4.tcp_rmem=4096 4194304 4194304
net.ipv4.tcp_wmem=98304 4194304 4194304
net.ipv4.tcp_window_scaling=1
```

All of the preceding network parameters have a lower limit configured as the default value and a max value. The default value is the startup value: the minimum allocation per socket immediately at socket creation. The max value determines how much memory each socket is allowed to dynamically consume. As a best practice, it is advised to set the default at the recommended values just listed and set the max to the maximum value supported by the O/S. This would help conserve memory when possible and would allow dynamic growth if additional memory is required by the sockets.

tcp_wmem

This variable takes three different values, which hold information on how much TCP send buffer memory space each TCP socket has to use. Every TCP socket is allocated this buffer space to use before the buffer is filled up. Each of the three values is used under different conditions.

The first value in this variable tells the minimum TCP send buffer space available for a single TCP socket; the second value tells the default buffer space allowed for a single TCP socket to use; and the third value tells the kernel the maximum TCP send buffer space. The /proc/sys/net/core/wmem_max value overrides this value.

tcp_rmem

The tcp_rmem variable tells the kernel the minimum receive buffer for each TCP connection. This variable takes three different values, just the same as the tcp_wmem variable. The first value is for the TCP connection; the second value specifies the default receive buffer allocated for each TCP socket; and the third value specifies the maximum receive buffer that can be allocated to a TCP socket.

This value overrides the /proc/sys/net/core/rmem_default value.

tcp_mem

The tcp_mem variable defines how the TCP stack should behave when it comes to memory usage. It consists of three values, just as the tcp_wmem and tcp_rmem variables. The three values define the low, medium, and maximum threshold values for the TCP sockets. If the maximum value is reached, TCP streams, and we see packets being dropped until the system stabilizes and the threshold reaches the lower value again.

Device Queue Sizes

Similar to tuning the network buffer sizes, it is important to look into the size of the queue between the kernel network subsystems and the driver for network interface card. Inappropriate sizing can cause loss of data due to buffer overflows, which in turn cause retransmission consuming resources and delays in performance. There are two queues to consider in this area: the txqueuelen, which is related to the transmit/send queue size, and the netdev_backlog, which determines the receive queue size. The txqueuelen setting can be checked using ifconfig command on Linux and Unix systems.

```
[oracle@prddb1]$ /sbin/ifconfig -a
eth1      Link encap:Ethernet  HWaddr 00:0C:29:3A:F1:6E
          inet addr:172.35.1.11  Bcast:172.35.1.255  Mask:255.255.255.0
          inet6 addr: fe80::20c:29ff:fe3a:f16e/64 Scope:Link
          UP BROADCAST RUNNING MULTICAST  MTU:1500  Metric:1
          RX packets:42232 errors:0 dropped:0 overruns:0 frame:0
          TX packets:11 errors:0 dropped:0 overruns:0 carrier:0
          collisions:0 txqueuelen:1000
          RX bytes:3483899 (3.3 MiB)  TX bytes:678 (678.0 b)
          Base address:0x2440 Memory:d8960000-d8980000
```

The value of the netdev_max_backlog parameter can be viewed from the following:

```
[oracle@prddb1]$ cat /proc/sys/net/core/netdev_max_backlog  300
```

These values can be manually defined using the ifconfig command on Linux and Unix systems. For example, the following command will reset the txqueuelen to 2000:

```
/sbin/ifconfig eth1 txqueuelen 2000
```

Similarly, the receive queue size can be increased by setting the following parameter file:

```
/proc/sys/net/core/netdev_max_backlog = 2000 in the /etc/sysctl.conf
```

Normally, the transmit (send) and the receive queue lengths should be set identical to avoid send or receive bottlenecks.

Transport Unit Size

Ethernet traffic moves in units called *frames*. Ethernet's variable frame size of 46–1,500 bytes is the transfer unit between the all Ethernet participants, such as the hosts and switches. The upper bound, in this case 1,500, is called Maximum Transmission Unit (MTU) and is the largest packet a network device transmits. When an application sends a message greater than 1,500 bytes (MTU), it is fragmented (broken into smaller frames) into 1,500-byte frames or smaller; or as a worst case, it's dropped. As illustrated in the ifconfig output following, historically, Ethernet has a maximum frame size of 1,500 bytes;[3] so most devices use 1,500 as their default MTU. To maintain backward compatibility, the "standard" GigE also uses 1,500-byte frames. This is maintained so a packet to/from any combination of 10/100/1000/10000 Mbps Ethernet devices can be handled without any layer two fragmentation or reassembly. An Ethernet packet larger than 1,500 bytes is called a *jumbo frame*.

```
[oracle@prddb1]$ /sbin/ifconfig -a
eth1      Link encap:Ethernet  HWaddr 00:0C:29:3A:F1:6E
          inet addr:172.35.1.11  Bcast:172.35.1.255  Mask:255.255.255.0
          inet6 addr: fe80::20c:29ff:fe3a:f16e/64 Scope:Link
          UP BROADCAST RUNNING MULTICAST  MTU:1500  Metric:1
          RX packets:42232 errors:0 dropped:0 overruns:0 frame:0
          TX packets:11 errors:0 dropped:0 overruns:0 carrier:0
          collisions:0 txqueuelen:1000
          RX bytes:3483899 (3.3 MiB)  TX bytes:678 (678.0 b)
          Base address:0x2440 Memory:d8960000-d8980000
```

---

[3]The Ethernet packet consists of a 1,500-byte payload + 14 bytes for header + VLAN tag 4 bytes + CRC 4 bytes.

Jumbo frame support is designed to enhance Ethernet networking throughput and significantly reduce the CPU utilization of large file transfers such as large multimedia files or large data files by enabling more efficient, larger payloads per packet. Sending large frame sizes avoids reassembly and fragmentation costs for data blocks, reduces the overhead on CPU, and improves throughput. Larger frame sizes also reduces chances for lost blocks encountered during transfers on busy interconnects. By using jumbo frames, the transfer frame sizes for Ethernet could be increased to 9,000 bytes.

Verifying the Interconnect

Tuning the cluster interconnect should begin with verifying the hardware configuration. This basic check should ensure that the database is using the correct IP addresses or NICs for the interconnect.

Check 1

The following query provides a list of IP addresses registered with the Oracle database kernel:

Script:MVRACPDnTap_verifyic.sql

```
SELECT addr,
       indx,
       inst_id,
       pub_ksxpia,
       picked_ksxpia,
       name_ksxpia,
       ip_ksxpia
FROM   x$ksxpia;
```

ADDR	Indx	Public	Impl Type	Name	IP Address
00002ABF8F3EA550	0	N	OCR	bond2	172.30.0.16
00002ABF8F3EA550	1	Y	OCR	bond0	10.32.5.7

```
SELECT inst_id,
       name,
       ip_address,
       is_public
FROM   gv$cluster_interconnects
ORDER  BY inst_id;
```

Instance	Name	IP_ADDRESS	IS_	SOURCE
1	bond2	172.30.0.16	NO	Oracle Cluster Repository
2	bond2	172.30.0.17	NO	Oracle Cluster Repository
3	bond2	172.30.0.10	NO	Oracle Cluster Repository
4	bond2	172.30.0.11	NO	Oracle Cluster Repository
5	bond2	172.30.0.12	NO	Oracle Cluster Repository
6	bond2	172.30.0.13	NO	Oracle Cluster Repository

The preceding output illustrates there are two interfaces currently configured on the node: bond0 and bond2. Both of these interfaces have used NIC bonding for high availability. Both of the interfaces are registered in the OCR. In the preceding output, bond0 has the value Y in column Public (PUB_KSXPIA), indicating it's the public interface; and bond2 is the private interface (identified by the value N). If the correct IP addresses are not visible, it is an indication of incorrect installation and configuration of the RAC environment.

■ **Note**   Yet another method to validate the interconnect configuration is to use the oifcfg utility.

```
[oracle@ssky1l3p1 ~]$ oifcfg iflist -p -n
eth0  192.168.2.0  PRIVATE  255.255.255.0
eth1  10.2.4.0  PRIVATE  255.255.255.0
eth1  169.254.192.0  UNKNOWN  255.255.192.0
eth1  169.254.0.0  UNKNOWN  255.255.192.0
eth2  10.2.4.0  PRIVATE  255.255.255.0
eth2  169.254.64.0  UNKNOWN  255.255.192.0
eth3  10.2.4.0  PRIVATE  255.255.255.0
eth3  169.254.128.0  UNKNOWN  255.255.192.0
```

In Oracle Database 11g Release 2 (11.2.0.2), the configuration has changed. If the installation is a new install using this version, Oracle assigns an HAIP for the private interconnect as well. If the RAC configuration is an upgrade from 11.2.0.1 to 11.2.0.2, Oracle retains the existing configuration unless manually modified.

The private interconnect is no longer recorded in the OCR file; instead, Oracle keeps the information locally in "GPnP" (Grid Plug and Play) profiles.

For every network available on the host servers, Oracle provides the list and allows for multiple networks to be selected as the private network. During the grid infrastructure (GI) installation (Figure 14-2), these private networks are all assigned IPs called HAIPs similar to the VIPs assigned to the public networks during the GI configuration.

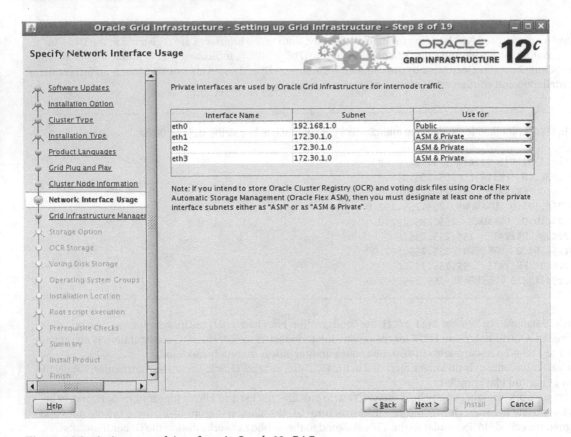

Figure 14-2. *Assign network interfaces in Oracle 12c RAC*

The number of HAIP addresses is decided by how many private network adapters are active when Oracle clusterware gets started on the first node in the cluster. If there's only one active private network, Grid will create one; if two, Grid will create two; and if more than two, Grid will create four HAIPs.

■ **Note** The number of HAIPs won't change even if more private network adapters are activated later; a restart of clusterware on all nodes is required for new adapters to become effective.

Grid automatically selects link local addresses from reserved 169.254.*.* subnet for HAIP, and it will not attempt to use any 169.254.*.* address if it's already in use for another purpose. With HAIP, by default, interconnect traffic will be load balanced across all active interconnect interfaces, and corresponding HAIP addresses will be failed over transparently to other adapters if one fails or becomes noncommunicative.[4]

The database now records the private interconnect with the IP address 169.254.x.x.

---

[4]Metalink Note # 1210883.1, 11gR2 Grid Infrastructure Redundant Interconnect, and ora.cluster_interconnect.haip.

Script:MVRACPDnTap_verifyic.sql

```
SELECT addr,
       indx,
       inst_id,
       pub_ksxpia,
       picked_ksxpia,
       name_ksxpia,
       ip_ksxpia
FROM   x$ksxpia;
                                  Impl
ADDR                 Indx  Public  Type       Name        IP Address
----------------     ----  ------  ----------  ----------  ---------------
00002B02FB7F89A0        0  N       GPnP       bond2:1     169.254.183.5
00002B02FB7F89A0        1  Y       GPnP       bond0       10.32.5.43
00002B02FB7F89A0        2  Y       GPnP       bond0:1     10.32.5.48
00002B02FB7F89A0        3  Y       GPnP       bond0:4     10.32.5.56

SELECT inst_id,
       name,
       ip_address,
       is_public
FROM   gv$cluster_interconnects
ORDER  BY inst_id;

Instance  Name        IP_ADDRESS        IS_   SOURCE
--------  ----------  ----------------  ---   -------------------------------
       1  bond2:1     169.254.183.5     NO
       2  bond2:1     169.254.250.200   NO
       3  bond2:1     169.254.129.142   NO

[oracle@prddb1]$ /sbin/ifconfig -a
bond2     Link encap:Ethernet  HWaddr 00:22:64:0F:B9:9B
          inet addr:172.30.0.143  Bcast:172.30.0.255  Mask:255.255.255.0
          inet6 addr: fe80::222:64ff:fe0f:b99b/64 Scope:Link
          UP BROADCAST RUNNING MASTER MULTICAST  MTU:9000  Metric:1
          RX packets:16277881 errors:0 dropped:0 overruns:0 frame:0
          TX packets:13903957 errors:0 dropped:0 overruns:0 carrier:0
          collisions:0 txqueuelen:0
          RX bytes:15725195854 (14.6 GiB)  TX bytes:13853391629 (12.9 GiB)
bond2:1   Link encap:Ethernet  HWaddr 00:22:64:0F:B9:9B
          inet addr:169.254.183.5  Bcast:169.254.255.255  Mask:255.255.0.0
          UP BROADCAST RUNNING MASTER MULTICAST  MTU:9000  Metric:1
```

■ **Note** In the preceding outputs, note the bond2:1, indicating that this is an upgrade from Oracle 11g Release 1; bonding of interfaces for the interconnect is not required when Grid Infrastructure version 11.2.0.2 is installed new on the cluster.

LINK LOCAL BLOCK

`169.254.0.0/16`—This is the "link local" block. It is allocated for communication between hosts on a single link. Hosts obtain these addresses by auto-configuration, such as when a DHCP server may not be found. This is a 16-bit address, class B subnet and can support up to 65,534 interfaces.[5]

Column `PICKED_KSXPIA` indicates the type of Oracle clusterware implemented on the RAC cluster, where the interconnect configuration is stored and the cluster communication method. The valid values in this column are the following:

- OCR = Oracle Clusterware is configured.

- OSD = Operating System dependent, meaning a third party cluster manager is configured, and Oracle Clusterware is only a bridge between Oracle RDBMS and the third party cluster manager.

- CI = Interconnect is defined using the `CLUSTER_INTERCONNECT` parameter in the instance.

- GPnP = Configured using Grid Plug and Play in Oracle Database 11g Release 2 (11.2.0.2).

Check 2

From the O/S level, check if the configuration is correct by verifying if the right NIC cards are being used for data transfer. This can be done using the `netstat` utility (`netstat -i`):

```
# netstat -i
Kernel Interface table
Iface      MTU Met   RX-OK RX-ERR RX-DRP RX-OVR    TX-OK TX-ERR TX-DRP TX-OVR Flg
bond0     1500   0 7144585      0    893      0 10645931      0      0      0 BMmRU
bond0:1   1500   0      - no statistics available -                           BMmRU
bond0:3   1500   0      - no statistics available -                           BMmRU
bond0:4   1500   0      - no statistics available -                           BMmRU
bond1     1500   0  233067      0      0      0      609      0      0      0 BMmRU
bond2     9000   0 2857345      0      0      0  2630894      0      0      0 BMmRU
bond2:1   9000   0      - no statistics available -                           BMmRU
eth20     1500   0 7138790      0    893      0 10645931      0      0      0 BMsRU
eth21     1500   0    5795      0      0      0        0      0      0      0 BMsRU
eth22     1500   0  233067      0      0      0      609      0      0      0 BMsRU
eth24     9000   0 2857345      0      0      0  2630894      0      0      0 BMsRU
lo       16436   0 1527642      0      0      0  1527642      0      0      0 LRU
```

bond0: is the public interconnect created using the bonding functionality.

bond0:1, bond0:3, bond0:4 are all SCAN VIPs.

bond2: is the private interconnect alias created using the bonding functionality.

bond2:1 is the private interconnect VIP. Because VIPs are logical, there are no direct NICs attached to them; hence, there is no traffic or statistics visible.

---

[5]Internet Assigned Numbers Authority (IANA): `http://tools.ietf.org/html/rfc3330`.

eth20 and eth21 are the physical public interfaces; however, they are bonded/paired together (bond0).

eth24 and eth25 are the physical private interfaces; however, they are bonded/paired together (bond2).

lo0: in the output also indicates that there is a loopback option configured. Verification of whether Oracle is using the loopback option should also be verified using the ORADEBUG command and is discussed later in this section. The use of the loopback IP depends on the integrity of the routing table defined on each of the nodes. Modification of the routing table can result in the inoperability of the interconnect.

In the previous netstat output, there are two types of NIC configurations. The public NIC has an MTU set at 1,500 bytes, but the private NIC has an MTU set to 9,000 bytes.

■ **Note**   In the previous output, NIC pairing/bonding is used for both public (bond0) and private (bond2) networks.

Check 3

The database and ASM alert logs show entries related to the interconnect.
    Both the RDBMS and ASM alert logs can also be sources to confirm this information:

```
Starting ORACLE instance (normal)
LICENSE_MAX_SESSION = 0
LICENSE_SESSIONS_WARNING = 0
Private Interface 'eth22:1' configured from GPnP for use as a private interconnect.
  [name='eth22:1', type=1, ip=169.254.62.94, mac=00-23-7d-36-5b-90, net=169.254.0.0/18,
mask=255.255.192.0, use=haip:cluster_interconnect/62]
```

After instance is started, Oracle then provides the IP addresses configured for the interconnect also in the alert log files:

```
Cluster communication is configured to use the following interface(s) for this instance
   169.254.62.94
   169.254.122.73
   169.254.155.149
   169.254.238.3
cluster interconnect IPC version:Oracle UDP/IP (generic)
IPC Vendor 1 proto 2
```

Check 4

The next important check would be to determine the transfer rate vs. the actual implemented packet size to ensure the installation has been carried out per specification.

The speed of the cluster interconnect solely depends on the hardware vendor and the layered O/S. Oracle depends on the O/S and the hardware for sending packets of information across the cluster interconnect. For example, one type of cluster interconnect supported on Solaris (Sun 4800s) had an O/S limitation of a 64 KB buffer size. To transfer a 256-KB packet across the interconnect would mean the packet would have to be broken into four smaller sized packets before the entire packet reaches the destination. Comparing this to another O/S, for example, Linux, where the supported packet size is 256 K, would mean just one send for the packet to be transmitted to the destination.

This may not raise an issue where the workload contains small data requests, typically in an OLTP environment. However, this could be a concern in high concurrent transaction-intensive environments with a high workload. On a high-transaction system where there is a large amount of interconnect traffic, because of user activity on the various instances participating in the clustered configuration, limitations on the packet size could cause serious performance issues.

Tools such as IPTraf on Linux environments (Figure 14-3), glance on HP-UX environments, or utilities such as netstat should help monitor network traffic and transfer rates between instance and client configurations.

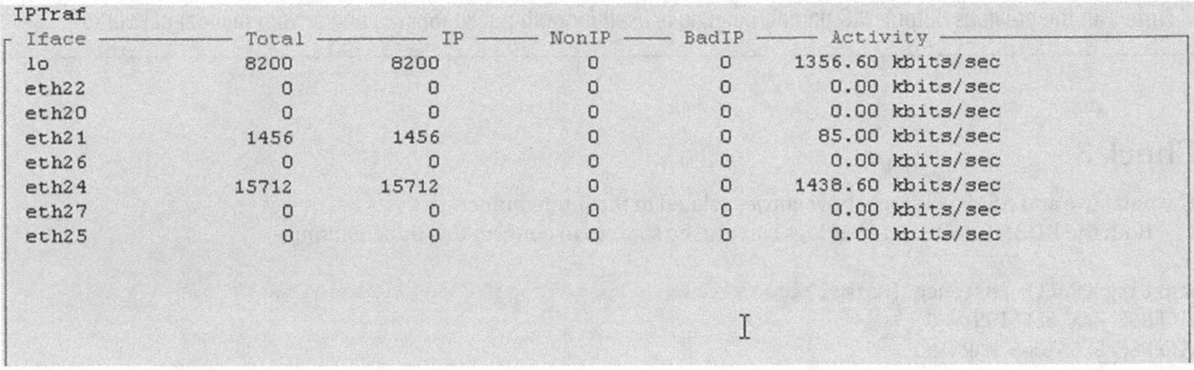

```
IPTraf
 Iface              Total            IP        NonIP        BadIP          Activity
 lo                  8200          8200            0            0    1356.60 kbits/sec
 eth22                 0             0             0            0       0.00 kbits/sec
 eth20                 0             0             0            0       0.00 kbits/sec
 eth21              1456          1456             0            0      85.00 kbits/sec
 eth26                 0             0             0            0       0.00 kbits/sec
 eth24             15712         15712             0            0    1438.60 kbits/sec
 eth27                 0             0             0            0       0.00 kbits/sec
 eth25                 0             0             0            0       0.00 kbits/sec
```

Figure 14-3. *IPTraf general network traffic*

IPTraf also helps to look into a specific network interface and monitor its performance in detail by the type of protocol used for network traffic. For example, in Figure 14-4, the network traffic by protocol (TCP and UDP) giving outgoing and incoming rates is displayed.

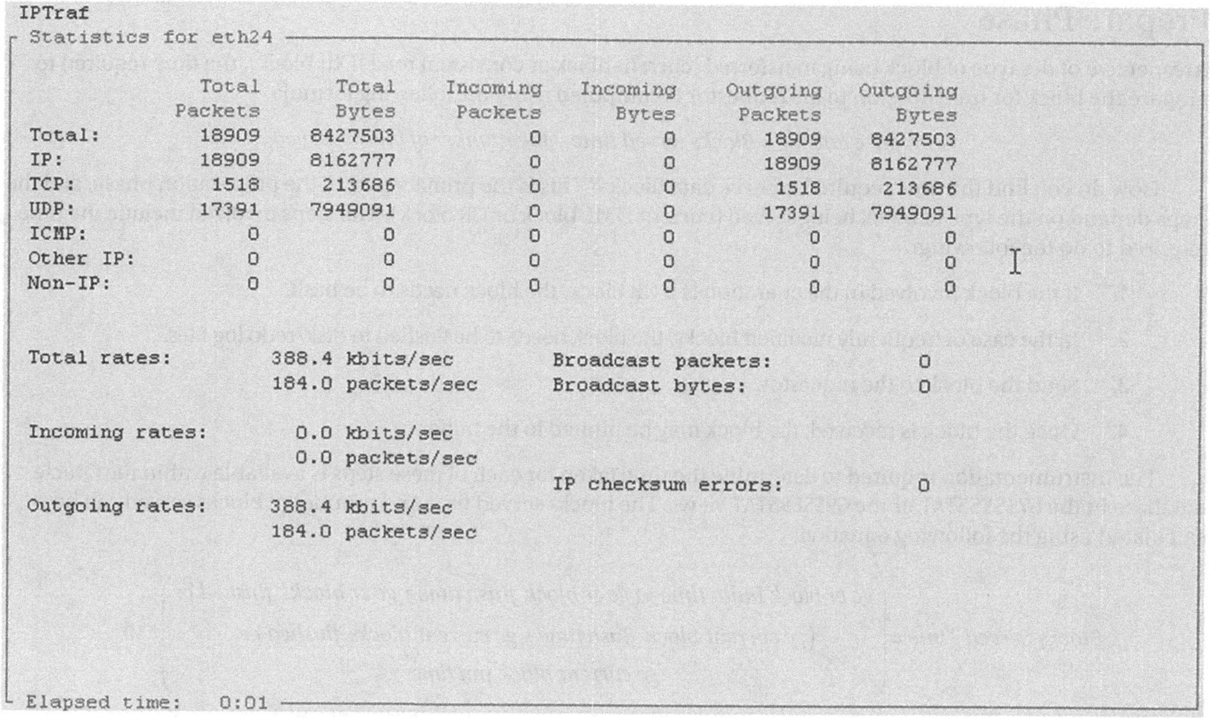

```
IPTraf
 Statistics for eth24

               Total        Total     Incoming    Incoming    Outgoing    Outgoing
             Packets        Bytes      Packets       Bytes     Packets       Bytes
 Total:        18909      8427503            0           0       18909      8427503
 IP:           18909      8162777            0           0       18909      8162777
 TCP:           1518       213686            0           0        1518       213686
 UDP:          17391      7949091            0           0       17391      7949091
 ICMP:             0            0            0           0           0            0
 Other IP:         0            0            0           0           0            0
 Non-IP:           0            0            0           0           0            0


 Total rates:          388.4 kbits/sec       Broadcast packets:            0
                       184.0 packets/sec      Broadcast bytes:              0

 Incoming rates:         0.0 kbits/sec
                         0.0 packets/sec
                                              IP checksum errors:           0
 Outgoing rates:       388.4 kbits/sec
                       184.0 packets/sec




 Elapsed time:    0:01
```

Figure 14-4. IPTraf statistics for eth24

Check 5

Yet another method of verifying that the right interconnect is used is to dump the contents of the IPC stack from inside the database is using the ORADEBUG utility. This method is illustrated later in the chapter as part of a troubleshooting workshop.

Think Inside the Interconnect

In the previous chapter, we looked at scenarios of why the interconnect may not be the reason for the slow performance. Here we look at the contrary: why interconnect can be one of the reasons for slow performance. Not because the bandwidth of the GigE or 10GigE was not sufficient for the load, but due to several other factors that caused the interconnect to be the reason for the poor performance.

With regard to Figure 14-1, we discussed that the request for a block may not be satisfied by the local instance or the master instance and may require a message to a third instance. We discussed in Chapter 13 how in a RAC configuration there are two main message protocol types; one involves just two instances in the cluster, and the entire communication process to request the block and find the block requires two hops. The other type is when the data is not available in the local cache, with the master, but on a third instance. The communication in this type of operation requires three hops to complete the request. In Chapter 13, we discussed these behaviors in Figures 13-3 and 13-5, respectively.

We also discussed in Chapter 13 that the request for a block of data by one instance may require GCS to complete two operational phases to get the block from the current holder to the requestor. Just to recap, we discuss these phases briefly here and drill down into the transfer phase that involves the interconnect.

Prepare Phase

Irrespective of the type of block being transferred (current block or consistent read [CR] block), the time required to prepare the block for transmission to the requestor is computed using the following formula:

Prepare latency = Blocks served time ÷ the number of blocks served

How do you find the time required to serve data blocks? This is the primary part of the preparation phase, and the steps depend on the type of block being served (current DML block or CR block). The steps involved include the time required to do the following:

1. If the block involved in the operation is a CR block, the block needs to be built.

2. In the case of frequently modified blocks, the block needs to be flushed to disk/redo log files.

3. Send the block to the requestor.

4. Once the block is received, the block may be pinned to the buffer.

The instrumentation required to determine the time taken for each of these steps is available within the Oracle database in the GV$SYSSTAT or the GV$SESSTAT views. The blocks served time and number of blocks served can be calculated using the following equation:

$$Blocks\ Served\ Time = \left(\begin{array}{c} gc\ cr\ block\ build\ time + \left(gc\ cr\ block\ flush\ time \div gc\ cr\ blocks\ flushed \right) + \\ \left(gc\ current\ block\ flush\ time \div gc\ current\ blocks\ flushed \right) + \\ gc\ current\ block\ pin\ time \end{array} \right) * 10$$

$$Blocks\ Served = \left(gc\ current\ blocks\ served + gc\ cr\ blocks\ served \right)$$

■ **Note**   Please review Chapter 13 before continuing further on this chapter.

Transfer Phase

Similar to the prepare latency, we also need to compute the transfer latency to determine what part of the operation is slowing down the system. The transfer latency is computed as follows:

Transfer latency = Interconnect latency ÷ prepare latency

We have found the components involved in a prepare latency. What about the interconnect latency? Interconnect latency depends on the number of data blocks received and the time required to receive these data blocks.

Interconnect latency = Blocks receive time ÷ blocks received

Data blocks received is the sum of both the current blocks received and the CR blocks received. Similarly, the time taken to receive these blocks is also the time taken to receive a current block and the CR block.

Once again, all the instrumentation required to compute the transfer latency is also available with the Oracle database in the GV$SYSSTAT and GV$SESSTAT views.

*Blocks received time = (gc cr block receive time + gc current block receive time) * 10*
Blocks received = (gc cr blocks received + gc current blocks received)

The statistics collected will give directions as to where the performance concerns may be: the prepare phase or the transfer phase. If the statistics on the transfer phase are significantly on the higher side, causing concern, for obvious reasons the interconnect configuration and setup may have to be looked at. However, if the prepare phase is of concern, the root cause of the problem should be identified by looking at what is causing these high numbers. The reasons could be resource contention, lack of resources, or the process is simply waiting or hung.

■ **Note**　We discussed the concerns around the prepare phase in Chapter 13. In this chapter, we just focus on the transfer phase.

Workshop

Figure 14-5 illustrates a six-node RAC cluster running a mixed distributed workload system. The cluster contains two separate databases, and the servers have been logically partitioned using server pools.

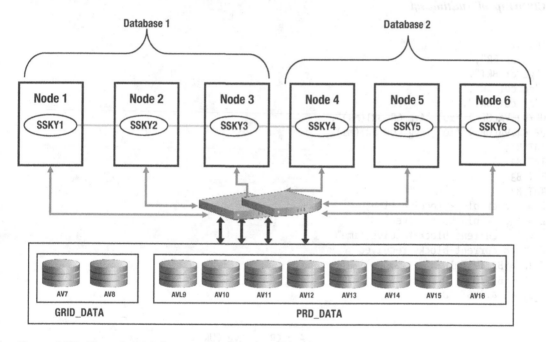

Figure 14-5. *Six-node RAC cluster – Distributed Workload*

Users have been complaining about poor performance of the cluster and the DBA's look at the general health of the database and analyze the environment.

Step 1

Does the cluster have the interconnect configured correctly?

```
Instance  Name       IP Address         IS_
--------  ---------- ---------------    ---
       1  eth2:1     169.254.14.121     NO
       1  eth3:1     169.254.140.97     NO
       2  eth2:1     169.254.12.119     NO
       2  eth3:1     169.254.246.237    NO
```

Step 2

The interconnect has been configured correctly, and the interconnect definitions are recorded in the GPnP file. In checking the data transfer rates across the interconnect, the following latency numbers are seen:

Script: MVRACPDnTap_blksndtime.sql

```
SELECT
    B1.INST_ID INT,
    B2.VALUE "gc cr BR",
    B1.VALUE "gc cr BRT",
    B4.VALUE "gc cur BR",
    b3.value "gc cur BRT",
    ((B1.VALUE/B2.VALUE ) *10) "Avg CR BRT(ms)",
    ((B3.VALUE/B4.VALUE ) *10) "Avg CUR BRT(ms)"
FROM GV$SYSSTAT B1,
     GV$SYSSTAT B2,
     GV$SYSSTAT B3,
     GV$SYSSTAT B4
WHERE B1.NAME = 'gc cr block receive time'
AND    B2.NAME = 'gc cr blocks received'
AND    B3.NAME = 'gc current block receive time'
AND    B4.NAME = 'gc current blocks received'
AND    B1.INST_ID = B2.INST_ID
AND    B1.INST_ID = B3.INST_ID
AND    B1.INST_ID = B4.INST_ID
ORDER BY 1
/
```

In	gc cr BR	gc cr BRT	gc cur BR	gc cur BRT	Avg CR BRT (ms)	Avg CUR BRT (ms)
1	164525	168021	50238	84114	10.21	16.74
2	178217	198596	53490	60261	11.14	11.27
3	112649	180146	40128	58259	15.99	14.52
4	108053	251629	48928	69379	23.29	14.18
5	249861	312446	41881	71759	12.50	17.13
6	461630	794437	170375	184664	17.21	10.84

From the preceding output, the transfer times are significantly high for both the CR and the current blocks. Investigating further, it was also noticed that a few of the servers (Servers 1, 2, and 3) had high CPU utilization. However, the block prepare time on these servers was low. This is likely an indication that the high CPU utilization and system load influenced the latencies. Reasons for high latency of the interconnect could be

- Poorly written SQL statements causing large blocks to be queried from the disk and loaded into buffer. When users on other instances execute the same query, the blocks are transferred over the interconnect, causing high traffic. This normally happens when the capacity of the interconnect is exceeded due to high traffic.

- Network bandwidth is not sufficient or a low bandwidth network is used. Speed of the network is low, causing slower movement of blocks over the interconnect.

- The database is using the public network for the cache fusion traffic. Normally, public networks are low-speed networks; and besides this, the public networks carry other user data, causing network contention and slower data movement. It's a requirement that a dedicated private network be used for cache fusion/interconnect.

- There are wrongly sized network buffers. The data traffic on the private network can be bursty and cause network waits for receive buffers which in turn cause high CPU utilization. The effect of low buffer sizes can also be packet loses at the O/S or blocks lost inside the database. Almost always lost blocks and poorly configured interconnects are the reason for poorly performing interconnect and high latencies caused by the interconnect itself.

Step 3

The next step is to monitor the network utilization using O/S level utilities such as netstat and IPTraf.

ifconfig –a on the private NIC showed that there are no errors at the NIC level. In the output following, errors, dropped, overrun, and collision counts columns all have zero values, indicating there are probably no errors with the NIC card configuration:

```
[oracle@prddb1]$ /sbin/ifconfig -a
eth1      Link encap:Ethernet  HWaddr 00:0C:29:3A:F1:6E
          inet addr:172.35.1.11  Bcast:172.35.1.255  Mask:255.255.255.0
          inet6 addr: fe80::20c:29ff:fe3a:f16e/64 Scope:Link
          UP BROADCAST RUNNING MULTICAST  MTU:1500  Metric:1
          RX packets:42232 errors:0 dropped:0 overruns:0 frame:0
          TX packets:11 errors:0 dropped:0 overruns:0 carrier:0
          collisions:0 txqueuelen:1000
          RX bytes:3483899 (3.3 MiB)  TX bytes:678 (678.0 b)
          Base address:0x2440 Memory:d8960000-d8980000
```

Similar to the ifconfig, which gives you the current configuration, the NIC card, and some of the statistics collected, the ethtool can also be helpful in getting this information:

```
[root@prddb1 ~]# ethtool -S eth24
NIC statistics:
     rcvd bad skb: 0
     xmit called: 2225012436
     xmited frames: 0
     xmit finished: 2225012436
     bad skb len: 0
     no cmd desc: 0
```

```
polled: 3056035547
uphappy: 2164405573
updropped: 0
tx dropped: 0
csummed: 2164406731
no rcv: 2164406784
rx bytes: 1305880876649
tx bytes: 1621856900611
```

Step 4

If there are no errors at the NIC level, how about errors during communication? This can be determined using the netstat -su command at the O/S level. The following output shows errors while receiving packets; however, compared to the total packets received, the errors are minimal and not much of a concern:

```
Udp:
    2417572082 packets received
    352524 packets to unknown port received.
    41277 packet receive errors
    2439175462 packets sent
```

Step 5

From Steps 2 to 4, we have not found any significant reason for what could be slowing down the network traffic and causing high latency. RAC uses the private network for most of the data transfers between instances. Only when the block is not present in one of the instances in the cluster will a disk I/O be performed. A good rule of thumb to follow is to ensure that network latency of the private interconnect is much lower compared to the disk I/O latency. If this is not the case, it probably defeats the purpose of using a RAC configuration.

■ **Note** One primary advantage of the clustered solution is to save on physical I/O against a storage system, which is expensive. This means that the latency of retrieving data across the interconnect should be significantly lower compared to getting the data from disk. For the overall performance of the cluster, 95% for immediate block transfers should be between 200 and 700 microseconds, depending on block size, protocol, and hardware when the system load is moderate. *The average latency of a consistent block request is the average latency of a consistent-read request round trip from the requesting instance to the holding instance and back to the requesting instance.*

When are such high latencies experienced over the interconnect? Another good test is to perform a test at the O/S level by checking the actual ping time. This will help to determine if there are any issues at the O/S level. After all, the performance issue may not be from data transfers within the RAC environment.

As discussed earlier in this chapter, the interconnect is used by the clusterware and the GCS for sending messages of various kinds. These messages include request for blocks, request for locks, heartbeats, and so forth. Such messages should also be taken into account when looking at the reasons for slow performance.

When sending and receiving messages between the nodes in the cluster, the GCS and the clusterware use a method called ticketing.

Every instance in the cluster has a pool of tickets allocated to it during instance startup. The number of tickets that an instance is allocated depends on the amount of buffer assigned at the O/S level, using the parameters we discussed earlier. At the database level, Oracle controls the total number of tickets available using the parameter _lm_tickets[6] and _cgs_tickets[7] for RAC-related messages. Both these parameters default to 1,000. When a message needs to be sent, the process needs to acquire a ticket from the pool and return the ticket back to the pool once the message has been transmitted. When there is a message flooding, there may not be a sufficient amount of tickets in the pool, and the process requesting the ticket will have to wait for the ticket. The allocation and usage of tickets can be verified in the view V$DLM_TRAFFIC_CONTROLLER:

Script:MVRACPDnTap_dlmtrafficcntrl.sql

```
SELECT inst_id    INT,
       local_nid  LNID,
       remote_nid RNID,
       remote_rid RRID,
       remote_inc RINC,
       tckt_avail,
       tckt_limit,
       tckt_rcvd,
       tckt_wait,
       snd_seq_no,
       snd_q_len,
       snd_q_max,
       snd_q_tot,
       snd_q_tm_base,
       snd_q_tm_wrap
FROM   gv$dlm_traffic_controller
ORDER  BY inst_id,
          tckt_avail;
```

In	LNID	RNID	RRID	RINC	Tckt Avail	Tckt Limit	Tckt Rcvd	Wait	SND_SEQ_NO	SND_Q_LEN	SND_Q_MAX	SND_Q_TOT	SND_Q_TM_BASE	SND_Q_TM_WRAP
1	0	7	4	142	3	142	0	YES	539802	0	11	320122	12397	0
	0	5	4	134	7	142	0	NO	532063	0	10	374045	6983	0
	0	6	4	138	96	142	1	YES	600074	0	8	366882	8371	0
	0	5	3	134	77	142	0	NO	525477	0	14	368271	6886	0
	0	6	3	138	105	142	1	NO	565620	0	13	352695	7946	0
	0	7	0	142	107	142	0	NO	1951677	0	30	607743	9007	0
	0	7	2	142	107	142	0	NO	456536	0	9	257905	9948	0
	0	7	1	142	107	142	0	NO	445955	0	15	262209	9750	0
	0	6	1	138	108	142	1	NO	581798	0	9	354269	6763	0
	0	6	0	138	108	142	1	NO	1485620	0	17	1096454	7420	0
	0	6	2	138	108	142	1	NO	570329	0	9	351729	8066	0
	0	5	0	134	109	142	0	NO	1023217	0	21	594179	7175	0
	0	5	2	134	109	142	0	NO	517306	0	8	369578	6787	0
	0	5	1	134	109	142	0	NO	529314	0	12	370442	6343	0

In the output, there are few processes that have the TCKT_WAIT(wait) columns that say YES. This indicates that the pool has run out of tickets. When several processes go into the wait state, it could cause GCS to hang. It is important to monitor the ticket usage and ensure that there are enough tickets available, which is indicated in the TCKT_AVAIL column.

---

[6]Underscore parameters should be modified only with consent from Oracle support.
[7]Underscore parameters should be modified only with consent from Oracle Support.

INTERCONNECT TRAFFIC TICKETS

As more and more instances are allocated to the cluster, the number of tickets allocated to every instance diminishes, thus hindering the actual number of tickets available to the instance. This indirectly causes contention on the packets being sent across the interconnect. The amount of buffer allocated is shared by

- ASM

- Database

Table 14-2 illustrates the ticket allocation from the pool of tickets defined by the _lm_tickets parameter (default value of 1,000). The table illustrates how the number of tickets available is reducing every time a new instance is added to the cluster. In a single-node cluster, there is no interconnect traffic, so no tickets are used or allocated. When the second node/instance is added to the cluster, the 1,000 tickets are used by both instances. Subsequently, starting with the third instance, the number of tickets reduces to 500 per instance and reduces further as more and more instances are added to the cluster.

Table 14-2. *Diminishing Allocation of Tickets*

Number of Instances	Tickets Allocated	Tickets Available
1	0	0
2	1,000	750
3	500	375
4	333	250
5	250	188
6	200	160
7	166	125
8	142	107

Tickets allocated = _lm_tickets/ (#number of instances -1)

Tickets Available = 0.75 * tickets allocated

Applying the preceding formula to the scalability of the cluster, the _lm_tickets should be increased (so should the buffer size) if the cluster has more than 8 instances in the cluster. The graph in Figure 14-6 illustrates how the ticket allocation reduces with the addition of instances to the cluster.

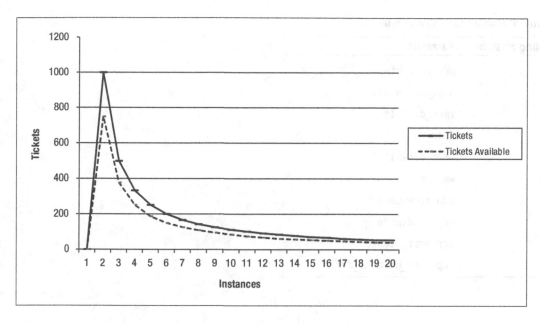

Figure 14-6. *Scale down on tickets when instances are increased*

Step 6

We now examine the TCP buffer sizes. A good rule of thumb to follow here is to set the network buffer sizes to the maximum size supported by the O/S.

The amount of buffers configured drives how much traffic and the size of packets that can be transmitted over the interconnect.

■ **Note** Oracle install guides suggest the initial value the TCP buffers need to be set to. These sizes have to be tuned based on the workload and the amount of data and messages being transmitted between the instance and servers in the cluster.

Table 14-3 gives a list of network-related parameters set at the O/S level used by RAC for cache fusion activity.

Table 14-3. *Network-Related Kernel Parameters*

Platform/Operating System	Parameter
SUN/Solaris	udp_recv_hiwat
	udp_recv_hiwat
Linux	rmem_default
	rmem_max
	wmem_default
	wmem_max
True 64	udp_recvspace
	udp_sendspace
HP	tcp_xmit_hiwater_def
	tcp_recv_hiwater_def

Step 7

Monitoring the interconnect traffic using tools such as EM and IPTraf gives the indication that there are large packets being transmitted, causing high latency of the interconnect. Figure 14-7 illustrates that the MTU size for the NIC is at the default 1,500, and jumbo frames have not been configured. As noticed in the IPTraf output, most of them are 1,426–1,500+ sizes. This is probably because the Oracle block size is 8 K.

```
IPTraf
┌ Packet Distribution by Size ────────────────────────────────

  Packet size brackets for interface eth24


  Packet Size (bytes)        Count       Packet Size (bytes)        Count
      1 to    75:             2827         751 to   825:             1809
     76 to   150:            33084         826 to   900:          1339561
    151 to   225:          1723285         901 to   975:             2087
    226 to   300:           222109         976 to  1050:             1447
    301 to   375:             8394        1051 to  1125:             1827
    376 to   450:           435289        1126 to  1200:             1287
    451 to   525:           925894        1201 to  1275:             4247
    526 to   600:             8392        1276 to  1350:             1037
    601 to   675:             1406        1351 to  1425:              838
    676 to   750:             4279        1426 to 1500+:           6666184


  Interface MTU is 1500 bytes, not counting the data-link header
  Maximum packet size is the MTU plus the data-link header length
  Packet size computations include data-link headers, if any
└ Elapsed time:    0:30 ────────────────────────────────────────
```

Figure 14-7. *IPTraf output, MTU set at default*

Low MTU size causes fragmentation of data, which indicates that data is split into several smaller packets, and it takes several transmissions to complete the operation. The following output is from IPTraf (network monitoring utility on Linux) and illustrates fragmentation of data transmitted on an Ethernet configuration without jumbo frames:

```
Thu Oct 24 12:12:38 2013; UDP; eth1; 1500 bytes; from ssky1l1p1-priv.summersky.biz to ssky1l1p3-priv.summersky.biz; fragment
Thu Oct 24 12:12:38 2013; UDP; eth1; 1500 bytes; from ssky1l1p1-priv.summersky.biz:11496 to ssky1l1p4-priv.summersky.biz:35052
Thu Oct 24 12:12:38 2013; UDP; eth1; 1500 bytes; from ssky1l1p1-priv.summersky.biz to ssky1l1p4-priv.summersky.biz; fragment
Thu Oct 24 12:12:38 2013; UDP; eth1; 1500 bytes; from ssky1l1p1-priv.summersky.biz to ssky1l1p4-priv.summersky.biz; fragment
Thu Oct 24 12:12:38 2013; UDP; eth1; 1500 bytes; from ssky1l1p1-priv.summersky.biz to ssky1l1p4-priv.summersky.biz; fragment
Thu Oct 24 12:12:38 2013; UDP; eth1; 1500 bytes; from ssky1l1p1-priv.summersky.biz to ssky1l1p4-priv.summersky.biz; fragment
Thu Oct 24 12:12:38 2013; UDP; eth1; 1500 bytes; from ssky1l1p1-priv.summersky.biz to ssky1l1p4-priv.summersky.biz; fragment
Thu Oct 24 12:12:38 2013; UDP; eth1; 1500 bytes; from ssky1l1p1-priv.summersky.biz to ssky1l1p4-priv.summersky.biz; fragment
Thu Oct 24 12:12:38 2013; UDP; eth1; 1500 bytes; from ssky1l1p1-priv.summersky.biz to ssky1l1p4-priv.summersky.biz; fragment
Thu Oct 24 12:12:38 2013; UDP; eth1; 1500 bytes; from ssky1l1p1-priv.summersky.biz to ssky1l1p4-priv.summersky.biz; fragment
Thu Oct 24 12:12:38 2013; UDP; eth1; 1500 bytes; from ssky1l1p1-priv.summersky.biz:35521 to ssky1l1p3-priv.summersky.biz:35871
Thu Oct 24 12:12:38 2013; UDP; eth1; 1500 bytes; from ssky1l1p1-priv.summersky.biz to ssky1l1p3-priv.summersky.biz; fragment
Thu Oct 24 12:12:38 2013; UDP; eth1; 1500 bytes; from ssky1l1p1-priv.summersky.biz to ssky1l1p3-priv.summersky.biz; fragment
Thu Oct 24 12:12:38 2013; UDP; eth1; 1500 bytes; from ssky1l1p1-priv.summersky.biz to ssky1l1p3-priv.summersky.biz; fragment
Thu Oct 24 12:12:38 2013; UDP; eth1; 1500 bytes; from ssky1l1p1-priv.summersky.biz:35521 to ssky1l1p2-priv.summersky.biz:54336
Thu Oct 24 12:12:38 2013; UDP; eth1; 1500 bytes; from ssky1l1p1-priv.summersky.biz to ssky1l1p2-priv.summersky.biz; fragment
Thu Oct 24 12:12:38 2013; UDP; eth1; 1500 bytes; from ssky1l1p1-priv.summersky.biz to ssky1l1p2-priv.summersky.biz; fragment
Thu Oct 24 12:12:38 2013; UDP; eth1; 1500 bytes; from ssky1l1p1-priv.summersky.biz to ssky1l1p2-priv.summersky.biz; fragment
Thu Oct 24 12:12:38 2013; UDP; eth1; 1500 bytes; from ssky1l1p1-priv.summersky.biz:11496 to ssky1l1p3-priv.summersky.biz:12914
Thu Oct 24 12:12:38 2013; UDP; eth1; 1500 bytes; from ssky1l1p1-priv.summersky.biz to ssky1l1p3-priv.summersky.biz; fragment
```

Fragmented packets, on reaching the destination, need to be reassembled. High CPU utilization and inadequate UDP buffer space can cause packet reassembly failures. Also for the reassemble to complete successfully, these packets have to be available until such an operation completes. Depending on the availability of resources and the load on the network, this may or may not be successful. Packets that are not reassembled are dropped and requested again. All this adds to the network and user response delays.

Increasing the fragment reassembly buffers, allocating more space for reassembly, and increasing the time required to reassemble fragmented packets may be required. The reassembly buffer space is controlled by the following parameters. Its default values are

```
[oracle@prddb1 ~]# cat /proc/sys/net/ipv4/ipfrag_low_thresh
196608
[oracle@prddb1 ~]# cat /proc/sys/net/ipv4/ipfrag_high_thresh
262144
[oracle@prddb1 ~]# cat /proc/sys/net/ipv4/ipfrag_time
30
```

- ipfrag_high_thresh is used set the maximum memory used to reassemble IP fragments. When ipfrag_high_thresh bytes of memory are allocated for this purpose, the fragment handler will toss packets until ipfrag_low_thresh is reached.

- ipfrag_low_thresh is used to set the maximum memory used to reassemble IP fragments before the kernel begins to remove incomplete fragment queues to free up resources. The kernel still accepts new fragments for defragmentation.

- ipfrag_time is used to set the interval required to reassemble before the reassembly will fail or time out.

MTU definitions do not include the data-link header. However, packet size computations include data-link headers. Maximum packet size displayed by the various tools is the MTU plus the data-link header length. To get the maximum benefit from the interconnect, the MTU should be configured to the highest possible value supported. For example, a setting as high as 9K using jumbo frames would help in improved interconnect bandwidth and data transmission.

Configuring the MTU for the NIC improved the overall performance of the interconnect and reduced the waits for tickets. The output in Figure 14-8 illustrates that packet sizes higher than 1,500 using jumbo frames has improved the performance of the network traffic.

```
IPTraf
- Packet Distribution by Size

  Packet size brackets for interface eth24


  Packet Size (bytes)      Count      Packet Size (bytes)      Count
     1 to   450:          283012      4501 to 4950:             427
   451 to   900:           30622      4951 to 5400:             141
   901 to  1350:            1497      5401 to 5850:             217
  1351 to  1800:            1029      5851 to 6300:            6838
  1801 to  2250:             363      6301 to 6750:             441
  2251 to  2700:             193      6751 to 7200:              99
  2701 to  3150:             738      7201 to 7650:            1162
  3151 to  3600:             826      7651 to 8100:              14
  3601 to  4050:            4907      8101 to 8550:            3228
  4051 to  4500:           17333      8551 to 9000+:          44522


  Interface MTU is 9000 bytes, not counting the data-link header
  Maximum packet size is the MTU plus the data-link header length
  Packet size computations include data-link headers, if any


- Elapsed time:   0:30
```

Figure 14-8. *IPTraf output with jumbo frames configured*

Step 8

The overall interconnect latency did improve, and the performance was acceptable. The ethtool output illustrates that the current network setup is a GigE interface. Network technology today has improved several folds so that organizations now have several options to get the best throughput. One can increase the bandwidth of the interconnect by using higher speed networks such as 10GigE or InfiniBand.

```
[root@prddb1 ~]# ethtool eth24
Settings for eth24:
        Supported ports: [FIBRE]
        Supported link modes:
        Supports auto-negotiation: No
        Advertised link modes:  1000baseT/Full
        Advertised auto-negotiation: No
        Speed: 1000Mb/s
        Duplex: Full
        Port: FIBRE
        PHYAD: 1
        Transceiver: external
        Auto-negotiation: off
        Supports Wake-on: g
        Wake-on: g
        Current message level: 0x00000005 (5)
        Link detected: yes
```

Step 9

The overall performance of the interconnect significantly improved. The latency numbers were reduced considerably.

Script: MVRACPDnTap_blksndtime.sql

```
SELECT
    B1.INST_ID INT,
    B2.VALUE "gc cr BR",
    B1.VALUE "gc cr BRT",
    B4.VALUE "gc cur BR",
    b3.value "gc cur BRT",
    ((B1.VALUE/B2.VALUE ) *10) "Avg CR BRT(ms)",
    ((B3.VALUE/B4.VALUE ) *10) "Avg CUR BRT(ms)"
FROM GV$SYSSTAT B1,
     GV$SYSSTAT B2,
     GV$SYSSTAT B3,
     GV$SYSSTAT B4
WHERE B1.NAME = 'gc cr block receive time'
AND   B2.NAME = 'gc cr blocks received'
AND   B3.NAME = 'gc current block receive time'
AND   B4.NAME = 'gc current blocks received'
AND   B1.INST_ID = B2.INST_ID
AND   B1.INST_ID = B3.INST_ID
AND   B1.INST_ID = B4.INST_ID
ORDER BY 1
/
```

INT	gc cr BR	gc cr BRT	gc cur BR	gc cur BRT	Avg CR BRT (ms)	Avg CUR BRT (ms)
1	44380	3039	70899	4969	.68	.70
2	35247	11330	62471	10061	3.21	1.61
3	42207	7406	61169	10415	1.75	1.70
4	756530	88951	1050510	95022	1.18	.90
5	35808	10791	58142	9869	3.01	1.70
6	6558172	942731	2860932	227932	1.44	.80

If any of these changes did not help in the overall latency number of the interconnect, tuning the DB_FILE_MULTIBLOCK_READ_COUNT parameter should be considered. Latency can also be influenced by a high value of the DB_FILE_MULTIBLOCK_READ_COUNT (MBRC) parameter. This is because this parameter determines the size of the block that each instance would request from the other during read transfers; and a requesting process can issue more than one request for a block, depending on the setting of this parameter, and may have to wait longer.

The number of blocks or messages transferred depends on the DB_FILE_MULTI_BLOCK_READ_COUNT * DB_BLOCK_SIZE. Oracle transfers blocks as contiguous, and the blocks are optimized to have the same master. For a MBRC of 16 and the database block size of 8, the global cache would still send 16 * 8 K requests logically; but the requests can be physically batched into a few physical messages.

Although all of these are hardware level and configuration changes to the servers, the root cause of high interconnect traffic was due to badly written, inefficient SQL statements. As new code comes into the environment, it could worsen the network traffic, increasing latency, and this entire workshop will have to be repeated.

Linear Scalability of Private Interconnect

As mentioned earlier in this chapter, in Oracle Database 11g Release 2 (11.2.0.2), Oracle has enhanced the private interconnect configuration and now allows multiple IPs to be configured as private interconnects.

This is compared to the traditional method of providing redundancy to the NIC configurations using bonding/pairing and so forth where only one NIC is used at any given time. The new HAIP feature provides load balancing and close to linear scalability to the network component, as additional private networks are added to the configuration.

The following output illustrates where a single private NIC is configured on the cluster; the output also illustrates that Oracle stores this information in the GPnP profile instead of the OCR (as done in the previous releases of Oracle):

Script:MVRACPDnTap_verifyic.sql

```
SELECT addr,
       indx,
       inst_id,
       pub_ksxpia,
       picked_ksxpia,
       name_ksxpia,
       ip_ksxpia
FROM   x$ksxpia;
```

ADDR	Indx	Public	Impl Type	Name	IP Address
00002B8010E5AA10	0	N	GPnP	eth23:1	169.254.240.242

```
SELECT inst_id,
       name,
       ip_address,
       is_public
FROM   gv$cluster_interconnects
ORDER  BY inst_id;
```

Instance	Name	IP Address	IS_PUBLIC	Source
1	eth23:1	169.254.240.242	NO	
2	eth23:1	169.254.170.5	NO	

Figure 14-9 illustrates the traffic across a single interconnect configured in a RAC cluster, with an average load of 114/028 kbits/sec, averaging about 1,800 packets/sec. This is pretty much the kind of load average expectancy when NIC bonding or pairing is configured for high availability of the interconnect. In this case of bonding (illustrated in Table 14-4), irrespective of the number of NICs that are bonded together at any given point in time, only one NIC is really being used.

```
IPTraf
┌ Iface ──────── Total ──────── IP ── NonIP ─ BadIP ── Activity ────────┐
  lo             161186        161186       0        0     5169.80 kbits/sec
  eth22               0             0       0        0        0.00 kbits/sec
  eth23          344510        344510       0        0   114028.20 kbits/sec
  eth20           18448         18448       0        0      615.00 kbits/sec
  eth21               0             0       0        0        0.00 kbits/sec




└ Elapsed time:   0:01 ─────────── Total, IP, NonIP, and BadIP are packet counts ┘
```

Figure 14-9. *IPTraf output with one interconnect configured*

Table 14-4. *Private Interconnect Throughput Comparison*

# of Interconnects	eth21 kbits/sec	eth22 kbits/.sec	eth23 kbits/sec	bond2 kbits/sec	HAIP kbits/sec
1			114028.20	132325.80	114028.20
2	170556.60	174490.80		132325.80	345047.39
3	177897.20	177897.20	178936.80	132325.80	534731.20

When multiple NICs are configured on the RAC cluster using the new HAIP feature available in Oracle Database 11g Release 2 (11.2.0.2), all NICs configured as private interconnects are put to use, giving almost double the throughput compared to the previous single NIC configuration (see Figure 14-10).

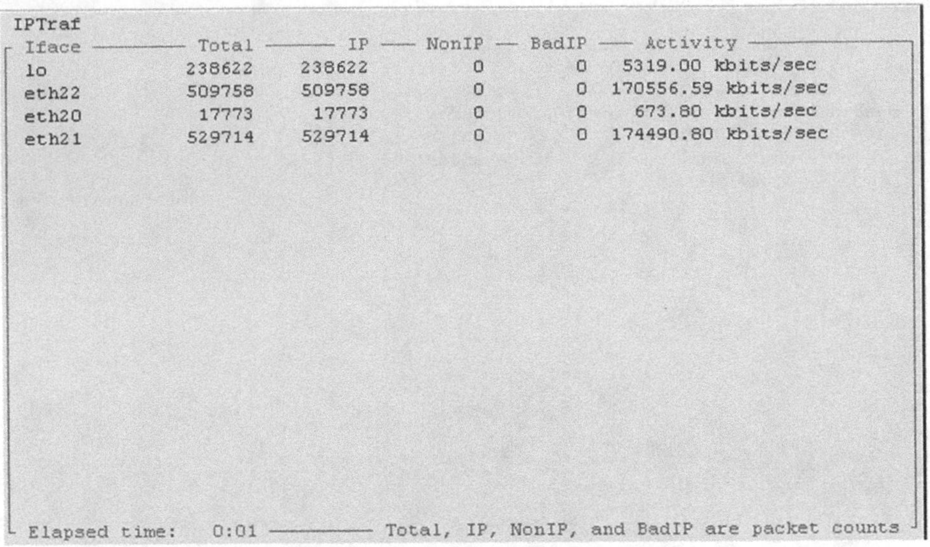

```
IPTraf
┌ Iface ────────── Total ─────── IP ──── NonIP ── BadIP ──── Activity ──────
  lo              238622       238622         0        0    5319.00 kbits/sec
  eth22           509758       509758         0        0  170556.59 kbits/sec
  eth20            17773        17773         0        0     673.80 kbits/sec
  eth21           529714       529714         0        0  174490.80 kbits/sec




└ Elapsed time:    0:01 ─────────── Total, IP, NonIP, and BadIP are packet counts ┘
```

Figure 14-10. *IPTraf output with dual interconnects configured*

Script:MVRACPDnTap_verifyic.sql

```
SELECT addr,
       indx,
       inst_id,
       pub_ksxpia,
       picked_ksxpia,
       name_ksxpia,
       ip_ksxpia
FROM   x$ksxpia
```

ADDR	Indx	Public	Impl Type	Name	IP Address
00002B8010E5AA10	0	N	GPnP	eth22:1	169.254.13.80
00002B8010E5AA10	1	N	GPnP	eth23:1	169.254.240.242

```
SELECT inst_id,
       name,
       ip_address,
       is_public
FROM   gv$cluster_interconnects
ORDER  BY inst_id;
```

Instance	Name	IP Address	IS_PUBLIC	Source
1	eth22:1	169.254.13.80	NO	
1	eth23:1	169.254.240.242	NO	
2	eth22:1	169.254.34.4	NO	
2	eth23:1	169.254.170.5	NO	

Figure 14-11 shows the global cache coherency screen from Enterprise Manager (EM), which illustrates that with three private interconnects, the latency is considerably low while maintaining high block transfers utilizing all three private interconnects.

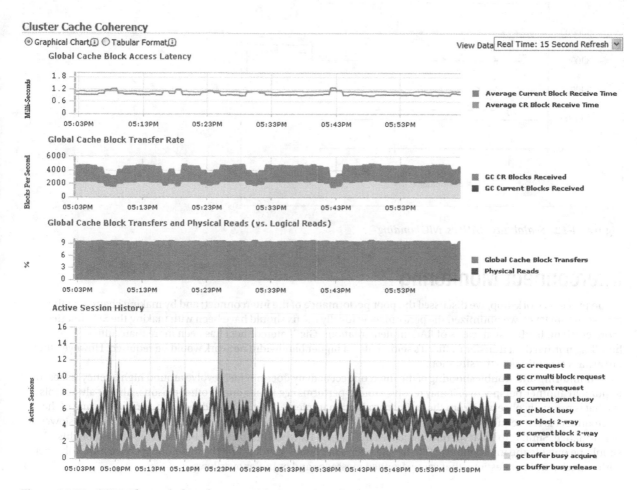

Figure 14-11. *OEM. Cluster cache coherency with three private interconnects*

Table 14-4 is a compilation of the various tests performed using the old method (NIC bonding) and the new HAIP option. The output generated and illustrated in Figure 14-12 indicates an almost close to perfect linear scalability. These results are from a controlled test environment, and in real life scenarios some variations are possible. However, the overall benefit of higher throughput compared to NIC bonding can be achieved using the HAIP feature.

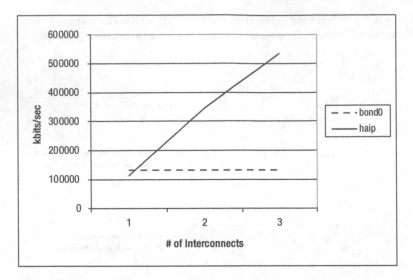

Figure 14-12. *Scalability HAIP vs. NIC bonding*

Interconnect Monitoring

In the previous workshop, we discussed the poor performance of the interconnect; and by making changes at the infrastructure level, we optimized the performance. Ideally the fix should have been with making the SQL queries more efficient. In almost all cases of RAC implementations, GigE interconnect has been more than sufficient for handling normal data transfer traffic. It's seldom that a higher bandwidth network would be required. However, there are always exceptions to the situation.

Monitoring and troubleshooting of the interconnect activity does not just revolve around high latency issues; or to put it in another perspective, it may revolve around performance issues due to other reasons. Almost always this is what is normally observed from the various production implementations. This does not mean monitoring of the interconnect is not required, but interconnect should not be the primary focus when the RAC cluster shows slower performance. Similar to what we have discussed in Chapter 13, when performance issues are noticed, thoughts should be outside the interconnect. That having been said, issues surrounding the interconnect have primarily been with capacity and congestions that cause dropped messages and or buffer overflows.

Workshop

One of the production clusters had seen several issues such as slow performance and occasional node evictions over the past several months. A production cluster running smoothly, giving extremely good performance all of a sudden has issues and causes real concerns to the DBA team. On analyzing the history of events to the servers, the only change the DBAs could recollect making to the production servers since the go live several years ago was the data center move from one city to another.

Checking through various statistics, the DBAs noticed that there was a significantly high amount of lost blocks. The amount of lost blocks where so high, it significantly affected production. The following output gives you the lost blocks for just one day of up time:

Script: MVRACPDnTap_raclostblocks.sql

```
SELECT
        A1.INST_ID ,
        A3.INSTANCE_NAME,
        A3.STARTUP_TIME,
        ROUND (SYSDATE - STARTUP_TIME) "Days",
        A1.VALUE ,
    A2.VALUE
FROM  GV$SYSSTAT A1,
        GV$SYSSTAT A2,
        GV$INSTANCE A3
WHERE A1.NAME = 'gc blocks lost'
AND   A2.NAME = 'gc blocks corrupt'
AND   A1.INST_ID = A2.INST_ID
AND   A1.INST_ID = A3.INSTANCE_NUMBER
ORDER BY 1;
```

Instance	Instance Name	Instance Startup Time	Up Days	Blocks Lost	Blocks Corrupt
1	MVP1	11-OCT-10 12:55:38	1	34263	0
2	MVP2	11-OCT-10 12:56:27	1	30413	0
3	MVP3	11-OCT-10 12:56:33	1	2265	0
4	MVP4	11-OCT-10 12:56:43	1	137	0
5	MVP5	11-OCT-10 12:51:23	1	18886	0

To solve the lost blocks issue, the following troubleshooting steps were taken:

Step 1

The first step is to understand if the cluster interconnect was configured correctly. Did the database really use the correct interconnect? A dump of the OCR file was taken using the following command:

```
$GRID_HOME/bin/ocrdump   < output file name>
$GRID_HOME/bin/ocrdump /home/oracle/mvallath/ocrdumpIC11oct10.dmp
```

Step 2

The private network alias (highlighted following) was rightly being referenced. For example, the OCR file output (following) showed the correct entries:

```
[SYSTEM.css.node_numbers.node1.nodename]
ORATEXT : oradb3
SECURITY : {USER_PERMISSION : PROCR_ALL_ACCESS, GROUP_PERMISSION : PROCR_READ, OTHER_PERMISSION :
PROCR_READ, USER_NAME : root, GROUP_NAME : root}
[SYSTEM.css.node_numbers.node1.privatename]
ORATEXT : oradb3-priv
SECURITY : {USER_PERMISSION : PROCR_ALL_ACCESS, GROUP_PERMISSION : PROCR_READ, OTHER_PERMISSION :
PROCR_READ, USER_NAME : root, GROUP_NAME : root}
```

Step 3

If the OCR file is correct, where is the problem? The next step was to ensure that the database understood the right IP address for the interconnect. For this, a dump of the IPC buffer from SQL*Plus indicated that the Oracle database was not aware of the private interconnect; the IP address registered, that is, 10.32.8.35, was the public IP address:

```
SQL> oradebug setmypid
Statement processed.
SQL> oradebug ipc
Information written to trace file.
SQL> exit
```

The trace file output had the following entries:

```
user cpu time since last wait 0 sec 0 ticks
system cpu time since last wait 0 sec 0 ticks
locked 1
blocked 0
timed wait receives 0
admno 0x5b0dce1b admport:
SSKGXPT 0xf684b80 flags SSKGXPT_READPENDING         socket no 7      IP 10.32.8.35     UDP 1131
context timestamp 0
        no ports
```

The output indicates that the IP address is a public IP used by users to access the database. However the database is also uses this as a private network. The public IP address was a 100 BaseT network, indicating it was all the more reason for slow performance. Oracle used UDP to transfer data blocks between instances.

HAIP VERIFICATION USING ORADEBUG

In Oracle Database 11g Release 2 (11.2.0.2), the oradebug ipc will give all the private interconnects configured and registered with the database:

```
wait delta 60 sec (60287 msec) ctx ts 0x0 last ts 0x0
user cpu time since last wait 0 sec 140733193388032 ticks
system cpu time since last wait 0 sec 140733193388032 ticks
locked 2
blocked 0
timed wait receives 0
fast reaps since last wait 0
context timestamp 0
flags=1 flags1=30 zcpyflg=15824 iflags=820 aflags=80 trcflags=0 trclevel=3
rcvbuf=131072 sndbuf=262144
admno 0x5a449d81 admport:
SSKGXPT 0x2b18269e4170 flags 0x5 { READPENDING } sockno 5 IP 169.254.2.61 UDP 31955 lerr 0
SSKGXPT 0x2b18269e4198 flags 0x0  sockno 8 IP 169.254.73.36 UDP 20886 lerr 0
SSKGXPT 0x2b18269e41c0 flags 0x0  sockno 10 IP 169.254.133.38 UDP 41693 lerr 0
SSKGXPT 0x2b18269e41e8 flags 0x0  sockno 11 IP 169.254.223.49 UDP 36434 lerr 0
 post port:
SSKGXPT 0x2b18269e45c8 flags 0x0  sockno 13 IP 127.0.0.1 UDP 25820 lerr 0
```

Step 4

Further investigation of the traffic on the network adapters using IPTraf indicated the following:

- There was traffic moving between the network configured for the interconnect using the TCP protocol. Clusterware uses TCP for heartbeat checks and clusterware-level messages. From Step 1 previously, the OCR file had the right entries for the CSS, indicating the clusterware was using the private network for heartbeat verification.

- There was no UDP traffic on the network configured for the interconnect. However, there was a large amount of UDP traffic on the public interface. This cross-verified the finding in Step 3 previously that the database had a wrong configuration and was using the public interface.

Step 5

Where did the database get the private IP address? The following query output indicated that the IP address for the cache fusion should have been coming from the OCR file but was coming from the O/S:

```
SELECT  inst_id,
        name,
        ip_address,
        is_public
FROM    gv$cluster_interconnects
ORDER   BY inst_id;


Instance  NAME             IP_ADDRESS        IS_  SOURCE
--------  ---------------  ----------------  ---  ----------------------
       1  bond0            10.32.8.35        NO   OS dependent software
       5  bond0            10.32.8.43        NO   OS dependent software
       4  bond0            10.32.8.41        NO   OS dependent software
       3  bond0            10.32.8.39        NO   OS dependent software
       2  bond0            10.32.8.37        NO   OS dependent software
```

Step 6

The private interfaces are not visible to the database for cache fusion. The oifcfg command can also help verify if the private interface is visible to the database. The following command returned no entries:

```
$GRID_HOME/bin/oifcfg getif
```

Step 6(a)

Because this was a production environment, to keep the downtime to a minimum, a quick temporary solution is possible using the CLUSTER_INTERCONNECTS parameter. On each instance in the cluster, the local private IP address is assigned to this parameter, and the database is restarted. This will route all cache fusion traffic via the private interconnect.

Why not use this parameter as a permanent solution? Using this parameter does not give all the HA features supported, for example, failover and so forth. This parameter was originally made available for SUN clusters and is not really used in other environments.

CLUSTER_INTERCONNECTS

This parameter provides Oracle with information on the availability of additional cluster interconnects that could be used for cache fusion activity. The parameter overrides the default interconnect settings at the O/S level with a preferred cluster traffic network. This parameter provides certain advantages on systems where there is high interconnect latency by helping reduce such latency. Configuring this parameter could affect the interconnect high-availability feature. An interconnect failure that is normally unnoticeable would instead cause an Oracle cluster failure, as Oracle still attempts to access the network interface.

Step 7

Using the $GRID_HOME/bin/oifcfg setif, the private interface definitions were set, and the OCR file was updated:

```
[oracle@oradb1 ~]$ $GRID_HOME/bin/oifcfg setif -global bond2/192.168.1.0:cluster_interconnect
[oracle@oradb1 ~]$ $GRID_HOME/bin/oifcfg getif
bond2  192.168.1.0  global  cluster_interconnect
```

Step 8

The update using the setif made the database aware of the right IP address and also made updates to the OCR file:

```
SELECT inst_id,
       name,
       ip_address,
       is_public
FROM   gv$cluster_interconnects
ORDER  BY inst_id;
```

INST_ID	NAME	IP_ADDRESS	IS_	SOURCE
1	bond2	192.168.1.46	NO	Oracle Cluster Repository
5	bond2	192.168.1.50	NO	Oracle Cluster Repository
4	bond2	192.168.1.49	NO	Oracle Cluster Repository
3	bond2	192.168.1.48	NO	Oracle Cluster Repository
2	bond2	192.168.1.47	NO	Oracle Cluster Repository

Step 9

A total of 17 days after the fix, there are no lost blocks in the production environment. The output does show a block corruption entry for instance one. Such occasional errors can be due to several unknown reasons and can be safely ignored. Oracle will retransmit the block back to the requestor:

Script: MVRACPDnTap_raclostblocks.sql

```
SELECT
      A1.INST_ID ,
      A3.INSTANCE_NAME,
      A3.HOST_NAME,
      A3.STARTUP_TIME,
      ROUND (SYSDATE - STARTUP_TIME) "Days",
      ROUND ((SYSDATE - STARTUP_TIME) *24) "Hours",
      A1.VALUE "BLKL",
      A1.VALUE/(ROUND((SYSDATE - STARTUP_TIME) *24)) "Perhr",
      A2.VALUE "BLKC"
FROM  GV$SYSSTAT A1,
      GV$SYSSTAT A2,
      GV$INSTANCE A3
WHERE A1.NAME = 'gc blocks lost'
AND   A2.NAME = 'gc blocks corrupt'
AND   A1.INST_ID = A2.INST_ID
AND   A1.INST_ID = A3.INSTANCE_NUMBER
ORDER BY 1;
```

Instance	Instance Name	Instance Startup Time	Up Days	Blocks Lost	Blocks Corrupt
1	MVP1	16-OCT-10 06:00:17	17	0	1
2	MVP2	16-OCT-10 06:00:18	17	0	0
3	MVP3	16-OCT-10 06:00:17	17	0	0
4	MVP4	16-OCT-10 06:00:19	17	0	0
5	MVP5	16-OCT-10 06:00:19	17	0	0

Data Dictionary Views to Monitor Cluster Interconnect

Like any feature of Oracle, the interconnect and RAC-related features can be monitored by a set of views. In this section, we discuss some of the important views that would help monitor and troubleshoot issues.

GV$DYNAMIC_REMASTER_STATS

This view gives the object re-master statistics from the time the object re-master has been initiated to its completion. All tasks involved in the process are recorded in the appropriate columns. This helps to determine how much of network traffic occurs during re-mastering activity. Using the steps illustrated to manually relocate an object master in Chapter 13, the individual re-master latencies can be obtained.

During peak network usage, re-mastering can also be delayed, which would indirectly affect the overall performance of the RAC environment. Apart from the delay during high interconnect activity, the re-mastering operation can also be impacted by high CPU utilization by the LMS process.

It's to be noted that although there are multiple factors that can influence the remastering activity, no one reason, such as the interconnect latency, can be the only cause for this delay. The data in the output following is an indication of the overall activity of remaster operations and the time spent at various stages of the operation:

Script:MVRACPDnTap_Dynamicmastersats.sql

```
SELECT inst_id,
       remaster_ops,
       remaster_time,
       remastered_objects,
       quiesce_time,
       freeze_time,
       cleanup_time,
       replayed_locks_sent,
       replayed_locks_received,
       current_objects
FROM   gv$dynamic_remaster_stats
ORDER  BY inst_id;
```

Inst	Remaster Operations	Remaster Time	Remaster Objects	Quiesce Time	Freeze Time	Cleanup Time
1	765	73676	872	7795	949	5433
2	765	73627	872	7799	765	5365
3	765	73652	872	7756	738	5216
4	10357	666977	12421	116083	12546	74389
5	765	73626	872	8365	778	4793
6	8387	539807	10168	122256	10538	44871

In the preceding output, instance 4 and 6 involve high remaster operations; and quite a bit of time is spent with related operations. There are potentially volatile objects, and its affinity keeps shifting between the two instances. The reasons for such high remastering could be two of many reasons: (1) Batch application performing high INSERT operations causing block movement between instances; (2) Same database services configured on two instances that access the same set of objects, but the load average keeps shifting between the two instances. If this is a read-only application, this would be of less concern; however, if this is a highly volatile set of objects that involves high DML operations, some additional tuning at the object level by distributing data using data partitioning should be considered.

GV$DLM_TRAFFIC_CONTROLLER

Traffic controller manages the allocation of tickets to processes that need to send messages. The traffic controller manages a pool of tickets allocated during instance startup and issues tickets to requests from processes sending messages; once the messages are sent, the ticket is released back into the pool. If there is delay in message communication and when tickets are not returned back to the pool, the pool may run out of tickets, and the processes wait to get tickets. At this time, the messages wait in a flow control queue until outstanding messages have been acknowledged and more tickets are available:

Script:MVRACPDnTap_dlmtrafficntrl.sql

```
SELECT inst_id   INT,
       local_nid  LNID,
       remote_nid RNID,
```

```
          remote_rid RRID,
          remote_inc RINC,
          tckt_avail,
          tckt_limit,
          tckt_rcvd,
          tckt_wait,
          snd_seq_no,
          snd_q_len,
          snd_q_max,
          snd_q_tot,
          snd_q_tm_base,
          snd_q_tm_wrap
FROM      gv$dlm_traffic_controller
ORDER  BY inst_id,
          tckt_avail;
```

In	LNID	RNID	RRID	RINC	Tckt Avail	Tckt Limit	Tckt Rcvd	Wait	Send Q Max	Send Q Total
1	0	1	0	4	484	500	119	NO	3	1664213
	0	1	1	4	485	500	119	NO	267	925932
	0	1	2	4	485	500	119	NO	266	1076223
	0	2	0	4	500	500	20	YES	3	1479461
	0	2	1	4	485	500	20	NO	252	4913920
	0	2	2	4	498	500	20	YES	249	4889374
2	1	0	2	4	483	500	1	NO	133	1064615
	1	0	1	4	484	500	1	NO	187	975192
	1	2	2	4	485	500	5	NO	244	4577424
	1	0	0	4	485	500	1	NO	11	2557942
	1	2	1	4	499	500	5	YES	238	4604011
	1	2	0	4	499	500	5	YES	6	2648164
3	2	0	2	4	481	500	0	NO	256	2927869
	2	1	2	4	491	500	0	NO	777	3200388
	2	1	1	4	484	500	0	NO	266	3093160
	2	0	1	4	494	500	0	NO	249	2896103
	2	1	0	4	495	500	0	YES	15	1757213
	2	0	0	4	500	500	0	YES	9	1169226

In the preceding output, there are several processes that have the TCKT_WAIT columns that say YES. This indicates that the pool has run out of tickets. When several processes go into the wait state, it could cause the GCS to hang. It is important to monitor the ticket usage and ensure that there are enough tickets available, indicated in the TCKT_AVAIL column.

GV$DLM_MISC

Although the view is called miscellaneous, it contains some of the most vital statistics related to messages. It's probably the only view that gives detailed statistics on the message traffic between instances. Earlier in this chapter, we discussed AST, BAST, and AAST type of messages. These statistics are all maintained in this view.

The following output gives the list for a three-node RAC cluster:

Script: MVRACPDnTap_dlmmisc.sql

```
SELECT * FROM (SELECT INST_ID, NAME, VALUE FROM GV$DLM_MISC) PIVOT (SUM(value) for  INST_ID IN
(1,2,3)) ORDER BY NAME;
```

NAME	1	2	3
messages flow controlled	55822	84833	96642
messages queue sent actual	5453201	7641557	6619674
messages queue sent logical	10441169	9808352	10101283
messages received actual	16978118	18765414	15525485
messages received logical	39326500	42175391	46091899
messages sent directly	6695061	6116041	8963878
messages sent indirectly	13049447	12369993	13557761
messages sent not implicit batched	1062	1099	1347
messages sent pbatched	24555803	26937853	36002459
msgs causing lmd to send msgs	4354994	6659117	3991411
msgs causing lms(s) to send msgs	2750828	2594875	1362431
msgs received queue time (ms)	12957956	13543472	9815095
msgs received queued	39326365	42175626	46091875
msgs sent queue time (ms)	858676	880076	1419012
msgs sent queue time on ksxp (ms)	53097467	58007840	77175847
msgs sent queued	14943725	16421747	15029984
msgs sent queued on ksxp	14755004	16571618	19910123
number of broadcasted resources	0	0	0
number of ges deadlock detected	0	0	0
process batch messages received	7265951	6886496	7716180
process batch messages sent	14623640	15792805	7610679

Enterprise Manager to Monitor Cluster Interconnect

The cluster database performance page in Figure 14-13 gives a glimpse of the overall performance of the database. This EM page has four sections:

> **Cluster host load average:** This shows maximum, average, and minimum values for available hosts in the cluster for the previous hour.

> **Global cache block access latency:** This chart gives the access latency for a block request between all instances in the cluster.

> **Average active sessions:** Probably one of the most important charts in the page shows potential problems inside the cluster database. The chart displays wait classes showing how much time the cluster database is waiting for a resource.

> **Through charts:** This section of the page displays throughput by I/O parallel execution, services, and instances.

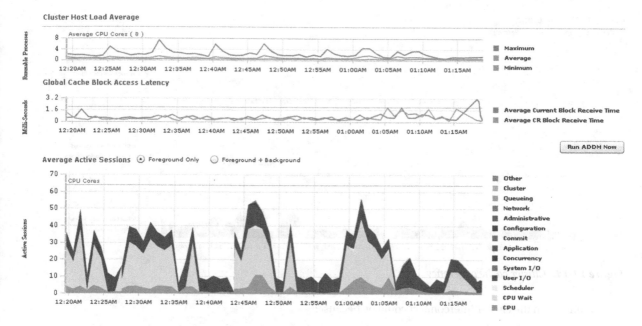

Figure 14-13. Cluster database performance

The EM cluster cache coherency screen (Figure 14-14) is also a tool to monitor cluster interconnect performance. The figure displays three important matrixes:

Global Cache Block Access Latency: This represents the elapsed time from when the block request was initiated until it completes. However, when a database block of any class is unable to locate a buffered copy in the local cache, a global cache operation is initiated by checking if the block is present in another instance. If it is found, it is shipped to the requestor.

Global Cache Block Transfer Rate: If a logical read fails to find a copy of the buffer in the local cache, it attempts to find the buffer in the database cache of a remote instance. If the block is found, it is shipped to the requestor. The global cache block transfer rate indicates the number of blocks received.

Block Access Statistics: This indicates the number of blocks read and the number of blocks transferred between instances in a RAC cluster.

Cluster Cache Coherency

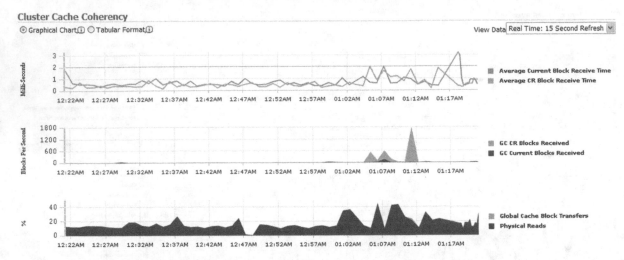

Figure 14-14. Cluster cache coherency

Latencies on the cluster interconnect could be because:

- No dedicated interconnect for cache fusion activity has been configured

- A large number of processes in the run queues waiting for CPU or due to processor scheduling delays

- Incorrect platform-specific O/S parameter settings that affect IPC buffering or process scheduling

- Slow, busy, or faulty interconnects

The packet rates being transferred over the interconnect can also be determined using the ping command and can be generated by the AWR global report[8] (Figure 14-15) or using the tcpdump command from the O/S.

```
tcpdump –ni eth24
17:49:08.019260 IP 169.254.100.30.65166 > 169.254.73.36.54220: UDP, length 192
17:49:08.019561 IP 169.254.100.30.55896 > 169.254.73.36.15879: UDP, length 8328
17:49:08.019585 IP 169.254.100.30.41485 > 169.254.73.36.50818: UDP, length 192
17:49:08.019721 IP 169.254.73.36.10368 > 169.254.100.30.49351: UDP, length 192
17:49:08.020410 IP 169.254.100.30.55896 > 169.254.73.36.16941: UDP, length 192
17:49:08.020679 IP 169.254.100.30.55896 > 169.254.73.36.18966: UDP, length 8328
17:49:08.021046 IP 169.254.100.30.49351 > 169.254.73.36.29081: UDP, length 440
17:49:08.021126 IP 169.254.73.36.13329 > 169.254.100.30.43241: UDP, length 5768
```

---

[8]This is generated using `$ORACLE_HOME/rdbms/admin/awrgrpt.sql`.

Ping Statistics

- Latency of the roundtrip of a message from Src Instance to the Target instances

Instance#		500 bytes				8 Kbytes			
Src	Target	Ping Count	Ping Time(s)	Avg Time(ms)	Std Dev	Ping Count	Ping Time(s)	Avg Time(ms)	Std Dev
1	1	1,875	0.37	0.20	0.11	1,875	0.34	0.18	0.11
	2	1,875	0.88	0.47	0.37	1,875	1.38	0.73	0.43
2	1	1,875	0.87	0.47	0.38	1,875	1.37	0.73	0.44
	2	1,875	0.32	0.17	0.10	1,875	0.30	0.16	0.09

Figure 14-15. *AWR ping statistics*

This helps determine the latency encountered at the database level vs. any overheads at the operating system level. Apart from the basic packet transfer tests that can be performed at the O/S level, there are other checks and tests that can be done to ensure that the cluster interconnect has been configured correctly:

1. There should be redundant, private, high-speed interconnects between the nodes participating in the cluster. Either implementing NIC bonding or pairing or by configuring multiple interconnects (HAIP) in Oracle Database Version 11.2.0.2 will help provide load balancing and failover when one of the interconnects fail.

2. The user network connection does not interfere with the cluster interconnect traffic, keeping the network traffic isolated from each other.

Conclusion

In this chapter, we looked at why performance problems centered around the interconnect may not always be related to the reasons why RAC cannot be the solution to highly available machine critical scalable architecture. Most of the interconnect-related issues are centered on bad configuration and/or bad and faulty interconnect infrastructures such as switches, NICs, and so forth.

With the technology advancement and improvement in networking configuration options available from the industry, high-speed interconnect options are possible for applications such as data warehouses where there is a high volume of data that is transmitted and where throughput is a concern, and high-speed interconnects such as 10GigE and Infiniband options are available.

Oracle also has been making considerable improvements on the configuration options, providing scalable interconnect options with the HAIP feature in Oracle database 11g Release 2 (11.2.0.2).

■■■

## CHAPTER 15

Optimize Distributed Workload

Business systems' infrastructure has become seriously fragmented and diverse, increasing its complexity and making it insecure, fragile, and difficult to maintain. The complexity of compounded functionality changes that have been implemented over the years has made it harder and less productive to implement any further changes. The business rules and functionalities that have been built into the application have made organizations think twice before rewriting these systems to be easily manageable. Reinventing several years of development and business knowledge that have gone into these business systems has been a huge investment that organizations are seldom interested in.

The growth toward a more loosely coupled composite solution has brought into existence a new wave in the technology architecture that focuses on functionality in the enterprise system as a service. For example, the dot-com and Internet-based solutions had brought the web services into existence. Whereas web services provided loose coupling at the interface level, the business systems did not propagate this architecture to the middle and database tier of the enterprise systems. The new wave is to take this service-oriented approach across the entire stack of the business or enterprise system.

Therefore, services are geared toward integrating systems not from an enterprise perspective but from a business values perspective, that is, by taking a coarse-grained step into a business transaction and grouping components that belong to its transaction boundaries. Thus service-oriented architecture (SOA) should design and build business services that easily and effectively plug into real business processes to deliver a composite business application.

Service Framework

The concept of services is not new in Oracle. Oracle introduced services in Oracle Database Version 8i, where client load balancing used services. Although client load balancing continues to be supported in Oracle Database 12c, the concept of services has as improved significantly. Apart from the database being a single service that applies to all instances in the cluster, several different types of services can now be created that will help in workload management across instances. A service is a group of related tasks within the database with common functionality, quality expectations, and priority definitions. Examples of services could be payroll, accounts payable, order entry, and so on. Some of the advantages of using services are the following.

Manageability

The legacy systems where one large application provides all business functions for an organization implemented as a single system image brought about complexity in its management and administration. When slow performance was noticed, one large monolithic application made troubleshooting and performance diagnosis difficult as well as not knowing which module or functional area in the application was the cause of the problem. However, services enable each workload to be managed in isolation and as a unit. This is made possible because services can span one or more instances of a RAC environment. Load balancing and other features available to the database service can be implemented at a more controlled and functional level.

Availability

Failure of a smaller component or subcomponent is acceptable in most cases compared to failure of the entire system. When a service fails, recovery of resources is much faster and independent because only a subset of functional users are affected, and this prevents restarting of the entire application stack. When several services fail, recovery can also happen in parallel. When the failed instances are brought online, the services that are not running (services that are not configured for failover) start immediately, and the services that failed over can be restored/relocated back to their original instance.

Performance

Prior to Oracle Database 10g, performance tuning was based on the statistics collected either at the system level or at the session level. This means that irrespective of the number of applications running against a given database, there was no instrumentation to provide any performance metric at the application or component level. With services and the enhancements to the database, performance metrics can now be collected at a service level, meaning more finite component-level troubleshooting. By grouping sessions performing similar kinds of activity on the database to connect using the same service name, they can be offered on a subset of instances, which helps limit the amount of cache transfers among instances. When services are configured to access only a single instance, this provides performance benefits by reducing block transfers and allowing object affinity to take place.

Services offer another level of troubleshooting the system when analyzing performance statistics. Apart from looking at statistics at the session level (V$SESSSTAT) and or the system level (V$SYSSTAT), using services provides an opportunity to measure the performance and metrics of a group of sessions connecting using the same service (V$SERVICE_STATS and V$SERVICEMETRIC). Using the DBMS_MONITOR, package tracing and stats collection can be enabled for a service, and trace files generated across multiple instances can be consolidated using the trcess utility.

Types of Services

Services can be broadly classified based on their usage and ownership into two main categories: application services and internal services.

Application Services

Application services are normally business related and are planned to describe business applications, business functions, and database tasks. These services can be either data dependent or functional dependent.

- Data-dependent services are based on database or data-related key values. Applications are routed to these services based on keys. Such services are normally implemented on databases that are shared by multiple applications and are associated with data partitioning. When meaning is based on the key values, the application will attach itself to a specific partition in the database server. This could be either a set of instances or a section of the database within an instance. Defining services for a specific area of the application and connections could be routed to one or more instances in the cluster depending on where the service is currently configured and could implement data-dependent services. Transaction monitors such as Tuxedo from BEA Systems (now Oracle) also support data-dependent services; and this type of service is called "data-dependent routing."

- Functional-dependent services are based on business functions, for example, Oracle applications, Accounts Receivable(AR), Accounts Payable(AP), General Ledger(GL), Bill of Materials(BOM), and so forth. Here the services create a functional division of work within the database. Such services are also termed "functional-dependent routing."

- The third type of service that has been in use with the earlier versions of Oracle is the PRECONNECT option in which a service spans a set of instances in the cluster. Such a service will pre-establish a connection to more than one instance in the Oracle database to support failover when the primary instance that the user session was originally established to fails.

Internal Services

Internal services are required and administered by Oracle for managing its resources. Internal services are primarily two: SYS$BACKGROUND, which is used by the Oracle background processes, and SYS$USERS, which is used by user sessions that are not associated with any service. Internal services are created by default and cannot be removed or modified.

Server Pools

While using services gave us an opportunity to look into the application at a functional level (users performing similar functions connect to the database as a service), in Oracle Database 11g, Oracle provides a paradigm shift by giving us yet another option to group nodes or severs as pools of resources. A group of servers can be grouped into pools and databases or services running in each pool can be prioritized based on the criticality of the functional areas that access the database using that pool. What if a pool is short on resources, in this case servers, because a server crashed or failed or the number of servers in the pool is not able to provide the resources required completing the job? Servers from other server pools can be dynamically provisioned into the pool that needs more resources.

Figure 15-1 illustrates a server pool configuration. The configuration has three pools; each pool has three distinct database services configured (SSKY, OLTP, TAPS). Pool sskypool1 and sskypool2 requires having the same number of server definitions; however, the importance level for sskypool3 is higher compared to all other pools. This means if a server failed in the sskypool3 and in sskypool2, the spare server in sskypool1 is moved to sskypool3.

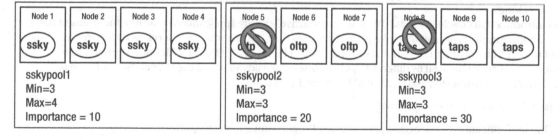

Figure 15-1. Server pool configuration

Distributed Workload Management (DWM)

Workloads on systems can be different depending on the day of the month or they can also vary based on the period of the year. To ensure sufficient resources are available based on demand for resources, they need to be balanced through some kind of internal mechanism, for example, prioritizing resources to the order processing systems during holiday season when customers tend to place online orders and at the same time, not limiting the resources required for the non-seasonal applications. Similarly, the payroll application would require more resources during payroll processing, which could be either weekly, biweekly or monthly. All these varying seasonal demands for resources could be a challenge for several organizations.

Oracle has enhanced and integrated some of its existing technology into RAC architecture for efficient workload management by allowing the control and allocation of resources required by the various processes and by efficiently managing them and allocating them based on the priority and importance. Two main areas of incorporation are included.

Resource Manager

Provisioning resources to database users, applications, or services in an Oracle database allows DBAs to control the allocation of available resources between the various users, applications, or services. This ensures each user, application, or service gets a fair share of the available computing resources. This is achieved by determining predefined resource plans that allocate resources to various consumer groups based on resource usage criteria such as CPU utilization or number of active sessions.

Fast Application Notification (FAN)

Traditionally, applications connect to the database based on user requests to perform an operation such as retrieve or update information. During the process of connecting to the database, if the database is not accepting any connection requests because a node, instance, database, service, or listener is down, the connection manager will have to return an error back to the application, which in turn will determine the next action to be taken. In the case of a RAC implementation, the next step (if the node, instance, or listener is down) would be to attempt connecting to the next available instance on the host address, defined in the address list in the TNS connection descriptor. The time taken to react to such connection failures and the application to subsequently retry the connection to another node, instance, or listener is often long.

FAN was introduced in Oracle Database 10g RAC to proactively notify applications regarding the status of the cluster and any configuration changes that take place. FAN uses the Oracle notification services (ONS) for the actual notification of the event to its other ONS clients. As illustrated in Figure 15-2, ONS provides and supports several callable interfaces that could be used by different applications to take advantage of the HA solutions offered in Oracle RAC. Applications supported and illustrated in Figure 15-2 include:

- Java Database Connectivity (JDBC)

- Oracle Notification Service (ONS) Application Programming Interface(API)

- Oracle Call Interface (OCI)

- Oracle Data Provider(ODP).NET Oracle Data Provider

- Simple Network Management Protocol(SNMP) Console

- Simple Mail Transfer Protocol (SMTP) email services

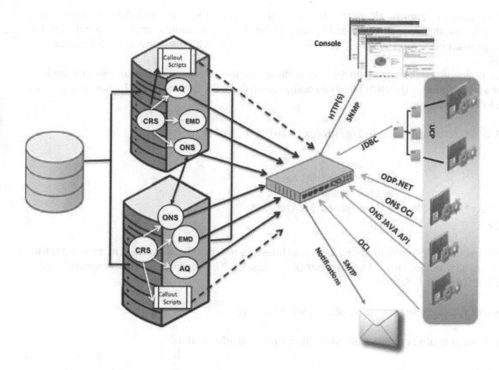

Figure 15-2. FAN event notification overview

FAN and ONS

ONS allows users to send SMS (short message system) messages, e-mails, voice notifications, and fax messages in an easy to access manner. Oracle Clusterware uses ONS to send notifications about the state of the database instances to mid-tier applications that use this information for load balancing and for fast failure detection.

ONS is a daemon process that communicates with other ONS daemons on other nodes informing it of the current state of the database components on the database server. For example, if a listener or node or service is down, a DOWN event is triggered by the EVMD process, which is then sent by the ONS daemon to the ONS daemon process on other nodes, including all clients and application servers participating in the network. Only nodes or client machines that have the ONS daemon running and have registered with each other will receive such notification. Once the ONS on the client machines receive this notification, the application (if using Oracle provided API [Application Programming Interface]) will determine, based on the notification, which nodes and instances have had a state change and appropriately send a new connection request. ONS helps the application to understand state changes proactively instead of the traditional reactive method.

ONS Configuration

ONS is installed and configured as part of the Oracle Grid Infrastructure (GI) installation. Execution of the root.sh file installation will create and start the ONS daemon process on all nodes participating in the cluster:

```
[[oracle@ssky1l1p1 ~]$ ps -ef | grep ons
oracle   5677      1  0 Feb03 ?        00:00:00 /u01/app/12.1.0.1/grid/opmn/bin/ons -d
oracle   5678   5677  0 Feb03 ?        00:00:02 /u01/app/12.1.0.1/grid/opmn/bin/ons -d
```

Configuration of ONS involves registering all nodes and servers that will communicate with the ONS daemon on the database server. During GI installation, all nodes participating in the cluster are automatically registered with the ONS. Subsequently, during restart of the Clusterware, ONS will register all nodes with the respective ONS processes on other nodes in the cluster.

To add additional members or nodes that should receive notifications, the hostname or IP address of the node should be added to the ons.config file or the OCR file. The configuration file is located in the $GRID_HOME/opmn/conf directory and carries the following format:

```
[oracle@ssky1l1p1 ~]$ more /u01/app/12.1.0.1/grid/opmn/conf/ons.config
usesharedinstall=true
allowgroup=true
localport=6100                        # line added by Agent
remoteport=6200                       # line added by Agent
nodes=ssky1l1p1:6200,ssky1l1p2:6200   # line added by Agent
 [oracle@ssky1l1p1 ~]$
```

The localport is the port that ONS binds to on the local host interface to talk to local clients. The remoteport is the port that ONS binds to on all interfaces for talking to other ONS daemons. The logcomp parameter specifies the ONS components to log. The format is as follows:

```
<component>[<subcomponent>,...];<component>[<subcomponent>,...];...
```

For example, to enable logging of all components with SSL operational information:

```
logcomp=ons[all,!secure]
```

The logcomp parameter replaces the loglevel parameter that existed in the earlier versions. Here is a list of components that could be logged. In the format for logcomp just mentioned, the valid values for components are:

- internal

- ons

If the component is internal, then there are no valid values for a subcomponent. However, if the component is specified as ons, then the following values could be used for subcomponents:

- all: Specifies all messages

- ons: ONS local information

- listener: ONS listener information

- discover: ONS discover (server or multicast) information

- servers: ONS remote servers currently up and connected to the cluster

- topology: ONS current cluster-wide server connection topology

- server: ONS remote server connection information

- client: ONS client connection information

- connect: ONS generic connection information

- subscribe: ONS client subscription information

- message: ONS notification receiving and processing information

- `deliver`: ONS notification delivery information

- `special`: ONS special notification processing

- `internal`: ONS internal resource information

- `secure`: ONS SSL operation information

- `workers`: ONS worker threads

The `logfile` specifies the log file to be used by ONS to log messages. If no `logfile` is specified, messages are written to the `$GRID_HOME/opmn/logs` directory. The `useocr` parameter (valid values `on`/`off`) indicates whether ONS should use the OCR to determine which instances and nodes are participating in the cluster. The `walletfile` is used by the Oracle Secure Sockets Layer (SSL) to store SSL certificates. If a wallet file is specified to ONS, then it uses SSL when communicating with other ONS instances and requires SSL certificate authentication from all ONS instances that try to connect to it. The nodes parameter lists all nodes in the network that will need to receive or send event notifications. It specifies the list of other ONS daemons to talk to. This list should include all RAC ONS daemons and all middle-tier ONS daemons. Listing the nodes ensures that the middle-tier node can communicate with the RAC nodes. Node values are given as either host names or IP addresses followed by their `remoteport`. This includes all RAC nodes client machines where ONS is also running to receive FAN events for applications.

Port information can also be verified using the following:

```
[oracle@ssky1l1p1 ~]$ $GRID_HOME/bin/srvctl config nodeapps -onsonly
ONS exists: Local port 6100, remote port 6200, EM port 2016
```

■ **Note**   The nodes listed in the nodes lines are public IP addresses and not VIP addresses.

A similar configuration is also to be performed on all client machines, and all node addresses should be cross-registered in the `ons.config` file on the respective machines.

ONS Communication

As mentioned earlier, ONS communicates all events generated by the EVMD processes to all nodes registered with the ONS. Figure 15-3 illustrates the notification channels that ONS will follow when an Oracle-related state change occurs on any of the nodes participating in the clustered configuration.

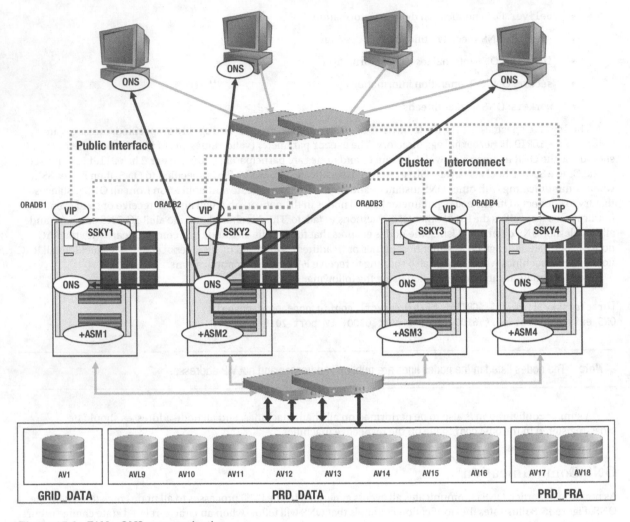

Figure 15-3. *FAN—ONS communication*

As illustrated in Figure 15-3, FAN uses ONS for server to server and server to client notification of state changes, which includes up, down, and restart events for all components of the RAC cluster. For example, in Figure 15-3, ONS daemon on node oradb2 notifies of any state changes with respect to components on that node to all other nodes in the cluster and to all client machines running ONS. The node sends all events, with the exception of a node failure event, where the event is generated; in the case of a node failure, then one of the surviving nodes will send the notification.

Based on the notification received, the FAN calls inside the application will proactively react to the situation, which includes failover of connections to another instance where the service is supported.

Oracle uses the advanced queuing (AQ; illustrated previously in Figure 15-2) technology for event notifications between various servers and clients.

FAN Events

When a state change occurs on a cluster or node or instance in a RAC environment, the Event manager triggers an event propagated by the ONS to the client machines. Such events that communicate state changes are termed as FAN events and consist of a predefined structure. Every FAN event consists of a header and payload information sent in name-value pairs from the origination to the respective targets participating in the framework. The name-value pair describes the actual name, type, and nature of the event. On receipt of this information, the recipient or the target application will take appropriate steps, such as routing the connection to another instance and so forth, based on the type of notification received.

Oracle supports two types of events:

1. Service event: Service events are application events and contain state changes that would only affect clients that use the service. Normally such events only indicate database, instance level, and application service failures.

2. System events. System events are more of a global nature and represent events such as node and communication failures. Such events affect all services supported on the specific system, for example, cluster membership changes, such as a node leaving or joining the cluster.

3. Both of the preceding types of events contain the following structure:

```
<Event_Type> VERSION=<n.n> service=<serviceName.dbDomainName>
[database=<db_unique_name> [instance=<instance_name>]] [host=<hostname>]
status=<Event_Status> reason=<Event_Reason>[card=<n>] timestamp=<eventDate>
<eventTime>
```

The various attributes used in the event and the descriptions can be found in Table 15-1.

Table 15-1. *ONS Event Descriptions*

Event Identifier	Description	
<Event_Type>	There are several types of events that belong to either the service type or system type of event:	
	SERVICE	Indicates it's a primary application service event, e.g., database service.
	SERVICEMEMBER	Application service on a specific instance event.
	DATABASE	Indicates it's an Oracle database event.
	INSTANCE	Indicates it's an Oracle instance event.
	NODE	Belongs to the system type event and indicates an Oracle cluster node event.
VERSION	This is an event payload version. This normally reflects the version of the database or Clusterware. When an environment supports several databases and they have different Clusterware versions, the payload version would help determine what actions to take depending on the features supported by the version.	
SERVICE	Name of the database service.	
DATABASE	Unique name of the RAC database for which the event is being raised. The name matches the DB_UNIQUE_NAME, which defaults to DB_NAME parameter.	

(*continued*)

Table 15-1. (*continued*)

Event Identifier	Description
INSTANCE	Name of the RAC instance for which the event is being raised.
HOST	Name of the cluster node from where such an event was raised; the value matches the node name known to Cluster Synchronization services (CSS).
STATUS	The current status of the event type indicates what has occurred for the event type. The valid status values are the following:

UP	Managed resource is now up and available.
DOWN	Managed resource is now down and is currently not available for access.
PRECONN_UP	The pre-connect application services is now up and available.
PRECONN_DOWN	The pre-connect application service has failed or is down and is not currently available.
NODEDOWN	The Oracle RAC cluster node indicated by the host identifier is down and is not reachable.
NOT_RESTARTING	Indicates that one of the managed resources that failed will not restart either on the failed node or on another node after failover. For example, VIP should failover to another and restart when a node fails.
UNKNOWN	Status is unknown and no description is available.

REASON	Indicates the reason for the event being raised and is normally related to the status. The following are the possible reasons:

USER	Indicates that the down or up event raised is use initiated. Operations performed using `srvctl` or from `sqlplus` belong to this category. This is a planned type of event.
FAILURE	During constant polling of the health of the various resources, when a resource is not reachable, a failure event is triggered. This is an unplanned type of event.
DEPENDENCY	Availability of certain resources depends on other resources in the cluster being up. For example, the Oracle instance on a specific node depends on the database application being available. This is also an unplanned event.
UNKNOWN	State of the application was not known during the failure to determine the actual cause of failure. This is also an unplanned event.
SYSTEM	Change in system state, for example, when a node is started. This reason is normally associated with only system events. For other event types, the reason would be "boot."
BOOT	The initial startup of the resource after the node was started, for example, once all system related resources are started such as VIP, ONS, etc. All user defined database services events have a reason code of boot.
AUTOSTART	Unable to perform autorestart of the resource.
MEMBER_LEAVE	Member of the resource has left the cluster, causing the resource to fail.
PUBLIC_NW_DOWN	The public network interface is not reachable/responding or is down.

(*continued*)

Table 15-1. (*continued*)

Event Identifier	Description
CARDINALITY	It represents the service membership cardinality. It is the number of members that are running the service. It can be used by client applications to perform software-based load balancing.
INCARNATION	Every time a member or node goes down and gets restarted, it gets a new cluster incarnation.
TIMESTAMP	Server side date and time when the event was detected.
TIMEZONE	The time zone given in GMT plus /minus value of Oracle Clusterware where the event occurred.

The example following is an event structure when an instance is brought down by a user operation:

```
INSTANCE VERSION=1.0 service=scdb database=scdb instance=SCDB_2 host=ssky1l1p1 status=down
reason=USER timestamp=2014-02-04 00:39:07 timezone=-05:00 db_domain= reported=date
```

When the preceding event is received by an ONS client machine, the application will use this information to reroute any future connections to this instance until the load profile defined for the service has been met.

Oracle defines services for all components within the RAC environment to monitor its state and to notify the application or client nodes of state changes. Figure 15-4 illustrates the relationship between the various components that affect the application servers directly and are all monitored by ONS for state change notifications.

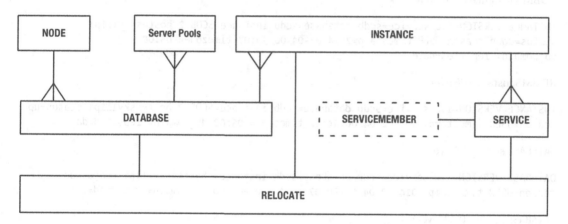

Figure 15-4. *ERD (entity relationship diagram) and dependency relationship of application services*

The number of components or subcomponents affected by a DOWN event depends on the component or service that has failed. For example, if a node fails or is removed from the cluster membership, then the NODE event is sent to all clients registered with the ONS of the failed node. All components that have a direct or indirect dependency to the NODE are all affected. For instance, illustrated in Figure 15-4, all entities database, instance, and the services that the instance supports are all affected. Whereas a node or server pool cannot failover in the cluster, certain services, database instance, including the database, can failover or relocate to another node in the cluster.[1] The type of service defined as SINGLETON can failover or relocate when a node fails. Similarly, if the database is down or has relocated itself to another node, then all services that depend on the database service will fail, and ONS will send that many notifications to all participating nodes.

---

[1]This requires that the database be configured as policy managed and not admin managed.

■ **Note**   Instance failover is only available with the policy-managed configuration. It is not available if the database is configured with the admin-managed option.

As illustrated in Figure 15-4, all components depend on the NODE service. For the DATABASE application, the instances and all services created on the instance will be affected should the DATABASE service fail. For an INSTANCE, all services are affected.

How do you monitor and track when these events are fired? Oracle has provided options where a script or utility or application (called server side callouts), if placed in the $GRID_HOME/racg/usrco directory, will be executed automatically. For example, the following shell script, when placed in the directory, will write out events generated by the event manager to the directory specified in the script:

```
[oracle@prddb2 oracle]$ more callout.sh
#!/bin/ksh
FAN_LOGFILE=$GRID_HOME/racg/log/fan_log_'hostname'.log
echo $* "reported="'date' >> $FAN_LOGFILE &
```

Similarly, any script or executable that could be invoked automatically when an ONS event condition occurs can be located in this directory and will be executed. A few example events from a Oracle Database 12c implementation (formatted for clarity) generated by the preceding callout script includes the following:

- RDBMS instance DOWN event

  ```
  INSTANCE VERSION=1.0 service=scdb database=scdb instance=SCDB_2 host=ssky1l1p1
  status=down reason=USER timestamp=2014-02-04 00:39:07 timezone=-05:00
  db_domain= reported=date
  ```

- RDBMS instance UP event

  ```
  INSTANCE VERSION=1.0 service=scdb database=scdb instance=SCDB_2 host=ssky1l1p1 status=up
  reason=USER timestamp=2014-02-04 00:44:12 timezone=-05:00 db_domain= reported=date
  ```

- DATABASE service UP event

  ```
  DATABASE VERSION=1.0 service=scdb database=scdb instance= host=ssky1l1p1 status=up
  reason=USER timestamp=2014-02-04 00:39:07 timezone=-05:00 db_domain= reported=date
  ```

- DATABASE service DOWN event

  ```
  DATABASE VERSION=1.0 service=scdb database=scdb instance= host=ssky1l1p1 status=down
  reason=USER timestamp=2014-02-04 00:39:07 timezone=-05:00 db_domain= reported=date
  ```

- SERVICEMEMBER UP event

  ```
  SERVICEMEMBER VERSION=1.0 service=TAPS database=scdb instance=SCDB_2 host=ssky1l1p1
  status=up reason=USER card=1 timestamp=2014-02-04 00:44:25 timezone=-05:00
  db_domain= reported=date
  ```

- Application SERVICE TAPS UP event

  ```
  SERVICE VERSION=1.0 service=TAPS database=scdb instance=SCDB_2 host=ssky1l1p1 status=up
  reason=USER timestamp=2014-02-04 00:44:25 timezone=-05:00 db_domain= reported=date
  ```

ONS Logging

ONS events can be tracked via logs both on the server side and the client side. ONS logs are written to the $GRID_HOME/opmn/logs directory. Logging can be enabled by setting the logcomp parameter in the ons.config file located in the $GRID_HOME/opmn/conf directory discussed earlier, under the ONS Configuration section.

The preceding extract from the ONS log file illustrates three notifications received from the ONS server node ssky1l1p1 containing instance SCDB_1 and application service TAPS. The three notifications received at different timeframes indicate various stages of the service TAPS. The first message indicates a notification regarding failure of TAPS on instance SCDB_1. The second message indicates a notification regarding a restart attempt of service TAPS on the same node ssky1l1p1. This restart also illustrates that the Instance and node are healthy or else it would not attempt to restart on the same node. The third message is an up event notification from the server to the client indicating that the service has started on node ssky1l2p2 (instead of its original node). Once this message is received, the application can resume connections using the service TAPS. This illustrates that the service TAPS has relocated from node ssky1l1p1 to ssky1l2p2. Details or events received can also be tracked at the application tier using the Oracle provided FAN APIs. Application TAPS requires additional resources; however, the current instances do not have the capacity to provide these resources. In this case, based on the threshold values defined, the event manager will notify the monitoring station. Once this notification is received, through a manual operation an additional instance could be added to process requests from application TAPS or scripts could be written to handle such notifications and automatically start them on other available instances.

When the node supporting the application service TAPS fails, an event is sent to the application client from node ssky1l2p2, at which time Oracle performs two operations in parallel:

1. Migrates the service or fails over the service to another instance allocated during service definition.

2. Sends a node down event to the application server.

The application on receipt of the event will start directing all connections allocated to the failed node to the new instance. Because the listener on the new node already establishes the service, the application server or client running this specific service will be able to establish connections and complete the required operations.

When an instance, either ssky1l3p3 or ssky1l4p4, fails, the following two operations are executed in parallel:

3. TAPS service is migrated from the failed instance to another backup/available instance.

4. ONS will send a notification to all clients known to ONS regarding the SERVICE down event. When such an event is received by the application, all connections are directed to the new instance.

Fast Connect Failover (FCF)

When using connection pooling, failover can also be implemented using a feature called FCF. While FAN is the technology and ONS is the method of physical notification mechanism, FCF is an implementation of FAN at the connection pool level.

Based on the notification received, the FCF calls inside the application will proactively react to the situation, which includes failover of connections to another instance or node where the services are supported. Under this architecture, failover is detected by listening to the UP or DOWN failover events generated by the database and the client is notified by the ONS daemon on the server to the ONS daemon on the client machine.

FCF and ONS

The architecture that Oracle uses to send events about the state change of each node to interested listeners is the ONS. This is required for using FCF. ONS daemons reside on all the nodes. Whenever the state change occurs, the server sends asynchronous notifications to all other ONS daemons (servers and clients, illustrated in Figure 15-2) and the JVM (Java virtual machine) where the JDBC (Java Database Connectivity) application is running.

How Does the JDBC Application Get These Notifications?

To understand the behavior of all components of FAN and FCF, we discuss this through a scenario:

1. The setFastConnectionFailoverEnabled method is used to enable FCF.

2. The connection cache manager starts the failover event-handler thread. This happens every time a connection cache is created.

3. The event-handler thread subscribes to ONS events of type "database/event."

4. When an event or state change occurs on any of the nodes on the database server, ONS daemon sends a notification of the following structure to all clients registered with the daemon:

   ```
   <Event_Type> VERSION=<n.n> service=<serviceName.dbDomainName>
   [database=<db_unique_name> [instance=<instance_name>]] [host=<hostname>]
   status=<Event_Status> reason=<Event_Reason>[card=<n>] timestamp=<eventDate>
   <eventTime>
   ```

5. ONS daemon on the client server receives this notification.

6. The instance name indicates whether a specific instance is down or if the entire service is down. If the instance value is null, it indicates that the entire service is down. If a specific instance is down, it is identified by the instance name. Applications that have connections to the instance that failed will roll back all open transactions.

7. The application will receive a connection-closed exception ORA-17008. The application is responsible for handling the errors.

8. When the last of the connection caches are closed, the connection cache manager terminates the event-handler thread by calling the connection close () method to release the connection back to the cache. On receiving the node down event, all connections in a connection cache that are on the node that went down are removed.

9. The cache is refreshed with new connections to the stable/backup node. When the cache is refreshed, the initial properties used to create the cache are used.

10. When the failed node is brought back online, the subscriber receives the notification, and the cache distributes the connections to load balance the connections.

FCF message traffic can be tuned using the parameters that influence the notification services, described in Table 15-2.

Table 15-2. *FCF API Parameters*

Parameter	Description
MinLimit	The minimum number of connection (default value is 0) instances the cache holds at all times. This value will not initialize the cache with the specified number of connections. The InitialLimit is used for the initial number of connection instances for the cache to hold.
MaxLimit	The maximum number (default 0) of connection instances the cache can hold.
MaxStatementsLimit	The maximum number of statements that a connection keeps open.
InactivityTimeout	The maximum time that a physical connection can be idle in connection cache. Value specified is in seconds (default 0).
TimeToLiveTimeout	The maximum time in seconds that a logical connection can remain open. When TimeToLiveTimeout expires, the logical connection is unconditionally closed, the relevant statement handles are canceled, and the underlying physical connection is returned to the cache for reuse.
AbandonedConnectionTimeout	The maximum time (default 0) that a connection can remain unused before the connection is closed and returned to the cache.
PropertyCheckInterval	The time interval (default value of 900 seconds) at which the cache manager inspects and enforces all specified cache properties.
ConnectionWaitTimeout	Specifies cache behavior when a connection is requested and there are already MaxLimit connections active. If ConnectionWaitTimeout is greater than 0, each connection request waits for the specified number of seconds, or until a connection is returned to the cache. If no connection is returned to the cache before the timeout elapses, the connection request returns null. This parameter has a default value of 0 and basically no timeout occurs.
ValidateConnection	Setting this to true causes the connection cache to test every connection it retrieves against the underlying database (default = false).
ClosestConnectionMatch	Setting this to true causes the connection cache to retrieve the connection with the closest approximation to the specified connection attributes. This can be used in combination with AttributeWeights to specify what is considered a "closest match" (default = false).
AttributeWeights	Sets the weights for each connection attribute used when ClosestConnectionMatch is set to true to determine which attributes are given highest priority when searching for matches. An attribute with a high weight is given more importance in determining a match than an attribute with a low weight. AttributeWeights contains a set of key/value pairs that set the weights for each connection attribute for which the user intends to request a connection.
	The key is a connection attribute and the value is the weight; a weight must be an integer value greater than 0. The default weight is 1.

■ **Note** Dynamic cleaning of the connections to the failed node eliminates the delay in realizing that the connections are stale and to establish the connections to stable/backup node, thus improving the failover time dramatically.

For the application to be ONS aware, the application using FAN should specify the system property –oracle.ons.oraclehome = < location-of-ons-home> and ensure that the ons.jar file is located on the application CLASSPATH. The ons-home must be the $GRID_HOME where ONS is installed on the client machine.

Transaction Guard

As discussed in the previous sections, in-flight transactions fail, and users tend to get notified by the application through a return message that a transaction was not completed successfully or they are falsely notified that a transaction did complete. The persistence layer of the application is not able to provide the right response back to the user. The user ends up guessing or falsely trying to create the transaction again.

In Oracle Database Version 12c (12.1.0), Oracle has introduced a feature called the transaction guard that makes several attempts on failed transactions before actually declaring it could not be processed successfully.

Transaction guard provides a new protocol and API for application developers to include in their code to monitor and react to any planned and unplanned outages and protects the persistence layer from repeated submissions by the users. This new logical transaction ID (LTXID) will help determine the outcome of the last transaction that was left open in the database after an instance or database failure.

Database services can participate in the logical transaction process by including the –commit_outcome and –retention parameters. These parameters are included in the database service definition process using the srvctl command.

Load Balancing

Apart from providing system availability and failover functions, a clustered solution should also be able to balance the available resources on all instances against the various user sessions and their workload. Meaning, based on the intensity of the process on hand on the various nodes and the availability of resources, a clustered configuration should be able to distribute load across all nodes in the cluster.

In a clustered database environment such as RAC, load balancing could be based on several criteria or goals: for example, the number of physical connections to each instance in the cluster; the throughput of the various instances in the cluster; the throughput (CPU) of the database servers on the cluster; the user traffic on a database a listener to accept more connections; and so forth. Although all of these are potential methods in which the nodes and or instances in a cluster could be load balanced, the most common and desired option is to load balance based on response time of the instances. Under this method, the load is not balanced based on the number of sessions but based on the amount of resources available on the respective instances.

RAC provides several types of load balancing that are broadly classified based on the type of user connections to the database server.

Client Load Balancing

When a user makes a connection to the database using the definitions provided in the tnsnames.ora file on the client machine, the connection is routed to one of the available nodes. This routing is based on the listeners on the respective nodes being able to accept the connection request from the user or application:

```
TAPS =
  (DESCRIPTION=
    (ADDRESS_LIST=
      (FAILOVER=ON)
      (LOAD_BALANCE=ON)
      (ADDRESS=(PROTOCOL=TCP)(HOST=PRODDB-SCAN.SUMMMERSKY.BIZ)(PORT=1521))
    )
```

```
(CONNECT_DATA=
  (SERVER=DEDICATED)
    (SERVICE_NAME=TAPS)
    (FAILOVER_MODE=(TYPE=SELECT)
                   (METHOD=BASIC)
                   (RETRIES=20)
                   (DELAY=15))
  )
)
```

When several users connect to the database, the listener in any of these nodes could be busy accepting requests from some other user on the network, at which point the client machine is notified. When a callback is received, the SQL*Net will attempt to make a connection to another IP address defined in the scan IP list. If this listener on this node is also busy, another address in the list is attempted, and so on until a connection is established.

Client load balancing is not based on the availability of resources on the database servers but on the availability of the listener to accept the users' connection request. To overcome this constraint, Oracle introduced another level of load balancing called connection load balancing or server side load balancing.

Connection Load Balancing

Client load balancing is between the user session on the client machine and the listener and does not provide any resource level load balancing. Client load balancing only distributed users across the various listeners picking an address from the list available, when several users connected close to one another. If the clients connected at various intervals, there was a potential that all users ended on the same node/instance. To help resolve this issue, Oracle introduced server side or connection load balancing.

Under this method, connections are routed to different instances (least loaded) in the cluster based on load information available to the listener. The PMON (Process Monitor) process on the respective nodes updates load information to the listener. The frequency or update interval is based on the load on the respective nodes. For example, if the load is very low, the update may take up to 10 minutes; on the other hand, on heavily loaded nodes, updates may occur in as little as 1-minute intervals.

To implement this load-balancing feature, the parameters listed in Table 15-3 have to be defined.

Table 15-3. *Instance Parameters*

Parameter	Description
LOCAL_LISTENER	This parameter informs the instance regarding the local listener name defined for the node. This parameter is only required to be defined if the listener on the local node is registered on a non-default port (1521).
REMOTE_LISTENER	This parameter, when defined, informs the instance regarding all other listeners defined on other nodes participating in the cluster.

The PMON will register with the listeners identified by the preceding two parameters defined in the server parameter file. Once registered, the PMON will update the listener with profile statistics that allow the listener to route incoming connections to the least loaded instance.

When an instance starts, the PMON registers itself with the listener. This could be verified by checking the listener log file located at $ORACLE_BASE/diag/tnslsnr/<hostname>/listener/trace/ directory for the service_register string.

When the PMON updates the listener with the profile statistics, it also makes an entry in the listener log file. This could be tracked by the service_update string. The frequency of update could also be tracked using the timestamp found against the service_update entries. For example, the following output indicates that the PMON has been updating the listener:

```
02-FEB-2014 23:06:50 * service_register * +APX1 * 0
03-FEB-2014 18:18:56 * service_register * LsnrAgt * 0
03-FEB-2014 18:19:01 * service_register * -MGMTDB * 0
03-FEB-2014 18:19:15 * service_register * +ASM1 * 0
03-FEB-2014 18:19:26 * service_register * -MGMTDB * 0
03-FEB-2014 18:19:43 * service_register * +ASM1 * 0
03-FEB-2014 18:22:13 * service_register * SCDB_2 * 0
03-FEB-2014 18:23:36 * service_register * +APX1 * 0
03-FEB-2014 18:23:48 * service_register * SCDB_2 * 0
04-FEB-2014 00:40:21 * service_register * SCDB_2 * 0
```

The load statistics available on the listener on the respective nodes is used to reroute any connection to the node that has the least load.

The following steps are performed to reroute connection requests based on user workload:

1. A user connection is established to a listener using the client load balancing options discussed earlier.

2. The listener where the connection was originally established will, based on the load statistics available, reroute the connection to another listener on another node. (The listener information is obtained from the REMOTE_LISTENER parameter).

With the introduction of services and distribution of services across various instances and based on user(s) business requirements, load balancing criteria will vary. This will depend on having a symmetric distribution or an asymmetric distribution of services and on the capacity of the nodes participating in the cluster. For symmetric services and nodes with similar capacity, the absolute session count by instance evenly distributes the sessions across the nodes; and if the service distribution is asymmetric or the nodes do not have a similar capacity, then the run queue length of the respective nodes is used to determine the least loaded node.

Oracle provides the DBAs the option of defining goals and determining load-balancing criteria. Load balancing goals could be:

1. Based on elapsed time: Under this method, a new ranking referred to as goodness of service is used in the load-balancing algorithm. Under this method, the load balancing is driven by the actual service time that would be experienced by the session on a given instance. Ranking compares service time, referred to within the database as the metric "Elapsed Time Per User Call."

2. Based on the number of sessions: Under this method, the load across the various nodes is balanced based on the number of Oracle sessions connected to the database. In this case, the actual resource load or response time or service time is not considered. However, the basic count on the number of sessions is considered to determine the least loaded node and where the next session should be connected.

   ```
   $GRID_HOME/bin/srvctl modify service -d SCDB -s FIPS -clbgoal SHORT -rlbgoal
   THROUGHPUT -notification TRUE
   ```

Applications Using Connection Pooling

For applications using connection pooling, Oracle provides a more robust, cleaner, and proactive method of load balancing called run-time connection load balancing (RCLB).

Instead of a using the old methods, where the application makes a connection to the database server to determine the actual load on the system, under the new method, events are used to notify the application regarding the load. Based on this information, connections are established to the least loaded machine.

RCLB relies on the ONS event mechanism (discussed in the previous sections) and FCF in applications using Java, and OCI or ODP.NET subscribe via Oracle's advanced queuing feature. The RCLB feature provides assignment of connections based on feedback from the instances in the RAC cluster. The connection cache assigns connections to clients based on a relative number indicating what percentage of requested connections each instance's service should handle. It is enabled automatically when RAC starts to post service metrics. Service metrics provide service levels and percentage distributions for each instance of a service. Connections to specific instances in the cluster are based on the service metrics available.

Oracle uses the services metrics values calculated and stored in the automatic workload repository (AWR) to determine current load characteristics on the various instances. The service metrics is thus forwarded to the master MMON background process. The MMON in turn builds the required load advisory and posts the required advice to AQ, PMON, and the ONS.

Notification mechanisms are based on one of two definitions:

1. Service time measures the elapsed time vs. the demand. When this option is selected, Oracle examines all of the time consumed in the service from an efficiency and delay perspective and rates this data against the service-level goals set for the service. Using service time or response time for load balancing recognizes machine power differences, sessions that are blocked in wait, failures that block processing, as well as competing services of different importance. Using the proactive propagation method ensures that work is not sent to overwork, hung, or failed nodes.

2. Throughput measures the efficiency of the system rather than delay. Throughput measures percentage of the goal response time that the CPU consumes for the service. Basically, throughput is the number of user calls completed in a unit of time.

■ **Note**   RCLB of work requests is enabled by default when FCF is enabled. There is no additional setup or configuration of ONS required to benefit from RCLB.

Load Balancing Definition

Load balancing can be configured using the OEM or srvctl command line utility. Connection load balancing is enabled by setting the CLB_GOAL parameter to appropriate values.

Valid values for CLB_GOAL are listed in Table 15-4.

Table 15-4. *Client Load Balancing Parameters*

Goal Type	Value	Description
CLB_GOAL_SHORT	1	Connection load balancing based on elapsed time.
CLB_GOAL_LONG	2	Connection load balancing based on number of sessions.

Valid goal types are listed in Table 15-5.

Table 15-5. *Load Balancing Goal Types*

Goal Type	Value	Description
GOAL_NONE	0	No load-balancing goal has been defined.
GOAL_SERVICE_TIME	1	Load balancing based on the service or response time.
GOAL_THROUGHPUT	2	Load balancing based on throughput.

Defining Thresholds

Apart from defining goals for load balancing the cluster, users can define thresholds that will verify activity in the notification service and inform the DBAs when such thresholds are reached.

Thresholds can be defined either using the OEM interface or using the PL/SQL procedures following:

```
SQL> exec DBMS_SERVER_ALERT.SET_THRESHOLD( -
> METRICS_ID => dbms_server_alert.elapsed_time_per_call,-
> WARNING_OPERATOR=> dbms_server_alert.operator_ge,-
> WARNING_VALUE=>'500',-
> CRITICAL_OPERATOR=>dbms_server_alert.operator_ge,-
> CRITICAL_VALUE=> '750',-
> OBSERVATION_PERIOD=> 15,-
> CONSECUTIVE_OCCURRENCES =>3,-
> OBJECT_TYPE=>dbms_server_alert.object_type_service,-
> OBJECT_NAME => 'TAPS');
PL/SQL procedure successfully completed.
```

The preceding definition defines a threshold on elapsed time, with a warning level of 500 seconds indicated by the variable WARNING_VALUE and a critical value of 750 seconds indicated by the variable CRITICAL_VALUE. The definition further stipulates that a notification should be sent only if the threshold is reached three consecutive times (indicated by CONSECUTIVE_OCCURRENCES), with an interval of 15 seconds apart (indicated by OBSERVATION_PERIOD).

Threshold Verification

Load-balance definitions could be verified using the following query:

```
SQL> COL inst format 999
COL name format a20
SELECT inst_id INST,
name,
goal,
clb_goal,
aq_ha_notification
FROM gv$services;
```

```
SQL>
INST NAME                    GOAL            CLB_G AQ_
---- --------------------    ------------    ----- ---
2    FIPS                    THROUGHPUT      SHORT YES
2    TAPS                    THROUGHPUT      SHORT YES
2    SCDBXDB                 NONE            LONG  NO
2    SCDB                    NONE            LONG  NO
2    SYS$BACKGROUND          NONE            SHORT NO
2    SYS$USERS               NONE            SHORT NO
1    FIPS                    THROUGHPUT      SHORT YES
1    TAPS                    THROUGHPUT      SHORT YES
1    SCDBXDB                 NONE            LONG  NO
1    SCDB                    NONE            LONG  NO
1    SYS$BACKGROUND          NONE            SHORT NO
1    SYS$USERS               NONE            SHORT NO
```

The preceding output service TAPS has not been configured for run time load balancing, and the connection time load-balancing option defined is SHORT. Using the following procedure, the run time load-balancing goal is changed to THROUGHPUT:

```
srvctl modify service -d SPDB -s TAPS -j SHORT -B THROUGHPUT
```

The following new output from the GV$ACTIVE_SERVICES view illustrates this change. This can also be viewed from V$SERIVCES:

```
SQL> COL inst format 999
COL name format a20
SELECT inst_id INST,
name,
network_name,
goal,
blocked,
aq_ha_notification AQ,
clb_goal
FROM gv$active_services;
SQL>
INST NAME                 NETWORK_NA GOAL          BLO AQ  CLB_G
---- -------------------- ---------- ------------  --- --- -----
2    FIPS                 FIPS       THROUGHPUT    NO  YES SHORT
2    TAPS                 TAPS       THROUGHPUT    NO  YES SHORT
2    SCDBXDB              SCDBXDB    NONE          NO  NO  LONG
2    SCDB                 SCDB       NONE          NO  NO  LONG
2    SYS$BACKGROUND                  NONE          NO  NO  SHORT
2    SYS$USERS                       NONE          NO  NO  SHORT
1    FIPS                 FIPS       THROUGHPUT    NO  YES SHORT
1    TAPS                 TAPS       THROUGHPUT    NO  YES SHORT
1    SCDBXDB              SCDBXDB    NONE          NO  NO  LONG
1    SCDB                 SCDB       NONE          NO  NO  LONG
1    SYS$BACKGROUND                  NONE          NO  NO  SHORT
1    SYS$USERS                       NONE          NO  NO  SHORT

12 rows selected.
```

How Do You Verify Whether the RCLB Feature Is Working?

When MMON generates load advices, it is stored in GV$SERVICEMETRIC view and is used to communicate with the client of the current load. For example, the following query displays the load characteristics as updated by MMON in GV$SERVICEMETRIC view. The view is joined with GV$INSTANCE and GV$ACTIVE_SERVICES to obtain additional information:

```
set pagesize 60 space 2 numwidth 8 linesize 132 verify off feedback off
column SERVICE_NAME format a20 truncated heading 'Service'
column INSTANCE_NAME heading 'Instance'  format a10
column SERVICE_TIME heading 'Service Time|mSec/Call' format 999999999
column CPU_TIME heading 'CPU Time |mSec/Call' 99999999
column DB_TIME heading 'DB Time |mSec/Call' 99999999
column THROUGHPUT heading 'Calls/sec' format 99.99 break on SERVICE_NAME skip 1
SELECT SERVICE_NAME,
       INSTANCE_NAME,
       ELAPSEDPERCALL  SERVICE_TIME,
       CPUPERCALL      CPU_TIME,
       DBTIMEPERCALL   DB_TIME,
       CALLSPERSEC     THROUGHPUT
FROM   GV$INSTANCE        GVI,
       GV$ACTIVE_SERVICES GVAS,
       GV$SERVICEMETRIC   GVSM
WHERE  GVAS.INST_ID   = GVSM.INST_ID
AND    GVAS.NAME_HASH = GVSM.SERVICE_NAME_HASH
AND    GVI.INST_ID    = GVSM.INST_ID
AND    GVSM.GROUP_ID  = 10
ORDER  BY
    SERVICE_NAME,
    GVI.INST_ID;
```

		Service Time Elapsed mSec/Call	CPU Time mSec/Call	DB Time mSec/Call	
Service	Instance				Calls/sec
TAPS	SCDB_1	1360	329	1360	232.07
	SCDB_2	1444	385	1444	222.71
	SCDB_3	1918	240	1918	161.55
	SCDB_4	736	254	736	678.04
	SCDB_5	2292	772	2292	27.09
FIPS	SCDB_2	60317	23490	60317	79.88
	SCDB_3	46358	12926	46358	105.18
	SCDB_4	52800	13701	52800	44.31
	SCDB_5	54303	13607	54303	71.31

In the preceding output, service TAPS on both instances does not seem balanced. The service time on SCDB_2 is high, the overall throughput is low; however, the DB time and CPU time values seem lower. When a message is received by the application server using the FAN technology regarding the current state of the instance, new sessions will be directed by FAN to instance SCDB_2.

GV$SERVICEMETRIC

This contains metric values measured for all the services defined in the database. The MMON process updates these values as it captures load and other service-related information from the SGA. Updates to this view happen in 5-second and 1-minute intervals.

Apart from making updates to the GV$SERVICEMETRIC view, MMON also updates the operating system statistics and uses this information to determine the load characteristics on the various nodes in the cluster. The following query output from GV$OSSTAT provides the operating system statistics:

```
SELECT * FROM (SELECT INST_ID,STAT_NAME,VALUE FROM GV$OSSTAT)
PIVOT (SUM(VALUE) FOR INST_ID IN (1,2,3,4)) ORDER BY STAT_NAME
```

STAT_NAME	1	2	3	4
BUSY_TIME	68523311	137810899	69100616	63652298
FREE_MEMORY_BYTES	1.36E+08	1.06E+08		
GLOBAL_RECEIVE_SIZE_MAX	4194304	4194304	4194304	4194304
GLOBAL_SEND_SIZE_MAX	4194304	4194304	4194304	4194304
IDLE_TIME	2263573618	2194213550	2848860288	2854392901
INACTIVE_MEMORY_BYTES	1.79E+09	1.72E+09		
IOWAIT_TIME	15425632	40378746	10725915	6031263
LOAD	1.01953125	2.07910156	1.19921875	.639648438
NICE_TIME	236916	447162	932710	16292
NUM_CPUS	24	24	24	24
NUM_CPU_CORES	24	24	24	24
NUM_CPU_SOCKETS	4	4	4	4
PHYSICAL_MEMORY_BYTES	1.3527E+11	1.3527E+11	1.3527E+11	1.3527E+11
RSRC_MGR_CPU_WAIT_TIME	189	1550	185	131
SYS_TIME	10010888	19905107	12695839	10304209
TCP_RECEIVE_SIZE_DEFAULT	4194304	4194304	4194304	4194304
TCP_RECEIVE_SIZE_MAX	4194304	4194304	4194304	4194304
TCP_RECEIVE_SIZE_MIN	4096	4096	4096	4096
TCP_SEND_SIZE_DEFAULT	4194304	4194304	4194304	4194304
TCP_SEND_SIZE_MAX	4194304	4194304	4194304	4194304
TCP_SEND_SIZE_MIN	98304	98304	98304	98304
USER_TIME	54526555	105473193	51760395	51184651
VM_IN_BYTES	3.3496E+12	2.8286E+12	2.1828E+12	3.5692E+12
VM_OUT_BYTES	2.5269E+12	3.6358E+12	2.4633E+12	7.8788E+11

GV$OSSTAT

This contains O/S statistics updated by the MMON process and is used to determine the load on the nodes/servers. The values are in hundredths of a second as a processor has been busy executing code and is averaged over all processors.

Workshop

To understand how such a distribution could be implemented, we discuss a typical workload configuration and management scenario using an example. A global operational organization has five applications that they would like to configure on a four-node RAC. Defined by the business needs, the applications are required to meet the following requirements:

- TAPS: This application is used by the client services to record customer interactions that happen throughout the day. It's an OLTP application and requires a 24/7 uptime.

- FIPS: This is a homegrown application used by various members of the organization. Considering the various time zones, except for a few hours between 3:00 AM and 7 AM EST, this application is also required to be functional most of the time.

- SSKY: This is another reporting batch application that runs two or three times a week and during weekends.

- GRUD: This online reporting system is a subcomponent of both TAPS and FIPS. These reports are triggered subprocesses and should support both applications. The load or usage of this application is not very high, and an infrastructure to queue all reporting requests is in place; hence, small outage of this system is acceptable.

- TICKS: This is a critical seasonal application that runs twice a month. The application's criticality is high such that during these two periods of execution, it should complete on time and should have a very minimal to no failure rate.

All the previous applications are to be configured over a four-node RAC cluster. Each node in the cluster has a public IP address, private IP address, and a VIP address. The cluster-level scan address has been configured. The database is configured using the policy managed option and has two server pools defined. Table 15-6 details the various characteristics of the application configuration across the available instances in the cluster.

Table 15-6. *Application to Instance Mapping*

Applications	Database Services	Type of Service	Server Pool	Preferred Instances	Pool Credentials	Priority/Criticality
TAPS	TAPS	Client Application	SCDB_POOL	SCDB_1, SCDB_2, SCDB_3	Max 3 Min 3	HIGH
FIPS	FIPS	Client Application	SCDB_POOL2	SCDB_4	Max 1 Min 0	STANDARD
SSKY	SSKY	Scheduler Job	SCDB_POOL2	SCDB_4	Max 1 Min 0	STANDARD
GRUD	GRUD	Client Application	SCDB_POOL	SCDB_1, SCDB_2, SCDB_3	Max 3 Min 3	LOW
TICKS	TICKS	Seasonal Application	SCDB_POOL	SCDB_1, SCDB_2, SCDB_3	Max 3 Min 3	HIGH

Using the services concept discussed in the previous sections, all applications in Table 15-6 are services in the clustered database SCDB, that is, all applications will have a different service definition in the database.

1. In Table 15-6, it should be noted that TAPS is a high priority service application and is set up to start on SCDB_1, SCDB_2, and SCDB_3 instances. If any of these instances fail, the service from that instance will migrate to instance SCDB_4. If all three preferred instances become unavailable, the service is available on instance SCDB_4. When all three instances or nodes are not available, SCDB_4 will be busy with all services executing off this one instance. However, because the priority of TAPS is HIGH, it will get a higher percentage of the resources compared to other services running on the same node with the exception of when TICKS is running (TICKS is discussed in Step 6 following). SCDB_4 will be shared by both TAPS and FIPS.

2. FIPS is a standard service and is set up to run on instance SCDB_4; if SCDB_4 fails, it would run on either SCDB_2 or SCDB_3 based on the current workload conditions. After failover, this service will not affect the existing services, especially service TAPS, because TAPS runs at a higher priority.

3. SSKY is a standard scheduled job (batch) that runs during the night and weekends. Because this is not an application continuously running, it is configured to run on SCDB_4. From the previous step, FIPS is also configured on instance SCDB_4. Like FIPS, when the instance SCDB_4 fails, SSKY will failover to either SCDB_3 or SCDB_1 depending on the current workload conditions. As an alternative solution, FIPS could be set to failover to SCDB_2, and SSKY could be set to failover to SCDB_1.

4. GRUD is a low priority triggered reporting job spawned from both TAPS and FIPS services. Because of this architecture, it is set up to run across all instances: SCDB_1, SCDB_2, and SCDB_3. If any of the nodes/instances fail, the surviving nodes will continue to execute the service; in other words, no failover has been configured.

5. TICKS are a high priority, seasonal application; they are executed twice a month. TICKS are configured to run on SCDB_3 and SCDB_4. If there are not sufficient resources to allow TICKS to complete on time or if one of the preferred instances fails, it has two other spare instances: SCDB_2 and SCDB_1.

Once the configuration and layout architecture has been defined, the RAC environment is to be updated to reflect these settings. Whereas most of the network interface definition and mapping them to their respective nodes is completed during the Oracle Clusterware configuration, the service to instance mapping is done using one of three methods listed in the service framework section earlier.

■ **Note** In the workshop, the example used is to implement a distributed workload system using the requirements listed in Table 15-6, which uses server pools. However, it should be noted that it is not a requirement to have a policy-managed (server pools) database to implement resource manager.

Step 1

The first step in the process is to ensure that the server pools required for the workshop have been configured using the following commands:

```
[oracle@sskyl1p1 -]$ $GRID_HOME/bin/srvctl config  srvpool
Server pool name: Free
Importance: 0, Min: 0, Max: -1
Category:
Candidate server names:
Server pool name: Generic
Importance: 0, Min: 0, Max: -1
Category:
Candidate server names:
Server pool name: SCDB_POOL
Importance: 0, Min: 3, Max: 3
Category:hub
Candidate server names:
Server pool name: SCDB_POOL2
Importance: 0, Min: 0, Max: 1
Category:
Candidate server names:
```

Step 2

The next step in configuring the applications defined in Table 15-5 is to map them to their respective instances and implement the preferred/available rules. For our example, we define these services to database mapping using the srvctl utility:

```
[oracle@ssky1l1p1 ~]$ srvctl modify service -d SCDB -service TAPS -pdb SPDB -g SCDB_POOL
[oracle@ssky1l1p1 ~]$ srvctl modify service -d SCDB -service FIPS -pdb SPDB -g SCDB_POOL
[oracle@ssky1l1p1 ~]$ srvctl modify service -d SCDB -service SSKY -pdb SPDB -g SCDB_POOL
[oracle@ssky1l1p1 ~]$ srvctl modify service -d SCDB -service TICKS -pdb SPDB -g SCDB_POOL2
[oracle@ssky1l1p1 ~]$ srvctl modify service -d SCDB -service GRUD -pdb SPDB -g SCDB_POOL
```

Step 3

At this point, the user has to decide if the applications will use the FAN feature called FCF or the standard Transparent Application Failover (TAF) feature or both. If the application will use the TAF feature to enable failover, then based on the criticality of the application the appropriate TAF policies, it should be added to the service definition using the srvctl utility. The remainder of the applications will be configured to have the BASIC policy.

```
srvctl modify service -d SCDB -s FIPS -P BASIC -failovertype SELECT -failovermethod BASIC
-failoverdelay 25 -failoverretry 125
srvctl modify service -d SCDB -s SSKY -P BASIC -failovertype SELECT -failovermethod BASIC
-failoverdelay 25 -failoverretry 125 -notification TRUE
srvctl modify service -d SCDB -s GRUD -P NONE -failovertype SELECT -failovermethod BASIC
-failoverdelay 25 -failoverretry 125 -notification TRUE
```

Step 4

Service definitions and failover policies defined using SRVCTL can also be verified using `srvctl`. For example

```
$GRID_HOME/bin/srvctl config service -d SCDB
```

■ **Note**   While the connection descriptions used by FAN can contain the TAF definitions, they are ignored by the default FAN operation. However, they can be programmatically used as a backup option. When the application service does not receive any event indicating a service failure, the application connection can use TAF.

Step 5

For service failover and load balancing, the client side TNS connection description has to be updated with the appropriate entries either with or without using the TAF feature. Applications connect to an HA service using the TNS connect descriptor. The service names used in the TNS names configuration should match the service names defined in Step 1 previously using the `srvctl` utility.

```
TAPS =
  (DESCRIPTION =
    (ADDRESS=(PROTOCOL=TCP)(HOST=prddb-scan.summersky.biz)(PORT=1521))
    (CONNECT_DATA =
      (SERVER = DEDICATED)
      (SERVICE_NAME = TAPS)
    )
)
```

Step 6

Listeners should be cross-registered using the REMOTE_LISTENER parameter; this is to ensure all listeners are aware of all services. Similar to the TNS names configuration, the listener should use scan addresses instead of physical host names.

Step 7

Based on the previous definitions, several applications are sharing instances; each application is to be configured to run at a specific priority level. Priorities should be defined for the service to enable workload management to set up when the scheduler should start the job and for configuration of resources.

The first step in the setting up of priorities is the creation of the various consumer groups. In our preceding example, we would require three different consumer groups: HIGH_PRIORITY, which will support all applications defined in Table 15-5 as having high priority; STD_PRIORITY, which will support all applications defined in Table 15-5 as having standard priority; and LOW_PRIORITY for low priority. These consumer groups map to the database resource plan. This is done using the Oracle provided PL/SQL packages using the following steps:

Step 7.1 Create a Pending Work Area

While defining ODRM (Oracle dynamic resource mastering) policies irrespective of the type of policy being defined, it's required that an initial workspace or working area be defined. This allows for validation and testing of the policies before committing or saving them for actual usage. The pending/work area is created using the following:

```
BEGIN
    DBMS_RESOURCE_MANAGER.CREATE_PENDING_AREA();
END;
/
```

■ **Note**   In an Oracle Database 12c multitenant database environment, if the resource manager is added to the PDB database, prior to setting the pending area, the control should be moved to the PDB database.

```
SQL> show con_name
CON_NAME
------------------------------
CDB$ROOT
SQL> ALTER SESSION SET CONTAINER=SPDB;
```

If the resource manager is added to the container database, the appropriate PL/SQL packages should be used. For example, instead of using the DBMS_RESOURCE_MANAGER.CREATE_PLAN used in a PDB or non-CDB database, when creating a plan at the container level, the DBMS_RESOURCE_MANAGER.CREATE_CDB_PLAN procedure would be used. A step-by-step description of implementing the DBRM (database resource manager) at the container database can be found in the appendix section.

Step 7.2 Define the Consumer Group

Once a working area has been created, the next step is to create all the different levels of priority. This is done using the CREATE_CONSUMER_GROUP procedure:

```
BEGIN
    DBMS_RESOURCE_MANAGER.CREATE_CONSUMER_GROUP
                (CONSUMER_GROUP=>'HIGH_PRIORITY',
                 COMMENT=>'High Priority group');
END;
/
BEGIN
    DBMS_RESOURCE_MANAGER.CREATE_CONSUMER_GROUP
                (CONSUMER_GROUP=>'STD_PRIORITY',
                 COMMENT=>'Standard Priority group');
END;
/
```

```
BEGIN
    DBMS_RESOURCE_MANAGER.CREATE_CONSUMER_GROUP
                (CONSUMER_GROUP=>'LOW_PRIORITY',
                 COMMENT=>'Low Priority group');
END;
/
```

Step 7.3 Map Consumer Groups to Services

Once the consumer groups are defined, the next step is to map the consumer group to its respective services; for example, consumer group HIGH_PRIORTY will be used by both TAPS and TICKS:

```
BEGIN
 DBMS_RESOURCE_MANAGER.SET_CONSUMER_GROUP_MAPPING
                (ATTRIBUTE=>DBMS_RESOURCE_MANAGER.SERVICE_NAME,
                 VALUE=> 'TAPS',
                 CONSUMER_GROUP=>'HIGH_PRIORITY');
END;
/
```

In the preceding output, service TAPS is mapped to HIGH_PRIORITY, indicating that it's governed by the resource criteria defined for consumer group HIGH_PRIORITY.

```
BEGIN
 DBMS_RESOURCE_MANAGER.SET_CONSUMER_GROUP_MAPPING
                (ATTRIBUTE=>DBMS_RESOURCE_MANAGER.SERVICE_NAME,
                 VALUE=> 'SSKY',
                 CONSUMER_GROUP=>'STD_PRIORITY');
END;
/
```

In the preceding output, service SSKY is mapped to STD_PRIORITY, indicating that it's governed by the resource criteria defined for consumer group STD_PRIORITY.

```
BEGIN
 DBMS_RESOURCE_MANAGER.SET_CONSUMER_GROUP_MAPPING
                (ATTRIBUTE=>DBMS_RESOURCE_MANAGER.SERVICE_NAME,
                 VALUE=> 'GRUD',
                 CONSUMER_GROUP=>'LOW_PRIORITY');
END;
/
```

In the preceding output, service GRUD is mapped to LOW_PRIORITY, indicating that it's governed by the resource criteria defined for consumer group LOW_PRIORITY.

Step 7.4 Resource Plans

To ensure that critical applications such as TAPS and TICKS can obtain sufficient resources from the Oracle resource pool, the ODRM functionality supports definition of resource plans where applications can be assigned resource limits such as % of CPU that would be available and so forth. The resource plan is created using the following PL/SQL definition (or through OEM):

```
BEGIN
    DBMS_RESOURCE_MANAGER.CREATE_PLAN (PLAN=>'SSKY_SCDB_PLAN',
                                       COMMENT=>'high priority plan');
END;
/
BEGIN
   DBMS_RESOURCE_MANAGER.CREATE_PLAN_DIRECTIVE
        (PLAN                        =>'SSKY_SCDB_PLAN',
         GROUP_OR_SUBPLAN            => 'HIGH_PRIORITY',
         COMMENT                     => 'High priority group ',
         MGMT_P1                     => 50,
         PARALLEL_DEGREE_LIMIT_P1    => 4,
         ACTIVE_SESS_POOL_P1         => 4);
   DBMS_RESOURCE_MANAGER.CREATE_PLAN_DIRECTIVE
        (PLAN                        =>'SSKY_SCDB_PLAN',
         GROUP_OR_SUBPLAN            => 'STD_PRIORITY',
         COMMENT                     => ' ',
         MGMT_P1                     => 25);

   DBMS_RESOURCE_MANAGER.CREATE_PLAN_DIRECTIVE
        (PLAN                        =>'SSKY_SCDB_PLAN',
         GROUP_OR_SUBPLAN            => 'LOW_PRIORITY',
         COMMENT                     => ' ',
         MGMT_P1                     => 15);
   DBMS_RESOURCE_MANAGER.CREATE_PLAN_DIRECTIVE
        (PLAN                        =>'SSKY_SCDB_PLAN',
         GROUP_OR_SUBPLAN            => 'OTHER_GROUPS',
         COMMENT                     => 'common catch all group',
         MGMT_P1                     => 10);
END;
/
```

Step 7.5

Once the consumer group definitions have been verified, the next step is to save and enable these definitions using the following procedure:

```
BEGIN
    DBMS_RESOURCE_MANAGER.VALIDATE_PENDING_AREA();
END;
/
BEGIN
    DBMS_RESOURCE_MANAGER.SUBMIT_PENDING_AREA ();
END;
/
```

```
BEGIN
   DBMS_RESOURCE_MANAGER.CLEAR_PENDING_AREA();
END;
/
```

This will save all the ODRM definitions created in the workspace area to disk.

In the preceding definition, we have three groups for which plans are defined. Group OTHER_GROUP is an Oracle-provided default group for every resource plan definition. The HIGH_PRIORITY and LOW_PRIORITY are groups created based on Table 15-5 in Step 7.2 previously. Based on the application distribution in Table 15-5, GRUD is defined under resource group LOW_PRIORITY (running under low priority) on instances SCDB_1, SCDB_2, and SCDB_3. Application TAPS and TICKS are defined under resource group HIGH_PRIORITY and share instances with application GRUD. Based on the requirements, the resource plan shares the resources between the two resource groups HIGH_PRIORITY and LOW_PRIORITY, giving resource group HIGH_PRIORITY more resources.

The default group, OTHER_GROUP, should not be ignored. At times, when there are runaway processes and both resource groups consume all the resources, it would be in the best interest of the DBA to allocate some resources under the OTHER_GROUP category to allow the DBA to interview and perform any administrative operation.

Step 7.6

The consumer group and priority definitions could be verified by querying against the DBA_RSRC_GROUP_MAPPINGS view:

```
SELECT ATTRIBUTE,
       VALUE,
  CONSUMER_GROUP
FROM   DBA_RSRC_GROUP_MAPPINGS
WHERE  ATTRIBUTE LIKE '%SERVICE%';


ATTRIBUTE                  VALUE     CONSUMER_GROUP
------------------------   -------   ----------------
SERVICE_NAME               TAPS      HIGH_PRIORITY
SERVICE_NAME               GRUD      LOW_PRIORITY
SERVICE_NAME               FIPS      STD_PRIORITY
SERVICE_NAME               SSKY      STD_PRIORITY
```

Step 7.7 Job Class Definition

One application listed in Table 15-5 is a batch job (reporting) that is triggered by other applications on other services in the cluster. Batch jobs are normally scheduled to run at predefined intervals and a predefined frequency. DBMS_SCHEDULER can schedule a batch job. One prerequisite to define a batch job using the DBMS_SCHEDULER is to define a job class using the CREATE_JOB_CLASS procedure:

```
EXECUTE DBMS_SCHEDULER.CREATE_JOB_CLASS -
            (JOB_CLASS_NAME => 'SSKY', -
             RESOURCE_CONSUMER_GROUP => NULL, -
             SERVICE=> 'SSKY', -
             LOGGING_LEVEL=> DBMS_SCHEDULER.LOGGING_RUNS,-
             LOG_HISTORY => 30);
```

The preceding definition will create a job class called SSKY. The parameters for the CREATE_JOB_CLASS procedure include the name identified by JOB_CLASS_NAME, the consumer group that the job class belongs to, and the service name (SERVICE) that is being mapped to the job class. The definition also contains a logging level (LOGGING_LEVEL) and a log history period (LOG_HISTORY).

The RESOURCE_CONSUMER_GROUP is NULL because the service was mapped to a resource consumer group in the previous step. Oracle supports three different levels of logging:

1.   No logging using DBMS_SCHEDULER.LOGGING_OFF

2.   Detailed logging using DBMS_SCHEDULER.LOGGING_RUNS

3.   Complete logging that records all operations performed by all jobs in the job class using DBMS_SCHEDULER.LOGGING_FULL

The job definitions could be verified using the following query DBA_SCHEDULER_JOB_CLASSES view:

```
SELECT JOB_CLASS_NAME,
       SERVICE
FROM DBA_SCHEDULER_JOB_CLASSES
WHERE SERVICE LIKE '%SSK%';

JOB_CLASS_NAME     SERVICE
------------------ ----------
SSKY               SSKY
```

Step 7.8 Job Definition

Once the job class has been defined, the next step is to add the batch job to the scheduler from where the job could be executed by the application by submitting it in the background. The Job is scheduled using the following command:

```
EXEC DBMS_SCHEDULER.CREATE_JOB-
(JOB_NAME=>'SSKY_REPORTING_JOB', -
JOB_TYPE=>'EXECUTABLE', -
JOB_ACTION=>'/usr/apps/batch/SSKYnightlybatch;', -
JOB_CLASS=>'SSKY',-
ENABLED=>TRUE, -
AUTO_DROP=>FALSE, -
COMMENTS=>'Batch Reporting');
```

Step 7.9 Performance Thresholds Definition

Performance thresholds may be defined for each instance participating in this cluster using the following PL/SQL package:

```
EXECUTE DBMS_SERVER_ALERT.SET_THRESHOLD -
(METRICS_ID => DBMS_SERVER_ALERT.ELAPSED_TIME_PER_CALL, -
 WARNING_OPERATOR => DBMS_SERVER_ALERT.OPERATOR_GE, -
 WARNING_VALUE => '500',-
 CRITICAL_OPERATOR => DBMS_SERVER_ALERT.OPERATOR_GE,-
 CRITICAL_VALUE => '7500', -
 OBSERVATION_PERIOD => 1,-
```

```
CONSECUTIVE_OCCURRENCES => 5,-
INSTANCE_NAME => NULL,-
OBJECT_TYPE => DBMS_SERVER_ALERT.OBJECT_TYPE_SERVICE,-
OBJECT_NAME => 'RAPTEST');
```

Step 7.10 Set the Plan to Be Used

Once the plan definition has been created and all the required attributes defined, the plan is ready for use. To allow the right resource manager plan to be used for each instance in the cluster, the appropriate default plan for the respective instances should be set by setting the RESOURCE_MANAGER_PLAN initialization parameter:

```
BEGIN
   EXECUTE IMMEDIATE 'ALTER SYSTEM SET resource_manager_plan =''SSKY_SCDB_PLAN'' SID=''SCDB_2''';
   EXECUTE IMMEDIATE 'ALTER SYSTEM SET resource_manager_plan =''SSKY_SCDB_PLAN'' SID=''SCDB_1''';
END;
```

At this point, a RAC cluster with distributed workload is implemented per Table 15-6 previously.

■ **Note**   In Step 7.10, the parameter is set specifically only on two instances because the resource manager setting is for the two instances in the pool. If the plan applies to all the instances in the cluster, it's advisable to use the SID='*'.

Step 8 Monitoring Workload

Service level monitoring of workload distribution can be monitored using V$SERVICEMETRIC view. Oracle has provided additional packages and views for monitoring of this functionality. Monitoring is set up using the following PL/SQL package. Once set up, the configuration information could be verified using the DBA_ENABLED_AGGREGATIONS view.

To avoid overloading this section, monitoring and troubleshooting is discussed in the next section.

Locating the Problem

With the support for SOA and Oracle's implementation of a layer of abstraction to the application as services, Oracle had also introduced in Oracle Database 10g a new dimension for performance tuning. With services, workloads are visible and measurable; and statistics gathered can be attributed to specific applications and or modules within applications. Services provide another level of performance optimization, meaning connecting a specific poor-performing SQL operation to a service instead of the traditional approach in which an SQL was always related to a session. Apart from wait events at the service level (discussed in Chapter 17) available through the GV$SERVICE_EVENT view, the statistics are also collected at the service level.

Oracle provides additional levels of data collection by defining modules within applications or actions within modules. This helps in easy identification of performance areas within the application. Module- and action-level monitoring can be enabled using the following PL/SQL definition:

```
DBMS_MONITOR.SERV_MOD_ACT_STAT_ENABLE (<SERVICE_NAME>, <MODULE NAME>)
```

For example, to enable statistics collection for module ORDERS in service SRV1, the following should be executed on the database server on any of the available instances:

```
EXEC DBMS_MONITOR.SERV_MOD_ACT_STAT_ENABLE ('SRV1', 'ORDERS');
```

Once monitoring has been enabled, it remains active until such time it is disabled using the following procedure:

```
EXEC DBMS_MONITOR.SERV_MOD_ACT_STAT_DISABLE (null,null);
```

These definitions can be verified by querying the DBA_ENABLED_AGGREGATIONS table:

```
SELECT AGGREGATION_TYPE,
       QUALIFIER_ID1 MODULE,
       QUALIFIER_ID2 ACTION
FROM DBA_ENABLED_AGGREGATIONS;

AGGREGATION_TYPE       MODULE      ACTION
---------------------- ----------  ---------
SERVICE_MODULE_ACTION  ORDERS      Mixed
SERVICE_MODULE_ACTION  ORDERS      Multiple
SERVICE_MODULE_ACTION  ORDERS      Read
SERVICE_MODULE_ACTION  ORDERS      Update
```

Before monitoring the performance statistics, the application connecting to the database should connect to the SERVICE_NAME being monitored, and the application should have the module identified in the code. The module name can be set in the application using the following procedure:

```
DBMS_APPLICATION_INFO.SET_MODULE (<MODULE NAME>, <ACTION TYPE>);
```

For example, to let the database know which module is being monitored, the following procedure should be executed from inside the application module:

```
EXEC DBMS_APPLICATION_INFO.SET_MODULE ('ORDERS');
```

Apart from monitoring individual modules, performance-related statistics could also be collected for any specific action. For example, the performance of various users executing update statements can also be monitored executing the following procedure:

```
EXEC DBMS_MONITOR.SERV_MOD_ACT_STAT_ENABLE ('SRV1', 'ORDERS', 'UPDATE');
```

Similarly, inside the application ORDERS module, the specific action ('UPDATE') being modified should also be identified using the following procedure:

```
EXEC DBMS_APPLICATION_INFO.SET_MODULE ('ORDERS', 'UPDATE');
```

Once the statistics collection has been enabled on the database server and on the client side, the performance metrics can be collected or monitored. For example, the output from the following script against the GV$SERVICE_STATS view provides a high level indication that DB Time for SRV1 on instance 2 is significantly high:

```
COL STAT_NAME FORMAT A35
COL MODULE FORMAT A10
COL SERVICE FORMAT A15
COL INST FORMAT 999
SELECT INST_ID INST,
       SERVICE_NAME SERVICE,
       STAT_NAME,
       VALUE
```

```
FROM  GV$SERVICE_STATS
WHERE VALUE > 0
AND   SERVICE_NAME ='SRV1'
ORDER BY VALUE;

INST SERVICE         STAT_NAME                                    VALUE
---- --------------- ----------------------------------------- ----------
   2 SRV1            parse count (total)                         114332
   2 SRV1            opened cursors cumulative                   114574
   2 SRV1            execute count                               252873
   2 SRV1            session logical reads                      5254843
   2 SRV1            redo size                                 21199172
   2 SRV1            cluster wait time                         27815562
   2 SRV1            application wait time                     87809921
   2 SRV1            user I/O wait time                        98546228
   2 SRV1            concurrency wait time                   2055384221
   2 SRV1            DB CPU                                  2156249531
   2 SRV1            sql execute elapsed time               6912286900
   2 SRV1            parse time elapsed                     8681424580
   2 SRV1            DB time                                9845032706
```

To identify the module and action type that caused the high DB time values, use the following script against the view GV$SERV_MOD_ACT_STATS:

```
COL STAT_NAME FORMAT A35
COL MODULE FORMAT A10
COL SERVICE FORMAT A10
COL INST FORMAT 999
COL ACTION FORMAT A8
SELECT INST_ID INST,
       AGGREGATION_TYPE,
       SERVICE_NAME SERVICE,
       MODULE,
       ACTION,
       STAT_NAME,
       VALUE
FROM GV$SERV_MOD_ACT_STATS;
```

The benefits provided for monitoring activity at the service level do not stop here. Tracing user operations is also available at the module and action level. Oracle generates one trace file per session connecting to the database using the SERVICE_NAME. Users connecting to the database may get attached to any of the available instances supporting the service. The advantage of tracing at this level is that when multiple trace files are generated from the current instance or across instances in the cluster, data related to a specific action type can be grouped together. For example, the following procedure will enable tracing of a service at the module and action level:

```
DBMS_MONITOR.SERV_MOD_ACT_TRACE_ENABLE (<SERVICE_NAME>,<MODULE NAME>,<ACTION TYPE>);
EXEC DBMS_MONITOR.SERV_MOD_ACT_TRACE_ENABLE ('SRV1', 'ORDERS', 'MIXED');
```

529

Apart from the basic SQL-level trace information, additional information such as wait events encountered (collected by default), bind variables and values used, and so forth, can also be collected. For example

```
EXEC DBMS_MONITOR.SERV_MOD_ACT_TRACE_ENABLE (
  SERVICE_NAME  => 'SRV1',
  MODULE_NAME   =>  'ORDERS ',
  ACTION_NAME   => DBMS_MONITOR.ALL_ACTIONS,
  WAITS         => TRUE,
  BINDS         => TRUE);
```

■ **Note** The SERV_MOD_ACT_TRACE_ENABLE utility generates trace files similar to the trace files generated using event 10046 at Level 1. Enabling wait events and binds will be similar to generating tracing using 10046 at Level 12.

Once these procedures are executed on the database server, the trace files are generated in the USER_DUMP_DEST directory on the respective instances. Oracle generates one trace file for every session connecting to the database using the service SRV1. The trace files can then be consolidated based on different criteria.

Based on the example, the trace file will contain information (SQL statements, wait events encountered, bind variables, and bind values). This trace information can be

- Analyzed directly using the tkprof (Transient Kernel Profiler) utility.

```
tkprof ssky1.ora.*.trc trcSRV1.prf explain=bmf/bmf table=bmf.temp sys=noFo
```

- Scanned through and extracted by action type using the trcsess utility. Once these have been extracted into a single file, it can be analyzed using the tkprof utility.

```
trcsess output=trcMixed.trc service=SRV1 module='ORDERS' action=Mixed  ssky1_ora_*.trc
```

```
trcsess [output=<output file name >] [session=<session ID>] [clientid=<clientid>]
[service=<service name>] [action=<action name>] [module=<module name>] <trace file names>
```

Following are the descriptions for the various parameters used in the trcsess utility:

<output file name> Output destination default being standard output.

<sessionID> Session to be traced. Session ID is a combination of session index and session serial number.

<clientid> To be traced.

<service name> Service to be traced.

<action name> Action to be traced.

<module name> Module to be traced.

<trace file names> Space separated list of trace files with wild card '*' supported.

The following trcsess command will extract trace information from the trace file that pertains to service SRV1 but contains all modules and actions:

```
trcsess output=trcSRV1.trc service=SRV1 ssky1_ora_*.trc
```

Similarly, the following `trcsess` command will extract trace information from the trace files that pertain to service SRV1 and module ORDERS but will contain all actions:

```
trcsess output=trcRead.trc service=SRV1 action=Mixed module=ORDERS ssky1_ora_*.trc
```

Workshop

The areas of applications experiencing problems cannot always be identified. Many times, slow response times are reported, however, not the module or action that caused the problem. Many times a small operation by one user can cause the entire system to go slow.

Step 1

Troubleshooting a performance issue to drill down to specific areas of the application can be done in one of two ways: first by adding tags into the application and logging every step of the application with a timestamp to measure the elapsed time every step of the code took; then from the log file, analyze the step that took the longest elapsed time.

Another simpler and more permanent method would be to use the `DBMS_APPLICATION_INFO` package, and the procedures to name the module and action are implemented.

GV$SESSION is a view that provides insight into what modules and actions are being executed at a given point in time:

Script: MVRACPDnTap whoractive.sql

```
SELECT  S.inst_id,
        s.service_name,
        To_char(s.logon_time, 'mm/dd hh24:mi ') logon_time,
        s.module,
        s.action,
        s.program
FROM    gv$session s
WHERE   username IS NOT NULL
        AND status = 'ACTIVE'
ORDER   BY logon_time,
        inst_id;
Ins
 ID SERVICE  LOGON_TIME   MODULE                 ACTION_PROGRAM
--- -------- ------------ ---------------------- --------------------------
  1 TAPS     11/26 18:12  CRE_BULK_DATA_LOADER   SSK_INST_BULK_DATA_LOADER
  2 TAPS     11/26 18:12  CRE_BULK_DATA_LOADER   SSK_INST_BULK_DATA_LOADER
  2 TAPS     11/26 18:12                         JDBC Thin Client
  1 TICKS    11/26 18:13  CRE_BULK_DATA_LOADER   SSK_INST_XML_DATA_STATUS J
  2 TICKS    11/26 18:13  CRE_BULK_DATA_LOADER   SSK_INST_FILE_PROCESS_STAT
  2 TICKS    11/26 18:14  CRE_BULK_DATA_LOADER   SSK_INST_FILE_PROCESS_STAT
  4 FIPS     11/26 19:58  CRE_BULK_DATA_LOADER   SSK_INST_FILE_PROCESS_STAT
  4 FIPS     11/28 09:00  JDBC Thin Client       JDBC Thin Client
  1 TAPS     11/28 09:36  CRE_BULK_DATA_LOADER   SSK_INST_BULK_DATA_LOADER
  3 QRTZ     11/28 10:40  JDBC Thin Client       JDBC Thin Client
  4 FIPS     11/28 10:45  CRE_BULK_DATA_LOADER   SSK_INST_FILE_PROCESS_STAT
  4 FIPS     11/28 08:45  JDBC Thin Client       JDBC Thin Client
  4 FIPS     11/28 09:00  JDBC Thin Client       JDBC Thin Client
  4 FIPS     11/28 09:18  JDBC Thin Client       JDBC Thin Client
```

```
4 FIPS      11/28 10:43 CRE_BULK_DATA_LOADER SSK_INST_FILE_PROCESS_STAT
4 FIPS      11/28 10:45 CRE_BULK_DATA_LOADER SSK_INST_FILE_PROCESS_STAT
4 FIPS      11/28 10:46 CRE_BULK_DATA_LOADER SSK_INST_FILE_PROCESS_STAT
```

Step 2

In the output listed in Step 1, there are connections grouped under different services. Each service further has several modules, and each module has several actions. From the output, it's also understood that the modules and actions are shared between the various services.

Results of the analysis identified shared modules and actions that were used by all services. This means if an inefficient code is found, the performance gains from optimizing the code will be to all services. To understand the overall performance of the various sections of the application and drill down to programmatic areas, it's important to enable aggregation of statistics. This can be done either using enterprise manager or directly from the SQL plus prompt.

In Chapter 1, breaking down the application into quadrants to help analyze the problem area was discussed. Breaking down the application based on the connection type, such as a database service (identified by SERVICE_NAME), could be the high-level quadrant. Once the quadrant with the performance issue has been identified, the quadrant can be further broken down into sub-quadrants; here the module will be the sub quadrants and will help by further drilling down to the specific problem area. Once the problem module is identified, the next step is to drill down to a specific action that could be causing performance issues.

The next step should be finding out services that are heavily utilized and checking against the GV$SERVICEMETRIC_HISTORY view:

Script: MVRACPDnTap_svcstatshist.sql

```
SELECT  SERVICE_NAME,
        INSTANCE_NAME,
        ELAPSEDPERCALL SERVICE_TIME,
        CPUPERCALL      CPU_TIME,
        DBTIMEPERCALL   DB_TIME,
        CALLSPERSEC     THROUGHPUT
FROM    GV$INSTANCE        GVI,
        GV$SERVICEMETRIC_HISTORY GVSM
WHERE   GVI.INST_ID     = GVSM.INST_ID
AND     GVSM.GROUP_ID   = 10
AND     GVSM.SERVICE_NAME NOT IN ('SYS$BACKGROUND')
ORDER   BY
    SERVICE_NAME,
    GVI.INST_ID;
```

Service	Int	Elapsed mSec/Call	CPU Time mSec/Call	DB Time mSec/Call	Calls/sec
TP	1	114021	25245	114021	2953.89
TP	2	36969442	460485	36969442	835.58
TQC	1	37822273	4808064	37822273	1021.07
TQC	2	63958174	9283369	63958174	722.73
TQI	1	12075688	338101	12075688	437.44
TQI	2	30649094	387219	30649094	270.62
SQH	5	807323	119198	807323	162.59
SQS	4	2124545	34642	2124545	8188.80

SQS	5	1374787	72728	1374787	10273.62
SYS$USERS	1	1653405	286593	1653405	22.71
SYS$USERS	2	95729887	7191936	95729887	39.40
SYS$USERS	3	192615	184326	192615	25.55
SYS$USERS	4	34397286	22534832	34397286	26.67
SYS$USERS	5	102555733	67790131	102555733	27.11

From the preceding output, DQC (data quality control) has the highest activity, and the elapsed time numbers are really high.

Step 3

Because the database service associated with the application has been identified, the next step is to analyze and check the data to understand which MODULE in the service requires performance optimization:

Script: MVRACPDnTap_SrvModSum.sql

```
SELECT INST_ID INT,
       MODULE,
       STAT_NAME,
       SUM(VALUE)
FROM   GV$SERV_MOD_ACT_STATS
GROUP  BY INST_ID, MODULE, STAT_NAME;
```

INST	SERVICE	MODULE	STAT_NAME	SUM(VALUE)
1	TAPS	TAP_BULK_DATA_LOADER	DB CPU	9999
1	TAPS	TAP_BULK_DATA_LOADER	DB time	10066
1	TAPS	TAP_BULK_DATA_LOADER	sql execute elapsed time	1018
1	TAPS	TAP_BULK_DATA_LOADER	DB CPU	3653014175
1	TAPS	TAP_BULK_DATA_LOADER	DB time	2.5375E+11
1	TAPS	TAP_BULK_DATA_LOADER	application wait time	2793563
1	TAPS	TAP_BULK_DATA_LOADER	cluster wait time	1.9224E+11
1	TAPS	TAP_BULK_DATA_LOADER	concurrency wait time	2.8272E+10
1	TAPS	TAP_BULK_DATA_LOADER	db block changes	11579470
1	TAPS	TAP_BULK_DATA_LOADER	execute count	4663044
1	TAPS	TAP_BULK_DATA_LOADER	gc cr block receive time	797861
1	TAPS	TAP_BULK_DATA_LOADER	gc cr blocks received	790623
1	TAPS	TAP_BULK_DATA_LOADER	gc current block receive time	1743295
1	TAPS	TAP_BULK_DATA_LOADER	gc current blocks received	1270908
1	TAPS	TAP_BULK_DATA_LOADER	opened cursors cumulative	3200379
1	TAPS	TAP_BULK_DATA_LOADER	parse count (total)	1111111
1	TAPS	TAP_BULK_DATA_LOADER	parse time elapsed	49286200
1	TAPS	TAP_BULK_DATA_LOADER	physical reads	47766
1	TAPS	TAP_BULK_DATA_LOADER	redo size	2074354084
1	TAPS	TAP_BULK_DATA_LOADER	session cursor cache hits	1.5891E+11
1	TAPS	TAP_BULK_DATA_LOADER	session logical reads	149803130
1	TAPS	TAP_BULK_DATA_LOADER	sql execute elapsed time	2.3728E+11
1	TAPS	TAP_BULK_DATA_LOADER	user I/O wait time	849885638
1	TAPS	TAP_BULK_DATA_LOADER	user calls	1462272
1	TAPS	TAP_BULK_DATA_LOADER	user commits	1333064

1	TICKS	CRE_BULK_DATA_LOADER	DB CPU	3040543
1	TICKS	CRE_BULK_DATA_LOADER	DB time	153181110
1	TICKS	CRE_BULK_DATA_LOADER	cluster wait time	123924946
1	TICKS	CRE_BULK_DATA_LOADER	concurrency wait time	5333193
1	TICKS	CRE_BULK_DATA_LOADER	db block changes	4911
1	TICKS	CRE_BULK_DATA_LOADER	execute count	13035
1	TICKS	CRE_BULK_DATA_LOADER	gc cr block receive time	858
1	TICKS	CRE_BULK_DATA_LOADER	gc current block receive time	5605
1	TICKS	CRE_BULK_DATA_LOADER	gc current blocks received	647
1	TICKS	CRE_BULK_DATA_LOADER	opened cursors cumulative	9123
1	TICKS	CRE_BULK_DATA_LOADER	parse count (total)	1289
1	TICKS	CRE_BULK_DATA_LOADER	parse time elapsed	271372
1	TICKS	CRE_BULK_DATA_LOADER	redo size	901224
1	TICKS	CRE_BULK_DATA_LOADER	session cursor cache hits	4294909653
1	TICKS	CRE_BULK_DATA_LOADER	session logical reads	32741
1	TICKS	CRE_BULK_DATA_LOADER	sql execute elapsed time	152791384
1	TICKS	CRE_BULK_DATA_LOADER	user I/O wait time	20580395
1	TICKS	CRE_BULK_DATA_LOADER	user calls	3163
2	TAPS	TAP_BULK_DATA_LOADER	DB CPU	20996
2	TAPS	TAP_BULK_DATA_LOADER	DB time	23571
2	TAPS	TAP_BULK_DATA_LOADER	concurrency wait time	1853
2	TAPS	TAP_BULK_DATA_LOADER	sql execute elapsed time	1561
2	TAPS	TAP_BULK_DATA_LOADER	DB CPU	3409137796
2	TAPS	TAP_BULK_DATA_LOADER	DB time	2.4099E+11
2	TAPS	TAP_BULK_DATA_LOADER	application wait time	2184882
2	TAPS	TAP_BULK_DATA_LOADER	cluster wait time	1.2299E+11
2	TAPS	TAP_BULK_DATA_LOADER	concurrency wait time	2.4219E+10
2	TAPS	TAP_BULK_DATA_LOADER	db block changes	10156572
2	TAPS	TAP_BULK_DATA_LOADER	execute count	4131093
2	TAPS	TAP_BULK_DATA_LOADER	gc cr block receive time	232311
2	TAPS	TAP_BULK_DATA_LOADER	gc cr blocks received	746592
2	TAPS	TAP_BULK_DATA_LOADER	gc current block receive time	858191
2	TAPS	TAP_BULK_DATA_LOADER	gc current blocks received	1209331
2	TAPS	TAP_BULK_DATA_LOADER	opened cursors cumulative	2825101
2	TAPS	TAP_BULK_DATA_LOADER	parse count (total)	882390
2	TAPS	TAP_BULK_DATA_LOADER	parse time elapsed	40182318
2	TAPS	TAP_BULK_DATA_LOADER	physical reads	45364
2	TAPS	TAP_BULK_DATA_LOADER	redo size	1807920872
2	TAPS	TAP_BULK_DATA_LOADER	session cursor cache hits	1.2455E+11
2	TAPS	TAP_BULK_DATA_LOADER	session logical reads	132062344
2	TAPS	TAP_BULK_DATA_LOADER	sql execute elapsed time	1.5694E+11
2	TAPS	TAP_BULK_DATA_LOADER	user I/O wait time	2934858941
2	TAPS	TAP_BULK_DATA_LOADER	user calls	1301025
3	RACGRUD	Toad.exe	DB time	916476497
3	RACGRUD	Toad.exe	application wait time	20135
3	RACGRUD	Toad.exe	cluster wait time	22852151
3	RACGRUD	Toad.exe	concurrency wait time	14291
3	RACGRUD	Toad.exe	gc cr block receive time	971
3	RACGRUD	Toad.exe	gc cr blocks received	60114
3	RACGRUD	Toad.exe	parse time elapsed	1250097
3	RACGRUD	Toad.exe	physical reads	14203147

3	RACGRUD	Toad.exe	session logical reads	14284994
3	RACGRUD	Toad.exe	sql execute elapsed time	916439031
3	RACGRUD	Toad.exe	user I/O wait time	777296854
3	SSKYPRD	backup incr datafile	concurrency wait time	567628
3	SSKYPRD	backup incr datafile	opened cursors cumulative	1327
3	SSKYPRD	backup incr datafile	session cursor cache hits	1225
3	SSKYPRD	backup incr datafile	user I/O wait time	11993832

Analyzing the preceding output, it's an indication that module TAP_BULK_DATA_LOADER has more resource utilization compared to the other module and now high DB CPU and DB Time on both instances in the cluster (recall that the database service is only configured to run on instance 1 and instance 2 of the cluster).

Step 4

Once the highly resource-intensive MODULE of the application has been identified, the next step is to drill down further to determine what part(s) of the code could be consuming a high amount of resources or having slow response times.

Script: MVRACPDnTap_SrvActSum.sql

```
SELECT INST_ID INT,
       ACTION,
       STAT_NAME,
       SUM(VALUE)
FROM   GV$SERV_MOD_ACT_STATS
GROUP  BY INST_ID,ACTION,STAT_NAME;
```

INST	SVI	ACTION	STAT_NAME	SUM(VALUE)
1	TAPS	FILE_NON_BULK_DATA_LOADER	DB CPU	9999
1	TAPS	FILE_NON_BULK_DATA_LOADER	DB time	10066
1	TAPS	FILE_NON_BULK_DATA_LOADER	sql execute elapsed time	1018
1	TAPS	SSK_INST_FILE_PROCESS_STATUS	DB CPU	3652942186
1	TAPS	SSK_INST_FILE_PROCESS_STATUS	DB time	2.5375E+11
1	TAPS	SSK_INST_FILE_PROCESS_STATUS	application wait time	2793563
1	TAPS	SSK_INST_FILE_PROCESS_STATUS	cluster wait time	1.9224E+11
1	TAPS	SSK_INST_FILE_PROCESS_STATUS	concurrency wait time	2.8272E+10
1	TAPS	SSK_INST_FILE_PROCESS_STATUS	db block changes	11579205
1	TAPS	SSK_INST_FILE_PROCESS_STATUS	execute count	4662872
1	TAPS	SSK_INST_FILE_PROCESS_STATUS	gc cr block receive time	797851
1	TAPS	SSK_INST_FILE_PROCESS_STATUS	gc cr blocks received	790614
1	TAPS	SSK_INST_FILE_PROCESS_STATUS	gc current block receive time	1743286
1	TAPS	SSK_INST_FILE_PROCESS_STATUS	gc current blocks received	1270887
1	TAPS	SSK_INST_FILE_PROCESS_STATUS	opened cursors cumulative	3200371
1	TAPS	SSK_INST_FILE_PROCESS_STATUS	parse count (total)	1111103
1	TAPS	SSK_INST_FILE_PROCESS_STATUS	parse time elapsed	49285922
1	TAPS	SSK_INST_FILE_PROCESS_STATUS	physical reads	47759
1	TAPS	SSK_INST_FILE_PROCESS_STATUS	redo size	2074315644
1	TAPS	SSK_INST_FILE_PROCESS_STATUS	session cursor cache hits	1.5891E+11
1	TAPS	SSK_INST_FILE_PROCESS_STATUS	session logical reads	149802353
1	TAPS	SSK_INST_FILE_PROCESS_STATUS	sql execute elapsed time	2.3728E+11
1	TAPS	SSK_INST_FILE_PROCESS_STATUS	user I/O wait time	849840546

1 TAPS	SSK_INST_FILE_PROCESS_STATUS	user calls	1462108
1 TAPS	SSK_INST_FILE_PROCESS_STATUS	user commits	1333015
2 TAPS	FILE_NON_BULK_DATA_LOADER	DB CPU	20996
2 TAPS	FILE_NON_BULK_DATA_LOADER	DB time	23010
2 TAPS	FILE_NON_BULK_DATA_LOADER	concurrency wait time	1853
2 TAPS	FILE_NON_BULK_DATA_LOADER	sql execute elapsed time	1497
1 TAPS		DB CPU	44398241
1 TAPS		DB time	4281592766
1 TAPS		cluster wait time	2873017407
1 TAPS		concurrency wait time	386393096
1 TAPS		db block changes	150845
1 TAPS		execute count	42158
1 TAPS		gc cr block receive time	14266
1 TAPS		gc cr blocks received	6701

The output from the preceding query indicates there are two actions that are part of the module identified in the previous step that are candidates for investigation. Both actions have high DB Time and DB CPU time apart from cluster wait time and concurrency wait time.

To drill down further into the code and identify the problem, a closer look at the code that is part of the action is required. If the process is currently active, then this information could be obtained from either GV$SESSION or GV$ACTIVE_SESSION_HISTORY by checking the ACTION, MODULE, SERVICE_NAME, and the SQL_ID against the view. If the application is structurally written with each ACTION identified by a separate name, information from the GV$SESSION view would be helpful. Otherwise, more than one SQL_ID may be associated with the ACTION, and further investigation may be required.

Step 6

With the information collected from the previous steps, we try to identify the query. Because there are several actions for the given module, it may be practical to identify queries associated with this ACTION.

Querying the GV$ACTIVE_HISTORY_SESSION for the action revealed several queries executed from multiple modules all having the same ACTION.

```
SELECT COUNT(*),
       inst_id,
       sql_id,
       action,
       event,
       wait_time,
       wait_class
FROM  gv$active_session_history
GROUP BY inst_id,
         sql_id,
         action,
         event,
         wait_time,
         wait_class
ORDER BY sql_id;
```

The preceding query revealed several SQL_IDs used commonly across many modules and actions. Further investigation into wait events and row level locking issues associated to the various SQL operations indicated potential issues with the SQL statement with SQL_ID 'dhp8kqqkag9tq'.

```
SELECT inst_id INT,
       event,
       p1,
       p2,
       wait_class
FROM   gv$active_session_history
WHERE  sql_id = 'dhp8kqqkag9tq'
       AND event IS NOT NULL
ORDER  BY p2,
          p1;
 INT  EVENT                               P1        P2  WAIT_CLASS
 ---- ------------------------------ --------- --------- -------------
    1 latch: cache buffers chains    5.42E+10        155 Concurrency
    2 latch: cache buffers chains    5.42E+10        155 Concurrency
      latch: cache buffers chains    5.42E+10        155 Concurrency
      latch: cache buffers chains    5.46E+10        155 Concurrency
      latch: row cache objects       5.43E+10        279 Concurrency
      latch: row cache objects       5.43E+10        279 Concurrency
      gc cr block 2-way                   150       6324 Cluster
      gc buffer busy acquire              149       7164 Cluster
      gc cr block 3-way                   149       7164 Cluster
      gc buffer busy acquire              149       7164 Cluster
      gc buffer busy acquire              140      10096 Cluster
      gc buffer busy acquire              151      11419 Cluster
      gc buffer busy acquire              138      12617 Cluster
      gc current block 3-way              143      18008 Cluster
      gc buffer busy acquire              160      18808 Cluster
      gc cr block 2-way                   159      20536 Cluster
```

Step 7

The cluster-related statistics following also indicate that the query was executed across multiple instances in the cluster:

Script: MVRACPDnTap_sqlstats.sql

```
SELECT inst_id                INT,
       sql_id,
       application_wait_time awt,
       concurrency_wait_time conwt,
       cluster_wait_time     clwt,
       user_io_wait_time     uiwt
FROM   gv$sqlstats
WHERE  cluster_wait_time > 10000
ORDER  BY inst_id,
          user_io_wait_time desc;
```

INT	SQL_ID	AWT	CONWT	CLWT	IOICBYTES
1	9q7k9nbpvk8pv	1303	8681215	3833115628	12166062080
	7p9s66ud42nmw	1607	14135556	1966278932	5832507392
	dhp8kqqkag9tq	**2401**	**213355467**	**54421595**	**0**
	7x5s1cjq1dd8z	1882	7169	35940718	1099939840
	bq829z449nhfu	3130756	1651536	32660485	23085375488
	6h85ar3uzms52	926053	7850711	29252830	28858040320
2	7p9s66ud42nmw	87597709	11132035	1985073170	6146048000
	dhp8kqqkag9tq	**1.11E+08**	**214990704**	**376465304**	**8192**
	7x5s1cjq1dd8z	785755	12371906	84915341	52792958976
	bq829z449nhfu	629	19779	14628380	1275248640
3	3v6dt7mn41xb3	1878	1403328	11742867534	6319423488
	8104kxuj6f3hp	1559	9791612	748775808	1299734528
	106crpma4qfu9	574	22560	20996170	1303863296
4	3v6dt7mn41xb3	4043	964909	10298084731	9079422976
	8104kxuj6f3hp	2126	5922086	104678129	12071821312
	1q931v7v7skp7	1727773	10161297	53504995	28051447808
	cfzuc2bt9kk4s	605709	10428350	45948917	33957453824

Querying GV$SQLSTATS indicated the application used database sequence numbers to populate the primary key column during INSERT operations:

```
SELECT  inst_id INT,
        sql_id,
        sql_text
FROM    gv$sqlstats
WHERE   sql_id = 'dhp8kqqkag9tq';
```

INT	SQL_ID	SQL_TEXT
1	dhp8kqqkag9tq	SELECT INST_FILE_UPLOAD_SEQ.NEXTVAL FROM DUAL
2	dhp8kqqkag9tq	SELECT INST_FILE_UPLOAD_SEQ.NEXTVAL FROM DUAL
3	dhp8kqqkag9tq	SELECT INST_FILE_UPLOAD_SEQ.NEXTVAL FROM DUAL
4	dhp8kqqkag9tq	SELECT INST_FILE_UPLOAD_SEQ.NEXTVAL FROM DUAL

Step 8

Almost always, due to movement of blocks between the holding instance and the requesting instance (reasons discussed in Chapter 2), highly insert-intensive applications that generate surrogate keys using database sequence numbers are creating significant contention issues at the index leaf block level. The contention can be at the leaf block level when inserting rows into the table and can also be delayed if there are concurrent requests for sequence due to depilation of the sequence cache (default 20). Typically, instance-level contention issues for sequences measured in frequent gets (GETS), misses (GETMISSES), and updates (MODIFICATIONS) can be obtained by checking the dc_sequences parameter from GV$ROWCAHCE view; similarly, cluster-level contentions can also be obtained from the same view by querying the DLM_REQUESTS, DLM_CONFLICTS, and DLM_RELEASES columns.

In the output following, dc_sequences shows 51.6% success in getting the next sequence number. This means that 50% of the time the sequences cache was empty and had to be refreshed:

Script: MVRACPDnTap_rowcache.sql

```
SELECT inst_id                            INT,
       parameter,
       SUM(gets)                          gets,
       SUM(getmisses)                     misses,
       100 * SUM(gets - getmisses) / SUM(gets) pgets,
       SUM(modifications)                 updates
FROM   gv$rowcache
WHERE  gets > 0
HAVING SUM(modifications) > 0
GROUP  BY inst_id,
          parameter
ORDER BY inst_id,
          6 DESC; d
```

INT	PARAMETER	GETS	MISSES	PGETS	UPDATES
1	dc_sequences	153802	126036	51.6	153802
	dc_rollback_segments	3054224	258	100.0	167
	dc_segments	31636	2325	92.7	158
	dc_objects	180114	3333	98.1	156
	dc_histogram_defs	87711	6224	92.9	55
	dc_constraints	36	19	47.2	36
	outstanding_alerts	267	237	11.2	21
	dc_awr_control	334	5	98.5	6
	dc_users	243669	186	99.9	2
2	dc_sequences	160079	126035	56.7	160079
	dc_segments	24599	2258	90.8	399
	dc_objects	108531	2847	97.4	334
	dc_rollback_segments	2849803	367	100.0	296
	dc_constraints	92	47	48.9	92
	dc_histogram_defs	43679	5286	87.9	49
	outstanding_alerts	298	254	14.8	47
	dc_awr_control	334	7	97.9	4
	dc_global_oids	39576	106	99.7	1
	dc_files	98	14	85.7	0

Similar to the preceding output, the cluster level also indicates high requests and conflicts. It indicates high cluster level contention due to concurrency issues.

```
SELECT inst_id INT,
       parameter,
       dlm_requests  requests,
       dlm_conflicts   conflicts,
       dlm_releases   releases
FROM   gv$rowcache
WHERE  dlm_requests > 1000
ORDER  BY inst_id,
          dlm_requests desc,
          dlm_conflicts desc;
```

INT	PARAMETER	REQUESTS	CONFLICTS	RELEASES
1	dc_sequences	1107598	126029	0
	dc_histogram_defs	6304	45	0
	dc_objects	3604	27	0
	dc_segments	2704	92	0
2	dc_sequences	1120159	126024	0
	dc_histogram_defs	5361	0	0
	dc_objects	3425	6	0
	dc_segments	2999	75	0
	dc_rollback_segments	2442	170	0

Step 9

Increasing the cache size to a higher number to reduce the number of get misses increases the percentage of successful gets:

```
ALTER SEQUENCE INST_FILE_UPLOAD_SEQ CACHE SIZE 4000;
```

INDEX LEAF BLOCKS

Initially each index tree has one level. If the data in the table is very small, there may be only one index block. In that case, the leaf block is the same as the branch block (Figure 15-5). As the data grows, the level increases; and then there is a branch block and a leaf block with a parent–child relationship. The maximum number of levels that the B-tree index can grow to is 24 (i.e., 0–23), which means that with two rows per index block, it can hold approximately 18 billion leaf blocks.

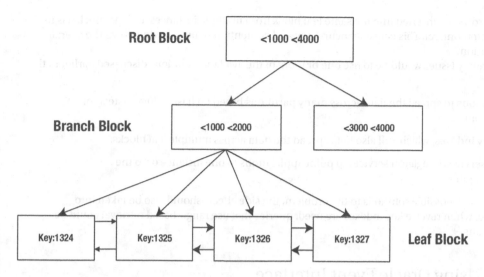

Figure 15-5. *Index leaf blocks for B-tree index*

The root block contains data that points to the branch block, which in turn points to the lower level leaf block. The lowest level contains the indexed data values and corresponding ROWIDs required for locating the row.

B-tree indexes provide considerable performance benefits where the index key value is unique across the database. Performance degradation of the B-tree index can be noticed when the index key value is non-unique and the number of rows per value gets higher.

B-tree indexes are useful in a RAC environment provided there is no collision of index key values, and the inserts into the leaf blocks are not adjacent to each other. If the values being inserted are sequential in nature, which means they are most likely to be inserted into the same leaf block, performance degradation occurs due to frequent index leaf block splits. Under such situations, it would be advisable to use the reverse key index option.

Various index types carry different structures. The B-tree structure has the following advantages:

- All leaf blocks of the tree are at the same depth, so retrieval of any record from anywhere in the index takes approximately the same amount of time. It is important that the index tree does not get very deep; and hence, a tree structure that is more than four levels deep would be inefficient.

- B-tree indexes automatically stay balanced.

- All blocks of the B-tree are three-quarters full on the average.

- B-trees provide excellent retrieval performance for a wide range of queries, including exact match and range searches.

Step 10

Monotonously increasing surrogate keys can cause high amounts of contention when leaf blocks splits occur and when the blocks need to be transferred over the interconnect, for new rows need to be inserted from other instances in the cluster.

Figure 15-5 illustrates the branch block and leaf block structure. Every time a new row is inserted, it will be stored in the rightmost leaf block of the index. As more and more rows are inserted into the table, this will cause the rightmost leaf block to fill and will cause the leaf block to split into two leaf blocks. The contention in a RAC environment occurs when rows are inserted into the same leaf block from multiple instances and the block has to be transferred across the interconnect. This causes concurrency and contention issues, slowing down the overall performance of the application.

To reduce the concurrency issues would be to use one or more of the available solutions discussed earlier in the previous chapters:

- Use hash partitions to spread the data across many partitions based on hash values instead of the actual key value.

- Use reverse key indexes, which will also help spread the data across multiple leaf blocks.

- Use database services (singleton service) to point applications to one instance or to the database server pool.

Although these options are possible solutions to the problem, the side effects should also be taken into consideration. For example, when reverse key indexes are used, queries that use range-based retrieval could be affected due to full table scans.

Troubleshooting Using Oracle Event Interface

RCLB can also be verified by enabling tracing at the database level using event 10735 at Level 3. Tracing can be enabled using the following statement:

```
SQL> ALTER SYSTEM SET EVENTS '10735 TRACE NAME CONTEXT FOREVER, LEVEL 3';
```

The trace file contains the activities involving the cluster and or services that are being monitored. This provides the insight into how the client machines using this metric will react. The output of the trace file resembles the following:

```
/usr/app/oracle/admin/SSKYDB/udump/ssky1_ora_23316.trc
Oracle Database 10g Enterprise Edition Release 10.2.0.1.0 - Production
With the Partitioning, Real Application Clusters, OLAP and Data Mining options
ORACLE_HOME = /usr/app/oracle/product/10.2.0/db_1
............
Instance name: SSKY1
Redo thread mounted by this instance: 1
Oracle process number: 70
Unix process pid: 23316, image: oracleSSKY1@oradb3.sumsky.net

kswsgsnp : length of KSWS_SYSTEM_SVC is 14
kswsgsnp : length of KSWS_DATABASE_SVC is 9
         Both should be less than 64 to avoid overrun
*** SERVICE NAME:(SRV1) 2005-09-24 23:58:31.636
*** SESSION ID:(91.1) 2005-09-24 23:58:31.635
###session count for SRV1=33
###session count for SRV1=34
*** 2005-09-24 23:59:32.626
SKGXPSEGRCV: MESSAGE TRUNCATED user data 40 bytes payload 200 bytes
SKGXPSEGRCV: trucated message buffer data skgxpmsg meta data header 0x0xbfff54e0 len 40 bytes
SKGXPLOSTACK: message truncation expected
SKGXPLOSTACK: data sent to port with no buffers queued from
```

```
SSKGXPID 0xbfff559c network 0    Internet address 10.168.2.140    UDP port number 54589
SSKGXPID 0xbfff559c network 1    Internet address 220.255.187.12        UDP port number 3260
SKGXPLOSTACK: sent seq 32763 expecting 32764
SKGXPLOSTACK: lost ack detected retransmit ack
*** 2005-09-25 00:02:38.927
###session count for SRV1=31
###session count for SRV1=30
```

The preceding output illustrates that the MMON's statistics collection is working and configured for the default type and that the load balance on session is counted. In this case, TAPS is the service; and Oracle updates the MMON process; which in turn builds the advisory and posts the required advice to AQ, PMON, and the ONS. The trace output could also provide indications regarding retransmissions and so forth if there are issues with the interconnect.

Conclusion

In this chapter, we discussed an in depth look at service-based architecture with DWM. In the chapter, we discussed about the load balancing and failover features available in RAC. In the workshop, we discussed the distributed workload management and monitoring of workload, integrating it with the resource manager to prioritize services and allocation of resources.

■ ■ ■

## CHAPTER 16

Oracle Clusterware Diagnosis

Webster's Dictionary's definition for a cluster is "a number of similar things that occur together." A clustered system occurs when things of the same sort are organized together or growing together to form or represent a group of their respective kind. For example, a number of people, flowers, or things grouped together forms a cluster. Similarly, a group of independent hardware systems or nodes that is interconnected to provide a single computer source is referred to as a hardware cluster. Unlike with flowers and other objects, if one node in a cluster fails, its workload is automatically distributed among the surviving nodes. This process of automatically distributing the workload to other available nodes reduces the downtime of the entire system. Clustering is an architecture that keeps systems running in the event of a single-system failure. Clustering provides maximum scalability by grouping separate servers into a single computing facility. Clusters have the potential to provide excellent price and performance advantages over traditional mainframe systems in many areas, such as availability, scalability, manageability, and recoverability.

Clustering has proven to be a successful architecture of choice for providing high availability (HA) and scalability in business-critical computing applications. Clients interact with a cluster as though it were a single entity or a single high-performance, highly reliable server. If a cluster fails, its workload is automatically distributed among the surviving nodes.

Oracle Clusterware

Oracle Clusterware is an application stack that resides on top of the basic operating system (O/S). Apart from the primary function of managing the nodes participating in the cluster, Oracle's clusterware offers additional services that provide a more comprehensive solution compared to third-party cluster managers. It's the clusterware component that's responsible for restarting RAC instances and listeners upon process failures and relocating the VIPs upon node failure. Oracle provides various utilities and commands to manage the various tiers of the clusterware.

Figure 16-1 illustrates the Oracle Grid Infrastructure (GI) stack in Oracle Clusterware 11g Release 2. There are several high availability daemons introduced in this release.

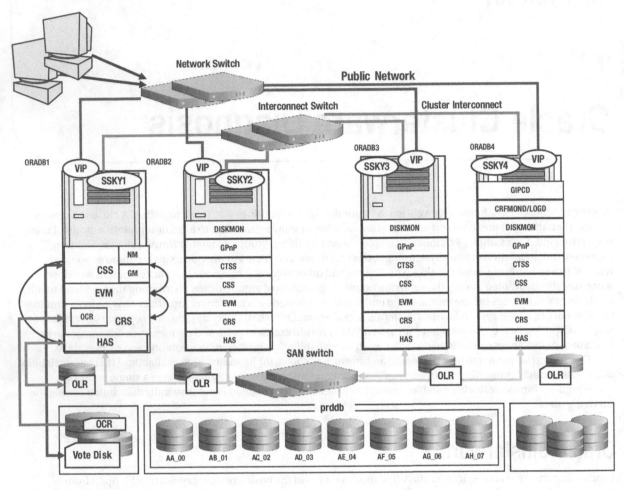

Figure 16-1. *Grid Infrastructure stack*

■ **Note** In the following sections only the primary components are discussed. Discussions of all the components are beyond the scope of this book.

The Oracle Cluster Registry (OCR)

OCR is a cluster repository used to maintain application resources and their availability within the RAC environment. The repository is a file created on the shared-storage subsystem (illustrated in Figure 16-1) during Oracle GI installation.

OCR contains the high availability (HA) rules for the various resources managed by the clusterware. These rules are maintained and updated by one of several client applications: server control utility (srvctl), cluster-ready services utility (crsctl),[1] Oracle Enterprise Manager (OEM), ASM Configuration Assistant (asmca), Database Configuration Assistant (dbca), and the network configuration assistant (netca).

---

[1]Cluster-ready services utility provides several command-line functions such as register, unregister, start, stop, etc.

OCR also maintains application resources defined within the Oracle Clusterware; specifically, database, instances, services, and node applications[2] information. Oracle Clusterware reads the ocr.loc file (ocr.loc file is located in the /etc/oracle/ directory on Linux and Unix systems; on Windows systems the pointer is located in the registry) for the location of the OCR file and to determine what applications resources need to be started as well as the nodes on which to start them.

```
[root@ssky3l11p1 ~]# cat /etc/oracle/ocr.loc
ocrconfig_loc=+GRID_DATA
local_only=FALSE
```

Here is an extract from the OCR file.

```
[SYSTEM.crs.user_default_dir]
ORATEXT : /u01/app/12.1.0/grid/crs/public
SECURITY : {USER_PERMISSION : PROCR_ALL_ACCESS, GROUP_PERMISSION : PROCR_READ,
OTHER_PERMISSION : PROCR_READ, USER_NAME : root, GROUP_NAME : root}
[SYSTEM.ORA_CRS_HOME]
ORATEXT : /u01/app/12.1.0/grid
SECURITY : {USER_PERMISSION : PROCR_ALL_ACCESS, GROUP_PERMISSION : PROCR_READ,
OTHER_PERMISSION : PROCR_READ, USER_NAME : root, GROUP_NAME : root}
```

Oracle uses distributed shared-cache architecture during cluster management to optimize queries against the cluster registry. Each node maintains a copy of the OCR in memory. Oracle Clusterware uses a background process to access the OCR cache. Only one OCR process (designated as the master) in the cluster performs any disk read/write activity. Once the master OCR process reads any new information, it performs a refresh of the local OCR cache and the OCR cache on other nodes in the cluster. Since the OCR cache is distributed across all nodes in the cluster, OCR clients communicate directly with the local OCR process on the node to obtain required information. While reading from the registry is coordinated through the master process across the cluster, any write (update) to disk or registry activity is not centralized—it is performed by the local OCR process, where the client is attached.

The Oracle Local Registry (OLR)

In Oracle Database 11g Release 2, Oracle introduced a different kind of registry called the OLR. OLR files contain information pertaining to all tiers of the clustered database for a specific node. OLR resides on every node (Figure 16-1) in the cluster and manages clusterware configuration information for each particular node. A dissection of the OLR file would reveal various parameters stored as name-value pairs, which are used and maintained at different levels of the architecture.

While the OLR contains a subset of the information contained in the OCR, the OLR file is maintained on the local storage under the GRID_HOME. Oracle Clusterware reads the olr.loc file (olr.loc file is located in the /etc/oracle/ directory on Linux and Unix systems; on Windows systems the pointer is located in the registry) for the location of the local registry.

```
[root@ssky3l11p1 ~]# cat /etc/oracle/olr.loc
olrconfig_loc=/u01/app/12.1.0/grid/cdata/ssky3l11p1.olr
crs_home=/u01/app/12.1.0/grid

[root@ssky3l11p1 ~]# ls -ltr  $GRID_HOME/cdata/ssky3l11p1.olr
-rw------- 1 root oinstall 503484416 Jan 14 20:31 /u01/app/12.1.0/grid/cdata/ssky3l11p1.olr
```

---

[2]The various processes such as the VIP, ONS, GSD, and listener are called *node applications*.

Here is an extract from the OLR file. Compare this data with the data illustrated earlier from the OCR file.

```
[SYSTEM.crs.user_default_dir]
ORATEXT : /u01/app/12.1.0/grid/ohasd/public
SECURITY : {USER_PERMISSION : PROCR_ALL_ACCESS, GROUP_PERMISSION : PROCR_READ,
OTHER_PERMISSION : PROCR_READ, USER_NAME : root, GROUP_NAME : root}
[SYSTEM.ORA_CRS_HOME]
ORATEXT : /u01/app/12.1.0/grid
SECURITY : {USER_PERMISSION : PROCR_ALL_ACCESS, GROUP_PERMISSION : PROCR_READ,
OTHER_PERMISSION : PROCR_READ, USER_NAME : root, GROUP_NAME : root}
```

Each tier is managed and administrated by Oracle's high availability services daemon (OHASD) processes, which use appropriate privileges to manage them. For example, all SYSTEM-level resources or application definitions would require "root," or super user, privileges to start, stop, and execute resources defined at this level. However, those defined at the DATABASE level will require "DBA" privileges to execute.

Apart from the difference mentioned previously, the following are some of the other differences:

1. OLR is configured on local storage and only contains the resource-related information pertaining to the local server or node in the cluster.

2. Unlike the OCR, the clusterware does not automatically back up the OLR. It's a good practice to add the OLR file from all nodes into the backup strategy.

3. Unlike OCR, OLR cannot be stored on ASM or on shared storage—it would defeat the purpose of having an OLR file. The OLR file is maintained locally on each node to help the clusteware start some of the critical resources while it waits for the ASM disks to be mounted, and the OCR files are visible to the clusterware.

OLR plays an important role during the startup process of the cluster on each node. The following output illustrates the first few steps that take place when the OHASD process is started and reads the OLR file to get the node-level information.

```
Oracle Database 12c Clusterware Release 12.1.0.1.0 - Production Copyright 1996, 2013 Oracle.
All rights reserved.
2014-01-17 22:39:21.
689: [ default][1666246176] OHASD Daemon Starting. Command string :reboot
689: [ default][1666246176] OHASD params []
753: [ default][1666246176]
753: [ default][1666246176] Initializing OLR
753: [ default][1666246176]proa_init: OLR Abstraction layer initialization. Bootlevel:[1]
876: [  OCRAPI][1666246176]a_init: Successfully initialized the patch management context.
876: [  OCRAPI][1666246176]a_init: Successfully initialized the OLR specific states.
876: [  OCRAPI][1666246176]a_init:13: Clusterware init successful
876: [  OCRAPI][1666246176]a_init:15: Successfully initialized the Cache layer.
876: [  OCRRAW][1666246176]proprioo: opening OCR device(s)
876: [  OCRRAW][1666246176]proprioo: Successfully opened the non-ASM locations if configured.
876: [  OCRRAW][1666246176]proprioo: for disk 0 (/u01/app/12.1.0/grid/cdata/ssky3l11p1.olr), id match (1),
total id sets, (1) need recover (0), my votes (0), total votes (0), commit_lsn (30), lsn (30)
877: [  OCRRAW][1666246176]proprioo: my id set: (745565135, 1028247821, 0, 0, 0)
877: [  OCRRAW][1666246176]proprioo: 1st set: (745565135, 1028247821, 0, 0, 0)
877: [  OCRRAW][1666246176]proprioo: 2nd set: (0, 0, 0, 0, 0)
877: [  OCRRAW][1666246176]proprinit: Successfully initialized the I/O module (proprioini).
```

```
877: [ OCRRAW][1666246176]proprinit: Successfully initialized the backend handle (propribctx).
877: [ OCRAPI][1666246176]proa_init: Successfully initialized the Storage Layer.
879: [ OCRAPI][1666246176]proa_init: Successfully initlaized the Messaging Layer.

979: [ OCRAPI][1666246176]a_init:18: Thread init successful
979: [ OCRAPI][1666246176]a_init:19: Client init successful
2014-01-17 22:39:22.
024: [  OCRAPI][1666246176]a_init:21: OLR init successful. Init Level [1]
```

What if the OLR file is missing or has been accidently removed from its current location listed in the /etc/oracle/olr.loc file? The following workshop discusses this scenario and what's required to get the node functional again.

Workshop

A missing or corrupted OLR file only affects the node of the cluster from which it is missing or on which it is corrupted. Other nodes remain functional. As discussed earlier, OLR is used by the OHASD to read the resources that are to be started on each specific node during clusterware and node startup. This means the file is only required once during node reboot and clusterware startup. This file is not later read—even for stopping and starting the clusterware stack using the crsctl utility (crsctl stop cluster -all) provided the OHASD demaon is still up and running. However if the OHASD crashes or is stopped for some reason, the clusterware would not start without the OLR file being present.

Step 1

The systems administrator had shut down the clusterware stack to complete a regular maintenance using

```
crsctl stop cluster -all
```

After maintenance was complete, the system administrator tried to restart the clusterware using the following crsctl command. However, the clusterware failed to start.

```
crsctl start cluster -all
```

The first step in Oracle Database 11g Release 2 and higher is to look for any entries in the clusterware alert log and OHASD log files. In prior releases the OCSSD log would report any startup issues.

Unfortunately, the OHASD log does not contain any information pertaining to the error. This may be because the OHASD has not started and the daemon is unable to write any information to the log files.

Step 2

An important prerequisite for the OHASD process to start is the availablility of the OLR file. The first step is to check whether the OLR file exists or not.

Using the definition contained in the olr.loc file, the current location of the OLR file can be determined. The olr.loc file is stored in /etc/oracle directory on the respective nodes of the cluster.

```
[root@ssky1l4p2 ]# cat /etc/oracle/olr.loc
olrconfig_loc=/u01/app/12.1.0.1/grid/cdata/ssky1l4p2.olr
crs_home=/u01/app/12.1.0.1/grid
```

Step 3

Since the olr.loc file still exists, the next step is to look for any entries in the client directory. Before the actual start of the OHASD process, the init.d tries to read the OLR file as a client process. During this step, it opens a log file in the $GRID_HOME/log/<node name>/client/ folder. Verifying the client log files indicates that the client process was unable to locate the OLR file.

```
[root@ssky1l4p2 client]# more crsctl_29422.log
Oracle Database 12c Clusterware Release 12.1.0.1.0 - Production Copyright 1996, 2013 Oracle.
All rights reserved.
2014-09-06 16:33:32.103: [    GIPC][2565203488] gipcCheckInitialization: possible incompatible
non-threaded init from [prom.c : 730], original from [clsCrsctlUtil.cpp : 2934]
2014-09-06 16:33:32.105: [  OCRMSG][2565203488]prom_waitconnect: CONN NOT ESTABLISHED (0,29,1,2)
2014-09-06 16:33:32.105: [  OCRMSG][2565203488]GIPC error [29] msg [gipcretConnectionRefused]
2014-09-06 16:33:32.105: [  OCRMSG][2565203488]prom_connect: error while waiting for connection
complete [24]
2014-09-06 16:33:32.105: [  OCROSD][2565203488]utopen:6m': failed in stat OCR file/disk
/u01/app/12.1.0.1/grid/cdata/ssky1l4p2.olr, errno=2, os err string=No such file or directory
2014-09-06 16:33:32.105: [  OCROSD][2565203488]utopen:7: failed to open any OCR file/disk,
errno=2, os err string=No such file or directory
2014-09-06 16:33:32.105: [  OCRRAW][2565203488]proprinit: Could not open raw device
2014-09-06 16:33:32.105: [ default][2565203488]a_init:7!: Backend init unsuccessful : [26]
[root@ssky1l4p2 client]#
```

Step 4

As seen in Step 3, it's clear that the clusterware stack on the ssky1l4p2 node would not start because of an issue with the OLR file.

Based on the information obtained from Step 2, verify whether the OLR file exists in the specified location. From the following command, it's determined that the OLR file is missing from the location.

```
[root@ssky1l4p2 client]# ls -ltr /u01/app/12.1.0.1/grid/cdata/ssky1l4p2.olr

ls: /u01/app/12.1.0.1/grid/cdata/ssky1l4p2.olr: No such file or directory
```

Step 5

Based on the information collected thus far, it's understood that the clusterware would not start because of the missing OLR file. At this stage, ideally, it would be good if a backup of the OLR file were available. The backups are verified using the following command:

```
ocrconfig -local -showbackup
```

No backups of the OLR file are found. Unlike the OCR file, the clusterware does not back up the OLR file on a regular basis. In this situation, the only backup of the OLR file available was from the time of the installation; which is outdated and does not contain the updates to the clusterware performed on the node.

■ **Note**   It's critical to include the backup of the OLR file from each node in the cluster in the backup strategy.

Step 6

Since no backups are available, the OLR file could be recovered by recreating the file. The first step is to perform a clean-up operation to remove any references to the clusterware files on the node. Then the root.sh script that was executed during GI installation could be rerun.

1. Execute the rootcrs.pl script located in the $GRID_HOME/crs/install/ directory to clear the current definitons.

```
[root@ssky1l4p2 oracle]# $GRID_HOME/crs/install/rootcrs.pl -deconfig -force
Using configuration parameter file: /u01/app/12.1.0.1/grid/crs/install/crsconfig_params
PRCR-1119 : Failed to look up CRS resources of ora.cluster_vip_net1.type type
PRCR-1068 : Failed to query resources
Cannot communicate with crsd
PRCR-1070 : Failed to check if resource ora.helper is registered
Cannot communicate with crsd
PRCR-1070 : Failed to check if resource ora.ons is registered
Cannot communicate with crsd
error: package cvuqdisk is not installed
2014/09/06 16:40:06 CLSRSC-336: Successfully deconfigured Oracle clusterware stack on this node
```

2. Step 6, sequence 1 cleared all existing pointer information, to the olr.loc file as well as the ocr.loc file and remove entries from the system startup files.

```
[root@ssky1l4p2 oracle]# cat /etc/oracle/ocr.loc
cat: /etc/oracle/ocr.loc: No such file or directory
[root@ssky1l4p2 oracle]#
[root@ssky1l4p2 oracle]# cat /etc/oracle/ocr.loc
cat: /etc/oracle/ocr.loc: No such file or directory
[root@ssky1l4p2 oracle]#
```

3. Now run the root.sh file from the $GRID_HOME/ directory.

```
[root@ssky1l4p2 oracle]# $GRID_HOME/root.sh
```

This will reconfigure the pointers, recreate the OLR file, and automatically start the clusterware stack.

```
...........................
...........................
...........................
```

```
Now product-specific root actions will be performed.
Using configuration parameter file: /u01/app/12.1.0.1/grid/crs/install/crsconfig_params

2014/09/06 16:41:03 CLSRSC-363: User ignored prerequisites during installation
OLR initialization - successful
2014/09/06 16:41:29 CLSRSC-330: Adding Clusterware entries to file '/etc/inittab'
```

4. The file pointers created from executing root.sh could be verified under /etc/oracle.

```
[root@ssky1l4p2 oracle]# cat /etc/oracle/olr.loc
olrconfig_loc=/u01/app/12.1.0.1/grid/cdata/ssky1l4p2.olr
crs_home=/u01/app/12.1.0.1/grid
```

5. Verify whether the OLR file listed in the olr.loc file in Step 6 sequence 4 is present.

```
 [root@ssky1l4p2 oracle]# ls -ltr /u01/app/12.1.0.1/grid/cdata/ssky1l4p2.olr
-rw------- 1 root root 503484416 Sep  6 16:41/u01/app/12.1.0.1/grid/cdata/ssky1l4p2.olr
[root@ssky1l4p2 oracle]#
```

This completes the recovery of the OLR file—the entire clusterware stack is operational and the instances will start up automatically once the clusterware components have been started.

■ **Note** There is another scenario in which a missing or corrupted OLR could be determined based on an ohasd.log file. When the clusterware does not start on system reboot or when the OHASD demaon is shut down as part of the process. The ohasd.log file contains the information seen in the following. The process required to restore the OCR file is the same as discussed in the earlier workshop.

```
2014-09-06 12:00:04.443: [ default][2829522464] OHASD Daemon Starting. Command string :restart
2014-09-06 12:00:04.443: [ default][2829522464] OHASD params []
2014-09-06 12:00:04.462: [ default][2829522464] Initializing OLR
2014-09-06 12:00:04.463: [ default][2829522464]proa_init: OLR Abstraction layer initialization.
Bootlevel:[1]
2014-09-06 12:00:04.542: [  OCRAPI][2829522464]a_init: Successfully initialized the patch management
context.
2014-09-06 12:00:04.542: [  OCRAPI][2829522464]a_init: Successfully initialized the OLR specific
states.
2014-09-06 12:00:04.542: [  OCRAPI][2829522464]a_init:13: Clusterware init successful
2014-09-06 12:00:04.542: [  OCRAPI][2829522464]a_init:15: Successfully initialized the Cache layer.
2014-09-06 12:00:04.542: [  OCRRAW][2829522464]proprioo: opening OCR device(s)
2014-09-06 12:00:04.542: [  OCROSD][2829522464]utopen:6m': failed in stat OCR file/disk
/u01/app/12.1.0.1/grid/cdata/ssky1l4p2.olr, errno=2, os err string=No such file or directory
2014-09-06 12:00:04.542: [  OCROSD][2829522464]utopen:7: failed to open any OCR file/disk, errno=2,
os err string=No such file or directory
2014-09-06 12:00:04.543: [  OCRRAW][2829522464]proprinit: Could not open raw device
2014-09-06 12:00:04.543: [  OCRAPI][2829522464]a_init:16!: Backend init unsuccessful : [26]
2014-09-06 12:00:04.543: [  CRSOCR][2829522464] OCR context init failure. Error: PROCL-26: Error
while accessing the physical storage Operating System error [No such file or directory] [2]
2014-09-06 12:00:04.544: [ default][2829522464] Created alert : (:OHAS00106:) :  OLR initialization
failed, error: PROCL-26: Error while accessing the physical storage Operating System error
[No such file or directory] [2]
2014-09-06 12:00:04.544: [ default][2829522464][PANIC] OHASD exiting; Could not init OLR
2014-09-06 12:00:04.544: [ default][2829522464] Done.
```

High Availability Service (HAS)

Pre–Oracle 11g, the RAC clusterware stack consisted primarily of three daemon processes: the cluster synchronization services (CSS), cluster ready services (CRS), and the event manager (EVM). Starting with Oracle Clusterware 11g Release 2, the stack has been streamlined to two primary stacks: the upper stack, called the Cluster Ready Services Daemon (CRSD), and the lower-level stack, called the Oracle High Availability Services Daemon (OHASD).

As illustrated in Figure 16-2, OHASD is the primary cluster boot process when a server that contains Oracle clusterware is started; it gets the cluster stack components started. While there are no real built-in levels within the clusterware stack, for easy understanding the entire startup process is grouped into four levels in Figure 16-2. Level 0 contains the clusterware boot process handled by OHASD.

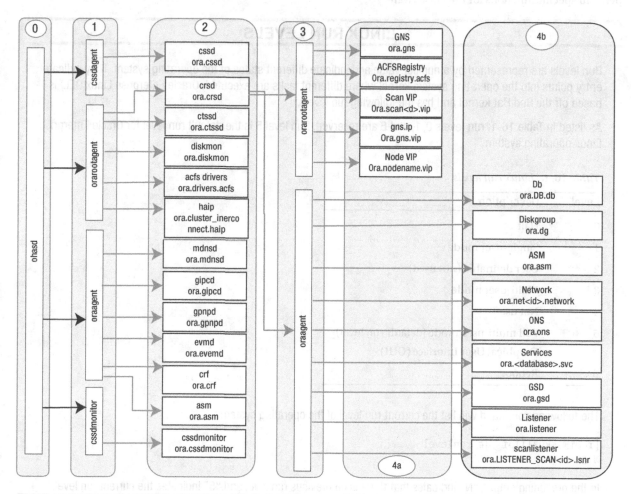

Figure 16-2. *Clusterware boot-up process flow* [3]

---

[3]Sandesh Rao and Bob Caldwell, "Troubleshooting and Diagnosing RAC and GI," www.oracleracsig.org.

The entry point for the OHASD is when the node is started or restarted through /etc/initab. This executes the /etc/init.d/ohasd and /etc/init.d/init.ohasd control scripts. This Linux script is a run-level (RC) script and contains controls to start, stop, enable, and disable actions. The control script in turn spawns the ohasd.bin executable.

Figure 16-2 illustrates several daemons involved in a clusterware startup. The figure illustrates how each daemon is responsible for the startup and administration of the other lower-level daemon processes. Some of these daemons are assocated with agents.

Agents are a new concept introduced in Oracle Clusterware 11g Release 2. These agents are multi-threaded, meaning they are responsible for the startup of multiple resource types, which in turn spawn processes to perform functions as required. Figure 16-2 illustrates two main agents, the oraagent and the orarootagent.

Figure 16-2 and Table 16-2 show the association of OHASD with various agent processes and other resources that perform specific functions for the clusterware.

LINUX RUN LEVELS

Run levels are represented by a number value and indicate different states of the operating system. They indicate entry points into the operating system kernel where different tasks are executed. Oracle Enterprise Linux(OEL) is based off the Red Hat kernel and has the following run levels.

As listed in Table 16-1, run levels 0, 1, and 6 are reserved. Run level 5 is the default run level for Oracle Enterprise Linux operating system.

Table 16-1. *Linux run levels*

Level	Description
0	Halt
1	Single-user mode
2	User definable (not used)
3	Multi-user mode
4	Not used
5	Full multi-user mode (default run level)
	Graphical User Interface (GUI)
6	Reboot

The following command will list the current run level of the operating system.

```
[root@ssky3l11p1 ~]# runlevel
N 5
```

In the preceding output, "N" indicates that there is no previous run level and "5" indicates the current run level.

Table 16-2. *Association between daemons and agents[4]*

Resource Name	Agent Name	Owner
ora.gipcd	oraagent	crs user
ora.gpnp	oraagent	crs user
ora.mdnsd	oraagent	crs user
ora.cssd	cssdagent	root
ora.cssdmonitor	cssdmonitor	root
ora.diskmon	orarootagent	root
ora.evmd	oraagent	crs user
ora.crsd	orarootagent	root
ora.asm	oraagent	crs user
ora.driver.acfs	orarootagent	root
ora.crf	orarootagent	root

A list of daemon resources can be listed using the following command:

```
[root@ssky3l11p1 ~]# /u01/app/12.1.0/grid/bin/crsctl stat res -init -t
--------------------------------------------------------------------------------
Name           Target  State       Server           State Details
--------------------------------------------------------------------------------
Cluster Resources
--------------------------------------------------------------------------------
ora.asm
      1        ONLINE  ONLINE      ssky3l11p1       Started,STABLE
ora.cluster_interconnect.haip
      1        ONLINE  ONLINE      ssky3l11p1       STABLE
ora.crf
      1        ONLINE  ONLINE      ssky3l11p1       STABLE
ora.crsd
      1        ONLINE  ONLINE      ssky3l11p1       STABLE
ora.cssd
      1        ONLINE  ONLINE      ssky3l11p1       STABLE
ora.cssdmonitor
      1        ONLINE  ONLINE      ssky3l11p1       STABLE
ora.ctssd
      1        ONLINE  ONLINE      ssky3l11p1       OBSERVER,STABLE
ora.diskmon
      1        OFFLINE OFFLINE                      STABLE
ora.drivers.acfs
      1        ONLINE  ONLINE      ssky3l11p1       STABLE
```

---

[4]Sandesh Rao and Bob Caldwell, "Troubleshooting and Diagnosing RAC and GI," www.oracleracsig.org.

```
ora.evmd
      1            ONLINE  ONLINE       ssky3l11p1                STABLE
ora.gipcd
      1            ONLINE  ONLINE       ssky3l11p1                STABLE
ora.gpnpd
      1            ONLINE  ONLINE       ssky3l11p1                STABLE
ora.mdnsd
      1            ONLINE  ONLINE       ssky3l11p1                STABLE
ora.storage
      1            ONLINE  ONLINE       ssky3l11p1                STABLE
--------------------------------------------------------------------------
```

The Cluster Synchronization Service (CSS)

CSS is a subcomponent of Oracle Clusterware. It maintains membership in the cluster through a special file called a voting disk (also referred to as a quorum disk), which is also on a shared-storage subsystem visible to all nodes participating in the cluster.

```
[oracle@ssky3l11p1 ~]$ $GRID_HOME/bin/crsctl query css votedisk
##  STATE    File Universal Id               File Name Disk group
--  -----    -----------------               --------- ----------
1. ONLINE   8ee93e68dfdb4fdfbf20036e0e42af51 (ORCL:AVOL1) [GRID_DATA]
2. ONLINE   82506bd06acf4f3bbfcb7dc6a89e256e (ORCL:AVOL2) [GRID_DATA]
3. ONLINE   b43b8039540f4f03bfee5a99b06bd918 (ORCL:AVOL3) [GRID_DATA]
Located 3 voting disk(s).
```

Oracle Clusterware Stack

At the cluster level, the main processes of Oracle Clusterware provide a standard cluster interface on all platforms and perform high availability operations on each node in the cluster. Figure 16-1 illustrates the various processes that compose the Oracle GI stack.

Initiated by the CSS process after nodes start up, the Oracle Cluster Synchronization Service Daemon, or CSSD, is a process that performs basic synchronization services between the various resources in the cluster. With the help of the voting disk, it arbitrates ownership of the cluster among cluster nodes in the event of a complete private network failure. CSSD is a critical daemon process and a failure of this process causes the node (server) to reboot.

cssdagent (Figure 16-1, section 1) is a new agent process introduced in Oracle Clusterware 11g Release 2 to start the CSSD process and tracks its activities by logging into the agent directory within the $GRID_HOME/log/ <node name>/agent/ directories.

cssdmonitor (Figure 16-1, section 1) is responsible for monitoring the health of the CSSD and replaces the OPROCD process that existed in the earlier versions of RAC.

Both cssdagent and cssdmonitor track the state information from the CSSD. These CSS services are performed by the node membership (NM) service and the group membership (GM) services.

The NM checks the heartbeat across the various nodes in the cluster every second across the private network (network heartbeat, or NHB). It also alternates to check the disk heartbeat (DHB) by performing a read/write operation every second to the voting file. If the heartbeat/node members do not respond within 30 seconds, as defined by the miscount parameter, the node (among the surviving nodes) that was started first (a.k.a., the master) will start evicting the other node(s) in the cluster.

```
2014-01-15 00:21:18.
453: [ CSSD][1109969216]clssnmvDiskVerify: Successful discovery for disk
/dev/oracleasm/disks/SAVOL1, UID 8cccacc5-d4eb4ff7-bf541125-3ef008ae, Pending CIN 0:1389748088:0,
Committed CIN 0:1389748088:0
453: [ CSSD][1109969216]clssnmvDiskVerify: Pending CIN of the potential voting file for CIN
0:1389748088:0
465: [ CSSD][1109969216]  misscount        30     reboot latency      3
465: [ CSSD][1109969216]  long I/O timeout 200    short I/O timeout  27
465: [ CSSD][1109969216]  rim hub timeout  30     grace period        0
465: [ CSSD][1109969216]  hub size         32  active version 12.1.0.1.0
465: [ CSSD][1109969216]  Listing unique IDs for 1 voting files:
465: [ CSSD][1109969216]      voting file 1: 8cccacc5-d4eb4ff7-bf541125-3ef008ae
465: [ CSSD][1109969216]clssnmvDiskVerify: Committed CIN of the potential voting file for CIN
0:1389748088:0
465: [ CSSD][1109969216]  misscount        30     reboot latency      3
465: [ CSSD][1109969216]  long I/O timeout 200    short I/O timeout  27
465: [ CSSD][1109969216]  rim hub timeout  30     grace period        0
465: [ CSSD][1109969216]  hub size         32  active version 12.1.0.1.0
465: [ CSSD][1109969216]  Listing unique IDs for 1 voting files:
465: [ CSSD][1109969216]      voting file 1: 8cccacc5-d4eb4ff7-bf541125-3ef008ae
465: [ CSSD][1109969216]clssnmvCloseDiskHandle: Closing handle (0x25068b0)
465: [ SKGFD][1109969216]Lib :UFS:: closing handle 0x2506c50 for disk :/dev/oracleasm/disks/SAVOL1:
465: [ CSSD][1109969216]clssnmvDiskVerify: Successful discovery of 1 disks
466: [ CSSD][1109969216]clssnmvDiskVerify: exit
```

Important parameters are highlighted in the preceding output. Misscount refers to the number of times the NHB could be missed before the clusterware decides to evict the member from the cluster. If the heartbeat is restored before the 30-count value is reached, the member continues to be part of the cluster.

Similar to the misscount value used by the NHB mechanism, the DHB mechanism uses the long I/O timeout to determine the health of the storage subsystem. If the I/O cannot complete in 200 seconds to a specific voting file, the voting file is considered to be unhealthy and is taken offline. The voting disk is referenced by the clusterware with a unique ID. This ID could also be obtained by querying the vote disk using the crsctl command-line utility.

By increasing the logging level of the CSSD daemon process, the details of the NHB activity can be tracked. For example, as seen in the following, the first failure to connect to remote node two happened at 22:44:05.427. The biggest misstime recorded in the cssd.log file was 1980 milliseconds (1.98 seconds). The NHB continues between the nodes every second, and at 22:44:33.659 the biggest misstime was 29990 millseconds (29.99 seconds). If the NHB receives a successful HB back from node 2 at this time, the node would be back in business. Unfortunately, in this specific example the node is evicted from the cluster.

```
2014-01-15 22:44:05.
427: [ CSSD][1090533696]clssgmConnectToNode: Failed to connect to remote node(2)
427: [ CSSD][1090533696]clssgmPeerListener: connected to 1 of 2
635: [ CSSD][1115601216]clssnmWaitThread: thrd(1), timeout(1000), elapsed 1000
635: [ CSSD][1115601216]clssscAllocAsyncMsg: msg(0x7f142c0aceb8), len(124), asqhd(0x7f142c0ace90),
flags(0x083)
635: [ CSSD][1115601216]clssnmsendmsg: sending msg type 3 size 124 to node 2 endp 0x7f140007525e
635: [ CSSD][1115601216]clssnmSendGIPC: cookie 0x7f1434027340 - endp 0x7525e type 3 size 124 dst 0
635: [ CSSD][1115601216]clssnmsendmsg: msg type 3 sent to node 2
635: [ CSSD][1115601216]clssnmHBInfo: css timestmp 1389843845 635 slgtime 8312654 DTO 27790
(index=0) biggest misstime 1980 NTO 26520
```

```
635: [ CSSD][1115601216]clssscAllocAsyncMsg: msg(0x7f142c099ac8), len(68), asqhd(0x7f142c099aa0),
flags(0x081)
635: [ CSSD][1115601216]clssscagSendMsg: min 0 max 2 flags 13 15
635: [ CSSD][1115601216]clssscagSendMsg: sending to endp 0x22

657: [ CSSD][1115601216]clssnmHBInfo: css timestmp 1389843870 657 slgtime 8337664 DTO 28260
(index=0) biggest misstime 26990 NTO 1510
658: [ CSSD][1115601216]clssnmHBInfo: css timestmp 1389843871 658 slgtime 8338664 DTO 28260
(index=0) biggest misstime 27990 NTO 510
658: [ CSSD][1115601216]clssnmHBInfo: css timestmp 1389843872 658 slgtime 8339664 DTO 28260
(index=0) biggest misstime 28990 NTO 0
659: [ CSSD][1115601216]clssnmHBInfo: css timestmp 1389843873 659 slgtime 8340664 DTO 28260
(index=0) biggest misstime 29990 NTO 0

661: [ CSSD][1117178176]clssscFreeAsyncMsg: freeing msg (0x7f14341ad758), asqhd (0x7f14341ad730),
sendct 0, flags 0x00000002
661: [ CSSD][1117178176]clssnmWaitForAcks: done, syncseq(285282724), msg type(11)
661: [ CSSD][1117178176]clssnmSetMinMaxVersion:node1  product/protocol (12.1/1.4)
661: [ CSSD][1117178176]clssnmSetMinMaxVersion: properties common to all nodes: 1,2,3,4,5,6,7,8,9,
10,11,12,13,14,15,16,17
661: [ CSSD][1117178176]clssnmSetMinMaxVersion: min product/protocol (12.1/1.4)
661: [ CSSD][1117178176]clssnmSetMinMaxVersion: max product/protocol (12.1/1.4)
661: [ CSSD][1117178176]clssnmNeedConfReq: No configuration to change
661: [ CSSD][1117178176]clssnmDoSyncUpdate: Terminating node 2, ssky3l12p2, misstime(30000) state(5)
661: [ CSSD][1117178176]clssnmDoSyncUpdate: Wait for 0 vote ack(s)
661: [ CSSD][1117178176]clssnmCheckDskInfo: Checking disk info...
```

NM also checks the voting disk to determine if there is a failure on any other nodes in the cluster. During this operation, NM will make an entry in the voting disk to inform its vote on availability. Similar operations are performed by other instances in the cluster. The three voting disks configured also provide a method to determine who in the cluster should survive. For example, if the eviction of one of the nodes is necessitated by an unresponsive action, then the node that has two voting disks will start evicting the other node. NM alternates its action between the heartbeat and the voting disk to determine the availability of other nodes in the cluster.

The GM provides group membership services. All clients that perform write I/O operations register with the GM; for example, the LMON, DBWR, etc. Reconfiguration of instances (when an instance joins or leaves the cluster) happens through the GM. When there are issues with the communication layer because of either NHB or DHB failure, which could require a node eviction, the GM services will fence off all I/O clients registered with it to avoid any I/O issues or in-transition activities. When a node fails, the GM sends out messages, through the EVM, to other instances regarding the status.

As illustrated in Figure 16-1, event manager daemon, or EVMD, is an event-forwarding daemon process that propagates events via the Oracle notification service (ONS). It also scans the node callout directory and invokes callouts in reaction to detected events; for example, node up and node down events. While this daemon is started subsequent to the OCSSD, EVMD is the communication bridge between the CRSD and OCSSD. All communications between the CRS and CSS happen via the EVMD.

The cluster ready service daemon (CRSD) function is to define and manage resources. A resource is a named entity whose availability is managed by the clusterware. Resources have profiles that define metadata about them. This metadata is stored in the OCR. CRS reads the OCR. The daemon itself manages the application resources: starts and stops, the failover of application resources, generation of events during cluster state changes, and maintenance configuration profiles in the OCR. If the daemon fails, it automatically restarts. The OCR information, described earlier in the section "The Oracle Cluster Registry (OCR)," is cached inside the CRS.

Resources that are managed by the CRS include global service daemon (GSD), Oracle notification services (ONS) daemon, virtual Internet Protocol (VIP), listeners, databases, instances, and services. Resources are grouped based on the level at which they apply to the environment. For example, some of these resources are referred to as node applications (nodeapps) and pertain to individual nodes in the cluster. Nodeapps are needed on a per-node basis independent of the number of databases on the node. GSD, ONS, VIPs, and listeners are nodeapps. Nodeapps are created and registered with the OCR during installation of the Oracle Clusterware. Listener, database, and service resources are formed during the database creation process.

Cluster/Node Failures/Evictions

Like any hardware and software component, clusters, nodes in the cluster, or clusterware components can fail due to various reasons. For example, when a specific node does not have sufficient resources (CPU starvation) for the clusterware components to complete its activity, it could be evicted from the cluster. There are several reasons for evictions and reboots to occur in an Oracle clusterware.

Node eviction due to missing NHB

When the CSS on one of the nodes sends a heartbeat message to another node indicating its health, a similar heartbeat is received back from the other node. If this does not happen in the set misscount interval, a potential node eviction is possible. The following output (formatted to fit the page) is extracted from the cssd.log file. The misscount entries in the log file are visible when the CSSD logging is set to level 3 and is searching for "PolllingThread" string.

```
cat ocssd.log | grep PollingThread.

2014-01-15 22:44:14.640: [    CSSD][1114024256]
clssnmPollingThread: node 2, ssky3l12p2, ninfmisstime 10980, misstime 10980, skgxnbit 4, vcwmisstime 0, syncstage 0
clssnmPollingThread: node 2, ssky3l12p2, ninfmisstime 11980, misstime 11980, skgxnbit 4, vcwmisstime 0, syncstage 0
clssnmPollingThread: node 2, ssky3l12p2, ninfmisstime 12980, misstime 12980, skgxnbit 4, vcwmisstime 0, syncstage 0
clssnmPollingThread: node 2, ssky3l12p2, ninfmisstime 13980, misstime 13980, skgxnbit 4, vcwmisstime 0, syncstage 0
clssnmPollingThread: node 2, ssky3l12p2, ninfmisstime 14980, misstime 14980, skgxnbit 4, vcwmisstime 0, syncstage 0
clssnmPollingThread: node ssky3l12p2 (2) at 50% heartbeat fatal, removal in 14.020 seconds
clssnmPollingThread: node 2, ssky3l12p2, ninfmisstime 15980, misstime 15980, skgxnbit 4, vcwmisstime 0, syncstage 0
clssnmPollingThread: node ssky3l12p2 (2) is impending reconfig, flag 2228224, misstime 15980
clssnmPollingThread: local diskTimeout set to 27000 ms, remote disk timeout set to 27000, impending reconfig status(1)
clssnmPollingThread: node 2, ssky3l12p2, ninfmisstime 16980, misstime 16980, skgxnbit 4, vcwmisstime 0, syncstage 0
clssnmPollingThread: node 2, ssky3l12p2, ninfmisstime 17980, misstime 17980, skgxnbit 4, vcwmisstime 0, syncstage 0
clssnmPollingThread: node 2, ssky3l12p2, ninfmisstime 18980, misstime 18980, skgxnbit 4, vcwmisstime 0, syncstage 0
clssnmPollingThread: node 2, ssky3l12p2, ninfmisstime 19980, misstime 19980, skgxnbit 4, vcwmisstime 0, syncstage 0
clssnmPollingThread: node 2, ssky3l12p2, ninfmisstime 20980, misstime 20980, skgxnbit 4, vcwmisstime 0, syncstage 0
clssnmPollingThread: node 2, ssky3l12p2, ninfmisstime 21980, misstime 21980, skgxnbit 4, vcwmisstime 0, syncstage 0
clssnmPollingThread: node ssky3l12p2 (2) at 75% heartbeat fatal, removal in 7.020 seconds
clssnmPollingThread: node 2, ssky3l12p2, ninfmisstime 22980, misstime 22980, skgxnbit 4, vcwmisstime 0, syncstage 0
clssnmPollingThread: node 2, ssky3l12p2, ninfmisstime 23980, misstime 23980, skgxnbit 4, vcwmisstime 0, syncstage 0
clssnmPollingThread: node 2, ssky3l12p2, ninfmisstime 24980, misstime 24980, skgxnbit 4, vcwmisstime 0, syncstage 0
clssnmPollingThread: node 2, ssky3l12p2, ninfmisstime 25980, misstime 25980, skgxnbit 4, vcwmisstime 0, syncstage 0
clssnmPollingThread: node 2, ssky3l12p2, ninfmisstime 26980, misstime 26980, skgxnbit 4, vcwmisstime 0, syncstage 0
clssnmPollingThread: node ssky3l12p2 (2) at 90% heartbeat fatal, removal in 2.010 seconds, seedhbimpd 1
clssnmPollingThread: node 2, ssky3l12p2, ninfmisstime 27990, misstime 27990, skgxnbit 4, vcwmisstime 0, syncstage 0
clssnmPollingThread: node 2, ssky3l12p2, ninfmisstime 28990, misstime 28990, skgxnbit 4, vcwmisstime 0, syncstage 0
clssnmPollingThread: node 2, ssky3l12p2, ninfmisstime 29990, misstime 29990, skgxnbit 4, vcwmisstime 0, syncstage 0
clssnmPollingThread: Removal started for node ssky3l12p2 (2), flags 0x220000, state 3, wt4c 0
2014-01-15 22:44:34.661: [    CSSD][1114024256]clssnmPollingThread: node(2) inactive
2014-01-15 22:44:35.661: [    CSSD][1114024256]clssnmPollingThread: node(2) inactive
2014-01-15 22:44:36.662: [    CSSD][1114024256]clssnmPollingThread: node(2) inactive
```

In the preceding output, (formatted to fit the page) the critical lines to be looked at are those with "fatal" in the message.

```
node ssky3l12p2 (2) at 50% heartbeat fatal, removal in 14.020 seconds
node ssky3l12p2 (2) is impending reconfig, flag 2228224, misstime 15980
local diskTimeout set to 27000 ms, remote disk timeout set to 27000, impending reconfig status(1)
node ssky3l12p2 (2) at 75% heartbeat fatal, removal in 7.020 seconds
node ssky3l12p2 (2) at 90% heartbeat fatal, removal in 2.010 seconds, seedhbimpd 1
Removal started for node ssky3l12p2 (2), flags 0x220000, state 3, wt4c 0
node(2) inactive
```

The NHB failure and corresponding node eviction is a countdown process—from 50% fatal to 90% fatal—before the node is finally removed from the cluster. If within this time, the NHB is restored, the node eviction is canceled and the cluster returns to normal function.

Node Eviction Due to Missing DHB

Normally, DHB is a continuation of the NHB error condition (split network) and is considered as a second check to verify the health of the node that is not responding. In this case, the timestamp of the NHB is compared to the recent DHB time to determine if the node is still alive, i.e., the short I/O timeout (SIOT). The following output (formatted to fit the page) is extracted from the cssd.log file. The entries in the log file are visible when the CSSD logging is set to level 3 and is searching for "CheckSplit" string.

cat ocssd.log | grep CheckSplit.

```
2014-01-15 22:34:08.960: [CSSD][1117178176]clssnmCheckDskInfo: Checking disk info...

clssnmCheckSplit: No wait for node 0, , defined 0, killnode 0, network state 0, disk state 0, disk status 0 shutdown 0, removal reconfig 1
clssnmCheckSplit: No wait for node 1, ssky3l11p1, defined 10, killnode 0, network state 2, disk state 3, disk status 3 shutdown 0, removal
reconfig 1
clssnmCheckSplit: Node 2, ssky3l12p2, dead, last DHB (1389843221, 3521704) after NHB (1389843221, 3522004), but within reboot time 3000
clssnmCheckSplit: No wait for node 3, , defined 0, killnode 0, network state 0, disk state 0, disk status 0 shutdown 0, removal reconfig 1
clssnmCheckSplit: No wait for node 4, , defined 0, killnode 0, network state 0, disk state 0, disk status 0 shutdown 0, removal reconfig 1
clssnmCheckSplit: No wait for node 5, , defined 0, killnode 0, network state 0, disk state 0, disk status 0 shutdown 0, removal reconfig 1
clssnmCheckSplit: No wait for node 6, , defined 0, killnode 0, network state 0, disk state 0, disk status 0 shutdown 0, removal reconfig 1
clssnmCheckSplit: No wait for node 7, , defined 0, killnode 0, network state 0, disk state 0, disk status 0 shutdown 0, removal reconfig 1
clssnmCheckSplit: No wait for node 8, , defined 0, killnode 0, network state 0, disk state 0, disk status 0 shutdown 0, removal reconfig 1
clssnmCheckSplit: No wait for node 9, , defined 0, killnode 0, network state 0, disk state 0, disk status 0 shutdown 0, removal reconfig 1
clssnmCheckSplit: No wait for node 10, , defined 0, killnode 0, network state 0, disk state 0, disk status 0 shutdown 0, removal reconfig 1
clssnmCheckSplit: No wait for node 11, , defined 0, killnode 0, network state 0, disk state 0, disk status 0 shutdown 0, removal reconfig 1
clssnmCheckSplit: No wait for node 12, , defined 0, killnode 0, network state 0, disk state 0, disk status 0 shutdown 0, removal reconfig 1
clssnmCheckSplit: No wait for node 13, , defined 0, killnode 0, network state 0, disk state 0, disk status 0 shutdown 0, removal reconfig 1
clssnmCheckSplit: No wait for node 14, , defined 0, killnode 0, network state 0, disk state 0, disk status 0 shutdown 0, removal reconfig 1
clssnmCheckSplit: No wait for node 15, , defined 0, killnode 0, network state 0, disk state 0, disk status 0 shutdown 0, removal reconfig 1
clssnmCheckSplit: No wait for node 16, , defined 0, killnode 0, network state 0, disk state 0, disk status 0 shutdown 0, removal reconfig 1
clssnmCheckSplit: No wait for node 17, , defined 0, killnode 0, network state 0, disk state 0, disk status 0 shutdown 0, removal reconfig 1
clssnmCheckSplit: No wait for node 18, , defined 0, killnode 0, network state 0, disk state 0, disk status 0 shutdown 0, removal reconfig 1
clssnmCheckSplit: No wait for node 19, , defined 0, killnode 0, network state 0, disk state 0, disk status 0 shutdown 0, removal reconfig 1
clssnmCheckSplit: No wait for node 20, , defined 0, killnode 0, network state 0, disk state 0, disk status 0 shutdown 0, removal reconfig 1
clssnmCheckSplit: No wait for node 21, , defined 0, killnode 0, network state 0, disk state 0, disk status 0 shutdown 0, removal reconfig 1
clssnmCheckSplit: No wait for node 22, , defined 0, killnode 0, network state 0, disk state 0, disk status 0 shutdown 0, removal reconfig 1
clssnmCheckSplit: No wait for node 23, , defined 0, killnode 0, network state 0, disk state 0, disk status 0 shutdown 0, removal reconfig 1
clssnmCheckSplit: No wait for node 24, , defined 0, killnode 0, network state 0, disk state 0, disk status 0 shutdown 0, removal reconfig 1
clssnmCheckSplit: No wait for node 25, , defined 0, killnode 0, network state 0, disk state 0, disk status 0 shutdown 0, removal reconfig 1
clssnmCheckSplit: No wait for node 26, , defined 0, killnode 0, network state 0, disk state 0, disk status 0 shutdown 0, removal reconfig 1
clssnmCheckSplit: No wait for node 27, , defined 0, killnode 0, network state 0, disk state 0, disk status 0 shutdown 0, removal reconfig 1
clssnmCheckSplit: No wait for node 28, , defined 0, killnode 0, network state 0, disk state 0, disk status 0 shutdown 0, removal reconfig 1
clssnmCheckSplit: No wait for node 29, , defined 0, killnode 0, network state 0, disk state 0, disk status 0 shutdown 0, removal reconfig 1
clssnmCheckSplit: No wait for node 30, , defined 0, killnode 0, network state 0, disk state 0, disk status 0 shutdown 0, removal reconfig 1
clssnmCheckSplit: No wait for node 31, , defined 0, killnode 0, network state 0, disk state 0, disk status 0 shutdown 0, removal reconfig 1
2014-01-15 22:34:08.961: [CSSD][1117178176]clssnmRemove: Start
clssnmrRemoveNode: Removing node 2, ssky3l12p2, from the cluster in incarnation 285282722, node birth incarnation 285282721, death
incarnation 285282722, stateflags 0x220000 uniqueness value 1389842617
```

The other situation is the split-brain scenario in which the voting disk does not respond to the timestamp write from a node. This happens when there are two or more nodes with no communication between them. In Figure 16-1, showing a four-node cluster, oradb1 and oradb2 can communicate with each other and oradb3 and oradb4 are able to communicate with each other. However, `oradb1` and `oradb2` are not able communicate with `oradb3` and `oradb4`. That is, one set of nodes in the cluster is unable to communicate with the other set of nodes in the cluster. The cluster creates a invisible grouping (cohorts) between nodes, which could potentially cause corruption and should be resolved.

Oracle Clusterware handles the split-brain scenario by terminating all the nodes in the *smaller* cohort. If both of the cohorts are the same size, the cohort with the lowest-numbered node in it survives. The clusterware identifies the *largest* cohort and aborts all the nodes that do *not* belong to that cohort. In a split-brain node eviction, the following message is present in the OCSSD log (`$GRID_HOME/log/ssky3l12p2/cssd/ocssd.log`) of the evicted node:

```
2014-01-15 22:34:08.960: [CSSD][1117178176] clssnmCheckDskInfo: Aborting local node to avoid splitbrain.
```

Node Reboots

Evictions are caused due to system faults, such as being unable to reach the participating node in the cluster, while reboots occur due to a lack of resources, for example, high CPU utilization. There are several reasons for a node reboot.

- Node reboot due to losing access to the majority of voting disks (loss of quorum). To create a quorum during conflict resolution, having an odd number of voting disks will help resolve decision-making scenarios by allowing the clusterwares to vote. It's for this reason that, as a best practice, voting disks should be configured in groups of 3 or 5, depending on the number of nodes participating in the cluster.

- Node reboots due to a node hang or perceived/false node hang. This situation can arise when networks or disk I/O channels are busy and the heartbeats are not able to complete in the required time. If this happens, the misscount and timeout numbers would be false information, thus causing the nodes to reboot. Busy interconnects or networks are caused by high-latency, low-bandwidth networks or because of inefficient SQL statements. SQL optimization, instance affinity, and service affinity could help reduce some of the busy interconnect/network traffic.

- Node reboots due to Global Cache/Enqueue Service Heartbeat Monitor, also called Lock Manager Heartbeat (LMHB) group member kill request. LMHB is an RAC database background process. Apart from forcing a node eviction during database hangs, the function of LMHB is to monitor the heartbeats of LMON, LMD, and LMSn processes. Like other background processes, the activities of LMHB are recorded in the trace directory of the RDBMS instance.

  The kill request from LMHB occurs when any critical background (LMON, LMD, LMSn) process is hung or stuck during operation. Searching the background process trace files for StatCheckCPU could capture this.

  ```
  cat SSKYDB_1_lmhb_7768.trc | grep StatCheckCPU

  kjgcr_StatCheckCPU: cpu based load is high, currently 56, average 18
  kjgcr_StatCheckCPU: cpu based load is high, currently 53, average 18
  kjgcr_StatCheckCPU: cpu based load is high, currently 48, average 18
  kjgcr_StatCheckCPU: cpu based load is high, currently 56, average 18
  kjgcr_StatCheckCPU: cpu based load is high, currently 51, average 18
  kjgcr_StatCheckCPU: cpu based load is high, currently 65, average 16
  kjgcr_StatCheckCPU: cpu based load is high, currently 65, average 16
  kjgcr_StatCheckCPU: runq based load is high, currently 212, average 44
  kjgcr_StatCheckCPU: runq based load is high, currently 276, average 44
  kjgcr_StatCheckCPU: runq based load is high, currently 253, average 44
  kjgcr_StatCheckCPU: runq based load is high, currently 232, average 44
  kjgcr_StatCheckCPU: runq based load is high, currently 317, average 44
  ```

LMHB sends a message to LMON to terminate the instances. When LMON is unable to complete the operation because the machine is busy, these processes get scheduled and the instances do not die. This delays the entire reconfiguration and causes the system to be in a hung state. To avoid this, LMHB escalates to a reboot scenario in CSSD in order to create a node eviction. The sequence of steps is

1.   LMHB tries to kill LMON, but does not succeed.

```
LMON (ospid: 7705) has not moved for 31 sec (1410129684.1410129653)
LMON (ospid: 7705) has not moved for 29 sec (1410129823.1410129794)
LMON (ospid: 7705) has not moved for 28 sec (1410129872.1410129844)
```

2.   LMHB escalates the request to CSSD to kill the node; however, the node kill request may not be successful because the system is overloaded.

3.   CSSD escalates the priority of the request to evict the machine from the cluster. If installed CSSD sends request to Intelligent Platform Management Interface (IPMI) to evict the machine from the cluster.

The next sections will discuss a few of the utilites available for troubleshooting the GI/clusterware environment is discussed.

Node Verification Using olsnodes

The olsnodes command provides the list of nodes and other information for all nodes participating in the cluster.

Additional cluster-related information could be obtained by adding one or more of the following parameters to the olsnodes command. To log cluster verification information with more details, options –g (log), -v (verbose), can be used:

```
[oracle@ssky3l11p1 ~]$ $GRID_HOME/bin/olsnodes -v -g
lang init : Initializing LXL global
main: Initializing CLSS context
memberlist: No of cluster members configured = 256
memberlist: Allocated mem for lease node vector.
memberlist: Leased NodeList entries used = 1.
memberlist: Getting information for nodenum = 1
memberlist: node_name = ssky3l11p1
memberlist: ctx->lsdata->node_num = 1
print data: Printing the node data
ssky3l11p1
main: olsnodes executed successfully
term: Terminating LSF
[oracle@ssky3l11p1 ~]$
```

It should be noted that the olsnodes utility could be executed with a combination of the preceding options. For example, for a summarized view of all the information, it could be executed as shown in the following:

```
[oracle@ssky3l11p1 ~]$ $GRID_HOME/bin/olsnodes -n -i -g -v
lang init : Initializing LXL global
main: Initializing CLSS context
memberlist: No of cluster members configured = 256
memberlist: Allocated mem for lease node vector.
```

```
memberlist: Leased NodeList entries used = 1.
memberlist: Getting information for nodenum = 1
memberlist: node_name = ssky3l11p1
memberlist: ctx->lsdata->node_num = 1
get node vip: Retrieving the virtual IP for node = ssky3l11p1
get node vip: prsr_vpip_key_len = 281
get node vip: Opening the OCR key DATABASE.NODEAPPS.ssky3l11p1.VIP
get node vip: OCR key value length = 27
get node vip: Virtual IP = ssky3l11p1-vip.localdomain
print data: Printing the node data
ssky3l11p1      1          ssky3l11p1-vip.localdomain
main: olsnodes executed successfully
term: Terminating LSF
[oracle@ssky3l11p1 ~]$
```

Cluster Services Control (crsctl) utility

Oracle provides a utility called crsctl for dynamic debugging, tracing, checking, and administration of various sub-components of the clusterware.

1.   Checking the health of the Oracle Clusterware daemon processes

```
[root@ssky3l11p1 ~]# /u01/app/12.1.0/grid/bin/crsctl check crs
CRS-4638: Oracle High Availability Services is online
CRS-4537: Cluster Ready Services is online
CRS-4529: Cluster Synchronization Services is online
CRS-4533: Event Manager is online
```

The preceding output shows the health of the three clusterware processes. The health of each individual process could also be checked using crsctl check css, evm.

2.   Querying and administering CSS voting disks

In a situation where less than three vote disks are available or when the vote disk location needs to be moved, the preceding command would be useful. It adds a new vote disk and then copies the contents from the existing vote disk at the specified location.

```
[oracle@ssky3l11p1 ~]$ $GRID_HOME/bin/crsctl query css votedisk
##  STATE   File Universal Id                File Name Disk group
--  -----   ----------------                --------- ---------
1. ONLINE  8ee93e68dfdb4fdfbf20036e0e42af51 (ORCL:AVOL1) [GRID_DATA]
2. ONLINE  82506bd06acf4f3bbfcb7dc6a89e256e (ORCL:AVOL2) [GRID_DATA]
3. ONLINE  b43b8039540f4f03bfee5a99b06bd918 (ORCL:AVOL3) [GRID_DATA]
Located 3 voting disk(s).
```

The preceding output lists all vote disks currently configured and in use by the CSS.

3.   Performing a dynamic state dump of the CRS

```
[root@ssky3l11p1 ~]# /u01/app/12.1.0/grid/bin/crsctl debug statedump crs
Dumping State for crs objects
```

State dynamic dump information is appended to the CRSD log file located in $GRID_HOME/log/ssky3l11p1/crsd directory:

```
2014-01-20 20:05:13.798: [    CRSD][1103345984] Dump State Starting ...
2014-01-20 20:05:13.850: [    CRSD][1103345984] State Dump for RTILock
2014-01-20 20:05:14.065: [   CRSPE][1103345984] Dumping PE Data Model...:DM has
[27 resources][44 types][3 servers][4 spools][2 categories]
------------- RESOURCES:
--------------------RESOURCE ora.ASMNET1LSNR_ASM.lsnr --------------
------------------- Attribs -------------------
CONFIG_VERSION=1
CHECK_INTERVAL=60
RESTART_ATTEMPTS=5
START_TIMEOUT=180
STOP_TIMEOUT=0
UPTIME_THRESHOLD=1d
AUTO_START=restore
DEGREE=1
ENABLED=1
LOAD=1
SCRIPT_TIMEOUT=60
AGENT_FILENAME=%CRS_HOME%/bin/oraagent%CRS_EXE_SUFFIX%
ACTION_SCRIPT=%CRS_HOME%/bin/racgwrap%CRS_SCRIPT_SUFFIX%
OFFLINE_CHECK_INTERVAL=0
DELETE_TIMEOUT=60
MODIFY_TIMEOUT=60
CHECK_TIMEOUT=120
CLEAN_TIMEOUT=60
ACTION_TIMEOUT=60
INSTANCE_FAILOVER=1
INTERMEDIATE_TIMEOUT=0
STATE=8
TARGET=8
LAST_SERVER=
RESTART_COUNT=0
LAST_RESTART=0
FAILURE_COUNT=0
FAILURE_HISTORY=
STATE_DETAILS=
INCARNATION=0
STATE_CHANGE_VERS=0
LAST_FAULT=0
LAST_STATE_CHANGE=0
INTERNAL_STATE=15
TARGET_SERVER=
NAME=ora.ASMNET1LSNR_ASM.lsnr
TYPE=ora.asm_listener.type
DESCRIPTION=Oracle ASM Listener
2014-01-20 20:05:14.065: [   CRSPE][1103345984] resource
START_DEPENDENCIES=weak(global:ora.gns)
```

```
STOP_DEPENDENCIES=
ACL=owner:oracle:rwx,pgrp:oinstall:rwx,other::r--
CREATION_SEED=9
STATE_CHANGE_TEMPLATE=
PROFILE_CHANGE_TEMPLATE=
ACTION_FAILURE_TEMPLATE=
NOT_RESTARTING_TEMPLATE=
DEFAULT_TEMPLATE=PROPERTY(RESOURCE_CLASS=listener) PROPERTY(LISTENER_NAME=PARSE(%NAME%, ., 2))
LOGGING_LEVEL=1
SERVER_CATEGORY=ora.hub.category
USER_WORKLOAD=no
STOP_CONCURRENCY=0
START_CONCURRENCY=0
ACTIONS=
ALERT_TEMPLATE=
INSTANCE_COUNT=3
ALIAS_NAME=
DEGREE_ID=0
ID=ora.ASMNET1LSNR_ASM.lsnr
TYPE_ACL=owner:root:rwx,pgrp:root:r-x,other::r--
TYPE_NAME=ora.asm_listener.type
BASE_TYPE=ora.listener.type
NLS_LANG=
TYPE_VERSION=1.1
USR_ORA_ENV=
VERSION=12.1.0.1.0
ENDPOINTS=TCP:1521
ORACLE_HOME=%CRS_HOME%
PORT=1521
USR_ORA_OPI=false
SUBNET=10.1.4.0
-------------------- PER-SERVER values -------------------
TARGET@ssky3l11p1 =7
LAST_SERVER@ssky3l11p1 =ssky3l11p1
TARGET_SERVER@ssky3l11p1 =
DEGREE_ID@ssky3l11p1 =1
ID@ssky3l11p1
2014-01-20 20:05:14.065: [   CRSPE][1103345984] =ora.ASMNET1LSNR_ASM.lsnr ssky3l11p1 1
TARGET@ssky3l12p2 =7
LAST_SERVER@ssky3l12p2 =ssky3l12p2
TARGET_SERVER@ssky3l12p2 =ssky3l12p2
DEGREE_ID@ssky3l12p2 =1
ID@ssky3l12p2 =ora.ASMNET1LSNR_ASM.lsnr ssky3l12p2 1
TARGET@ssky3l13p3 =7
LAST_SERVER@ssky3l13p3 =ssky3l13p3
TARGET_SERVER@ssky3l13p3 =
DEGREE_ID@ssky3l13p3 =1
ID@ssky3l13p3 =ora.ASMNET1LSNR_ASM.lsnr ssky3l13p3 1
Starting RIs : 0, stopping RIs : 0, waiting to start: 0, waiting to stop: 0
------------------------Per-server Joints:-------------------
```

```
<---------BEGIN OF JOINT for ssky3l11p1------->
Degree Joint [Resource=ora.ASMNET1LSNR_ASM.lsnr Cardinality=0]   Instances:
Resource Instance ID[ora.ASMNET1LSNR_ASM.lsnr ssky3l11p1 1]. Values:
STATE=ONLINE
TARGET=ONLINE
LAST_SERVER=ssky3l11p1
RESTART_COUNT=0
LAST_RESTART=1390231672
FAILURE_COUNT=0
FAILURE_HISTORY=
STATE_DETAILS=
INCARNATION=1
STATE_CHANGE_VERS=1
LAST_FAULT=0
LAST_STATE_CHANGE=1390231672
INTERNAL_STATE=15
TARGET_SERVER=ssky3l11p1
DEGREE_ID=1
ID=ora.ASMNET1LSNR_ASM.lsn
2014-01-20 20:05:14.065: [    CRSPE][1103345984]r ssky3l11p1 1
Lock Info:
Write Locks:none
ReadLocks:|STATE INITED||INITIAL CHECK DONE|
<----------END OF JOINT ---------->

<---------BEGIN OF JOINT for ssky3l12p2------->
Degree Joint [Resource=ora.ASMNET1LSNR_ASM.lsnr Cardinality=0]   Instances:
Resource Instance ID[ora.ASMNET1LSNR_ASM.lsnr ssky3l12p2 1]. Values:
STATE=ONLINE
TARGET=ONLINE
...........
...........

ID=ora.ASMNET1LSNR_ASM.lsnr ssky3l12p2 1
Lock Info:
Write Locks:none
ReadLocks:|STATE INITED||INITIAL CHECK DONE|
<----------END OF JOINT ---------->

<---------BEGIN OF JOINT for ssky3l13p3------->
Degree Joint [Resource=ora.ASMNET1LSNR_ASM.lsnr Cardinality=0]   Instances:
Resource Instance ID[ora.ASMNET1LSNR_ASM.lsnr ssky3l13p3 1]. Values:
2014-01-20 20:05:14.065: [    CRSPE][1103345984]
STATE=ONLINE
TARGET=ONLINE
...........
...........
ID=ora.ASMNET1LSNR_ASM.lsnr ssky3l13p3 1
```

```
Lock Info:
Write Locks:none
ReadLocks:|STATE INITED||INITIAL CHECK DONE|
<----------END OF JOINT ---------->

<------Aliases: ------->
---------------------------------------------------------
```

The preceding output is the state dump of the CRS activity, listing all the current resident resources and their current thread IDs. The descriptions of the parameters are self-explanatory. For example:

RESTART_ATTEMPT – Number of times Oracle Clusterware attempts a restart a resource on a node before attempting to relocate the resource to another node (if specified)

SCRIPT_TIMEOUT – Seconds (default 60) to wait for a return from the action script

CHECK_INTERVAL – The time (in seconds) between repeated executions of a resource's action program

UPTIME_THRESHOLD – The time (in seconds) that the resource should be functional before the clusterware considers it as a stable resource.

4. Verifying the Oracle Clusterware version

```
[root@ssky3l11p1 ~]# /u01/app/12.1.0/grid/bin/crsctl query crs softwareversion
Oracle Clusterware version on node [ssky3l11p1] is [12.1.0.1.0]
```

The preceding output shows the current version of Oracle Clusterware installed and available on the cluster.

5. Verifying the current version of Oracle Clusterware being used

```
[root@ssky3l11p1 ~]# /u01/app/12.1.0/grid/bin/crsctl query crs activeversion
Oracle Clusterware active version on the cluster is [12.1.0.1.0]
```

6. Debugging. Oracle Clusterware has several modular sub-components that perform specific actions on behalf of the cluster services. To debug the activities performed by these modules and sub-components, the crsctl utility provides several options.

    a. Few of the CRS modules and the functionalities performed are listed in Table 16-3.

Table 16-3. *CRS Modules*

Modules	Functions / Description
CRSUI	User interface module
CRSCOMM	Communication module
CRSRTI	Resource management module
CRSMAIN	Main module/driver
CRSPLACE	CRS placement module
CRSAPP	CRS application
CRSRES	CRS resources
CRSOCR	OCR interface/engine
CRSTIMER	Various CRS-related timers
CRSEVT	CRS–EVM/event interface module
CRSD	CRS daemon

Depending on the module and the functionality provided by it, the debug operation can be performed at different levels. Based on the usefulness of the output provided, setting the operation to level two would provide the most useful information. Outputs of several of these modules are illustrated in the following:

b. Debug all CRS application–level activity. The debug output is generated using the following:

```
[root@ssky3l11p1 ~]# /u01/app/12.1.0/grid/bin/crsctl get log crs CRSAPP
Get CRSD Module: CRSAPP Log Level: 0
[root@ssky3l11p1 ~]# /u01/app/12.1.0/grid/bin/crsctl set log crs CRSAPP:2
Set CRSD Debug Module: CRSAPP  Level: 2
[root@ssky3l11p1 ~]# /u01/app/12.1.0/grid/bin/crsctl get log crs CRSAPP
Get CRSD Module: CRSAPP Log Level: 0
```

The preceding output is the debug information for the CRS application activity. The output provides the frequency of the context construction and destruction.

c. Debug all CRS timer activity. The debug output is generated using the following:

```
[root@ssky3l11p1 ~]# /u01/app/12.1.0/grid/bin/crsctl get log crs CRSTIMER
Get CRSD Module: CRSTIMER Log Level: 0
 [root@ssky3l11p1 ~]# /u01/app/12.1.0/grid/bin/crsctl set log crs CRSTIMER:2
Set CRSD Debug Module: CRSTIMER  Level: 2
[root@ssky3l11p1 ~]# /u01/app/12.1.0/grid/bin/crsctl get log crs CRSTIMER
Get CRSD Module: CRSTIMER Log Level: 2
```

The output from this module generates scheduler-related information for all the resources executed by the CRS on the cluster.

d. Debug all CRS log activity. The debug output is generated using the following:

```
[root@ssky3l11p1 ~]# /u01/app/12.1.0/grid/bin/crsctl set log crs CRSD:3
Set CRSD Debug Module: CRSD  Level: 3
```

Oracle Clusterware has several sub-components (one being the event manager) that are modules and perform specific actions on behalf of the cluster services. The crsctl utility provides several options for debugging the activities performed by these modules and sub-components.

A few of the EVM-related modules and their functionalities are listed in Table 16-4. Debug data for these modules can be generated similar to the CRS modules discussed earlier.

Table 16-4. EVM modules and descriptions

Module Name	Function
EVMD	EVM daemon
EVMDMAIN	EVM main module
EVMCOMM	EVM communication module
EVMEVT	EVM event module
EVMAPP	EVM application module
EVMAGENT	EVM agent module
CRSOCR	OCR interface/engine
CLUCLS	EVM cluster/CSS information
OCRMSG	OCR message module
OCRAPI	OCR API module
OCRCLI	OCR command-line interface

7. Starting cluster in exclusive mode

A new troubleshooting method introduced in Oracle Clusterware 11g Release 2 is to start the clusterware in exclusive mode. When doing so, clusterware ignores some of the required components such as the voting disk and networking requirements. This mode is useful for maintenance and troubleshooting purposes.

To use the exclusive feature, all clusterware components should be shut down on all participating members of the cluster. Compare this output with a full stack startup output using crsctl start crs -all:

```
[root@ssky1l4p1 oracle]# crsctl start crs -excl
CRS-2672: Attempting to start 'ora.cssdmonitor' on 'ssky1l4p1'
CRS-2676: Start of 'ora.cssdmonitor' on 'ssky1l4p1' succeeded
CRS-2672: Attempting to start 'ora.cssd' on 'ssky1l4p1'
CRS-2672: Attempting to start 'ora.diskmon' on 'ssky1l4p1'
CRS-2676: Start of 'ora.diskmon' on 'ssky1l4p1' succeeded
CRS-2676: Start of 'ora.cssd' on 'ssky1l4p1' succeeded
CRS-2672: Attempting to start 'ora.ctssd' on 'ssky1l4p1'
CRS-2672: Attempting to start 'ora.cluster_interconnect.haip' on 'ssky1l4p1'
CRS-2676: Start of 'ora.ctssd' on 'ssky1l4p1' succeeded
CRS-2676: Start of 'ora.cluster_interconnect.haip' on 'ssky1l4p1' succeeded
CRS-2672: Attempting to start 'ora.asm' on 'ssky1l4p1'
CRS-2676: Start of 'ora.asm' on 'ssky1l4p1' succeeded
CRS-2672: Attempting to start 'ora.storage' on 'ssky1l4p1'
CRS-2676: Start of 'ora.storage' on 'ssky1l4p1' succeeded
CRS-2672: Attempting to start 'ora.crsd' on 'ssky1l4p1'
CRS-2676: Start of 'ora.crsd' on 'ssky1l4p1' succeeded
[root@ssky1l4p1 oracle]#
```

OCR Administration Utilities

There are a few utilities that are installed as part of the GI to help validate the OCR.

OCR Verification (ocrcheck) Utility

This utility checks the health of the OCR. Apart from generating information regarding the OCR, the ocrcheck utility generates a log file in the directory from which this utility is executed.

```
[oracle@ssky3l11p1 ~]$ $GRID_HOME/bin/ocrcheck
Status of Oracle Cluster Registry is as follows :
         Version                  :          4
         Total space (kbytes)     :     409568
         Used space (kbytes)      :       1264
         Available space (kbytes) :     408304
         ID                       : 1817192482
         Device/File Name         : +GRID_DATA
                                    Device/File integrity check succeeded
                                    Device/File not configured
                                    Device/File not configured
                                    Device/File not configured
                                    Device/File not configured

         Cluster registry integrity check succeeded
         Logical corruption check bypassed due to non-privileged user
[oracle@ssky3l11p1 ~]$

[root@ssky3l11p1 ~]# /u01/app/12.1.0/grid/bin/ocrcheck
Status of Oracle Cluster Registry is as follows :
         Version                  :          4
         Total space (kbytes)     :     409568
         Used space (kbytes)      :       1264
         Available space (kbytes) :     408304
         ID                       : 1817192482
         Device/File Name         : +GRID_DATA
                                    Device/File integrity check succeeded
                                    Device/File not configured
                                    Device/File not configured
                                    Device/File not configured
                                    Device/File not configured

         Cluster registry integrity check succeeded
         Logical corruption check succeeded
```

■ **Note** In the preceding output, while the basic OCR check can be performed as "oracle" user, the logical corruption check is only performed when the ocrcheck utility is executed as "root" user.

If additional OCR files need to be created, there are two ways of doing so.

1. Create a new diskgroup with Normal or High redundancy and create or relocate the current OCR file to this new diskgroup. Oracle Clusterware will maintain mirrored images of the OCR file.

2. Create a new diskgroup with external redundancy and, using the ocrconfig utility, add a new OCR file using the ocrconfig -add command.

```
[root@ssky3l11p1 ~]# /u01/app/12.1.0/grid/bin/ocrconfig -add +GRID_DATA2
[root@ssky3l11p1 ~]# /u01/app/12.1.0/grid/bin/ocrcheck
Status of Oracle Cluster Registry is as follows :
         Version                  :          4
         Total space (kbytes)     :     409568
         Used space (kbytes)      :       1264
         Available space (kbytes) :     408304
         ID                       : 1817192482
         Device/File Name         : +GRID_DATA
                                    Device/File integrity check succeeded
         Device/File Name         : +GRID_DATA2
                                    Device/File integrity check succeeded
                                    Device/File not configured
                                    Device/File not configured
                                    Device/File not configured
         Cluster registry integrity check succeeded
         Logical corruption check succeeded
```

OCR Configuration (ocrconfig) Utility

This utility provides various options for configuration and administration of the OCR, such as export, import, restore, and so forth.

1. Export of the OCR could be performed while the registry is online or offline. To perform an export the following syntax is used:

```
ocrconfig -export <filename > [-s online]
    [root@ssky3l11p1 ~]# /u01/app/12.1.0/grid/bin/ocrconfig -export OCRExpPostSRV.dmp
-s online
```

In the preceding output, an export of the OCR is taken while the OCR is in an online state by using ocrconfig.

2. An OCR could be restored from either an export dump file or from a backup file. To import from an OCR file the following syntax is used:

```
ocrconfig -import <filename>
```

The OCR is restored to a previous state by the import operation (from a previously exported file). In certain situations, it may be required to bounce the clusterware.

3. Oracle performs an automatic backup of the OCR once every four hours while the system is up. While performing automatic backups, Oracle maintains three previous versions of the backup from that day as well a backup copy taken at the beginning of the day and another taken at the beginning of the week before purging the rest.

Oracle performs these automatic backups to the cluster directory (for example, $GRID_HOME/cdata/SSKYCW, as illustrated in the following example) on one of the nodes. To check previous backups, the following syntax is used:

```
[root@ssky1l2p2 ~]# /u01/app/12.1.0.1/grid/bin/ocrconfig -showbackup
ssky3l11p1    2014/01/19 08:08:36    /u01/app/12.1.0/grid/cdata/ssky1lp-cluster/backup00.ocr
ssky3l11p1    2014/01/19 04:08:34    /u01/app/12.1.0/grid/cdata/ssky1lp-cluster/backup01.ocr
ssky1l2p2     2014/01/03 15:43:59    /u01/app/12.1.0/grid/cdata/ssky1lp-cluster/backup02.ocr
ssky3l11p1    2014/01/19 04:08:34    /u01/app/12.1.0/grid/cdata/ssky1lp-cluster/day.ocr
ssky3l11p1    2014/01/19 04:08:34    /u01/app/12.1.0/grid/cdata/ssky1lp-cluster/week.ocr
PROT-25: Manual backups for the Oracle Cluster Registry are not available
```

Starting with Oracle Clusterware 11g, there is an option to take manual backups of the OCR file. Previous releases only supported automatic backups.

```
[root@ssky3l11p1 ~]# /u01/app/12.1.0/grid/bin/ocrconfig -manualbackup
ssky3l11p1    2014/01/14 21:13:30    /u01/app/12.1.0/grid/cdata/sskylc3-cluster/
                                     backup_20140114_211330.ocr
ssky3l11p1    2014/01/14 21:13:20    /u01/app/12.1.0/grid/cdata/sskylc3-cluster/
                                     backup_20140114_211320.ocr


[root@ssky3l11p1 ~]# /u01/app/12.1.0/grid/bin/ocrconfig -showbackup
PROT-24: Auto backups for the Oracle Cluster Registry are not available
ssky3l11p1    2014/01/14 21:13:30    /u01/app/12.1.0/grid/cdata/sskylc3-cluster/
                                     backup_20140114_211330.ocr
ssky3l11p1    2014/01/14 21:13:20    /u01/app/12.1.0/grid/cdata/sskylc3-cluster/
                                     backup_20140114_211320.ocr

[root@ssky3l11p1 ~]#

[root@ssky3l11p1 ~]# ls -ltr /u01/app/12.1.0/grid/cdata/sskylc3-cluster/
total 2692
-rw-r--r-- 1 root root 1359872 Jan 14 21:13 backup_20140114_211320.ocr
-rw-r--r-- 1 root root 1388544 Jan 14 21:13 backup_20140114_211330.ocr
[root@ssky3l11p1 ~]#
```

The following gives a list of the backup files found in the cluster directory:

```
[root@ssky3l12p2 ~]# ls -ltr /u01/app/12.1.0/grid/cdata/sskylc3-cluster/
total 9140
-rw-r--r-- 1 root root 1867776 Jan  2 03:43 day.ocr
-rw-r--r-- 1 root root 1867776 Jan  3 03:43 day_.ocr
-rw-r--r-- 1 root root 1867776 Jan  3 07:43 backup02.ocr
-rw-r--r-- 1 root root 1867776 Jan  3 11:43 backup01.ocr
-rw-r--r-- 1 root root 1867776 Jan  3 15:43 backup00.ocr
```

In the preceding output, a listing of all backups taken by the CRS is listed. It should be noted that there are three backups taken during the day (listed as backup00.ocr, backup01.ocr, and backup02.ocr). The listing also contains a backup refreshed at the beginning of each day (day.ocr) and another taken weekly (week.ocr).

■ **Note**   Backups performed to individual nodes become a single point of failure when the nodes are not down yet are not reachable. It is advised that the backups be moved to the shared storage to provide access to this file from any node in the cluster.

Unlike the OCR files, OLR files are not backed up by the clusterware. A manual backup is required to keep copies of the OLR files, as follows:

```
[root@ssky3l12p2 ~]# /u01/app/12.1.0/grid/bin/ocrconfig -local -manualbackup
ssky3l12p2    2014/01/19 10:22:50    /u01/app/12.1.0/grid/cdata/ssky3l12p2/backup_20140119_102250.olr
ssky3l12p2    2013/12/22 17:43:41    /u01/app/12.1.0/grid/cdata/ssky3l12p2/backup_20131222_174341.olr

[root@ssky3l12p2 ~]# /u01/app/12.1.0/grid/bin/ocrconfig -local -showbackup
ssky3l12p2    2014/01/19 10:22:50    /u01/app/12.1.0/grid/cdata/ssky3l12p2/backup_20140119_102250.olr
ssky3l12p2    2013/12/22 17:43:41    /u01/app/12.1.0/grid/cdata/ssky3l12p2/backup_20131222_174341.olr

[root@ssky3l12p2 ~]# ls -ltr /u01/app/12.1.0/grid/cdata/ssky3l12p2/
total 1932
-rw-r--r-- 1 root root  860160 Dec 22 17:43 backup_20131222_174341.olr
-rw-r--r-- 1 root root 1110016 Jan 19 10:22 backup_20140119_102250.olr
```

■ **Note**   It's good practice to include backing up the OLR files into the backup and recovery strategy for all nodes in the RAC cluster.

---

4. The automatic backup (default) location could be changed using the following syntax:

    ```
    ocrconfig -backuploc < new location of backup>
    ```

5. OCR could be restored from a previous backup using the following syntax/option:

    ```
    ocrconfig -restore <backup filename>
    [root@ssky3l12p2 ~]# /u01/app/12.1.0/grid/bin/ocrconfig -restore backup01.ocr
    ```

6. Other options supported by the ocrconfig utility include the following:

To replace the current OCR and create a new one in another location:

```
ocrconfig -replace  ocrmirror <new location>
```

To repair the current OCR and to automatically fix issues with the registry:

```
ocrconfig -repair -add < ocr location>
```

OCR Dump (ocrdump) Utility

The primary function of this utility is to dump the contents of the OCR into an ASCII readable format file. The output file is created in the directory where the utility is executed. If no file name is specified, the dump is created in OCRDUMPFILE within the same directory. The utility also generates a log file in the directory from which the ocrdump was executed.

```
[root@ssky3l12p2 ~]# /u01/app/12.1.0/grid/bin/ocrdump [<filename>]
```

In addition, partial dump outputs can be generated by specifying –keyname <keyword> with the ocrdump command. For example, to generate a dump of all SYSTEM-level definitions, the following syntax should be followed:

```
[root@ssky3l12p2 ~]# /u01/app/12.1.0/grid/bin/ocrdump -keyname SYSTEM OCRsystemDUMP
```

Workshop

There could be several reasons why the Oracle-related resources managed by the clusterware do not start on reboot. As a normal practice, one should check the clusterware-related log files. Figure 16-3 illustrates the list of log files generated by the various daemon processes running at the clusterware level. Most logs have a retention policy of capping at 50MB per file and keeping 10 logs per log type. For example, the list of logs created for CSSD are listed below.

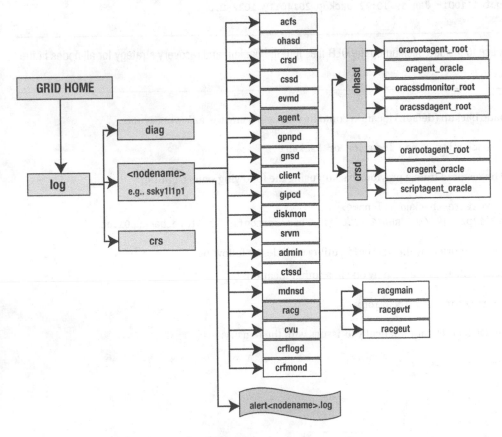

Figure 16-3. *Clusterware-related log directories*

The size of these logs could be increased using the crsctl command. The get attribute in the following lists the current logfile size while the set attribute allows changing the size to a new value.

```
[oracle@ssky1l3p1 ~]$ $GRID_HOME/bin/crsctl get css logfilesize
CRS-4676: Successful get logfilesize 52428800 for Cluster Synchronization Services.

[root@ssky1l4p2 client]# $GRID_HOME/bin/crsctl set css logfilesize 62428800
CRS-4686: Successful set logfilesize 62428800 for Cluster Synchronization Services.
```

Step 1

If the various resources did not start on reboot of the clusterware, the first step would be to verify whether the clusterware alert logs have any messages indicating errors. Most of the time the alert logs would have some indication as to where to look. In this case, the clusterware alert file had the following message:

```
[crsd(14620)]CRS-0804:Cluster Ready Service aborted due to Oracle Cluster Registry error
[PROC-26: Error while accessing the physical storage
]. Details at (:CRSD00111:) in /u01/app/12.1.0.1/grid/log/ssky1l1p1/crsd/crsd.log.
2014-01-28 10:10:02.030:
[ohasd(3970)]CRS-2771:Maximum restart attempts reached for resource 'ora.crsd'; will not restart.
2014-01-28 10:10:03.806:
[ohasd(3970)]CRS-2769:Unable to failover resource 'ora.crsd'.
```

Step 2

Subsequent to this would be to check if all the components of the clusterware stack are up and running. This can be done using the crsctl check crs command, as follows:

```
[root@ssky3l11p1 ~]# /u01/app/12.1.0/grid/bin/crsctl check crs
CRS-4638: Oracle High Availability Services is online
CRS-4535: Cannot communicate with Cluster Ready Services
CRS-4529: Cluster Synchronization Services is online
CRS-4533: Event Manager is online
```

Step 3

Verification of the clusterware indicated that all components of the stack were healthy with the exception of the CRSD daemon process. This gave a clear indication as to why the resources managed by the CRS did not start. The next step would be to verify whether the clusterware-related O/S processes were running. This could be verified using the following:

```
[root@ssky3l11p1 ~]# ps -ef | egrep "crsd|cssd|evmd|ohasd"
root     14148     1  0 20:05 ?        00:00:00 /bin/sh /etc/init.d/init.ohasd run
root     16470     1  1 20:09 ?        00:00:50 /u01/app/12.1.0/grid/bin/ohasd.bin reboot
_ORA_BLOCKING_STACK_LOCALE=AMERICAN_AMERICA.AL32UTF8
oracle   16593     1  0 20:09 ?        00:00:22 /u01/app/12.1.0/grid/bin/evmd.bin
oracle   16625 16593  0 20:09 ?        00:00:00 /u01/app/12.1.0/grid/bin/evmlogger.bin -o
/u01/app/12.1.0/grid/log/[HOSTNAME]/evmd/evmlogger.info -l /u01/app/12.1.0/grid/log/[HOSTNAME]
/evmd/evmlogger.log
root     16659     1  0 20:09 ?        00:00:02 /u01/app/12.1.0/grid/bin/cssdmonitor
root     16671     1  0 20:09 ?        00:00:02 /u01/app/12.1.0/grid/bin/cssdagent
oracle   16682     1  0 20:09 ?        00:00:19 /u01/app/12.1.0/grid/bin/ocssd.bin
```

Step 4

In our example, both verifications indicated that the CRSD was down. $GRID_HOME/bin/crs_stat -t would give the current state of the application stack managed by the clusterware. This verification returned the following error, which indicates that the CRS was not able to activate the resources:

```
[root@ssky3l11p1 crsd]# $GRID_HOME/bin/crs_stat -t
CRS-0184: Cannot communicate with the CRS daemon.
```

Step 5

Verifying the alert log file in Step 1 indicated that issues existed in reaching the OCR file. Since the OCR file is managed on the ASM storage, the next obvious step would be to verify whether the ASM diskgroup is visible and reachable, as follows:

```
SQL> SELECT NAME, STATE, TYPE FROM V$ASM_DISKGROUP;

NAME                              STATE         TYPE
------------------------------    -----------   ------
SSKYDB_FRA                        MOUNTED       EXTERN
SSKYDB_DATA                       MOUNTED       EXTERN
GRID_DATA                         MOUNTED       NORMAL
```

Step 6

The next step would be to verify the CSSD and CRSD log files, looking for any errors related to the problem.

■ **Note**   In a similar, earlier situation, a reboot of all servers fixed the locking and the clusterware then started without any hiccups.

Step 7

Based on an analysis of the preceding steps, the next step would be to repair the OCR file using the following steps, being sure to act as user "root":

    a.   In order to replace/repair and add a new OCR file, the CRS stack should be down not the entire clusterware stack, however, as only the CRS daemon needs to be down. Use the following command to do this:

```
$GRID_HOME/bin/crsctl stop crs
```

    b.   However, since the additional OCR file will be added to an ASM diskgroup, ASM on just one of the instances should be up.

    c.   Add the OCR file using the following command:

```
[root@ssky3l11p1 ~]# /u01/app/12.1.0/grid/bin/ocrconfig -repair -add +GRID_DATA2
```

d. Oracle will update the ocr.loc file with the appropriate information and make an entry into the cluster alert log file on the node, as follows:

```
[root@ssky3l11p1 ~]# cat /etc/oracle/ocr.loc
#Device/file  getting replaced by device +GRID_DATA2
ocrconfig_loc=+GRID_DATA
ocrmirrorconfig_loc=+GRID_DATA2
local_only=false
```

e. Verify the OCR file using the ocrcheck utility, as seen here:

```
[root@ssky3l11p1 ssky3l11p1]# /u01/app/12.1.0.1/grid/bin/ocrcheck
Status of Oracle Cluster Registry is as follows :
        Version                  :          4
        Total space (kbytes)     :     409568
        Used space (kbytes)      :       1764
        Available space (kbytes) :     407804
        ID                       : 1514747975
        Device/File Name         : +GRID_DATA
                                   Device/File integrity check succeeded
        Device/File Name         : +GRID_DATA2
                                   Device/File integrity check succeeded

                                   Device/File not configured

                                   Device/File not configured

                                   Device/File not configured

        Cluster registry integrity check succeeded

        Logical corruption check succeeded
```

Step 8

Now that both OCR files are fixed, restart the clusterware stack by using the /etc/init.d/init.ohasd start or the $GRID_HOME/bin/crsctl start cluster commands. This will start the clusterware and the complete stack.

Step 9

If during the process the OHASD daemons were disabled to avoid a crash, they should now auto restart. One could reset OHASD daemons to enable auto restart on reboot, as follows:

```
/etc/init.d/init.ohasd enable
/etc/init.d/init.ohasd start
```

Step 10

The ocr.loc file on the other nodes in the cluster will be automatically updated during subsequent restart of the clusterware on the respective nodes.

■ **Note**   Occasionally, once the restore or import is completed, clusterware could go into a panic mode and reboot the server. This is normal behavior, and it happens when CRS has not completely shut down and has a hanging daemon on one of the servers.

This should restart the clusterware and all of the applications managed by the CRS. Once the clusterware components have been verified and the database has been checked, it would be a good practice to export or manually back up the OCR and archive it as a good copy.

EVMD Verification

EVMD plays a very important function in the RAC architecture; it sends and receives actions regarding resource state changes to and from all other nodes in the cluster. To determine whether the EVMD for a node can send and receive messages from other nodes, the set of tests outlined here should help.

Activities of the EVMD could be verified using the evmwatch monitor utility. The evmwatch monitor is a background process that constantly watches for actions, which are then parsed to the evmshow utility for formatting and display.

For example, evmwatch -A -t "@timestamp @@" will monitor for actions sent and received, and such information will be displayed on standard output. The display in this example is from evmshow; however, it is automatically started when the –A switch is specified. @timestamp will list the date and time at which actions are sent and received by the node.

Additional details regarding the actions received or sent could also be obtained using additional switches. For example, evmwatch -A -t "@timestamp @priority @" will return the designated priority of the event received, and the third "@name" will display the name (shown in the following output) of the service, resource, or application. See the following:

```
[root@PRDDB1 home]# $GRID_HOME/bin/evmwatch -A -t "@timestamp @priority @name"
"05-Apr-2011 22:00:51 200 sys.ora.clu.cluster_evt"
"05-Apr-2011 22:01:22 200 sys.ora.clu.cluster_evt"
"05-Apr-2011 22:01:52 200 sys.ora.clu.cluster_evt"
"05-Apr-2011 22:02:22 200 sys.ora.clu.cluster_evt"
"05-Apr-2011 22:02:53 200 sys.ora.clu.cluster_evt"
```

This output illustrates two types of actions sent and received. An imcheck action is sent to determine the state of the resources defined in the OCR, and a subsequent response is received that provides the current state (imup) of the resource (similar to a reply message for the initial verification request). All action/responses are user-defined (user is identified by ora) HA services (identified by ha), and all communications are performed at priority 200.

Other types of actions sent and received by the EVMD are listed in Table 16-5.

Table 16-5. EVMD actions

Action	Priority	Function
Error	500	No response is received for the action sent
Transition	300	The event is in a state change process. Normally the action is received when a resource or service is initially started, stopped, or failing over.
Down	200	Indicates that the resource or service is currently down
Running	300	Indicates that the service or resource is currently in execution state. This state is normally seen in cluster services or applications managed by the Oracle Clusterware, for example, CRS
Up	200	Indicates that the service or resource specified is up.
Imstop	200	Indicates an HA service stop action
relocatefailed	300	Indicates an attempt to relocate a service or resource from one node to another; however, such relocation attempt has failed. This action normally follows other actions such as "imstop" or "stopped"
Stopped	300	Indicates that the application has completely stopped execution

Grid Plug and Play

Starting with Oracle Clusterware 11g Release 2, Oracle has introduced a new feature called Grid Plug and Play, which is managed by the Grid Plug and Play daemon (GPnPD). During installation, Oracle creates and makes copies of the Oracle universal installer, called the GPnP profile. The profile is stored in the GPnP cache on all nodes in the cluster. Unless the profile is changed using of the client interfaces, the data in the cache should be identical on all nodes in the cluster. The Profile Sequence number identifies the version of the profile.

Figure 16-4 is a snapshot of the GPnP profile, which contains bootstrap information that is required in order to form the cluster. The following is a list of information found in the profile:

- Profile sequence
- Cluster UID
- Cluster name
- Host network
- CSS profile
- ASM profile
- Wallet information, such as the public and private RSA keys

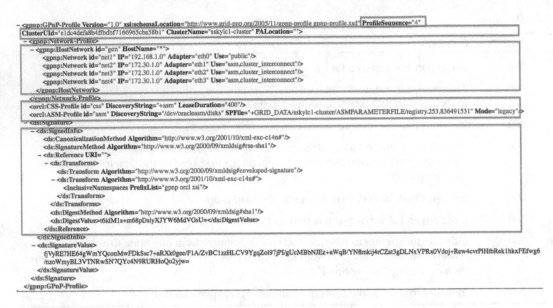

Figure 16-4. GPnP profile

The GPnP daemon is spawned by the OHASD oraagent (illustrated in levels 2 and 3 in Figure 16-2). Since most of the clusterware-related information is contained in this profile, it is crticial for the GPnP daemon process to run in order for the clusterware stack to begin.

Oracle provides a GPnP tool to look at the contents of the profile, seen here:

```
[oracle@ssky3l11p1 ~]$ /u01/app/12.1.0.1/grid/bin/gpnptool
Oracle GPnP Tool
Usage:
"gpnptool <verb> <switches>", where verbs are:
create   Create a new GPnP Profile
edit     Edit existing GPnP Profile
getpval  Get value(s) from GPnP Profile
get      Get profile in effect on local node
rget     Get profile in effect on remote GPnP node
put      Put profile as a current best
find     Find all RD-discoverable resources of given type
lfind    Find local gpnpd server
check    Perform basic profile sanity checks
c14n     Canonicalize, format profile text (XML C14N)
sign     Sign/re-sign profile with wallet's private key
unsign   Remove profile signature, if any
verify   Verify profile signature against wallet certificate
help     Print detailed tool help
ver      Show tool version
```

a. To check the sanity of the profile, use this code:

```
[oracle@ssky3l11p1 ~]$ /u01/app/12.1.0.1/grid/bin/gpnptool check
-p=/u01/app/12.1.0.1/grid/gpnp/ssky3l11p1/profiles/peer/profile.xml
Profile cluster="ssky1lp-cluster", GUID="f11ea7cce6e1df31ff1456d7bbf76823",
version=9
GPnP profile signed by peer, signature valid.
Checking target profile networks.
Got GPnP Service current profile to check against.
Current GPnP Service Profile cluster="ssky1lp-cluster", GUID="f11ea7cce6e1d
f31ff1456d7bbf76823", version=9
Warning: profile version 9 is older than- or duplicate of- GPnP Service
current profile version 9.
Profile appears valid, but basic push will not succeed.
 [oracle@ssky3l11p1 ~]$
```

b. To check if the profile has been cached and found in the local node, use this code:

```
[oracle@ssky3l11p1 ~]$ /u01/app/12.1.0.1/grid/bin/gpnptool lfind
Success. Local gpnpd found.
```

c. To check if the profile can be found in other nodes in the cluster, use the following:

```
[oracle@ssky3l11p1 ~]$ /u01/app/12.1.0.1/grid/bin/gpnptool find
Found 3 instances of service 'gpnp'.
mdns:service:gpnp._tcp.local.://ssky1l2p2:41523/agent=gpnpd,cname=ssky1lp-
cluster,guid=f11ea7cce6e1df31ff1456d7bbf76823,host=ssky1l2p2,pid=4547/gpnpd
h:ssky1l2p2 c:ssky1lp-cluster u:f11ea7cce6e1df31ff1456d7b
mdns:service:gpnp._tcp.local.://ssky1l3p3:62850/agent=gpnpd,cname=ssky1lp-
cluster,guid=f11ea7cce6e1df31ff1456d7bbf76823,host=ssky1l3p3,pid=4588/gpnpd
h:ssky1l3p3 c:ssky1lp-cluster u:f11ea7cce6e1df31ff1456d7b
mdns:service:gpnp._tcp.local.://ssky3l11p1:59756/agent=gpnpd,cname=ssky1lp-
cluster,guid=f11ea7cce6e1df31ff1456d7bbf76823,host=ssky3l11p1,pid=4542/gpnpd
h:ssky3l11p1 c:ssky1lp-cluster u:f11ea7cce6e1df31ff1456d7b
 [oracle@ssky3l11p1 ~]$
```

■ **Note** Situations can occur in which errors are encountered and are not fixable using only the messages contained in the various log files. Under these circumstances, open an SR with Oracle support. Collect all relevant log files required for analysis by Oracle support. Oracle has provided a PERL script (diagcollection.pl) to complete this process. Once the data is collected, upload the zip file.

Monitoring Resource Utilization in the Cluster

Once the cluster is configured as a component of the GI and assigned a name, it's identified as such and is monitored by the Enterprise Manager agent. Statistics are measured and collected under that name and can be viewed from the Database Express or cloud control. The advantage of monitoring the cluster from the cloud control console is having the ability to drill down from the O/S level to other layers of the stack, including the database.

Figure 16-5 illustrates the current O/S-level performance statistics for a 4-node cluster. As noted earlier, the CPU usage overall across the cluster is high and needs further investigation.

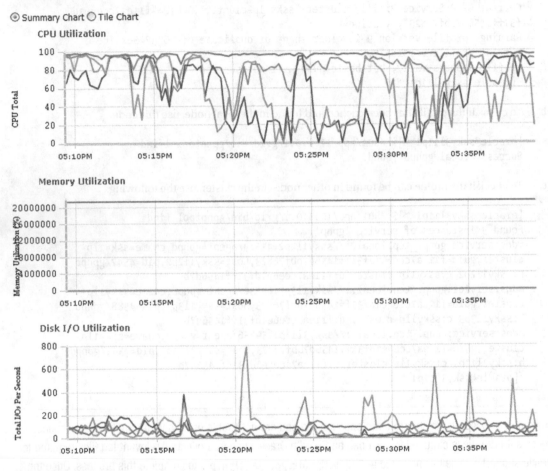

Figure 16-5. *Oracle 11g OEM: Cluster-level monitoring*

Step 1

In Figure 16-5, CPU utilization is high across most of the servers in the 4-node cluster. Server 1 is the highest. Drilling down into server 1 by selecting the legend that appears on the right side of the chart provides a detailed view (illustrated in Figure 16-6) of the statistics that have been collected on that server.

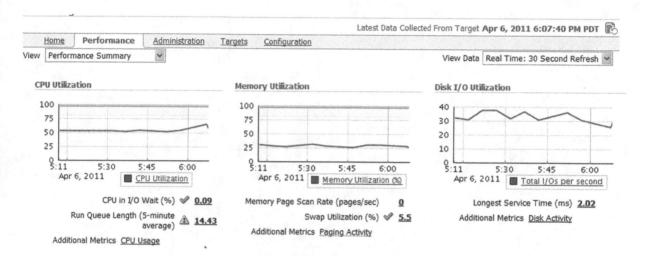

Figure 16-6. *Oracle11g performance statistics*

Step 2

Once the resource (CPU, memory, disk I/O) that needs further investigation is identified, selecting the legend below the chart will provide a historical chart for the specific resource going back to when the server was last restarted. This chart gives an indication of whether the resource utilization has been consistent over a period of time or is being noticed for the first time, in which case it could bc considered as a spike.

Step 3

The information collected helps drill down into the instance-level statistics. The node-level monitoring of the database shows that there was high virtual memory paging earlier.

As advised by the ADDM analysis report on investigating the allocations, Figure 16-4 shows that memory utilization is not even at 50%. Adding memory is not always possible and may not solve the problem. Apart from that, paging can occur when processes are created, and sometimes ADDM offers nothing about the root cause, so presumably no action is required.

Conclusion

The clusterware is the backbone of having all servers in the configuration work in conjunction with each other. The efficiency and functioning of the clusterware is important. This chapter discusses the various diagnosis options available. While the clusterware consists of more than just the various daemons covered here, we leave other components, such as the interconnect and storage, to be discussed in their respective chapters.

CHAPTER 17

∎∎∎

Waits, Enqueues, and Latches

When optimizing Oracle database systems, the SQL statement, its explain plan, adding indexes, or changing the optimizers access paths, using hints, and so forth are just methods of helping Oracle to perform user operations. When all these tuned and optimized SQL statements are executed, there are other types of potential bottlenecks such as contention, concurrency, locking, and resource availability that could cause applications to run slow and provide slow response times to the users. Contention for resources could be measured or interpreted at the various levels of the systems processing cycle. Such resources could be lack of CPU, lack of network bandwidth, lack of memory, issues with the storage subsystem, and so forth. Oracle provides instrumentation into the various categories of resource utilization levels and provides methods of interpreting them. In this chapter, we look at some of these critical statistics that help optimize the database.

Latches

Latches are low-level serialization mechanisms used to protect shared data structures in the SGA.[1] A latch is a type of lock that is very quickly acquired; and when the work is complete, it is freed. Latches are used by Oracle to prevent multiple processes executing the same piece of code at the same time and to prevent dead locks. Depending on the type of data structure accessed, Oracle uses different types of latches.

Once a process acquires a latch at a certain level, it cannot subsequently acquire a latch at a level that is equal to or less than that level.[2] When trying to acquire a latch, if the latch is not available, the process spins on the CPU for a short while and then it sleeps for a while before trying again. The number of times a process will spin when trying to acquire a latch before waiting on the CPU and going to sleep is controlled by the _SPIN_COUNT parameter. This parameter defaults to 2,000. Based on if the latch is obtained, it increments the SPIN_GETS and MISSES counters. However, if it is not available, it increments the wait counter and tries again. Waiting for latches can be either a short wait (no-wait) or a long wait (willing-to-wait); most of the latches fall under the willing-to-wait category.

Willing-to-Wait Mode

If the process attempts to get a latch in the willing-to-wait mode and finds out the latch is not available; it would spin (loop) briefly and try to make the request again until the latch is obtained. The process/session is still in active wait because from the O/S perspective, the process continues to consume CPU cycles.

---

[1]Metalink Note # 22908.1. "What Are Latches and What Causes Latch Contention." Accessed at metalink.oracle.com.
[2]Ibid.

No-Wait Mode

If a process attempts to get a latch in no-wait mode and finds out that the latch is not available, instead of spinning and trying again, it would make a request for the latch again immediately.

Oracle database provides instrumentation on the various types of latches. To be precise, in Oracle Database 12c Release 1 Oracle provides instrumentation through 703 types of latches (compared to 553 in Oracle 11g Release 2 and 394 in Oracle 10g Release 2). When optimizing database operations, special attention should be given to latch statistics. Tuning database operations and reducing latch contention would help improve the overall response times; that having been said, many of the latches are required latches for Oracle to complete its operation. While V$LATCH provides latch statistics for the overall database behavior, V$GES_LATCH[3] filters latch statistics for a RAC environment. Like the generic latches, RAC-related latches are also measured by hits, misses—the number of spins before which the process was able to acquire a latch—and the total time it waited to get the latch. The higher number of misses could indicate the operation had to spin several times, which in turn potentially indicates a higher wait time to acquire a latch. The higher spin and wait times for a latch would indicate shortage of resources mostly centered on contention for the CPU.

The output following is the number of times the latch was acquired by sessions on one of the instances in a RAC cluster in an Oracle Database 12c Release 1 environment:

Script: MVRACPDnTap_dlmlatch.sql

```
SELECT inst_id              INT,
       latch#,
       level#,
       name,
       gets,
       misses,
       gets / misses        RATIO,
       sleeps,
       spin_gets,
       immediate_gets       Igets,
       immediate_misses     Imisses,
       wait_time / 1000000  "WT"
FROM   gv$latch
WHERE  misses > 1000
ORDER  BY inst_id,
          spin_gets DESC;
```

Inst	Latch	Level	Name of Latch	Gets	Misses	Gets:Misses Ratio	Sleeps	Gets After Spinning	Immediate Gets	Immediate Misses	Wait Time (Seconds)
1	203	1	cache buffers chains	138844758	324380	428.03	55528	269429	57637	113	7.67
	120	1	ges resource hash list	134966315	298080	452.79	120049	178724	238875	510	6.17
	123	5	ges enqueue table freelist	76351930	173215	440.79	17224	156064	0	0	2.27
	65	5	channel operations parent latch	102738317	113733	903.33	13486	100757	0	0	1.33
	241	5	redo allocation	7878359	54612	144.26	7864	46791	80211629	283494	1.12
	249	3	oc element	103021035	86056	1197.14	44483	43571	5779626	8094	4.95
	35	4	enqueue hash chains	1179195433	56556	20850.05	15337	41506	55058933	11184	1.06
	149	6	KJCT flow control latch	47449209	16730	2836.18	858	15905	0	0	.06
	153	4	ocs resource hash	85226904	22141	3849.28	6810	15622	4658	8	.62
	314	5	undo global data	18793997	13579	1384.05	433	13154	0	0	.07
	33	8	messages	77005996	12857	5989.42	992	11913	0	0	.26
	66	6	message pool operations parent l	40772796	11594	3516.72	1783	9893	0	0	.21
	358	4	row cache objects	39100298	9937	3934.82	723	9289	26280	14	.04
	14	5	session allocation	8609374	8977	959.05	363	8614	8414027	1853	.03
	344	0	space background task latch	2849387	74725	38.13	66278	8491	263823	61	8.08
	17	1	session idle bit	16994100	8940	1900.91	507	8433	0	0	.05
	198	2	cache buffers lru chain	27925103	12944	2157.38	5023	8006	48856193	47881	.71

---

[3]V$GES_LATCH is depreciated in Oracle Database 12c Version 1.

In the preceding output, the columns

- Gets indicates the number of times the latch was requested in willing-to-wait mode;

- Misses indicate the number of times the latch was requested in willing-to-wait mode and the requester had to wait;

- Sleeps indicate the number of times a willing-to-wait latch request resulted in a session sleeping while waiting for the latch;

- Immediate Gets indicate the number of times a latch was requested in no-wait mode;

- Immediate Misses indicate number of times a no-wait latch request did not succeed;

- Wait Time is the elapsed time displayed in seconds spent waiting for the latch.

In the preceding output, few of the latches show high wait time. We look at drilling down into the reasons for high waits in these latches.

Cache Buffers Chains

This latch is acquired whenever a block in the buffer cache is accessed, normally due to high logical I/O (LIO). SQL statements reading more buffers than required; and when multiple sessions are trying to access the same block, this causes sessions to wait on this latch.

Reducing contention for the cache buffer chains latch will usually require reducing logical I/O rates by tuning and minimizing the I/O requirements of the SQL involved. Optimizing the access paths, such as adding additional indexes, could reduce I/O rates. High I/O rates could also be a sign of a hot block, which would mean looking at storage distribution; and tuning access paths would benefit in reducing these latch times.

Typical solutions include the following:

- Look for SQL statements that access the blocks in question and determine if the repeated reads are necessary. This may be within a single session or across multiple sessions.

- Check for suboptimal SQL. Look at the execution plan for the SQL being run and try to reduce the gets per executions, which will minimize LIO, the number of blocks being accessed, and therefore reduce the chances of multiple sessions contending for the same block.

How do we find what blocks or objects are hot and are the cause for this high latch contention? We try to analyze through the following workshop how to troubleshoot and identify the hot blocks.

Workshop

For the output discussed previously, lets try to understand the details a little.

Step 1

To find the various latches currently having high wait times, execute the following query to get the latch details:

Script: MVRACPDnTap_dlmlatch.sql

```
SELECT inst_id           INT,
       latch#,
       level#,
       name,
       gets,
       misses,
```

```
        gets / misses          RATIO,
        sleeps,
        spin_gets,
        immediate_gets         Igets,
        immediate_misses       Imisses,
        wait_time / 1000000 "WT"
FROM    gv$latch
WHERE   misses > 1000
ORDER   BY inst_id,
           spin_gets DESC;
```

Inst	Latch	Level	Name of Latch	Gets	Misses	Gets:Misses Ratio	Sleeps	Gets After Spinning	Immediate Gets	Immediate Misses	Wait Time (Seconds)
1	203	1	cache buffers chains	138844758	324380	428.03	55528	269429	57637	113	7.67
	120	1	ges resource hash list	134966315	298080	452.79	120049	178724	238875	510	6.17
	123	5	ges enqueue table freelist	76351930	173215	440.79	17224	156064	0	0	2.27
	65	5	channel operations parent latch	102738317	113733	903.33	13486	100757	0	0	1.33
	241	5	redo allocation	7878359	54612	144.26	7864	46791	80211629	283494	1.12
	249	3	gc element	103021035	86056	1197.14	44483	43571	5779626	8094	4.95
	35	4	enqueue hash chains	1179195433	56556	20850.05	15337	41506	55058933	11184	1.06
	149	6	KJCT flow control latch	47449209	16730	2836.18	858	15905	0	0	.06
	153	4	gcs resource hash	85226904	22141	3849.28	6810	15622	4658	8	.62
	314	5	undo global data	18793997	13579	1384.05	433	13154	0	0	.07
	33	8	messages	77005996	12857	5989.42	992	11913	0	0	.26
	66	6	message pool operations parent l	40772796	11594	3516.72	1783	9893	0	0	.21
	358	4	row cache objects	39100298	9937	3934.82	723	9289	26280	14	.04
	14	5	session allocation	8689374	8977	959.05	363	8614	8414027	1853	.03
	344	0	space background task latch	2849387	74725	38.13	66278	8491	263823	61	8.08
	17	1	session idle bit	16994100	8940	1900.91	507	8433	0	0	.05
	198	2	cache buffers lru chain	27925103	12944	2157.38	5023	8006	48856193	47881	.71

The preceding V$LATCH output gives you details about misses and gets across various latches. To understand the memory structure and for what memory address these latches are being requested, we query the V$LATCH_CHILDREN views.

Step 2

The task here is to determine the memory address that is consistently being missed and that has the highest miss rate. Querying the view V$LATCH_CHILDREN can help us arrive at the address that has the highest miss rate.

Script: MVRACPDnTap_latchchildren.sql

```
SELECT inst_id INT,
       latch#,
       level#,
       child#  "Child",
       addr    "Address",
       name    "Name",
       gets    "Gets",
       misses  "Misses",
       sleeps  "Sleeps"
FROM   gv$latch_children
WHERE  misses > 1000
ORDER  BY 1,
          6,
          2,
          3;
```

Inst	Latch	Level	Child	Address	Name of Latch	Gets	Misses	Sleeps
1	203	1	306	00000000A51B4058	cache buffers chains	3716256	3946	510
	203	1	5152	00000000A54F32D8	cache buffers chains	33185081	1794	34
	203	1	7302	00000000A5667F58	cache buffers chains	6391335	24320	11702
	203	1	7478	00000000A5684358	cache buffers chains	36464190	13925	13

From the preceding output, Address 00000000A5667F58 has the highest miss and sleep rates. We now try to understand what hot objects in memory are causing these high misses and sleeps.

Step 3

Using the address from Step 2, we can query the X$BH table, joining with DBA_EXTENTS and V$LATCH_CHILDREN to get the hot objects in buffer.

Script: MVRACPDnTap_HotSegments.sql[4]

```
SELECT /*+ ordered */ e.owner
                      ||'.'
                      || e.segment_name        segment_name,
                      e.extent_id              extent#,
                      x.dbablk - e.block_id + 1 block#,
                      x.tch,
                      l.child#
FROM   sys.v$latch_children l,
       sys.x$bh x,
       sys.dba_extents e
WHERE  l.name = 'cache buffers chains'
       AND l.sleeps > &sleep_count
       AND x.hladdr = l.addr
       AND e.file_id = x.file#
       AND x.dbablk BETWEEN e.block_id AND e.block_id + e.blocks - 1;
```

SEGMENT_NAME	EXTENT#	BLOCK#	TCH	CHILD#
RAPUSR.STOCK	77	5	157	7302
RAPUSR.CUSTOMER	81	26	44	7302
SYS._SYSSMU14_4287170308$	2	68	8	7302
SYS.C_OBJ#	21	110	7	7302
SYS._SYSSMU14_4287170308$	7	54	7	7302
RAPUSR.CUSTOMER	63	40	3	7302
RAPUSR.WAREHOUSE	1	1	1	7302
RAPUSR.WAREHOUSE	1	1	1	7302
XDB.SYS_IL0000018294C00007$$	0	3	1	7302
XDB.SYS_IL0000018294C00007$$	0	3	1	7302
SYS.I_JIJOIN$	0	1	1	7302
SYS.I_JIJOIN$	0	1	1	7302

---

[4]Script source is *Oracle Wait Interface: A Practical Guide To Performance Diagnostics & Tuning* (2004, Oracle Press) by Richmond Shee, Kirtikumar Deshpande, and K. Gopalakrishnan.

RAPUSR.ORDERS	93	582	1	7302
RAPUSR.WAREHOUSE	1	1	1	7302
RAPUSR.WAREHOUSE	1	1	1	7302
RAPUSR.WAREHOUSE	1	1	1	7302
RAPUSR.WAREHOUSE	1	1	1	7302
SYS.WRH$_ACTIVE_SESSION_HISTORY	92	843	0	7302
RAPUSR.IORDL	285	526	0	7302
RAPUSR.IORDL	292	5404	0	7302
RAPUSR.WAREHOUSE	1	1	0	7302
RAPUSR.WAREHOUSE	1	1	0	7302

From the previous output, there are several objects in the buffer that are being accessed from the same address spot: the hot block is indicated by the highest TCH count. In this situation, it would be the STOCK table. There is another view that could help potentially identify the current holder of the latch; however, because the request (get) for latch, misses, sleep, and retry are all steps that happen instantaneously, it sometimes is difficult to identify the current latch holder. Repeatedly querying the view V$LATCHHOLDER could potentially help identify the holder.

Step 4

Query the GV$LATCHHOLDER view to determine the current holder of the lock.

```
SELECT inst_id,
       pid,
       sid,
       name,
       gets,
       con_id
FROM   gv$latchholder;
```

Ins ID	PID	SID	NAME	GETS	CON_ID
2	65	269	cache buffers chains	74784	0
2	72	42	cache buffers chains	123802	0
2	72	42	redo copy	12838407	0
1	73	285	cache buffers chains	141940	0
1	73	285	cache buffers lru chain	59778528	0
1	73	285	cache buffers chains	166841	0

From the preceding GV$LATCHHOLDER output, there are several sessions holding the same latch on the buffer. It should be noted from the query output that the cache buffer chains latch is reported from both instance 1 and instance 2. Unlike session blockers, latches are instance specific; and latches are placed on the local buffer. That having been said, it should be noted that because blocks may currently be used by one instance, there could potentially be cases where another instance (requestor) is currently waiting for the block. A block that is a hot block on one instance (holder) may be required by another instance (requestor). Although there would be latch-related contentions on the requesting instance, the requestor waiting for the block is not directly interpreted in the latch wait times; it should be analyzed with the related GCS resource wait. RAC resource waits are discussed later in the chapter.

Step 5

It's good to understand the details of SIDs holding the buffer. A query against the GV$SESSION and GV$PROCESS views would help list the currently active sessions and the SQL_ID for the statements executed.

Script: MVRACPDnTap_whoractivep.sql

```
select
        s.inst_id,
        s.username,
        ' '||to_char(s.SID)||','|| to_char(s.serial#) "SID_SER",
        to_char(s.logon_time,'mm/dd hh24:mi ') logon_time,
        SUBSTR(s.status,1,1) status,
        s.service_name,
        p.pid    ppid,
        p.spid,
        s.process,
        s.sql_id,
        s.blocking_session,
        s.event,
        s.machine
from    gv$session s,
        gv$process p
where   s.paddr       = p.addr
and     s.inst_id     = p.inst_id
and     s.username is not null
and     s.username not in ('SYS','SYSTEM')
and     s.status ='ACTIVE'
and     s.type <> 'BACKGROUND'
order by logon_time,s.inst_id
;
```

Ins ID	User Name	SesID,Ser#	Logon Time	Stat us	Service	PPID	SPID	Process	Sql ID	Blocker	Wait Event	Machine
1	RAPUSR	42,8909	06/10 21:30	A	FIPS	70	2665	10624	gwcvcq87cn4sc		db file sequential r	ssky1l4p1.su
1	RAPUSR	274,17181	06/10 21:30	A	FIPS	71	2669	10624	gwcvcq87cn4sc		db file sequential r	ssky1l4p1.su
1	RAPUSR	285,35437	06/10 21:30	A	FIPS	73	2673	10624	69gxtaqr1vk8j		gc cr request	ssky1l4p1.su
2	RAPUSR	269,23955	06/10 21:30	A	FIPS	65	10888	10624	f9rutjmvjm8j7		db file sequential r	ssky1l4p1.su
2	RAPUSR	42,16211	06/10 21:30	A	FIPS	72	10892	10624		246	log file sync	ssky1l4p1.su
2	RAPUSR	279,48997	06/10 21:30	A	FIPS	73	10896	10624	gwcvcq87cn4sc		db file sequential r	ssky1l4p1.su

From the preceding output, the session details and the SQL_ID for the SQL operations could be obtained; and for further analysis, an XPLAN (Explain Plan) could be generated. Based on the XPLAN generated and the type of SQL being executed, appropriate optimization could be done.

gc element

In a RAC environment, there are global operations. Global operations may require changes to be made to the distributed lock manager (DLM) lock elements. When such changes are made, the lock element array is protected by the gc element latch. Due to the nature of the architecture, with high global operations, there are bound to be several latch requests. Closer understanding of the transaction behavior of the application would help determine the amount of global cache traffic. Reducing the amount of global cache traffic by implementing service to instance affinity and object to instance affinity would help reduce the gc element latch waits. High gc element latches could be of serious concern and should be reported to Oracle support. For the curious minds, a trace using event 10899 or gc_elements dump of the global cache element could help in identifying the problem areas.

Redo Allocation

Redo log buffers hold information about changes made to the database. Changes are stored in redo entries. These entries contain information required to reconstruct or redo the changes made to the database. The server process copies these redo entries from the users memory area into the redo log buffer area. The LGWR process writes the redo log buffer data into the redo log files.

When a user process needs to make a change to the data block, it creates a redo record in the redo log buffer by executing the following steps:

- Ensure no other process has generated a higher SCN.

- Find buffer space to write the redo record. If no sufficient space is available, it forces LGWR write operation or issues a log switch.

- Allocate sufficient space required to write the redo log record to the buffer.

- Copy the redo record to the log buffer and link it to the appropriate structures for recovery purposes.

Any time buffer activity is involved, and Oracle processes need to determine if the buffer is free or if the buffer can be written or cleaned, the process would need a latch. A redo allocation latch is required to allocate space in the log buffer for each transaction entry. Subsequently, during a log switch operation or when buffer space needs to be freed for other redo entries, the latch is released.

Similar to the redo allocation latch, there are two other latches associated with redo: redo copy latch and redo writing latch. The redo copy latch is acquired in "no-wait" mode for the entire duration of the operation and released when a log switch is initiated to free up buffer space. It indicates that a process is copying redo into the log buffer and that the LGWR should wait until the copy has finished before writing the target log buffer blocks to disk. Redo writing latch is to prevent multiple LGWR processes requesting for log switches simultaneously. When a process needs to free redo log buffer space, it acquires this latch before the LGWR can perform a write operation. Latch waits may show high waits when writes take longer than expected. This is normally reflected as a resource issue when Oracle triggers "log file sync" wait event. The log file sync wait event is discussed later in the chapter.

As discussed earlier, if a latch is not available, the process goes into sleep mode for 1 centi-second and tries again; if not found, it goes into sleep again for 1 centi-second and then for 2 centi-seconds, with the wait time increasing through several iterations until such time the latch is obtained. Most of the time during a second or third iteration, the O/S makes the latch available to the process; however, this may not be always the case. Latches assigned to the process by the O/S also depend on the level of priority that the process is currently scheduled to run.

In an O/S such as Linux kernel 2.6, CPU and other resources are allocated to tasks or processes that are scheduled. Like memory, CPU is a shared resource for which processes contend for a slice of time to complete their operations. The O/S decides how to apportion this resource among all the processes. The scheduler is a component of the O/S that determines which process to run at any given time and how long to let it run. The scheduler gives the CPU to each process with highest priority for a brief period of time before switching to another process. This period is called a time quantum or time slice.[5]

The scheduler makes it possible to execute multiple programs at the same time, thus sharing the CPU with users of varying needs. Each task has a time slice that determines how much time it is permitted to execute and utilize the CPU resources. The first 100 priority lists of the run queue are reserved for real-time tasks, and the last 40 are used

---

[5]Uresh Vahalia, *UNIX Internals: The New Frontiers* (Prentice Hall, 1996).

for user tasks. During periods of heavy activity, if there is a shortage or high demand for resources, which process gets the available resource—such as CPU cycles—depends on where in the run queue the process is currently located, and this depends on the priority of the process. This means that scheduling delays and run queue lengths of the operating system affects the execution of tasks.

```
[oracle@ssky1l4p1 ~]$ ps -flcae | egrep "TTY|ora_d"

F S UID        PID  PPID CLS PRI ADDR SZ WCHAN  STIME TTY        TIME CMD

0 S oracle    6206     1 TS   19 - 382802 poll_s 01:53 ?      00:00:59 ora_diag_SSKYDB_2

0 S oracle    6212     1 TS   19 - 382177 semtim 01:53 ?      00:00:04 ora_dbrm_SSKYDB_2

0 S oracle    6224     1 TS   19 - 385078 poll_s 01:53 ?      00:02:56 ora_dia0_SSKYDB_2

0 S oracle    7616     1 TS   19 - 384140 semtim 01:57 ?      00:00:12 ora_dbw0_SSKYDB_2

0 S oracle    7671     1 TS   19 - 381931 epoll_ 01:57 ?      00:00:00 ora_d000_SSKYDB_2
```

Here is the description of the various columns:

- UID—The user that created the O/S process. In this case, Oracle user on the database cluster created the process.

- PID—Process ID. The PID is assigned by the O/S when the process is added to the run queue.

- PPID—Parent process ID. This Indicates these processes are children to those listed in the PID.

- CLS—Class of the process. The class is assigned to the process when the process starts execution by the application that starts it. In this case, Oracle assigns at what class the process should run. TS ("Time Sharing") is the default class. The other types of classes are RT ("Real Time"), RR ("Round Robin"), and FF (FIFO).

- PRI—Priority of the process. PRI indicates at what priority the process is currently executing. The priority also determines where in the run queue the process is placed and how soon and how much CPU the scheduler will assign the process.

- CMD—The actual command being executed by the process.

Classes

Depending on the O/S, UNIX or Linux, or the flavor of UNIX, there are several types of classes:

- Time sharing (TS)

- Fixed priority (FX)

- System (SYS)

- Real Time (RT)

- Round Robin (RR)

- First in First Out (FF)

Time Sharing

This is the default class for a process. When processes with the same priority are in run time mode, it changes the priorities dynamically to use the RR method. As discussed earlier, the scheduler allocates slices of time to a process, and this depends on the scheduling priority. Under this class, the processes that are scheduled with higher priority get larger time slices. This is based on the assumption that lower priority processes do not run often and should be given a larger quantum.

Fixed Priority

The priorities associated with the processes under this class are fixed. They did not dynamically change over the lifetime of the process. FX is normally present in operating systems such as Solaris and has a range of 0–59.

System

This class is used to schedule kernel processes. Processes in this class are bound, which means they run until they block or complete. SYS has a range of 60–99.

Real Time

The real time class uses priorities in the range of 100–159. They are higher compared to the time-sharing processes, which means the real time process will be scheduled before any kernel process.

Round Robin

Like the name "round robin," the different program/process takes turns using the resources of the computer to limit each process to a certain short time period, then suspends that process to give another process a turn (or "time slice").

First in First Out

This is probably the simplest type of scheduling algorithms available; and as the name suggests, the process or requests for CPU resources are queued in the order in which they arrive. Because of the nature in which they are received and processed, the rules are fixed, and no prioritization of the processes is possible. Each CPU has a run queue made up of 140 priority lists that are serviced in FIFO order. Every time a new task is scheduled for execution, it's added to the end of the task's respective run queue.

CPU utilization by a process can be determined using the "top" command on Linux and UNIX systems or with more details using the collectl, mpstat, sar, or the iostat commands.

```
[oracle@ssky1l4p1 ~]$ collectl -i 5
waiting for 5 second sample...
#<----CPU[HYPER]----><----------Disks----------><---------Network---------->
#cpu sys inter  ctxsw KBRead  Reads KBWrit Writes   KBIn  PktIn KBOut  PktOut
   1   0  1284  11041    100      8    338     33     75    157    60     144
   0   0  1329  10691     68      6    309     28     67    182    69     165
   0   0  1169  10590     97      8    123     12     69     96    53      83
```

```
[oracle@ssky1l4p1 ~]$ mpstat -P ALL
Linux 2.6.18-128.el5 (ssky1l4p1)        11/15/2013
12:10:27 PM  CPU  %user  %nice  %sys  %iowait  %irq  %soft  %steal  %idle   intr/s
12:10:27 PM  all   5.88   0.01  1.30    2.93   0.05   0.22   0.00   89.61  5684.01
12:10:27 PM    0   2.57   0.01  0.68    0.07   0.00   0.01   0.00   96.67  1000.20
12:10:27 PM    1   6.35   0.01  1.40   10.15   0.04   0.15   0.00   81.90   100.27
12:10:27 PM    2   3.03   0.01  0.75    3.59   0.01   0.05   0.00   92.56    38.04
12:10:27 PM    3   5.92   0.01  1.17    7.17   0.03   0.12   0.00   85.58    64.51
12:10:27 PM    4   1.83   0.01  0.56    0.69   0.00   0.02   0.00   96.90    18.18
12:10:27 PM    5   6.12   0.00  1.34    3.29   0.00   0.10   0.00   89.14     3.17
12:10:27 PM    6   1.89   0.01  0.55    0.72   0.00   0.01   0.00   96.81    17.04
12:10:27 PM    7   6.20   0.01  1.31    5.26   0.01   0.11   0.00   87.10    35.39
12:10:27 PM    8   2.45   0.01  0.63    0.05   0.00   0.01   0.00   96.85     0.00
12:10:27 PM    9   4.64   0.01  0.87    1.48   0.00   0.03   0.00   92.97    26.45
12:10:27 PM   10   4.22   0.01  1.83    0.37   0.00   0.04   0.00   93.53     1.48
12:10:27 PM   11   8.85   0.01  2.33    1.58   0.07   0.33   0.00   86.84   657.63
12:10:27 PM   12   2.96   0.01  0.86    0.10   0.00   0.01   0.00   96.06     1.69
12:10:27 PM   13  19.36   0.00  3.27    7.76   0.34   1.52   0.00   67.75  1531.39
12:10:27 PM   14   3.01   0.01  0.69    0.09   0.00   0.01   0.00   96.19     8.24
12:10:27 PM   15  14.61   0.01  2.62    4.59   0.22   0.96   0.00   76.99  2180.31

[mvallath@prddb1 mysql]$ sar -u 2 5
Linux 2.6.18-128.el5 (prddb1)     11/15/2010
01:07:03 PM    CPU   %user  %nice  %system  %iowait  %steal  %idle
01:07:05 PM    all   11.03   0.00    0.88    6.12    0.00   81.97
01:07:07 PM    all   12.43   0.00    1.81    6.28    0.00   79.48
01:07:09 PM    all   12.37   0.00    2.53    6.50    0.00   78.60
01:07:11 PM    all   13.78   0.00    1.84    6.22    0.00   78.16
01:07:13 PM    all   14.58   0.00    2.65    6.03    0.00   76.73
Average:       all   12.84   0.00    1.94    6.23    0.00   78.99
```

In the preceding output, **-u 2 5** reports CPU utilization. The following values are displayed:

- %user: Percentage of CPU utilization that occurred while executing at the user level (application)

- %nice: Percentage of CPU utilization that occurred while executing at the user level with nice priority

- %system: Percentage of CPU utilization that occurred while executing at the system level (kernel)

- %iowait: Percentage of time that the CPU or CPUs were idle, during which the system had an outstanding disk I/O request

- %idle: Percentage of time that the CPU or CPUs were idle and the system did not have an outstanding disk I/O request

While tuning, database systems latches are the least of anyone's concerns. Very little attention is given to tuning latches. Most of the time, resource contention and latch-related wait times would reduce when overall wait times are reduced, certain types of latches cannot be ignored.

As discussed earlier, high ratio value between gets and misses should be indicators to give closer attention to the latch-related wait numbers. The LOCATION column in V$LATCH_MISSES view provides better indication of the area where the latch contention occurs.

■ **Tip** Tanel Poder has an excellent latch profiler scripts (`latchprof.sql` and `latchprofx.sql`) on his web site (www.tanelpoder.com). These scripts help get to the data for analyzing these latch dependencies and contention.

Enqueues

Enqueues are also a type of locking mechanism used in Oracle. An enqueue is a more sophisticated mechanism that permits several concurrent processes to have varying degrees of sharing of "known" resources.[6] A lock is a resource that is used to get access to a resource that is requested by a process or session. Oracle has two kinds of locks: enqueues and latches. Although a request for a latch is quick and inexpensive type of lock, enqueues are more sophisticated locks for managing access to shared resources, for example, tables, rows, segments, transactions, and so forth. Enqueues help prevent more than one process from accessing the same data structure at a given time. Enqueues are queues, and using the FIFO method, requests are serviced in an arbitrary order. Similar to acquiring a latch (discussed later), Oracle tries to acquire an enqueue.

When access is required by a session, a lock structure is obtained and a request is made to acquire access to the resource at a specific level (mode). The lock structure is a three-level link lists placed on the acquirer, the waiter, and the convertor. The user lock details of the enqueue (TX [transaction], TM [DML], and UL [user defined]) are defined by the type of resource that requires the lock; the two lock identifier columns ID1 and ID2 have values that depend on the type of enqueue. Apart from this, there is a lock mode used by both the holder and requestor. The following are the different modes/requests (which is the description for the values from LMODE and REQUEST columns in V$LOCK view, in the script below):

- 0 = none
- 1 = null (NULL)
- 2 = row-S (SS)
- 3 = row-X (SX)
- 4 = share (S)
- 5 = S/Row-X (SSX)
- 6 = exclusive (X)

Script: MVRACPDnTap_lockmodes.sql

```
SELECT inst_id,
       sid,
       type,
       id1,
       id2,
       lmode,
       request,
       ctime,
       block
```

---

[6]Metalink Note # 22908.1. "What are Latches and What Causes Latch Contention." Accessed at metalink.oracle.com.

```
FROM   gv$lock;
```

INST_ID	SID	TY	ID1	ID2	LMODE	REQUEST	CTIME	BLOCK
1	10	RS	25	1	2	0	183030	2
1	239	XR	0	0	1	0	183148	2
1	10	XR	4	0	1	0	183148	2
1	10	RD	1	0	1	0	183146	2
1	9	DM	1	0	4	0	183021	2
1	9	MR	201	0	4	0	183023	2
1	10	CF	0	0	2	0	183038	2
1	247	RT	2	1	6	0	183023	2
1	9	RT	2	2	6	0	183023	2
1	249	TS	3	1	3	0	183004	2
1	241	KT	16749	0	4	0	48798	2
1	14	AE	133	0	4	0	182993	2
1	282	PS	1	32766	4	0	1	2
2	10	RS	25	1	2	0	183791	2
2	239	XR	0	0	1	0	183959	2
2	10	XR	4	0	1	0	183959	2
2	10	RD	1	0	1	0	183956	2
2	9	DM	1	0	4	0	183463	2
2	10	CF	0	0	2	0	183824	2
2	9	MR	201	8	4	0	183805	2
2	247	RT	1	0	6	0	183799	2
2	9	RT	1	2	6	0	183473	2
2	**269**	**TM**	**93128**	**0**	**3**	**0**	**0**	**2**
2	**37**	**TM**	**93128**	**0**	**3**	**0**	**0**	**2**
2	**289**	**TM**	**93128**	**0**	**0**	**3**	**0**	**0**
2	**280**	**TM**	**93120**	**0**	**3**	**0**	**0**	**2**

CTIME, displayed in seconds, is the time since the current lock mode was acquired/converted. The value of this column keeps increasing until such time that the lock is not converted.

The following query will give an overview of the locking and enqueue activity since the instance startup:

```
SELECT statistic#,
       name,
       class,
       value
FROM   v$sysstat
WHERE  class = 4;
```

STATISTIC#	NAME	CLASS	VALUE
38	enqueue timeouts	4	1057
39	enqueue waits	4	254192
40	enqueue deadlocks	4	0
41	enqueue requests	4	29103432
42	enqueue conversions	4	124263
43	enqueue releases	4	29102329
72	max cf enq hold time	4	65700
73	total cf enq hold time	4	2615250
74	total number of cf enq holders	4	8104

In the preceding output, the enqueue timeouts gives the total number of enqueue operations that could not complete successfully and was timed out before the request was completed. The counters include both the get and convert requests.

Enqueue waits show the total number of times the sessions had to wait for an enqueue.

Enqueue deadlocks output shows the number of times a deadlock had occurred. This value should not be ignored; the system/application/trace files should be checked to understand what's causing the deadlocks. Almost always, deadlocks indicate inefficient SQL operations and poor business logic.

Enqueue requests and enqueue releases show how many locks are currently requested and released. The difference between the two values should be the total number of locks currently being held. This value should normally be close to the number of locks received from V$LOCK view.

Enqueue conversions indicate the number of lock conversions that have occurred. Basically, this indicates the number of times the lock was requested in a mode and then later converted to another mode due to operation change requirements, for example, when the session changed its SQL operation from a SELECT to an UPDATE operation.

In an Oracle RAC environment, there are two types of enqueues: the enqueues that are specific to a RAC environment and those that apply to a single-instance environment. However, both types of enqueues can have a higher impact in a RAC environment. In this section, we try to analyze few of the enqueues.

Script: MVRACPDnTap_EnqStats.sql

```
SELECT inst_id       INT,
       eq_name,
       eq_type       EQ,
       req_reason    RR,
       total_req#    TR,
       total_wait#   TW,
       succ_req#     SR,
       failed_req#   FR,
       cum_wait_time CWT
FROM   gv$enqueue_statistics
WHERE  total_req# > 100
ORDER  BY inst_id,
          cum_wait_time DESC;
```

INT	EQ NAME	EQ	RR	TR	TW	SR	FR	CWT
2	Transaction	TX	row lock conte	10450	10417	10450	0	1153800
	Multiple Object Reuse	RO	fast object re	1520	414	1520	0	125560
	Process Startup	PR	contention	588	14	588	0	114140
	KSV slave startup	PV	syncstart	355	3	355	0	84290
	PX Process Reservation	PS	contention	4261	2302	4249	12	11630
	DML	TM	contention	434473	120	434468	0	10080
	Controlfile Transaction	CF	contention	12899	178	12875	24	9950
	Transaction	TX	index contenti	171	168	171	0	8000
	Format Block	FB	contention	484	224	484	0	2490
	Reuse Block Range	CR	block range re	1162	12	1162	0	1890
	SGA Log Operation	MC	Securefile log	2318	5	2318	0	1020
	Transaction	TX	contention	106432	1	106405	35	430
	Job Scheduler	JS	queue lock	62151	5	62151	0	230
	Temp Object	TO	contention	542	57	542	0	180
	Segment High Water Mark	HW	contention	289	23	289	0	90

In a RAC environment, the LMD background process demonstrates enqueue activity. When more and more users submit requests that are to be completed by the LMS process while the LMS is busy catering to other user requests, the LMD will enqueue/queue these requests until such time that the LMS has completed its requests and is ready to accept new requests. Some of the commonly encountered enqueues are listed in Table 17-1.

Table 17-1. *Enqueues*

Enqueue	Name	Resource	Description
TS	Temporary Segment	Contention	Serializes accesses to temp segment
WF	AWR Flush	Contention	The enqueue is used to serialize the flushing of snapshots
CF	Control file Transaction	Contention	Synchronizes accesses to the control file
PS	PX Process Reservation	Contention	Parallel Execution Server Process reservation and synchronization
PV	KSV slave startup	Syncstart	Synchronizes slave start_shutdown
TX	Transaction	Index Contention	Lock held on an index during a split to prevent other operations on it
SQ	Sequence cache	Contention	Lock to ensure that only one process can replenish the sequence cache
PS	PX Process Reservation	Contention	Parallel Execution Server Process reservation and synchronization
DF	Datafile Online in RAC	Contention	Enqueue held by foreground or DBWR when a datafile is brought online in RAC
RD	RAC Load	RAC Load	Update RAC load info
HW	Segment High Water Mark	Contention	Lock used to broker the high water mark during parallel inserts

We now discuss a few of the common enqueues found in a RAC environment.

TX—Transaction

As soon as a transaction is started, a TX enqueue is needed. A session can be waiting on a TX enqueue for several reasons:

- **row lock contention**—Another session is locking the requested row. These locks are more prominently visible in a RAC environment when multiple instances try to access the same row from the block.

- **index contention**—When a transaction is inserting a row in an index, it would have to wait for an index block split operation being done by another transaction.

- **allocate ITL entry**—There is no free ITL (interested transaction list) in the block header because one or more other sessions have rows locked in the same block.

Among the various reasons listed, lack of ITLs could be the initial reason for high TX enqueues. Normally, ITLs are added dynamically; however, there could be insufficient free space in the block to add an ITL.

Large objects with several concurrent transactions and with a high DML operation are candidates for low ITLs. Normal practices followed by administrators to help reduce ITL related latch or contention is to increase the INITRANS parameter at the object level. INITRANS is set by default to 1 for the table and 2 for indexes. For very large objects, this should be increased after checking the V$SEGMENT_STATISTICS view for segments with high "ITL waits." Almost always a small increase in the INITRANS should help resolve this issue. On the contrary, increasing this to very large numbers could also have impacts in other areas of performance.

DATA BLOCK FORMAT

Figure 17-1 illustrates the data block format dissection. The data block consists of two major sections: the header and the body or data layer. The header contains the cache layer, a fixed transaction layer, and a variable transaction layer. The body consists of various sections of the physical data and free space. The variable transaction layer is of importance in our discussion here. The variable transaction layer consists of 24 bytes and represents one ITL.

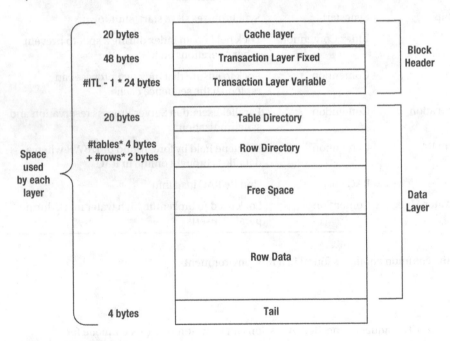

Figure 17-1. *Data block structure*

The number of ITLs allocated is determined by the parameter INITRANS. This happens during a CREATE/ALTER TABLE/CLUSTER/INDEX DDL operations. If no value is specified, Oracle allocates a default value of 1 for tables and 2 for indexes. After the initial allocation, subsequent changes will take effect only on new data blocks. Whereas INITRANS limits the initial number of transactions, the maximum number of transactions is preset by Oracle to 255 (in earlier releases, the MAXTRANS parameter helped set this value; the MAXTRANS parameter is now depreciated).

Increasing the value of INITRANS would mean the space would be moved from the data block free space into the header section, leaving less room to contain the physical data.

Less data in each block would mean more blocks to be read from disk and more data transfers when blocks are transferred over the interconnect.

When the ITL area cannot be extended, either because there is no additional space in the block or the max preset value of 255 is reached, the process waits for an existing ITL to be freed. This wait time is reflected as TX enqueue waits.

INITRANS should be selectively increased for segments that have high ITL waits when the V$SEGMENT_STATISTIC view is queried.

TM—DML (Table)

Every time a session wants to lock a table, a TM enqueue is requested. If a session deletes a row in the parent table (DEPT), and a referential constraint (foreign key) is created without an index on the child table (EMP), or if the session is updating the column(s) that the foreign key references to, a share lock (level 4) is taken on the child table. If another session tries to make changes to the child table, the requesting session will have to wait (the enqueue request is in row exclusive mode). If an index is created on the child table's foreign-key column, then no share lock is required on the child table.

ST—Space Management Transaction

The ST enqueue is held every time the session is allocating/de-allocating extents. Operations such as coalescing, drop/ truncate segments, and disk sorting are candidates that require Oracle to create an ST enqueue lock. If the session gets a timeout when requesting the ST enqueue, "ORA-1575 timeout waiting for space management" is returned.

HW—Segment High Water Mark

High water marks are markers placed by Oracle on the storage segments to indicate the highest point in the segment that has been used. When a table is created for the first time, and there are no rows, the high water mark is in the beginning of the segment. As more and more rows get inserted, the high water mark will be moved up to the highest used segment. However, as illustrated in Figure 17-2, when rows are deleted the high water mark will not be moved down until such time that the table is rebuilt, truncated, or shrunk (reorganized).

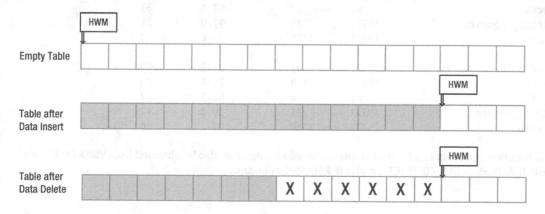

Figure 17-2. *Depiction of high water mark (HWM)*

This enqueue is used by the space management layer of the Oracle kernel. High water mark enqueues are locks placed on segments while this occurs it acquires free spaces /extent the segment to insert rows into the table.

SQ—Sequence Number

Sequence numbers are used to generate surrogate keys when inserting data into tables to form primary key indexes. To help improve overall performance, the cache clause preallocates a set of sequence numbers on respective instances in the cluster. This helps keep sequence numbers in memory to help with faster access when required by user sessions. However, when these cache values are depleted, a new set of values will be cached. Frequent cache duplication from multiple instances and frequent requests for new values to be cached causes Oracle to generate SQ enqueues when the dictionary needs to be updated with the new max value.

Applications that perform high insert operations to the database need to have higher values of sequence numbers to reduce contention when updates are made to the dictionary. The sequence refresh rates could be determined by checking the V$ROWCACHE view. In the following output, dc_sequences show high updates almost equal to the GETS column, which means that almost always, every time a sequence was required, the database sequence had to be accessed:

Script: MVRACPDnTap_rowcache.sql

```
SELECT inst_id int
     , parameter
     , sum(gets) gets
     , sum(getmisses) misses
     , 100*sum(gets - getmisses) / sum(gets)  pct_succ_gets
     , sum(modifications)  updates
  FROM GV$ROWCACHE
 WHERE gets > 0
   HAVING sum(modifications) > 0
 GROUP BY INST_ID, parameter
 ORDER BY inst_id,
        6 desc;
```

In	PARAMETER	GETS	MISSES	PCT_SUCC_GETS	UPDATES
1	dc_histogram_defs	93039	8807	90.5	815
	dc_sequences	23432	5480	76.6	23432
	dc_objects	63	27	57.1	63
	dc_rollback_segments	16549	21	99.9	21
	dc_segments	17404	1771	89.8	4
2	dc_histogram_defs	109521	6293	94.3	1060
	dc_sequences	16049	4159	74.1	16049
	dc_objects	67	26	61.2	67
	dc_rollback_segments	19312	31	99.8	42
	dc_segments	15475	1510	90.2	16

RAC level contention and global cache related row cache information can also be obtained from V$ROWCACHE view by querying the DLM_REQUESTS, DLM_CONFLICTS, and DLM_RELEASES columns.

Script: MVRACPDnTap_dlmrowcache.sql

```
SELECT  inst_id INT,
        parameter,
        dlm_requests,
        dlm_conflicts,
        dlm_releases
FROM    gv$rowcache
WHERE   dlm_requests > 1000
ORDER   BY inst_id,
           dlm_requests desc,
           dlm_conflicts desc;
```

In	PARAMETER	DLM_REQUESTS	DLM_CONFLICTS	DLM_RELEASES
1	dc_histogram_defs	8429505	61653	1917642
	dc_objects	1507367	14260	511584
	dc_segments	1246299	10924	377148
	outstanding_alerts	851238	413316	5270
	dc_tablespace_quotas	520598	27608	215
	dc_sequences	46137	5052	410
	dc_constraints	14669	89	1017
	dc_users	4713	12	4512
2	dc_histogram_defs	3349862	69089	1284916
	dc_objects	1083807	13353	706857
	dc_segments	1016777	10883	556050
	outstanding_alerts	848524	416058	1172
	dc_tablespace_quotas	332066	24337	134
	dc_sequences	31688	3808	325
	dc_constraints	12665	118	821
	dc_users	4000	21	3764

CF—Control File Transaction

The CF enqueue is placed by Oracle during any operation that requires reading or making changes to the control file. CF enqueues are used to serialize control file transactions and read write operations on shared operations of the control file. This is more prominently visible in a RAC environment when multiple instances share one control file and need to update/write to the control file when there are structure changes to the database such as adding tablespace and or datafile, during redo log switch or checkpoint, and during startup and shutdown of the database. The SCN information for all transactions required for data recovery and the master SCN number is also managed and maintained in the control file.

Waits

A wait event in Oracle is a situation when a session puts itself to sleep to wait for some external event to happen. Wait events are classified based on what resource level the wait has occurred at: system, service, CPU, and so forth. Wait events can also be classified based on what type of resource it's waiting for; idle waits occur when a session is waiting for a work request to be issued. Non-idle or Service wait events are waits for the system to perform asynchronous operations such as I/O or process creation.

Oracle provides visibility and instrumentation to these resource related matrix via the Oracle wait interface (OWI). OWI is driven by the three primary views—GV$SYSTEM_EVENT, GV$SESSION_EVENT, and GV$SESSION_WAIT. These views provide wait times at the system level or at the individual session level. To isolate waits, a specific set of modules or sessions grouped into services within application wait times could be queried using GV$SERVICE_EVENT.

Wait events are classified into wait classes; this helps in grouping wait events and helps directing tuning efforts to the various areas of the environment. The following query (Table 17-2) illustrates the number of wait events grouped under the various wait classes.

```
SELECT WAIT_CLASS,
       COUNT(*)
FROM   V$SYSTEM_EVENT
GROUP BY WAIT_CLASS;
```

Table 17-2. *Wait Count by Wait Class*

WAIT_CLASS	12cR1 Count	11gR2 Count	12cR1 Count
Concurrency	20	12	14
User I/O	17	12	14
System I/O	14	11	10
Administrative	11	1	1
Configuration	12	6	8
Scheduler	2	1	1
Other	203	152	160
Application	8	9	7
Cluster	24	24	21
Idle	43	33	40
Commit	1	1	1
Network	3	3	1

Almost all wait events have direct or indirect impact in a RAC environment; however, for our purposes, we discuss few of the wait events[7] that belong to the Cluster class.

Oracle RAC events have some intelligence built into their structure, meaning there is a built-in format to the structure. Figure 17-3 illustrates the format of the wait event.

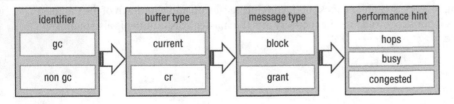

Figure 17-3. *RAC wait event structure*

---

[7]For single-instance-related wait events, please refer to the book *Oracle Wait Interface: A Practical Guide To Performance Diagnostics & Tuning* (2004, Oracle Press) by Richmond Shee, Kirtikumar Deshpande, and K. Gopalakrishnan.

Figure 17-3 illustrates four sections of the wait event. Section 1 is a basic identifier, which shows if the wait event is RAC related. RAC related wait events start with an identifier of gc. The second section differentiates what kind buffer the wait event is related to: current or consistent read (cr). The third section provides an indication on the type of message the wait event will cover: if the wait event is block activity related or privilege and access related such as grants. The fourth section of the event name indicates/reflects on the type of operation, such as network-related hops (two way and three way), busy or congested.

As discussed earlier, wait event information can be obtained by querying three primary views: GV$SYSTEM_EVENT, GV$SESSION_EVENT, and GV$SESSION_WAIT. The V$SESSION_WAIT event has a few important columns, described in Table 17-3.

Table 17-3. *Structure of V$SESSION_WAIT View*

Column Name	Description
WAIT_CLASS	Name of class the event is grouped under
EVENT	Name of event
P1	File #
P2	Block #
P3	Mode requested/mode held/block class
SECONDS_IN_WAIT	Amount of time waited for the current event
STATE	Current wait state

The following query will extract the preceding information for the current wait events:

```
SELECT  inst_id,
        sid,
        event,
        wait_class,
        p1,
        p2,
        p3,
        seconds_in_wait
FROM    gv$session_wait
WHERE   event LIKE 'gc%'


  INST_ID   SID EVENT                    WAIT_CLASS              P1          P2          P3 SWAIT
---------- ----- ------------------------ --------------- ---------- ---------- ---------- -----
        2    37 gc current request       Cluster                  7         306    33554433     0
        2   240 gcs log flush sync       Other                   30           0         138     0
        2   269 gc buffer busy acquire   Cluster                  7         306           1     0
        2   280 gc buffer busy release   Cluster                  7         159           1     0
        1    27 gc buffer busy acquire   Cluster                  7         159           1     0
        1   244 gcs log flush sync       Other                   30           0         138     0
        1   265 gc current request       Cluster                  7         159    33554433     0
```

From the preceding output, using the data in P1 and P2, the related object information could be obtained using the following query:

```
SELECT segment_name
FROM   dba_extents
WHERE  file_id = &file
       AND &block BETWEEN block_id AND block_id + blocks - 1
       AND ROWNUM = 1;
Enter value for file: 7
Enter value for block: 159
old   3: where file_id = &FILE and &BLOCK between block_id and block_id + blocks - 1 and rownum = 1
new   3: where file_id = 7 and 159 between block_id and block_id + blocks - 1 and rownum = 1

SEGMENT_NAME
----------------------------------------------------------------------------
WAREHOUSE
```

Current and CR (consistent read) waits are based on current and CR blocks in the buffer of various instances. What is the difference between CR and current waits?

Consistent Read vs. Current

The very first time a block is read into a buffer of any participating instance, it's termed a current block, no matter what the purpose of the user accessing the block may be: meaning it could be a SELECT operation or a DML operation. The first access is always termed a current operation. Subsequently, a CR block is when the block is transferred from one instance to another instance because a session on that instance requested the block.

As discussed in Chapter 2, when a block is required by a process for read purposes, it accesses the block in shared mode. When the block is to be modified, the processes would require a grant from the GCS to access this block in exclusive mode. The frequency of state/grant changes to the block can be obtained by querying STATE column from GV$BH view. The RAC-related state changes are the following:[8]

- XCUR—exclusive current

- SCUR—shared current

- CR—consistent read

- READ—reading from disk

- WRITE—write clone mode

- PI—past image

When blocks are required by more than one process on the same instance, Oracle will clone the block. The number of times a block can be cloned is defined by the parameter _DB_BLOCK_MAX_CR_DBA[9] and defaults to six, meaning only six cloned copies of the same block of the same DBA (data block address) can exist in the local buffer of an instance. The CR blocks are treated like any other data block and use the Touch Count Algorithm (TCA). Under *TCA, the block read is placed at midpoint (insertion point) in the buffer cache and will have to gain creditability when sessions access or touch the block to climb up the stack to reach the hot buffer area. If the block is not touched by other sessions, it will move down the stack and finally get flushed out when new blocks need the buffer.*

---

[8]Tierney, Brian L., Jason R. Lee, Dan Gunter, Martin Stoufer, and Tom Dunigan, "Improving Distributed Application Performance Using TCP Instrumentation." Berkeley, CA: Lawrence Berkeley National Laboratory, May 2003.
[9]Underscore parameters should be modified only after consulting with Oracle support.

Similarly, when blocks are required by more than one other instance, Oracle will ship an image of the CR block (if it has not already done so) to the requesting instance. As we discussed in Chapter 2, blocks are shipped from one instance to another (illustrated in Figure 17-4); and the details regarding which instance contains the block are maintained in the GRD. The number of instances a block can exist is determined by the parameter _FAIRNESS_THRESHOLD[10] parameter and defaults to four, meaning only four images of the same block of a particular DBA can exist in a RAC cluster (irrespective of the number of instances) at any given point in time.

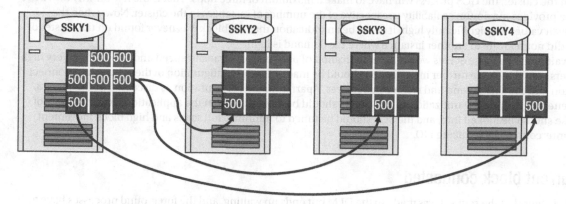

Figure 17-4. *Block cloning and imaging*

Once the holder reaches the threshold defined by the parameter _FAIRNESS_THRESHOLD, it stops making more copies, flushes the redo to the disk, and downgrades the locks.[11]

■ **Note**   Whereas data movement in a RAC environment is at the block level, data modifications are all at the row level (same as in a single-instance configuration).

Cluster Waits

In this section, we discuss a few of the common cluster-related wait events.

gc cr/current block two-way/three-way

One primary function of a cluster environment is to share blocks between instances, minimizing access to the physical storage. When a block is required by a session and it's not found in the local cache, it has to be requested either from another instance (current holder) or the disk. The time the session has to wait for the block is recorded in one of the transfer wait events depending on where the block was currently being held and how many hops the request passed through to complete the operation. For example, a two-way event indicates that there was a two-way shipment to transfer the block and that the requester sends a message to the master and the master ships the block back to the requestor. Similarly, a three-way event indicates that there were three hops before the block was received by the requestor.

---

[10]Underscore parameters should be modified only after consulting with Oracle support.
[11]Tierney, Brian L., Jason R. Lee, Dan Gunter, Martin Stoufer, and Tom Dunigan, "Improving Distributed Application Performance Using TCP Instrumentation." Berkeley, CA: Lawrence Berkeley National Laboratory, May 2003.

In the RAC architecture, to get a block, the GCS may usually have to perform two hops if the block requested cannot be found on the local instance: two hops because if the master is located on the instance where the demand for the blocks concerning a specific object is the highest, and hence most likely, the block is going to be present where the master is located. When the demand for the blocks concerning the object increases on another instance, the master will dynamically move/relocate to this new instance. Only when blocks are not found on the master does the GCS need to direct the transfer from another instance or from disk (three hops). Irrespective of the number of instances in the cluster, the GCS process will have to make a maximum of three hops. That is the reason why the RAC's architecture provides maximum scalability irrespective of the number of instances in the cluster. Now, when the three-way wait values are significantly high, it could be an indication that the block was never found on the master or the master did not relocate to another instance where the demand is high.

High wait times for these events would be an indication of poor network transfer speed and bandwidth. Very high wait numbers would indicate further investigation should be made into the configuration of the private interconnect configuration and the socket send and receive buffer sizes. Apart from the configuration as discussed in Chapter 13, the run queue length and CPU utilization of the servers should be looked at. From the application level, hot spots of the database should be looked into, and the SQL should be tuned to minimize full scans and high block movement across the interconnect by reducing LIO.

gc cr/current block congested

This wait indicates that the request was made to the DLM but ends up waiting, and the foreground processes have to retry the request. Under these circumstances, the "gc cr/current block congested" wait counter is incremented.

Normally this indicates that the GCS process (LMSn background) is not able to keep up with the requests. LMSn is a single threaded synchronous process and follows the FIFO algorithm to complete block requests. This means that when multiple requests are received, the GES will place the requests in a queue and send the request to the LMSn process when it has completed a previous operation. In such situations, considerations should be given to increase the number of LMSn processes using the parameter GCS_SERVER_PROCESSES. Performance implications of setting a high value for this parameter are discussed in Chapter 13.

LMSn processing delays due to frequent interrupts by other high priority processes and LMS being overloaded, making it unable to keep up with requests, could be indications for high wait times. Almost always this is the result of scheduling delays and high queue lengths experienced by the node at the O/S level.

RAC has several other types of wait events. For a better understanding, in Figure 17-5 the global cache related wait events have been grouped by the resource area they impact.

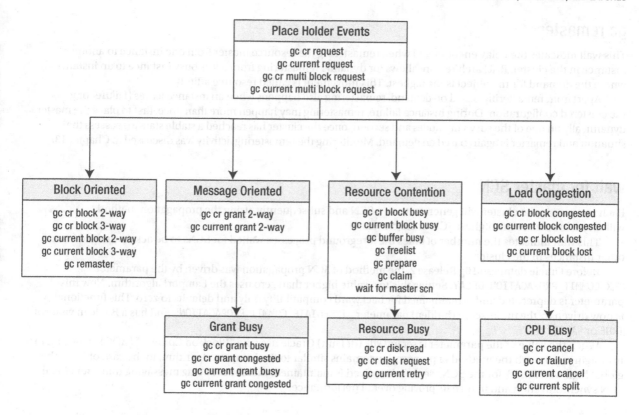

Figure 17-5. *Wait events grouped*[12]

gc buffer busy

gc buffer busy waits are normally global-level issues of buffer busy waits noticed on single-instance Oracle databases. Buffer busy waits are caused by frequent requests for buffer space, and Oracle is unable to acquire such buffer space and goes into wait mode. Poorly written SQL statements that perform high LIO are the reasons for high wait times.

In a RAC environment, multiple waiters maybe queuing for the same block that has a global operation pending for both the requestor and holder of the block. The wait times could also be caused by high network latencies and slow service times of the servers. A user trying to pin a buffer that is globally busy will have to wait until the block has arrived and the waiter at the head of the queue has released the buffer or the remote user has given up the buffer.

Whereas in the earlier releases of Oracle, buffer busy waits in a RAC environment were grouped under this wait event, starting with Oracle database 11g Release 2, the "gc buffer busy" waits are categorized into two new wait categories:

- gc buffer busy acquire
- gc buffer busy release

The classification here is based on if the request was made from the local instance of the requestor, in which case the session will wait on "gc buffer busy acquire." If the request was made from the remote instance, the current instance will wait on "gc buffer busy release" event.

---

[12]Vallath, Murali. *Oracle 10g RAC Grid, Services & Clustering*. Digital Press, 2007.

gc remaster

This wait indicates the delay encountered when remastering the resource master from one instance to another instance in the cluster. RAC architecture allows for dynamic remastering from a less busy instance to an instance where the demand for the object is the highest. This movement is called resource affinity.

Apart from remastering based on demand, remastering also happens when an instance leaves (failure) or joins the clustered configuration. During instance failure, remastering may happen more than once, first to place the master dynamically on one of the surviving nodes and second, once the cluster has reached a stable state to reassess the situation and remaster is again based on demand. Monitoring the remastering activity was discussed in Chapter 13.

wait for master SCN

Each instance in the cluster will generate its own SCN and subsequently, using the propagation method, will resynchronize to the highest SCN in the cluster.

This wait indicates the number of times the foreground processes waited for SCNs to be acknowledged from other instances in the cluster.

Before Oracle database 10g Release 2, the method of SCN propagation was driven by the parameter MAX_COMMIT_PROPAGATION_DELAY. Setting this to a value higher than zero uses the Lamport algorithm. Now this parameter is deprecated and is maintained for backward compatibility only and defaults to zero. This functionality is now driven by the underscore (hidden) parameter _IMMEDIATE_COMMIT_PROPAGATION[13] and has a Boolean value of TRUE or FALSE.

When the value of the parameter is set to TRUE (default) Oracle uses the "Block on Commit" (BOC) algorithm for messaging. Although the method of propagation remains similar to the Lamport algorithm, in the case of BOC, the global high water mark for the SCNs sent and received is maintained, thereby reducing messaging traffic for global SCN synchronization and in turn improving overall performance.

gc cr/current request

This event indicates the time waited when a session is looking for a CR version of a block and cannot find it in its local cache and so has made a request to a remote instance for the block. However, the transferred block has not yet arrived at the requesting instance. The event ends when the requesting session gets the block or permission to read the block from disk. This is normally a placeholder event, and the times here are cumulative of wait times for all other wait events that had an impact on the operations. Placeholder wait events are transient (illustrated in Figure 17-5) and are part of every view that captures active wait information.

gc current/cr block busy

This wait indicates that a current or CR block was requested and received but was not sent immediately by LMSn because some special condition that delayed the sending was found. Wait times for these events are dominated by block flush times (log file sync) and the defer time for the current blocks. Increased wait times are indications of high concurrency and block contention and are caused by high I/O and overall system load.

Querying GV$INSTANCE_CACHE_TRANSFER view would help determine instances involved in high current and CR block activity. Reducing log file sync times by monitoring the LGWR I/O and DBWR latencies would also help in determining some of the performance bottlenecks that are causes for high wait times.

At the database level, tuning SQL statements by using sparse blocks, sequence number ranges, or by hash partitioned indexes would help improve wait times.

---

[13]Underscore parameters should be modified only after consulting with Oracle support.

DEFER TIME

When a current block is requested, LMS may defer the shipping of the block to the requestor if the cleanout of the block is pending. This defer time maybe as high 30 ms or the value specified by the GC_DEFER_TIME parameter. The default value of this parameter is 3 milliseconds.

The hidden parameter _GC_DEFER_TIME defines the time that a LMS process grants to a user process to complete the transaction before starting to down-convert the lock and sending the block to a requestor on another instance.

---

gc current/cr grant

This wait indicates that the block access grant was received. However, the block was not present on the local instance of the requestor. The wait time only indicates the time to provide access from the remote instance or read the block from disk.

High wait times would indicate network transfer speed and bandwidth, high context switching at the O/S level of the instances involved in the transfer, and overall load on the servers. Tuning SQL statements to reduce high buffer activity due to high LIO would help reduce wait times for this event.

gc current grant busy

This wait indicates that a current block was requested and a grant message received. The busy hint implies that the request was blocked because others were ahead of it or it could not be handled immediately. This normally occurs when the current block is shared by several instances, and the requestor is waiting for exclusive access to this block. All holders of the block would have to release this block before exclusive access (S to X conversion) can be granted to the requestor.

High wait times on this event would indicate tuning SQL statements and database objects involved in frequent block activity (hot blocks) should be monitored. Almost always environments where multiple instances are inserting rows (highly insert intensive batch loads) could cause index block splits and could be the primary reason for high wait times for this event.

gc current/cr multiblock request

Oracle is attempting to read multiple blocks into one message to save on CPU. This read process may include either grants or blocks. These requests are usually caused by a full table scan or index full scan. If the request involves "current" blocks, the space management layer would setup multiblock requests when viewing blocks with contiguous data block addresses.

Multiblock requests normally don't cause any additional performance issues unless there are transmission issues over the interconnect and blocks are lost. In that case, there would be performance degradation, followed by gc cr failure and cr request retry activities.

gc current/cr lost blocks

Data is transferred over the interconnect; however, the data does not reach the target server, but the data was lost during transmission. When blocks are lost or corrupt over the interconnect, the GCS process will retransmit the block to the requestor; this would mean the requestor would wait for a longer duration until such time as the block is received.

Occasionally, a few blocks being lost ("hiccups") over the interconnect may not affect the overall performance. It's when blocks are consistently being lost on a continuous basis that diagnosis should look at getting to the root cause of the issue. Blocks lost over the interconnect could be due to one or more of many reasons and should be addressed to avoid poor response times for the users. The following query will help check for lost blocks:

Script: MVRACPDnTap_lostblocks.sql

```
SELECT A1.inst_id,
       A3.instance_name,
       A3.host_name,
       A3.startup_time,
       ROUND(SYSDATE - startup_time)                        "Days",
       ROUND(( SYSDATE - startup_time ) * 24)               "Hours",
       A1.value                                             "BLKL",
       A1.value / ( ROUND(( SYSDATE - startup_time ) * 24) ) "Perhr",
       A2.value                                             "BLKC"
FROM   gv$sysstat A1,
       gv$sysstat A2,
       gv$instance A3
WHERE  A1.name = 'gc blocks lost'
AND    A2.name = 'gc blocks corrupt'
AND    A1.inst_id = A2.inst_id
AND    A1.inst_id = A3.instance_number
ORDER  BY 1;
```

Ins ID	Instance Name	Host Name	Instance Startup Time	Uptime (Days)	Uptime (Hours)	Blocks Lost	Blks Lost Per Hour	Blocks Corrupt
1	SSKYDB_1	ssky4l4p3.localdomain	28-MAR-14 11:56:42	1	35	839	24	0
2	SSKYDB_2	ssky4l4p2.localdomain	28-MAR-14 12:06:49	1	35	36	1	0
3	SSKYDB_3	ssky4l4p4.localdomain	28-MAR-14 12:26:43	1	35	101	3	0
4	SSKYDB_4	ssky4l4p1.localdomain	28-MAR-14 12:15:59	1	35	98	3	0

There are several areas that may be the reason for blocks being lost over the interconnect:

- Faulty or poorly configured cables/cards/switches

- Poorly sized UDP receive buffer sizes and/or UDP buffer socket overflows

- Poor interconnect performance and high CPU utilization: netstat -s reports packet reassembly failures

- Network packet corruption resulting from UDP checksum errors and/or send/receive transmission errors

- Mismatched MTU sizes in the communication path

- Interconnect LAN non-dedicated

- Lack of server/switch adjacency

- Outdated network driver or NIC firmware

- Proprietary interconnect link transport and network protocol

- Misconfigured bonding/link aggregation

- Misconfigured jumbo frames

- NIC force full duplex and duplex mode mismatch

- Flow control mismatch in the interconnect communication path

- Packet drop at the O/S, NIC, or switch layer

- NIC driver/firmware configuration

- NIC send and receive queue lengths

- High CPU usage and scheduling latencies

gc current retry

A current block was requested; however, the requested block was not received due to a failure status either because the block was corrupted or the block was lost during transmission over the interconnect. Reasons for the failure to receive the block could be one or many of the reasons listed previously under the "gc current/cr blocks lost" event.

gc cr failure

This is similar to the gc current retry wait event, but in this case, "cr" block was requested. However, a failure status was received either because the block was corrupted or the block was lost during transmission over the interconnect. Reasons for the failure to receive the block could be one or many of the reasons listed previously under the "gc current/cr blocks lost" event.

Mutex Waits

Mutex waits refers to waits resources associated with the management of cursor objects in the shared pool during parsing. Mutex is a type of latch and was introduced with Oracle Database 10g Release 2. Similar to latches and other type of waits, these are excessive waits causing contention and performance problems in Oracle database systems.

Mutex contention is normally a CPU-using resource; and high mutex-related contention can cause excessive CPU usage and impact user response times. Mutexes are local to the instance in a RAC environment. Mutex waits are characterized by sessions waiting for one or more of the following events:

- cursor: mutex X—Cursor is being parsed and is trying to get the cursor mutex in exclusive mode.

- cursor: mutex S—Cursor is parsed and is trying to get the cursor mutex in share mode.

- cursor: pin S—Cursor is being parsed and trying to get the cursor pin in shared mode. There are currently no concurrent X holders, but the cursor could not acquire the mutex immediately. The wait time indicates the sessions have to increment the mutex reference count and requires performing an exclusive atomic update to the mutex structure.

- cursor: pin X—Cursor is being parsed and trying to get the cursor pin in exclusive mode.

- cursor: pin S wait on X—Cursor is being parsed and has the cursor pin and is trying to get the mutex in shared mode; however, another session is currently holding the same mutex in exclusive mode. The session continues to wait for the current holder to release the mutex.

The following query will help determine the current number of gets and sleeps for the various mutex wait events just described:

```
SELECT  to_char(SYSDATE, 'HH:MI:SS')  time,
        kglnahsh                       hash,
        SUM(sleeps)                    sleeps,
        location,
        mutex_type,
        substr(kglnaobj, 1, 40)        object
FROM    x$kglob,
        v$mutex_sleep_history
WHERE   kglnahsh = mutex_identifier
GROUP   BY kglnaobj,
        kglnahsh,
        location,
        mutex_type
ORDER   BY sleeps
```

Similar to latches we discussed earlier, when resources are not available, sessions requesting for a mutex also go into a sleep mode. If a session tries to get a mutex but another session is already holding it, then the get request cannot be granted, and the session requesting the mutex will "spin" for the mutex a number of times in the hope that it will be quickly freed. During each spin, the session will check if the mutex has been freed. If not freed by the end of the spinning, the session waits.[14]

Conclusion

In this chapter, we looked at three primary performance areas. Oracle provides sufficient instrumentation into these areas to help diagnose and troubleshoot the resource limitations. Performance of systems is affected by lack of resources. When a session is unable to complete a request because it is not able to obtain the required resource, it waits. The session waits, hoping it will get the required resources in a sufficiently fair amount of time. However, when this does not happen, it waits for a period of time. When the wait period increases, it can begin a chain of events causing several sessions to wait and thus slowing the entire system down. OWI is almost always sufficient to get to the bottom of most of the performance concerns. However, other areas discussed in this chapter, such as the mutex waits, latches, and enqueues, are all types of waits and have their own roles; and Oracle provides instrumentation to collect statistics to support their findings. Although this chapter provides overall guidance to the various interfaces, and more specifically toward RAC, it does not provide complete reference. Readers are advised to refer to the *Oracle Wait Interface: A Practical Guide To Performance Diagnostics & Tuning* (2004, Oracle Press) by Richmond Shee, Kirtikumar Deshpande, and K. Gopalakrishnan book from for a more detailed discussion on this subject.

---

[14]Metalink Note # 1377998.1. "Troubleshooting: Waits for Mutex Type Events."

CHAPTER 18

■ ■ ■

Problem Diagnosis

How many times did DBAs have to open priority one service requests with Oracle support for critical errors faced while supporting their production environments? Errors are bound to happen, and as much as we would all like to see it, there is no such thing as the perfect application that is bug free. Critical errors can be caused by a misconfiguration or uncontrolled environments or due to human error; but when it occurs, they interrupt production, cause downtime, and slow performance that affects the credibility of the DBA, the system administrators, or the application in general. So it's important that when problems do arise there is an immediate remedy, the database is operational immediately, and that the error has fixes in the form of patches or code, operational procedures, or configuration changes that ensure the errors do not happen again.

RAC is a multi-instance clustered configuration. As discussed in the previous chapters, apart from single-instance-related issues, RAC could have issues across multiple instances; or a problem on one node can cause a problem on another node However, on the positive side, the advantage of using RAC over single-instance configuration is that if one instance fails or is unhealthy, there is always another instance that users can connect to and use the database.

To help the DBA troubleshoot issues with the environment, Oracle provides utilities that help gather statistics across all instances. Most of the utilities that focus on database performance-related statistics were discussed in Chapter 6. There are other scripts and utilities that collect statistics and diagnostic information to help troubleshoot and get to the root cause of problems.

The data gathered through these utilities will help diagnose where the potential problem could be.

Health Monitor

Probably ever since the database was invented, the DBA's everyday routine task has been to check the health of the database. On certain days like Mondays, there were additional checks and scripts that got executed compared to the others. A task that every DBA continues to perform or performed during some part of his or her career irrespective of whether the database was Oracle, DB2, or SQL Server or Sybase. To complete these routine everyday tasks, several types and flavors of scripts have been written. Starting with scanning the alert logs for ORA error messages, purging of trace files and opening service requests with Oracle support has been a regular task of the day. In the 11g Release 2 of the database, Oracle has introduced a few new features that help in making some of the DBA tasks easier than before.

Similar to the DBA writing scripts to check the various areas of the database—for space, for errors, for locks, and so forth—the health monitor (HM) provided by Oracle validates most of the areas and components of the database. Checks performed by the HM include file corruptions, physical and logical corruptions, undo and redo corruptions, and so forth. Besides just identifying problems, the HM also provides a report of its findings and recommendations. The HM can be invoked in one of two ways: reactive mode where the checks are performed automatically by the database when a critical error is encountered, or manually by the DBA when he/she desires to execute any specific routine at any specific desired time when they get suspicious about issues with certain areas of the database.

Apart from the reactive checks and checks that are performed manually, there are checks that can be done when the database is online and others that can be executed when the database is offline. The list of tests and their execution type can be viewed using the V$HM_CHECK query.

V$HM_CHECK

Use the following query to view the tests and their execution types:

Script Name: MVRACTnTop_HMChecksList.sql

```
SQL> SELECT name,
        cls_name,
        internal_check,
        offline_capable
FROM   v$hm_check;
```

NAME	CLS_NAME	I	O
HM Test Check	GENERIC	Y	Y
DB Structure Integrity Check	PERSISTENT_DATA	N	Y
CF Block Integrity Check	PERSISTENT_DATA	N	Y
Data Block Integrity Check	PERSISTENT_DATA	N	Y
Redo Integrity Check	PERSISTENT_DATA	N	Y
Logical Block Check	PERSISTENT_DATA	Y	N
Transaction Integrity Check	PERSISTENT_DATA	N	N
Undo Segment Integrity Check	PERSISTENT_DATA	N	N
No Mount CF Check	PERSISTENT_DATA	Y	Y
Mount CF Check	PERSISTENT_DATA	Y	Y
CF Member Check	PERSISTENT_DATA	Y	Y
All Datafiles Check	PERSISTENT_DATA	Y	Y
Single Datafile Check	PERSISTENT_DATA	Y	Y
Tablespace Check Check	PERSISTENT_DATA	Y	Y
Log Group Check	PERSISTENT_DATA	Y	Y
Log Group Member Check	PERSISTENT_DATA	Y	Y
Archived Log Check	PERSISTENT_DATA	Y	Y
Redo Revalidation Check	PERSISTENT_DATA	Y	Y
IO Revalidation Check	PERSISTENT_DATA	Y	Y
Block IO Revalidation Check	PERSISTENT_DATA	Y	Y
Failover Check	PERSISTENT_DATA	Y	Y
Txn Revalidation Check	PERSISTENT_DATA	Y	N
Failure Simulation Check	PERSISTENT_DATA	Y	Y
Dictionary Integrity Check	PERSISTENT_DATA	N	N
ASM Mount Check	ASM	Y	Y
ASM Allocation Check	ASM	N	Y
ASM Disk Visibility Check	ASM	Y	Y
ASM File Busy Check	ASM	Y	Y
ASM Toomanyoff Check	ASM	Y	Y
ASM Insufficient Disks Check	ASM	Y	Y
ASM Insufficient Mem Check	ASM	Y	Y
ASM DGFDM Check No DG Name	ASM	Y	Y
ASM DG Force Dismount Check	ASM	Y	Y
ASM Sync IO Fail Check	ASM	Y	Y

34 rows selected.

DB-online mode means the check can be run while the database is open (i.e., in OPEN mode or MOUNT mode).

DB-offline mode means the check can be run when the instance is available but the database itself is closed (i.e., in NOMOUNT mode).

Not all checks can be run online and offline. Some checks can be run only internally (database is online), indicated by the INTERNAL_CHECK column, and some when the database is offline, indicated by the OFFLINE_CAPABLE column. Checks that are marked as "ASM" in the CLS_COLUMN should be run from an ASM instance.

The following output lists all the checks and their descriptions:

```
NAME                           DESCRIPTION
-----------------------------  -------------------------------------
HM Test Check                  Check for health monitor functionality
DB Structure Integrity Check   Checks integrity of all database files
CF Block Integrity Check       Checks integrity of a control file block
Data Block Integrity Check     Checks integrity of a data file block
Redo Integrity Check           Checks integrity of redo log content
Logical Block Check            Checks logical content of a block
Transaction Integrity Check    Checks a transaction for corruptions
Undo Segment Integrity Check   Checks integrity of an undo segment
No Mount CF Check              Checks control file in NOMOUNT mode
Mount CF Check                 Checks control file in mount mode
CF Member Check                Checks a multiplexed copy of the control
All Datafiles Check            Checks all datafiles in the database
Single Datafile Check          Checks a data file
Tablespace Check Check         Checks a tablespace
Log Group Check                Checks all members of a log group
Log Group Member Check         Checks a particular member of a log group
Archived Log Check             Checks an archived log
Redo Revalidation Check        Checks redo log content
IO Revalidation Check          Checks file accessibility
Block IO Revalidation Check    Checks file accessibility
Txn Revalidation Check         Revalidate corrupted transaction
Failure Simulation Check       Creates dummy failures
Dictionary Integrity Check     Checks dictionary integrity
ASM Mount Check                Diagnose mount failure
ASM Allocation Check           Diagnose allocation failure
ASM Disk Visibility Check      Diagnose add disk failure
ASM File Busy Check            Diagnose file drop failure
```

Running Checks

HM checks can be executed either online using EM, or manually using Oracle provided PL/SQL packages. Oracle provides two procedural language PL/SQL procedures to manually execute this operation: 1) DBMS_HM.RUN_CHECK and 2) DBMS_HM.GET_RUN_REPORT (discussed under "V$HM_RUN" later in this section).

1. DBMS_HM.RUN_CHECK

The RUN_CHECK procedure is used to manually execute checks at the component level of the database. The RUN_CHECK is executed using the following syntax:

```
EXEC DBMS_HM.RUN_CHECK('Dictionary Integrity Check','MV_DFRUN1');
```

Although most of the checks can be executed without using any parameters, others require parameters. In the preceding execution, 'MV_DFRUN1' is the name of the run. The V$HM_CHECK_PARM script gives a list of checks and the required parameters to complete the operation.

V$HM_CHECK_PARM

To access the list of checks and requirements, use the following query:

Script Name: MVRACTnTop_hmparmlist.sql[1]

```
SELECT   c.NAME CHECK_NAME     ,
         p.NAME PARAMETER_NAME,
         p.DESCRIPTION
FROM     V$HM_CHECK_PARAM p,
         V$HM_CHECK c
WHERE    p.CHECK_ID         = c.ID
         AND c.INTERNAL_CHECK = 'N'
ORDER BY c.NAME;
CHECK_NAME                        PARAMETER_NAME      DESCRIPTION
--------------------------------  ------------------  --------------------
ASM Allocation Check              ASM_DISK_GRP_NAME   ASM group name
CF Block Integrity Check          CF_BL_NUM           Control file block number
Data Block Integrity Check        BLC_DF_NUM          File number
Data Block Integrity Check        BLC_BL_NUM          Block number
Dictionary Integrity Check        CHECK_MASK          Check mask
Dictionary Integrity Check        TABLE_NAME          Table name
Redo Integrity Check              SCN_TEXT            SCN of the latest good redo (if known)
Transaction Integrity Check       TXN_ID              Transaction ID
Undo Segment Integrity Check      USN_NUMBER          Undo segment number
```

V$HM_RUN

The status of the execution can be viewed from V$HM_RUN view:

Script Name: MVRACPDnTap_HMRunStatus.sql

```
SELECT   INST_ID INT     ,
         NAME            ,
         CHECK_NAME      ,
         RUN_MODE        ,
         STATUS          ,
         SRC_INCIDENT SI,
         NUM_INCIDENT NI,
         ERROR_NUMBER EN
FROM     GV$HM_RUN
WHERE    RUN_MODE <> 'REACTIVE'
ORDER BY INST_ID;
```

---

[1]Source: Oracle Corporation.

In	NAME	CHECK_NAME	RUN_MODE	STATUS	SrcIn	#inc	Err
1	MV_RUN1	Dictionary Integrity Check	MANUAL	COMPLETED	0	0	0
	MV_RUN10	DB Structure Integrity Check	MANUAL	COMPLETED	0	0	0
	MV_DFRUN1	Dictionary Integrity Check	MANUAL	COMPLETED	0	0	0
	MV_RUN2	Dictionary Integrity Check	MANUAL	COMPLETED	0	0	0

In the preceding output, if there are checks that have incident count higher than 0, this indicates they require further investigation. Details of the incident can be viewed using the PL/SQL procedure DBMS_HM.RUN_REPORT.

2. **DBMS_HM.GET_RUN_REPORT**

```
SQL> SET LONG 100000
SET LONGCHUNKSIZE 1000
SET PAGESIZE 1000
SET LINESIZE 512
SQL> SELECT DBMS_HM.GET_RUN_REPORT('mv_runcf3') from dual;
DBMS_HM.GET_RUN_REPORT('MV_RUNCF3')
---------------------------------------------------------------------
Basic Run Information
  Run Name                    : mv_runcf3
  Run Id                      : 20301
  Check Name                  : CF Block Integrity Check
  Mode                        : MANUAL
  Status                      : COMPLETED
  Start Time                  : 2010-12-10 21:04:21.142783 -08:00
  End Time                    : 2010-12-10 21:04:21.264650 -08:00
  Error Encountered           : 0
  Source Incident Id          : 0
  Number of Incidents Created : 0
Input Paramters for the Run
  CF_BL_NUM=4949
Run Findings and Recommendations
```

The report lists all findings and recommendations. Findings and recommendations can also be found by querying the various Oracle provided views.

V$HM_FINDING

V$HM_FINDING displays all findings from the various checks executed from the HM. This view provides details such as type of error, what level of criticality (PRIORITY), and the extent of damage (DAMAGE_DESCRIPTION) that has occurred to the specific area of check performed:

Script MVRACPDnTap_HMfinding.sql
```
SELECT  FINDING_ID FI,
        RUN_ID RI    ,
        NAME         ,
        TIME_DETECTED,
        PRIORITY     ,
        STATUS       ,
```

```
        TYPE
FROM    V$HM_FINDING
ORDER BY TIME_DETECTED DESC;
Finding Run
    id   id  NAME                 TIME_DETECTED    PRIORITY STATUS
------- ----- -------------------- --------------- -------- --------
  17801 17761 Dictionary Inconsist 09-DEC-10 02.19 CRITICAL OPEN
  17798 17761 Dictionary Inconsist 09-DEC-10 02.19 CRITICAL OPEN
  17795 17761 Dictionary Inconsist 09-DEC-10 02.19 CRITICAL OPEN
  17792 17761 Dictionary Inconsist 09-DEC-10 02.19 CRITICAL OPEN
  17789 17761 Dictionary Inconsist 09-DEC-10 02.19 CRITICAL OPEN
  17786 17761 Dictionary Inconsist 09-DEC-10 02.19 CRITICAL OPEN
  17783 17761 Dictionary Inconsist 09-DEC-10 02.19 CRITICAL OPEN
  17780 17761 Dictionary Inconsist 09-DEC-10 02.19 CRITICAL OPEN
  17777 17761 Dictionary Inconsist 09-DEC-10 02.19 CRITICAL OPEN
     17     1 Datafile is old      21-AUG-10 10.11 HIGH     CLOSED
      8     1 Old Data Files       21-AUG-10 10.11 HIGH     CLOSED
     11     1 Datafile is old      21-AUG-10 10.11 HIGH     CLOSED
      5     1 System datafile is o 21-AUG-10 10.11 CRITICAL CLOSED
      2     1 Control File needs r 21-AUG-10 10.11 CRITICAL CLOSED
```

The preceding output gives a list of all findings for the various incidents that have occurred in this environment.

V$HM_RECOMMENDATION

For the incidents and the reported findings, HM normally provides recommendations provided there is sufficient data available. This view helps to display these recommendations:

```
SQL> DESC V$HM_RECOMMENDATION
Name                                     Null?    Type
---------------------------------------- -------- -------------------
RECOMMENDATION_ID                                 NUMBER
FDG_ID                                            NUMBER
RUN_ID                                            NUMBER
NAME                                              VARCHAR2(32)
TYPE                                              VARCHAR2(7)
RANK                                              NUMBER
TIME_DETECTED                                     TIMESTAMP(6)
EXECUTED                                          TIMESTAMP(6)
STATUS                                            VARCHAR2(7)
DESCRIPTION                                       VARCHAR2(1024)
REPAIR_SCRIPT                                     VARCHAR2(512)
```

This view can be joined with V$HM_FINDING to get more detailed information.

HM Using EM

The discussions so far have been about using HM in an interactive mode using SQLplus. As usual, for most manual interfaces, Oracle has a graphical interface through EM. To view, check, or run HM reports from the EM console, the steps are as follows:

1. Select Advisor Central from DB home page. Figure 18-1 illustrates the advisor central page in OEM. The tab next to the Advisors tab is the Checkers tab.

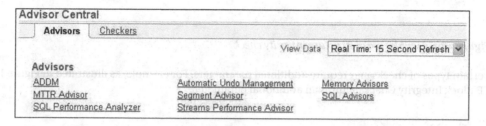

Figure 18-1. *OEM—Advisor central page*

2. Select Checkers to view the checkers page. Figure 18-2 illustrates the checkers page. This page contains the various types of checks that can be executed manually or internally by the database kernel.

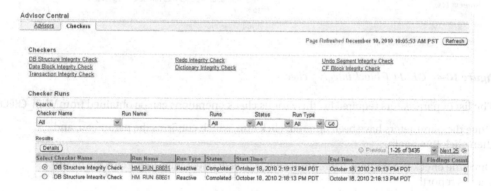

Figure 18-2. *OEM HM checkers page*

3. Select the appropriate check that needs to be executed. In this specific example, the DB Structure Integrity Check has been selected.

4. From the various checks listed in Figure 18-2, select the type of check to be executed. Figure 18-3 illustrates the input screen to enter the required parameters for DB Structure Integrity Check.

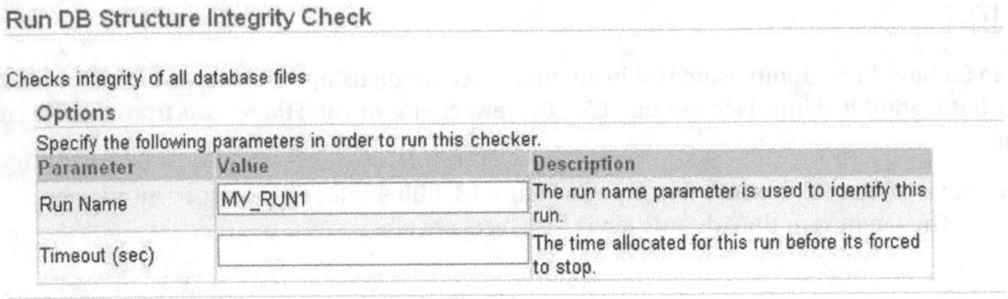

Run DB Structure Integrity Check

Checks integrity of all database files

Options

Specify the following parameters in order to run this checker.

Parameter	Value	Description
Run Name	MV_RUN1	The run name parameter is used to identify this run.
Timeout (sec)		The time allocated for this run before its forced to stop.

Figure 18-3. *OEM run DB structure integrity check*

Certain types of checks may require additional parameters. For example, as illustrated in Figure 18-4, the CF Block Integrity Check requires an additional parameter.

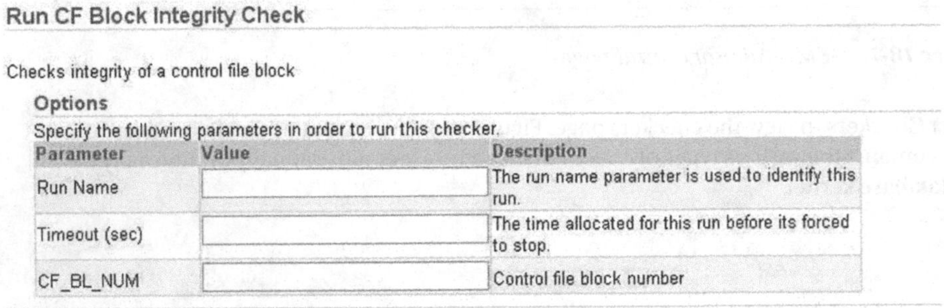

Run CF Block Integrity Check

Checks integrity of a control file block

Options

Specify the following parameters in order to run this checker.

Parameter	Value	Description
Run Name		The run name parameter is used to identify this run.
Timeout (sec)		The time allocated for this run before its forced to stop.
CF_BL_NUM		Control file block number

Figure 18-4. *OEM CF block integrity check*

The list of parameters required for the various check operations can be obtained from V$HM_CHECK_PARM.

5. Once the parameters have been entered, click Run, which confirms the parameter, and then click Run again.

6. Once the check is complete, the report can be viewed: select View Report for the health checks report.

Automatic Diagnostic Repository

In Oracle Database Release 9i, Oracle had introduced a new background process called DIAG for the RAC environment. The function of the DIAG background process is to collect memory statistics when process state changes happened within the Oracle memory structures or other RAC-related background processes. The DIAG process collected trace into separate directories every time a state change occurred; however, the data saved in these files could not be read by the DBAs. The output in these directories was only useful to Oracle support. When database errors such as ORA-0600 occurred of the instance crashed, these directories along with other trace files were uploaded to the support site for a service request.

In Oracle Database 11g Release 1, besides making the DIAG process available on both a single instance and a RAC database, Oracle has enhanced the entire diagnostic process by storing all information for tracking and analysis in a repository called Automatic Diagnostic Repository (ADR). The ADR contains all trace, dump, and other information related to any incident or error encountered by the instance.

Like most utilities and tools, Oracle provides two types of interfaces to query the ADR: command line interface using adrci or using EM.

ADR Actions

The ADR is a file-based repository for database diagnostic data such as traces, dumps, the alert log, HM reports, and more. It has a unified directory structure across multiple instances and multiple products. The Oracle database, ASM, and other Oracle products or components store all diagnostic data in the ADR. ADR uses an internal methodology (illustrated in Figure 18-5) to manage these diagnostic data and consists of the actions described following.

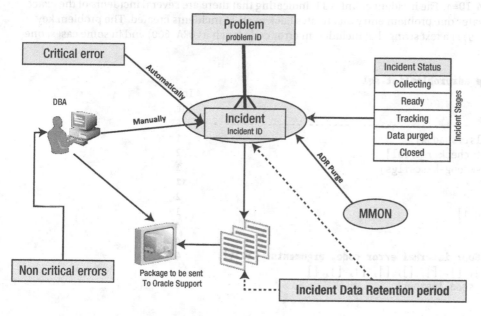

Figure 18-5. *Incident tracking process flow*

Problem

ADR is used to track problems. Each problem has a problem key and a unique problem ID that is a sequence number to the problems reported in the ADR. An example of a problem could be a critical error generated by the database such as an ORA-600 error.

Incident

An incident is a single occurrence of a problem. When a problem occurs multiple times, an incident is created for each occurrence. When an incident occurs, the database makes an entry in the alert log, sends an *incident alert* to EM, gathers diagnostic data about the incident in the form of dump files (incident dumps), tags the incident dumps with the incident ID, and stores the incident dumps in an ADR subdirectory created for that incident.

Problem Key

Every problem identified and created by the ADR has a problem key. The problem key is a text string that includes an error code (such as ORA 600) and in some cases, one or more error parameters. Whereas PROBLEM IDs are unique to the database, problem keys are not. There could be many occurrences of the similar problem and they may have the same problem key.

V$DIAG_PROBLEM

This view lists all the problem keys associated with incidents for a database instance. Please note the incident count column for PROBLEM_ID=4. The incident count is 11, indicating that there are several incidents of the exact same error and Oracle creates one problem entry that relates back to all 11 incidents created. The problem key (for example, PROBLEM_ID=9) is a text string that includes an error code (such as ORA 600) and in some cases, one or more error parameters:

Script Name:MVRACPDnTap_adrproblemlist.sql

P-id	PROBLEM_KEY	Inc Cnt
1	ORA 600 [kjbmprlst:shadow]	1
2	ORA 600 [rwoirw: check ret val]	2
3	ORA 600 [kksfbc-wrong-kkscsflgs]	1
4	**ORA 600 [4193]**	**11**
5	ORA 1578	2
6	ORA 600 [kewrose_1]	1
7	ORA 600 [2023]	4
8	ORA 600 [4136]	4
9	**ORA 600 [ORA-00600: internal error code, arguments: [2023],** [o], [o], [], [], [], [], [], [], [], [], []	**4**
10	ORA 600 [kcratr_scan_lastbwr]	1

Incident Package

All incidents that are critical in nature have to be reported to Oracle support for resolution. Before sending incident data to Oracle Support, it must be collected into a package using the Incident Packaging Service (IPS).

When an incident occurs, the database server makes an entry in the alert log, gathers diagnostic data about the incident, tags the diagnostic data with the incident ID, and stores the data in an ADR subdirectory created for that incident. As mentioned previously, each incident has a problem key and is mapped to a single problem. Incidents that have the same problem keys have the same root cause or identical PROBLEM_KEY.

In certain cases, there could be a large number of errors being generated (when a specific feature causing the problem is repeatedly being used). This could indicate a large number of incidents that belong to the same root cause and could cause flooding of the ADR. To avoid this, Oracle controls the number of dumps that could be generated for a given problem to five.

ADR Configuration

An ADR base is the base directory identified during Oracle database installation (in prior versions of Oracle, this directory was identified as the admin directory). Because Oracle uses the ADR to store diagnostic information related to multiple products and components, there are several ADR homes: one for each component. All ADR homes are grouped under the ADR base directory and are identified by the parameter DIAGNOSTIC_DEST. In a RAC environment, each instance will have a separate base directory:

```
SQL> show parameter diagnostic_dest
NAME                                 TYPE        VALUE
------------------------------------ ----------- -------------------
diagnostic_dest                      string      /app/oracle
```

From the same ADR base, ADR can support multiple homes and is managed by how many products are configured on the server. In the output following, there are several homes: one for ASM, another for the database, and the others for the LISTENER:

```
adrci> show homes
ADR Homes:
diag/asm/+asm/+ASM1
diag/rdbms/prddb/PRODDB_1
diag/tnslsnr/prddb1/listener_scan3
diag/tnslsnr/prddb1/listener
diag/tnslsnr/prddb1/listener_scan1
diag/tnslsnr/prddb1/listener_scan2
```

ADR is enabled by default and the different ADR destination homes can be identified by querying the view V$DIAG_INFO:

Script Name: MVRACPDnTap_ADRDiagInfo.sql
```
SELECT INST_ID INT, NAME, VALUE
FROM   GV$DIAG_INFO
ORDER BY INST_ID, NAME;
In  NAME                    VALUE
--- ----------------------- -------------------------------------------------
  1 ADR Base                /app/oracle
    ADR Home                /app/oracle/diag/rdbms/prddb/PRDDB_1
    Active Incident Count   3
    Active Problem Count    2
    Diag Alert              /app/oracle/diag/rdbms/prddb/PRDDB_1/alert
    Diag Cdump              /app/oracle/diag/rdbms/prddb/PRDDB_1/cdump
    Diag Enabled            TRUE
    Diag Incident           /app/oracle/diag/rdbms/prddb/PRDDB_1/incident
    Diag Trace              /app/oracle/diag/rdbms/prddb/PRDDB_1/trace
    Health Monitor          /app/oracle/diag/rdbms/prddb/PRDDB_1/hm
..... . . . . . .
 . . . . . . . .
  5 ADR Base                /app/oracle
    ADR Home                /app/oracle/diag/rdbms/prddb/PRDDB_5
    Active Incident Count   37
    Active Problem Count    6
    Diag Alert              /app/oracle/diag/rdbms/prddb/PRDDB_5/alert
```

```
Diag Cdump              /app/oracle/diag/rdbms/prddb/PRDDB_5/cdump
Diag Enabled            TRUE
Diag Incident           /app/oracle/diag/rdbms/prddb/PRDDB_5/incident
Diag Trace              /app/oracle/diag/rdbms/prddb/PRDDB_5/trace
Health Monitor          /app/oracle/diag/rdbms/prddb/PRDDB_5/hm
```

■ **Note** This is the only view that supports a RAC configuration. All other views discussed are all instance specific and do not have a corresponding GV$ view.

In the preceding output, the ADR monitors one product (e.g., RDBMS) home. Also in the preceding output, there are several directories under the home directory:

alert: This directory contains the extensible markup language (XML) alert log.

cdump: Core dumps generated by the Oracle kernel when it encounters critical errors are stored in this directory.

trace: Process trace files and the database alert log are stored in the trace directory.

incident: The incident directory stores dump files created when critical errors are encountered. Each occurrence of a critical error is given its own incident directory with the incident ID used to form the directory name.

metadata: The metadata directory stores a series of files that contain diagnostic metadata.

hm: The hm directory contains reports for health checks.

incpkg, ir, lck, sweep: These directories contain the internal diagnostic framework state.

Like most utilities and tools, Oracle provides two types of interfaces to query the ADR, command line interface using adrci or using EM.

Retention Policy

The time frame for which the various incidents and problems are retained before being purged by the MMON process is based on the retention policy defined. ADR stores two types of files:

1. Files that have short duration, such as the dump trace and log files, which are retained by default for 30 days. These files are controlled through the parameter SHORTP_POLICY.

2. Files that have a longer duration, such as the metadata information, which is retained by default for 365 days. The purges for long duration files are controlled through the parameter LONGP_POLICY.

These values can be modified using ADR command line interface or using the EM. To modify these parameters using command line interface, the following steps are the followed:

```
adrci> show control
ADR Home = /app/oracle/diag/rdbms/prddb/PRDDB_1:
*******************************************************************
ADRID                 SHORTP_POLICY        LONGP_POLICY         LAST_MOD_TIME
-------------------------------------------------------------------------------
2673816947            720                  8760                 2010-08-21 19:44:43.295761
1 rows fetched
adrci> SET CONTROL (SHORTP_POLICY=168);
adrci> SHOW CONTROL
ADR Home = /app/oracle/diag/rdbms/prddb/PRDDB_1:
*******************************************************************
ADRID                 SHORTP_POLICY        LONGP_POLICY         LAST_MOD_TIME
-------------------------------------------------------------------------------
2673816947            168                  8760                 2010-12-12 19:48:05.604658
1 rows fetched
adrci>
```

V$DIAG_ADR_CONTROL

The short-term policy and the long-term policy parameters, along with other control information, can be viewed from inside the database using this view:

Script Name: MVRACPDnTap_adrcontrol.sql

ADR Home	Short Pck Policy	Long Pck Policy
diag/asm/+asm/+ASM1	720	8760
diag/rdbms/prddb/PRDDB_1	168	8760
diag/tnslsnr/prddb1/listener	720	8760
diag/tnslsnr/prddb1/listener_scan1	720	8760
diag/tnslsnr/prddb1/listener_scan2	720	8760
diag/tnslsnr/prddb1/listener_scan3	720	8760

■ **Note** In the preceding output, the short-term purge (retention policy) has been modified to 7 days or 168 hours. Similarly, the retention policy for the long-term files can also be modified by setting the parameter LONGP_POLICY.

Because these control parameters apply to each ADR home, in a RAC environment, these changes have to be made separately for each ADR home.

ADR HOME: Each product stores diagnostic data underneath its own ADR home directory. For example, in an Oracle RAC environment with shared storage and ASM, each database instance and each ASM instance has a home directory within the ADR. The ADR's unified directory structure helps correlate and analyze diagnostic data across multiple instances and multiple products. All ADR homes share the same hierarchical directory structure. Some of the standard subdirectories in each ADR home include alert (for the alert log), trace (for trace files), and incident. ADR homes are located within the ADR base directory.

Homepath: The homepath determines the ADR homes that are current. It does so by pointing to a directory within the ADR base hierarchy. If it points to a single ADR home directory, that ADR home is the only current ADR home. If the homepath points to a directory that is above the ADR home directory level in the hierarchy, all ADR homes that are below the directory that is pointed to become current.

With multiple components (database, ASM, etc.), there are multiple locations where diagnostic data is collected by Oracle. ADR home by default points to more than one location as illustrated here:

```
adrci> show homes
ADR Homes:
diag/tnslsnr/prddb3/listener_scan1
diag/tnslsnr/prddb3/listener_scan3
diag/tnslsnr/prddb3/listener_scan2
diag/tnslsnr/prddb3/listener_prd
diag/tnslsnr/prddb3/listener
diag/rdbms/prddb/PRDDB_1
diag/asm/+asm/+ASM1
```

To change this to one specific location, the homepath definition needs to be reset using `set homepath <path>` command:

```
adrci> set homepath diag/rdbms/prddb/PRDDB_1
adrci> show homes
ADR Homes:
diag/rdbms/prddb/PRDDB_1
```

Similar to the show home, show control, and set control commands discussed earlier, ADR command line interface provides several commands that can be executed from the command line. To get a list use the help command or help extended command, use the following:

```
[mvallath@prddb3]$ adrci
ADRCI: Release 11.2.0.2.0 - Production on Fri Dec 17 17:24:13 2010
Copyright (c) 1982, 2009, Oracle and/or its affiliates. All rights reserved.
ADR base = "/app/oracle"
adrci> HELP EXTENDED
 HELP [topic]
    Available Topics:
        BEGIN BACKUP
        CD
        CREATE STAGING XMLSCHEMA
        CREATE VIEW
        DDE
        DEFINE
```

```
DELETE
DESCRIBE
DROP VIEW
END BACKUP
INSERT
LIST DEFINE
MERGE ALERT
MERGE FILE
MIGRATE
QUERY
REPAIR
SELECT
SET COLUMN
SHOW CATALOG
SHOW DUMP
SHOW SECTION
SHOW TRACE
SHOW TRACEMAP
SWEEP
UNDEFINE
UPDATE
VIEW
```

Viewing Alert Logs

Beginning with Oracle Database 11*g*, the alert log is written as both an XML-formatted file and as a text file. You can view either format of the file with any text editor, or you can run an ADRCI command to view the XML-formatted alert log with the XML tags stripped. By default, ADRCI displays the alert log in your default editor. You can use the SET EDITOR command to change your default editor:

```
SHOW ALERT -TAIL
```

This displays the last portion of the alert log (the last 10 entries) in your terminal session.

```
SHOW ALERT -TAIL 50
```

This displays the last 50 entries in the alert log in your terminal session.

```
SHOW ALERT -TAIL -F
```

This displays the last 10 entries in the alert log and then waits for more messages to arrive in the alert log. As each message arrives, it is appended to the display. This command enables you to perform "live monitoring" of the alert log. Press CTRL-C to stop waiting and return to the ADRCI prompt:

```
adrci> SHOW ALERT -TAIL -F
2010-05-12 00:05:39.881000 -07:00
database, requires manual RMAN intervention to resolve OMF
datafile pathnames.
NOTE: Please refer to the RMAN documentation for procedures
describing how to manually resolve OMF datafile pathnames.
2010-05-12 00:06:09.996000 -07:00
```

```
alter database backup controlfile to trace
Backup controlfile written to trace file /app/oracle/diag/rdbms/prddb/PRDDB_1/trace/PRDDB_1_
ora_1963.trc
Completed: alter database backup controlfile to trace
2010-05-12 02:00:00.097000 -07:00
Clearing Resource Manager plan via parameter
2010-05-12 13:37:06.902000 -07:00
Thread 1 advanced to log sequence 205 (LGWR switch)
  Current log# 1 seq# 205 mem# 0: +PRDDB_DATA/prddb/onlinelog/group_1.261.715810991
2010-05-12 13:37:10.393000 -07:00
Archived Log entry 727 added for thread 1 sequence 204 ID 0xaff834aa dest 1:
```

Workshop—Monitoring Incidents and Problems

In this workshop, we will try to track and collect information required to help Oracle support complete their tasks of diagnosing the problem. The workshop uses ADRCI (automatic diagnostic repository command interface).

Step 1

DBA gets an alert from the EM that the Instance 1 has crashed. DBA gets on the server to investigate the reason for the crash. Browsing through the alert log, DBA notices that the instance had reported an ORA-0600 error. Being a production database, the DBA's first primary task is to see if the instance will start and look at investigating the problem as soon as possible. Because other instances in the cluster are up and running, the DBA is certain that the database should be in good shape and there should be some sort of bug that the database must have been encountered. After making some quick checks on the ASM instance, database listener, scan listener, and a good check on the health of the clusterware on the instance, he/she moves to the next step of starting the instance.

Step 2

DBA finds all components on the server are in good health and starts the failed instance using the srvctl command line interface. After the instance starts, the DBA verifies if the instance is useable and sessions are able to connect to the database.

Step 3

Now that the instance is up and running, it's time to investigate the root cause of the problem and try to find a permanent fix. Checking the alert log once again, and locating any trace files associated with the error is a good place to start and get details regarding the error.

As a practice, it's good to check metalink if there are any bugs or situations reported by other customers. Illustrated in Figure 18-6 is a lookup tool to identify ORA-00600 and ORA-07445 errors and the possible fixes. If this is a known issue and a solution has already been identified, the tool provides the fixes and patches that maybe available.

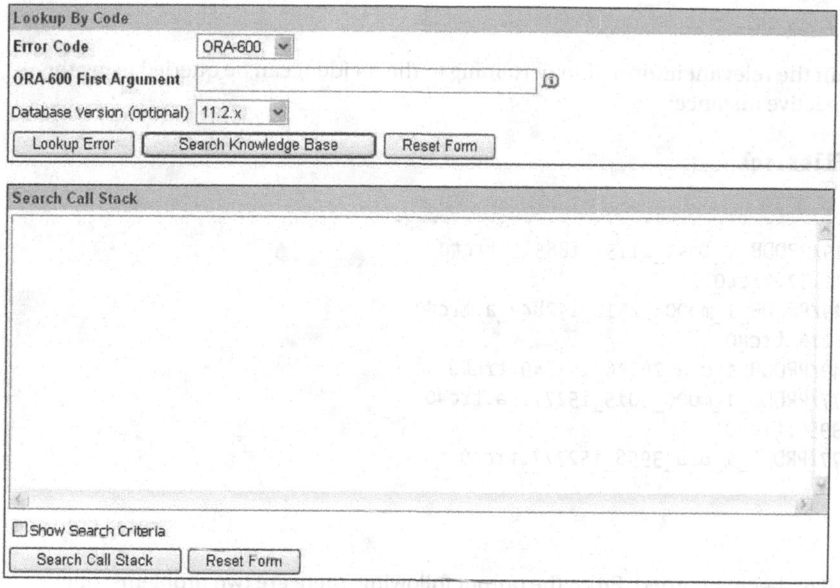

Figure 18-6. ORA-600 and ORA-7445 error lookup tool

If no errors have been reported, the DBA needs to open a service request with Oracle support. This is where the ADR gives a helping hand.

The ORA-600 and ORA-7445 error lookup is accessible via Oracle metalink Note 153788.1.

Step 4

All errors encountered by the various components of the database are stored in the repository as incidents. A list of incidents can be viewed from the ADR command line utility using the SHOW INCIDENT command:

```
adrci> SET HOME /app/oracle/diag/rdbms/prddb/PRDDB_1
adrci> SHOW INCIDENT
ADR Home = /app/oracle/diag/rdbms/prddb/PRDDB_1:
*****************************************************************
INCIDENT_ID          PROBLEM_KEY                                CREATE_TIME
------------         -----------------------------  ---------------------------
52777                ORA 600 [kkqsMapExp:badleaf]               2010-11-19 16:58:13.938000
52849                ORA 600 [kkqsMapExp:badleaf]               2010-11-19 17:12:28.076000
88515                ORA 600 [kjbrasr:pkey]                     2010-12-02 01:04:06.313000
3 rows fetched
```

From the preceding incident list, there are two identical incidents that occurred on 2010-11-19 and a new incident that occurred on 2010-12-02. All the incidents listed in the preceding output are critical ORA-600 errors.

■ **Note**   Incidents 52777 and 52849 are SQL-related errors and will be discussed in a later section.

V$DIAG_INCIDENT_FILE

Trace and user dump files that contain the relevant information pertaining to the incident can be queried using the V$DIAG_INCIDENT_FILE from the respective instance:

Script Name:MVRACPDnTap_adrincfiles.sql

```
BFILE
-----------------------------------------------------------------------
<ADR_HOME>/incident/incdir_88515/PRDDB_1_lms1_11152_i88515.trc#0
<ADR_HOME>/trace/PRDDB_1_lms1_11152.trc#0
<ADR_HOME>/incident/incdir_52849/PRDDB_1_m000_32510_i52849_a.trc#0
<ADR_HOME>/trace/PRDDB_1_ora_26216.trc#0
<ADR_HOME>/incident/incdir_52849/PRDDB_1_ora_26216_i52849.trc#0
<ADR_HOME>/incident/incdir_52777/PRDDB_1_m000_5015_i52777_a.trc#0
<ADR_HOME>/trace/OBIPRD_1_ora_3956.trc#0
<ADR_HOME>/incident/incdir_52777/PRDDB_1_ora_3956_i52777.trc#0
```

Step 5

Now we check how many problems have been recorded. From the output following, there are two problems: one for each type of incident. Considering there is only one incident for the error that occurred on 2010-12-02, the DBA decides to create the IPS using the incident ID:

■ **Note**   IPS, which is a utility within the ADR, helps in creating logical incident packages, adding the required diagnostic data and generating the physical package that could then be uploaded or sent to Oracle support.

```
adrci> show problem
ADR Home = /app/oracle/diag/rdbms/prddb/PRDDB_1:
*************************************************
P_ID  PROBLEM_KEY                    LAST_IN  LASTINC_TIME
----- ------------------------------ -------- ------------------------
2     ORA 600 [kjbrasr:pkey]         88515    2010-12-02 01:04:06.313000
1     ORA 600 [kkqsMapExp:badleaf]   52849    2010-11-19 17:12:28.076000
2 rows fetched
```

Step 6

First step is to create the package for the incident so we could collect all relevant information for Oracle support:

```
adrci> IPS CREATE PACKAGE INCIDENT 88515 CORRELATE ALL
Created package 2 based on incident id 88515, correlation level all
adrci> ips show package
    PACKAGE_ID            1
    PACKAGE_NAME          ORA600kjb_20101213212018
    PACKAGE_DESCRIPTION
    DRIVING_PROBLEM       2
    DRIVING_PROBLEM_KEY   ORA 600 [kjbrasr:pkey]
    DRIVING_INCIDENT      88515
```

```
DRIVING_INCIDENT_TIME    2010-12-02 01:04:06.313000 -08:00
STATUS                   New (0)
CORRELATION_LEVEL        All (4)
PROBLEMS                 1 main problems, 0 correlated problems
INCIDENTS                1 main incidents, 0 correlated incidents
INCLUDED_FILES           3
```

The show package command lists all the incidents and the problems associated with this package.

Step 7

Once the package has been created, the next step is to generate the package. This step can be completed in one step or can be completed in increments, meaning that in the future when more incidents occur with the same error or any related incidents occur, they could be added to the same package. In this specific example, the package is closed with the complete clause:

```
adrci> IPS GENERATE PACKAGE 1 IN /home/oracle/mvallath
Generated package 1 in file /home/oracle/mvallath/ORA600kjb_20101213212018_COM_1.zip, mode complete
adrci> ips show incidents package 1
MAIN INCIDENTS FOR PACKAGE 1:
    INCIDENT_ID          88515
    PROBLEM_ID           2
    EXCLUDE              Included
CORRELATED INCIDENTS FOR PACKAGE 1:
```

V$DIAG_IPS_FILE_METADATA

When generating a package for the incident or problem, ADR collects all the related metadata information. This view lists the metadata related to the incident:

Script Name:MVRACPDnTap_adripsmetadata.sql

BFILE	INCIDENT_ID
<ADR_HOME>/incident/incdir_88515/PRDDB_1_lms1_11152_i88515.trc#0	88515
<ADR_HOME>/incpkg/pkg_1/seq_2/crs/alertprddb1.log#0	0
<ADR_HOME>/trace/PRDDB_1_lms1_11152.trc#0	0
<ADR_HOME>/alert/log.xml#0	0
<ADR_HOME>/trace/alert_PRDDB_1.log#0	0
<ADR_HOME>/incpkg/pkg_1/seq_1/export/IPS_CONFIGURATION.dmp#0	0
<ADR_HOME>/incpkg/pkg_1/seq_1/export/IPS_PACKAGE.dmp#0	0
<ADR_HOME>/incpkg/pkg_1/seq_1/export/IPS_PACKAGE_INCIDENT.dmp#0	0
<ADR_HOME>/incpkg/pkg_1/seq_1/export/IPS_PACKAGE_FILE.dmp#0	0
<ADR_HOME>/incpkg/pkg_1/seq_1/export/IPS_PACKAGE_HISTORY.dmp#0	0

Step 8

After generating the package, which brings together all the required files, the next step is to finalize the package so the output can be sent to Oracle support:

```
adrci> IPS FINALIZE PACKAGE 1
Finalized package 1
```

This step makes the package ready for upload to Oracle support. The ADR keeps track of all components used at the point in time when the error occurred. The zip file generated in Step 7 has a complete list of all log files required by Oracle support for analyzing of the problem.

SQL Test Case Builder

In Oracle Database 11g Release 2, Oracle has introduced a SQL Test Case Builder (TCB). The test case builder helps in gathering and reproducing as much information as possible about a problem and the environment in which the problem had occurred. This helps to reproduce the problem on a separate Oracle database.

The incident-related files are stored in the ADR, and the incident directories are under the ADR_HOME. In the case of incidents in which an SQL query was involved, the trace files also include the query being executed, table and index definitions, PL/SQL functions, procedures and packages, optimizer statistics, and initialization parameter settings.

Step 1

There could be several incidents that happen in a production database environment. Not all incidents need to be related to an SQL query. Whereas all incidents get listed as incidents at the top level under the SHOW INCIDENT command, incidents that are related to an SQL query need to be isolated:

```
adrci> SET HOME /app/oracle/diag/rdbms/prddb/PRDDB_1
adrci> SHOW INCIDENT
ADR Home = /app/oracle/diag/rdbms/prddb/PRDDB_1:
*****************************************************************
INCIDENT_ID   PROBLEM_KEY                CREATE_TIME
------------- -------------------------- --------------------------
52777         ORA 600 [kkqsMapExp:badleaf] 2010-11-19 16:58:13.938000
52849      ·  ORA 600 [kkqsMapExp:badleaf] 2010-11-19 17:12:28.076000
88515         ORA 600 [kjbrasr:pkey]     2010-12-02 01:04:06.313000
3 rows fetched
```

There are two incidents with an identical problem key. When ADR encounters more than one incident with the same problem key, it maintains just one problem entry for up to five incidents.

Step 2

1. One way to determine if there are any SQL statements associated with the incident is to check all the trace files generated during the process and examine those moved to the "incident" directory. For example, the incident directory created for 52777 contains relevant trace files and can be examined manually if it contains any SQL statements:

```
[oracle@prddb1 incdir_52777]$ ls -ltr
total 5648
-rw-r----- 1 oracle dba   413783 Nov 19 16:58 PRDDB_1_ora_3956_i52777.trm
-rw-r----- 1 oracle dba  5339461 Nov 19 16:58 PRDDB_1_ora_3956_i52777.trc
-rw-r----- 1 oracle dba      206 Nov 19 16:58 PRDDB_1_m000_5015_i52777_a.trm
-rw-r----- 1 oracle dba     1299 Nov 19 16:58 PRDDB_1_m000_5015_i52777_a.trc
[oracle@prddb1 incdir_52777]$ more PRDDB_1_ora_3956_i52777.trc
Dump file /app/oracle/diag/rdbms/prddb/PRDDB_1/incident/incdir_52777/PRDDB_1_ora_3956_
i52777.trc
Oracle Database 11g Enterprise Edition Release 11.2.0.1.0 - 64bit Production
With the Partitioning, Real Application Clusters, Automatic Storage
. . . . . . . . . .
. . . . . . . . . .
*** 2010-11-19 16:58:13.942
*** SESSION ID:(750.2230) 2010-11-19 16:58:13.942
*** CLIENT ID:() 2010-11-19 16:58:13.942
*** SERVICE NAME:(BIAPPS) 2010-11-19 16:58:13.942
*** MODULE NAME:(nqsserver@prdapp3 (TNS V1-V3)) 2010-11-19 16:58:13.942
*** ACTION NAME:() 2010-11-19 16:58:13.942
Dump continued from file: /app/oracle/diag/rdbms/prddb/PRDDB_1/trace/PRDDB_1_ora_3956.trc
ORA-00600: internal error code, arguments: [kkqsMapExp:badleaf], [], [], [], [], [], [],
[], [], [], [], []
========= Dump for incident 52777 (ORA 600 [kkqsMapExp:badleaf]) ========
*** 2010-11-19 16:58:13.943
dbkedDefDump(): Starting incident default dumps (flags=0x2, level=3, mask=0x0)
----- Current SQL Statement for this session (sql_id=c7x8nxwzf42ac) -----
select distinct T537387.SRV_REQ_NUM as c1,
     T537387.INCIDENT_TYPE_CD as c2,
     T534609.DAY_DT as c3,
     T501320.NAME as c4,
     T512643.INSTANCE_NUM as c5,
     T512643.SERIAL_NUM as c6,
     T32069.X_PROD_HIER8_NAME as c7,
     T595543.NOTE_TYPE_NAME as c8,
. . . . . . . . . . .
. . . . . . . . . . .
```

2. Another method of checking if there are SQL queries associated with the incident is to query the V$DIAG_DDE_USER_ACTION:

```
Script Name:MVRACTnTop_adrddeuseraction.sql
                            Action   Incident invocation
     ADR Home               Name          id         id
---------------------------  ---------- --------  ----------
diag/rdbms/prddb/PRDDB_1     SQLTCB      52777          1
diag/rdbms/prddb/PRDDB_1     SQLTCB      52849          1
```

The preceding output contains the action names SQLTCB (SQL Test Case Builder) associated with each incident, indicating that both these incidents involve SQL statements.

> ■ **Note**   Either way, the trace file will have to be checked to determine the actual query. However, if we use the V$ views as the method, this would could help us get to the exact trace files.

Querying the V$DIAG_INCIDENT_FILE will get us the list of trace files associated with this incident. From the trace files, the SQL statement can be obtained.

Step 3

We have determined that the incident is associated with an SQL statement, and the SQL statement is part of the following trace file:

```
/app/oracle/diag/rdbms/prddb/PRDDB_1/trace/PRDDB_1_ora_3956.trc
```

The next step is to create a diagnosis task using the PL/SQL procedure DBMS_SQLDIAG.CREATE_DIAGNOSIS_TASK. This will help build the SQL repair advisor.

Step 4

When creating the diagnosis task, we assign the task a name for easy identification and also associate the problem type with the task:

```
DECLARE
    rep_out         CLOB;
    MV_id           VARCHAR2(50);
  BEGIN
   MV_id := DBMS_SQLDIAG.CREATE_DIAGNOSIS_TASK(
      sql_text =>
'SELECT DISTINCT T537387.SRV_REQ_NUM  AS c1 ,
       T537387.INCIDENT_TYPE_CD     AS c2 ,
       T534609.DAY_DT               AS c3 ,
       T501320.NAME                 AS c4 ,
       T512643.INSTANCE_NUM         AS c5 ,
       T512643.SERIAL_NUM           AS c6 ,
       T32069.X_PROD_HIER8_NAME     AS c7 ,
       T595543.NOTE_TYPE_NAME       AS c8 ,
       T595543.NOTES                AS c9 ,
       T595543.NOTES_DETAIL         AS c10,
       T595543.CREATED_ON_DT        AS c11,
       SUM(T537323.ROW_WID / NULLIF( T537323.ROW_WID, 0)) AS c12
   FROM   W_ORG_D T501320              ,
          W_CUSTOMER_LOC_D T501866 ,
          W_DAY_D T534609             ,
          W_PRODUCT_D T32069         ,
          X_SRV_INSTALL_BASE_D T512643   ,
          X_SRV_REQ_F T537323         ,
          X_SRV_REQ_D T537387 left outer join X_SRV_NOTES_V T595543  On T537387.ROW_WID = T595543.
PARENT_WID
```

```
where ( T32069.ROW_WID = T537323.PRODUCT_WID and T501320.ROW_WID = T501866.CUSTOMER_WID and T501866.
ROW_WID = T537323.INSTALL_LOC_WID and T512643.ROW_WID = T537323.INSTALL_BASE_WID and T534609.ROW_WID
= T537323.INCIDENT_DT_WID and T537323.EFFECTIVE_TO_DT_WID = 47121231 and T537323.SRV_REQ_WID =
T537387.ROW_WID and T537387.INCIDENT_TYPE_CD = '8-Telephone Support' and T595543.NOTE_TYPE_NAME is
not null and T595543.CREATED_ON_DT between TO_DATE('2010-07-26 00:01:45' , 'YYYY-MM-DD HH24:MI:SS')
and TO_DATE('2010-07-27 00:01:45' , 'YYYY-MM-DD HH24:MI:SS') )
group by T32069.X_PROD_HIER8_NAME, T501320.NAME, T512643.INSTANCE_NUM, T512643.SERIAL_NUM, T534609.
ROW_WID, T534609.DAY_DT, T537387.SRV_REQ_NUM, T537387.INCIDENT_TYPE_CD, T595543.CREATED_ON_DT,
T595543.NOTES, T595543.NOTES_DETAIL, T595543.NOTE_TYPE_NAME
order by c1, c2, c3, c4, c5, c6, c7, c8, c9, c10, c11 ',
    task_name => 'ERR_INC_52777_TASK',
    problem_type => DBMS_SQLDIAG.PROBLEM_TYPE_EXECUTION_ERROR);
```

The problem-type parameter can have the following values:

- `PROBLEM_TYPE_COMPILATION_ERROR`
- `PROBLEM_TYPE_WRONG_RESULTS`
- `PROBLEM_TYPE_EXECUTION_ERRORS`

Step 5

Once the procedure has been created, the next step is to execute the diagnosis task by calling DBMS_SQLDIAG.EXECUTE_
DIAGNOSIS_TASK with the task ID returned by the CREATE_DIAGNOSIS_TASK from Step 4. After a short delay, the SQL
Repair Advisor returns. As part of its execution, the SQL Repair Advisor keeps a record of its findings, which can be
accessed through the reporting facilities of SQL Repair Advisor.

```
DBMS_SQLDIAG.EXECUTE_DIAGNOSIS_TASK (MV_id);
```

Step 6

Once the task is executed, the next step is to report the task using DBMS_SQLDIAG.REPORT_DIAGNOSIS_TASK. If the
SQL Repair Advisor was able to find a work-around, it recommends an SQL patch. An SQL patch is similar to an SQL
profile; but unlike the SQL profile, it is used for work-around compilation or execution errors:

```
BEGIN
  REP_OUT:= DBMS_SQLDIAG.REPORT_DIAGNOSIS_TASK (MV_id, DBMS_SQLDIAG.TYPE_TEXT);

  DBMS_OUTPUT.PUT_LINE ('Report: ' || REP_OUT);

END;
/
```

Step 7

From Step 6, if the patch was found, the next step is to apply the patch using the DBMS_SQLDIAG.ACCEPT_SQL_PATCH
procedure, which takes the task_name as an argument:

```
EXECUTE DBMS_SQLDIAG.ACCEPT_SQL_PATCH (task_name => ' ERR_INC_52777_TASK ', task_owner => 'SYS',
REPLACE => TRUE);
```

Step 8

After the patch has been accepted, the next step is to rerun the SQL statement. This time, it should not give the critical error. An "explain plan" for this statement should show that the SQL patch was used.

Step 9

After the official patch from Oracle to fix an error is received, the patch that was applied using the previous steps should be dropped using DBMS_SQLDIAG.DROP_SQL_PATCH with the patch name. The patch name can be obtained from the explain plan section or by querying the view DBA_SQL_PATCHES.

ORADEBUG Utility

ORADEBUG is an undocumented but powerful utility and helps identify and troubleshoot a wealth of information regarding the database, its components, and interfaces. This utility comes in handy to step deep into the internal structures of Oracle and understand the actual problem. One of the great benefits of using this utility is to get a jump start into investigating problems encountered with the performance or failure of instances in the cluster. The information gathered using this is also useful when calling Oracle Support. The information puts the problem closer to resolution. The ORADEBUG utility is invoked from an SQL*Plus session by simply connecting to it and executing the specific ORADEBUG command. For example, the following code is to get help on the various commands available through ORADEBUG:

```
SQL> oradebug help
HELP            [command]                    Describe one or all commands
SETMYPID                                     Debug current process
SETOSPID        <ospid>                      Set OS pid of process to debug
SETORAPID       <orapid> ['force']           Set Oracle pid of process to debug
SETORAPNAME     <orapname>                   Set Oracle process name to debug
SHORT_STACK                                  Get abridged OS stack
CURRENT_SQL                                  Get current SQL
DUMP            <dump_name> <lvl> [addr]     Invoke named dump
DUMPSGA         [bytes]                       Dump fixed SGA
DUMPLIST                                     Print a list of available dumps
EVENT           <text>                       Set trace event in process
SESSION_EVENT   <text>                       Set trace event in session
DUMPVAR         <p|s|uga> <name> [level]     Print/dump a fixed PGA/SGA/UGA variable
DUMPTYPE        <address> <type> <count>     Print/dump an address with type info
SETVAR          <p|s|uga> <name> <value>     Modify a fixed PGA/SGA/UGA variable
PEEK            <addr> <len> [level]         Print/Dump memory
POKE            <addr> <len> <value>         Modify memory
WAKEUP          <orapid>                     Wake up Oracle process
SUSPEND                                      Suspend execution
RESUME                                       Resume execution
FLUSH                                        Flush pending writes to trace file
CLOSE_TRACE                                  Close trace file
TRACEFILE_NAME                               Get name of trace file
LKDEBUG                                      Invoke global enqueue service debugger
NSDBX                                        Invoke CGS name-service debugger
-G              <Inst-List | def | all>      Parallel oradebug command prefix
-R              <Inst-List | def | all>      Parallel oradebug prefix (return output
```

```
SETINST        <instance# .. | all>       Set instance list in double quotes
SGATOFILE      <SGA dump dir>           Dump SGA to file; dirname in double quotes
DMPCOWSGA      <SGA dump dir> Dump & map SGA as COW; dirname in double quotes
MAPCOWSGA      <SGA dump dir>        Map SGA as COW; dirname in double quotes
HANGANALYZE    [level] [syslevel]         Analyze system hang
FFBEGIN                                   Flash Freeze the Instance
FFDEREGISTER                              FF deregister instance from cluster
FFTERMINST                                Call exit and terminate instance
FFRESUMEINST                              Resume the flash frozen instance
FFSTATUS                                  Flash freeze status of instance
SKDSTTPCS      <ifname> <ofname>          Helps translate PCs to names
WATCH          <address> <len> <self|exist|all|target>  Watch a region of memory
DELETE         <local|global|target> watchpoint <id>    Delete a watchpoint
SHOW           <local|global|target> watchpoints        Show watchpoints
DIRECT_ACCESS  <set/enable/disable command | select query> Fixed table access
CORE                                      Dump core without crashing process
IPC                                       Dump ipc information
UNLIMIT                                   Unlimit the size of the trace file
PROCSTAT                                  Dump process statistics
```

This tool helps in identifying any specific issues with the database, such as the following examples:

1. In Chapter 13, we used this tool to relocate the master from one instance in the cluster to another:

```
SQL> oradebug lkdebug -m pkey 492984
Statement processed.
```

The preceding command will relocate the object identified by 492984 mastered on another instance to the current instance. LKDEBUG is a RAC-specific command to collect global cache data:

2. In Chapter 14, we discussed how this tool could be helpful to understand what IP address for interconnect is registered with the database:

```
SQL> ORADEBUG SETMYPID
  ORADEBUG IPC
  EXIT
```

The preceding command will dump the interconnect details registered with the Oracle kernel.

```
SSKGXPT 0x3671e28 flags SSKGXPT_READPENDING info for network
        socket no 9    IP 172.16.193.1        UDP 59084
        sflags SSKGXPT_WRITESSKGXPT_UP
        info for network 1
        socket no 0    IP 0.0.0.0      UDP 0
        sflags SSKGXPT_DOWN
context timestamp 0x4402d
        no ports
```

3. When servers are running slow and there are users complaining of slow sessions, ORADEBUG helps the DBA collect session trace information for user sessions:

```
sqlplus '/as sysdba'
sqlplus> oradebug setospid 7010
sqlplus>oradebug event 10046 trace name context forever, level 12
sqlplus>
sqlplus '/as sysdba'
sqlplus> oradebug setospid 7010
sqlplus> oradebug event 10046 trace name context off
sqlplus>
```

In the preceding output, 10046 trace is collected for session 7010 by setting the operating system process identifier (OSPID) to the current session.

4. Several times when critical issues arise in a production environment and the management keeps looking over the shoulders of the DBA to get the database up, the DBAs do not have sufficient time to do any preliminary investigation. Under these circumstances or when additional information needs to be dumped from the memory structures of Oracle, it could be useful to freeze the instance and dump out instance information for analysis later.

By invoking the flash freeze feature available from ORADEBUG, DBAs can take a diagnostic snapshot of the entire system at the time of failure and quickly restart the database. This helps to complete the analysis offline:

```
SQL> oradebug ffbegin
Statement processed.
```

FFBEGIN (flash freeze begin) will freeze the database instance, including all background processes. When this command is issued, the database will record the freeze information in the alert log:

```
Fri Dec 17 18:01:27 2010
Issuing ORADEBUG FFBEGIN to: Unix process pid: 20344, image: oracle@prddb1 (PMON)
Issuing ORADEBUG FFBEGIN to: Unix process pid: 20346, image: oracle@prddb1 (PSP0)
Issuing ORADEBUG FFBEGIN to: Unix process pid: 20348, image: oracle@prddb1 (VKTM)
Error (ORA-00072) failed to issue ORADEBUG FFBEGIN to: Unix process pid: 20348, image: oracle@prddb1
(VKTM)
Errors in file /app/oracle/diag/rdbms/prddb/PRDDB_1/trace/PRDDB_1_ora_23646.trc:
ORA-00072: process "VKTM" is not active
Issuing ORADEBUG FFBEGIN to: Unix process pid: 20352, image: oracle@prddb1 (GEN0)
Fri Dec 17 18:01:27 2010
Unix process pid: 20344, image: oracle@prddb1 (PMON) flash frozen [ command #1 ]
Issuing ORADEBUG FFBEGIN to: Unix process pid: 20354, image: oracle@prddb1 (DIAG)
Fri Dec 17 18:01:27 2010
Unix process pid: 20346, image: oracle@prddb1 (PSP0) flash frozen [ command #1 ]
Issuing ORADEBUG FFBEGIN to: Unix process pid: 20356, image: oracle@prddb1 (DBRM)
Issuing ORADEBUG FFBEGIN to: Unix process pid: 20358, image: oracle@prddb1 (PING)
Issuing ORADEBUG FFBEGIN to: Unix process pid: 20360, image: oracle@prddb1 (ACMS)
Unix process pid: 20701, image: oracle@prddb1 (TNS V1-V3) flash frozen [ command #1 ]
Fri Dec 17 18:01:27 2010
Unix process pid: 20747, image: oracle@prddb1 (CJQ0) flash frozen [ command #1 ]
Fri Dec 17 18:01:27 2010
Unix process pid: 20706, image: oracle@prddb1 (TNS V1-V3) flash frozen [ command #1 ]
```

```
Fri Dec 17 18:01:27 2010
Unix process pid: 20780, image: oracle@prddb1 (Q000) flash frozen [ command #1 ]
Fri Dec 17 18:01:27 2010
Unix process pid: 20782, image: oracle@prddb1 (Q001) flash frozen [ command #1 ]
```

While the database instance is in freeze mode, DBAs can collect relevant statistics, such as system state dumps and so forth, which could be used for offline analysis:

```
SQL> alter session set events 'immediate trace name systemstate level 10';
Session altered.

*** 2010-12-17 18:01:27.423
Oradebug command 'ffbegin' console output: <none>
*** 2010-12-17 18:02:59.651
=====================================================
SYSTEM STATE (level=10)
------------
System global information:
     processes: base 0x67c3f5cf0, size 150, cleanup 0x6843d4078
     allocation: free sessions 0x68c3dedd0, free calls (nil)
     control alloc errors: 0 (process), 0 (session), 0 (call)
     PMON latch cleanup depth: 0
     seconds since PMON's last scan for dead processes: 141
     system statistics:
0 OS CPU Qt wait time
275 logons cumulative
42 logons current
25367 opened cursors cumulative
```

Once the trace is complete, the instance can be put back to normal operation using the flash freeze resume instance command (FFRESUMEINST):

```
SQL> oradebug ffresumeinst
Statement processed.
FFRESUMEINST (flash freeze resume instance) will unfreeze the database instance allowing normal
operations.
Fri Dec 17 18:07:32 2010
Issuing ORADEBUG FFRESUMEINST to: Unix process pid: 20344, image: oracle@prddb1 (PMON)
Issuing ORADEBUG FFRESUMEINST to: Unix process pid: 20346, image: oracle@prddb1 (PSP0)
Issuing ORADEBUG FFRESUMEINST to: Unix process pid: 20348, image: oracle@prddb1 (VKTM)
Error (ORA-00072) failed to issue ORADEBUG FFRESUMEINST to: Unix process pid: 20348, image: oracle@
prddb1 (VKTM)
```

■ **Note**   In a RAC environment, this should be a quick operation; if the instance where the freeze was issued does not come back to normal operation in approximately 60 seconds, the clusterware will attempt to evict the nonresponding instance from the cluster. This is illustrated in the output from the alert log file.

```
Fri Dec 17 18:05:47 2010
LMS1 (ospid: 18144) has detected no messaging activity from instance 1
LMS1 (ospid: 18144) issues an IMR to resolve the situation
Please check LMS1 trace file for more detail.
Fri Dec 17 18:05:47 2010
Communications reconfiguration: instance_number 1
Fri Dec 17 18:06:05 2010
LMS0 (ospid: 18140) has detected no messaging activity from instance 1
LMS0 (ospid: 18140) issues an IMR to resolve the situation
Please check LMS0 trace file for more detail.
Fri Dec 17 18:06:33 2010
minact-scn master exiting with err:12751
Fri Dec 17 18:06:43 2010
IPC Send timeout detected. Sender: ospid 18172 [oracle@prddb2 (MMON)]
Receiver: inst 1 binc 447836989 ospid 20366
Fri Dec 17 18:06:45 2010
Evicting instance 1 from cluster
Waiting for instances to leave: 1
IPC Send timeout to 1.0 inc 4 for msg type 8 from opid 27
IPC Send timeout: Terminating pid 27 osid 18172
Fri Dec 17 18:06:56 2010
IPC Send timeout detected. Sender: ospid 18138 [oracle@prddb2 (LMD0)]
Receiver: inst 1 binc 447836989 ospid 20366
Fri Dec 17 18:06:57 2010
Restarting dead background process MMON
Fri Dec 17 18:06:57 2010
MMON started with pid=27, OS id=20073
IPC Send timeout to 1.0 inc 4 for msg type 65521 from opid 12
Fri Dec 17 18:07:05 2010
Remote instance kill is issued with system inc 6
Remote instance kill map (size 1) : 1
LMON received an instance eviction notification from instance 2
The instance eviction reason is 0x20000000
The instance eviction map is 1
Reconfiguration started (old inc 4, new inc 8)
List of instances:
 2 (myinst: 2)
 Global Resource Directory frozen
 * dead instance detected - domain 0 invalid = TRUE
 Communication channels reestablished
 Master broadcasted resource hash value bitmaps
 Non-local Process blocks cleaned out
Fri Dec 17 18:07:06 2010
 LMS 0: 0 GCS shadows cancelled, 0 closed, 0 Xw survived
Fri Dec 17 18:07:06 2010
 LMS 1: 0 GCS shadows cancelled, 0 closed, 0 Xw survived
 Set master node info
 Submitted all remote-enqueue requests
 Dwn-cvts replayed, VALBLKs dubious
 All grantable enqueues granted
 Post SMON to start 1st pass IR
```

```
Fri Dec 17 18:07:06 2010
Instance recovery: looking for dead threads
 Submitted all GCS remote-cache requests
 Post SMON to start 1st pass IR
 Fix write in gcs resources
Reconfiguration complete
Beginning instance recovery of 1 threads
 parallel recovery started with 23 processes
Started redo scan
Completed redo scan
 read 1670 KB redo, 628 data blocks need recovery
Started redo application at
 Thread 1: logseq 6, block 35939
Recovery of Online Redo Log: Thread 1 Group 5 Seq 6 Reading mem 0
 Mem# 0: +PRD_DATA/prddb/onlinelog/group_5.263.737994533
 Mem# 1: +PRD_FRA/prddb/onlinelog/group_5.259.737994535
Fri Dec 17 18:07:09 2010
minact-scn: Inst 2 is now the master inc#:8 mmon proc-id:20073 status:0x7
minact-scn status: grec-scn:0x0000.00000000 gmin-scn:0x0000.00108c8e gcalc-scn:0x0000.00108c99
minact-scn: master found reconf/inst-rec before recscn scan old-inc#:8 new-inc#:8
Completed redo application of 1.52MB
Completed instance recovery at
 Thread 1: logseq 6, block 39279, scn 1105982
 604 data blocks read, 610 data blocks written, 1670 redo k-bytes read
Thread 1 advanced to log sequence 7 (thread recovery)
minact-scn: master continuing after IR
Fri Dec 17 18:07:33 2010
Dumping diagnostic data in directory=[cdmp_20101217180733], requested by (instance=1, osid=20398
(ASMB)), summary=[abnormal instance termination].
Fri Dec 17 18:07:58 2010
Reconfiguration started (old inc 8, new inc 10)
List of instances:
 1 2 (myinst: 2)
 Global Resource Directory frozen
 Communication channels reestablished
```

When the instance is released from the freeze, it joins the cluster immediately.

Critical ORA Errors

DBAs, when paged for critical production issues and the message received on the page/e-mail/notification is an ORA-0600 error, will allmost always get on the the database server to get an understanding of how critical or what kind of immediate impact it has on the system and then starts working on creating a support request (SR) with Oracle support. In this section, we discuss two important such errors: ORA-0600 and ORA-7445.

ORA-600: Internal error code, arguments: [...], [...]

An ORA-600 error indicates a kernel exception. When such an error is encountered, Oracle records certain details related to this error in the alert log file and also in a trace file.

This error message could mean errors in different areas of the Oracle kernel. The actual area is identified by the arguments listed in the error message. For example

```
ORA-600: internal error code, arguments: [784], [0x3BE577248], [0x3BE578B88],
```

In the ORA-600 error message, the first argument 784 indicates that the error is related to the service layer. Similarly, depending on the range that the first argument falls into, the error is grouped under a specific category, as shown in Table 18-1.

Table 18-1. *ORA-600 Argument and Layer Information*

Argument	Layer
0000	Service layer
2000	Cache layer component base
4000	Transaction layer
6000	Data layer
8000	Access layer
9000	Parallel server
10000	Control layer
12000	User/Oracle interface layer
14000	System-dependent layer (port specific)
15000	Security layer
17000	Generic layer
18000	K2 (2-phase commit)
19000	Object layer
21000	Replication layer
23000	OLTP layer

If an ORA-600 error is encountered and a solution to the problem is not available internally or from search on metalink, Oracle Support needs to be notified by opening a service request. During the notification process, all related information, including copies of the alert log and trace files referenced in the alert log, needs to be uploaded for Oracle to analyze and provide the appropriate fix[2].

■ **Note**   As discussed in the earlier sections, starting with Oracle Database 11g, the ADR should be used to package all related information required for Oracle support.

---

[2]Source: Oracle Corporation.

Before notifying Oracle of the error message, as DBAs, the first step is to determine if others have encountered this error. Such information could be obtained from metalink. Oracle has provided an ORA-600 error lookup utility that will help in obtaining this.

Figure 18-6, shown earlier in this chapter, is an input screen for the ORA-600 argument lookup. On selecting the Oracle version and providing the first argument, the lookup will search through metalink and provide any information that is available on the specific error argument. Based on the message, the fix may already be explained.

In certain cases, depending on the type of error and occurrence of the message, information pertaining to the argument may not be available. In this case, a technical assistance request (TAR) or a service request (SR) is opened with Oracle Support.

ORA-7445: exception encountered core dump [...][...]

ORA-7445 is also a critical error; however, the criticality is not grouped at the same level as the ORA-600 errors. The ORA-7445 error indicates that the process may have performed an illegal operation and hence was terminated by the operating system.

Like the ORA-600 error, ORA-7445 also reports arguments to the error message. Unlike the ORA-600 error argument, the ORA-7445 argument is alphanumeric rather than numeric and normally reflects an Oracle-related internal function call. The Oracle error lookup tool[3] (shown previously in Figure 18-6) is a good starting point to look at ORA-7445 errors.

DBA Support Utilities

In the preceding section, when critical errors are encountered and an SR is opened with Oracle support, to help, the Oracle support staff—to better understand the environment and diagnose the issues—would like to understand the current state of the environment: for example, the patches applied, the current version levels, any third-party utilities/applications configured, and so forth. In this section, we discuss some of these utilities.

Remote Diagnostic Agent (RDA)

RDA is a command line utility to gather diagnostic information about an Oracle environment. The scripts are focused to collect information that will aid in problem diagnosis; however, the output is also very useful to see the comprehensive view of an environment.

When reporting critical errors to Oracle Support, it is encouraged that the RDA be used because it gives a comprehensive picture of the environment. This can greatly reduce TAR resolution time by minimizing the number of requests from Oracle Support Services for more information. RDA does not modify your system in any way; it merely collects data useful for Oracle Support Services.

Because the operation of these scripts is system specific, Oracle provides different sets of scripts and downloadable scripts for the various operating systems.

When installing RDA for gathering information from a RAC implementation, depending on whether Oracle and the operating system files are installed individually for each node, it is good to download and configure RDA on all instances. If Oracle and the operating systems files are shared among all instances (e.g., in HP Tru64), only one installation of RDA is required. My Oracle support (MOS) 314422.1 gives details on how to download, install, configure, and collect required information.

---

[3]Troubleshoot on ORA-600 or ORA-7445 error using lookup tool—Metalink Note: 153788.1.

RAC DIAG

RACDIAG.SQL is a script downloadable from Oracle support MOS 135714.1. This script contains queries that will help diagnose various areas of the RAC instance and the cluster. The script was originally intended to diagnose hung sessions; however, its potential is much greater.

Among these scripts and outputs generated by the RACDIAG.SQL utility, the section that contains information regarding WAITING SESSIONS is very important in providing details of any serious issues.

Apart from the RAC diagnostic scripts, which help capture performance-related data, Oracle also provides another set of diagnostic steps for troubleshooting inter-instance performance. Although Oracle metalink Note 18489.1 is titled "Tuning inter-instance performance in RAC and OPS," it has a good amount of detail that helps troubleshoot interconnect issues.

ORACHK

ORACHK (Oracle check) is a new utility available from Oracle support to validate the Oracle environment and collect configuration information. The tool currently supports single instance, RAC, Exadata, and Oracle E-Business (EBS) suite implementations. The utility could be implemented to run as a single run or can be scheduled to run automatically at predefined intervals. The utility provides the following capabilities:

- It runs one node at a time and runs across all nodes in the cluster, checking all required configuration parameters and O/S-level prerequisites.

- The proactive method helps, simplifies, and streamlines how to investigate and analyze which known issues present a risk to you.

- The utility is itself lightweight. It runs as user Oracle and does not require any configuration or schemas to be created.

- The report produced by this tool allows you to drill down to specific areas of the configuration and validate information.

- When the utility is configured to run automatically at predefined intervals, it can be configured to send e-mail notifications when it detects problems.

- Collection Manager, a companion Application Express web app, provides a single dashboard view of collections across your entire enterprise.

The utility can be downloaded from Oracle support MOS 1268927.2. Once the utility is downloaded to the appropriate cluster node, assign the execute privileges and invoke it using the following command. The output following is cluster information from a five-node 12c RAC implementation:

```
oracle@ssky1l4p1]$ ./orachk -a -o V

CRS stack is running and CRS_HOME is not set. Do you want to set CRS_HOME to /u01/app/12.1.0.1/
grid?[y/n][y]y

Checking ssh user equivalency settings on all nodes in cluster
```

Node ssky1l4p2 is configured for ssh user equivalency for oracle user
Node ssky1l4p3 is configured for ssh user equivalency for oracle user
Node ssky1l4p4 is configured for ssh user equivalency for oracle user
Node ssky1l4p5 is configured for ssh user equivalency for oracle user

Searching for running databases . . . . .
. . .
Checking Status of Oracle Software Stack - Clusterware, ASM, RDBMS

. . . .

Oracle Stack Status

Host Name	CRS Installed	ASM HOME	RDBMS Installed	CRS UP	ASM UP	RDBMS UP	DB Instance Name
ssky1l4p1	Yes	Yes	Yes	Yes	Yes	No	
ssky1l4p2	Yes	Yes	Yes	Yes	Yes	No	
ssky1l4p3	Yes	Yes	Yes	Yes	Yes	No	
ssky1l4p4	Yes	Yes	Yes	Yes	Yes	No	
ssky1l4p5	Yes	Yes	Yes	Yes	Yes	No	

Copying plug-ins

. . . .
. . . . . .
123 of the included audit checks require root privileged data collection . If sudo is not configured
or the root password is not available, audit checks which require root privileged data collection
can be skipped.
1. Enter 1 if you will enter root password for each host when prompted
2. Enter 2 if you have sudo configured for oracle user to execute root_orachk.sh script
3. Enter 3 to skip the root privileged collections
4. Enter 4 to exit and work with the SA to configure sudo or to arrange for root access and run the
tool later.
Please indicate your selection from one of the above options for root access[1-4][1]:- 1

*** Checking Best Practice Recommendations (PASS/WARNING/FAIL) ***
Collections and audit checks log file is
/media/sf_Downloads/orachk_ssky1l4p1_051914_170031/log/orachk.log

Running orachk in serial mode because expect(/usr/bin/expect) is not available to supply root
passwords on remote nodes
NOTICE: Installing the expect utility (/usr/bin/expect) will allow orachk to gather root passwords
at the beginning of the process and execute orachk on all nodes in parallel speeding up the entire
process. For more info - http://www.nist.gov/el/msid/expect.cfm. Expect is available for all major
platforms. See User Guide for more details.

Checking for prompts in /home/oracle/.bash_profile on ssky1l4p1 for oracle user...
Checking for prompts in /home/oracle/.bash_profile on ssky1l4p2 for oracle user...
Checking for prompts in /home/oracle/.bash_profile on ssky1l4p3 for oracle user...
Checking for prompts in /home/oracle/.bash_profile on ssky1l4p4 for oracle user...
Checking for prompts in /home/oracle/.bash_profile on ssky1l4p5 for oracle user...

```
================================================================
                    Node name - ssky1l4p1
================================================================


Collecting - ASM DIsk I/O stats
Collecting - ASM Disk Groups
Collecting - ASM Diskgroup Attributes
Collecting - ASM disk partnership imbalance
. . . . . . . . . . . . . . . . . . . . . . .
. . . . . .
Collecting - DiskMount Information
Collecting - Huge pages configuration
Collecting - Kernel parameters
Collecting - Linux module config.
Collecting - Maximum number of semaphore sets on system
. . . . . . . . . . . . . . . . . . . . . . .
. . . . . .
Collecting - Operating system release information and kernel version
Collecting - Oracle Executable Attributes
Collecting - Voting disks (clusterware)
Collecting - number of semaphore operations per semop system call
Collecting - slabinfo
Preparing to run root privileged commands  ssky1l4p1.  Please enter root password when prompted.
root@ssky1l4p1's password:
Collecting - Broadcast Requirements for Networks
. . . . . . . . . . . . . . . . . . . . . . .
. . . . . .
Collecting - OCFS2 disks
Collecting - OLR Integrity
Collecting - Root user limits
Collecting - ocsf status
Collecting - root time zone check

Data collections completed. Checking best practices on ssky1l4p1.

WARNING => /tmp is NOT on a dedicated filesystemPASS =>   ORA_CRS_HOME environment variable is not
set
PASS =>    net.core.wmem_default Is Configured Properly
PASS =>    net.core.wmem_max Is Configured Properly
PASS =>    net.core.rmem_default Is Configured Properly
PASS =>    None of the hostnames contains an underscore character
PASS =>    Interconnect is configured on non-routable network addresses
PASS =>    net.core.rmem_max is Configured Properly
PASS =>    OCR is being backed up daily
INFO =>    $CRS_HOME/log/hostname/client directory does not have too many older log files
PASS =>    The number of async IO descriptors is sufficient (/proc/sys/fs/aio-max-nr)
PASS =>    Kernel Parameter kernel.shmall OK
PASS =>    Kernel Parameter SEMOPM OK
PASS =>    Kernel Parameter SEMMNI OK
PASS =>    Kernel Parameter SEMMSL OK
PASS =>    Kernel Parameter kernel.shmmni OK
```

```
PASS =>    Kernel Parameter SEMMNS OK
INFO =>    Number of SCAN listeners is NOT equal to the recommended number of 3.
FAIL =>    Operating system hugepages count does not satisfy total SGA requirements
WARNING => NIC bonding is not configured for interconnect
WARNING => NIC bonding is NOT configured for public network (VIP)
WARNING => OSWatcher is not running as is recommended.
. . . . . . . . . . . . . . . . . . . . . . . . . . . . . .
. . . . . .
INFO =>    Jumbo frames (MTU >=8192) are not configured for interconnect
WARNING => NTP is not running with correct setting
INFO =>    Information about hanganalyze and systemstate dump
. . . . . . . . . . . . . . . . . . . . . . . . .
WARNING => Network interfaces for cluster_interconnect are NOT on separate subnets
WARNING => TFA Collector is either not installed or not running
WARNING => vm.min_free_kbytes should be set as recommended.
INFO =>    Consider increasing the COREDUMPSIZE size
WARNING => Shell limit hard nproc for root is NOT configured according to recommendation
. . . . . . . . . . . . . . . . . . . . . . . . . . . . . .
. . . . . .


Best Practice checking completed.Checking recommended patches on ssky1l4p1.
-------------------------------------------------------------------------------
. . . . . . . . . . . . . . . . . . . . . . . . .
. . . . . .
=================================================================
                  Node name - ssky1l4p2
=================================================================


Collecting - /proc/cmdline
. . . . . . . . . . . . . . . . . . . . . . . . . . .
. . . . . .
```

OLS

The OLS (Oracle LiSt) is a Perl script that helps get consolidated information/configuration of the RAC cluster. It helps get a list of installed components on the cluster. Although the utility was originally developed to give a consolidated list of cluster information for Oracle Database 12c RAC environment, the utility also works on the lower versions of Oracle. The Perl script/utility can be downloaded from Oracle support MOS 1568439.1.

Once the utility is downloaded to the appropriate cluster node, assign the execute privileges and invoke it using the following command. The output following is cluster information from a five-node Oracle Database 12c RAC implementation:

oracle@ssky4l4p1]$ ./ols.pl

```
Local Time Now :        2014-04-08 14:26:19

The Cluster Nodes are :                 ssky4l4p2, ssky4l4p3, ssky4l4p4, ssky4l4p5
The Local Node is :                     ssky4l4p2
The Remote Nodes are :                  ssky4l4p3, ssky4l4p4, ssky4l4p5
```

```
Major Clusterware Software Version is :        12.1.0.1.0
Major Clusterware Active Version is :          12.1.0.1.0
Major Clusterware Release Version is :         12.1.0.1.0


CRS_HOME is installed at :                     /u01/app/12.1.0.1/grid
CRS_BASE is installed at :                     /u01/app/oracle
CRS_OWNER is :                                 oracle
CRS_GROUP is :                                 oinstall


ORACLE_HOMES[0] is installed at :              /u02/app/oracle/product/12.1.0/db_1
ORACLE_BASES[0] is installed at :              /u02/app/oracle
ORACLE_OWNERS[0] is :                          oracle
ORACLE_GROUPS[0] is :                          oinstall


All databases created : EMCCDB, SSKYDB
```

DB_NAME	MANAGEMENT	DB_TYPE	DB_VERSION	DB_HOME	DG_USED
EMCCDB	administrator	SINGLE	12.1.0.1.0	/u02/app/oracle/product/12.1.0/db_1	'+SEMCC_DATA'
SSKYDB	policy	RAC	12.1.0.1.0	/u02/app/oracle/product/12.1.0/db_1	'+SSKYDB_DATA'

NODE_NAME	NODE_ID	NODE_STATE	NODE_ROLE
ssky4l4p2	1	Active	Hub
ssky4l4p5	2	Active	Hub
ssky4l4p3	3	Active	Hub
ssky4l4p4	4	Active	Hub
semcc1l1p1	5	Inactive	None

```
WARNING: Error occurred during running "/u01/app/12.1.0.1/grid/bin/srvctl config gns -clustername" :
PRKF-1110 : Neither GNS server nor GNS client is configured on this cluster
256
Cluster Name :              ssky4l4-cluster
SCAN Name :                 ssky4l4p-scan
SCAN Listeners :            LISTENER_SCAN1 (Port: TCP:1521)
GNS Status :                not configured

Node VIP Version :          12.1.0.1.0
Local Node VIPs :           ora.ssky4l4p2.vip       ssky4l4p2-vip.localdomain       (static)
                            ora.ssky4l4p3.vip       ssky4l4p3-vip.localdomain       (static)
                            ora.ssky4l4p4.vip       ssky4l4p4-vip.localdomain       (static)
                            ora.ssky4l4p5.vip       ssky4l4p5-vip.localdomain       (static)

Oracle Interfaces :         eth0    192.168.1.0     global  public
                            eth1    10.1.4.0        global  asm
                            eth2    10.1.4.0        global  cluster_interconnect
                            eth3    10.1.4.0        global  cluster_interconnect
```

OCR Location :   '+GRID_DATA'

Voting Disk Location :   '+GRID_DATA'

Cluster Mode :   Standard Cluster with Flex ASM

Hub Node	attaches	Leaf Node
ssky4l4p2(1,Active)	<---	None
ssky4l4p5(2,Active)	<---	None
ssky4l4p3(3,Active)	<---	None
ssky4l4p4(4,Active)	<---	None
semcc1l1p1(5,Inactive)	<---	None

MGMTDB Status :   enabled and is running on ssky4l4p3
MGMTDB HOME :   /u01/app/12.1.0.1/grid
MGMTDB Spfile :   '+GRID_DATA/_mgmtdb/spfile-MGMTDB.ora'
MGMTDB Instance :   '-MGMTDB'

DISKGROUP PATH	REDUNDANCY	AU	COMPATIBILITY	DB_COMPATIBILITY	SIZE_MB	FREE_MB	USABLE_MB
GRID_DATA /dev/oracleasm/disks/ASMVOL2	NORMAL	1MB	12.1.0.0.0	10.1.0.0.0	15342	7555	1220
/dev/oracleasm/disks/ASMVOL3							
/dev/oracleasm/disks/ASMVOL1							
SEMCC_DATA /dev/oracleasm/disks/ASMVOL7	EXTERN	1MB	12.1.0.0.0	10.1.0.0.0	51199	48045	48045
SEMCC_FRA /dev/oracleasm/disks/ASMVOL5	EXTERN	1MB	12.1.0.0.0	10.1.0.0.0	10228	9911	9911
/dev/oracleasm/disks/ASMVOL4							
SSKYDB_ACFS /dev/oracleasm/disks/ASMVOL9	EXTERN	1MB	12.1.0.0.0	10.1.0.0.0	12284	12146	12146
SSKYDB_DATA /dev/oracleasm/disks/ASMVOL6	EXTERN	1MB	12.1.0.0.0	10.1.0.0.0	102398	94721	94721
SSKYDB_FRA /dev/oracleasm/disks/ASMVOL8	EXTERN	1MB	12.1.0.0.0	10.1.0.0.0	20473	19692	19692

ASM Host	connects	Client
ssky4l4p2.localdomain(+ASM1)	<---	'+APX1(ssky4l4p2)'
ssky4l4p2.localdomain(+ASM1)	<---	'+APX2(ssky4l4p5)'
ssky4l4p2.localdomain(+ASM1)	<---	'+ASM1(ssky4l4p2)'
ssky4l4p2.localdomain(+ASM1)	<---	'EMCC(ssky4l4p5)'
ssky4l4p3.localdomain(+ASM3)	<---	'+APX3(ssky4l4p3)'
ssky4l4p3.localdomain(+ASM3)	<---	'+ASM3(ssky4l4p3)'
ssky4l4p3.localdomain(+ASM3)	<---	'-MGMTDB(ssky4l4p3)'
ssky4l4p3.localdomain(+ASM3)	<---	'SSKYDB_1(ssky4l4p3)'

```
ssky4l4p4.localdomain(+ASM4)          <---                    '+APX4(ssky4l4p4)'
ssky4l4p4.localdomain(+ASM4)          <---                    '+ASM4(ssky4l4p4)'
ssky4l4p4.localdomain(+ASM4)          <---                    'SSKYDB_2(ssky4l4p4)'


OCR/CRSD Master :  ssky4l4p3

CRSD PE Master :     ssky4l4p3

CRSD PE Standby :    ssky4l4p4

CTSS Master :        ssky4l4p3

UI Master :          ssky4l4p3

ONS Master :         ssky4l4p4

CHM Master :         ssky4l4p3

CHM Replica :        REPLICA has been deprecated from 12c

OCR Local/Writer                     connects                ASM Instance
================                     ========                ============
ssky4l4p2(Hub,OCR Local)             --->                    ssky4l4p4(+ASM4)
ssky4l4p5(Hub,OCR Local)             --->                    ssky4l4p2(+ASM1)
ssky4l4p3(Hub,OCR Writer)            --->                    ssky4l4p3(+ASM3)
ssky4l4p4(Hub,OCR Local)             --->                    ssky4l4p4(+ASM4)
```

Conclusion

In this chapter we looked at the various problem-solving diagnosis methods for different kinds of error situations. ORA-0600 and ORA-7445 are errors that normally cause great concern to the DBAs. Such concerns are genuine because these errors are critical and could mean downtime for the production instance in certain cases.

Oracle has provided various methods of troubleshooting the instance and the database to gather information. If any of the previously mentioned errors occur, it is advisable to collect the following information irrespective of what is already generated by Oracle:

1. Use the HM and ADR for creating problem definitions.

2. Gather information from all instances using the RDA utility.

3. If required, use ORADEBUG to freeze the instance and collect the system state dump as illustrated in the flash freeze section previously.

4. If a query is involved during the operation, the SQL Diagnosability functionality can be used to create the required test case so that Oracle support can reproduce the problem.

5. Zip these files and upload them to Oracle Support when the TAR is initially created.

APPENDIX A

■ ■ ■

The SQL Scripts Used in This Book

This appendix lists and documents the various scripts referenced and/or used in the various chapters of this book.

Please note that the scripts are provided for illustration/example purposes only. The author does not intend to support these scripts. The scripts have been tested and appear to work as intended. It is advised that all scripts should be run in a test environment before executing the same in a production environment.

All scripts are suffixed with the following string: "MVRACPDnTap" (Murali Vallath, RAC Performance Diagnostics and Tuning, Apress). It's just a method to keep generic scripts from those written specifically for this book.

Chapter 3—Testing for Availability

No.	Script Name	Description
1	MVRACPDnTap_verifyic.sql	Script helps to list the interconnects configured and currently in use by the database for cache fusion activity.
2	MVRACPDnTap_taftest.sql	Check if the connections made to the database are using the TAF feature. Also, during an instance crash, the script can be used to check on how many connections have failed over from the failed instance to one of the surviving instances.
3	MVRACPDnTap_dgsynchcheck.sql	The script is used to verify if the database is synchronized between the primary and the standby site. Useful during a scheduled maintenance operation when the data guard switchover operation is planned between the primary and standby site.

Chapter 4—Testing for Scalability

No.	Script Name	Description
1	MVRACPDnTap_iocalcheck1.sql	I/O calibration check. Script helps to check if calibration has been completed for the database and what the current IOPS (I/Os per second) is for the number of physical disks provided to the calibration operation.

Chapter 5—Real Application Testing

No.	Script Name	Description
1	MVRACPDnTap_extractsql.pl	Sample perl script to help extract SQL statements from 10046 trace file and help replace bind variables with bind values. The output could be used for load/stress testing the environment.

Chapter 6—Tools and Utilities

No.	Script Name	Description
1	MVRACPDnTap_ServiceStats.sql	Script lists database service stats. The script helps to isolate top activity on the database by service name.
2	MVRACPDnTap_enableAgg.sql	Lists the aggregation type enabled at the module/action level.
3	MVRACPDnTap_ServModActStats.sql	Script lists statistics enabled at the service/module/action level from GV$SERV_MOD_ACT_STATS view.

Chapter 9—Tuning the Database

No.	Script Name	Description
1	MVRACPDnTap_EnqStats.sql	The query/script gives a list of the top enqueue statistics from all instances in the cluster. It helps to understand the current enqueue activity and potential contention areas.
2	MVRACPDnTap_rowcache.sql	The row cache statistics from the output help to understand the database configuration settings. Higher refresh or reload activity for a specific row cache item could be an indication to look at optimizing it, for example, in the case of sequences (identified by dc_sequences) to increase the cache size.
3	MVRACPDnTap_dlmrowcache.sql	It's a variation of the previous query. The primary difference between the two is from what level the data is reported. This query reports data from a RAC level, across instances, and reflects cache fusion activity.
4	MVRACPDnTap_seqcachebal.sql	When monitoring the cache size requirements for database sequences, the script helps to understand how frequently the database sequences are consumed and how often they have to be reloaded. This helps to size the cache and to understand the contentions when the database sequences are defined with the order clause.
5	MVRACPDnTap_hardparses.sql	The script gives a count of the total number of hard parse operations from the database.
6	MVRACPDnTap_rcobjectcount.sql	The script gives a list of objects currently stored in the result cache section of the shared pool.
7	MVRACPDnTap_rcobjects.sql	The query gives a list of objects involved in a result cache operation.
8	MVRACPDnTap_rcutil.sql	The query gives the current result cache statistics. It gives the current space utilization of the results section of the operation.
9	MVRACPDnTap_clsqlstats.sql	The script gives cluster-level stats for an SQL Statement.
10	MVRACPDnTap_impopcheck.sql	The script lists the current segment statistics of the in-memory area.

Chapter 11—Tuning Oracle Net

No.	Script Name	Description
1	MVRACPDnTap_svcloadstats.sql	The query displays the current load distribution across the various database services. The load characteristics are updated by MMON and can be viewed from GV$SERVICEMETRIC view.

Chapter 12—Tuning the Storage Subsystem

No.	Script Name	Description
1	MVRACPDnTap_iostat.sql	The script displays information regarding disk I/O statistics of database files. Statistics for data files and temp files are listed for each file. However, for other types of files, such as archive logs and backup sets, statistics are consolidated into one entry.

Chapter 13—Tuning Global Cache

No.	Script Name	Description
1	MVRACPDnTap_reslimit.sql	The query lists the current utilization of the global cache section of the instance memory. When the current utilization equals or nears the value of the initial allocation, it's an indication to resize the appropriate memory parameters.
2	MVRACPDnTap_sharedpooladvice.sql	The scripts checks against the shared_pool_advice view and indicates the current utilization of the shared pool. Based on the frequent need for a higher shared pool, increasing the start value to 30 G provided improved performances.
3	MVRACPDnTap_blkpreptime11g.sql	The query will help determine the average time spent to prepare the block for the requestor.
4	MVRACPDnTap_blksndtime.sql	The query will help determine the average time spent by the process to send the block to the requestor.
5	MVRACPDnTap_gesLockBlockers.sql	This script shows GES locks and blockers with grants and acquires.
6	MVRACPDnTap_policyhistory.sql	The script helps to understand what type of policy was used while the objects where remastered from one instance to the other. The query looks at historical behavior by querying the V$POLICY_HISTORY view.
7	MVRACPDnTap_sqlstats.sql	The script gives the wait times experienced by the query during various stages of the operation. It helps to understand cluster-related waits and IO-related waits for the query.
8	MVRACPDnTap_findhotobjmasters.sql	The script lists the current master (CM) and previous master (PM) instances for a few of the objects. The output has been sorted by the number of times it has been remastered (CNT column) since the instances were started.

(continued)

No.	Script Name	Description
9	MVRACPDnTap_objpolicystats.sql	The script against the X$OBJECT_POLICY_STATISTICS gives current statistics on the type of access the objects have on the instances they are currently being mastered. SOPENS column indicates the number of times the object has been mastered on the instance in shared mode. XOPENS indicates exclusive mode, and XREFS indicates exclusive reference.
10	MVRACPDnTap_blockers.sql	The script helps to identify lockers and the sessions that are blocked from due to chained waits.
11	MVRACPDnTap_latch_childrencbc.sql	The script lists the CBC (cache buffer chains) latch statistics.
12	MVRACPDnTap_seglatchstats.sql	The query helps determine the objects and the number of times that the object has been touched.
13	MVRACPDnTap_instCacheTrans.sql	The query displays statistics for blocks transferred among instances in the cluster; the view captures data based on where the data had originated.
14	MVRACPDnTap_gesLockBlockers.sql	The script displays all locks currently maintained by the Global Enqueue Service and helps in identifying global lockers and waiters across the cluster.
15	MVRACPDnTap_crblksrvr.sql	The script list the CR blocks served statistics.
16	MVRACPDnTap_curblksrvr.sql	The script lists the current block served statistics.
17	MVRACPDnTap_ConvertLocal.sql	The script displays statistics for local GES enqueue operations and records average convert times, count information, and timed statistics for global enqueue requests for current and consistent read requests/operations.
18	MVRACPDnTap_ConvertRemote.sql	The script displays average convert times, count information, and timed statistics for global enqueue requests for CURRENT blocks. The script helps to determine the type of locks conversions that did not occur locally on the instance and had happened on one of the remote instances in the cluster.
19	MVRACPDnTap_dlmlibcache.sql	The script displays statistics showing library cache performance and activities. When looking at RAC from each individual instance in the cluster, the RELOADS and INVALIDATIONS columns should be monitored. RELOADS indicates the number of times the objects had to be reloaded into the library cache.
20	MVRACPDnTap_rowcache.sql	This script displays statistics showing the cache behavior of the dictionary cache. The dictionary cache is part of the shared pool and does not have any tunable parameters other than the \SHARED_POOL initialization parameter itself. This means that if the shared pool has not been sized correctly, there is a direct impact on the dictionary cache.
21	MVRACPDnTap_svcstats.sql	The script list the statistics for the database services with active sessions. The script is identical to the MVRACPDnTap_svcloadstats.sql script used in Chapter 11.

Chapter 14—Tuning the Cluster Interconnect

No.	Script Name	Description
1	MVRACPDnTap_dlmmisc.sql	The script gives you the distributed lock manager activity across the network and specifically around the message traffic.
2	MVRACPDnTap_verifyic.sql	The script helps to verify the Interconnect configuration to check if the right interconnect addresses have been registered or are visible from inside the database instance.
3	MVRACPDnTap_blksndtime.sql	The script helps calculate the time required to send the block from the holder to the requestor across all instances in the cluster.
4	MVRACPDnTap_dlmtrafficntrl.sql	When a message needs to be sent, the process needs to acquire a ticket from the pool and return the ticket back to the pool once the message has been transmitted. When there is a message flooding, there may not be a sufficient amount of tickets in the pool, and the process requesting for the ticket will have to wait for the ticket. The script displays the current usage of tickets.
5	MVRACPDnTap_raclostblocks.sql	Blocks can be corrupted or lost during transfer across the interconnect. This script helps determine the number of blocks lost/corrupted over the interconnect since the instance was started.
6	MVRACPDnTap_Dynamicmasterstats.sql	The data from the query provides an indication of the overall activity of remaster operations and the time spent at various stages of the operation.

Chapter 15—Optimizing Distributed Workload

No.	Script Name	Description
1	MVRACPDnTap_rowcache.sql	This script displays statistics showing the cache behavior of the dictionary cache. The dictionary cache is part of the shared pool and does not have any tunable parameters other than the SHARED_POOL initialization parameter itself. This means that if the shared pool has not been sized correctly, there is a direct impact on the dictionary cache.
2	MVRACPDnTap_sqlstats.sql	The script lists SQL run time statistics.
3	MVRACPDnTap_whoractive.sql	This script will list details for active sessions.
4	MVRACPDnTap_dbrm.sql	This script will define DBRM packages and the various services used in Chapter 15.
5	MVRACPDnTap_svcstatshist.sql	Script will list all statistics for services from the service metrics history view.
6	MVRACPDnTap_SrvActSum.sql	Script lists the summary of all actions by services.
7	MVRACPDnTap_SrvModSum.sql	Script lists the summary of all modules by services.

Chapter 17—Waits, Enqueues, and Latches

No.	Script Name	Description
1	MVRACPDnTap_dlmlatch.sql	The script shows the number of times the latch was acquired by sessions on one of the instances in a RAC cluster in an Oracle Database 12c Release 1 environment.
2	MVRACPDnTap_latchchildren.sql	This script against the view V$LATCH_CHILDREN can help us arrive at the address that has the highest miss rate.
3	MVRACPDnTap_hotsegments.sql	The script helps identify the segments most often subject to cache buffer chains latch statistics.
4	MVRACPDnTap_whoractivep.sql	The script helps list all the current active sessions and the process information.
5	MVRACPDnTap_lockmodes.sql	The script helps list all the current lock modes for the enqueues on the database.
6	MVRACPDnTap_enqstats.sql	The script helps understand the enqueue stats from the database.
7	MVRACPDnTap_rowcache.sql	The row cache statistics from the output helps to understand the database configuration settings. The higher the refresh or reload activity for a specific row cache item could be an indication one should look at optimizing it, for example, in the case of sequences (identified by dc_sequences) to increase the cache size.
8	MVRACPDnTap_dlmrowcache.sql	This is a variation of the pervious query. The primary difference between the two is from what level the data is reported. This query reports data from a RAC level, across instances, and reflects cache fusion activity.
9	MVRACPDnTap_lostblocks.sql	Blocks can be corrupted or lost during transfer across the interconnect. This script helps determine the number of blocks lost/corrupted over the interconnect since the instance was started.

Chapter 18—Problem Diagnostics

No.	Script Name	Description
1	MVRACPDnTap_HMChecksList.sql	Script lists all the currently configured health monitor checks.
2	MVRACPDnTap_hmparmlist.sql	Script provides a list of parameters required to execute the various health monitor checks.
3	MVRACPDnTap_HMRunSatus.sql	Script helps check the status of the various health monitor checks.
4	MVRACPDnTap_HMfinding.sql	Script provides a listing of the findings from the health monitor check.
5	MVRACPDnTap_adrproblemlist.sql	Script provides a summary of the currently encountered problems on the various instances in the cluster.

(*continued*)

No.	Script Name	Description
6	MVRACPDnTap_ADRDiagInfo.sql	Script provides a list of all the ADR destinations in the environment.
7	MVRACPDnTap_adrcontrol.sql	Script helps list the currently set retention parameters for the both the short-term and long-term policies.
8	MVRACPDnTap_adrincfiles.sql	Script provides details on the trace and user dump files that contain the relevant information pertaining to the incident.
9	MVRACPDnTap_adripsmetadata.sql	Script lists all the metadata related to the incident.
10	MVRACPDnTap_adrddeuseraction.sql	Script lists SQL queries associated with any incident.

Bibliography

"Designing Disaster Tolerant High Availability Clusters." HP Invent, March 2004.

"Linux Ethernet Bonding Driver Mini How-To Page." The Linux Kernel Archives. www.kernel.org.

"Parallel Execution Fundamentals in Oracle Database 11g Release 2." Oracle White Paper, November 2009, www.oracle.com.

Adams, Steve. "IXORA." http://www.ixora.com.au/tips/

Chien, Timothy, and Greg Green. "Recovery Manager (RMAN) Configuration and Performance Tuning Best Practices." Oracle Open World 2010.

Deshpande, Kritikumar. "Oracle 10g: Data Replication Made Easy." RMOUG Training Days, 2006. www.rmoug.org

Fink, Daniel. "Rollback Segment and Undo Internals." UKOUG 2002 conference. www.ukoug.org

Foster, Ian, and Carl Kesselman. *The Grid: Blueprint for a New Computing Infrastructure*. San Francisco: Morgan Kaufmann, 1999.

Foster, Ian, Carl Kesselman, and Steven Tuecke. "Anatomy of the Grid: Enabling Scalable Virtual Organizations." http://arxiv.org/ftp/cs/papers/0103/0103025.pdf

The Globus Alliance. www.globus.org

Gongloor, Prabhaker, Graham Wood, and Karl Dias. "Performance Diagnosis Demystified: Best Practices for Oracle 10g." Oracle Open World 2005, Oracle Corporation.

Goodman, Joel. "Managing Sequences in a RAC Environment." Oracle University UK, Oracle Corporation, May 2008. www.oracleracsig.org

Haisley, Stephen. "Transaction Management in Oracle 9i." UKOUG Presentation, 2002. www.ukoug.org

Harrison, Guy. *Oracle SQL High Performance Tuning*. Upper Saddle River, NJ: Prentice Hall, 2001.

HP OpenVMS Systems Documentation. OpenVMS Programming Concepts Manual. June 2002. http://h71000.www7.hp.com/doc/731final/5841/5841pro.html

Internet Assigned Numbers Authority (IANA). http://tools.ietf.org/html/rfc3330

Lamba, Rajiv. "Grid Computing and Future Trends." Technical White Paper, Tata Consultancy Services. www.tcs.com

Lewis, Jonathan. "Buffer sorts." Oracle Scratchpad. http://jonathanlewis.wordpress.com/2006/12/17/buffer-sorts/

Lewis, Jonathan. *Cost-Based Oracle Fundamentals*. Berkeley, CA: Apress, 2005.

Li, Tong, Dan Baumberger, and Scott Hahn. "Efficient and Scalable Multiprocessor Fair Scheduling Using Distributed Weighted Round-Robin." White Paper, Intel Corporation, 2009. http://dl.acm.org/citation.cfm?id=1504188

Loaiza, Juan. "Optimal Storage Configuration Made Easy." `www.oracle.com/technetwork/database/performance/opt-storage-conf-130048.pdf`

Metalink Note 22908.1 "What Are Latches and What Causes Latch Contention." `metalink.oracle.com`

Metalink Note 294430.1 "CSS Timeout Computation in Oracle Clusterware." `metalink.oracle.com`

Microsoft Corporation. "Performance Tuning Guidelines for Windows Server 2008." White Paper, May 20, 2009. `www.microsoft.com`

Millsap, Cary. "Why a 99%+ Database Buffer Cache Hit Ratio Is *Not* OK." Hotsos Enterprises, Ltd., 2001. `www.hotsos.com`

Millsap, Cary. *Optimizing Oracle Performance*. Sebastopol, CA: O'Reilly, 2003.

Morle, James. "Brewing Benchmarks." White Paper, Scale Abilities, December 2003. `www.oaktable.net/sites/default/files/BrewingBenchmarks.pdf`

Morle, James. "Connection Management in Oracle RAC Configuration." Scale Abilities, October 2006. `www.scaleabilities.co.uk/wp-content/uploads/downloads/2011/11/RAC_Connection_Management.pdf`

Morle, James. *Scaling Oracle 8i*. Reading, MA: Addison-Wesley, 2000.

Multiple articles and papers from Metalink and Tech Net, Oracle Corporation. `http://metalink.oracle.com`.

Oracle Database 11g Release 2 Documentation. `http://docs.oracle.com/cd/E11882_01/index.htm`

Oracle Documentation (Version 10.1.0, Version 10.2.0, Version 11.2.0, Version 12.1.0). Oracle Technology Network, Oracle Corporation. `http://technet.oracle.com`

Oracle Technology Network. "Best Practices for a Data Warehouse on Oracle Database 11g." Oracle White Paper, Oracle Corporation, November 2010. `www.oracle.com/technetwork/database/bi-datawarehousing/twp-dw-best-practies-11g11-2008-09-132076.pdf`

Oracle Technology Network. "Oracle Real Application Clusters in Oracle VM Environments." Oracle White Paper, Oracle Corporation, March 2012. `www.oracle.com/technetwork/products/clustering/oracle-rac-in-oracle-vm-environment-131948.pdf`

Oracle Technology Network. "SQL Plan Management in Oracle Database 11g." Oracle White Paper, Oracle Corporation, October 2010. `www.oracle.com/technetwork/database/bi-datawarehousing/twp-sql-plan-management-11gr2-133099.pdf`

Oracle Technology Network. "Upgrading from Oracle Database 10g to 11g: What to Expect from the Optimizer." Oracle White Paper, Oracle Corporation, November 2010. `www.oracle.com/technetwork/database/bi-datawarehousing/twp-upgrading-10g-to-11g-what-to-ex-133707.pdf`

Postel, J. "Internet Protocol." RFC 760, USC/Information Sciences Institute, January 1980.

Postel, J. "Transmission Control Protocol." RFC 761, USC/Information Sciences Institute, January 1980.

Pujol, Hector. "Case Study: Resolving High CPU Usage on Oracle Servers." White Paper, Center of Expertise, Oracle Corporation. `https://levipereira.files.wordpress.com/2011/01/cs_highcpu.pdf`

Shee, Richmond. "Got Waits? A Wait Approach to Performance Tuning and Optimization." IOUG Live 2001. `www.ioug.org`

Shee, Richmond, Kirtikumar Deshpande, and K. Gopalakrishnan. *Oracle Wait Interface: A Practical Guide to Performance Diagnostics and Tuning*. Emeryville, CA: Oracle Press, 2004.

Spragins, John. "Analytical Queueing Models." Oregon State University, April 1980. `http://ieeexplore.ieee.org/xpl/articleDetails.jsp?reload=true&arnumber=1653570`

Tierney, Brian L., Jason R. Lee, Dan Gunter, Martin Stoufer, and Tom Dunigan. "Improving Distributed Application Performance Using TCP Instrumentation." May 2003. Lawrence Berkeley National Laboratory.

Vahalia, Uresh. *Unix Internals: The New Frontiers*. Upper Saddle River, NJ: Prentice Hall, 1996.

Vaidyanatha, Gaja Krishna. "Implementing RAID on Oracle Systems." Proceedings of Oracle Open World 2000. www.oracle.com.

Vaidyanatha, Gaja Krishna, Kirtikumar Deshpande, and John A. Kostelac, Jr. *Oracle Performance Tuning 101*. Berkeley, CA: Oracle Press, 2001.

Valerio, Jose. "Global Cache Waits." Technical White Paper, Oracle Corporation, June 2010. www.oracleracsig.org

Vallath, Murali. "High Availability Using Transparent Application Failover on Real Application Clusters." Technical Feature, Oracle Scene. *UKOUG Journal*, Issue 12, Winter 2002. www.ukoug.org

Vallath, Murali. *Oracle 10g RAC: Grid, Services and Clustering*. Boston: Elsevier Digital Press, 2006.

Vallath, Murali. *Real Application Clusters*. Boston: Digital Press, 2004.

Vallath, Murali. "Think Outside the Interconnect." Oracle Open World 2011, Oracle Corporation.

Vallath, Murali. "Using 11gR2 Result Cache features in a RAC Environment." Oracle Open World 2011, Oracle Corporation.

Vallath, Murali. "Using Oracle Database 11g Release 2 Result Cache in an Oracle RAC Environment." Oracle Technology Network, January 2011. www.oracle.com/technetwork/articles/datawarehouse/vallath-resultcache-rac-284280.html

Vengurlekar, Nitin. "ASM Technical Best Practices." MyOracleSupport Note: 265633.1. http://support.oracle.com

Vengurlekar, Nitin, Murali Vallath, and Rich Long. *Oracle Automatic Storage Management: Under-the-Hood & Practical Deployment Guide*. New York: Oracle Press, 2008.

Zafar, Mahmood, Anthony Fernandez, Bert Scalzo, and Murali Vallath. "Testing Oracle 10g RAC Scalability." DELL PowerSolutions, March 2005. www.dell.com/downloads/global/power/ps1q06-20050300-Quest.pdf

Index

■ A

Active Session History (ASH), 159
Architecture *See* RAC architecture
Automatic Database Diagnostic Monitor (ADDM)
    Advisor Central selection, 157
    database activity, 157
    error report, 158–159
    issues, 156
    process flow diagram, 156
Automatic diagnostic repository (ADR), 622
    actions, 623
    ADRCI command, 629
    configuration, 625
    home directory, 626
    incident, 623–624
    MMON process, 626
    problem keys, 623–624
    retention policy, 626
    SQL test case builder (TCB), 634
    V$DIAG_ADR_CONTROL, 627
        ADR HOME, 628
        alert log, 629
        command line interface, 628
        homepath, 628
    working principles, 630
        V$DIAG_INCIDENT_FILE, 632
        V$DIAG_IPS_FILE_METADATA, 633
Automatic Segment Space Management (ASSM), 282
Automatic Storage Management (ASM)
    architecture, 376
    background and foreground processes, 376–377
    clustered file system, 375
    disk structure, 375
    JBOD, 374
    OEM, 382
        diskgroup-level statistics, 383–384
        disk-level statistics, 384

    SGA, 379
    V$ASM_OPERATION view, 380
    V$IOSTAT_FILE view, 381–382
Automatic workload repository (AWR), 513
    CREATE_SNAPSHOT procedure, 150
    DB_HIST_BASELINE table, 150
    foreground events, 152
    Global Cache Load Profile Formula, 153–154
    Global Cache Transfer Statistics, 153–154
    scripts, 151
    SYSAUX tablespace, 150
    top timed events, 154
    warehouse, 155
    workload characteristics, 152
Automatic Workload Repository Warehouse
        (AWRW), 155
AUTOTRACE feature, 176
Average seek time, 359

■ B

Backup process, 319
Block request, RAC
    prepare phase, 405
    transfer phase, 407
    2-way cache fusion, 399
        AWR report, 400
        wait events, 402
    3-way cache fusion, 402
    working principles, 407
        AWR reports, 411
        OBIEE, 408
        prepare phase, 409
        serialization issue, 413
        slow down process, 410
        top timed events, 411
Block written record (BWR), 51, 323
B-tree index, 279

■ C

Cache fusion, 387
    addresses transaction concurrency, 34
    resource mode, 35
    resource role, 35
Capacity planning, 21
    benefits of, 23
    business requirements, 24
    clustering
        configuration, 24
        intangible factors, 26
        measurement, 25–26
        process, 25
    computer system stack, 22
    DBMS_SPACE.CREATE_TABLE_COST function, 28
    DBMS_SPACE.OBJECT_GROWTH_TREND
        function, 27
    factors influence, 24
    measurement, 25
    simulation model, 24
Client connection, 345
    TCP parameters
        array size, 348
        fetch size, 348
        session data unit (SDU), 346
        tcp_rmem, 346
        tcp_Wmem, 346
        trace analyzer, 348, 351
    wait events
        SQL*Net message from client, 351
        SQL*Net message to client, 351
        SQL*Net more data from client, 353
        SQL*Net more data to client, 353
Cluster communication method, 462
Clustered file systems (CFS), 374
Cluster Health Monitor (CHM)
    architecture, 172
    Berkeley DB (BDB)/Management DB, 173
    logger daemon, 173
    primary daemon, 172
    proxy daemon, 172
    statistics, 173
Cluster interconnect, 451, 657
    advantage of, 470
    block transfers, 453
    device queue sizes, 456–457
    Gigabit Ethernet, 454
    Infiniband technology, 454–455
    interconnect monitoring (see Interconnect
        monitoring)
    jumbo frame, 457
    linear scalability
        global cache coherency, 481
        GPnP profile, 478

        HAIP vs. NIC bonding, 482
        IPTraf output with, 479–480
    network buffer sizes
        tcp_mem variable, 456
        TCP protocol, 455
        tcp_rmem variable, 456
        tcp_wmem variable, 456
    prepare latency, 466
    sequence diagram, 451–452
    transfer latency, 466
    verification
        ASM alert logs, 463
        Oracle database kernel, IP addresses, 458
        ORADEBUG utility, 465
        O/S level, 462–463
        transfer rate checking, 463–465
    workshop
        buffer, 472
        EM and IPTraf, 474–476
        GCS, 470
        GigE interface, 476
        GPnP file, 468–469
        ifconfig command, NIC card configuration, 469
        interconnect configuration, 468
        lm_tickets parameter, 472–473
        netstat-su command, 470
        performance of, 477
        RAC cluster, 467
        TCKT_AVAIL column, 471
        TCP buffer sizes, 473–474
        V$DLM_TRAFFIC_CONTROLLER view, 471
Cluster ready service daemon (CRSD), 558
Cluster synchronization service (CSS)
    CRSD function, 558
    cssdagent, 556
    CSSD daemon process, 557
    cssdmonitor, 556
    disk heartbeat (DHB), 556
    NM checks, 556
    Nodeapps, 559
    ONS, 558
Clusterware diagnosis, 545
    boot-up process flow, 553
    cluster synchronization service (CSS)
        CRSD function, 558
        cssdagent, 556
        CSSD daemon process, 557
        cssdmonitor, 556
        disk heartbeat (DHB), 556
        NM checks, 556
        Nodeapps, 559
        ONS, 558
    crsctl utility, 563
    EVMD verification, 578
    grid infrastructure (GI) stack, 545

Grid Plug and Play, 579
High availability service (HAS), 553
monitoring resources, 582
node eviction, DHB, 560
node eviction, NHB, 559
node reboots, 561
OCR utilities
    alert logs, 575
    ASM storage, 576
    crsctl check crs command, 575
    CRSD daemon process, 575
    log directories, 574
    ocrcheck utility, 570, 577
    ocrconfig utility, 571
    ocrdump utility, 574
    OHASD daemons, 577
olsnodes command, 562
Oracle Cluster Registry (OCR), 546
Oracle local registry (OLR), 547
    crcstl command, 549
    differences, 548
    GI installation, 551
    OHASD process, 548–549
    system-level resources, 548
run levels, 554
service control utility
    CRS modules, 567
    dynamic state dump, 563
    EVM modules, 568
    query and administering, 563
    self-explanatory parameters, 567
Cost-based optimizer (CBO), 149
    goals, 217
    join types, 233
    operations, 216
    OPTIMIZER_MODE, 217
        ALTER SESSION command, 220
        execution paths, 219
        parameters, 221
        SQL automatic tuning, 221
        SQL hints, 219
        SQL plan management, 227–228
        SQL tuning advisor, 222
    statistics, 231

■ D

Database tuning, 654
    features, 277
    hard parses
        bind variables/prepared statements, 294
        CURSOR_SHARING parameter, 294
        inefficient queries, 294
        SESSION_CACHED_CURSORS parameter, 294
        V$SHARED_POOL_ADVICE view, 295
        WHERE clause, 293

in-memory cache (see In-memory cache)
partitioning
    benefits of, 280
    B-tree index, 279
    composite, 278
    definition, 278
    global indexes, 280
    hash, 278
    indexing methods, 279
    list, 278
    local index, 280
    range, 278
result cache (see Result cache)
sequence numbers
    ASSM, 282
    cache size, 282
    LMT, 282
    reverse key indexes (see Reverse key indexes)
    usage, 281
undo block considerations, 293
Data block format, 600
Datafiles
    data warehouse, 366
    INSERT/DELETE/UPDATE operations, 365
    RAID01, 366
    RAID5, 367–368
    RAID 10, 366
DB_CONNECT_STRING parameter, 167
DBMS_SQLTUNE package
    graphical form, 179
    methods and descriptions, 180
    procedures, 177–178
DB_USERID parameter, 167
Degree of parallelism (DOP), 238
DIAG process, 622
Distributed workload management (DWM), 658
    FAN (see Fast application notification (FAN))
    FCF
        connections failure detection, 507
        ONS, 508
        transaction guard, 510
    load balancing (see Load balancing)
    payroll application, 498
    PL/SQL definition, 527
        advantages, 541
        B-tree index, 541
        DBA_ENABLED_AGGREGATIONS table, 528
        DBMS_APPLICATION_INFO package, 531
        GV$ACTIVE_HISTORY_SESSION, 536
        GV$SERVICEMETRIC_HISTORY view, 532
        GV$SERVICE_STATS view, 528
        hash partitions, 542
        monitoring activity, benefits, 529
        MVRACPDnTap, 531
        MVRACPDnTap_rowcache.sql, 539–540
        MVRACPDnTap_sqlstats.sql, 537–538

Distributed workload management (DWM) (*cont.*)
  MVRACPDnTap_SrvActSum.sql, 533, 535–536
  TAP_BULK_DATA_LOADER, 535
  trcsess utility, 530
  troubleshooting, 542
  USER_DUMP_DEST directory, 530
  wait events and row level locking, 537
  resource manager, 498
  server pools configuration, 497
  service framework
    availability, 496
    data-dependent service, 496
    functional-dependent services, 497
    internal services, 497
    management, 495
    performance benefits, 496
    pre-establish services, 497
Dynamic resource mastering (DRM), 40

■ **E**

Enqueues, 585, 596, 658
  control file transaction, 603
  high water marks, 601
  sequence numbers, 602
  space management transaction, 601
  TM-DML, 601
  TX transaction, 599
Entity relationship diagram (ERD), 505
Event 10046, 182
Event 10053, 185
Event interface, 447–449

■ **F**

Fast application notification (FAN)
  cluster status, 498
  ERD, 505
  event notification, 498–499
  and ONS
    communication, 501–502
    configurations, 499
    event descriptions, 503
    logging, 507
    working process, 499
  service event, 503
  system events, 503
Fast connect failover (FCF)
  connections failure detection, 507
  ONS, 508
  transaction guard, 510
Fast recovery area, 335
Fiber channel (FC)switch, 357

■ **G**

Global cache, 655
Global cache optimization
  blockers and deadlocks, 429
  data access patterns, 424
  data dictionary views
    enterprise manager, 445
    GV$CR_BLOCK_SERVER, 436
    GV$CURRENT_BLOCK_SERVER, 439
    GV$GES_CONVERT_LOCAL, 441
    GV$GES_CONVERT_REMOTE, 441
    GV$GES_ENQUEUE, 435
    GV$INSTANCE_CACHE_TRANSFER, 434
    GV$LIBRARYCACHE, 442
    GV$ROWCACHE, 443
    lock conversion types, 440
    troubleshooting, 447
  hot blocks (*see* Hot blocks)
  logical I/O operations, 425
  queries, 427
  wait events, 426
Group membership (GM) services, 34
GV$INSTANCE view, 198
GV$SERVICE_STATS view, 192
GV$SERV_MOD_ACT_STATS view, 193–194
GV$SESSION_WAIT view, 197
GV$SYSSTAT and GV$SESSTAT views, 466
GV$SYSTEM_EVENT views, 197

■ **H**

Health monitor (HM) checks
  DBMS_HM.GET_RUN_REPORT, 619
  DBMS_HM.RUN_CHECK, 617
  using OEM
    advisor central page, 621
    CF block integrity check, 622
    checkers page, 621
    DB structure integrity check, 622
  V$HM_CHECK, 616
    DB-offline mode, 617
    DB-online mode, 617
  V$HM_CHECK_PARM, 618
  V$HM_FINDING, 619
  V$HM_recommendation, 620
  V$HM_RUN view, 618
Hot blocks, 430

■ **I**

ifconfig command, 456
Incident packaging service (IPS), 624

In-memory area *See* In-memory cache
In-memory cache
    alert log file, 313
    alter table, 313
    AWR report, 315–316
    buffer cache, 316–317
    column descriptions, 314
    definition, 311
    INMEMORY attribute, 313
    INMEMORY_MAX_POPULATE_SERVERS, 314
    SGA, 312, 314
    TABLE ACCESS INMEMORY FULL, 316
    V$SESSION_WAIT view, 316
    WHERE condition, 317
Input/output operations per second (IOPS), 24
INSERT statement, 293
INSTANCE parameter, 167
Instance recovery
    alert log file, 322
    background process, 320
    BWR process, 323
    cache recovery, 324, 326
    checkpoint counter, 320, 329
    crash recovery, 333
    failures, 320
    fast-start fault recovery, 324
    Fast-start parallel rollback, 325
    LMON process, 320
    online block recovery, 333
    parallelism, 328
    performance optimization, 326
    recovery process, 321
    redo log files, 330
    redo log switches, 326
    SHUTDOWN ABORT command, 320–321
    SMON process, 323
    system change number (SCN), 320
    thread recovery, 333
    transaction recovery, 326
Institute of Electrical and Electronics Engineers (IEEE), 100
Interconnect monitoring
    data dictionary views
        GV$DLM_MISC, 490
        GV$DLM_TRAFFIC_CONTROLLER, 488–489
        GV$DYNAMIC_REMASTER_STATS, 487–488
    enterprise manager
        cluster cache coherency, 491–492
        database performance, 490–491
        tcpdump command, 492–493
    troubleshooting of, 482
    workshop
        $GRID_HOME/bin/oifcfg setif, 486
        CLUSTER_INTERCONNECTS parameter, 486
        IPC buffer, 484

    IPTraf indication, 485
    lost blocks, 482–483
    occasional errors, 487
    OCR file, 483, 485
    oifcfg command, 485
    private network, 483
    setif command, 486
Interprocess communication (IPC)
    protocol, 31

■ J, K

Jumbo frame, 457

■ L

Latches, 658
    buffer cache, 587
    classes, 593
        FIFO order, 594
        fixed priority, 594
        real time, 594
        round robin, 594
        system, 594
        time sharing, 594
    gc element, 592
    no-wait mode, 586
    Redo log buffers, 592
    willing-to-wait mode, 585
Light Onboard Monitor (LTOM)
    configuration of, 166
    creation, 166
    directory structure, 166
    properties file
        automatic hang detection, 169
        automatic session tracing, 171
        connection parameters, 167
        event trigger rules section, 169
        execution process, 168
        Hang detection directives, 168, 170–171
        sequencing rules, 170
        session recorder, 168
        system profiler, 167, 171
    UNIX and Linux environments, 165
Listener registration process (LREG), 342
Listeners
    database listeners, 342
    scan listeners
        domain name system (DNS), 341
        local area network (LAN), 341
        RAC configuration, 341
        SCAN VIPs, 341
        virtual memory system (VMS), 341
SDU settings, 347

Load balancing
    applications, connection pooling
        CREATE_CONSUMER_GROUP
            procedure, 522–523
        database mapping, srvctl utility, 520
        DBA_RSRC_GROUP_MAPPINGS view, 525
        DBA_SCHEDULER_JOB_CLASSES view, 526
        DBMS_SCHEDULER, 525
        definition, 513
        failure, SRVCTL, 521
        FAN feature, 520
        FIPS, 518–519
        GRUD, 518–519
        GV$OSSTAT, 517
        GV$SERVICEMETRIC, 517
        HIGH_PRIORTY, 523
        instance mapping, 518
        job scheduling, 526
        pending/work area, 522
        PL/SQL package, 526
        RCLB working, 516
        REMOTE_LISTENER parameter, 521
        RESOURCE_CONSUMER_GROUP, 526
        RESOURCE_MANAGER_PLAN initialization
            parameter, 527
        resource plans, 524
        server pools, 520
        SSKY, 518–519
        TAPS, 518–519
        thresholds, 513–514
        TICKS, 518–519
        TNS connection description, 521
        workload monitoring, 527
        workspace area, 525
    client load balancing, 510
    connection load balancing, 511
    threshold
        GV$SERVICEMETRIC, 517
        RCLB feature, working, 516
Locally Managed Tablespaces (LMT), 282

■ M

Manageability Monitor (MMON)process, 343–344
Maximum transmission unit (MTU), 457
Media recovery
    backup destination, 334
    determine throughput, 334
    optimal performance, 334
    RMAN tuning, 334

■ N

netdev_max_backlog parameter, 457
netstat utility, 462

Network bandwidth, 469
Node membership (NM) service, 33
Non-container database (non-CDB), 116
N-tier computing model, 111

■ O

Object affinity, 38
oifcfg utility, 63, 459
Operating system (O/S), 93
Oracle 12c RAC, 460
Oracle BI Enterprise Edition (OBIEE), 408
Oracle Cluster Registry (OCR), 546
Oracle Cluster Synchronization Service Daemon
        (OCSSD), 33
Oracle Clusterware stack, 29, 32
Oracle dynamic resource mastering (ODRM), 522
Oracle Enterprise Manager (OEM)
    Advisor Central selection, 157
    ASH report, 159
    AWR (see Automatic Workload Repository (AWR))
    AWRW, 155
    Cloud Control, 146
    database activity, 157
    error report, 158–159
    front tier, 146
    grid control, 145
    issues, 156
    performance screen, 147–148
    process flow diagram, 156
    SQL Advisory, 148
    target tier, 146
    three-tier architecture, 147
Oracle local registry (OLR), 547
    crcstl command, 549
    differences, 548
    GI installation, 551
    OHASD process, 548–549
    system-level resources, 548
Oracle Net, 655
Oracle notification services (ONS)
    FAN
        callable interfaces, 498
        communication, 501–502
        configuration, 499
        logging, 507
        working process, 499
    FCF, 508
Oracle's wait interface (OWI)
    BEFORE LOGOFF ON DATABASE trigger, 197
    data dictionary views, 196
    GV$INSTANCE view, 198
    GV$SYSTEM_EVENT views, 197
    system-level activities, 198
    table creation, 197

ORDER clause, 286
OSWATCHER (OSW)
    configuration, 162
    data collection, 163
    directory structure, 161
    nohup option, 161
    OS-specific performance metrics, 160

■ P

Parallel processing
    advantages, 237
    ALTER operation, 240
    characteristics, 238
    clustered solutions, 237
    default values, 241
    description, 235
    dynamic performance views
        GV$PX_BUFFER_ADVICE, 265
        GV$PX_PROCESS, 271
        GV$PX_PROCESS_SYSSTAT, 266
        GV$PX_SESSION, 267
        GV$PX_SESSTAT, 266, 268
        GV$PX_TQSTAT, 266
    hints, 242
        NOPARALLEL, 245
        PARALLEL, 243
        PQ_DISTRIBUTE, 245
    intra and inter operations, 249
    metaphor discussion, 237
    optimization
        I/O requirements, 264
        relevant statistics, 264
        slave activity, 264
        troubleshooting, 263
    parameters
        adaptive algorithm, 246
        default DOP, 246
        maximum servers, 245
        message size, 246
        minimum percentage, 246
        minimum servers, 245
    performance, 238
    query architecture, 248
        degree of parallelism (DOP), 238, 240
        pictorial view, 240
        PX processes, 239
        query coordinator (QC), 238
        query slaves, 239
        queue references, 238
        sort operation, 239
    query coordinator (QC), 247
    RAC environment
        aggregated buffer cache, 251
        controls, 260
        DDL operations, 261

degree limits, 257
DML operations, 261
fragments, 251
minimum execution, 257
multiple nodes, 250
server process, 260
slave distribution, 251
valid values, 257
XPlan (see XPlan)
recovery, 262
session level, 242
table/index creation, 240
table queues (TQ), 247
wait events
    events 10391, 274–275
    execution, 272, 274
    fragmentation, 272
    Join ACK, 273
    need buffer, 272
    parsing, 274
    PX qref latch, 273
    queuing statement, 273
    reap credit, 273
    send blkd, 272
Parallel server (PX) processes, 238
Partition pruning, 280
Partition-wise join, 281
Problem-solving diagnosis methods
    ADR (see Automatic diagnostic
        repository (ADR))
    DBA troubleshoot, 615
    DBA utilities
        OLS, 649
        ORACHK utility, 646
        RACDIAG, 646
        Remote diagnostic agent (RDA), 645
    HM checks, 615 (see also Health monitor (HM)
        checks)
    ORADEBUG utility, 638
        LKDEBUG, 639
        operating system process identifier (OSPID), 640
        preceding command, 639
    ORA errors
        argument and layer information, 644
        internal error code, 643
        ORA-7445, 645
    RAC, 615
Problem soving diagnostics methods, 653

■ Q

Query architecture, 248
Queue depth
    definition, 362
    EMC storage array, 362
    iostat utility, 362–363

■ R

RAC architecture
   cluster components, 31
   cluster management
      cache fusion (*see* Cache fusion)
      communication software layer, 31
      high-level system stack, 30
      monitoring processes, 32
      network layer, 32
      Oracle Clusterware/cluster manager, 32
      Oracle Clusterware stack, 32
   Heartbeats
      Disk Heartbeat (DHB), 36
      Local Heartbeat (LHB), 37
   lock management, 40
   oracle single-instance *vs.* clustered
      configuration, 29
   read/read behavior
      with no transfer, 42
      possibilities, 41
      SSKY3, 42
      with transfer, 42–43
   read/write behavior, 44
   resource master, 37
   SCN, 37
   write/read behavior, 47–48
   write to disk behavior
      activity, 49–50
      block request instance, 51–53
      BWR, 51
      circumstances, 49
      DML operation, 51
   write/write behavior, 46
RAC environment
   aggregated buffer cache, 251
   controls, 260
   degree limits, 257
   fragments, 251
   multiple nodes, 250
   parameters
      DDL operations, 261
      DML operations, 261
      minimum execution, 257
      server process, 260
      valid values, 256
   slave distribution, 251
   XPlan
      column description, 252
      operation column, 254
Read/read behavior
   with no transfer, 42
   possibilities, 41
   SSKY3, 42
   with transfer, 42–43
Read/write behavior, 44

Real application cluster (RAC)
   architecture (*see* RAC architecture)
   background process, 388
      ACMS process, 390
      global cache resources, 391
      IPCO process, 391
      LCKO process, 390
      LDDn process, 391
      LMDn process, 390
      LMHB process, 390
      LMON process, 389
      LMSn process, 389
      PING process, 391
      RMSn process, 391
      RSMN process, 391
   block requests, 398
      prepare phase, 405
      transfer phase, 406
      2-way cache fusion, 399
      3-way cache fusion, 402
      working principles, 407
   environment (*see* RAC environment)
   global cache optimization (*see* Global cache
      optimization)
   global cache service (GCS)
      cache fusion, 388
      global resource directory (GRD), 387
      synchronization, 388
   global enqueue services (GES), 387
   latch, 405
   mastering resources, 414
   remastering resources, 416
      clustered configuration, 417
      dynamic statistics, 418
      enterprise manager, 421
      LMD process, 423
      manual performance, 422
      mointoring, 417
Real application testing (RAT), 111
   database replay, 113–114
      non-container database (non-CDB), 116
      transportable tablespace, 130
      workload (*see* Workload)
   RAC environment, 114
   SQL performance analyzer, 113, 132
      capture process, 134
      options, 133
      parameter change, 137
      regression impact, 141
      run comparsion, 135
      SPA report, 136
      trial comparsions, 140
      tuning advisor, 142
      tuning set, 133
      tuning statements, 135
      workflow process, 134

Redolog files, 368
Remote Direct Memory Access (RDMA), 455
Result cache
    buffer cache, 295
    client_result_cache_lag and client_result_
        cache_size, 295
    data warehouse, 296
    function
        creation, 307
        DBMS_RESULT_CACHE, 310
        definition, 306
        RELIES_ON, 306
        shared pool, 309–310
        V$RESULT_CACHE_OBJECTS
            view, 307–309
        validation, 307
    limitations, 311
    Oracle RAC environment, 296, 306
        cache fusion, 303
        CPU and network, 303
        factors, 304
        GV$RESULT_CACHE_OBJECTS view, 304
        memory structure, 303
        objects, 298
        ORDER_LINE table, 305
        shared pool, 302
        tkprof, 298
        trace file, 299
        V$RESULT_CACHE_OBJECTS view, 300–302
        v$sgastat view, 297
    result_cache_max_result parameter, 295
    result_cache_max_size parameter, 295
Reverse key indexes
    cluster-related overhead methods, 292
    DML operation, 289
    drawback of, 283
    enqueue statistics view
        DLM_* columns, 285–286
        GV$ROWCACHE, 284–285
        NEXTVAL, 287
        NOORDER, 287
        ORDER clause, 286
        sequence cache, 283–284
        V$_SEQUENCES, 286
        wait events, 287
    INSERT operation, 288
    srvctl utility, 289
    structure, 282
    surrogate key, 282
    usage, 282
    V$ACTIVE_SESSION_HISTORY, 290–292
    V$DATAFILE, 291
    V$SQLSTATS view, 288–289
Run-time connection load
        balancing (RCLB), 513

■ S

Scalability, 87
    aix, 91
    application testing, 102
    ASM, 92
    characteristics, 98
    CHM disk latency alarms, 98
    cluster utilization and demand on 2-node
        RAC cluster, 97
    database testing, 102
    end-to-end testing, 107
    Hammerora tool, 95
    hammerora workload generator, 94
    hardware testing, 93
    instance, 92
    interconnect, 89
    I/O calibration
        8 Eight-node cluster study, 101
        issues, 100
        iterations and testing, 100
        netstat and ifconfig, 100
        procedure, 99
        scalability load on two servers, 101
    jumbo frames, 90
    N/A = not applicable, 108
    N/A = not available, 109
    RAC configuration, 89
    RAP Phase I, 95
    RAP Phase II, 95
    RAP Phase V Hardware, 93
    RAP phase VII application, 102
        application server's to db server's
            user workload, 107
        consolidated list of tests, 106
        data collection table, 103
        LoadRunner, 103
        load test on one server, 104–105
        load test on six servers, 105
        primary bottlenecks, 106
        testing, 103
    RAP Phase VIII Recorder, 108
    RAP phaseVIII recording test progress, 109
    RAP testing phase VIII burnout tests, 107
    RAP VIII recording, 110
    rules, 98
    scalability load on two servers, 98
    scalable components, 89
    scale-out, 87–88
    scale-up, 87
    solaris, 92
    SQL*Net, 92
    transactions counter 2-node cluster test, 96
    workload-testing tools, 94
    workshop, 93

SELECT statement, 293
Self-developed utilities
    dump destination directory, 112
    iterative process, 113
    multiple sessions, 113
    production environment, 112
    trace file identifier, 112
Service-Module-Action
    DBA_ENABLED_AGGREGATIONS table, 192
    GV$SERVICE_STATS view, 192
    GV$SERV_MOD_ACT_STATS view, 193–194
    PL/SQL definition, 191
    statistics collection, 191
Service-oriented architecture (SOA), 495
Session data unit (SDU), 346
setFastConnectionFailoverEnabled method, 508
Single Client Access Name (SCAN), 341
SQL execution life cycle, 201
    bind variables, 207
    close the cursor, 208
    cursor, 203
    fetch rows, 208
    hard parsing
        flow diagram, 204
        SQL_ID, 204
        SQL parsing and execution, 206
        steps, 203
        variations, 204
    library cache feature, 203
    parallelism, 207
    query output, 207
    soft parsing, 207
    SQL statement execution, 208
SQL statement, EXPLAIN PLAN, 176
SQL Test case builder (TCB), 634
SQL trace utility, 180–182
SQL tuning, 201, 216
    CBO (see Cost-based optimizer (CBO))
    execution times
        STATISTICS_LEVEL, 209
        TIMED_OS_STATISTICS, 210
        TIMED_STATISTICS, 208
        V$STATISTICS_LEVEL, 209
    life cycle (see SQL execution life cycle)
    logical I/O, 211–212
    physical I/O, 211, 215
Storage subsystem, 369, 655
    allocation units, 377–379
    array, 357
    ASM (see Automatic Storage Management (ASM))
    CFS, 374
    considerations, 355–356
    contention
        access paths, 360
        HBA device, 360–361

queue depth (see Queue depth)
    read cache, 364
    SAN switch, 360
    write cache, 364
datafiles (see Datafiles)
disk drive performance
    database applications, 359
    factors, 358
    rotational latency, 358–359
    seek time, 358–359
diskgroups, 379
I/O characteristics
    data retrieval, 372
    Oracle RDBMS, 371
    random data access, 373
    sequential data access, 372
    variables, 373
I/O operations
    disk performance characteristics, 371
    Oracle kernel, 370
    segment size, 370
mixed workloads, 356
redolog files, 368
throughput-based workload, 356
transaction-based workload, 356
System change number (SCN), 37, 281

■ T

Testing
    availability, 653
    scalability, 653
TKPROF utility, 182–183, 196
Tools and utilities, 654
Transmission control protocol (TCP), 32
Transparent application failover (TAF), 520
Transparent network substrate (TNS) technology, 340
Trcsess utility, 195–196
Tuning, 339
    client connection (see Client connection)
    user connection (see User connection)
Tuning recovery, 319
    Fast recovery area, 335
    instance recovery
        alert log file, 322
        background process, 320
        BWR process, 323
        cache recovery, 324, 326
        checkpoint counter, 321, 329
        crash recovery, 333
        failures, 320
        fast-start fault recovery, 324
        Fast-start parallel rollback, 325
        LMON process, 320, 331
        online block recovery, 333

parallelism, 328
performance optimization, 326
recovery process, 321
redo log files, 330
redo log switches, 326
SHUTDOWN ABORT
  command, 320–321
SMON process, 323
system change number (SCN), 320
thread recovery, 333
transaction recovery, 326
media recovery, 333
  backup destination, 334
  backup methods, 334
  determine throughput, 334
  optimal performance, 334
  RMAN tuning, 334

■ U, V

UNION ALL clauses, 149
User connection
  connectivity drivers, 340
  Java Database Connectivity (JDBC), 339
  listeners
    database listener/Oracle Net listener, 342
    scan listeners, 341
  load balancing
    enterprise manager, 343
    GV$OSSTAT, 344
    GV$SERVICEMETRIC, 343
    manageability monitor (MMON), 343
    MMNL process, 344
    server control (SRVCTL), 343
  network layers, 340
  Oracle Net Foundation Layer (ONFL), 340–341
  protocol layer, 341

■ W

Wait event, 585, 603
  cluster waits
    block access grant, 611
    buffer busy, 609
    CR block busy, 610
    current block congested, 608
    current block request, 611
    current request, 610

    failure status, 613
    lost blocks, 611
    multiblock request, 611
    mutex, 613
    resource master, 610
    retry current block, 613
    SCN number, 610
    two-way/three-way blocks, 607
  consistent read *vs.* current, 606
  defer time, 611
  RAC events, 604
Wait events, 658
Workload
  capture process, 114
    AWR Data, 119
    EM requests, 116
    filters, 117
    job schedule, 119
    options, 115
    parameters, 118
    production environment, 115
    review screen, 118
  processing
    capture section, 121
    directory selection, 121
    execution process, 123
    job status review, 122
    preceding process, 123
    prepare test database, 120
    RATDIR, 120
    replay operations, 124
  replay process, 124
    analysis report, 129
    AWR ststistics, 130
    client preparation, 127
    clustered environment, 130
    connection mappings, 126
    directory identification, 125
    parameter settings, 127
    test database, 125
Write/read behavior, 47–48
Write/write behavior, 46

■ X, Y, Z

XPlan
  column description, 253
  operation column, 254

Get the eBook for only $10!

> Now you can take the weightless companion with you anywhere, anytime. Your purchase of this book entitles you to 3 electronic versions for only $10.

This Apress title will prove so indispensible that you'll want to carry it with you everywhere, which is why we are offering the eBook in 3 **formats** for only $10 if you have already purchased the print book.

Convenient and fully searchable, the PDF version enables you to easily find and copy code—or perform examples by quickly toggling between instructions and applications. The MOBI format is ideal for your Kindle, while the ePUB can be utilized on a variety of mobile devices.

Go to www.apress.com/promo/tendollars to purchase your companion eBook.

Apress®

THE EXPERT'S VOICE™